The Great Ideas

Man
Mathematics
Matter
Mechanics
Medicine
Memory and Imagination
Metaphysics
Mind
Monarchy
Nature
Necessity and Contingency
Oligarchy
One and Many
Opinion
Opposition
Philosophy
Physics
Pleasure and Pain
Poetry
Principle
Progress
Prophecy
Prudence
Punishment
Quality
Quantity

Reasoning
Relation
Religion
Revolution
Rhetoric
Same and Other
Science
Sense
Sign and Symbol
Sin
Slavery
Soul
Space
State
Temperance
Theology
Time
Truth
Tyranny
Universal and Particular
Virtue and Vice
War and Peace
Wealth
Will
Wisdom
World

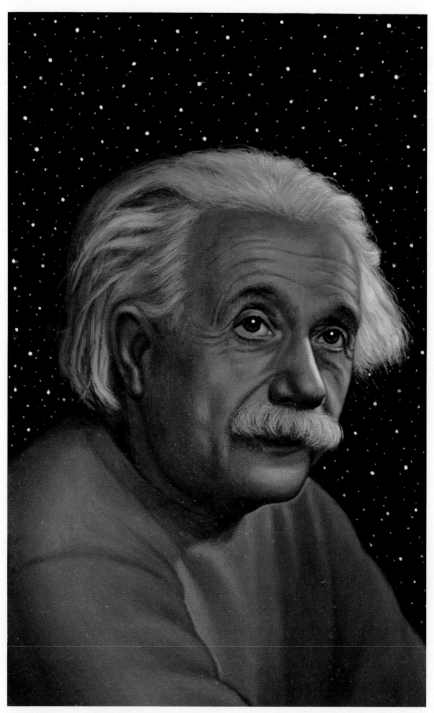

Albert Einstein (1879-1955)

The
Great Ideas
Today

1979

The
Great Ideas
Today

1979

Encyclopædia Britannica, Inc.

Chicago • London • Toronto • Geneva • Sydney • Tokyo • Manila • Seoul

Tables 1 and 2 in "The Social Sciences Since the Second World War—Part
One," by Daniel Bell are reprinted from the article, "Conditions Favoring
Major Advances in Social Science," by K.W. Deutsch *et al.* They appeared as
Tables 1 and 2 in *Science*; Vol. 171, pp. 450–459, 5 February 1971; Copyright
© 1971 by the American Association for the Advancement of Science.
Reprinted by permission of *Science* and the authors.

"Two Old Men" is reprinted from *Twenty-Three Tales* by Leo Tolstoy, translated
by Louise and Aylmer Maude and published by Oxford University Press.
Reprinted by permission of Oxford University Press.

Printed in the U.S.A. Library of Congress Catalog Number: 61-65561
International Standard Book Number: 0-85229-364-X
International Standard Serial Number: 0072-7288

Contents

A NOTE ON REFERENCE STYLE

In the following pages, passages in *Great Books of the Western World* are referred to by the initials *'GBWW,'* followed by volume, page number, and page section. Thus, *'GBWW,* Vol. 39, p. 210b' refers to page 210 in Adam Smith's *The Wealth of Nations,* which is Volume 39 in *Great Books of the Western World.* The small letter 'b' indicates the page section. In books printed in single column, 'a' and 'b' refer to the upper and lower halves of the page. In books printed in double column, 'a' and 'b' refer to the upper and lower halves of the left column, 'c' and 'd' to the upper and lower halves of the right column. For example, 'Vol. 53, p. 210b' refers to the lower half of page 210, since Volume 53, James's *Principles of Psychology,* is printed in single column. On the other hand, 'Vol. 7, p. 210b' refers to the lower left quarter of the page, since Volume 7, Plato's *Dialogues,* is printed in double column.

Gateway to the Great Books is referred to by the initials *'GGB,'* followed by volume and page number. Thus, *'GGB,* Vol. 10, pp. 39-57' refers to pages 39 through 57 of Volume 10 of *Gateway to the Great Books,* which is James's essay, "The Will to Believe."

The Great Ideas Today is referred to by the initials *'GIT,'* followed by the year and page number. Thus *'GIT* 1968, p. 210' refers to page 210 of the 1968 edition of *The Great Ideas Today.*

Preface

This issue of *The Great Ideas Today* is largely devoted to science. In observance of the centennial of Albert Einstein's birth, our symposium deals with modern cosmology, which is to say, cosmology as it has evolved since Einstein published his theory of general relativity some sixty years ago. An extended discussion of this theory and of its bearing on cosmology is further provided in the present volume by S. Chandrasekhar, the distinguished astrophysicist. Also, among our Additions to the Great Books Library this year are six "Popular Scientific Lectures" by Ernst Mach, who is among other things the eponymous source of a principle which is of great importance in relativity theory. And a special feature of the volume is a discussion by Gerald Holton and Katherine R. Sopka of great books of science (with special reference to physics) which have appeared in the twentieth century.

With respect to this last, it may be noted that the editors had for years sought without success to find someone who would agree to identify and comment upon the great books of twentieth-century science. Professor Holton and Dr. Sopka undertook this task (still with misgivings) only after the suggested title had been changed with thought to the way in which scientific information is actually disseminated in our time. While admitting that there existed few if any twentieth-century scientific publications that could be compared to those in *Great Books of the Western World*, Professor Holton and Dr. Sopka, with the help of others whom they consulted, were able to compile a list of writings in physics, at least, which are perhaps of only lesser importance than that, and which in any case are very interesting to contemplate. Even nonphysicists, who can read some of the listed books only with great difficulty and others not at all, will be glad, we think, to know of them.

In other fields, we are publishing this year the first part of a two-part essay by Daniel Bell on developments in the social sciences since the Second World War; Part Two of this essay will appear next year. Included also in the present volume is an essay by Donald Merriell on the idea of beauty that was written under the direction of the Institute for Philosophical Research in Chicago, whose permission to publish it we hereby gratefully acknowledge.

This year also we commence a new feature consisting of reviews of recent books which we think our subscribers may wish to know about. Our reviewer is William Gorman, a consultant to the Center for the Study of Democratic Institutions, who was formerly our contributing editor. The books Mr. Gorman has chosen to comment upon this year are *The Life of the Mind,* by Hannah Arendt, and *On Human Nature,* by Edward O. Wilson.

Among our Additions to the Great Books Library in this issue, besides Mach's lectures, are J. B. Bury's lectures on Thucydides from *The Ancient Greek Historians;* a selection from the *Lives of the Poets,* by Samuel Johnson; and two short stories, one of which, "Young Goodman Brown," is by Nathaniel Hawthorne, and the other, "Two Old Men," is from Tolstoy's *Twenty-Three Tales.*

In connection with these writings and the articles previously mentioned, readers who own earlier issues of *The Great Ideas Today* may wish to consult certain of their contents. Thus, with respect to the symposium on cosmology, it will be interesting to look up Hermann Bondi's discussion of developments in astronomy in the volume for 1966 and the essay by Owen Gingerich entitled "A Fresh Look at Copernicus" in the 1973 issue. With respect to the essay here by Professor Holton and Dr. Sopka, it should be noted that Einstein's *Relativity: The Special and General Theory* was reprinted in our first issue (1961); that Max Planck's *The Universe in the Light of Modern Physics* was published in 1962, and that Erwin Schrödinger's *What Is Life?* appeared in our volume for 1967. And in connection with Professor Bell's discussion of recent developments in the social sciences, a reader may wish to consult his earlier essay written for our 1964 issue, along with the essay by Henry Steele Commager entitled "The Discipline of History" that appeared in 1972, and also the symposium on the world economy that was a feature of our volume for 1976.

Among writings in *Gateway to the Great Books* that are of relevance to the contents of this volume are: Sir Francis Bacon, "Of Beauty" (*GGB,* Vol. 5, p. 94); Kees Boeke, "Cosmic View" (Vol. 8, pp. 600–644); Sir Arthur Eddington, "The Running-Down of the Universe" (Vol. 8, pp. 565–80); Albert Einstein and Leopold Infeld, "The Rise and Decline of Classical Physics" (Vol. 8, pp. 490–560); Galileo's "The Starry Messenger" (Vol. 8, pp. 330–55); Sir James Jeans, "Beginnings and Endings" (Vol. 8, pp. 585–96); W. K. Clifford, "The Postulates of the Science of Space" (Vol. 9. pp. 243–59); Henri Poincaré, "Space" (Vol. 9, pp. 265–93); and J. B. Bury, "Herodotus" (Vol. 6, pp. 364–83).

PART ONE

A Symposium on Modern Cosmology

Introduction

The editors have selected modern cosmology as the focus of their annual symposium this year. In so doing they had in mind the fact that the study of the cosmos (as we say if we are being Greek), or the universe (if we prefer Latin), while something very old in the tradition of the Great Books, has been transformed in our time by new theories and fresh observations. As a result, current conceptions of the subject are radically different from what they were at the beginning of this century, and even in some respects from what they were at the end of the Second World War. It is to the end that we may hear what scientists now think they know about the universe, and why they think they know it, that the contributors to the symposium have been asked to speak.

Of these contributors, three—Dennis Sciama, Stephen Hawking, and Paul Davies—are British theorists who in various ways, either through their researches or by their writings, or both, have achieved reputation in the field. A fourth contributor, James E. Gunn of the California Institute of Technology, is well known as an astronomer. The fifth contributor, Owen Gingerich of Harvard University, is a distinguished historian of science who has appeared in the pages of *The Great Ideas Today* before, and who on this occasion was asked to say something about the cosmology of earlier times.

A silent but acknowledged presence in all but Professor Gingerich's article is that of Albert Einstein, whose centennial we celebrate this year, and whose own contribution to modern cosmology can hardly be exaggerated. Indeed, the fundamental theory of cosmology was provided by Einstein's paper of 1916 on the general theory of relativity. A discussion of relativity theory and of the role it plays in cosmology as that subject is now understood will be found not only in our symposium articles but in the essay by S. Chandrasekhar which appears elsewhere in this volume. Professor Chandrasekhar's essay was originally scheduled to appear last year but could not be completed in time for publication and was therefore available for inclusion here, where it is eminently appropriate.

In any perusal of these writings on cosmology, the reader of the Great Books will realize that (to simplify, perhaps to oversimplify, some very complex theories) the conception that underlies them is distinct from earlier conceptions—of which something may be gathered from the works of Ptolemy, Copernicus, Kepler, and Newton—in both a quantitative and a qualitative sense. With respect to the first of these, what is important is that quantity exists throughout. The universe as contemplated here is of staggering size, having in it not merely a great number of solar systems like our own within what is nowadays called the "home Galaxy," but a great many galaxies—millions of them, in fact—each of which is of an extent comparable to our own if not much greater, though we perceive them, if at all, merely as spots or smudges of light in the distant heavens. And this uncounted and uncountable multitude of immense systems is not only vast as we look out upon it but is continually expanding even as we do so, for every one of those systems is now receding from every other in the wake of the great explosion—the so-called big bang—with which the existing order of things is now thought to have commenced some ten billion to twenty billion years ago. But the point is that this arrangement, however great the extent of it may be, has size, is something of which certain measurements are possible, though perhaps only in very approximate terms. This is so even if the expansion is taken to be infinite (still the great question, of course). However far our theory reaches, there is extent, there is increase.

That is the point also with respect to the qualitative aspect of modern cosmology. It is not that the universe as we now conceive it, with its myriad parts understood in terms of a single event with which the general movement of all began, and within which innumerable cyclical motions such as that of our solar system and even our Galaxy can repeat themselves, has about it an organic character; such an idea is as old as Plato, who propounds it in the *Timaeus*. Nor is it that the whole has about it something also of the features of a machine, each of whose parts moves obedient to the same laws; we can find that conception in the *Principia* of Newton. It is that the universe as we now regard it is conceived of as having its existence in time, or coincident with time, so that it and everything within it is in a state of continuous development from a beginning which we can pinpoint, all things considered, with astonishing accuracy, to an end which is as yet altogether conjectural, but which may eventually be possible to formulate with some assurance. And the point in this case is that dimly remote as its beginning is supposed to have been, and unimaginably distant as its end must for the moment be assumed to be, if it ever has an end, the universe as we now contemplate it no longer wears the aspect of eternity that was once thought to be represented by the fixed stars or the Newtonian absolutes. It, or its present arrangement, which is the only arrangement of which we can have a scientific grasp, is temporal if not mortal, however large may be the scale of its continuance, and the only thing fixed or constant about it is its rate of change.

Our realization of these things may only prove, of course, that we are finally Kantian creatures. While it may be true that space and time are coextensive and coexistent with the universe as now conceived, it may also be true that that is the only way in which we can perceive it, that space and time are a priori coordinates of our minds, which are unable to perceive the world of phenomena except in their terms. If that is so, we may be looking no further than ourselves when we think we contemplate the wheeling galaxies, the aging fires, of what we take to be the universe. It has been remarked of Dante that his vast conception of eternal heaven, set forth in the pages of the *Divine Comedy,* was in a sense no larger than his skull. And we remember the poet Andrew Marvell, who spoke of the mind as

> *that ocean where each kind*
> *Does straight its own resemblance find;*
> *Yet it creates, transcending these,*
> *Far other worlds and other seas,*
> *Annihilating all that's made*
> *To a green thought in a green shade.*

Yet it may be, too, that it is our minds which are created in the image of cosmic laws, rather than the other way around. The fundamental fact about the cosmos would appear to be that it *is* a cosmos, *i.e.,* an order, and not chaos. And if that is really the case instead of the mere appearance of the case, there is nothing inherently impossible in the attempt by minds that have evolved consistent with such an order to understand it. There doubtless will always be an immense amount that we do not know about the universe, but one is struck reading the papers by these contributors at the things which with tolerable certainty we can now say that we do know, or may know, within a relatively brief further space of time. And perhaps that in the end is what Einstein did for us. He could not himself make the cosmos known, but he defined it in a way that made it knowable to an extent that was not imagined before. We are still at the work he started, which was of great prescience, and of which the end has not yet been reached.

Observations in Cosmology: The Shape of Space and the Totality of Time

James E. Gunn

James Edward Gunn was born in Livingston, Texas, in 1938. He earned his Ph.D. in astronomy and physics from the California Institute of Technology in 1965, and from 1966 to 1968 was a senior space scientist with the Jet Propulsion Laboratory there while serving with the United States Army's Corps of Engineers.

After a brief term at the University of California at Berkeley, Dr. Gunn became an assistant professor at Princeton University, where he worked on theoretical pulsar models, the formation and dynamics of clusters of galaxies, and background radiation from such clusters. The next three years were spent at Caltech in a similar capacity, continuing the same type of research and extending it to cover broader areas such as the physics of strong electromagnetic waves, cosmic ray acceleration, and observations of quasar-galaxy associations. At the same time Dr. Gunn was devising further advances in instrumental techniques. In 1972 he was appointed professor of astronomy at Caltech and became a staff member of Hale Observatories.

Professor Gunn is much in demand as a lecturer and writer. His articles and lectures on cosmology, which are often directed to the lay public, include such titles as "A Worm's-Eye View of the Mass Density of the Universe," and "On the Dynamics of Globular Clusters." He is among the authors of the *Scientific American* article, "Will the Universe Expand Forever?" (1976) and of articles in the *Astrophysical Journal*.

The most difficult questions which science has asked thus far deal with the very small and the very large, the very short and the very long. What are the ultimate building blocks of matter and what are the rules governing their behavior, rules which we know operate on a time scale of a trillionth of a trillionth (10^{-24}) of a second, and length scales smaller than a trillionth of a centimeter? At the other extreme, what is the geometry of space? How did the universe begin, and how will it end, and what, indeed, are the rules by which we might determine such things? We know the rules at this extreme operate on length scales of billions of light-years and on time scales of billions of years.

The goal of physics is to evolve one set of rules which governs the very small, the very large, and everything in between—a simple set of rules which, when properly applied and interpreted, predicts all physical phenomena. One "understands" a phenomenon when one understands how it follows from the mathematical rules. The goal of thus understanding all phenomena is still a distant one, but there have been giants in human history who have carried us a number of steps along the way. One of these giants was Albert Einstein, whose ideas about the nature of time and space and gravitation have taken us closer to understanding the nature of the universe on the largest scales than all those whose work preceded him, and it is very fitting in this centennial celebration of his birth to explore our current ideas about the structure of the universe and the data which have shaped them.

Cosmology as a science

Cosmology is the study of the large-scale properties of the universe, its structure, and its evolution. It is often claimed by its detractors that it is not in fact a scientific pursuit; one can do no experiments, and the cornerstone of the scientific method, *repeatability*, is inapplicable—we have only one universe to study, and we cannot perturb it (for which fact we should be profoundly grateful) and see how it reacts. For these reasons the philosophical approach to the subject is a little different from that used in experimental sciences. Our basic goal is to understand the universe as we see it, *applying the physical laws which we know govern smaller-scale phenomena.*

This approach inevitably contains a desperate hope—viz., that such an application holds. We have no assurance that the rules governing the evolution of the universe are the same as those which operate in the laboratory and in the solar system and in the Galaxy. On the other hand, neither (as of now) do we have any evidence to the contrary. It would seem that our only hope of understanding, in the scientific sense, is to follow this path. One day it may become painfully clear that our hope has failed. If that happens, I think our chances of understanding disappear. Let us take this approach and see where it has led.

The fundamental data

The three pieces of data on which our current ideas of the structure of the universe rest are very simple. I shall state them here, and the rest of this article will mostly serve to expand on them and explore their consequences.
1. The sky at night is dark.
2. The universe looks pretty much the same in all directions.
3. The universe is expanding, in the sense that distant galaxies are receding from us.

The Olbers paradox

The first of these phenomena has, of course, been evident to human observers for a long time. It was long ago realized, by de Cheseaux and later by Wilhelm Olbers (though the situation is usually called "Olbers' paradox"), that the classical idea that the universe is infinite and unchanging is inconsistent with such a fact. A very simple geometrical argument shows that if the stars and galaxies stretch out in unchanging numbers to infinity, the sky should be as bright as the surface of a typical star, for the stars would *eventually* overlap one another. A "typical" star is like the Sun, and it is quite clear that the night sky is not as bright as the surface of the Sun. Thus, either the universe is not infinite, or it is not everywhere the same. Of course, if there were no star beyond some finite distance, there would be no problem. But there is another possibility. As light does not travel infinitely rapidly, it takes some time for it to reach us. This means that we see distant objects in the universe as they were long ago, not as they are now. Thus, if there were no stars *before* some time, that would do as well as if there were no stars *beyond* some distance. We will see that this is almost certainly a major part of the resolution of Olbers' paradox.

Isotropy and the cosmological principle

Before discussing the very important data regarding the seeming sameness of the universe in different directions, let us review briefly our understanding of the various kinds of structure we see in the universe around us.

The Earth and other planets circle the Sun, a typical dwarf star in the

Figure 1. A nearby galaxy (number 7331 in the *New General Catalogue*) very much like our own, about fifty million light-years distant. Recent work has shown that much of the matter in systems like this one is in some unknown dark form distributed around the luminous body of the galaxy.

Galaxy, which in turn is an assemblage of some 100 billion such stars. The Galaxy, a structure typical of many others, is about 100,000 light-years in diameter, and most of its stars are arranged in a thin circular disk about 2,000 light-years thick. (A light-year, of course, is the distance light travels in one year in a vacuum—about six trillion miles, or about 60,000 times the mean distance from the Earth to the Sun. The *nearest* stars are some tens of light-years distant; the solar system is about ten *light-hours* across.) The nearest external galaxy of any significance is the great Andromeda spiral, about two million light-years away. It is a system similar to our own, but probably somewhat larger. It and our own Galaxy are the dominant members of a small assemblage of galaxies called the local group. Most galaxies are members of such groups and somewhat larger clusters. Galaxies and clusters and groups of galaxies are sometimes congregated loosely in giant structures which have come to be called superclusters and may be as large as 100 million light-years across. The most distant galaxies we have been able to study are, by comparison, nearly ten billion light-years away, some one hundred times the diameter of the superclusters. There does not appear to be any grouping on scales larger than superclusters. There are, out to a distance of ten billion light-years, about a billion large galaxies and

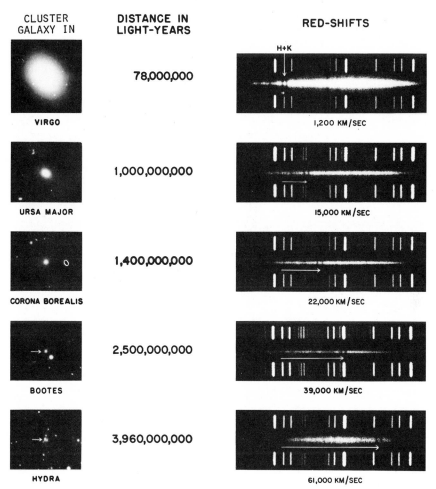

CLUSTER GALAXY IN	DISTANCE IN LIGHT-YEARS	RED-SHIFTS
VIRGO	78,000,000	H+K 1,200 KM/SEC
URSA MAJOR	1,000,000,000	15,000 KM/SEC
CORONA BOREALIS	1,400,000,000	22,000 KM/SEC
BOOTES	2,500,000,000	39,000 KM/SEC
HYDRA	3,960,000,000	61,000 KM/SEC

Figure 2. Five cluster galaxies in order of distance, showing the red shift of their spectra. The vertical bright lines on either side of the galaxy spectra are produced by a laboratory discharge lamp containing helium and are used as wavelength references. Blue light is recorded on the left, red on the right.

many more small ones like our Galaxy's own satellites, the Magellanic clouds.

Since the Galaxy (as we shall call the one in which we exist) is disk-shaped and contains not only stars but gas and dust, one cannot see beyond it easily if one looks along the plane of the disk; few external galaxies are seen in the direction of the Milky Way, which is the plane of the disk. This "zone of avoidance" is explained fully by the effects of gas, dust, and stars in the Galaxy. If one looks even a few degrees away from the plane and counts distant galaxies, or clusters, one finds very nearly the same number per square degree in any direction one looks. One sees local irregularities of course, since galaxies cluster, but the average number is the same in all directions. Some peculiar galaxies are strong emitters of radio noise. These radio sources have been counted by radio astronomers, and they, like the optical counts, show that the average numbers are independent of direction. Such a distribution, which does not depend on direction, is said to be isotropic.

The strongest evidence for this isotropy comes not from counts but from a remarkable probe of the distant past, the cosmic microwave background —probably the most significant single discovery in cosmology in all of history. In 1965 two Bell Telephone Laboratories scientists, Arno A. Penzias and Robert W. Wilson (who in 1978 received the Nobel Prize in physics for their work), discovered that there was a feeble radio signal which came into their antenna with the same strength no matter where it was pointed. Subsequent work over the past thirteen years has established that the radiation is characteristic of the thermal radiation emitted by a body at only three Celsius degrees above absolute zero, and that its intensity is the same in all directions to an accuracy of one part in a thousand. The only reasonable explanation for this radiation is that it is a relic of the very distant past in the universe, a time when the universe was dense and hot (we shall return to discuss conditions in the universe at such early times later). We believe that this radiation has been essentially undisturbed since the universe was only about one million years old, and its extreme smoothness indicates that the universe has, and has had, the same properties in all directions since then.

Consider for a moment the implications of all this. No matter how far we gaze, the universe looks the same in any direction we care to observe it. It thus appears that we, the observers, are at the *center* of the universe. This notion was, of course, current in ancient cosmologies, and we were only disabused of it painfully through the Copernican revolution. Are we then to accept it again? No. Another possibility is that there is no center—or, more accurately, *everywhere* is the center. Clearly, if the universe is homogeneous one can sit *anywhere* and see essentially the same things. The universe looks isotropic to anyone in it, anywhere, at any time.

This super-Copernican notion is called the "cosmological principle." The evidence for it is strong, but the principle is so far-reaching that we must be careful to verify the effects of assuming its truth each time we make a statement about the universe that we have deduced by using it.

The expansion

All of the foregoing accords very well with the ancient notions of an infinite, homogeneous, unchanging universe. We have seen, however, that such ideas must be wrong because of the Olbers paradox. That they *are* wrong was demonstrated graphically in the late 1920s when Edwin Hubble discovered (only shortly after it became clear that the other galaxies, which astronomers had studied for a century, were really distant external systems like our Galaxy) that the galaxies were moving away from us—the more rapidly, the more distant. This discovery was made using the Doppler shift, a very powerful astronomical technique. If the light of a galaxy or star is analyzed into its component pure colors using a spectrograph, it is found that in some colors—that is, at some wavelengths of light—there is very little energy. These dark spectral lines are caused by the characteristic absorption of certain atoms in the atmosphere of the stars in the Galaxy, primarily those of the abundant elements hydrogen, iron, calcium, sodium, and magnesium. When Hubble obtained spectra of galaxies, he found that these lines were present, but that they did not occur at the same wavelengths as lines in a laboratory source; instead, they were all shifted to longer wavelengths—the red. For the same reason that a whistle on a train appears higher-pitched when approaching and lower when receding, as compared with the pitch one hears when the train is at rest, frequencies and wavelengths of light shift to higher frequencies and shorter wavelengths (blue shift) when an object is approaching an observer and to lower frequencies and longer wavelengths (red shift) when receding. By measuring this Doppler shift, the velocity of recession or approach can be determined with high accuracy.

In this way, Hubble found the law which bears his name: namely that the velocity of recession is in direct proportion to the distance. We can write

$$\text{velocity} = H_0 \times \text{distance}.$$

The number H_0 is called "Hubble's constant." It has a simple geometrical significance which can be seen by considering a mundane example.

Suppose a group of people set out at a given time from a single place. All travel in straight lines at constant speeds, but not all move at the same speed. It is clear that at any given time later the fastest travelers have gone the farthest, and that if one measures the distance one finds that it is in direct proportion to the speed, or vice versa. If one looks at the travelers at time T hours after all left, one finds the relation

$$\text{velocity} = 1/T \times \text{distance};$$

if after two hours a traveler is found ten miles away, he must be traveling five miles per hour. The Hubble constant for this case is simply the reciprocal of the time since everybody started out.

Before we consider the implications of this simple analogy to the universe, let us ask an obvious question. Since expansion clearly demonstrates that the universe is not static, how can a changing, evolving universe satisfy the cosmological principle?

Consider again our example, but this time let the travelers be in spaceships in empty space, going in all directions. To the observer in a ship which never went anywhere, the others seem to be receding from him in the way discussed above. But to an observer in another ship which *did* go, the picture is precisely the same. Relative to him, faster ships recede in the direction *away* from home; slower ships recede from him in the direction

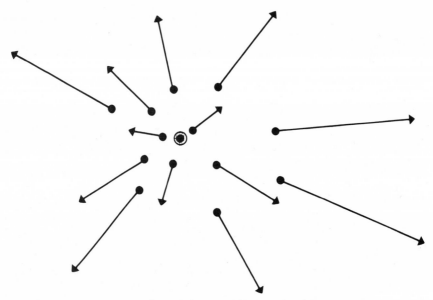

Figure 3. The expansion schematically illustrated. The lengths of the arrows represent expansion speeds, which increase in direct proportion to their distance from the center.

toward home. If our observer travels five miles per hour, a ship traveling six miles per hour is one mile distant after an hour; one traveling four miles per hour is one mile distant in the other direction after an hour; each has a speed of recession of one mile per hour relative to him.

The remarkable thing is that, if there is no marker for "home," it is impossible to tell which ships are traveling and which one is at rest. Einstein's special theory assures us that all motion is relative, so any observer on any ship can blithely assume that it is he who is in the privileged position of never having left home, and no one can ever produce any evidence to the contrary.

Hubble expansion is thus consistent with the cosmological principle—and, remarkably, it is the *only* motion which is so. An often used illustration is the balloon analogy—a two-dimensional universe. Imagine galaxies painted on a balloon which is being inflated slowly. To an observer on any one galaxy, the others seem to be expanding away from him as indicated by Hubble's law, and no one is in any way special.

Let us return for a moment to Hubble's constant. If the universe were like our analogy, all the galaxies would have been piled on top of one another at exactly one time in the past, and the time since that incredibly messy state would be what is measured by the Hubble constant. In practice the Hubble constant is difficult to measure precisely. Velocities from red shifts can be determined to high accuracy, but one must also know distances to individual galaxies in order to determine Hubble's constant. Distances

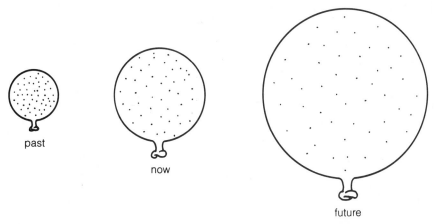

past

now

future

Figure 4. A balloon being inflated, with painted dots representing the galaxies, is a two-dimensional model for an expanding universe. To any dot, its neighbors recede from it with a Hubble expansion law.

are notoriously difficult to measure in astronomy, and the Hubble constant is therefore uncertain by perhaps as much as 20 percent to 30 percent. The best estimate is a number which corresponds to an "exodus from home" about sixteen billion or seventeen billion years ago. Note that the universe may be different from our analogy in one very important respect: the expansion might be slowing down or speeding up, and the time when everything was all piled up may not be exactly the Hubble time. Indeed, if the expansion accelerates with time in a suitable manner, that pile may never have existed at all.

The shape of space

The cosmological principle implies that we cannot tell one place in the universe from another. We must not, of course, take that too literally. There is (presumably—but see the remarks at the very end) only one Hoboken, New Jersey, only one Earth, and our Galaxy is probably not *exactly* like any other; but if we look at a large enough volume, a cube 100 million light-years or so on a side, any such cube will look pretty much like any other.

How is that centerless, featureless space arranged? That this is not a nonsensical question can be seen by restricting for a moment our perceptions to two dimensions only. Some hundreds of years ago, a controversy raged as to the shape of the surface of the Earth, a two-dimensional "space." Round or flat? If one inhabits a plane, one cannot tell by any geometric measurement where one is; likewise, if one inhabits the surface of a sphere, one cannot tell any place from any other. Both these two-dimensional figures satisfy the cosmological principle in two dimensions. In fact, our balloon with galaxies sprinkled uniformly over its surface is an *expanding* two-dimensional universe satisfying the cosmological principle. The global properties of the two figures are, however, very different. The sphere is finite, the plane infinite. If one travels far enough on the sphere, one returns to the place one started. How can one tell what kind of surface one lives on? The simplest way, supposing one cannot go far enough to circumnavigate (and circumnavigation can be heartbreaking inasmuch as one does not know a priori how big the sphere is; the starting place—which you better have marked—might always be just a little farther on), is to measure the circumference of circles. On the plane, the circumference of a circle is always 2π times the radius. On a sphere, very small circles have this property, but bigger ones clearly have circumferences which are smaller than this by an amount which grows larger as one draws bigger and bigger circles (remember that the "radius" is also measured along the sphere). At the equator (if one begins at either pole), the ratio is only four, instead of 6.28. Beyond the equator, the circumference begins to *decrease*, and it is *zero* at the opposite pole.

It happens that there is another sort of surface which is centerless, a construction called a pseudosphere. Any small place of a pseudosphere looks like a saddle, and it is clear that in this case the circumference of circles must be *bigger* than 2π times their radius, since one goes up hill and down dale to get around the circle. These three kinds of space—sphere, plane, and pseudosphere—are the *only* kinds of homogeneous spaces. The sphere is finite and closed: the distance between any two points measured along the surface is finite, and it has finite area. Both the plane and the pseudosphere are infinite.

What has all this to do with the three-dimensional universe? Mathematicians have known for a long time that these three kinds of geometry are the only possible kinds corresponding to homogeneous space in *any number* of dimensions. It is not easy to visualize the curvature of a three-dimensional space because we are three-dimensional creatures; the curvature of a sphere would be equally difficult to envisage to a two-dimensional being who had no notion of "thickness." He could nevertheless describe the sphere mathematically and even prove he lived on one by performing geometrical measurements.

Thus, space may be spherical, flat, or pseudospherical (also called hyperbolic, which is easier to say and shorter to write), and we can, in principle, tell which it is, though we are by no means yet able to do the necessary measurements. If it is spherical, it has finite volume and is said to be closed. Traveling in a straight line will eventually bring one back to one's starting place. Flat and hyperbolic space, barring some geometers' nightmarish variations which in any case violate the cosmological principle, are infinite and open. One of the pressing questions of cosmological inquiry is, then, to find out what kind of geometry the universe has: what is the shape of space?

We must inject a tiny note of caution before proceeding. It is the rigid

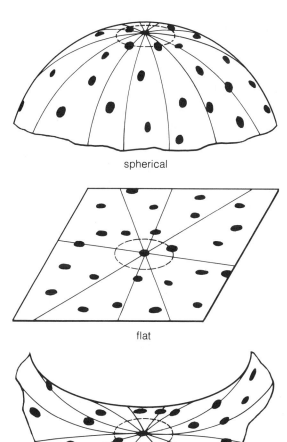

spherical

flat

hyperbolic

Figure 5. There are only three possible "shapes" for a universe which satisfy the cosmological principle. These are illustrated here in their two-dimensional analogues. An observer can in principle tell which sort he is living on by measuring the circumferences of circles (or by studying triangles or parallel lines).

application of the cosmological principle which has reduced the bewildering infinity of possible geometries to only three, and it is still possible that the cosmological principle is not strictly true—more on this point later.

Dynamics—the effects of gravitation

The cosmological principle has enabled us to discuss the geometry of space very simply, but there is still a question open, a question posed by the expansion. How does the universe behave with *time*? It is at this point that our hope of applying laboratory physics to the universe is most likely to meet with difficulty. The problem is to understand the forces which govern the behavior of the expansion. Newton's universal law of gravitation and

Einstein's beautiful extension of it, the general theory of relativity, state that there is attraction between all massive bodies. Both these theories, as well as many other gravitation theories, possess a property contained in a statement called "Birkhoff's theorem," which says that in a system isotropic about any given point—such as the universe is about us, or anyone else— the gravitational forces inside any sphere centered on that point depend only on the mass *inside* the sphere. That means that if we wish to understand the behavior of, say, the galaxies within 100 million light-years of here, we can forget about the galaxies farther away.

This simplifies the situation enormously, because it is clear what happens to the expanding galaxies at the edge of such a sphere: they are attracted by *all* the galaxies inside, and hence they are *slowed down* by gravity.

The situation for such a galaxy is exactly analogous to a ball thrown up from the Earth's surface. If we throw a ball, we know that it will rise for a while, just as the galaxies are receding from us now, but will eventually be slowed to a stop, and then will fall back. If, however, we persuade NASA to toss the ball, it can be thrown hard enough so that it will escape the gravitational field of the Earth and, finally, travel at still considerable and essentially unchanging speed very far away, where the Earth's gravity is negligible. If we reduce the speed with which the ball is thrown very carefully, we will find a speed at which the ball will just escape. Any slower, and it will fall back after a very long time; any faster, and it will escape easily. This critical speed is called the "escape velocity" and is about 25,000 miles

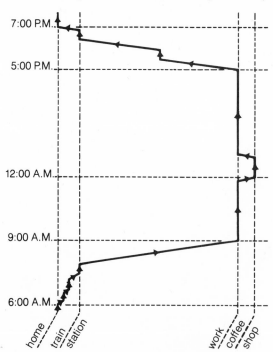

Figure 6. The space-time diagram for a day in the life of a typical commuter. Traffic is heavy on the way to the train station in the morning. The train in to work is an express; the one home makes one stop. Notice that high speeds are represented by lines which are nearly flat; vertical lines represent sitting in one place.

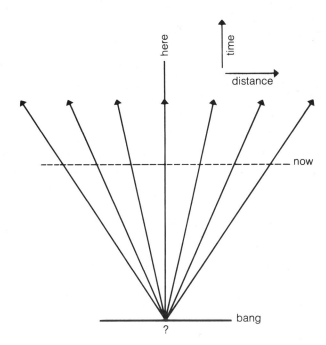

Figure 7. The space-time diagram for a universe with negligibly small mass density. There is no appreciable gravitational force, so the galaxy world lines are straight.

per hour for the Earth. It depends on the mass and size of the gravitating body and is very much smaller, for example, in the case of the Moon.

It is worth dispelling a small confusion shared by many at this point. We—you and I, dear reader—are not expanding, nor is the solar system, nor is the Galaxy. The chemical forces supporting organisms and planets, the gravitational forces in which the planets orbit the Sun and the Sun and other stars the Galaxy, are not changing, and so the sizes of these things are fixed. It is the *galaxies* which are separating, and even there, those in great clusters are in orbit about one another and are not separating; in this case, it is the clusters which are separating. Nothing pushes them; they are in free, coasting fall, like a thrown ball. What it is that threw them we will consider later.

Thus, we may understand the dynamics of the expansion. To the accuracy with which we know the Hubble constant, we know the speed of a galaxy at a given distance. What we do not know yet is what the escape velocity is at that distance. Knowing the escape velocity is equivalent to knowing the amount of *mass* within any given distance, and it is that which we do not know.

Consider, however, what would happen if we observed different hypothetical universes with different densities of mass. It is the mass *density*, the mass per unit volume, which is important, and the cosmological principle implies that it is the same everywhere at a given time, again if one averages over a large enough volume. The mass per unit volume must continually

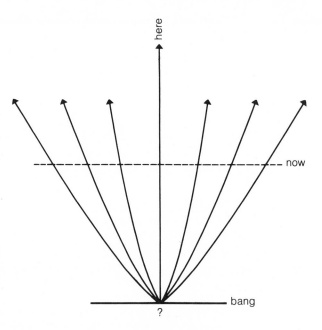

Figure 8. The space-time diagram for a universe with only a small mass density. Early in its history that mass is crowded together, and the gravitational effects cause the expansion to slow down; later, the gravity becomes negligible and the world lines are again nearly straight.

decrease with time, however, since a given number of galaxies occupied a smaller space in the past than they do today and will occupy a larger volume in the future because of the expansion.

A very useful visual tool for this discussion is the space-time diagram. Space-time diagrams are pictorial histories, with one space dimension to the left and right, and time going upward. A horizontal line in the diagram corresponds to the situation at a given *time*, a vertical line to a given *place*. A line following the location of a traveler is a generally upward line in the diagram and is called a *world line*. Figure 6 shows the space-time diagram with the world line of a typical commuter. Note that travel outward from the center (home) is represented by lines sloping away from the center; travel toward the center is represented by lines sloping toward the center. The more nearly horizontal the line, the higher the traveler's velocity. Uniform speeds are represented by straight lines.

Think first about a universe with a negligibly small amount of mass. There are no gravitational forces, and all galaxies travel at uniform speeds. The analogy we used when discussing the expansion is then quite exact; all the galaxies were piled up on each other exactly one Hubble time ago, about seventeen billion years, give or take a few billion. We may look at this pictorially in figure 7, a space-time diagram for this hypothetical universe. The universe is represented by the fan of straight galaxy world lines emanating from the great pileup one Hubble time ago. Since there is no gravity, there is no question of gravity stopping the expansion; it continues forever, unabated.

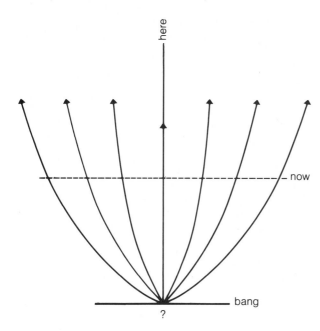

here

now

bang

?

Figure 9. The space-time diagram for a universe whose density is just the critical density. Gravity is *always* important and the expansion slows down continuously, though it never quite stops.

If we consider now a case with only a little mass, the effects are strong at the beginning, when the galaxies are close together, but they diminish later, and become negligible. This universe is expanding faster than its escape speed and also will expand forever.

If we now imagine a universe with exactly enough density so that it expands with just its escape velocity, we have the case in figure 9. It is always slowed down, and expands more and more slowly as time goes on, but never quite stops. It clearly also expands forever, but ever more slowly. A little more mass and the effect is dramatic. The expansion will stop sometime in the future, and the universe will *fall back together*, ending in a final catastrophe of unimaginable violence.

Which one of these last three cases is appropriate to the real universe we do not know, and it is the foremost question, along with that of the geometry, facing cosmology. Note that in all the cases considered here, the expansion is *always* slowed down by gravity; the universe was always expanding faster in the past than now. The effect is larger and larger as one imagines the matter density higher and higher. In figure 12, the effect is illustrated for a particular galaxy world line, and one sees, that, for a given (known) expansion speed now, real universes with mass are always *younger* than empty ones, and so the age of the universe is always *less* than the Hubble time.

Age? By this we mean the time since the initial pileup. All the cases we have discussed have it, and it *must* happen in any universe which is slowing down under the effect of gravitation. The starting event, in effect a mighty

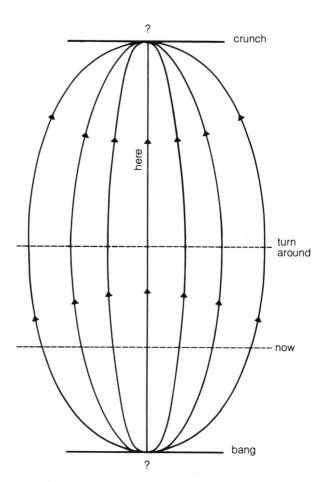

Figure 10. The space-time diagram for a universe with a mass density greater than the critical density. The expansion is halted by gravitation at some future time, and the universe collapses toward a final cataclysm.

explosion in which the expansion originated, is called the "big bang," and that it really occurred is attested to not only by the inconclusive speculations we have been indulging in, but by other evidence we shall discuss presently —most notably by the existence of the cosmic microwave background. Current thought maintains that this event was so violent that it is impossible to ask about *before*; time itself, and space, and matter, as well as the energy of expansion, were created in it. Thus, it is sensible to date the universe from it, and to speak of the *age* of the universe.

Let us discuss briefly the ever present question of whether we are on the right track. The question in this instance is whether we are using the correct gravitation theory—whether we *know* the correct gravitation theory. It is encouraging that the situation, again presented by the cosmological principle, is so simple that both Newtonian theory and the vastly more subtle Einstein theory give the same result, but it is just possible that we do not understand gravity on very large scales. Einstein himself proposed a modification of his theory which corresponds to space itself having a weak repulsive gravitational field, but this was done in order to make a static universe which would not collapse upon itself; he did not know of the expansion of the universe when he made the proposal! This "cosmological constant" is now generally discredited, but we have no real evidence that it does not exist. We have only some faith in the simplicity of nature, which may be unwarranted. This graphically illustrates the difficulty with cosmology as a science; there could be a force so weak that it only operates on the very largest scales, perhaps only after the universe has expanded to many times its present size, and we cannot even know of its existence, much less explain its properties. We generally assume, however, that the original, unadulterated form of the general theory is correct. This assumption is motivated as much by aesthetics as by the data, though such data as there are support the choice strongly. There is, however, a strong feeling that any theory so simple, so elegantly beautiful, so sensible, must be correct. There is no doubt that it must fail on very small scales because of quantum effects, which so far have eluded correct treatment, but there is no reason to suppose it does not correctly describe very large-scale phenomena.

The general theory makes a startling prediction concerning the connection between dynamics and geometry. It is a theory *about* dynamics and geometry, after all, and what it says is unambiguous. If the universe has so little mass density it will expand forever, it is open and hyperbolic and infinite. If it is so dense that it will end in a "big crunch," it is closed and spherical and finite. If it is delicately balanced between and just expanding at its escape velocity, space is open and flat and infinite. Thus, if we appeal to the general theory, our two big questions about the nature of the universe become one: open and unending, or closed and doomed?

Observational tests—an outline of methods

How does one attempt to decide the above question? The most direct way, one might think, would be somehow to measure the mass density in the universe in our immediate area over a volume large enough to constitute a fair sample of space. From the known expansion rate, one can calculate the *critical* density, that density which makes the observed expansion just at the escape velocity. If the measured density is bigger than the critical density, the expansion will stop, the universe will collapse, and the space is spherical and closed. If the density measured is smaller than the critical one, gravitation will be too weak to stop the expansion, and it will go on forever; space is infinite, open, and hyperbolic. If the density is just critical, space is infinite and flat, and still the expansion will continue forever (as there are always errors of measurement, one can never be *sure* the density is exactly critical; indeed, since Hubble's constant is imprecisely known, the critical density itself is not exactly known). We can only hope that the measure-

Figure 11. If the universe is closed, a galaxy at a given velocity is nearer and brighter than if the universe is open. World lines (1) and (2) are for a galaxy receding from us at the same velocity (and hence have the same distance) *now*. When the light we see now left them, (2) was closer in the closed case and is receding faster than (1). We must come still closer, to (3), to find a galaxy receding at the same velocity as (1).

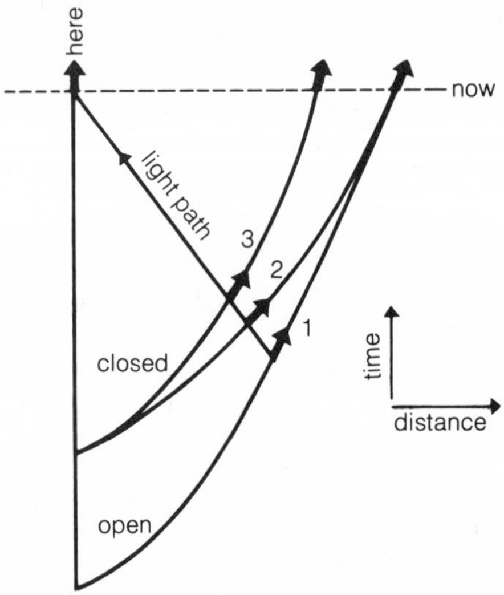

ments will give a density unambiguously either greater or smaller than the critical one.

Another way to proceed is to attempt to measure the rate at which the expansion is slowing down. This is not as absurd as it might seem, again because light does not travel with infinite rapidity. A galaxy five billion light-years away is seen as it was five billion years ago; in particular, it is seen traveling at the speed it had five billion years ago. Think for a moment about a galaxy which is a certain distance from us *now* (we cannot *see* it now, of course, because the light just leaving it will not reach us for a long time). Inasmuch as we know the expansion rate now, we know how fast the galaxy is receding now. The light we see from it, however, left a long time ago. Consider two hypothetical universes, one hardly decelerated at all and the other strongly so. In the second one—the dense, closed one—the galaxy was traveling much faster in the past, and in order that it be where it is now, it must have been closer to us at all times in the past than the galaxy in the universe which has experienced no deceleration, as an appeal to figure 11 shows. If we want to find a galaxy with the same velocity (red shift) in the dense universe as the galaxy in the low-density open one, we have to come even closer. Thus, a galaxy at a given red shift appears much closer and hence brighter in a closed universe than in an open one. The apparent brightness can be calculated for any red shift for any sort of hypothetical universe and the predictions compared with observations of real galaxies. This technique, the method of the Hubble diagram, is a classical way to decide what sort of universe we live in. In reality, its application is beset with great difficulty on many fronts, to which we shall return shortly.

A very direct test is to make use of the fact that highly decelerated, closed universes are younger (again, fig. 12) than open ones. If one can some-

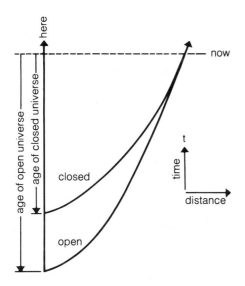

Figure 12. The world lines of galaxies curve more in closed universes than in open ones because of the larger mass density and hence gravitational forces in the closed ones. For a given expansion rate now, the universe is younger if it is closed than if it is open.

how measure the age of the universe and compare it with the Hubble time, one can decide what sort of universe we live in. It happens that ⅔ is the magic number. If the universe is older than ⅔ of the Hubble time (about eleven billion to twelve billion years), it is open; if younger, it is closed. The difficulty with this method is at once apparent. One can perhaps measure the ages of things in the universe—rocks, stars, radioactive elements, planets—but unless one knows when they were formed, one must add an unknown amount of time to get the age of the universe. Thus, one can prove that the universe is open by this technique, by finding something in it older than ⅔ the Hubble time, but never that it is closed unless one *knows* that the thing being dated was formed very early indeed, and one does not know that for any of the things currently considered.

There are also other indirect tests which we will discuss briefly, but these three are the important direct ones. It must be stressed that, because of the extremely shaky limb the cosmologist finds himself perched upon, it is not sufficient to obtain the answer from any one of these methods. Ideally, we must have answers from all three (answers which agree!), and from any indirect ones we can lay our hands on as well, before we count ourselves satisfied that we know what we are talking about.

The observational data—where do we start?

Let us discuss the three direct tests in the opposite order in which they were introduced. First, the ages. The Hubble time probably lies in the range of fifteen billion to nineteen billion years, with sixteen billion or seventeen billion the most likely values, but no one would be terribly surprised if it turned out as small as twelve billion or as large as, say, twenty billion years. The measurements are extremely difficult and rest upon a tedious step-by-step distance scale by which one has proceeded from the distances to the nearest stars, used them to obtain distances to brighter stars and star clusters, used these in turn to obtain distances to the nearest galaxies. Those nearby galaxies, however, are bound in the local group and are not taking part in the expansion relative to us, so one must make yet another step to more distant galaxies. One can, and does, make errors at each step in this process, and it is not surprising that the distances to galaxies, and hence the expansion rate and the Hubble time, are not known very accurately.

We must, therefore, compare measured ages with ⅔ of a number which we know very imprecisely. The measured ages are not much better. The two age-dating techniques which have been used for the universe involve the ages of certain radioactive elements, and the ages of very old stars. It is now thought that the chemical elements heavier than helium were all made by thermonuclear processes in stars. Some of the elements (like uranium and osmium) have radioactive isotopes which are very long-lived (several billion years) and have origins thought to be relatively well understood. These isotopes decay into other elements; in some cases one can measure the amounts of both *parent* radioactive and *daughter* decay product and, knowing the rate at which the daughter is produced, measure the age (*e.g.*, of a rock or a meteorite). The techniques for doing this are very difficult but relatively well developed and have been used to measure the ages of rocks on the Earth and Moon to quite phenomenal accuracy. The basic problem vis-à-vis the universe is that one does not know the *history* of element production in the Galaxy. When was the average atom of osmium or uranium *formed* in the fiery interior of some star? We don't know. Various guesses can be applied, and complex mathematical artifices raised upon them, but the answers are only as good as the guesses going in. The elements are probably between eight billion and eighteen billion years old, although some scientists say between twelve billion and eighteen billion years old. It is gratifying that the Hubble-time numbers and the ages are so consistent, but it is clearly impossible yet to say that the ages are greater than or smaller than ⅔ the Hubble time, though it *looks* as if greater might be the better bet. Two-thirds the Hubble time is unlikely to be bigger than thirteen billion years.

Another class of things which can be dated is stars. The oldest stars in our Galaxy, which are thought to have formed when the universe was less than one billion years old, are thought themselves to be about fourteen billion or fifteen billion years old. Again, this number is imprecisely known. It is unclear whether we understand fully the physics of the Sun even, and until we do, it may be a bit foolhardy to place too much confidence in our understanding of other stars. For what it is worth, the ages of these objects, plus a fraction of a billion years for their formation, would seem to be

Figure 13. The 200-inch (5-meter) Hale telescope at the Palomar Mountain Observatory. This instrument has been used for most of the cosmological measurements of distant galaxies to date.

greater than ⅔ of any likely value for the Hubble time; this would indicate again that the universe is open.

The most promising, and without a doubt the most frustrating, technique is to try to measure the expansion rate in the past via the Hubble diagram. The observations are enormously difficult. Red shifts must be obtained for galaxies which can scarcely be detected using the most modern electronic imaging devices, and observing conditions must be absolutely superb. The problem can be attacked only by the very largest telescopes. A great deal of time and effort at the 200-inch Hale telescope has been spent on the problem, with as yet rather uncertain results.

There are several difficulties, some in the observations, some in the interpretations. Since one measures the apparent brightness of the galaxy, and wishes to know how far away it is, the answer depends on how much energy the galaxy is emitting. If one thinks one is looking at a 100-watt light bulb and is really observing a flashlight bulb, one can make a very large error in the derived distance. Thus, one needs a set of "standard candles," galaxies one knows all have the same real brightness. Using them,

Figure 14. The central region of the great cluster of galaxies in Coma Berenices, located between Leo and Boötes in the northern hemisphere of the sky. This cluster is about 300 million light-years distant. The big galaxy in the middle is typical of the bright cluster galaxies used for the Hubble diagram.

one can measure distance just by measuring their apparent brightness. We are indeed fortunate that the very brightest galaxies in clusters seem to come in one "giant economy size" with a rather small total range in brightness. There is *some* variation from object to object, but if one averages over a suitable number of such galaxies, one should be able to obtain the answer.

The problems come from two sources. The fact that these bright galaxies are not *quite* all alike means that one must be very careful how one selects them. If one were to pick only the relatively faint members of the class nearby and only the brightest ones far away (an effect which one can see might, in fact, happen) one would obtain the wrong answer. This statistical question is as yet not well understood — rather, *how* to deal with it is not well understood. The second problem is even worse, and comes from the fact that a given galaxy does not, in all likelihood, remain at the same brightness for all time. It *evolves*, and since one observes distant galaxies as they were a very long time ago, one must understand this effect. If galaxies were brighter in the past, one would underestimate their distances and overestimate the deceleration and perhaps conclude wrongly that the universe is closed; if fainter, one could conclude the opposite.

Galaxies change in brightness because of two activities. First, the stars in them age and die. The full effect of this is complex but, as one might expect, the net effect is that the galaxy gets fainter as it ages. Second, big galaxies

Figure 15. A distant cluster in the constellation of Hydra, the largest constellation in the sky, some four billion light-years away. The limit set by current technology is about twice this distant.

exert a kind of frictional drag on their neighbors, causing them to spiral slowly into the big ones and amalgamate with them. Thus, big galaxies eat little ones and become brighter. The relative sizes of these effects are not, as of this writing, known with any accuracy. Different scientists obtain different *raw* results, before these corrections are applied, doubtless because of different statistical treatment of their (quite different) samples. The situation is depressingly unclear but will hopefully improve over the next few years with better data and better theoretical understanding.

By far the most decisive results, although the interpretation is by no means uncontroversial, come from direct attempts to measure the matter density in the universe. The mean averaged density required to close the universe (the critical density discussed before) is equivalent to only four hydrogen atoms per cubic meter. Typical densities on the Earth (*e.g.*, that of water) are a trillion trillion times bigger. Clearly one must try to measure this very low density by sensitive, indirect methods, and one must remember that we need to do the measurement over a large enough volume to ensure that we take a "fair sample" of the universe as a whole. It is this point which presents the greatest difficulty.

The most direct way to approach the problem is by means of a technique easy to do in astronomy: counting. If one could count the galaxies in some volume of space and could somehow *weigh* them (*i.e.*, measure their mass), one could find the density directly by dividing the total mass by the total volume. Finding the masses of galaxies is, in principle, not difficult. The disk galaxies, like our own, rotate; each star is in a very nearly circular orbit about the center of the galaxy, attracted to the center by the masses of all the stars inside. By measuring the difference in red shift from one side to the other, the velocity of rotation can be deduced (unless the galaxy is exactly face-on to us in the sky). From this rotation velocity one can deduce the mass, just as one can (and does) deduce the mass of the Sun by knowing the velocity of the Earth in its orbit.

It is found, not surprisingly, that bright galaxies are more massive than faint ones, and indeed that the ratio of mass to total light output is about the same from galaxy to galaxy. That fact suggests that one handle the problem a little differently: the amount of light produced in a volume of space is totaled up by measuring the brightnesses of all the galaxies therein and divided by the volume to get a luminosity density, a density of total light output. The luminosity density is then multiplied by the "universal" mass-to-light ratio to get the mass density. Since galaxies are made of stars, the convenient units to measure the mass-to-light ratio (usually just called M/L) is in solar units; if a galaxy were made of stars all exactly like the Sun and had no other mass, its M/L would be one. The values of M/L obtained from galaxies are typically about ten, which corresponds to the fact that most of the mass of a galaxy is in stars a little less massive but very much fainter than the Sun.

The mass density one obtains for the universe with this result is tiny—a factor of 200 smaller than the critical density. That would suggest that the universe is open indeed, and by a wide margin. Caution is in order, however. One can also measure the masses of clusters of galaxies by techniques not unlike those used for measuring the masses of galaxies, and one finds values of M/L about ten times larger, near one hundred. There is now evidence from many other sources that galaxies possess—associated with them but outside their main bodies which produce most of their light—dark matter which is about ten times as massive as the luminous stars in the galaxies. The evidence is also fairly strong that such matter is *always* about ten times the visible mass. If we include this "hidden" dark matter, the density estimate is increased by a factor of ten but is still only $\frac{1}{20}$ of the critical density.

Perhaps the outstanding question in extragalactic astronomy today is: what is the dark matter? It is disturbing, to say the least, for 90 percent of the mass of the universe to be in some completely unknown form, its existence made evident only by its gravitation. Guesses run from the prosaic low-mass dwarf stars (the most likely, in the author's estimation) to black holes made in the big bang, to some new unknown kind of stable, electrically neutral elementary particle. But they are only guesses. It is my guess that we will not know the answer any time soon.

For the question at hand, however, the nature of the "stuff" is immaterial. We need only know how much of it there is, and that seems fairly well determined. There are uncertainties, to be sure, but even allowing for them, the answer seems to be that the total density is between $\frac{1}{40}$ and $\frac{1}{10}$ the critical density. The conclusion, if we take this answer at face value, is that the universe is open, infinite, and will expand forever.

This technique has been applied from small groups to (with some modification) the superclusters of which the local group is a member, and to many large external clusters, all with consistent conclusions. The one nagging doubt is that there may be mass hidden *between* the clusters, but there are persuasive theoretical arguments that this should not be so. Basically, the idea is that the clusters have grown as the universe expands, and any other matter would have been pulled into them just as the galaxies have been.

A beautiful confirmation of these results comes from another distant corner in the astronomical data closet. We discussed in the beginning the cosmic microwave radiation, which is universally believed to be a relic of a time when the universe was very dense and very hot, a direct leftover of the big bang. One calculates that the universe was *so* hot, in fact, that nuclei could collide with enough energy to induce nuclear reactions. It is thought that most of the helium in the universe today was made of protons and neutrons in the universe only a couple of minutes after the big bang, when the temperature was about 100 million degrees. The helium can be accounted for in no other way, and the amount agrees very well with the calculated production. Traces of other elements are produced, most notably deuterium, the heavy isotope of the abundant element hydrogen. If the universe is closed, the matter density during those early epochs was higher than if the universe is open, and the result is that nearly all of the deuterium is destroyed only shortly after it is made. If the universe is open, some — although still only a very small amount — survives. The abundance of deuterium which presently exists in interstellar space has been measured recently by the Copernicus satellite and agrees well with the prediction for a universe whose density is about $\frac{1}{20}$ of the critical density. This same conclusion was reached, remember, from gravitational measurements of the total density.

Not everyone is willing to believe that these results can be taken at face value. Indeed, loopholes can be found individually in all the arguments, but it is clear that the simplest interpretation of the results is that the universe is open by a wide margin, is infinite, and will expand forever.

Prognosis for the future — and a dilemma or two

If we are willing to accept the results presented above, we still are in the uncomfortable position of having only part of a big puzzle put together. The other tests, the age and the deceleration, have yet to yield conclusive results, and they really must before we are really sure. Technology is rapidly coming to our rescue. Solid-state, televisionlike detectors called CCDs will make our present telescopes much more powerful instruments for working on faint galaxies. Development of detectors for the infrared and radio has made it possible to obtain much better distances for galaxies than ever before and will very likely result in a much more accurate determination of the Hubble time. Finally, the Space Telescope, when it is launched in late 1983, will allow more detailed study of distant galaxies than would ever be possible from the ground. These developments and ongoing advances in theoretical understanding bid to make the next ten or twenty years in cosmology exciting indeed.

What if our preliminary conclusions are verified by these studies? The universe is *infinite* and will exist for an *infinitely* long time. The implications of infinity are staggering and should give us a little pause. We see, even in the microwave background, only a finite part of the universe. Yet, we are claiming that the infinitely big remainder of the universe is like our little neighborhood—such is the thrust of the cosmological principle. Perhaps we should rethink that philosophical crutch. There are amusing aspects of infinite universes—we think of ourselves as unique, but in an infinite universe one can argue that nothing is unique, because nature has probably tried all experiments an infinite number of times. There is a planet somewhere *exactly* like Earth, with exactly the same people doing exactly the same things. There is also a planet exactly like this one except that everyone (or someone) wore a yellow shirt this morning instead of a white one, or any other variation one might think of. We will almost certainly never know of any of these worlds, but they exist.

It has often been claimed that a universe which lasts for an infinitely long time inevitably suffers a "heat death"—that is, all the sources of energy get used up. Even the feeblest, faintest stars exhaust their stores of nuclear fuel, and eventually, after perhaps thousands of billions of years, everything is dark and cold and dead, as the expansion carries the galaxies farther and farther apart in the cold void. Some find the fiery end of the closed universe in 50 billion or 100 billion years' time more satisfactory, but recently there has appeared a bright spark in the darkness at the cold end of the open, ever-expanding universe. Freeman Dyson, of the Institute for Advanced Study, has pointed out that, as the universe gets colder, it can be easier, at least for a properly designed machine, to think. If one is willing to allow a thinking machine (we don't have them yet, of course, but we have a very long time to develop them) to think more and more slowly as the universe expands, it can take less and less energy per thought, and can think an infinite number of thoughts and "live" forever with only a finite energy supply. "Forever" is also an idea which is fraught with problems. Our physical understanding now would suggest that *eventually* (the times are so long as not to be easily expressible, much less conceivable), everything material will have spontaneously evaporated into electromagnetic radiation. Whether the Dyson denizens of the universe at that advanced age will be able to cope, or will even care to, is something only they will know.

The Limits of Space and Time

Stephen W. Hawking

A theoretical physicist of recognized brilliance, Stephen W. Hawking is one of the world's foremost theorists on the subject of black holes. Among other findings, he has shown that a region of space-time called a black hole stabilizes rapidly, and that its surface can never decrease. He and Roger Penrose of the University of Cambridge have developed global techniques to show that "if general relativity [is] correct, and if certain physically reasonable conditions [are] satisfied, space-time singularities are inevitable in the gravitational collapse of a star and at the beginning of the expansion of the universe."

Professor Hawking, who graduated from University College, Oxford, with first class honors in 1962, when he was twenty, received his Ph.D. in 1966 from Cambridge, and served as a member of the graduate staff at the Institute of Theoretical Astronomy and in the Department of Applied Mathematics and Theoretical Physics, both at Cambridge, before becoming professor of gravitational physics there in 1977.

Among his numerous awards have been the Eddington Medal of the Royal Astronomical Society (1975), the Dannie Heinemann Prize for Mathematical Physics of the American Physical Society and the American Institute of Physics, the William Hopkins Prize of the Cambridge Philosophical Society, the Maxwell Medal and Prize of the Institute of Physics, the Hughes Medal of the Royal Society (1976), the Albert Einstein Award of the Lewis and Rosa Strauss Memorial Fund (1977), and the Albert Einstein Medal, Bern, Switzerland (1979). He was elected a fellow of the Royal Society in 1974.

Among his publications is *The Large Scale Structure of Space-Time* which he wrote with G. F. R. Ellis (1973).

Most early world pictures seem to have the common feature that man appeared or was created at some finite (and generally not very distant) time in the past. This was probably because it must have been apparent even in primitive societies that man was progressing both culturally and technologically. On the other hand, man would not have noticed much evolution in the physical surroundings such as mountains and rivers or in the heavenly bodies which were therefore regarded as essentially unchanging in time. In some cases the geographical and celestial surroundings were thought to have existed forever as an empty landscape into which life was introduced at some definite epoch, and in other cases they were believed to have been created at the same time as life itself. In nearly all cases, though, time was regarded as an entity which was independent of the physical universe and which extended infinitely both in the past and in the future.

The early cosmologies were of finite extent in space. In the Ptolemaic system, for example, the Earth was placed at the center and surrounded by a number of spheres which bore the Sun, the Moon, and the planets. The outermost sphere carried the fixed stars. What, if anything, was outside this sphere was never very clear, but it seemed that it was not a part of the observable universe as far as human beings were concerned. This model continued in general favor until the seventeenth century, when observations made by Galileo caused it to be replaced by the Copernican theory in which the Earth and the planets all revolved around the Sun. That theory was given a firm mathematical basis by Newton's law of gravitation. This postulated the existence of a space of infinite extent.

Newton and others realized that the so-called fixed stars must be other bodies like our Sun scattered throughout this infinite space. This raised a problem: according to Newton's theory of gravity, these bodies should attract each other and start falling toward each other. Yet it was still believed that the distribution of stars was unchanging with time. Newton attempted to resolve this paradox by postulating that there was an infinite number of stars distributed more or less uniformly throughout infinite space. If this were the case, he argued, the net gravitational force on any star would be zero and the stars could not fall together because there would be no preferred point for them to fall to. In fact, we now know that he was wrong: in an infinite distribution of stars that was initially at rest, each star would start to approach its neighbors even though there was not any preferred point to which they would all fall. Another attempt to maintain a static universe was the suggestion that maybe Newton's law of gravitation was modified at large distances to make it repulsive rather than attractive. Such a modification could indeed provide a static cosmological model, but it would be unstable: the least disturbance would cause it to collapse or to expand forever.

Despite these difficulties it was generally accepted that the universe was infinite in time and space. The question was extensively discussed by Kant in his monumental *Critique of Pure Reason** published in 1781. His arguments and reasoning are rather obscure (at least to me) but his final conclusion was that the universe could not have any limits in space or time. Interestingly enough, he discussed only the possibility that the universe had a beginning; he never considered that it might have an end. His argument was, basically, that if the universe had a beginning, there must have been an infinity of time before the beginning during which nothing happened. Why then should the universe have come into existence at a particular time? Similarly, if the universe were limited in spatial extent, it would be surrounded by an infinite region of empty space, which he considered to be absurd.

Neither Kant nor anyone else seems to have considered the possibility that the universe might not be static, but might be evolving in time. However, during the early 1920s Vesto Slipher and Edwin Hubble made a number of very important astronomical observations which showed that certain fuzzy objects which had been called nebulae and which were thought to be clouds of gas, were in fact systems composed of millions of stars at a great distance from us. These objects, which were called galaxies, exhibited the curious property that the light from them was systematically shifted toward the red or long wavelength end of the spectrum compared to the light from similar elements on Earth. The red shift was greater the further the galaxy was from us. Although there have been a number of attempts to account for the red shift in terms of "tired light" or other mechanisms in a static universe, the only workable explanation seems to be that other galaxies are moving away from ours with a velocity proportional to their distance from us. Such a motion would produce a red shift by the Doppler effect, which one can experience by listening to a car as it passes on a highway: when the car is approaching the engine note is raised, but when the car has passed the note is lowered.

One might think that if all the galaxies were moving away from us, this would imply that we were at the center of the universe, a position that we have been too modest to claim since the time of Copernicus. However, this is not the case and can be seen by the following analogy. Imagine a balloon with a number of spots painted on it. As the balloon is inflated the spots will

* *GBWW*, Vol. 42.

move further apart, but no spot will be in a preferred position. The case with the universe is similar: it can be expanding uniformly without any galaxy having a privileged position.

The first cosmological model to describe a universe that was the same at all points in space but evolving in time was constructed by the Soviet physicist Alexander Friedmann in 1922. He used Einstein's recently discovered general theory of relativity, but very similar models are possible using the Newtonian theory of gravity, only no one had thought of looking for them because everyone believed that the universe was static. Friedmann's model was spatially uniform and isotropic, *i.e.*, at a given time it looked the same at all points in space and in all directions. When it was formulated there was little observational evidence to show that the "real" universe possessed either of these properties; they were merely assumed for convenience. However, observations of the microwave background radiation discovered by the radio astronomers Arno Penzias and Robert Wilson in 1965 have indicated that the radiation is isotropic to a high degree of accuracy, indicating that the other galaxies in the universe must be distributed more or less isotropically about us. Since we are now too humble to believe that we occupy a special position in the universe, this is taken to imply that the distribution of matter is nearly isotropic about any point. This in turn implies that the universe is nearly uniform in space at the present time, at least on scales large compared with galaxies.

As one went back in time in the Friedmann model, the galaxies would have been nearer together and the density of matter in the universe would have been higher. About ten billion years ago there would have been a state of infinite density when all the particles were on top of each other. Many people found this "singularity" very distasteful because it seemed to imply that the universe had a beginning. There were several attempts to avoid this conclusion.

One idea, proposed in 1948 by Hermann Bondi, Thomas Gold, and Fred Hoyle in Great Britain, was that the universe was in a "steady state" and presented the same general appearance at all times as well as at all points in space. As the galaxies receded from each other, new matter was continually created in between to maintain the average density of the universe at a constant value. This theory was aesthetically very attractive and had the great merit of making definite testable predictions. Unfortunately, these predictions were inconsistent with observations of radio sources and of the microwave background radiation, so the theory had to be abandoned.

Another attempt to avoid singularities was the suggestion that maybe they were simply a consequence of the high degree of symmetry of the Friedmann models. The assumption of isotropy implied that the relative motion of any pair of particles had to be directed along the line joining them, while the assumption of spatial uniformity meant that the pressure could not have any effect. It was therefore not surprising that the trajectories of all particles should intersect each other at some instant of time.

However, in a realistic model one might expect random velocities and irregularities. As one goes back in time using the model, these would grow large and might prevent the occurrence of a singularity of infinite density, and might instead produce a "bounce" connecting the present expanding phase of the universe to a previous contracting one.

In 1963 two Soviet physicists, E. M. Lifshitz and I. M. Khalatnikov, claimed that according to general relativity, singularities would not occur in cosmological models that were fully general and did not have any exact symmetries. They based this on an analysis of a solution of Einstein's field equations of general relativity. The solution contained a singularity, but it obeyed a constraint that would not be satisfied in a general solution. The Soviets subsequently realized that there was a more general class of solutions with singularities which did not satisfy the constraint. They concluded therefore, that singularities *could* occur in general relativistic cosmological models.

Their methods, however, did not allow them to determine whether singularities necessarily *would* occur. This was done between 1965 and 1970 by Roger Penrose and the author using a rather different approach. They showed that a singularity was inevitable if general relativity was correct, if matter satisfied certain reasonable conditions such as positive density and pressure, and if there was more than a certain critical amount of matter in the universe. Observations of microwave background radiation mentioned above indicate that this last condition is satisfied. Thus, it seems that the universe ought to have an initial singularity, a "big bang," if the general theory of relativity is correct.

What is the evidence for general relativity? The first confirmation came in 1919 when an expedition led by the British astronomer Sir Arthur Eddington measured the apparent positions of stars nearly in line with the Sun during an eclipse. The expedition found that the light from the stars was deflected through a small angle by the gravitational field of the Sun, exactly as Einstein had predicted. In more recent years, the use of spacecraft, radar, and laser ranging have enabled us to verify the theory to a high degree of accuracy in the solar system. We also have direct observational evidence from the microwave background radiation about conditions in the universe at earlier times. The spectrum of the radiation indicates that the universe must have been much hotter and denser in the past and must have been composed of an almost featureless plasma of hot gas and radiation.

The picture we now have is that the universe began with a singularity, the big bang, of infinite density and temperature, about ten billion years ago. As the universe expanded, it would have cooled. After about a hundred seconds the temperature would have dropped to a billion degrees at which point nuclear reactions would have begun to convert some of the original hydrogen into deuterium (heavy hydrogen) and helium. The nuclear reactions would have continued for a few hours, after which about a quarter of the matter in the universe would have been helium and the rest hydrogen, apart from a small amount of deuterium. These abundances of helium and deuterium are more or less what we observe today, and it is very difficult to account for them in any other way.

The evidence therefore strongly suggests that the universe had a singular origin about ten billion years ago. But what of Kant's objection to a beginning in time? What happened before the big bang? One answer that can be given is that in general relativity, unlike earlier theories, space and time are not independent of the matter in the universe. It was Einstein's greatest stroke of genius to realize that they could be combined into a four-dimensional curved space. It is impossible (even for those who work in the subject) to visualize a four-dimensional curved space, but one can understand some of its properties by thinking of a two-dimensional curved space such as the Earth's surface. On the Earth, the nearest things to straight lines are so-called great circles which provide the shortest routes between pairs of points. Lines with this minimizing property in a curved space are called geodesics. According to general relativity, bodies like the Earth or Sun, which are acted upon only by gravity, move on geodesics in a four-dimensional space whose curvature is determined by the distribution of matter in the universe. This viewpoint transforms space-time from a fixed background to a dynamical entity on the same footing as other physical fields like the electromagnetic field. Because it is just a physical field, it is possible for space-time to become infinite in some sense, or to be undefined at some point. On this view the question of what happened before the big bang would have no operational meaning because there would be no way that one could communicate with events before the big bang. They would not be part of the observable universe.

Although one might be reasonably happy with the idea that time had a beginning ten billion years ago, because, after all, we were not around then, it is a lot more disturbing to think that time might have an end in the future. Yet this also is allowed by general relativity, and indeed it is predicted under certain conditions. The expansion of the universe is being slowed down all the time by the mutual gravitational attraction between the various galaxies. If the attraction is sufficiently strong, it will eventually stop the expansion and turn it into a contraction leading to another singularity. This will indeed be an end of time with a vengeance: everything will become extremely hot and will be crushed out of existence. Fortunately, this will not happen for at least twenty billion years or so. An interesting consequence of general relativity is that if the universe is going to recollapse eventually, then space is finite but unbounded, like the surface of an orange. On the other hand, the universe may be expanding so fast that it never stops but just carries on forever, with the galaxies getting further and further apart. In this case space would be infinite.

There are two possible ways to determine whether our universe is going to collapse again or whether it will expand forever. One method is to measure the rate at which the expansion is slowing down by observing how the red shift of galaxies increases with their distance from us. Unfortunately, the only way we have of determining the distance of faraway galaxies is their apparent brightness. This would be a reliable measure if the galaxies all had the same intrinsic luminosity. However, the finite speed of light means that we are observing distant galaxies at earlier epochs in the universe when they were probably brighter. Because we are not sure how much to allow for the evolution of the luminosities of galaxies, this method of determining whether or not the universe will recollapse has produced indeterminate results.

The other possible way to tell whether the universe is going to recollapse is to see if the density of matter is high enough to slow down and stop the present rate of expansion. In fact, if we add up the densities of all the forms of matter in the universe that we have detected, it falls short of this critical density by a factor of about ten. There may be other forms of matter that we have not been able to find, however. Possible examples include hot, ionized intergalactic gas, stars of very low mass and luminosity, and black holes. Thus, although it seems that the universe should expand forever, we cannot be quite sure.

Even if the universe as a whole does not recollapse, it seems certain that isolated regions of it, such as stars or galactic nuclei, will do so. A normal star supports itself against its own gravity by thermal pressure generated by burning hydrogen into helium. Eventually it will exhaust its nuclear fuel and will begin to contract. If it has a fairly low mass, it can settle down to be a white dwarf (radius, a few thousand miles) or a neutron star (radius, twenty miles) in which gravity is balanced by pressure created by electrons or neutrons respectively. However, this pressure is insufficient to support a cold body of more than about one and a half times the mass of the Sun. A star of more than this mass might explode as a supernova before it had used up all its nuclear fuel, but, in some cases at least, it seems that it will just collapse to a point—a singularity of infinite density. After the star has shrunk below a certain critical radius, its gravitational field will become so strong that it will drag back any further light emitted by the star and prevent it from escaping to an outside observer. According to the theory of relativity, nothing can travel faster than light. Thus, if light cannot get out, nothing else can either. One has then a region of space-time from which it is not possible to escape to infinity. This is called a black hole.

An observer who remains outside the black hole will never see or know about the singularity. The situation is very different from that of someone unfortunate or foolhardy enough to fall into a black hole. There are some solutions of the field equations of general relativity in which it is possible to avoid the singularity and pass through a "wormhole" into another region of the universe. It seems, however, that these solutions are special cases and that they are unstable: the least disturbance, such as the presence of an observer, would cause the wormhole to close off, and would produce an unavoidable singularity at which the observer would be torn to shreds and crushed out of existence. It is with some justification that gravitational collapse has been called "the greatest crisis in physics of all time" by physicist John A. Wheeler, who has pioneered its study within the general theory of relativity.

When a physical theory predicts that some measurable quantity should become infinite, it is generally a signal that the theory has broken down and has ceased to provide an accurate description of nature. This happened in the early years of this century with the classical model of the atom as a cloud of negatively charged electrons orbiting around a positively charged nucleus. According to the classical laws of electrodynamics, the electrons should emit radiation because of their motion and should lose energy and spiral into the nucleus producing a collapse of the atom. That problem was overcome by Niels Bohr, Erwin Schrödinger, and Werner Heisenberg when they developed the quantum theory, which is based on the uncertainty principle: one cannot simultaneously measure the position and velocity of a particle to arbitrary accuracy. This uncertainty meant that the lowest energy state of the electron is not to be located exactly on the nucleus (because then its position and velocity would both be precisely defined) but instead it is "smeared out" with some probable distribution in a region around the nucleus.

General relativity, as Einstein formulated it, is a purely classical theory—that is, it does not include the uncertainty principle. However, every other physical field that we have detected seems to be governed by quantum principles. It therefore seems necessary for consistency to extend general relativity to a quantum theory. One would expect that this would make very little difference to its predictions in the very weak gravitational fields in our neighborhood. But because the classical theory predicts very strong fields in black holes and the big bang, quantum gravitational effects should be very important in those situations. One might even hope that they could smear out the singularities and enable one to pass through to another region of space-time. This seems rather unlikely, however.

Although we have not yet managed fully to incorporate quantum mechanics into general relativity, we believe that we know how it will affect black holes. The uncertainty principle also applies to energy: one cannot precisely measure the energy of a system at a precise instant of time. A consequence of this is that the vacuum, the lowest energy state of space-time, is not completely empty (because then it would have precisely zero energy), but is filled with pairs of virtual particles and antiparticles which appear together at some instant, move apart, and then come together again and annihilate each other. They are called "virtual" because, unlike "real" particles or antiparticles, they cannot be observed directly with a particle detector, but their indirect effects have been measured in a number of experiments. When a black hole is present, one member of a particle-antiparticle pair may fall into the hole leaving the other member without a partner with whom to annihilate. The forsaken particle or antiparticle may follow its mate into the hole, but it may also escape to a distant observer to whom it will appear to have come from the black hole. An alternative way of looking at it is to regard the member of the pair that fell into the black hole (say, the antiparticle) as being a particle traveling backward in time and coming out of the black hole. When it reached the point at which the particle-antiparticle pair first appeared, it would be scattered by the gravitational field into a particle traveling forward in time and escaping to a distant observer.

It turns out, therefore, that when quantum mechanics is taken into account, a black hole is not completely black after all. In fact, it emits particles and radiation just as if it were a hot body. The temperature is inversely proportional to the mass. For a black hole of a mass equal to that of our Sun it is about one ten-millionth of a degree above absolute zero. Such black holes would therefore emit at a rate that we would be quite unable to detect. In fact, the radiation would be completely swamped by the microwave background, which has a temperature of three degrees above absolute zero. But if the universe continues to expand forever, the temperature of the microwave background radiation will eventually fall below that of any black hole. The black holes will then begin to lose energy and therefore mass, though at a very low rate. As their mass decreases, their temperature and their rate of emission will go up. Finally, it seems they will disappear completely in a tremendous explosion comparable to millions of H-bombs.

The total energy that a black hole emits during its lifetime corresponds with its original mass according to Einstein's famous equation $E = Mc^2$, where E is the energy, M is the mass, and c is the speed of light. Thus, if anything or anybody falls into a black hole, an amount of energy equivalent to its mass will eventually be re-emitted. However, the total energy, together with the state of rotation and the electric charge, seem to be the only features of what fell into the black hole that are returned to the rest of the universe; the emitted radiation is completely random apart from these three properties. This is because black holes "have no hair," as Wheeler puts it. A black hole "forgets" everything about what fell into it apart from its total energy or mass, its state of rotation, and its electric charge. Of course, it would be of little consolation to a hapless astronaut who fell into a black hole to know that his mass-energy would survive him and be recycled. His personal experience of time would come to an end inside the black hole. One might imagine that some similar process took place whereby the total energy of the universe, if it recollapsed, was recycled into a new expanding phase. But if the total energy was the only property that was preserved from the collapse to the expansion, one could not claim that time, in any sense that we experience it, continued without an end or a beginning.

It is clear from the classical general theory of relativity and from the observational evidence we have that something quite drastic happens both in the past in the big bang, and in the future with the collapse of stars or of the whole universe. Whether or not time has a beginning or an end at these events is something that we cannot give a definite answer to until we have a complete synthesis of general relativity and quantum mechanics. This is closely related to the problem of unifying gravity with the other interactions in physics. Einstein spent most of his later years working on this second problem. He failed for two reasons. First, he did not include quantum mechanics, which he distrusted because of its element of randomness or chance. Second, the time was not ripe for a unification because very little was known about the other forces in nature apart from the electromagnetic interaction. The twenty years or so that have elapsed since his death have seen great advances in our knowledge of the other two fundamental interactions, the weak and the strong nuclear forces. We now have a theory (the Salam/Weinberg model) that unites the electromagnetic and weak interactions. This has made a number of predictions which have been confirmed by experiment, though the theory has not yet been fully checked. We are now beginning to understand how the strong interactions might work and might be connected with the weak and electromagnetic forces, though we are still some way from having a proper theory, let alone experimental verification. Still, the stage now seems set for attempting a "grand unification" of everything in physics. If and when that is achieved, we will be in a position to answer the question: "Does time have a beginning and an end?"

Order and Disorder in the Universe

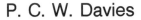

P. C. W. Davies

Paul Davies is a specialist in relativity, cosmology, and quantum field theory. He has written two undergraduate introductions, one on space-time physics and cosmology, entitled *Space and Time in the Modern Universe* (1977), and a second, *The Forces of Nature* (1979), which deals with subatomic and elementary particles, quantum theory, unified theories of the forces of nature, and so forth. *The Physics of Time Asymmetry* (1974), his single most important work, discusses the origin and nature of the past-future asymmetry of time in detail, including statistical mechanics, thermodynamics, electrodynamics, quantum theory, and relativity. The central role of cosmology, especially the big bang, in the origin of the asymmetry is established. His popular level book about the end of the universe and the place of life and technology in it, *The Runaway Universe,* appeared in 1978.

Dr. Davies has also been a regular contributor to journals and magazines in the United Kingdom and the United States. He has published over forty research papers on fundamental physics and cosmology.

Since 1972 Professor Davies has been a lecturer in mathematics at King's College, University of London. He was awarded his Ph.D. in theoretical physics from University College, also at the University of London, in 1970 and was a visiting fellow at the Institute of Theoretical Astronomy, University of Cambridge, from 1970 to 1972.

The most conspicuous and perhaps the most fundamental feature of the universe is the fact that it is not just a random and haphazard collection of matter and energy but a highly organized, integrated system. This is clearly true in the everyday world around us. People, technology, life, the weather—all of these represent highly ordered systems in which many component parts are organized together to act collectively. Even away from familiar experience, scientists uncover order wherever they look, from the deepest recesses of the atom, to the far-flung galaxies.

Order is of two types. The first is what we may call simple and is exemplified by the regular motions of the planets around the Sun, or the electrons in their orbit around the atom; it is an inherent tidiness in the elementary phenomena of the world, the result of nature's unfailing conformity with simple mathematical laws. The second kind of order, which we may call complex, is exemplified by the human observer. Here, vast numbers of simple units (atoms, molecules, cells) behave cooperatively in a hierarchy of structure and ordered activity. Such arrangements are not inherent; they may exist, but it is not necessary to the simple order of things that they should.

We cannot hope to account for the first of these orders, which lies at the very foundation of existence; we cannot know *why* nature obeys mathematical laws. Moreover, because these laws do not (by definition) change with time, this simple fundamental order cannot evolve. In contrast, the second and more complex order, which is structural, is observed to evolve with time, and the general principles which govern its evolution are understood.

What is order?

Complex organization and activity are so ubiquitous in our world that to attempt a unified discussion might appear hopelessly ambitious. Remarkably enough, physicists have invented a measure of order and disorder that can be universally applied to systems as diverse as a star and a crystal. As a simple illustration, consider a box divided into two compartments by a membrane (*see* figure). The left-hand compartment contains a gas of one type, the right-hand compartment that of another type. The membrane is then removed, and the gases quickly diffuse into each other, until after a

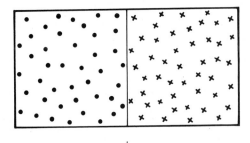

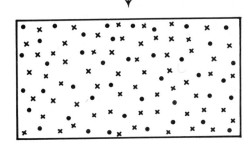

Example of an order-disorder transition. A sealed box is divided by a membrane which separates the two enclosed gases (the molecules of which are denoted by dots and crosses) into the neat arrangement shown. When the membrane is removed, the gases soon get completely mixed up as a result of molecular collisions.

short while they are thoroughly mixed up. This is a good example of an order-disorder transition. The initial state is clearly more orderly than the final state.

The explanation for this particular disordering tendency can be traced to the rapid, chaotic motions of the individual gas molecules. In particular, these microscopic particles rush around haphazardly, bouncing off each other and the container walls millions of times every second. The effect of the collisions is to "reshuffle" continually the molecular arrangement, thereby progressively destroying the initial orderly state, just as reshuffling a pack of cards breaks up the suit order. Very soon all semblance of the initial state dissolves; indeed, any other arrangement of the separated gases would end up, after mixing, looking much the same. It is not possible to gaze at the mixture and infer the initial state.

The reason why reshuffling always seems to convert order into chaos rather than the other way around can be understood with the help of an analogy. Suppose a troop of soldiers is marching in step in an orderly fashion, and they are then instructed to break step at random. It is exceedingly improbable, though not strictly impossible, that all the soldiers will simultaneously alter their stride in exactly the same way, so that the troop still remains in step afterward. The overwhelming likelihood is that the orderly collective marching will disintegrate into disorderly uncorrelated walking, with each individual soldier striding independently of the others. In the same way, provided the molecular collisions in a gas occur randomly, they will almost always disintegrate the orderly state into a chaotic one.

The tendency is no mystery. There are many ways that soldiers can walk independently, but only a very small number of ways that they can march in step. Any random change of step is far more likely to result in one of the former arrangements than in the latter one. Thus, there are many more ways to achieve chaos than to create order. It is precisely by counting the relative numbers of chaotic and orderly states that we arrive at a universal definition of disorder. The actual quantity of disorder is known as *entropy*, and its relation to the number of possible internal arrangements is a mathematical one that need not concern us here; it involves careful consideration of what constitutes distinguishable states, how to assess the statistical weights of different permutations, and so on. One general feature which emerges is that the most probable state is the most disordered. This is one step away from the consequence that the *equilibrium* state is also the most disordered. Once a system has achieved maximum disorder, it will, by definition, most probably remain that way. It follows that the equilibrium state is the state of maximum entropy.

It is important to realize, however, that equilibrium and disorder are only exceedingly *probable*, not absolutely certain. There is always a tiny probability that, in the box of gas for example, a random reshuffling will separate the two gases with each gas spontaneously rushing to opposite ends of the box. Similarly, there is a minute chance that a card player will shuffle the pack into suit or numerical order. In the real world, where the numbers of participating atoms are usually vast, spontaneous self-organizing events like this are considered as so wildly unlikely that their occurrence would be regarded as a miracle. However, small-scale departures from disorder are easy to observe. For example, microscopic particles immersed in a gas can be seen to execute an erratic zigzag motion as the gas momentarily organizes itself to bombard the surfaces of the particle slightly unequally. A very large fluctuation, in which a brick is hurled about under the impact of grossly uneven molecular bombardment, is exceedingly more unlikely. So too may a card player occasionally deal himself four aces.

A useful way of visualizing order is in terms of information. A highly ordered system requires a lot of information to describe it. Alternatively, we could say that it *contains* a great deal of information. The letters on this page that have been carefully ordered to communicate a message is an obvious example. When a system becomes disordered, information is lost, just as if the letters on this page were scrambled.

Armed with these concepts, we may now examine the principles which govern the evolution of disorder in the universe.

The triumph of disorder

Because there are many more ways of achieving disorder than order, we may say that ordering a system is difficult, whereas disordering it is easy. One has only to remember the fate of Humpty-Dumpty who, having disordered himself rather badly when tumbling from a wall, was impossible to reorder, even with the assistance of all the King's horses and men. The human body is perhaps the most familiar highly ordered system. Its constituents are simple chemicals, but what makes it so interesting is not what it contains but the way the contents are put together. The colossal information content of such a body is delicately encoded in the double helix structure of the DNA molecules. While we cannot hope to generate this incredibly organized system out of a pile of raw chemicals, we have little difficulty in effecting the opposite transition: it is necessary merely to step in front of a moving automobile.

The asymmetry between tendencies toward order and disorder is universal within nature. Sometimes it is expressed by saying that disordering is *irreversible*. Such a statement is not really correct. Certainly we cannot reverse the anatomical disintegration of a human being, but we can rebuild houses that fall down and restock libraries that are burned out. We can even use chemical reactions to separate two gases. But there is a price to be paid. It is never possible to get something for nothing, and a careful balance sheet reveals that to achieve order somewhere is inevitably to generate disorder somewhere else. Thus, rebuilding a bombed city requires the utilization of new materials and the expenditure of much energy. The disorder generated by the irreversible depletion of natural resources more than offsets the order represented by the rebuilt city itself.

These observations are encompassed in the celebrated second law of thermodynamics which, stated most compactly, says that the *total* disorder always increases. Thus, adopting a cosmic perspective, we may say that the entropy of the universe keeps rising; every day the universe becomes a slightly more disordered place. So fundamental is this universal increase of disorder that it provides the only known physical distinction between past and future (except for some exotic subatomic processes) and is therefore closely related to the nature of time. It is important to note that although called a *law*, the second law of thermodynamics is really only a statistical statement. As explained in the previous section, it is overwhelmingly likely to be correct in practice, but a "miraculous" violation of the law is possible in principle, though with negligible likelihood.

On the basis of the second law, it seems that the universe as a whole is faced with the inexorable destruction of its orderly arrangement and the relentless disintegration of all its organized activity. Facing up to this conclusion squarely provides a number of insights into the origin and ultimate fate of the cosmos.

Order out of chaos

If we accept the idea that order continually gives way to disorder, we are presented with the puzzle of where the order came from in the first place. Recall the example of the human body, so dauntingly complex that we could not hope to manufacture such a thing from its constituent chemicals. Yet nature has managed to produce human beings, apparently unaided and spontaneously. How did it do so? Where did the information come from?

The key to terrestrial order is the Sun. The heat energy of sunlight produces most of the complex organized activity on the Earth's surface. We should not regard terrestrial systems as isolated; they are coupled into the wider solar environment, as in the case of weather systems. Thus, human industrial activity mostly runs on fossil fuels which owe their existence ultimately to sunlight. And in a larger sense, so far as our local solar neighborhood is concerned, complex structures such as living organisms have been generated at the expense of the utilization of millions of years of sunlight. It is our proximity to this source of free energy that makes our immediate environment so rich in its activity.

The irreversible degradation of the Sun's energy is the entropic price paid for our existence. The second law of thermodynamics indicates that the Sun, while producing terrestrial organization, steadily loses the energy with which it does so, dispersing it into the surrounding universe as heat and light. Thus, the ordered energy trapped in the Sun's fuel is released and disordered as it plunges irretrievably into the depths of space.

This explanation, however, only pushes the problem of the origin of order back one step—from the Earth to the Sun; we still have to explain how the Sun acquired its fuel in the first place. It is clear that the whole universe is in a condition of thermodynamic disequilibrium, with hot, dense stars punctuating vast chasms of cold, empty space. How did such enormous quantities of energy get locked up in the stars when on the foregoing principles it would far more easily and with greater probability have been spread about the universe in random chaos?

These observations call to mind an analogy to a clock. This is a device which also manifests organized activity. While it does so, it slowly converts its orderly motion into disorderly motion, as its stored-up energy is dissipated among the cogs as heat and sound through friction. The clock runs down. Similarly, a star like our Sun—indeed, the entire universe—is rather like a clock slowly running down. So we may ask: how did it get wound up in the first place?

This question only makes sense if we understand the mechanism of the stars' energy. It is known that the cores of stars are huge nuclear furnaces in which the nuclei of light elements such as hydrogen are slowly reacting to form heavier elements. The process continues until much of the star is in the form of heavy substances, such as iron. Indeed, from the nuclear standpoint, iron is the most stable substance. Thus, converting the Sun (mainly hydrogen) into iron would squeeze out the greatest amount of available energy. Why then is the Sun not made of iron, with its enormous energy content exploded throughout the cosmos?

To find out why stars begin their lives made mainly of hydrogen rather than the more stable heavier elements, we must look to the early history of the universe for clues.

Fortunately, by looking into distant regions of the universe, astronomers can obtain information about its remote past, because the light we receive now started out from those regions many millions of years ago. According to current ideas of cosmology, the sort of universe we observe now cannot always have existed. There is good observational evidence that between ten billion and twenty billion years ago the universe was in an immensely hot and dense condition, with the entire cosmic panorama that we now see, out to the most distant known galaxies, compressed into a fireball barely a few light-years across. In this condition no atomic nuclei (let alone atoms) could exist in the enormous temperatures. Only individual subatomic particles existed in profusion, violently colliding and interacting in a complex network of activity.

It has been possible to reconstruct imaginatively this primeval phase of the universe, using mathematics and the known laws of subatomic particle physics. In the first moments the fireball expanded explosively fast; between one microsecond and one second after the beginning, it increased in size about one thousand times, and the temperature fell from ten thousand billion degrees to ten billion degrees. This hot, explosive origin of the universe has earned the name "big bang." In spite of the rapidity of change in the primeval conditions, the fireball remained so hot and dense that the "soup" of subatomic particles had no difficulty in adjusting its composition to the changing circumstances. Most of the cosmic material remained in thermodynamic equilibrium up to about one second.

The tremendous heat energy believed to have accompanied the birth of the universe has not entirely disappeared. The initial explosive expansion of the universe continued, and is still observed today, though it is now going on at a much slower rate. The expansion has cooled the primeval heat from many billions of degrees down to a mere three degrees above absolute zero—a last, fading remnant of the fiery cataclysm that marked the beginning of the cosmos as we know it. The discovery of this primeval heat radiation by the radio astronomers Arno A. Penzias and Robert W. Wilson in 1965 confirmed the basic idea of a hot big bang but presents us with something of a paradox. If the organized activity of the universe is slowly disintegrating in obedience to the second law of thermodynamics, we would expect that as we look to the early moments of the universe, we would see *more* rather than less order. Yet the evidence is just the opposite. The primeval cosmos was not orderly at all but chaotic. Indeed, as far as we know, it was locally in a condition of thermodynamic equilibrium, which, as explained in the previous sections, is the most *disorderly* state.

The paradox is resolved when we examine what happened after the first second or so in the big bang. The temperature, previously too high to allow heavy nuclei to exist, had by this time fallen far enough to allow the sort of nuclear reactions that are now occurring in the centers of stars to proceed. Crudely speaking, the way was open for the universe to turn into iron. For about three minutes this was beginning to happen, but at the end of that time the temperature and density of subatomic particles had fallen so low that the nuclear reactions switched off. As a result, the processes concerned being slow, the conversion never really got started. About one-quarter of the material ended up as helium (the lightest compound nucleus); the rest remained almost entirely in the form of the simplest and lightest element—hydrogen.

It is now possible to understand how, on the analogy of the clock, the universe became "wound up." It began "unwound," in a state of thermal equilibrium, with nuclear particles engaging only in the most rapid processes. Then, after one second or so, the much slower nucleosynthesis set in, commencing to build up heavy elements. Because it was so slow this process could not keep pace with the rapid cosmic expansion, and the initial equilibrium was destroyed, with the evolving material lagging further and further behind equilibrium conditions. Once nuclear reactions ceased, the material was left in a condition which is not really stable. Since that time, the stars have been trying to catch up with the expanding universe by converting the remaining unstable hydrogen into iron and other heavy elements. The winding mechanism can thus be identified with the explosion of the primeval fireball in the first few minutes. Although the winding still takes place, the rate is far too sluggish to have any significance. Consequently, in the universe we observe now, the rate of unwinding is much faster than the rate of rewinding. The order which was injected into the cosmos in these early moments is now being relentlessly dissipated.

With this explanation, we can understand how order has arisen from chaos in apparent defiance of the second law of thermodynamics. The material of the universe is not really an isolated system but is embedded in a rapidly changing background space-time. Thus, although the entropy of this material was at maximum for the conditions prevailing before the first second, these conditions changed with the subsequent expansion. Since that time the amount of entropy has risen, but so has the maximum amount of *possible* entropy.

Gravity and black holes

Although stellar structure and nuclear physics provide a straightforward account of the rise of order in the universe, they cannot provide the whole story. There are disordering processes familiar in daily life that clearly do not have their origin in the Sun's nucleosynthesis—for example, the tides which slowly erode the continental shores. Terrestrial tides are caused by the Moon's gravity, and astrophysics provides many other examples of the role of gravity in organizing the behavior of the cosmos. Gravity shapes the structure of the solar system and the Galaxy and controls the expansion of the universe. We look to gravity to explain the existence of discrete objects, such as stars, planets, and galaxies.

Though weak, gravity is a cumulative force which, given enough gravitating matter, can overwhelm all other forces of nature. It acts indiscriminately between all material and energy in the universe. Being always attractive, it operates universally to pull matter together into ever more compact lumps. In relatively low-mass objects like the Earth, the force of gravity is balanced by atomic forces. In the Sun, it is resisted by the huge interior pressure generated by the nuclear furnace in the core. In some stars that have expended their nuclear fuel the pressure support fails, and they implode under their own immense weight. For stars with masses comparable to the Sun, atomic or nuclear forces may still prevent total collapse, and the imploded star will settle down in a highly shrunken condition as a so-called white dwarf, or as a neutron star. However, if its mass is a few times greater, no known means of support exists, and it is widely supposed that the star will shrink rapidly (in a few microseconds, star-time) and without any limit that we know.

Whatever happens to the star, its surface gravity becomes so intense that it seriously distorts the structure of space and time in its vicinity, trapping all light and other objects inside a surface known as an event horizon. The empty region inside the horizon is known as a black hole. Many astronomers believe that most heavy stars will end their days inside a black hole.

Black holes represent the ultimate triumph of gravity. Objects like the Sun and stars are really only temporary, metastable interludes between a distended cloud of gas and totally imploded matter. This universal tendency of gravitating systems always to shrink is reminiscent of the second law of thermodynamics, and in recent years some spectacular discoveries by mathematicians and theoretical physicists about black holes have confirmed the close connection between the irreversible ubiquitous rise of entropy and the irreversible tendency toward gravitational collapse.

One easy way of understanding why a black hole is highly disordered, is to regard the concept of entropy as the negative of information in the sense of that term mentioned on page 46. When a black hole swallows matter, the matter becomes imprisoned. From the outside world, all information about the engulfed matter is lost except for its total mass (the black hole grows a little larger) and any electric charge or rotation it may have (which persists in the hole). Indeed, the black hole destroys information more completely than anything else known, so that it is impossible to decide whether such a hole was formed from an imploded star, or antimatter, or light, or green cheese: the information content of the matter (*e.g.*, its cheesiness) gets wiped out when it falls across the event horizon. It follows that there are many ways of making a black hole of a given mass, charge, and rotation. Thus, just as a box of gas is maximally disordered when its state can be achieved in the greatest variety of ways, so too is a black hole the maximally disordered *gravitating* system.

We may inquire how all the objects we see in the universe have avoided becoming black holes (observations suggest that the overwhelming majority of astronomical objects are something else). Just as matter would like to become iron so, when gravity is taken into account, we can see that it would like to become a black hole. Ordinary matter is restrained from converting into iron because of the strong electric barrier around the atomic nuclei, which prevents their coalescence except at very high temperatures. Likewise, ordinary matter is restrained from imploding under gravity to a black hole by its rigidity and internal pressure. Can we say that the big bang did not produce innumerable black holes for the same reason that it did not present us with an iron universe?

The problem here is that, whereas with earlier and earlier moments of the primeval fireball we can be more and more sure that iron did not exist (the temperature becomes progressively higher as we go back toward the bang), we cannot say the same about black holes. Indeed, the earlier the epoch considered, the more likely it is that black holes were able to form, because the density of material was higher at that time than at later epochs. It follows that the most important phase of black hole formation probably occurred at a very early time, about which our knowledge of the relevant physics is fragmentary. This makes any attempted explanation of how so much matter escaped falling into black holes extremely conjectural. We know almost nothing about ultra-hot, ultra-crushed matter. Conceivably it was so stiff that even when compressed very close to black hole densities, it resisted annihilation.

Could it be merely a lucky chance that the universe is not made up chiefly of black holes? We can compare the amount of entropy that would then exist with the state of affairs as we now have it. Most of the observed entropy in the universe is contained in the primeval heat radiation. If the observable universe were a single gigantic black hole, its entropy would exceed that of the cosmic heat that now exists by the colossal factor of 10^{30}. Moreover, the relationship between entropy and probability is an exponential one, so this number translates into the absurdly minute odds of one in about $10^{10^{30}}$ (that is, one followed by 10^{30} zeros!) against a chance origin for the present holeless arrangement. Either the universe is a miracle, or some as yet unknown mechanism stiffens the primeval matter.

If this latter conjecture is correct, it may explain another of the great mysteries of cosmology. It has long been wondered why the expansion of the universe is so *uniform*. As far as we can tell, whichever way we look into space, the rate of expansion is the same. This type of uniform expansion corresponds to a universal *dilation* of space. That is, the expansion is not haphazard or directional but behaves just as though the *scale* of cosmic distance were gradually stretching everywhere and in all directions at the same rate. Why, out of all the ways in which the universe could have expanded, did it choose such an orderly pattern of motion? In the primeval phase, had the expansion energy been shared randomly among all the available channels of expansion, we would have ended up with a highly turbulent, chaotic expansion.

In recent years some attempt has been made to explain the absence of turbulent disorder in the cosmic expansion as having come about through the dissipation of turbulent energy as heat in the primeval fireball. One problem is that the dissipation mechanisms investigated seem to be progressively more efficient at earlier epochs. But it can be shown that the heat produced for a given amount of turbulence rises without limit the earlier it is dissipated. Thus we would expect even a minute amount of turbulence to generate enormous heat. However, we know that the universe is actually very *cold*—about three degrees above absolute zero—which makes it seem unlikely that there was ever very much turbulence at all. Once again we are faced with the mystery of why the real universe chose such a remarkably orderly kind of behavior for itself from among the overwhelming number of chaotic possibilities that confronted it. If the primeval material possessed properties of stiffness which prevented it from degenerating into black holes, this might also account for the fact that it was able to avoid chaotic expansion.

The end of the universe

However the universe managed to survive its inception without plunging into cosmic anarchy, it seems inevitable that disorder will overtake it eventually. The relentless growth of entropy must in time destroy all the organized activity and orderly structure we now see, including intelligent life and everything that it has made. This conclusion has been known for over a century and is inescapable given the second law of thermodynamics. The second law cannot, however, tell us *how* the universe will end.

Modern cosmologists envisage two scenarios concerning the demise of the cosmos. In the first of these the stars slowly but surely burn out, as their nuclear fuel becomes exhausted and the supply of primeval hydrogen runs out. Some of the massive burnt-out stars implode into black holes, others into compact stars which slowly cool and fade. As the galaxies gradually dim, these two sorts of inert objects inexorably spiral together, as the orbital energy around their galaxy is dissipated in the form of gravity waves. One by one they collide and coalesce, with the black holes gradually absorbing all of the other objects that they encounter. Most of the atoms in the universe will end up inside black holes. The holes themselves will also eventually coalesce to form superholes. Even the matter that escapes them will not be safe, for subtle quantum effects can cause it to overcome its internal support and implode also.

Until recently it seemed that the ultimate end state of the universe would be mainly black holes. In 1974 Stephen W. Hawking discovered that this is probably not so. Black holes appear not to be *completely* black after all. A hole with a mass comparable to that of the Sun, Hawking suggests, should have a temperature of about one microdegree, and should therefore give off at least a feeble glow. Galactic-sized holes would radiate even more feebly, having temperatures of 10^{-17} K or less. That is very cold indeed. Nevertheless, as the universe continues expanding, the time would eventually be reached when the cosmic background heat radiation, now 3 K, would fall below such a temperature, and the black holes would then slowly start to radiate. As they lose energy, so they must shrink. The smaller they become the hotter they get, thus accelerating the rate of shrinkage. As far as can be judged, the process continues until the hole disappears altogether in a brief explosive flash of high-energy subatomic particles. After this has happened to all the black holes, all further activity in the universe will cease, and until the end of time all that will occur is the steady decline of the already minute background radiation.

This depressing state of affairs is sometimes referred to as heat death, though such a term might have been reserved for the alternative scenario. If the universe contains about one hundred times as much matter as we actually see (which is entirely possible), it will not have time to decay in the manner outlined above. The time required for the dispersion of a galactic-sized black hole, for example, is an unbelievable 10^{70} years, but according to our present theory the combined gravity of all the matter in the universe could halt the present expansion and cause it to collapse on a time scale very much shorter than this. In fact, present observations do not rule out cosmic collapse even before the stars have burnt out.

In this scenario, the universe suffers a more dramatic fate. It begins by shrinking slowly, then more rapidly, until it eventually is engulfed in a cataclysmic crunch similar to the big bang in reverse. The intense heat and pressure destroys all the orderly structure that survives until then, and it is even possible that the rising gravity will become so intense that space-time itself will be torn apart and the entire universe, including space and time, will be smashed out of existence.

Either of these two scenarios—slow refrigeration or fiery extinction—spells the end, eventually, for the complex order that we now observe in the universe. It may appear unpalatable that the cosmos has only a limited lifetime, because the range of possible activities which can occur is then limited in scope. But it may be that what is lost in available time is gained in available space, as will be explained below.

Order in space

The observed universe is nearly as big as the observable universe. We see nearly all that can be seen. Owing to the properties of light in an expanding space, it is not possible for us to observe beyond a definite distance in space (often called the Hubble radius, after Edwin Hubble who discovered the cosmological expansion in the 1920s), about ten billion or twenty billion light-years away. There we encounter a sort of horizon beyond which we cannot see, however powerful our instruments may be. This being the case, further advances in our understanding of the universe *as a whole* are necessarily speculative ones.

There is an almost unanimous assumption among cosmologists that the universe we observe is a *typical sample* of the whole. This expectation has in the past been confirmed with each increase in our instrumental power. The Earth, Sun, Milky Way, and our local cluster of galaxies all appear to be typical, unexceptional systems at their respective scale of sizes. If this remains true for the universe *beyond* the horizon too, then it has some profound implications. For example, if the universe looks much the same *wherever* it is observed, it can have no center or edge, for such places would be privileged, special locations. But if it is infinite in size (due to the possibility of curved space it could be finite and still have no edge, but here I shall assume that it is infinite and populated uniformly with galaxies), there will necessarily be an infinity of galaxies. It follows that any other feature of our environment which is not totally miraculous must also occur in an infinity of places. This includes Earth-like planets, intelligent life, technical civilizations and so forth. In fact as pointed out recently by the cosmologist George Ellis, the reasoning inevitably extends to DNA. There must be an infinity of duplicate people to the reader of this article and an infinity of duplicate Earth populations! The extraordinary and remarkable cosmic order which we think of as our own must, on the basis of elementary probability, be repeated ad infinitum throughout the cosmos!

The alternative to unlimited replication is to assume that the observed universe is not, after all, typical of the whole. It could be that we inhabit a sort of "Hubble bubble" of order amid cosmic chaos. Perhaps our own existence as biological systems is a function of our privileged location in the only inhabitable corner of the cosmos.

Whatever one thinks about these wider philosophical issues, the existence and behavior of order and disorder are firmly rooted in laboratory experiment. The second law of thermodynamics is perhaps the most thoroughly confirmed of all the laws of physics. In spite of its humble origins in the business of heat engines and industrial machinery and in a century of study of disorder, it has been seen to have literally cosmic implications.

Mach's Principle, 1879–1979

Dennis W. Sciama

Dennis W. Sciama, who appears here in the company of his former student at the University of Cambridge, Stephen Hawking, is a specialist in astrophysics, cosmology, and relativity. Now a member of the Department of Astrophysics at Oxford, where he was appointed a senior research fellow at All Souls College in 1970, he has since last year divided his time between Oxford and the Department of Physics at the University of Texas, Austin.

Dr. Sciama has been a frequent visiting lecturer on American campuses. Appointed a resident fellow of Trinity College, Cambridge, in 1952, he visited Princeton's Institute for Advanced Study in 1954, and was at Harvard in 1955. He was a visiting professor at Cornell in 1960 when he accepted an appointment as lecturer in mathematics at Cambridge and was made a fellow of Peterhouse College, where he remained until 1970.

His publications include *The Unity of the Universe* (1959), *The Physical Foundations of General Relativity* (1969), and *Modern Cosmology* (1971). He is a fellow of the Royal Astronomical Society, the Physical Society, and the Cambridge Philosophical Society.

Introduction

Albert Einstein was born on March 14, 1879. One of his greatest contributions to physics was to take up an idea which at that time Ernst Mach was stressing, to give it physical shape, and to make it the foundation stone of his general theory of relativity. Nevertheless, although that theory is itself now widely accepted by physicists, the original idea, which Einstein came to call Mach's principle, has remained controversial down to the present day. Inasmuch as the issues involved in this controversy are tied up with cosmology, and as this year is the centenary of Einstein's birth, it seems appropriate to give an account of the controversy in this issue of *The Great Ideas Today.*

The problem with which Mach's principle is concerned has a long history going back at least to Isaac Newton and his contemporary Bishop Berkeley. They debated the nature of space and of motion, the main issue between them being whether these concepts are purely relative or instead are in some sense absolute. That it is important to try and decide this is perhaps clear enough. We know from daily life that the universe possesses a dynamical structure which dictates the existence of different distinguishable states of motion. When a car moves steadily its occupants move with the car, but when it is suddenly braked they are thrown violently forward; it is tiring to sit in a bumpy airplane but not in an armchair at home, and so on. Obviously we have here two sorts of motion which are quite different from each other. To a physicist this difference presents a challenge. He is bound to ask what it signifies. Does it mean that we are always subject—without reference to anything else, simply as bodies existing in space—to an absolute, "real," motion, of which we are made aware in situations of the sort just described, and which is independent of any local, relative, or apparent motion that we happen to have?; or is the motion that we take to be absolute merely the effect upon us of other objects besides ourselves—the matter of the universe—with respect to which our local, real, or apparent motion is sometimes steady and sometimes not?

This question, which is still unresolved, is the subject of the present article. I shall introduce the relevant ideas in rough historical order beginning with Newton, and end on the theoretical side with Gödel and with Raine, and on the observational side with the recent measurements of the so-called 3 K cosmic black body background, which in the 1970s have transformed the empirical aspects of the problem.

Newton

Newton carried out an experiment which he offered as demonstrating the existence of absolute motion. The moving system he considered was that of a bucket of water in various states of rotation. When the water was not rotating its surface was flat; when rotating fast it would climb up the sides of the bucket to form a curved surface (in fact, roughly a paraboloid). The shape of the water surface thus provided an objective way of distinguishing between the different rates of rotation to which the water might be subjected.

The question which Newton considered was this: does the shape of the water surface depend on the motion of the water relative to other material objects, or is it independent of such a relation and so an absolute property of the water's own motion, relative only, as it were, to space? What Newton showed experimentally was that the rotation of the water relative to the bucket was irrelevant to the shape of the water surface. He did this by having the bucket rotate sometimes with the water and sometimes in the opposite direction. Also, he studied the situation when the bucket rotated and the water did not. In all cases the result was clear: the relative motion of the water and bucket in respect to each other had no effect on the shape of the water surface.

So far everything is straightforward (indeed, one wonders whether Newton actually bothered to do the experiment). It is at the next step that the trouble begins. Newton concluded from his experiment that the endeavor of the water to rise in the bucket was the result of an absolute rotational motion to which it had been subjected and was independent of any material object whatever. His actual words (in translation) were:

> And therefore this endeavor does not depend upon any translation
> of the water in respect of the ambient bodies, nor can true circular
> motion be defined by such translation. There is only one real circular
> motion of any one revolving body, corresponding to only one power
> of endeavoring to recede from its axis of motion, as its proper and
> adequate effect; but relative motions in one and the same body, are
> innumerable, according to the various relations it bears to external
> bodies, and, like other relations, are altogether destitute of any real
> effect, any otherwise than they may perhaps partake of that one only
> true motion.[1]

Berkeley

That there was an error in Newton's argument was pointed out by Berkeley a generation after the publication of Newton's *Principia*. One cannot argue,

---

[1] *GBWW*, Vol. 34, p. 12.

Berkeley said, from the irrelevance of the bucket's motion relative to the water to the irrelevance of its motion relative to all objects in the world. The bucket constitutes the object *nearest* to the water and is needed to hold the water and to set it in rotation, but it is not necessarily the only material object that is involved. There is much other matter in the universe whose greater abundance may compensate for its greater distance and cause it to have some effect. In fact, experiment has shown that it is *only when the water rotates relative to the stars* that the surface is curved.

Of course Newton could have replied that the rotation relative to the stars may not be the *cause* of the curvature of the water surface. If the system of stars is not rotating relative to absolute space, the observable effects of absolute rotation can be mistakenly ascribed to rotation relative to the stars. Because of this possibility, the question remains open whether there exists such a thing as absolute motion or not. But already here we meet a basic empirical problem which underlies the controversy: with what precision may we say it is true that an objectively nonrotating system (*e.g.*, a bucket of water with a flat surface) is also nonrotating relative to the system of stars? If we could establish experimentally that the precision is very high, we might decide that we had found empirical evidence favoring the contention that Berkeley went on to make, which was that things at rest or in motion are only so with respect to other things.

This contention was based on a view of the universe which led Berkeley to deny that empty space could have dynamical properties. Thus, in the absence of external matter there should be no objective effects of rotation. As Berkeley put it:

> I must confess it does not appear to me that there can be any motion other than *relative;* so that to conceive motion there must be at least conceived two bodies, whereof the distance or position in regard to each other is varied. Hence, if there was one only body in being it could not possibly be moved. . . . But philosophers . . . discover even the earth itself to be moved. In order therefore to fix their notions they seem to conceive the corporeal world as finite, and the utmost unmoved walls or shell thereof to be the place whereby they estimate true motions. If we sound our own conceptions, I believe we may find all the absolute motion we can frame an idea of to be at bottom no other than relative motion thus defined. For, as hath been already observed, absolute motion, exclusive of all external relation, is incomprehensible; and to this kind of relative motion all the above-mentioned properties, causes, and effects ascribed to absolute motion will, if I mistake not, be found to agree.[2]

We thus first meet here a question which was asked so often by nineteenth-century physicists struggling to understand electromagnetic and optical phenomena and their relation to the ether, namely what physical

---

[2] *GBWW*, Vol. 35, p. 435.

properties, if any, should we ascribe to space in order to account for natural phenomena?

Mach

The main objections to Berkeley's ideas came from mathematicians, physicists, and philosophers who regarded the proposed influence of the distant parts of the universe as astrological rather than astronomical or physical. Thus, Euler called the idea of such an influence "very strange and contrary to the dogmas of metaphysics." Later, Whitehead expressed himself as sure that "this ascription of the centrifugal force on the earth's surface to the influence of Sirius is the last refuge of a theory in distress. The point is that the physical properties, size, and distance of Sirius do not seem to matter." Whitehead meant that if Berkeley were right one would expect the curvature of the water surface to depend on the properties of the stars, but there was at that time no evidence of any such connection.

Mach was not impressed with objections of this kind. Like Berkeley, he was anxious to eliminate empty space in the problem as something unobservable and so he demanded that the same consequences should follow if (*a*) the bucket of water is regarded as rotating while the stars are at rest or, (*b*) the stars are regarded as rotating while the bucket of water is at rest. However, in case (*b*), Newtonian dynamics would predict that the water surface should be flat. This, Mach regarded as a crucial defect in the Newtonian scheme. "Obviously," he wrote,

> it does not matter if we think of the earth as turning round on its axis, or at rest while the fixed stars revolve round it. Geometrically these are exactly the same case of a relative rotation of the earth and the fixed stars with respect to one another. But if we think of the earth at rest and the fixed stars revolving round it, there is no flattening of the earth, no Foucault's experiment, and so on—at least according to our usual conception of the law of inertia. Now one can solve the difficulty in two ways. Either all motion is absolute, or our law of inertia is wrongly expressed. I prefer the second way. The law of inertia must be so conceived that exactly the same thing results from the second supposition as from the first. By this it will be evident that in its expression, regard must be paid to the masses of the universe.[3]

Mach meant that, if one argued that the Earth is at rest while the fixed stars rotate around it, one should be able to show that the rotation of the stars can in turn be regarded as giving rise to the flattening of the Earth and the behavior of the Foucault pendulum. This view, that the effects of rotation on a body have their physical origin in the rotation of the stars relative to that body, Einstein later came to call Mach's principle.

---

[3] Ernst Mach, *History and Root of the Principle of the Conservation of Energy* (1872), p. 76.

Einstein

The weakness of Mach's position was that he offered no *theory* as to how the rotating stars could influence the shape of the water surface. One would want to know more about the physical nature of this influence, how it depends on the properties of the stars and on their number and distance from the water, and so on. It is rather curious that before Einstein no one seems to have bothered to try to supply such a theory. There was no shortage of verbal argument but very little constructive physics.

Einstein changed all that. Moreover he did it with a stroke of genius. A supporter of Mach's principle might be willing to invent a new kind of force exerted by the stars on local matter. Einstein showed that this was unnecessary, for a well-known force would explain the effect, namely gravitation. The most remarkable aspect of this proposal was that the main reason for it stems from a property of gravitation that was well known to Galileo and Newton, namely that all bodies fall equally fast under gravity. This is the relevant property because the dynamical effects of acceleration which we are trying to explain (such as the shape of the water surface) depend only on the acceleration itself and not at all on the physical properties of the accelerating body. Thus, the effects of acceleration are either absolute, as Newton claimed—a function, that is, of absolute motion, independent of anything else—or arise from a force which produces the same acceleration in all bodies. Einstein made the proposal that the water surface is curved because of *gravitational* forces acting on the water and exerted by the rotating stars.

This was in 1907 and represented the first step toward a new theory of gravitation—the general theory of relativity. A new gravitational theory was needed because according to Newtonian theory the stars exert the same gravitational force whether they are rotating or nonrotating. What was needed was a theory in which the stars exert an *extra* gravitational force when they rotate, since this extra force could then be identified with the centrifugal force. Of course this extra force would have to have the properties necessary to account in detail for the shape of the water surface. It took Einstein eight years to construct this theory, and his famous field equations were published in 1916.

Of course a new theory of gravitation has to be studied from many points of view and its relation to observation investigated. Thus, in 1917 Einstein returned to the problem of Mach's principle. In the new gravitational theory it was easy to show that rotating stars would exert an extra force, as compared with fixed stars, and one of the correct general character in its dependence on the angular velocity of rotation. The question which Einstein studied was: are there enough stars in the universe for the *whole* of the dynamical effects of rotation to be attributable to them? This required solving his field equations for the whole universe, and this is how the first modern paper on cosmological theory came to be written.

At that time the expansion of the universe was unknown. It was not even known whether the spiral nebulae were members of the Milky Way system of stars, or whether they were external objects, each individually a Milky Way in its own right. This question was under debate by astronomers, and was not settled until 1924 when Edwin Hubble showed that the nebula in Andromeda lies outside the Milky Way. His announcement of the systematic expansion of the universe followed in 1929.

It was natural therefore for Einstein in 1917 to try to construct a static, nonexpanding model of the universe with a uniform distribution of stars for his study of cosmological theory. Nevertheless, this led immediately to a problem, because a static model is not possible in view of the gravitational forces which the stars would exert on one another. Einstein solved that problem by introducing an extra term into his field equations which involved a new factor, the so-called cosmological constant. The idea was that this extra term was too small to disturb the agreement with observation in the solar system, but could be important cosmologically since, if chosen with the appropriate sign, it has the same effect as that of a repulsive force which would oppose the self-gravitation of the universe and enable a static solution to be attained. This solution was the famous "Einstein universe" in which the volume of space is finite but unbounded—the three-dimensional analogue of the model of a sphere.

Mach's principle does seem to be satisfied by this model of the universe, in which there is enough matter for its rotation to produce a gravitational force sufficiently great to account for the whole dynamical effect of rotation. It was Einstein's hope that his new equations had no solution at all where such a distribution of matter did not exist. If such a solution did exist it would mean that the dynamical effects of rotation could also exist even in the absence of ambient matter, which of course would tend to prove that Newton had been right. In the absence of such solutions, Einstein's theory as a whole could be said to incorporate Mach's principle. His hope was not fulfilled, however. Willem de Sitter showed in the same year (1917) that the amended field equations did have another solution which was devoid of gravitating matter. The de Sitter model had the apparently curious property that small particles introduced into it would fly apart under the contrary influence of the cosmological constant. Thus, the first model of an expanding universe was discovered. This model is not Machian, of course; centrifugal forces within it would still act upon rotating bodies, but it is essentially empty. Einstein's field equations therefore seem to work even where Mach's principle does not apply.

This result weakens the argument for introducing the extra term into the field equations, since the amended equations are no more Machian than the original ones. This point was reinforced in 1922 with the discovery by Alexander Friedmann that expanding models of the universe can be constructed which are compatible with Einstein's original, unamended field equations. When in 1929 Hubble announced his observational discovery that the universe *is* actually expanding, Einstein advocated dropping the constant extra term and called its introduction "the biggest blunder of my life."

Where does this leave Mach's principle? All the Friedmann models are Machian in the sense that in them centrifugal forces act only on bodies which are rotating relative to the rest of the matter in the universe. There are other solutions of Einstein's equations in which rotating bodies experience centrifugal forces even in the absence of other matter. The question then arises whether all the solutions with widespread distributions of matter are Machian, that is, whether in each of them the whole of the centrifugal force acting on a rotating body is due to the distribution of matter. Thanks to a remarkable discovery by Kurt Gödel, it was found that there are non-Machian solutions despite the presence in them of a widespread, indeed uniform, distribution of matter.

Gödel

In 1949 Gödel showed that there are exact cosmological solutions of Einstein's field equations in which the whole material universe is rotating relative to absolute space. This means that if one were to observe the distant galaxies from a frame of reference in which a water surface is flat, one would find them to be in a state of rotation about a particular axis. It is important to realize that there is no question here of a single rotation axis passing through the center of the system as would be the case, say, for the rotating Earth. Gödel's model is homogeneous in space. This means that an observer anywhere in the universe would find the galaxies to be rotating relative to his local inertial frames. The axis of this rotation would pass through the observer himself and, in the Gödel model, all the rotation axes would be aligned parallel to one another.

Gödel's concern in constructing his model went beyond demonstrating that Einstein's theory does not rule out the possibility of absolute rotation for any cosmological distribution of matter. He was also interested in the behavior of time in general relativity. Gödel's model has the paradoxical property that it possesses closed time-like lines. This means that a suitably moving observer in such a model would, as time went on, find himself to be at an earlier epoch than at the "start" of his journey. Einstein was much disturbed that such paradoxical behavior was compatible with his theory, and he suggested that such solutions should be ruled out on the ground that they are physically impossible.

This idea of ruling out certain solutions of a theory as unphysical brings out a point which has also been used by several physicists, including myself, in an attempt to construct an argument reconciling Einstein's theory with Mach's principle. The point is that, in technical language, Einstein's equations are differential equations, and in order to obtain solutions they must be supplemented by boundary conditions. This means that the field equations tell one how the gravitational field varies as one goes from one point to a neighboring point or from one time to a neighboring time. But they do not tell one the actual value of the field at any particular point or at any particular time. To find a solution one must specify the field at certain places and times (the boundary conditions), and then the field equations tell one what the field must be everywhere else.

Einstein's equations are thus incomplete and must be supplemented by choosing appropriate boundary conditions. This is likewise the case with theories such as those set forth by James Clerk Maxwell in dealing with electromagnetism. The conventional attitude to this flexibility of field theory is that it is essential if the theory is to be applicable to all the different field configurations which are realized in nature. This makes good sense in local physics, but the flexibility becomes embarrassing in cosmology, for there is only one universe actually realized. The boundary conditions thus take on a unique character and should really become part of the laws of nature rather than essentially arbitrary constructs which vary from case to case.

A comprehensive theory of the universe should thus supply unique boundary conditions as well as a unique set of field equations. Perhaps in a future cosmological theory we will not deal with differential equations at all, but with some kind of integral equations in which the distinction between laws and boundary conditions is lost. As a step toward such a complete theory, my colleagues and I have investigated formulations of Einstein's equations in which some kind of integral representation is possible. This enables one to discuss the problem of selecting boundary conditions in a rather systematic way. Derek Raine, in particular, has shown how to characterize which boundary conditions are and which are not Machian. Because of the mathematical difficulties of the problem, this was a considerable technical achievement. If the universe conforms to Mach's principle, we can argue that the cosmological model appropriate to the real world must satisfy Raine's boundary conditions as well as Einstein's field equations.

According to our point of view, this last statement is a physical one—that is, it should be empirically verifiable. In the last section of this article I shall explain that we can make a definite set of predictions and that these predictions do seem to agree well with observation. However, I should stress here that at least one of these predictions is not specific to Raine's theory but would presumably be made in any reasonable theory of Mach's principle, namely, that inertial frames are determined by the universe as a whole and not by absolute space, so that one would expect the rotation of the universe relative to a local inertial frame to be precisely zero. We shall see that, to a very good approximation, this requirement is observed to be true of the actual universe.

Empirical considerations

To arrive at a definite prediction we note that, when averaged over a region containing many galaxies, the universe appears to be uniform in its structure. This uniformity has been elevated by some writers into a Copernican or cosmological principle which states that at any one cosmic epoch the universe has the same properties everywhere. Such a homogeneous universe could still be anisotropic as far as Einstein's field equations are concerned—that is, it could have different properties in different directions. Such anisotropy would result, for example, from Gödel-like absolute rotation, in which the rotation axis would define a preferred direction at each point. Another possibility is that the universe could be expanding at different rates in different directions. What Raine succeeded in showing was that, if we add to Einstein's field equations the Machian boundary conditions which he—that is, Raine—developed, then of necessity a homogeneous universe must be isotropic. Accordingly, there could be no absolute rotation, a conclusion which we might expect from any reasonable theory of Mach's principle. In addition, however, there is the less obviously expected prediction that the universe must be expanding at the same rate in all directions.

To compare these predictions with observation we must ask two questions: With what precision is it true that a fixed (*i.e.*, dynamically nonrotating) frame of reference is also fixed with respect to distant matter? With what precision is the expansion rate of the universe independent of direction?

We will consider these two questions in turn.

Observational limits on the absolute rotation and isotropy of the universe

To a terrestrial observer it appears that the Sun and the stars are rotating around him and that the rotation period is one day. According to Mach's principle we would expect the dynamical effects of this rotation to be evident on the Earth. Careful measurements do indeed show that the Earth is flattened at the poles and bulges at the equator as we would expect if it is rotating once a day relative to an inertial frame. More readily demonstrated is another consequence of such rotation, namely the behavior of a Foucault pendulum. Such a pendulum is suspended from a universal joint and, in accordance with Newton's laws of motion, swings in a fixed inertial frame. As the Earth rotates relative to such a frame, the plane of the pendulum swings around as observed by a terrestrial observer. Now we also know from observation that the motion of the pendulum does lie in a plane fixed with respect to the Sun and stars as Mach's principle would require.

Nevertheless, the precision involved in such an observation is not very great.

To arrive at greater precision we use the fact that the system of stars in our Galaxy is itself in rotation and that as a result the Galaxy is "flattened at the poles and bulges at the equator." This flattening is much greater for the Galaxy than it is for the Earth, although the rotation period is much longer, namely more than 100 million years. From the Newtonian point of view, the Galaxy could contain all the material in the universe and still be flattened by rotation; the associated centrifugal force would be absolute and independent of the presence of ambient matter. According to Berkeley and Mach, there would have to be a substantial distribution of material outside the Galaxy relative to which it is rotating in order to cause such an effect. Curiously enough, the existence of an extragalactic universe and the rotation of the Galaxy were both established by independent observations within a year of one another in 1924–25.

Using the rotation of the Galaxy, we can begin to interpret strictly the statement that the universe has no absolute rotation. As with the flattening of the Earth and the apparent motion of the Sun and stars, we can compare the shape of the Galaxy with the motion relative to the galaxy of extragalactic objects. From the flattened shape of our Galaxy we can infer its rotation. We can then compare this rotation with the motion of extragalactic objects relative to our Galaxy. This comparison tells us that if there is any *absolute* rotation of the universe, it must have a period exceeding several times the rotation period of our Galaxy, which is about one billion years. This implies that it is practically static, if it moves at all. The corresponding upper limit to the absolute angular velocity of the universe is about 10^{-4} seconds of arc per year. This is a far more stringent limit than one could obtain using the best available gyroscopes or the rotation of the Earth—not quite infinitesimal, but practically so.

A still better limit can be obtained using observations of the red shifts of distant galaxies which are ascribed to the Doppler effect arising from the motion of the galaxies directly away from us. If the system of galaxies was also rotating relative to absolute space, there would be an additional Doppler effect. Galaxies observed in directions making an angle to the axis of rotation would have a component of their motion transverse to the line of sight. This would introduce a Doppler shift additional to that due to their radial motion associated with the expansion of the universe, and this additional Doppler shift would vary systematically with the direction of observation. In particular, it would be zero if we looked along the axis of rotation. No such effect is observed, which places a lower limit on the rotation period of the distant galaxies of about 10^{10} years—again, not quite forever, but at least a ten times stronger limit than we obtained from the rotation of our own Galaxy.

This limit still does not provide very convincing evidence in favor of

Mach's principle. Since it takes light about 10^{10} years to cross the universe, one might heuristically argue that we need not be surprised if the rotation period of the universe were at least as long as the light-time associated with its size. Only if we could establish that the rotation period were several orders of magnitude larger could one regard the observations as indicating seriously that the universe may actually have no rotation at all.

Just such a stringent limit can now be placed on the rotation of the universe. Within the last few years, radio astronomers have established the existence in the universe of heat radiation which we believe is the cool remnant of the hot big-bang origin of the universe. This so-called 3 K cosmic black body radiation field is observed to be equally intense in different directions to a precision of about one part in three thousand. If the sources of this radiation were rotating relative to absolute space, there would again be a transverse Doppler effect which would vary with the direction of observation. This would show up in a variation of the temperature of the background radiation with direction. This effect is not observed, and so one can place a still more stringent limit on the rotation period of the universe. How stringent depends on which model of the universe one adopts, but in all cases one gains at least four powers of ten on the best previous argument. Thus, at last we have strong observational evidence that the absolute rotation of the universe is very slow indeed, essentially zero.

One can also use the 3 K background to test Raine's other prediction, that the universe should expand at the same rate in all directions. As a result of this expansion the heat radiation cools down with each increasing cosmic epoch, and if the rate of expansion were different in different directions, the temperature of the radiation would itself vary with direction. Since this effect is not observed, one can place a stringent limit on any anisotropy of the expansion rate. Thus, Raine's theory passes this test.

Of course, other explanations may be found for the isotropy of the universe. Nevertheless, these recent observations have aroused renewed interest in Mach's principle since this principle provides an explanation of the high isotropy of the universe. It is surely remarkable that a controversy in physics initiated by Newton and Berkeley should remain so active today. It reminds one very forcibly of the power of a Great Idea.

REFERENCES

BARROW, J. D. AND MATZNER, R. A., "The Homogeneity and Isotropy of the Universe," *Monthly Notices of the Royal Astronomical Society* 181 (1977):719.
RAINE, D. J., "Mach's Principle in General Relativity," *MNRAS* 171 (1975):507.
REINHARDT, M., "Mach's Principle—A Critical Review," *Zeitschrift für Naturforschung* 28a (1973):529.
SCIAMA, D. W., "The Physical Foundations of General Relativity," *Science Study Series* (1969).

The Aethereal Sky: Man's Search for a Plenum Universe

Owen Gingerich

Owen Gingerich is an astrophysicist at the Smithsonian Astrophysical Observatory in Cambridge, Massachusetts, and a professor of both astronomy and the history of science at Harvard University. A scholar of the first distinction, he is the author as well of many popular writings on astronomy and teaches a celebrated course in that subject at Harvard for nonscientists.

In recent years he has become a leading authority on both Copernicus and Kepler. He recently undertook a survey of extant copies of Copernicus's *De revolutionibus,* and having examined over 400 of these in libraries throughout Europe and North America he plans to publish an annotated census of them in the form of a 600-page monograph.

Professor Gingerich is a recent coeditor of a *Source Book in Astronomy and Astrophysics, 1900–1975* (1979) and is also involved in the editing of the twentieth-century volume of the International Astronomical Union's *General History of Astronomy*. Widely known as the editor of a collection of *Scientific American* articles entitled "New Frontiers in Astronomy," he has contributed articles to various encyclopedias and journals as well. He was awarded the American Philosophical Society's John F. Lewis Prize in 1976 for a paper entitled "From Copernicus to Kepler: Heliocentricism as Model and as Reality." His "A Fresh Look at Copernicus" appeared in *The Great Ideas Today, 1973*.

L uminiferous aether will prove to be superfluous," wrote Albert Einstein in his celebrated 1905 paper on special relativity. With this, he apparently sounded the death knell for one of the most intriguing ideas in the history of thought—the concept of a plenum universe completely full of something fundamental but invisible.

For the ancient Greek philosophers, that mysterious something was the weightless, transparent, permanent substance of the heavens. Lying above the terrestrial earth, water, air, and fire, it was literally the quintessence, a fifth element. Philosophers of the Middle Ages conceptually crystallized the aether into smooth, glassy, solid spheres, still weightless and invisible. Copernicus was ambivalent about their role, but before the end of the sixteenth century Tycho Brahe had shattered the crystal spheres with his geo-heliocentric cosmology. Scarcely had the celestial aether been exorcised when Descartes reintroduced it in the form of pervasive material vortices that drove the planetary rhythms. In turn, the Cartesian plenum gave way to the luminiferous aether of Newton and Huygens, a "subtle fluid" that bore the vibrations of light across space. For two centuries this luminiferous aether played an increasingly significant role in physics until Einstein with a stroke rendered it irrelevant.

In the Greek view, the celestial aether occupied the region of the stars and planets, filling every conceivable space beyond the zone of fire. Carved in concentric spheres, it provided the carriers for individual planets, which were envisioned as luminous nodules within the aethereal plenum. Because the heavens were eternal and because circular motion was seen as unending, the Greek philosophers associated uniform circular motions (or combinations thereof) with these aethereal spheres.

"Eudoxus was the first of the Greeks to concern himself with hypotheses of this sort," wrote Simplicius in his commentary to Aristotle's *De caelo*, "Plato having set it as a problem to all earnest students of this subject to find the uniform movements by which the motions of the planets can be explained."[1] Eudoxus, a brilliant mathematician who discovered much of what has become Euclid's *Elements*, proposed a nested series of spheres pegged together with different axes so that the individual motions of various spheres combined to produce the apparently irregular planetary motion. Eudoxus's theory was more to be admired than used, because it failed to provide reliable numerical predictions. Nevertheless, the homocentric spheres of Eudoxus became, in the next generation, a fundamental feature of Aristotle's cosmology.

Aristotle's medieval followers paraphrased his view of the plenum in an epigram: *Nature abhors a vacuum.* There is no evidence that Aristotle himself said this, but he would have known what it meant. To preserve the plenum and to ensure a smooth mechanical operation of the Eudoxian spheres within the high heavens, Aristotle added enough new spheres to counteract the motion of each planet, an inside-out set to reduce the motion back to the zero level so that one planet's spheres could be neatly linked to the next. This cost Aristotle about fifty-five spheres, not unduly many considering the apparent complexity of the planetary motions. Perhaps more disappointing was the failure of the scheme to account for the clearly different distances of the planets from the Earth. "This is indeed obvious," remarked Simplicius, "for the star called after Aphrodite [Venus] and also the star of Ares [Mars] seem, in the middle of their retrogressions, to be many times as large, so that the star of Aphrodite actually makes bodies cast shadows on moonless nights."[2]

An attempt to model the celestial motions accurately enough for future predictions came two centuries after Aristotle with the astronomer Hipparchus (fl. between 147 and 127 BC). Borrowing numerical parameters from the Babylonians and forging them into a geometric model, Hipparchus succeeded well enough with the Sun and Moon to predict the times of eclipses, but evidently he failed completely with the planets. The line of mathematical philosophers was so thin in those ancient times that not until AD 140, nearly three centuries after Hipparchus, did a sufficiently gifted theoretician emerge to establish a satisfactory system that could predict planetary positions. Ptolemy (Claudius Ptolemaeus), an astronomer of Alexandria, linked major circles to account for the motions of each planet. On the larger circle, called the deferent, moved a subsidiary circle, called the epicycle, and their combined movements roughly reproduced both the direct and the so-called retrograde motions of the planets.

To bring his model into closer agreement with the observed planetary motions, Ptolemy introduced several important auxiliary devices. Rather than center the deferent circle on the Earth itself, he placed it somewhat eccentric to the Earth, thereby generating the varying angular speed of the Sun and epicycles as seen from the Earth. Second, he proposed an off-centered axis of uniform angular motion, which brought the differing lengths of the retrogressions into agreement with observations. This latter device, known as the equant, violated the precept of uniform motion around the circumference of the circle and, as we shall see, provoked increasing philosophical criticism of Ptolemy in later centuries.

Ptolemy described his planetary models in a great handbook of mathematical astronomy originally entitled the *Syntaxis*, but generally known as the *Almagest* or "the Greatest," as it was designated by Islamic admirers. The *Almagest* thus provided the basis for what is often called the Ptolemaic

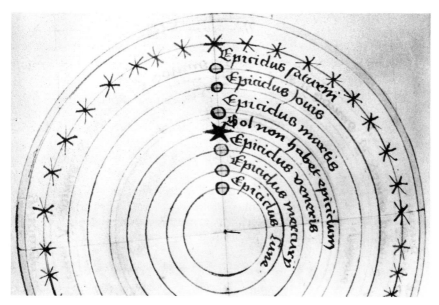

Drawn by a medieval scribe, this highly schematic Ptolemaic system shows the planetary circles and epicycles arranged around the Earth.

system; in fact, the book describes the individual parts with no attempt to fit the pieces together into a grand cosmological scheme, as Aristotle had done in his *De caelo*. However, about ten years ago a long overlooked section of another Ptolemaic treatise, the *Planetary Hypotheses,* was discovered in an Arabic translation.[3] This section, lacking in the surviving Greek text, showed that Ptolemy had indeed created the Ptolemaic system.

The heretofore missing text, although essentially mathematical in nature, fits beautifully into the Aristotelian scheme with its plenum of nested spheres. In it Ptolemy determines the ratio of the nearest and farthest approach of each planet, taking into account not only the epicycle but also the eccentric position of the deferent circle. In this scheme he arranged the nearest approach of Mercury to fall immediately beyond the farthest excursion of the Moon, the nearest approach of Venus immediately beyond the farthest excursion of Mercury, and so on through the spheres for the Sun, Mars, Jupiter, and Saturn. Since Ptolemy had already established the distance of the Moon in terrestrial units, he could then specify the dimensions of the remaining mechanisms in absolute terms. Furthermore, the arrangement satisfied the Aristotelian requirements, provided that invisible aether existed to fill all the gaps around the epicycles.

Nevertheless, Ptolemy's geometrical devices were compromised by three features which made it difficult to construct a mechanical model of pure aether. First, the motion of the Moon was sufficiently complicated so that he had been obliged to add a further circle, a kind of interior crank that brought the Moon closer to the Earth at first and third quarter. Second,

Mercury required an extra circle to account for certain observed positions. (The data had caused Ptolemy to suppose that this elusive planet had a closest approach to the Earth in two different places, an idiosyncrasy challenged neither by the Islamic astronomers nor by Copernicus, although it is now known to rest on faulty observations.) The interior circles required by the lunar and Mercury models clearly got in each other's way whenever anyone tried to diagram a comprehensive mechanical model of the system. Finally, the tidy picture of nested spheres was disturbed by the equant, an objectionable "additional center," which, if represented mechanically, required a linkage from an interior point through the intervening spheres to the planet in question.

The Ptolemaic-Aristotelian cosmology clearly fascinated the Islamic astronomers, who adopted it as their world view. But criticism of Ptolemy on philosophical grounds emerged in the eleventh century in the work of Ibn al-Haytham (Alhazen, 965–*c.* 1040). In his *Doubts on Ptolemy*, Ibn al-Haytham complained that the equant failed to satisfy the requirement of uniform circular motion. At the same time he objected to Ptolemy's lunar model, although he passed in silence over the complicated construction for Mercury. A more extreme criticism was launched in the following century by the Cordoban astronomer and philosopher, Averroës (Ibn Rushd, 1126–98), who wrote:

> In my youth I hoped it would be possible for me to bring this research
> to a successful conclusion. Now, in my old age, I have lost hope, for
> several obstacles have stood in my way. But what I say about it will
> perhaps attract the attention of future researchers. The astronomical
> science of our days surely offers nothing from which one can derive an
> existing reality. The model that has been developed in the times in
> which we live accords with the computations, not with existence.[4]

Averroës was thoroughly critical of the Ptolemaic theory; he found its eccentric epicycles, and above all its equant, completely unacceptable. Nevertheless, he failed to propose any satisfactory alternative.

Perhaps in response to these criticisms, the Moorish astronomer al-Bitrūjī attempted late in the twelfth century to formulate a strictly concentric geocentric model, somewhat reminiscent of the Eudoxian scheme and equally disastrous. Although Bitrūjī's system spread throughout much of Europe in the thirteenth century, it attracted no continuing support.

Elsewhere, at the other end of the Islamic world, a fresh critique of the Ptolemaic mechanism was undertaken in the thirteenth century by Naṣīr ad-Dīn at-Ṭūsī. In his *Tadhkira*, or "Memorandum," Ṭūsī launched a thorough exposition of the shortcomings of Ptolemaic astronomy. Ṭūsī found the equant particularly objectionable; he also found the Mercury and lunar models inadequate, presumably because of the difficulty of fitting their spheres together for a consistent plenum universe. In the *Tadhkira*, Ṭūsī proposed an ingenious linkage of two circles whose uniform motions together produced a straight-line reciprocating motion, and this device (now called the Ṭūsī couple) provided a replacement for the equant, a replacement that generated the same apparent angular motion by means of two additional epicyclets rather than by the interior off-center axis. Hence, Ṭūsī not only preserved the principle of uniform circular motion, but he achieved it with a mechanism that would fit neatly within each planet's own set of spheres. He also tried, apparently with less success, to eliminate the philosophically objectionable central mechanisms of the Moon and Mercury.

Mu'ayyad ad-Dīn al-'Urḍī and, later, Quṭb ad-Dīn ash-Shīrāzī, both workers at Ṭūsī's Marāgha observatory, offered an alternative arrangement of the Ṭūsī couple to provide another approach to the planetary models, but one that still retained the eccentric circles.[5] A completely concentric rearrangement of the planetary mechanisms was finally achieved by the Damascene astronomer, Ibn ash-Shāṭir, around 1350. He wrote:

> I found that the most distinguished of the later astronomers had
> adduced indisputable doubts concerning the well-known astronomy of
> the spheres according to Ptolemy. I therefore asked Almighty God to
> give me inspiration and help me to invent models that would achieve
> what was required, and God—may He be praised and exalted, all
> praise and gratitude to Him—did enable me to devise universal
> models for the planetary motions in longitude and latitude and all
> other observable features of their motions, models that were free from
> the doubts surrounding previous ones.[6]

By using the Ṭūsī couple, Ibn ash-Shāṭir succeeded in transferring not only the equant but the central circles in Ptolemy's constructions for the Moon and Mercury from the interior regions of the model to the outer parts, thereby clearing the way for a perfectly nested and mechanically acceptable set of celestial spheres. However, his solution remained generally unknown in medieval Europe, was eventually forgotten, and was ultimately rediscovered only in the late 1950s.

Meanwhile, although technical understanding of Ptolemy's astronomy had nearly vanished in Latin-speaking Europe, the concentric spheres of terrestrial elements and of crystalline celestial aether entered the artistic repertoire. Piero di Puccio's calm but majestic fresco on the wall of the Camposanto in Pisa adds spheres of angels and God himself beyond the crystal dome of stars—a typical Christianized version of the fourteenth century. Giovanni di Paolo's colorful nested spheres, now a prize of the Lehman Collection of the Metropolitan Museum of Art in New York City, depicts the same tradition in the fifteenth century; and by 1493 a lavishly illustrated book, the *Nuremburg Chronicle*, gave still greater currency to this tidy, compact view of the universe.

The *Sphaera* of the thirteenth-century cleric John of Holywood, or Sacrobosco, conveyed the principal knowledge of astronomy available in the

The nested aethereal spheres of the planets surround the terrestrial spheres of
earth, water, air, and fire in Giovanni di Paolo's *Expulsion from the Garden of Eden,*
a Christianized mid-fifteenth-century version of Aristotle's cosmos.

Middle Ages, but it dealt with planetary theory only in its unsatisfactory
final chapter. Hence a *Theorica planetarum* (anonymous, though often mistakenly attributed to Gerard of Cremona) was added to the standard "textbook" collection of Latin astronomical manuscripts. Brief and faulty as the
Theorica was, it established the astronomical vocabulary, and it gave a
preeminence to Ptolemy's geometric theory. Not until the mid-fifteenth
century was the old *Theorica* successfully overhauled and replaced by a new
and longer *Theoricae novae planetarum*, written by Georg Peurbach, professor
of astronomy at Vienna. What was new in Peurbach's little treatise was
principally a set of diagrams showing how crescent-shaped zones of crystalline aether could fill in the spaces and thus make geometric units from
Ptolemy's eccentric circles and epicycles. Such diagrams had already been
included in Ptolemy's *Planetary Hypotheses,* but precisely how Peurbach got
them remains a mystery. In any event, the introduction of printing in the
fifteenth century served to disseminate this arrangement, and the simple
machinery of the nested spheres became the standard iconography of the
astronomical Renaissance.

In 1473, the same year that Peurbach's "New Theories of the Planets" was first printed, Nicolaus Copernicus was born. When young Copernicus studied astronomy as an undergraduate at Cracow in the 1490s, he must have seen Peurbach's pictorial representation of the crystalline spheres. Whether his teachers expressed any doubt about the arrangement, as the Islamic astronomers had been doing for several centuries, we do not know. But it is highly suggestive that Copernicus attacked the Ptolemaic equant at the very beginning of his earliest extant tract on astronomy. Equally remarkable are the great pains Copernicus took to replace the interior circles of the lunar and Mercury models by alternative mechanisms at the perimeter of their orbits. Concerning these problems, he wrote:

> Our predecessors assumed a large number of celestial spheres
> principally in order to account for the apparent motion of the planets
> through uniform motion, for it seemed highly unreasonable that the
> heavenly bodies should not always move uniformly in a perfectly
> circular figure. Callippus and Eudoxus, who endeavored to solve this
> problem by the use of concentric spheres, were unable to account for
> all the planetary movements. . . . Therefore it seemed better to employ
> eccentrics and epicycles, a system which most scholars finally accepted.
> Yet the planetary theories of Ptolemy and most other astronomers,
> although consistent with the numerical data, also seemed quite
> doubtful. For these theories were not adequate unless certain equants
> were also conceived; it then appeared that a planet moved with
> uniform velocity neither on its deferent nor with respect to its proper
> center. Hence a system of this sort seemed neither perfect enough nor
> sufficiently pleasing to the mind.[7]

Copernicus, of course, did far more than replace the mechanical blemishes of the Ptolemaic system. He almost literally turned cosmology inside-out by proclaiming that the Sun, not the Earth, was the fixed center of the universe. In the most profound philosophical sense, the ultimate and most revolutionary consequences of his work were the twin recognitions that the Earth was but one of the planets and that the Sun was but one of the stars. Apparently Copernicus himself only vaguely grasped the implications of the first of these concepts, and not at all the second. Nevertheless, as the greatest cosmographer since Ptolemy, Copernicus recognized the intrinsic elegance of the heliocentric system. Ptolemy had used two major circles for each planet; Copernicus saw that the great Earth-Sun circle could serve in common for every pair. Thus, instead of ten major circles for the five planets and another for the Sun as Ptolemy had required, Copernicus needed only five major circles plus the Earth-Sun circle, which furnished the common measure and hence the distance scale for the entire scheme. The intrinsic economy of this rearrangement offered to sixteenth-century astronomers the most persuasive argument for heliocentric cosmology, and once glimpsed, the idea was too compelling to be abandoned. Furthermore, this ordering placed Mercury, the swiftest planet, closest to the Sun and the lethargically moving Saturn the most remote; "In no other way," wrote Copernicus, "do we perceive the clear harmonious linkage between the motions of the planets and the sizes of their orbs."[8]

But did Copernicus still envision the solar system filled with solid crystalline spheres? Unfortunately, he is virtually silent on this subject. The Ptolemaic blemishes seem minor compared to the radical reordering that he finally adopted. Yet the equant, the inner lunar circle, and the construction for Mercury, which Copernicus worked so hard to eliminate, are objectionable principally in the context of a plenum universe and with the Aristotelian spheres. Could it be that Copernicus had merely stumbled onto the heliocentric arrangement as he responded to a current philosophical problem concerning the physical reality of the Ptolemaic mechanism?

How and why Copernicus adopted the heliocentric cosmology remains a mystery. We can, however, glean a few shreds of evidence to support the following speculative reconstruction. Early in his career the young Copernicus somehow became aware of the inadequacy of the Peurbachian models for a physically acceptable universe of crystalline spheres (just as Ibn al-Haytham had perceived these inadequacies four centuries earlier). In tinkering with the arrangement of circles, Copernicus must surely have seen how the Earth-Sun motion kept recurring in each planetary model—indeed, the organization of the numbers in his well-thumbed copy of the *Alfonsine Tables* made this quite obvious. It was an easy step to transpose the epicycles for Mars, Jupiter, and Saturn to a common circle coincident with the solar orbit, all within a geocentric framework. This had the effect of placing the planets in orbit around the Sun, while the Sun in turn orbited the Earth. In fact, precisely such notes still exist—on one page of the handful of his surviving manuscripts.[9] But straightway a difficulty arose for Copernicus; the dimensions of the two primary circles for Mars were such that when the deferent and epicycle were interchanged, the circle carrying Mars around the Sun intersected the circle carrying the Sun around the Earth. How could the spheres be saved? By a still more radical transformation—choosing the Sun rather than the Earth as the fixed center! As Copernicus's disciple Rheticus remarked, Mars unquestionably comes closer to the Earth than the Sun does, "and therefore it seems impossible that the earth should occupy the center of the universe."[10] Rheticus's statement is a stark non sequitur unless seen in the context of the intersecting spheres.

At this point (as we may speculate) Copernicus revised his goal: instead of saving the physical reality of the spheres with a geocentric system, he would try a heliocentric system—not just heliostatic, but absolutely heliocentric, unblemished by eccentrics or equants. The program is entirely analogous to Ibn ash-Shāṭir's but converted to the heliocentric case, and in fact Copernicus's initial solution follows that of Ibn ash-Shāṭir so closely that many contemporary historians suppose that some currently missing link

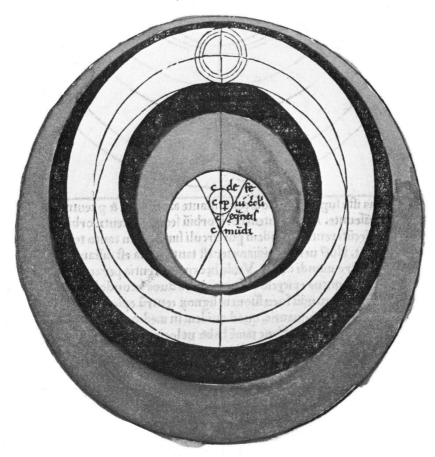

The space-filling spheres of Mercury in the original Regiomontanus edition of
Peurbach's *Theoricae novae planetarum* (1473).

accounted for the westward transmission of the Arabic ideas. Such was the
scheme outlined by Copernicus in his *Commentariolus,* a small tract closely
modeled on Peurbach's *Theoricae novae planetarum* and written sometime
prior to 1514.

But in 1515 the full text of Ptolemy's *Almagest* appeared in print for the
first time, and perhaps for the first time Copernicus recognized the formidable task awaiting a cosmologist who sought to supersede the Alexandrian.
The labor required nearly three more decades, and in the process Copernicus abandoned his attempt to set up a strictly heliocentric astronomy. In
his research Copernicus discovered that the eccentric orientation of the
planetary orbits slowly changed, and it seemed easier to him to represent
this with circles not centered on the Sun rather than with an additional
epicyclet at the perimeter of the planetary orbits. Thus, the order of circles

in his magnum opus, the *De revolutionibus*, paralleled the original arrangement of al-'Urḍī rather than that of Ibn ash-Shāṭir.

If Copernicus had indeed been motivated originally by a fervent ambition to save the crystalline spheres, he must have cooled to this idea as his thinking matured. The idea of a moving Earth composed of ponderous terrestrial elements and a fixed Sun made of weightless aether destroyed the coherence of Aristotelian physics. As the distinguished Danish observer Tycho Brahe was to complain later in the century, "Copernicus's theory in no way offends the principles of mathematics. Yet it gives to the earth, this lazy, sluggish body unfit for motion, a movement as fast as that of the aethereal torches."[11]

Only a few vestiges of Copernicus's original commitment to cosmic spheres remain in his *De revolutionibus*, as when he says: "The space remaining between Venus' convex sphere and Mars' concave sphere must be set apart as also a sphere or spherical shell, both of whose surfaces are concentric with those spheres."[12] In contrast, when he discusses the Earth-Sun mechanism, he describes three alternative modes quite indifferently as to whether the auxiliary wheels are placed in the center or at the perimeter of the model. Perhaps by the time he wrote this later section he was taking the role of the mathematician rather than that of the cosmographer, having failed at his attempt to achieve a physically acceptable celestial cosmology consistent with physics of his day.

Tycho Brahe, the number two astronomer of the sixteenth century, would have loved to go down in history as one of the all-time-great cosmographers. Born in the generation after Copernicus's death, Tycho understood the beauty of the heliocentric system as well as its contradiction with the accepted Aristotelian physics, and for this he criticized Copernicus. But in electing to save physics by abandoning heliocentrism, he made the wrong choice and an apparent step backward in cosmology. History has awarded Tycho laurels as an all-time-great instrument builder and observer, but not as a cosmographer.

Nevertheless, Tycho's insistence on a physically real model of the universe moved astronomy a major step closer to modern science. For years Tycho toyed inconclusively with various planetary arrangements, but not until 1583 did he finally adopt the Tychonic system, precisely the geo-heliocentric model used briefly by Copernicus, in which the Sun, while circling the Earth, carried the other planets in orbit around itself.

From a twentieth-century vantage point, the distinction between Copernicus's heliocentric system and Tycho's geo-heliocentric plan may seem to be only a matter of relativity: two geometrically identical schemes with different reference points. But, as this discussion attempts to make clear, each model was embedded in a larger view of the physical world. Because of the intersection of the circles for Mars and the Sun in the geo-heliocentric plan, accepting this geometry necessarily implied rejecting the solid

The heliocentric planetary spheres in the first edition of Copernicus's *De revolutionibus* (1543). Besides the circles shown for Mercury, Venus, Earth, Mars, Jupiter, and Saturn, two extra circles show schematically the bounds of the Moon's circle, which is centered on the Earth.

spheres, a consequence almost as radical as that for Copernicus in throwing the Earth into orbit.

With his analysis of the Great Comet of 1577, Tycho already had some evidence for doubting the existence of the crystal spheres, for the observations clearly placed the comet beyond the sphere of the Moon. Still, he considered the possibility that the comet could circle the Sun in the space left beyond the sphere of Venus. The sticking point, as it had been for Copernicus, was the "ridiculous penetration of orbs [of Mars and the Sun]", as Tycho called it. "It happened that my own discovery was suspect," he later wrote, "because I was so steeped in the opinion, approved and long accepted by nearly everyone, that the heavens were composed of solid spheres."[13]

A detailed study of Mars in its close approach of 1583 finally convinced Tycho that Mars indeed came nearer than the Sun, as the sphere-smashing Tychonic arrangement would require. The irony of all this, as Kepler later pointed out, was that in no way could Tycho's observations yield an accurate distance to Mars, and hence he made his decision on spurious grounds!

Faulty as Tycho's basis for accepting the geo-heliocentric system may have been, it nevertheless made a crucial and total impact on the young Kepler, who for ten months was Tycho's last but most brilliant understudy. History remembers Kepler for distilling from Tycho's data the elliptical shape of the planetary orbits, but he would probably have preferred to be

The Earth-centered Tychonic system (right) hangs more heavily in Urania's balance than the Sun-centered Copernican system (left) in this frontispiece from J. B. Riccioli's *Almagestum novum* (1651). Note in the Tychonic scheme the intersection of the larger circle of Mars with the smaller circle that carries the Sun and planets about the Earth.

known as the first astrophysicist. Like Tycho, Kepler noted the inconsistency between the heliocentric plan and the Aristotelian physics of his day, but unlike Tycho, Kepler accepted the Sun-centered arrangement and sought to rework the physics. For Kepler, the rejection of the solid aethereal spheres left the planets with no mechanical means to maintain their motion. As a searcher after physical causes, he naturally turned to magnetism, for

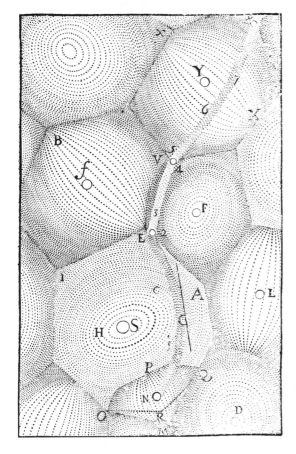

The sinuous path of a comet through the celestial vortices as depicted in Descartes's *Principia philosophiae* (1644).

he knew of the lodestone's mysterious ability to attract iron across seemingly empty space. Such a force emanating from the Sun could, Kepler believed, push the planets in their orbits.[14] Furthermore, his theory could be linked quantitatively to the fact that the closer the planets were to the Sun, the faster they completed their circuits.

Kepler's theory of action-at-a-distance was, in the eyes of many contemporaries, no proper substitute for the aether. Even Galileo labeled Kepler's notion occult,[15] and in the next generation Descartes hammered out an alternative world view based on a fluid plenum. Descartes agreed with Aristotle that nature abhors a void; he regarded space and substance as identical except in our mode of conception of them. "Space without matter is a contradiction," he once said. As a starting point for his geometry and physics, he imagined extension, and since matter was the essence of extension, matter must fill all of space. The subtle matter, set by God into vortical motion at creation, drove the planets and satellites. It also gave an easy out with respect to the troubling question of the center of the universe. The

Earth is at rest with respect to its own vortex, said Descartes sagely, and the Sun is at rest with respect to the solar vortex.

Like the Eudoxian spheres, Descartes's vortical theory was more to be admired than used. Several generations of continental scientists, soothed by the revival of the plenum, tried in vain to deduce mathematical consequences from it. Descartes had entitled his grand cosmological book *Principia philosophiae*; when Isaac Newton, who had for many years been attracted to the Cartesian philosophy, finally realized how dismally the vortices failed when dealing with elliptical orbits, he deliberately entitled his own work *Philosophiae Naturalis Principia Mathematica*—emphasizing that it was the *mathematical* principles of natural philosophy that concerned him.

Newton, of course, described his gravitational theory in the mathematics of geometry and of a nascent calculus. He described the consequences of gravity without saying what it was. Pricked by criticism that "action-at-a-distance" smacked of the occult, he added in later editions a scholium saying that as to the nature of gravity, he feigned no hypotheses. But privately, Newton wrote to Richard Bentley:

> That gravity should be innate, inherent and essential to matter so that
> one body may act upon another at a distance through a *vacuum*,
> without the mediation of anything else, by and through which their
> action and force may be conveyed from one to another, is to me so
> great an absurdity, that I believe no man who has in philosophical
> matters a competent faculty of thinking, can ever fall into it.[16]

Solid crystalline spheres were of course dead, and the material fluid of the Cartesian vortices had proved inadequate to explain the detailed phenomena of planetary motion. Nevertheless, like a phoenix rising from the ashes, an elusive aethereal plenum arose once more. In founding the wave theory of light, Newton's illustrious Dutch contemporary Christiaan Huygens introduced an aether in 1690 to explain the propagation of light. "One will see," Huygens wrote, "that it is not the same that serves for the propagation of sound. . . . It is not the same air, but another kind of matter in which light spreads; since if the air is removed from the vessel, the light does not cease to traverse it as before."[17] To have an aether to support the motion of light is necessary for the true philosophy, Huygens remarked elsewhere, "or else [we] renounce all hopes of ever comprehending anything in physics."[18]

Newton's *Optics* also carried a notice of the new aether:

> . . . Is not the heat of the warm room conveyed through the vacuum
> by the vibrations of a much subtiler medium than air, which after the
> air was drawn out remained in the vacuum? And is not this medium
> the same with that medium by which light is refracted and reflected,
> and by whose vibrations light communicates heat to bodies?. . . And is
> not this medium exceedingly more rare and subtile than the air, and
> exceedingly more elastic and active? And doth it not readily pervade

all bodies? And is it not (by its elastic force) expanded through all the heavens? (Query 18)[19]

And further:

> May not planets and comets, and all gross bodies, perform their
> motions more freely, and with less resistance in this aethereal medium
> than in any fluid, which fills all space adequately without leaving any
> pores, and by consequence is much denser than quick-silver or gold?
> And may not its resistance be so small, as to be inconsiderable?
> (Query 22)[20]

Thus, in the age of Newton and Huygens the luminiferous aether was born as the carrier of light. Remarking on the history of aether in the ninth edition of the *Encyclopædia Britannica* (c. 1860), James Clerk Maxwell wrote:

> Aethers were invented for the planets to swim in, to constitute electric
> atmospheres and magnetic effluvia, to convey sensations from one part
> of our bodies to another, and so on, till all space had been filled three
> or four times over with aethers. . . . The only aether which has
> survived is that which was invented by Huygens to explain the
> propagation of light. The evidence for the existence of the
> luminiferous aether has accumulated as additional phenomena of light
> and other radiations have been discovered; and the properties of this
> medium, as deduced from the phenomena of light, have been found to
> be precisely those required to explain electromagnetic phenomena.[21]

Maxwell himself studied the interaction of electric and magnetic fields in space. He discovered their wavelike behavior and showed theoretically that these electromagnetic waves propagated at the velocity of light. His contribution, in the words of Joseph Larmor in the eleventh edition of the *Encyclopædia Britannica*, "largely transformed theoretical physics into the science of aether."[22] Larmor's entry on "Aether" was long and technical. "Can we form a consistent notion of such a connecting medium?" he asks, almost in despair. "In carrying out this scientific procedure false steps will from time to time be made, which will have to be retraced, or rather amended," he adds; but though published in 1911, the article carries no hint of Einstein's iconoclastic statement of 1905, that the luminiferous aether will prove to be superfluous.

Writing partly in jest about a decade later, Einstein remarked:

> As regards the mechanical nature of Lorentz's ether, one might say of
> it . . . that immobility was the only mechanical property which Lorentz
> left it. It may be added that the whole difference which the special
> theory of relativity made in our conception of the ether lay in this, that
> it divested the ether of its last mechanical quality, namely immobility.[23]

With special relativity, Einstein did not so much "solve" the problem of the aether as to make it irrelevant. His radically different choices of

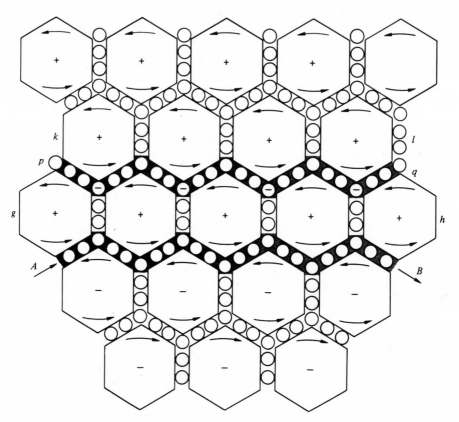

James Clerk Maxwell's molecular vortices and electrical particles, part of the nineteenth-century elaboration of the luminiferous aether (1861).

what were the pivotal points of physics essentially rendered aether a non-problem. Indeed the luminiferous aether, stripped of its essential properties, withered on the vine. In our modern conceptions, space has become emptier and emptier. Light waves inhabit space quite independently of any material or aethereal substratum. But, in fact, the aether has simply undergone another metamorphosis. No longer needed as the bearer of light, an entirely new aether can symbolize the physical properties of space specified by Einstein's general theory of relativity in 1916. As Einstein himself wrote in 1920: "To deny the existence of the ether means, in the last analysis, denying all physical properties to empty space. But such a view is inconsistent with the fundamental facts of mechanics."[24]

Among Einstein's contemporaries were scientists like Sir Oliver Lodge, who had made their scientific reputations by describing the aether. By 1926, when the thirteenth edition of the *Encyclopædia Britannica* appeared, not only had Einstein's theory been well established, but the idea of the nuclear atom as well; reluctant to abandon a concept once so firmly entrenched, Lodge could still write:

Meanwhile we must assume that the ether has a substantiality and
wave-conveying structure beyond our present clear imaginings, with
parts of it modified in an unknown way into electrons and protons. . . .
There is very little doubt that matter is not an alien substance, but is
essentially composed of it, being built up of the electrons and protons
whose constitution has not yet been ascertained, but which must
somehow be constituted of ether, perhaps in some sense analogous to
that in which a knot in a piece of string is constructed of string.[25]

Lodge went on to say:

The theory of Relativity has led some people—not many leaders of
thought—to doubt if the ether can really exist. . . . Einstein was led by
considerations of relativity to formulate a law of gravitation, not in
terms of force or of action at a distance, but in terms of something in
space, that is, in the ether, which results in a tendency of bodies to
approach each other. It might be called a warp in space, or it might be
called by other names: the names do not matter. . . .

The beauty of these results is overwhelming; but the idea that any
mathematical scheme is more than a powerful method of exploration,
and that a universe can be thus constructed in which physical
explanations can be dispensed with, involves too simple and
anthropomorphic a view of nature. The things calculated, and the
things observed, cannot exhaust reality; an explanation is bound to be
sought, and ultimately attained, in terms of the partially recognised but
largely unexplored properties of the entity which fills space.[26]

Because the word *aether* has been virtually banished from today's physics,
Lodge's statement has a curiously conservative ring; yet Einstein himself
would probably have agreed with much of it. As he grew older, Einstein
long pondered the relation of electromagnetism, atoms, and gravitation.
His unsatisfied search for a unified field theory was, in effect, an attempt
to reconcile the metrical properties of space (the "gravitational ether" as he
called it) and the electromagnetic properties of matter. "It would, of course,
be a great step forward if we succeeded in combining the gravitational field
and the electro-magnetic field into a single structure," Einstein wrote in the
article mentioned above. "The antithesis of ether and matter would then
fade away, and the whole of physics would become a completely enclosed
intellectual system, like geometry. . . ."[27]

Most of Einstein's contemporaries saw his search for a unified field theory
as a frustrating quest after a will-o'-the-wisp. To Einstein it remained a
compelling goal. To have two independent structures of space, one metric-
gravitational and the other electromagnetic, was, to him, "intolerable to the
theoretical spirit." Had Einstein lived to be a centenarian, he would undoubtedly be gratified to learn that his elusive objective is once more a
fashionable area of research. Whether gravitational, electrical, and nuclear
interactions can be encompassed within a unified theoretical structure, and
whether such a structure will be conceived as a plenary space with physical

properties, remains to be seen. But if the history of the successive dynasties of aether is any guide, we can eventually proclaim:

The luminiferous aether is dead!

Long live the aether!

---

[1] Paraphrased from Thomas L. Heath, *Greek Astronomy* (London: J. M. Dent & Sons, 1932), p. 67.

[2] Heath, *Aristarchus of Samos* (Oxford: Clarendon Press, 1913), p. 222.

[3] Bernard Goldstein, "The Arabic Version of Ptolemy's *Planetary Hypotheses*," *Transactions of the American Philosophical Society*, 57, part 4 (1967).

[4] Roger Arnaldez and Albert Z. Iskandar, "Ibn Rushd," in *Dictionary of Scientific Biography* (New York: Charles Scribner's Sons, 1975), Vol. 12, p. 3.

[5] For this information I am indebted to Dr. George Saliba who has recently discovered the treatise of My'ayyad ad-Dīn al-'Urdī.

[6] Adapted from the translation of Ibn ash-Shāṭir, by David A. King, in *Dictionary of Scientific Biography* (New York: Charles Scribner's Sons, 1975), Vol. 12, p. 358.

[7] Revised from the translations of Edward Rosen, *Three Copernican Treatises* (New York: Columbia University Press, 1939; Octagon Books, 1971), p. 57, and Noel Swerdlow, "The Commentariolous of Copernicus," *Proceedings of the American Philosophical Society*, 117, no. 6 (1973): pp. 433–34.

[8] *GBWW*, Vol. 34, p. 528.

[9] *See* Swerdlow, op. cit., pp. 427–29.

[10] In Rheticus's *Narratio prima; see* Rosen, op. cit., p. 137.

[11] Tycho Brahe, *De mundi aetherei recentioribus phaenomenis*, in *Tychonis Brahe opera omnia*, ed. J. L. E. Dreyer (Libraria Gyldendaliana: Copenhagen, 1922), Chap. 8, p. 156; for a translation of this chapter, *see* M. Boas and A. Rupert Hall, *Occasional Notes of the Royal Astronomical Society*, Vol. 3 (1959), pp. 253–63.

[12] Nicholas Copernicus, *On the Revolutions*, trans. Edward Rosen (Baltimore: Johns Hopkins University Press, 1978), p. 20; see also *GBWW*, Vol. 16, p. 525.

[13] Tycho Brahe to Caspar Peucer, 13 September 1588, in *Tychonis Brahe opera omina*, ed. J. L. E. Dreyer (Copenhagen, 1924), Vol. 7, p. 130. Trans. Christine Jones and quoted by Robert Westman in "Three Responses to the Copernican Theory," in *The Copernican Achievement*, ed. R. Westman (Berkeley: University of California Press, 1975) p. 329.

[14] *GBWW*, Vol. 16, pp. 888–905.

[15] Galileo Galilei, *Dialogue Concerning the Two Chief World Systems*, trans. Stillman Drake (Berkeley: University of California Press, 1953) p. 462.

[16] Isaac Newton to Richard Bentley, 25 February 1692/3, in *The Correspondence of Isaac Newton*, ed. H. W. Turnbull (Cambridge: Cambridge University Press, 1961), Vol. 3, p. 254; see also *GBWW*, Vol. 3, pp. 817–18.

[17] *GBWW*, Vol. 34, p. 558; see also *GBWW*, Vol. 3, p. 817.

[18] *GBWW*, Vol. 34, p. 554.

[19] *GBWW*, Vol. 34, p. 520.

[20] *GBWW*, Vol. 34, p. 521.

[21] Quoted in Joseph Larmor's article "Aether," in *Encyclopædia Britannica*, 11th edition (London and New York, 1911), Vol. I, p. 292.

[22] Ibid.

[23] Albert Einstein, "Relativity and the Ether" (1920), in *Essays in Science* (New York: Philosophical Library), p. 103.

[24] Ibid., p. 106.

[25] Oliver Lodge, "Ether," in *Encyclopædia Britannica*, 13th edition (London and New York, 1926), Vol. 29, pp. 1027–28.

[26] Ibid., p. 1028.

[27] Einstein, op. cit., pp. 110–11.

NOTE TO THE READER

While cosmology is not itself among the great ideas that make up the *Syntopicon*, its subject matter is comprehended by topics listed under several of those ideas. The most extensive discussion is in Chapter 102, WORLD. Three great conceptions of the universe are there distinguished. One conceives it as a living organism with a soul; another regards it as a mechanical system of moving parts; still another perceives in it an ordered community of beings diverse in kind. Of these conceptions, only the second would be recognized by the contributors to this symposium as of scientific interest; the first, which goes back to Plato, has long since been relegated to poetry and the third was always the province of the theologians. Yet the analogue of the organism is perhaps not altogether wrong in terms of modern cosmology. Consistent with such a notion are theories noted in the WORLD chapter in the *Syntopicon* to the effect that the universe was formed originally by a fortuitous concourse of atoms (Topic 4c); that there are other universes besides the one in which we now exist (Topic 5); that our own universe is structured in the same way throughout (Topic 6a); that it may be of greater or less extent (Topic 7); and that it may at some point have an end (Topic 8). Material on each of these proposals can be found in *GBWW*.

Additional relevant readings are listed in Chapter 5, ASTRONOMY, where the relation of astronomy and cosmology is taken up (Topic 5) along with the laws of celestial motion (Topic 8c [3]). *See also* Chapter 23, ETERNITY, the readings at Topic 2 dealing with issues raised by conceptions of the infinity of time and the possible eternity of the universe; also Chapter 40, INFINITY, Topics 3d and 3e dealing with space and time, and Topic 4a having to do with infinity as a function of any existing thing as well as of matter generally; also Chapter 93, TIME, the readings at Topic 2c which contemplate the prospect of an eternity prior to or outside time.

PART TWO

Current Developments in the Arts and Sciences

Einstein's General Theory of Relativity and Cosmology

S. Chandrasekhar

Indian born, S. Chandrasekhar was educated at the University of Cambridge, where he received his Ph.D. in theoretical physics in 1933. In 1937 he came to the University of Chicago, at which he has remained ever since. He is now the Morton D. Hull Distinguished Service Professor in the Departments of Astronomy and Physics and in the Enrico Fermi Institute at the university.

While Professor Chandrasekhar's current work is centered on general relativity in astrophysics, he has contributed to a number of different fields of astronomy as indicated in the titles of the books of which he is the author: *An Introduction to the Study of Stellar Structure* (1939), *Principles of Stellar Dynamics* (1942), *Radiative Transfer* (1950), and *Ellipsoidal Figures of Equilibrium* (1969). He is widely known for his astronomical theory called the "Chandrasekhar limit," an upper limit assigned to the mass of "white dwarf" stars—those which are in the later or final evolutionary stages of their lives.

Among his numerous honors have been the Bruce Gold Medal of the Astronomical Society of the Pacific (1952), the Gold Medal of the Royal Astronomical Society of London (1953), the Rumford Prize of the American Academy of Arts and Sciences for his work on radiative transfer in the interior of stars (1957), and India's Padma Vibhushan Decoration (1968). In 1962 he was awarded the Royal Medal of the Royal Society by Queen Elizabeth for distinguished research in mathematical physics; and in 1967, at a White House ceremony, he received the National Medal of Science from Pres. Lyndon B. Johnson for "numerous superb contributions to stellar astronomy, physics, and applied mathematics, and for his guidance and inspiration to his many students and colleagues."

Nature and Nature's laws lay hid in night:
God said, *Let Newton be!* and all was light.

> Alexander Pope (*Epitaph Intended for Sir Isaac Newton*)

The reality on which our space is based must form a discrete manifold, or else the reason for the metrical relationships is to be looked for externally in the binding forces acting upon it.

> Bernhard Riemann ("Concerning the Hypotheses Which Lie at the Base of Geometry," Inaugural address, Göttingen, 1854)

Scarcely anyone who has fully understood this theory can escape from its magic; the theory represents a genuine triumph of the methods of the absolute differential calculus founded by Gauss, Riemann, Christoffel, Ricci, and Levi-Civita.

> A. Einstein ("Zur allgemeinen Relativitätstheorie," in *Sitzungsberichte der Preussischen Akademie der Wissenschaften zu Berlin*, 1915)

Thus this theory, which is one of the greatest examples of the power of speculative thought, presents a solution not only of the problem of the relativity of all motion (the only solution which satisfies the demands of logic), but also of the problem of gravitation. We see how cogent arguments bring the ideas of Riemann and Einstein to a successful issue. . . . It is as if a wall which separated us from Truth has collapsed.

> Hermann Weyl (*Space, Time, Matter*, 1918)

This fusion of two previously quite disconnected subjects—metric and gravitation—must be considered as the most beautiful achievement of the general theory of relativity. . . . This fusion of gravity and metric leads to a satisfactory solution not only of the gravitational problem, but also that of geometry.

> W. Pauli ("Relativitätstheorie," in *Encyclopädie der mathematischen Wissenschaften*, 1921)

By his theory of relativity, Albert Einstein has provoked a revolution of thought in physical science.

> A. S. Eddington (*Space, Time and Gravitation*, 1921)

I. THE GENERAL THEORY OF RELATIVITY

Newton's *Philosophiae Naturalis Principia Mathematica* [Mathematical Principles of Natural Philosophy], 1687, occupies an honored place among the
Great Books of the Western World; and Einstein's general theory of relativity,
which necessitates some fundamental revisions in the conceptual framework of the Newtonian principles, certainly deserves to be included among
the great ideas of the twentieth century. But so much myth and legend have
surrounded Einstein's theory that it is not always possible to disentangle
(without being argumentative) its underlying concepts. On this account, the
present exposition will ignore the mass of irrelevant assertions, speculations, and dogmas which have accreted over the years and concentrate
instead on the basic ideas of the theory in the spirit of the statements of
Pauli and of Weyl which preface this essay.

A. The need for modifying the Newtonian theory

We begin by asking if there was any reason to feel dissatisfied with the
Newtonian theory of gravitation when Einstein founded his general theory
of relativity in 1915.

Observationally, the Newtonian theory had been subjected to the most
stringent tests and had come to be regarded as a perfect model for formulating exact laws of nature. The cases where possible failures could be
suspected were almost insignificant. Certain discrepancies had been found
in some irregularities in the motion of the Moon, but astronomers had
correctly sought reasons for these irregularities in other causes. Only one
failure had led to a serious questioning of the law: the discordance of the
motion of the planet Mercury. But the magnitude of this discordance was
no more than one part in ten million, and even in that instance astronomers
were looking for other causes.

What then were the grounds for being dissatisfied with the Newtonian
theory, as Einstein was for ten years following his formulation in 1905 of
the principles of what has come to be called the special theory of relativity?
Einstein believed that Newton's theory, besides being ambiguous, was inconsistent with the special theory of relativity.

The inconsistency derives from the fact that Newton's theory of gravitation postulates instantaneous action at a distance, and this postulate violates
the rule that no signal of any kind can be propagated with a velocity
exceeding that of light. The ambiguity derives from the fact that mass as
conceived by Newton—namely, as "the quantity of matter"—is not appropriate; the principles of special relativity require that we include in "mass"
the equivalent of other forms of energy such as the very kinetic energy of
the motion.

While one may concede the foregoing reasons for dissatisfaction, one is
at a loss to know how one might formulate a theory which would successfully modify the Newtonian principles without violating in any way their im-

pressive results. Yet, that is what Einstein did. The successful solution of this problem is his triumph.

B. Newton's laws of motion: their conceptual implications

In order to elucidate Einstein's reasoning in formulating his general theory of relativity, it is necessary that we first clarify the full implications of Newton's laws of motion. As Hermann Bondi has written:

> The really difficult step is the step taken by Newton and Galileo, and not the step taken by Einstein. Because we learn Newtonian physics at a stage of life when our receptive power is very high and our critical power not over-great, we tend to swallow these very difficult ideas without much questioning, and then think that the difficulty lies in what we happen to learn later when our receptive powers are poorer and our critical powers a little greater. But we find this difficulty in the Einsteinian picture only because we have not digested it sufficiently in the Newtonian picture.

And what is this difficult step that Newton and Galileo took? It is implied in the way in which Newton formulated his first two laws of motion. These laws, as stated in his *Principia*, are:

Law 1: Every body continues in its state of rest, or of uniform motion in a right line, unless it is compelled to change that state by forces impressed upon it.

Law 2: The change of motion is proportional to the motive force impressed; and is made in the direction of the right line in which that force is impressed.

Newton's first law requires us, for example, to distinguish observers in uniform relative motion. Observers distinguished by this fact, namely, that each one considers the other as moving with a uniform velocity relative to himself, are called *inertial observers*. Since each inertial observer can attribute causes (in terms of impressed force) only to *accelerations* (*i.e.*, rates of change of velocity), it follows that their description of external phenomena (described in terms of forces that may be impressed) must essentially be the same. In other words, the *world view of different inertial observers must be the same.* This requirement of the invariance of the world view is consistent with the fact that all the laws of physics which have been formulated (including Newton's own laws of gravitation) provide equations only for the accelerations of bodies (or, components of bodies) belonging to a system. This invariance of the laws of physics, as formulated by different inertial observers, underlies all of physics since Newton; and the special theory of relativity is no exception. But the special theory of relativity requires a far-reaching generalization of the basic concepts; and to this generalization we now turn.

C. The enlargement of the notion of inertial observers and the principles of the special theory of relativity

While Newton's first law of motion that "every body continues in its state of rest, or of uniform motion in a right line, unless it is compelled to change that state by forces impressed upon it" retains its universal validity, its base has yet to be broadened to allow for the important discovery of James Clerk Maxwell that the velocity of propagation of electromagnetic disturbances (in a vacuum) is that of light; and that on Maxwell's theory the velocity of light, c, is uniform and constant. If that is the case, with respect to what is this velocity, c? To this question, the answer of the physicists of the nineteenth century was that the constant velocity of propagation of light in a vacuum is with respect to a uniform luminiferous all-pervading ether. But all efforts to detect the motion of the Earth through the presumed all-pervading ether failed. The most celebrated of these experiments is that of A. A. Michelson and Edward Morley in 1887. The failure of that experiment to detect the motion of the Earth (or other material bodies) through the postulated ether left Maxwell's theory of electromagnetism in an ambiguous position. The basic question was how to reconcile Newton's first law of motion with Maxwell's theory and the belief in ether. Several heroic efforts were made toward this reconciliation, particularly by H. A. Lorentz; and the great mathematician and physicist H. Poincaré came very near to resolving the impasse to which the physics of the nineteenth century had reached. But an unexpectedly simple and direct solution was provided by Einstein in 1905.

As we have stated, the equivalence of inertial observers in uniform relative motion underlies Newtonian dynamics. That is Newton's principle of relativity. In making deductions from this principle, one makes a further assumption of *absolute time, i.e.,* that inertial observers, carrying with them clocks for timekeeping, can synchronize them in such a way that they can all assign the same time, t, unambiguously, to any external world event. In essence, what Einstein did was to abandon the notion of absolute time. The content of his argument is the following.

It is a logical consequence of Newton's first law of motion that there exists a class of observers in uniform relative motion, whom we call inertial observers, such that all of them find Newton's law to be correct, while no one else does. The converse of this statement is that all inertial observers are equivalent as far as Newton's first law of motion is concerned. In Newtonian dynamics the assumption is made that this equivalence obtains for all *dynamical* phenomena. Einstein widened the equivalence to all *physical* phenomena. This widening of the equivalence is Einstein's principle of relativity: it is a hypothesis and requires empirical confirmation.

A conceptual readjustment is needed to incorporate the constancy of the velocity of light into Einstein's principle of relativity. A direct (if somewhat naive) way of incorporating this fact would be to make the following assumption. Let two inertial observers in uniform relative motion encounter one another at a particular point and at a particular instant. Further, at the instant of encounter, let a flash of light be emitted. The two observers separate after the encounter. The crucial statement is that *both* observers will describe the advancing wave front of the emitted light (as each discerns it) as expanding spherically symmetrically about them with the *same* velocity, *c*. Clearly, this result cannot be obtained if the transformation between the two inertial observers is carried out in the usual manner (with the aid of the conventional "parallelogram of velocities") in three-dimensional space and consistent with the notion of absolute time. A transformation consistent with the stated assumption requires one to deal with space and time in a unified manner and to revise one's common notion of simultaneity. It is this unified way of treating inertial observers (with the underlying postulate of the constancy of the velocity of light with respect to all of them) that leads one directly to the special theory of relativity and its various ramifications, including Einstein's well-known equivalence of mass with energy. A detailed description of how all these deductions follow will require a mathematical treatment (albeit an elementary one) which we must forgo in this account.

D. Newton's and Einstein's principles of equivalence

We have already stated why Newton's laws of gravitation are ambiguous and inconsistent with the requirements of the special theory of relativity. We shall now outline the reasoning that led Einstein to his formulation of his general theory of relativity and his laws of gravitation.

In a gravitational field, particles are, of course, accelerated and the different particles, on that account, can no longer represent inertial observers. Einstein's desire was to show that there is, nevertheless, some equivalence among them, and further, that the equivalence need not wholly be restricted to inertial observers. In other words, he sought an equivalence extending to accelerated observers. Einstein was successful in his search by reason of the special character of motions in a gravitational field, which derives from Galileo's observation that *all bodies fall equally fast*. This observation of Galileo, in combination with Newton's second law of motion, implies the equality of what has generally been called the *inertial* and the *gravitational* masses of a body. Newton recognized the prime importance of this inference. Indeed his Definition I in Book I of the *Principia* is devoted to it. He states:

> *The quantity of matter is the measure of the same, arising from its density and bulk cojointly.*
>
> Thus air of a double density, in a double space, is quadruple in quantity: in a triple space, sextuple in quantity. The same thing is to be understood of snow, and fine dust or powders, that are condensed by compression or liquefaction, and of all bodies that are by any causes whatever differently condensed. I have no regard in this place to a medium, if any such there is, that freely pervades the interstices between the parts of bodies. It is this quantity that I mean hereafter

everywhere under the name of body or mass. And the same is known
by the weight of each body, for it is proportional to the weight, as I
have found by experiments on pendulums, very accurately made,
which shall be shown hereafter.

The accuracy of the equality stated by Newton and verified by him (by
his "experiments on pendulums") to one part in a thousand has been
improved by modern, more sophisticated experiments to one part in 10^{13}.
And this equality, as Weyl has emphasized, is an "enigmatic fact" which
obtrudes into Newton's theory as an element of magic.

The equality of the inertial and the gravitational masses of a body manifests itself, for example, in the following empirical fact: the direction of a
plumb line at a point of the Earth in no way depends on the constitution
(physical or chemical) of the bob; this independence was verified, for example, by Roland Eötvös to one part in 10^{11}. But the forces acting on the bob
of the plumb line derive from two sources: besides the gravitational field
of the Earth, it is subject to the centrifugal force derived from the rotation
of the Earth. On account of the centrifugal force, the bob experiences an
inertial force proportional to what Newton calls the "quantity of matter,"
i.e., its *inertial mass.* On the other hand, the force due to gravity, making the
plumb line point toward the center of the Earth, is proportional to what
Newton calls the "weight," *i.e.,* its *gravitational mass.* The fact that the direction of the plumb line is independent of the physical and the chemical
constitution of the bob attests to the precise equality of the two masses.

We can state the implications of the equality of the inertial and the
gravitational masses somewhat differently as follows: if an observer experiences a certain acceleration, he will see other bodies as having an acceleration that is opposite in sign with his own; and he will describe the other
bodies as experiencing a force proportional to their inertial masses. Since
these forces he attributes to them result from his describing them in his own
accelerated frame, they are "fictitious." But gravitational forces are also
proportional to the same masses. Why then should we suppose that the
gravitational forces are "real" while inertial forces are "fictitious"? Einstein's
argument is that there is no reason to suppose that one kind of force is any
more "real" or any less "fictitious" than the other; and this is the center and
the core of his reasoning.

In view of the importance of Einstein's conclusion, it may be profitable
to look at the matter in a somewhat different way.

Suppose we wish to verify the truth of Newton's first law of motion. We
should then seek a place where no external forces act on any of the inertial
observers that are postulated. In practice, we can compensate for most
forces that act on bodies: we can ensure that no strings, elastic or otherwise,
are attached to the inertial observers; we can compensate for whatever
electric or magnetic forces that may be acting. But to be free of gravitational
forces, we should have to go infinitely far from whatever gravitating bodies

that may be present. In a universe such as ours, in which matter is all pervasive, we cannot find such a haven. But Einstein showed that we can compensate for a prevailing gravitational field *without* finding such a haven.

A set of inertial observers enclosed in a box, for example, can free themselves of gravity by letting the box fall freely. In such a box, falling freely in a uniform gravitational field, two observers initially at rest with respect to each other will always remain so. Similarly, two observers with a certain relative velocity at a given instant will retain their relative velocity for all times (since they are equally accelerated by the gravitational field). For such freely falling observers in a uniform gravitational field, Newton's first law of motion will appear to be valid, and they will be justified in believing themselves to be inertial observers.

We may accordingly formulate Newton's first law of motion in two parts: *first* that there exists a standard motion such that for bodies following that motion, no force acts between them; and *second* that the standard motion prescribed is that of uniform relative motion. In Einstein's formulation of Newton's first law, the first part of the foregoing statement is retained; but in place of the second part, he substitutes that the standard motion prescribed is that of freely falling observers in a volume sufficiently small so that the *nonuniformity* of whatever gravitational field that may be present can be ignored. This is Einstein's principle of equivalence and it forms the corner-stone of his theory.

While we have tried to introduce the principle of equivalence in an intuitive fashion, it may be useful to state it in a more formal language in the manner of Pauli:

> For every infinitely small world region (*i.e.*, a world region which is so small that the space- and time-variation of gravity can be neglected in it) there always exists a coordinate system K_0 (x, y, z, t) in which gravitation has no influence either on the motion of particles or any other physical processes.

To repeat, the essential content of Einstein's principle of equivalence is that in every sufficiently small region of the world the gravitational field can always be transformed away; and this is possible only because a gravitational field has the fundamental property that it imparts the same acceleration to all bodies by virtue of the equality of the inertial and the gravitational mass.

On the basis of the principle of equivalence, it would be natural to assume that the special theory of relativity should be valid in the local frame K_0 (*i.e.*, in the local freely falling frame). The problem now is to extend the laws holding *locally* (*i.e.*, in small infinitesimal regions) to be valid *globally* (*i.e.*, to regions separated by finite space-time intervals).

The extension of the laws of physics as formulated by inertial observers (which we assume to be valid locally for freely falling bodies) to finite regions is fraught with ambiguity, and the passage from the foregoing general considerations to Einstein's particular formulation of his laws of gravitation requires mathematical reasoning somewhat beyond the scope of this essay. For the sake of completeness, we shall give a general account of the manner of Einstein's reasoning in the following section. (A reader not interested in this may omit Section E and pass on to Section F.) Let it suffice here to say that by arguments which are a mixture of physical reasonableness, mathematical simplicity, and aesthetic sensibility, Einstein was able to write down a set of equations whose consequences have been verified (within the accuracy of experiments or of observations) wherever such verification is possible. (We consider these verifications in Section F).

E. Einstein's laws of gravitation

As we have seen, an accelerated observer in a region of space, free of gravitational forces, will ascribe the acceleration of the bodies which he sees to the action of inertial forces upon them. These forces are "fictitious" because they arise from the motions of bodies not in a standard frame of Cartesian coordinates (x, y, z) but in a general frame of curvilinear coordinates; or, as one says, the inertial forces are *metrical* in origin. Since Einstein's principle of equivalence denies that gravitational forces are any less "fictitious" than inertial forces, one must conclude that *all acceleration, inertial and gravitational, must be metrical in origin*. This fundamental postulate of Einstein is stated in mathematical terms as follows.

In the freely falling frame K_0 (*see* Section D), the interval ds between two space-time events separated by a spatial interval dx, dy, dz, and a time interval dt is given by

$$ds^2 = dx^2 + dy^2 + dz^2 - c^2dt^2.$$

In this equation the differentials dx, dy, dz, and dt are to be determined directly by means of standard measuring rods and clocks. If we now consider some other frame of reference, K, in which the value of the coordinates $(x^1, x^2, x^3,$ and $x^4)$ are assigned to space-time events in a completely arbitrary manner, then at each space-time point the corresponding differentials dx^1, dx^2, dx^3, and dx^4 will be some linear combinations of dx, dy, dz, and cdt and the interval ds^2 will be transformed into

$$
\begin{aligned}
ds^2 = {} & g_{11} \, (dx^1)^2 + g_{22} \, (dx^2)^2 + g_{33} \, (dx^3)^2 + g_{44} \, (dx^4)^2 \\
& + 2g_{12}dx^1dx^2 + 2g_{13}dx^1dx^3 + 2g_{14}dx^1dx^4 \\
& + 2g_{23}dx^2dx^3 + 2dg_{24}dx^2dx^4 + 2g_{34}dx^3dx^4,
\end{aligned}
$$

where the ten coefficients g_{11}, g_{12}, etc., are functions of $x^1 \ldots x^4$. It is moreover obvious that a transition to a coordinate frame, different from $x^1, x^2, x^3,$ and x^4, will transform the ten coefficients g_{11}, etc., in such a way that the interval ds^2 remains the same. A space-time, described in terms of an expression for the interval of the form we have written, is governed by laws which are generalizations of the laws which govern our familiar three-dimensional Euclidian world in which the distance, dr, between two points at (x, y, z) and

$(x + dx, y + dy, z + dz)$ is given by

$$dr^2 = dx^2 + dy^2 + dz^2.$$

The laws governing these more general "geometries" were derived by Bernhard Riemann in 1854. Essentially, Einstein's description of space-time in terms of this geometry of Riemann is that one must contemplate the possibility of describing the physical world in all conceivable coordinate systems. The coordinates, in fact, will have to be thought of as associated with space-time events in some unique and continuous manner.

To pass from these very general premises to specific laws governing gravitation is, as we have said, fraught with ambiguities, and it requires exceptional aesthetic sensibility (or "the power of speculative thought," as Weyl has expressed) to obtain a unique solution to the problem. The main lines of Einstein's arguments, modeled on Newton's derivation of *his* laws of gravitation, are as follows.

The Newtonian laws of gravitation are formulated with increasing generality in three steps: *(1)* the laws of motion applicable in a field-free space; *(2)* the laws of gravitation and of motion applicable to regions free of matter but where gravitational forces of external bodies are operative; and *(3)* the laws of gravitation and of motion applicable to regions where matter is present.

These laws are the following:

1. In field-free space, Newton's first law of motion applies and bodies describe linear trajectories with a constant velocity.
2. In regions external to material bodies, the gravitational field is determined by a gravitational potential V; and the acceleration experienced by a particle, where the gravitational potential is V, is determined by the nonuniformity of V at that point and is in the direction of its maximum change and with an intensity proportional to the magnitude of this change. Symbolically, this fact is expressed by the equation

   acceleration = gradient of V.

   (When V = constant, the acceleration is zero as required by the first law.) And moreover, the potential V satisfies the equation,

   $$\frac{\delta^2 V}{\delta x^2} + \frac{\delta^2 V}{\delta y^2} + \frac{\delta^2 V}{\delta z^2} = 0$$

   —the so-called equation of Laplace.
3. In regions where matter is present, the gravitational potential is determined by the prevailing distribution of matter; and the force acting at any point is obtained by simply summing over the gravitational attraction of the different portions of the matter in accordance with Newton's law that "every particle of matter attracts every other particle of matter with a force proportional to their masses and inversely as the square of

the distances between them." Symbolically, the corresponding equation governing the gravitational potential V is written as

$$\frac{\delta^2 V}{\delta x^2} + \frac{\delta^2 V}{\delta y^2} + \frac{\delta^2 V}{\delta z^2} = -4\pi G\rho,$$

where ρ denotes the material density and G the constant of gravitation; and the acceleration that a particle will experience at any point is determined by V by the same equation as in the second law.

Einstein's formulation of his laws follows in analogous fashion in three steps:

1. While it is true that particles describe curved trajectories in noninertial frames, it is insisted that in the absence of a gravitational field one should be able to eliminate the "fictitious" inertial forces and reduce the trajectories of individual particles to "right lines" (as in Newton's first law) described with a constant velocity. This requirement is consistent with Einstein's description of motions, in an arbitrary coordinate system in the framework of Riemannian geometry, only if a certain complicated quantity—the Riemann-Christoffel tensor with twenty distinct components—vanishes identically. And this requirement is a restriction on the nature of the geometry that must obtain in field-free space.

2. In regions of space-time where no matter is present, but where a gravitational field derived from neighboring bodies is present, Einstein makes a lesser restriction on the possible forms of geometries than that all twenty components of the Riemann-Christoffel tensor be required to vanish identically. He adduces arguments of simplicity and mathematical similarity with Newtonian equations to require that certain ten linear combinations of the twenty components of the Riemann-Christoffel tensor—the so-called Ricci tensor—vanish. Further, he requires that the trajectories of free particles in such regions be arcs of minimum length in the appropriate geometry: in other words, the paths are the "straightest" possible, or "geodesics," as one says.

3. In regions of space where matter is present, one must enlarge the possible geometries to allow for the presence of matter. In the Newtonian theory, one relates the Newtonian gravitational potential, V, to the prevalent distribution of matter determined by the density, ρ. In general relativity, the density alone will not suffice to specify the prevalent distribution of matter *and* motions. A complete description of the latter requires ten quantities comprised under what one calls the energy-momentum tensor. Einstein's equations relate these ten components of the energy-momentum tensor to the ten components of the Ricci tensor. These equations make the distribution of matter and motions determine the geometry of space-time and conversely. It is in this sense that Einstein's theory provides a "fusion of the metric with gravitation" and unifies the geometry of space-time with the presence of matter.

We may add that there is no need to supplement Einstein's "field equations" with any separate "equations of motion."

F. Experimental and observational confirmations of the predictions of general relativity

In announcing his laws of gravitation in 1915, Einstein enunciated three tests for his theory. These tests have come to be known as the classical tests. They pertain, respectively, to: *(1)* the dependence of the rate of a clock on the gravitational potential at its location; *(2)* the deflection of light by a gravitational field; and *(3)* the precession of the fixed Keplerian orbits of the Newtonian theory.

We shall consider the extent to which these tests have confirmed the predictions of general relativity.

1. The first of the three tests enumerated is not really a test of the precise form of Einstein's equations; it is rather a test of the principle of equivalence. Indeed, as we shall presently show, Einstein's prediction with respect to the dependence of the rate of a clock on the gravitational potential at its location follows from extremely general considerations.

First, we observe that the frequency, ν, of a characteristic radiation emitted by an atom provides the basis for an atomic clock, even as any mechanical oscillator (such as a tuning fork) with a constant frequency. The frequency ν is related to the wavelength λ of the emitted radiation by $\nu = c/\lambda$; and according to the quantum theory, the emission of light by an atom can also be pictured as the emission of discrete light quanta, or photons, with an energy $h\nu$ where h denotes Planck's constant.

Einstein's prediction relative to his first test is that the frequency of the radiation emitted by an atom, in a location where the gravitational potential is V, differs from the frequency of the radiation emitted by the same atom, in field-free space, by the fractional amount $\Delta\nu/\nu = -V/c^2$. In particular, the frequency of the radiation emitted by two identical atoms, at two different heights on the Earth, should differ by the fractional amount gH/c^2, where g is the value of gravity, H is the difference in the heights, and c is the velocity of light. Also, it is the atom at the lower level which emits the radiation of lower frequency and, therefore, light quanta of lower energy. The following ideal experimental arrangement devised by Bondi shows how one can infer this predicted difference in energy from such elementary notions as the nonexistence of perpetuum mobile (*i.e.*, perpetual motion).

Consider a closed chain of buckets stretched between two pulleys whose axes, fixed relative to the Earth, are at different heights (and, therefore, at different gravitational potentials). (*See* fig. 1.) Let each bucket contain an atom which is capable of existing in two states—a ground state and an excited state of higher energy. Further, let the atoms in the buckets on the left-hand side be excited while those in the buckets on the right-hand side

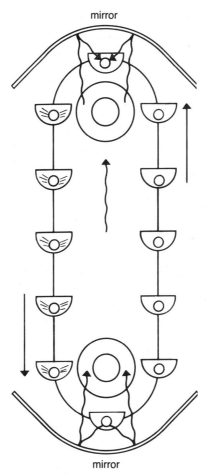

Figure 1. The endless bucket chain devised by Bondi. Extra energy in the excited atoms causes the chain to rotate.

are in the ground state. The excited atoms, being in states of energy higher than the atoms in the ground state, are (by virtue of the equivalence of mass and energy) more *massive* and therefore (by the equality of the inertial and gravitational masses) *heavier*. If we assume that there is no friction in the system (as we may, since the arrangement is an ideal one), it is clear that the chain will begin to rotate in a counterclockwise direction. We arrange that when each bucket reaches the bottom, the atom, which is in it, is de-excited with the emission of a photon with an energy derived from the atomic transition. We further arrange, by a suitable disposition of mirrors, that the emitted photon is reflected upward and made to impinge on the normal atom in the bucket which is then at the top. Now, *if* the reflected photon *could* be reabsorbed by the normal atom at the top and excited to the state of higher energy, we should have succeeded in constructing a perpetuum mobile, for the process envisaged could be repeated indefinitely, and energy could be extracted from the continuing rotation of the chain. But as no perpetuum mobile can be constructed, we must conclude that the photon which arrives at the top cannot be absorbed by the normal atom which is there. In other words, by Planck's formula relating the radiation of a photon with its energy, we must conclude that the energy of the reflected photon has insufficient energy to excite the normal atom. Therefore, the frequency of the radiation which is emitted when an excited atom is in the bucket at the bottom of the chain must be less than that which would be emitted by the same atom if it were at the top of the chain. Since the rate of a clock is determined (inversely) by the frequency of the oscillator that controls its rate, it follows that the clocks at the bottom of the chain must run more slowly than the clocks at the top. And this is in accordance with Einstein's prediction.

The foregoing is an idealized experimental arrangement. But the effect predicted is precisely that which has been directly observed on the Earth in some refined experiments carried out by R. V. Pound and G. A. Rebka. Their experiments confirm the predicted effect ($\Delta\nu/\nu = gH/c^2$) to one part in a hundred.

More recently, the same effect has been measured to much higher precision by making use of frequency standards of very high stability (of a few parts in 10^{15} to 10^{16} over time intervals of 10 to 100 seconds). Thus, a hydrogen-maser clock was flown on a rocket to an altitude of about 10,000 kms and its frequency compared to a similar clock on Earth. This experiment confirmed Einstein's prediction to about two parts in ten thousand.

2. The second of Einstein's tests relative to the deflection of light bears equally on the principle of equivalence and on the particular form of his equations (*see* below). Precisely, Einstein's theory predicts that light grazing the circumference of an object of mass M and radius R should be deflected by an angle,

$$\theta = 4GM/Rc^2,$$

measured in radians (one radian $\simeq 57.17°$). For a light ray grazing the Sun, this deflection amounts to 1.75 seconds of arc. As is well known, the first announcement of a positive confirmation of this prediction (within the limits of accuracy of the measurements), by the British expeditions to observe the solar eclipse of May 29, 1919, came under spectacular circumstances on the first observance of Armistice Day after World War I.

It is of interest to recall that in 1911, Einstein had calculated, on the basis of his principle of equivalence, the amount by which light would be deflected by a gravitational field. But this calculation gives only *half* the amount predicted by the full theory. An expedition planned to test this earlier prediction, by observations that were to be made during a solar eclipse in 1914 in Russia, was foiled by the outbreak of World War I. If that expedition had succeeded, Einstein's first prediction would not have been confirmed and his later revision of the prediction to twice the earlier value would not have had the same impact as, in fact, the confirmation of 1919 did have.

The most precise test to date of the prediction with respect to the deflection of light comes from long baseline interferometric radio observations of two quasars (3C 273 and 3C 279) which are only nine degrees apart and which are occulted by the Sun every year in early October. The occultations by these quasars have been observed systematically over the past seven or eight years. The principal source of error in these observations derives from the propagation of the radio waves through the plasma of the solar corona. Fortunately, this source of error can be compensated by making observations in different radio wavelengths. The latest analysis of these observations confirms the predictions of general relativity to a fraction of a percent.

3. On the Newtonian theory, the orientation of the Keplerian ellipse described by a planet (or by the components of binary stars) is fixed in space. But on the general theory of relativity, the ellipse, while it is described in an invariant (*i.e.*, fixed) plane, nevertheless, *precesses* in the sense that the major axis, instead of pointing in a fixed direction, rotates (in the direction in which the orbit is described) at a certain constant rate. In the case of Mercury, the planet closest to the Sun, the predicted rate of precession is 43 seconds of arc per century. This rate is in extremely good agreement with the rate deduced from observations, as indeed Einstein showed already in his first publication on the subject. (This agreement has lately come under some questionings by claims that the interior of the Sun is rotating sufficiently rapidly to make the very good agreement illusory. But the experiments purporting to provide evidence for the supposed rapid rotation of the Sun have not been confirmed by other independent experiments.)

The prediction of general relativity with regard to the precession of a Keplerian orbit has found some striking applications to the binary pulsar (PSR 1913 + 16), discovered by two radio astronomers, Russel A. Hulse and Joseph H. Taylor, in 1974, which has an orbital period of 27,908 seconds. It has been found that the orbit of this pulsar binary precesses at the rate of 4.2 degrees per year (in contrast to 43 seconds of arc per century of Mercury). This rate of precession, together with other data concerning the orbit, allows one to infer that the total mass of this binary pulsar is 2.83 solar masses. This is the first instance in which the general theory of relativity has been used to make a precise astronomical deduction.

G. Black holes

Given that light is affected by gravity, it is entirely reasonable to ask the question: "How strong must the gravitational field around a body be in order for a particle, projected with the velocity of light, to escape to infinity?" Exactly this calculation was made by Laplace in 1798, though at that time he had no reason to suspect that light would be affected by gravity. If light cannot escape from a body, the body can neither be self-luminescent nor capable of reflecting or scattering any particle incident on it with a velocity less than or equal to that of light. These are essentially the conditions for an object to become a black hole.

We have seen that light grazing the Sun is deflected by the minute amount of 1.75 seconds of arc. It can be calculated that if the entire mass of the Sun could be compressed into a sphere of radius 2½ km, the gravitational field around it would be strong enough to contain any light it may emit: it would, under the circumstances, have become a black hole.

The contraction of a star of a solar mass to a radius of 2½ km does not require us to postulate unfamiliar physical conditions: the mean density of matter at that radius is no different from what it is in ordinary atomic nuclei. The physical conditions that are required for stellar masses to become black holes are, therefore, entirely within the realm of reason. The question is whether such physical conditions can be realized in the natural course of events. Or, to state the question differently, can a star, in the natural course of its evolution, attain a state in which the surrounding gravitational field becomes sufficiently strong to prevent light from escaping? That such situations can occur, during the last stages in the evolution of stars more massive than four or five solar masses, is well known. We shall not consider the astrophysical aspects of the subject in this context; we shall rather turn to what sort of predictions the general theory of relativity makes with respect to black holes that may occur in nature.

One might have thought that black holes of diverse shapes and forms would be possible, even, as on the Newtonian theory, gravitating masses can have a diversity of shapes and forms depending on the internal stratification of density and temperature and on the state of internal motions such as rotation. But on the general theory of relativity, stationary black holes that one may expect in the present astronomical universe, can be of one kind and one kind only. More precisely, the geometry of space-time around a black hole is uniquely specified by just two parameters: the mass of the black hole and its angular momentum. The uniqueness of this description derives from certain theorems proved by Brandon Carter and David Robinson. The remarkable fact is that a solution of Einstein's equations satisfying the requirements of a black hole—namely that it partition space into two regions such that the inner region can in no way communicate to the world outside and, further, that far from the inner region, space becomes asymptotically what it is in a field-free region—was discovered by Roy Kerr in 1963 before the theorems of Carter and Robinson were established. It follows that by studying the properties of Kerr's solution we can, in principle, derive all that we can ever know about black holes.

A special case of Kerr's solution is when the angular momentum of the

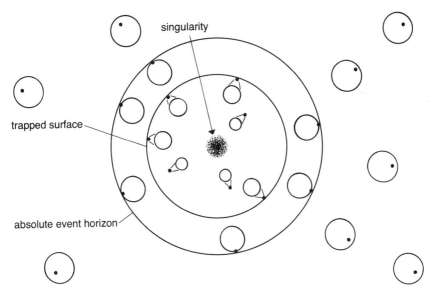

Figure 2. Effect of the curvature of space-time on the propagation of light from points in the neighborhood of a Schwarzschild (nonrotating) black hole.

black hole is zero; in this case the black hole is spherically symmetric. And this spherically symmetric solution, appropriate for nonrotating black holes, was discovered by Karl Schwarzschild in December 1915, within a month of Einstein's formulation of his theory.

We shall now briefly consider the nature of the space-times around black holes described by the Schwarzschild and the Kerr solutions. The best way to visualize them is to exhibit the "light-cone structure" in the manner of Roger Penrose.

Imagine that at a point in space, a flash of light is emitted. Consider the position of the wave front of the emitted flash of light at a fixed short interval of time later. In field-free space, the wave front will be a sphere about the point of emission. But in a strong gravitational field this will not be the case. The sphere will be distorted by the curvature of space-time about the point of emission.

Figure 2 displays these wave fronts at various distances from the center of symmetry of the Schwarzschild black hole. The section of the wave fronts by a plane through the center of symmetry is illustrated. One observes that the sections of the wave fronts are circles far from the center as one should expect; they are, however, progressively displaced asymmetrically inward as one approaches the center. And on the *horizon* (as the boundary of a black hole is called), the wave front is directed entirely inward toward the center with the point of emission on the wave front—the wave front has become tangential to the horizon. This is clearly the reason why light emitted from the horizon of a black hole does not escape to infinity. The situation in the interior of the horizon is even more remarkable. The wave front does not include the point of emission: the wave front has detached itself. And since no observer can travel with a speed faster than that of light, it follows that there can be no stationary observers within the horizon—the inexorable propulsion of every material particle toward the singularity at the center cannot be avoided.

Turning next to the geometry of the space-time in Kerr geometry, we illustrate in figure 3 sections of the wave fronts of light emitted at various points on the equatorial plane of the Kerr black hole. The singularity in this case is a ring around the center in the equatorial plane. In contrast to the Schwarzschild geometry, we have to distinguish, besides the horizon—where the wave front is entirely inside the horizon—a second surface where the wave front just manages to be attached to the source of emission. This second surface describes what has been called the ergosphere. In the region between the ergosphere and the horizon, while the wave front has detached itself from the point of emission, it is still possible for a particle, with a sufficient velocity suitably directed, to escape to infinity. The importance of this intermediate region is that it is possible for a particle entering this region from infinity to split in two in such a way that one of the pieces is absorbed by the black hole, while the other escapes to infinity with an energy which is in excess of that of the incident particle. This is the so-called Penrose process for extracting the rotational energy of the Kerr black hole. An analogous phenomenon occurs when electromagnetic or gravitational waves of sufficiently small frequencies are incident on the black hole in suitable directions. In these cases, the reflection coefficient for such incident waves exceeds unity and is called super-radiance.

H. Thermal emission by "mini" black holes

We have already referred to the possibility of extracting the rotational energy of a Kerr black hole. By a careful analysis of the manner in which energy can be extracted by incident test particles, it has been shown that the energy extracted must satisfy an equality of the form

change in mass = surface gravity × change in surface area + angular velocity of motion × change in the angular momentum.

A more general result is that the surface area of the black hole must always increase. While this restriction on the change in the surface area consequent to the extraction of energy was first established with respect to the Kerr black hole, Stephen Hawking was able to prove that the same restriction must apply quite generally. In other words, the surface area of the event horizon (that is, the boundary of a black hole) has as a property that it always increases when matter or radiation falls into the black hole. Moreover, if two black holes collide and coalesce to form a single black hole, the area of the event horizon around the resulting black hole must also be greater than the sum of the areas of the event horizons around the original

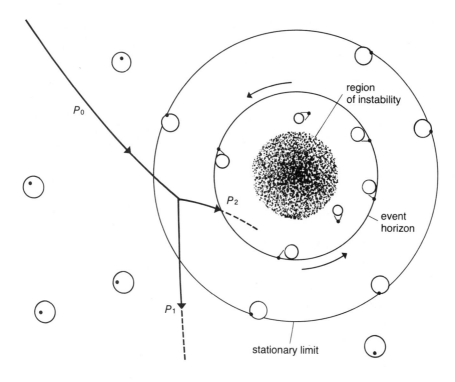

Figure 3. Equatorial cross-section of a Kerr (rotating) black hole. The positions of the wave fronts of light signals emitted at various points should be contrasted with those shown for the Schwarzschild black hole in figure 2. The rotational energy of the Kerr black hole can be extracted by a particle (P_0) that crosses the stationary limit from outside: the particle divides into two particles, one of which (P_2) falls into the black hole while the other (P_1) escapes from the ergosphere with more mass energy than the original particle (P_0).

black holes. These properties suggest an analogy between the area of the event horizon of a black hole and entropy in thermodynamics. (Entropy can be regarded as a measure of a lack of detailed information resulting from the averaging over the inherent coarse-grained character of a macroscopic system.)

The analogy between the laws governing black holes and the laws of thermodynamics has been extended by James Bardeen, Carter, and Hawking. They show that a small change in the surface area of a black hole is accompanied by a small change in its surface gravity, even as in a thermodynamic system a small change in entropy is accompanied by a small change in temperature. This analogy would suggest that we may formally identify the surface gravity with temperature. The analogy is strengthened by the fact that the surface gravity is the same at all points of the event horizon just as the temperature is the same at all points in a body in thermal equilibrium.

Although there is a similarity between entropy of a thermodynamic system and the surface area of the event horizon of a black hole and between the surface gravity on the event horizon and the temperature, it is not obvious what meaning, if any, one has to give to this analogy. These analogies remained a paradox until 1974 when Hawking was able to show, by applying the methods of the quantum theory to the formation of black holes by gravitational collapse, that there is a steady emission of particles from the horizon with a pure thermal spectrum; and further, that the temperature of the thermal radiation so emitted increases rapidly as the mass of the black hole decreases. For a black hole with a mass equal to that of the Sun, the temperature is only about a tenth of a millionth of a degree above absolute zero; the consequent rate of radiation is so insignificant that it can have no conceivable physical consequence. On the other hand, a black hole with a mass of a billion tons (which will have the size of a proton) would radiate at a temperature of some 120 billion degrees. At this temperature, the black hole would profusely emit pairs of electrons and positrons; and this emission would increase explosively as the mass of the black hole diminished.

The discovery of this purely quantal production of particles at the horizons of black holes has initiated what appears to be the first steps in the unification of relativity and quantum theory, a unification that has been sought for nearly a half century.

I. Cosmic censorship

Again in connection with the extraction of energy from a Kerr black hole, a question of considerable significance but of a different sort arises.

The Kerr solution represents a black hole with a smooth event horizon only so long as its angular momentum is less than an amount determined by its mass. If the angular momentum should exceed this limit, we should no longer have an event horizon which conceals the singularity in the interior. We would then have, as one says, a "naked" singularity, *i.e.*, a singularity with which one can communicate from the outside. Under these circumstances, the world around us would be quite unlike what we have always thought it to be: predictable with respect to the future in terms of the conditions which obtain at the present. For these reasons, Penrose has conjectured that:

> A system which evolves according to classical general relativity, with reasonable equations of state from generic non-singular initial data, does not develop any space-time singularity which is visible from infinity.

This conjecture is often referred to as the hypothesis of cosmic censorship.

The question arises, whether this hypothesis can be proved, or counterexamples to it be given. While no definite counterexamples have so far been given, a rigorous proof of its validity also remains to be given.

II. COSMOLOGY: FACTS AND PRINCIPLES

A rose-red city—'half as old as Time'!
—Rev. John William Burgon

In the study of cosmology, we seek a description and an understanding of the features of the largest scales in the observable astronomical universe. In seeking such a description, we must allow for the possibility that no volume is really large enough to make any reasonable extrapolation. By necessity, however, we must rather ask ourselves whether the observations extended over the largest scales provide indications or clues which, while suggesting a description of the universe consistent with our knowledge of other aspects of nature, enable us to draw inferences of wider scope and deeper significance. It appears that this question can be answered in the affirmative.

A. The basic facts of cosmology

Since cosmology deals with the largest observable scales, a prior question concerns the identification of the basic units of which the universe may be considered as being composed. While this question was, at one time, a matter of heated debate, it is now generally agreed that the basic units are the galaxies, each comparable, in size and in content, with our Milky Way system.

The galaxies occur in a wide diversity of shapes and forms. They are mostly of spiral or elliptical forms, of various degrees of oblateness, central condensations, and luminosities. Further, galaxies occur in clusters which are in turn of various sizes and richness. A description and classification of the various types of galaxies and their clusterings are beyond the scope of this essay. For our purposes, it will suffice to idealize the universe as a *substratum* (representing the smoothed out distribution of matter and radiation) in which the galaxies, playing the role of *fundamental observers*, trace out the motions prevailing in the substratum.

The basic observational fact, concerning the distribution of the galaxies, is that, to the extent to which the observations have been made, it is homogeneous and isotropic when averaged over local fluctuations (such as are present in the clusterings of the galaxies.) This homogeneity and isotropy of the distribution of the galaxies, combined with the near perfect isotropy (to one part in a thousand) of the universal cosmic microwave radiation of 3°K, strongly suggest that the universe is now and has been from its very early beginning—how "early," we shall specify later—homogeneous and isotropic. A further remarkable fact is that the homogeneity and isotropy are consistent with the observed motions of the galaxies as they have been measured. These measurements show that the galaxies are in a state of uniform expansion: they recede from one another with velocities

111

proportional to their mutual distances* (Hubble's law).

We may now summarize the basic facts which appear to be relevant to an understanding of the universe in the large.

1. The primary units of the universe, as presently constituted, are the galaxies.
2. The distribution of the galaxies, allowing for local clusterings and associated fluctuations, is homogeneous and isotropic. The smoothed out distribution of the galaxies may be idealized as a substratum in which the matter and the radiation are uniformly distributed and in which the galaxies are representative "points" which trace the motions of the substratum. The galaxies, then, may be considered as the "fundamental observers" of the universe.
3. The galaxies define a pattern of motions which is one of expansion; and, in a "local" neighborhood, the velocity of expansion is proportional to the distance. Thus, the measured velocity, V, of recession of a galaxy is, to a good first approximation, proportional to its distance, r, from us:

$$V = Hr \qquad (1)$$

where the constant of proportionality, H, is called the Hubble constant.

The present estimated value of H is (about) 150 km/sec per 10 million light-years. Departures from the simple linear relation (1), requiring an additional term in it which is quadratic in the separation r, are indicated by measurements made on galaxies observed at the farthest distances. A precise evaluation of these departures (not available at present) will provide information concerning the geometry of space-time—whether it is "open" or "closed" (*see* Section E below).

4. The existence of a background microwave radiation with a Planck thermal spectrum of 3°K with near perfect isotropy (discovered by Arno Penzias and Robert Wilson in 1965) enables us to extrapolate our present knowledge of the universe backward in time to its early beginnings, before the galaxies and the stars had been formed. (This extrapolation is made possible by a fundamental discovery by Roger Penrose on the necessary occurrence of singularities in the evolution of massive bodies in the framework of general relativity.)

While the foregoing are the principal facts which provide the basis for the extant cosmological theories, the following additional facts have proved to be of relevance.

5. The mean density, $\bar{\rho}$, of the matter in the universe (*i.e.*, the substratum), is of the order of

$$\rho_c = \frac{3}{8\pi G} H^2 \simeq 4 \times 10^{-29} \text{ gm/cm}^3, \qquad (2)$$

---

* There are measurable departures from this simple law when the distances become comparable to the "radius of the universe" (*see* Section E).

where G is the constant of gravitation and H is the Hubble constant. The best current estimate of $\bar{\rho}$ is, however, ten times smaller:

$$\bar{\rho} \sim 3 \times 10^{-30} \text{ gm/cm}^3.$$

6. The mean density, $\bar{\rho}$, combined with our knowledge of the all-pervasive thermal radiation of 3°K, implies that the ratio of the number of photons in the universe (or, light quanta) to the number of nucleons in the universe (*i.e.*, neutrons and protons bound in all the nuclei of all the atoms in the universe) is about 10^9—a number, which, as we shall see, is of crucial importance.

7. The abundance of helium of approximately 25 percent by weight, unlike the abundances of the other elements, appears to be independent of the cosmic sources from which it is derived. This fact, together with the impossibility of synthesizing appreciable amounts of helium in the interiors of stars during the course of their evolution, suggests that helium is of primordial origin and that it was synthesized during the early evolution of the universe.

The facts which we have enumerated suggest a cosmological principle on the basis of which we might hope to develop a theory of the universe. It should, however, be stated that the early discoveries of Hubble (concerning the velocity-distance relation and the homogeneity and the isotropy of the distribution of the galaxies) suggested, already, to the cosmologists of fifty years ago the formulation of such a principle. In fact the term "cosmological principle" was coined by Milne in 1931; he also clearly stated what it might signify.

B. General considerations; the cosmological principle

Before formulating the cosmological principle in precise terms, we shall consider certain elementary interpretations of the principal facts of cosmology which will lead us directly to its formulation.

Consider first this matter of the recession of the galaxies and Hubble's law. A simple model (due to Milne) which will account for the observed relation is the following:

Suppose that at some initial epoch, t_0, a large number of particles ("galaxies") are confined to a small volume (*see* fig. 4); and that at t_0 the different particles are moving in different directions with different velocities. After a certain length of time, an outward moving particle will just move outward into the originally unoccupied volume and will continue outward. An inward moving particle will cross the volume in which it was confined and move outward. Ultimately, recession will prevail. It is in fact clear that after a sufficient length of time, particles with an initial velocity, V, will find themselves at a distance, r, from the volume in which they had been confined, given approximately, by

$$r \sim V(t - t_0) \text{ or } V \sim r/(t - t_0). \tag{3}$$

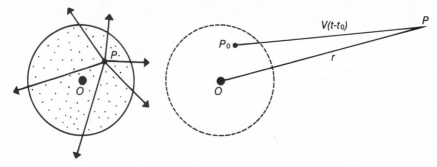

Figure 4. A simple model for interpreting a linear velocity-distance relation.

In other words, the eventual motions of the particles will conform to Hubble's law. As Milne stated, "the birds of a feather, flock together."

The foregoing simple model suggests that the observed expansion of the universe is the result of an early beginning of high mean density. But a system of particles for which a Hubble relation obtains has another interesting property.

Suppose that an observer at O (at $\vec{r}_O$, say) considers himself at rest at the center of a swarm of particles homogeneously distributed about himself and receding from him with velocities proportional to their distances from him with a constant of proportionality, H. Consider a particular particle P at location $\vec{r}_P$; then, in accordance with our assumption, its velocity $\vec{v}_{OP}$ relative to O will be given by (*see* fig. 5)

$$\vec{v}_{OP} = H(\vec{r}_P - \vec{r}_O) = H\vec{r}_{OP}. \tag{4}$$

Consider another particle Q at $\vec{r}_Q$; its velocity $\vec{v}_{OQ}$ relative to O will similarly,

Figure 5. Illustration of the fact that a cosmological principle is satisfied in a system in which velocity is proportional to distance. Particles P and Q are receding from point O at velocities proportional to their distance from O, but to an observer moving with particle Q, the only apparent motion at particle P is a recession from Q at a velocity proportional to the distance between P and Q.

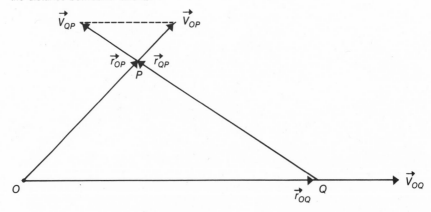

be given by

$$\vec{v}_{OQ} = H(\vec{r}_Q - \vec{r}_O) = H\vec{r}_{OQ}. \tag{5}$$

It follows from these relations that the velocity of P relative to Q will be (by the parallelogram law of the composition of velocities),

$$\vec{v}_{QP} = \vec{v}_{OP} - \vec{v}_{OQ} = H\,(\vec{r}_P - \vec{r}_Q) = H\vec{r}_{QP}. \tag{6}$$

From this last relation it follows that an observer at Q (sharing the local motion of the substratum) will consider himself, equally, as at the center of the swarm of particles and further that the particles of the swarm are receding from *him* (radially) with velocities proportional to their distances from him with the same constant of proportionality H. (Or, as Arthur Eddington stated, each observer can consider himself as the "plague spot" of the universe!)

We have thus shown that the descriptions of the motions, by virtue of the Galilean transformation used in passing from equations (4) and (5) to equation (6), as perceived by the different fundamental observers, are the same.

The preceding discussion is based on Newtonian concepts. An interpretation of the expansion of the universe in conformity with the principles of general relativity was first given by Weyl. In Weyl's interpretation, we consider the family of geodesics originating from a common point O in space-time (*see* fig. 6). (Geodesics are the trajectories described by freely falling particles as explained in Part I Section E.) Suppose, now, that these geodesics are being described by a set of fundamental observers starting simultaneously at O. And consider the locus of the points at which the observers will arrive after an interval of time, t, as measured by standard clocks, synchronized at O and carried by the observers; t is then the "proper time"

Figure 6. Weyl's interpretation of the expansion of the universe as originating in a swarm of particles emanating along geodesics from a point in space-time.

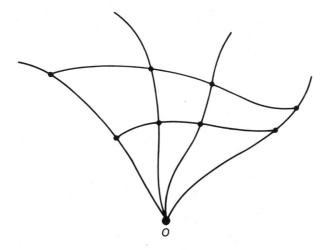

O

as measured and experienced by each of the observers. The locus will be a three-dimensional spatial surface. In this manner, we can construct an unfolding family of (initially) nonintersecting spatial surfaces with the property that these are the surfaces on which the fundamental observers will find themselves, simultaneously. It is clear from the construction that the mutual spatial distances between the observers will be increasing at rates depending on their separations. It is also clear that the description by the different observers of their relative motions and their distributions can in no essential way be different. Thus, a swarm of particles originating simultaneously at a common point and describing geodesics can very well serve as a model for an expanding universe.

The foregoing illustrations suggest that a universe which is homogeneous and isotropic, and in which the motions satisfy a Hubble relation are related facts which derive their common origin in a cosmological principle. It is, however, important to emphasize that the notions of homogeneity and isotropy, as we have used them hitherto, are intuitive ones and not free of inconsistency. For, in an expanding and an *evolving* universe of the kind we are envisaging, the notion of spatial homogeneity is not as simple as it is in a static or a stationary universe.

Normally, we think of homogeneity as meaning that all sufficiently large samples of the universe are equivalent. If, however, the universe is a changing one, there is ambiguity in the notion: how are samples by different observers at different times to be compared? A sample taken here and now may be, and in general will be, different from a sample taken here at a later time, and certainly will be different from a sample taken elsewhere at some other time. We must also remember that in general relativity one has to be cautious in using intuitive concepts such as "simultaneity," "later," and "earlier." On these accounts, we must define homogeneity in a somewhat different way. We define it as follows.

Homogeneity must be taken to mean that the totality of observations that any fundamental observer (sharing the motion of the substratum) can make on the universe is the same as the totality of the observations made by any other fundamental observer. More explicitly, if, through all time, we here, and others elsewhere, record all observations relating to the density and the directional distributions of the galaxies and their motions, as they evolve in time (as measured locally by standard clocks), homogeneity implies that the *histories* as recorded by us, and by the others, are identical. In other words, homogeneity should be taken to mean that the *world pictures* of all the fundamental observers are the same.

The notion of homogeneity as we have defined it implies, further, that the clocks of the different fundamental observers can be synchronized and a universal *cosmic time* can be established: one has only to reset the arbitrary origins of time reckoning and regraduate the clocks so that the same date is assigned to the same event by the different observers. Thus, a homogeneous universe, if it is evolving, acts as its own synchronizing agent.

Homogeneity, according to the definition given, does not imply that the instantaneous view of an observer will be the same in all directions: the distribution of the galaxies and the Hubble constant could well depend on the direction. On the other hand, if we assert that the view *is* the same in all directions, *i.e.*, if the universe is isotropic, then homogeneity is implied. For suppose that, at a given instant of time, the universe had different properties in the neighborhoods of two points A and B; then at a point C, equidistant from A and B, the difference will manifest itself as a lack of isotropy.

The assumption that the universe in the large is homogeneous and isotropic is the cosmological principle; it underlies most modern cosmological theories. It should, however, be emphasized that it is not a principle in the sense that the word is used in combinations such as "thermodynamic principles" or the "uncertainty principle": the cosmological principle can be violated without affecting any known law of nature. It is important to be aware of this fact, since the cosmological principle is, as we shall see, very restrictive in its implications.

C. The velocity-distance relation, the Hubble constant, and the local mean density

As we have explained, the observations pertaining to the large-scale distribution of the galaxies and the velocity-distance relation of Hubble suggest the adoption of the cosmological principle as a working hypothesis for developing a theory. However, before we turn to outlining the principles of relativistic cosmology based on the postulates of homogeneity and isotropy, it may be useful to derive some simple consequences of the theory which follow from some very general considerations.

It is clear that the cosmological principle requires that the world view of any observer relative to himself must have spherical symmetry about himself. Consider a sphere of radius R with the observer at the origin. Then according to a theorem of Newton which remains valid also in the framework of general relativity (by a theorem due to George Birkhoff), a particle at the boundary of the sphere (in a distribution of matter having spherical symmetry about the same origin) will be gravitationally acted upon only by the matter interior to the sphere. Consequently, so long as the velocities of expansion are small compared to the velocity of light, c, we may restrict ourselves to the Newtonian laws of gravitation and to Newtonian concepts in analyzing the dynamical motions in the sphere. And we should expect that the results so derived will be valid, also, in the wider framework of general relativity, within the stated limitations ($v \ll c$).

Consistent with the postulates of homogeneity and isotropy, the density, ρ, of the matter inside R must, at any instant of time, be uniform; and the mass inside the sphere of radius R, namely $\frac{4}{3} \pi R^3 \rho$, must remain the same as R varies with time, as required by the law of the conservation of mass. Accordingly, if ρ_0 and R_0 are the density and the radius of the sphere, respectively, at some initial epoch t_0, then

$$M_0 = \tfrac{4}{3}\pi\rho_0 R_0^3 = M_R = \tfrac{4}{3}\pi\rho R^3. \tag{7}$$

Consider now a particle (of mass m_0) at the boundary of the sphere R. By Newton's laws of gravitation and the theorem we have stated, the particle will be acted upon by the gravitational force only of the mass interior to R; and this force, again by a theorem due to Newton, is the same as if the entire mass M_R is concentrated at the center. Accordingly, the force acting on the particle is given by

$$\text{Force} = -G\frac{M_R}{R^2}\,m_0 = -G\frac{M_0}{R^2}\,m_0, \tag{8}$$

where G is the constant of gravitation; and this radial force will result in the particle experiencing the radial acceleration,

$$\frac{d^2R}{dt^2} = -\frac{GM_0}{R^2}. \tag{9}$$

From this equation, we readily infer (by integration) that

$$\frac{1}{2}\left(\frac{dR}{dt}\right)^2 = \frac{GM_0}{R} - \frac{1}{2}k = \frac{4}{3}\pi G\rho R^2 - \frac{1}{2}k, \tag{10}$$

where k is a constant. This last equation expresses no more than the fact that the sum of the kinetic and the gravitational potential energies of the particle remains constant during the motion.

The sign of the constant k in equation (10) is crucial. If k should be positive, it is clear that after a certain length of time, R will cease to increase: it will increase until R reaches the maximum value given by

$$\tfrac{4}{3}\pi G\rho R^2 = \tfrac{1}{2}k, \tag{11}$$

when $dR/dt = 0$; after this instant R will decrease, eventually to the value zero. But if k should be zero or negative, then R will continue to increase indefinitely.

So far, we have restricted ourselves to the motion of the particles which are instantaneously (at time t_0) on the surface of the sphere of radius R_0 and move radially outward as the sphere expands (or contracts). But it is clear that a particle at a distance $r\,(< R)$ at time t will move outward with the proportionate velocity,

$$V = \frac{r}{R}\frac{dR}{dt}. \tag{12}$$

Thus, we have a linear velocity-distance relation with a Hubble constant

$$H = \frac{1}{R}\frac{dR}{dt}. \tag{13}$$

Inserting this last relation in equation (10), we obtain

$$H^2 = \frac{8}{3} \pi G \rho - \frac{k}{R^2}, \tag{14}$$

or (cf. equation (2))

$$\rho = \frac{3}{8\pi G} H^2 \left[1 + \frac{k}{(dR/dt)^2} \right]. \tag{15}$$

To the extent that equation (15) is a local relation, it must obtain also in the framework of general relativity (as, in fact, we shall verify in Section E). And it is an important relation since, from a knowledge of the local mean density and the Hubble constant, we can determine the sign of k; and as we shall see in Section D, the sign of k determines the nature of the spatial geometry of the universe—whether it is "closed" or "open." The present estimate of $\bar{\rho}$ ($\simeq 3 \times 10^{-30}$ gm/cm^3) is about ten times smaller than $3H^2/8\pi G$ ($\simeq 4 \times 10^{-29}$ gm/cm^3); and on this evidence it would appear that $k < 0$.

The conclusion to be drawn from our discussion so far is that the cosmological principle provides a reasonable basis for developing more detailed theoretical models for the universe. It is important to emphasize that the conclusion could have been otherwise. Thus, it could have been that the large-scale distribution of the galaxies is so irregular that smoothing would not have left anything significant. If smoothing were significant, any theory of differential motions would have allowed a radial expansion linear with the distance; but there is no a priori reason for expecting the linearity to hold for velocities of recession approaching a tenth of the velocity of light, as is, in fact, the case. Even if the observed expansion were uniform for such large recessional velocities, it could well have been that the Hubble constant is different in different directions. And even if the Hubble constant is independent of direction, there is no compelling reason to expect that the mean density of the substratum, obtained by averaging over the largest measurable scales, would be, within a factor of ten, the value $3H^2/8\pi G$. The fact that none of these possibilities is realized is an indication that the cosmological principle has a deeper role to play in our taking a measure of the universe.

D. An outline of relativistic cosmology: the Friedmann models for the universe

The discussion in the preceding section, based on Newtonian concepts and Newtonian laws, is expected to provide a correct local description by virtue of Birkhoff's theorem which ensures its correctness, so long as the velocity of recession is small compared to the velocity of light (c) and the contribution of the pressure (p) to the inertial mass can be neglected compared to the contribution ρc^2 by the matter content. The discussion will cease to be valid when the velocities of recession (as measured by the fundamental observers) become comparable to the velocity of light and the pressure becomes comparable to ρc^2. We thus have no reason to expect that the linear velocity-distance relation will hold indefinitely. Departures from linearity must arise when measurements are extended to the farthest accessible sources. Indeed, the detection of such departures is an important part of the current efforts in observational cosmology.

A theory in which no restrictions, such as $v << c$ and $p << \rho c^2$, are made can be developed only in the framework of general relativity. In this section, we shall outline the method of construction of some basic relativistic models of the universe which lie at the base of most current cosmological discussions. But, unfortunately, even an outline requires a somewhat more technical treatment than in the earlier (or the subsequent) parts of this account. A reader not interested in these aspects of the theory may omit this section.

The cosmological principle, with its requirements of homogeneity and isotropy, already restricts the geometry of space-time drastically. Indeed, it can be shown that the metric, which epitomizes the geometry of space-time, can be reduced to the form

$$ds^2 = c^2\,(dt)^2 - \frac{R^2(t)}{(1 + \tfrac{1}{4}k\,r^2)^2}\left[(dr)^2 + r^2\,(d\theta)^2 + r^2\sin^2\theta\,(d\varphi)^2\right], \quad (16)$$

where $R(t)$ is a function of the cosmic time, t, only, k is a constant, and r, θ, and φ are the familiar polar coordinates. This form of the metric was deduced by H. P. Robertson and A. G. Walker from the postulates of homogeneity and isotropy (in the strict sense as we have defined them in Section C). But the metric itself (without deducing it from any general principle) was used by A. Friedmann in 1922 when he constructed the basic models of the universe of modern cosmology.

The metric which we have written down differs from the metric of the special theory of relativity (appropriate when no gravitational fields are present) only by the presence of the undetermined scale factor $R(t)$ (dependent on time) and the constant k. This fact becomes apparent when we consider the spatial section (or the spatial slice) of the geometry at some given instant of time, t_0, say. Then, the distance, dl, between neighboring points in the three-dimensional space, at this instant t_0, will be determined by

$$dl^2 = \frac{R^2(t_0)}{(1 + \tfrac{1}{4}k\,r^2)^2}\left[(dr)^2 + r^2\,(d\theta)^2 + r^2\sin^2\theta\,(d\varphi)^2\right]. \quad (17)$$

At a later time t_1 (say), the spatial intervals will be determined by a similar formula in which $R^2(t_0)$ is replaced by $R^2(t_1)$. Accordingly, the proper distances between two points at times t_1 and t_0 will be in the ratio $R(t_1)/R(t_0)$. It follows that if this factor is greater than one, then observers at different points will consider themselves as receding from one another (at rates dependent on time) and they would describe their universe as an expanding one.

We shall presently see that the constant k in the metric plays formally the same role as the constant k which appeared in equation (10) in the Newtonian discussion of Section C. The interpretation of k, in the framework of general relativity, is, however, different: it determines, as one says, the curvature of the spatial geometry. (The reason for this nomenclature will be made clear presently.)

We have the following three cases to distinguish:

(a) $k = 0$, when the three-dimensional space is Euclidean;

(b) $k > 0$, when the spatial geometry is said to be "closed" or spherical;

(c) $k < 0$, when the spatial geometry is said to be "open" or hyperbolic. (Parenthetically, we may note here that, since we have not specified the unit of distance, it will suffice to distinguish only the three cases, $k = 0$, $k = +1$, and $k = -1$.)

Suppressing one spatial dimension, we can visualize the spaces described by the metric (17) for $k = +1, 0$, and -1 by a sphere, an infinite plane, and an infinite surface which is everywhere locally like a saddle, respectively (*see* fig. 7). And since $R(t)$ may either increase or decrease (corresponding to an expanding or a contracting universe) we may think of the sphere as a rubber balloon which can be inflated or deflated, and of the other two surfaces as also made of elastic membranes which can be similarly stretched or contracted. The membrane in each case represents the substratum and a selected set of points, distributed uniformly on it, corresponding to the galaxies. The radius of curvature R corresponds to the radius of the sphere in the case $k = 1$ and the radius of either of the two spheres fitting into the saddle (one below and one above) in the case $k = -1$. In all cases, the distance between neighboring points (galaxies) will vary as $R(t)$ with time. (In the case $k = 0$, $R(t)$ has only this last interpretation.)

A further fact which we may notice from the illustrations is the following. In the case $k = 0$, the ratio of the circumference of a circle to its radius is always 2π (no matter where on the plane we draw the circle). But on a sphere ($k = 1$) distances are to be measured along great circles: these are the *proper* distances. A circle, whose co-latitude is θ, has a circumference $2\pi R\sin\theta$ while its proper radius is $R\theta$. The ratio of the circumference of the circle to its proper radius is, therefore, $2\pi\sin\theta/\theta$; this is always less than 2π, and its maximum departure from 2π occurs for $\theta = \pi/2$, on the "equator," when its value is 4. It should also be noted that the circumference is not a

Figure 7. The three spatial geometries: (a) spherical, (b) Euclidean, and (c) hyperbolic.

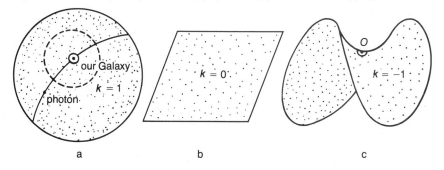

monotonic function of its proper radius $R\theta$: it attains a maximum value at the equator, and it vanishes at the poles $\theta = 0$ and $\theta = \pi$. Similarly, on the saddle ($k = -1$) the distances from the saddle point (O) are to be measured along the intersection of the surface with the meridian planes; and it can be shown that the circumference of a circle (which is the locus of points equidistant from O as measured on the surface) to its proper radius is always in excess of 2π; and, further, that the circumference is a monotonically increasing (*i.e.*, an ever increasing) function of its proper radius.

The foregoing description applies when one of the spatial dimensions is suppressed. In the three-dimensional case, we must consider the surface of a three-dimensional sphere in place of the circumference of a circle. And in the case $k = 0$, the surface of a sphere of radius R has an area $4\pi R^2$ no matter where the sphere is. But in the case $k = 1$, the surface area is always less than $4\pi R^2$, while in the case $k = -1$, the volume of the available three-dimensional space is finite (equal to $\pi^2 R^3$); on this account, the space is said to be "closed." On the other hand, the volume of the available three-dimensional space is infinite, both when $k = 0$ and $k = -1$; on this account, the space is said to be "open" in these cases.

So far, we have considered only the requirements of homogeneity and isotropy. As we have seen, these requirements drastically limit the form of the metric; but they leave $R(t)$ undetermined and leave open, also, the question of what determines the sign of k. To make the problem determinate, we must turn to the equations of Einstein which relate the metric to the pressure and the matter content (or, more generally, to the stress and the energy-density) of the universe.

In relativity, pressure, as derived from the fluctuating "thermal motions" of the constituent particles, contributes to the inertial mass and, therefore, is also a source of gravitation. We must accordingly include it in writing the relevant equations.

In the actual universe, the pressure is derived from diverse sources: the "peculiar motions" (representing the fluctuations from the mean motion of the substratum) of the galaxies themselves, radiation, intergalactic gas, etc. And we must allow for pressure even if, as at the present epoch, none of these sources contributes appreciably to the inertia.

On the assumption that the substratum can be idealized as a hydrodynamic fluid with pressure and energy-density as thermodynamic variables, we find that, for the chosen form of the metric, Einstein's equations yield the pair of equations

$$\left(\frac{dR}{dt}\right)^2 = \frac{8}{3}\pi G\rho\, R^2 - k \tag{18}$$

and

$$\frac{2}{R}\frac{d^2R}{dt^2} + \frac{1}{R^2}\left(\frac{dR}{dt}\right)^2 = -\frac{8\pi G}{c^2}\,p - \frac{k}{R^2}. \tag{19}$$

The first of the two foregoing equations is seen to be formally identical with equation (10) derived in Section C from local considerations under circumstances in which Newtonian concepts can be applied. But the equations are not entirely equivalent unless we ignore the term in the pressure in the second equation. For if $p = 0$, then it is easy to show that the second equation (combined with the first) gives

$$\rho\ R^3 = \text{constant} \tag{20}$$

—a relation which expresses the conservation of mass in the Newtonian considerations; and this last relation is a necessary one in the context of the considerations of Section C. But the extent to which the relation (20) is a consequence of neglecting the pressure as a source of inertia (which is permissible only so long as $p <\!< \rho c^2$), it is not general enough for our purposes. On the other hand, since equation (18) is formally the same as equation (10) derived from local considerations, the equation (*cf.* equation (15))

$$\rho = \frac{3}{8\pi G}\ H^2\left[1 + \frac{k}{(dR/dt)^2}\right], \tag{21}$$

relating the density to the Hubble constant H continues to hold so long as we restrict ourselves to the linear portion of the velocity-distance relation. But there are differences in the interpretation of this equation as well. Since the Newtonian considerations were strictly limited to the "immediate neighborhood," the density ρ refers to the average local density; but in the present relativistic framework ρ refers to the constant energy-density which prevails everywhere (at a given instant of cosmic time). A more important difference is in the meaning of k; in the relativistic theory, the sign of k determines the nature of space-time in the large: it determines whether the universe is closed or open.

Equations (18) and (19) are generally referred to as "Friedmann's equations."

In examining the implications of Friedmann's equations, we shall restrict our considerations to two cases: the *matter-dominated* universe (in which the role of the pressure is ignored) and the *radiation-dominated* universe (in which $p = \frac{1}{3}\rho c^2$). The first case is relevant to the present epoch of the universe and is, therefore, the most useful for comparisons with observations on the galaxies; the second case is relevant to discussions pertaining to the early universe (as we shall see in detail in Sections G and H).

In the matter-dominated universe, equation (20), expressing the conservation of mass, is valid and the only equation we have to consider is

$$\left(\frac{dR}{dt}\right)^2 = \frac{8}{3}\ \pi G\rho\ R^2 - k = \frac{8\pi G\rho_0 R^3_0}{R} - k, \tag{22}$$

where ρ_0 and R_0 may be assumed to refer to the present mean density and the present *radius of the universe* (as the radius of curvature R is generally referred to).

It is convenient to measure R in units of its present value R_0. With R measured in this unit, the basic equation is

$$\left(\frac{dR}{dt}\right)^2 = \frac{8}{3}\,\pi G\,\frac{\rho_0}{R} - k, \tag{23}$$

where k now is R_0^{-2} of the k in equation (22).

We shall now consider the three cases, $k = 0$, $k > 0$, and $k < 0$, separately.

(a) $k = 0$: In this case the solution of equation (23) is

$$R = (6\pi G\rho_0)^{\frac{1}{3}}t^{\frac{2}{3}}, \tag{24}$$

where we have chosen the origin of time at the instant $R = 0$. (We shall consider in Section F how seriously we are to take this predicted singularity.)

(b) $k > 0$: In this case the behavior of R as a function of time is not a

Figure 8. The variation of the radius of curvature, $R(t)$, of the universe as a function of time, t, in each of these three geometries. Top, $k > 0$ (spherical geometry); middle, $k = 0$ (Euclidean geometry); bottom, $k < 0$ (hyperbolic geometry).

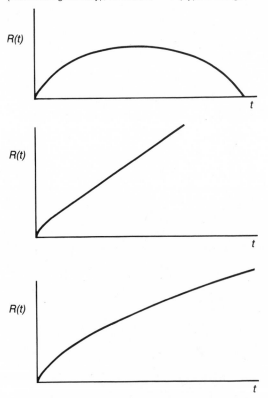

monotonic one: it attains the maximum value,

$$R_{\max} = 8\pi G\rho_0/3k, \tag{25}$$

when $dR/dt = 0$. The radius R of the universe is initially zero, and after attaining its maximum value it again goes to zero: the cosmic span of life for the universe is finite. And as we have stated earlier, the mass of the universe is also finite in this case. (Again, we postpone to Sections F and I the consideration of how seriously we are to take the predicted initial and final singularities.)

(c) $k < 0$: In this case, it is clear that R increases monotonically; and its behaviors, near $t = 0$ and $t \to \infty$, are

$$R \sim t^{\frac{2}{3}} \ (t \to 0) \text{ and } R \sim t \ (t \to \infty). \tag{26}$$

In figure 8, the behaviors of the radius of the universe as a function of time are illustrated for the three cases.

Finally, considering a radiation-dominated universe in which $p = \frac{1}{3}\rho c^2$, the equation governing R (obtained from adding the two Friedmann equations (18) and (19)) is

$$R\frac{d^2R}{dt^2} + \left(\frac{dR}{dt}\right)^2 + k = 0. \tag{27}$$

From this equation one finds that

$$R \sim t^{\frac{1}{2}}, \ \rho \sim t^{-2}, \text{ and Temperature} \sim t^{-\frac{1}{2}}, \tag{28}$$

where, under the circumstances contemplated, the temperature varies as $\rho^{\frac{1}{4}}$. (These formulae determine the variation of density and temperature in the very early universe; these formulae provide the basis for the considerations in Section H.)

E. The velocity-distance relation

Clearly, the most important verifiable prediction of a cosmological theory must relate to the velocity-distance relation. We shall now consider the nature of the predictions which follow from the cosmological principle, generally, and the Friedmann models in particular.

It is clear from symmetry considerations that light rays (as well as freely falling particles) must describe trajectories which lie in the meridian planes ($\varphi = $ constant). Thus, in figure 7a, the trajectories will be along arcs of great circles on the sphere; and for light rays, the trajectories will be further restricted by the requirement $ds^2 = 0$ (even as they are in the special theory of relativity, in accordance with the postulate of the constancy of the velocity of light in frames in uniform relative motion).

If we write the Robertson-Walker metric in the form

$$ds^2 = c^2dt^2 - dl^2, \tag{29}$$

then dl measures increments of proper lengths (*i.e.*, lengths measured by observers in frames in which they are at rest). From this relation it follows that light is propagated in accordance with the equation

$$\frac{dl}{dt} = c,$$

(30)

which expresses no more than that light is propagated with the velocity of light! In the illustrative model of the rubber balloon (fig. 7a), the photon (representing light) travels, from one point on the surface to another point on the surface, with the velocity of light along the arc of the great circle joining the two points.

Now consider an atom in a galaxy emitting, at a time t_0, one of its characteristic spectral radiations in the form of a wave train. The distance between the successive crests in such a wave train is the wavelength λ_* of the spectral radiation. Let the wave train arrive at another galaxy at a time t_1. For an observer at this galaxy, the distance λ_1 between the successive crests of the wave train will differ from λ_* on account of the universe having expanded meantime. In accordance with what we have stated earlier in Section D, about measurements of spatial distances in an expanding universe (with an underlying Robertson-Walker metric), his measurement will, in fact, yield a wavelength,

$$\lambda_1 = \lambda_* \, R(t_1)/R(t_0),$$

(31)

where $R(t_1)$ and $R(t_0)$ denote the radii of the universe at the time of receipt and at the time of emission of the wave train. Moreover, the observer receiving the wave train will be able to identify that the radiation he is receiving is the particular characteristic spectral radiation of an atom whose wavelength λ_* he knows from his own laboratory measurements. He will, therefore, conclude that this same radiation, emitted by an atom in the distant galaxy, has been red-shifted by an amount z given by

$$1 + z = 1 + \frac{\lambda_1 - \lambda_*}{\lambda_*} = \frac{R(t_1)}{R(t_0)}.$$

(32)

This is an exact relation dependent only on the postulates of homogeneity and isotropy.

If the two galaxies considered are sufficiently near that $z \ll 1$, then, in a first approximation,

$$z = \frac{\Delta\lambda}{\lambda_*} \simeq \left(\frac{1}{R}\frac{dR}{dt}\right)_{t_1} (t_1 - t_0);$$

(33)

and in this approximation, it will suffice to write

$$t_1 - t_0 \simeq r/c,$$

(34)

where r is the distance between the galaxies. The equation for the red shift in this linear approximation is, therefore,

$$c\frac{\Delta\lambda}{\lambda_*} = \left(\frac{1}{R}\frac{dR}{dt}\right)_{t_1}. \tag{35}$$

If we should now wish to interpret the red shift as due to a velocity of recession and a resulting Doppler shift, then the quantity on the left-hand side of the foregoing relation is precisely the velocity, V, which we should assign to the source. We thus recover the familiar relation,

$$V = Hr \quad \text{where} \quad H = \left(\frac{1}{R}\frac{dR}{dt}\right)_{t_1}. \tag{36}$$

The interpretation of the red shift as due to a velocity of recession (in the conventional sense) is neither useful nor possible if we should be dealing with values of z comparable to 1. (Values of $z > 3$ have been measured.) In any event, we should expect observations to show departures from linearity, when they are extended to galaxies at farther and farther distances and the measured red shifts become appreciable ($z \gtrsim 0.5$). On theoretical grounds, we should expect these departures to depend on d^2R/dt^2 even as the Hubble constant, in the linear relation, depends on dR/dt.

It is customary to express the departures from linearity of the basic relation in terms of the so-called deceleration parameter,

$$q = -\frac{1}{R}\frac{d^2R}{dt^2}\frac{1}{H^2} = -\frac{R}{(dR/dt)^2}\frac{d^2R}{dt^2}. \tag{37}$$

A simple theoretical expression for q can be given on the matter-dominated Friedmann models: even for $z = 3$, the radius of the universe, at the time the light was emitted at the distant galaxy (and which we are now receiving), was only four times smaller than it is at present, and it is entirely reasonable to suppose that homogeneity, isotropy, and matter domination prevailed then, as now. From Friedmann's equations, we find that,

$$\frac{1}{R}\frac{d^2R}{dt^2} = -\frac{4}{3}\pi G\rho; \tag{38}$$

accordingly

$$q = \frac{4\pi G\rho}{3H^2}. \tag{39}$$

If one could determine q with some degree of precision, then the foregoing relation combined with the earlier relation (cf. equation (14))

$$H^2 = \tfrac{8}{3}\pi G\rho - k \tag{40}$$

will enable us to deduce, directly from observations, whether our universe is open or closed. But so far, it has not been possible to derive from observations a sufficiently reliable value for q. Among other ambiguities that confront this problem, one must find a proper way of expressing the relation between distance and cosmic time which is more precise than $r = c(t_1 - t_0)$.

F. How seriously should we take the singularities predicted by the Friedmann models?

The usefulness of the Friedmann models cannot be denied for purposes of interpreting the observations bearing on cosmology and for obtaining the values of the constants and the parameters which characterize these models. Thus, an independently derived mean density of the universe, together with a knowledge of the Hubble constant, will determine whether the universe is open or closed; and this deduction, for the validity of the Friedmann models at this level, must be consistent with the deductions which one may, eventually, be able to draw from well-established departures from the simple Hubble relation. But these comparisons and deductions will still leave open two fundamental questions: *first*, as to how literally one should take the singularities predicted on the Friedmann models and to what extent one would be justified in extrapolating backward the observed velocity-distance relation (or, more precisely, the (R,t)-relation), to times when the radius of curvature tends to zero and the density tends to infinity; and *second*, even should the extrapolation be justified, how close to the singularity could we suppose that the assumed homogeneity and isotropy will prevail?

With regard to the first question, one could well be skeptical of extrapolating the Friedmann models to the time when $R = 0$ (and, in the case of the closed models, also to the future time, when R again goes to zero): for these models assume *strict* spherical symmetry, *strict* homogeneity, and *strict* isotropy, and none of these assumptions are *strictly* realized (or, can be realized). One can, therefore, argue that some slight inhomogeneity, some slight anisotropy, and some slight departures from spherical symmetry and strict radial flow will replace the singularity by a state of high mean density which need not transcend any "reasonable" limit which we may wish to impose. This skepticism was widespread during the 1950s and the early '60s, when it was maintained by some of the most perceptive cosmologists of the time (*e.g.*, E. M. Lifshitz and I. M. Khalatnikov). Thus, in a *Survey of Cosmological Theories*, published in 1963 by William H. McCrea, we find the statement: "There is no known feature of the universe that gives any indication of its ever having been in a state of extreme congestion as required by the [Friedmann] models."

One's views, with respect to the occurrence of singularities in solutions describing the evolution of gravitating physical systems in general relativity, changed radically in 1965 when Penrose proved that, so long as matter obeys certain very reasonable conditions (such as that the energy density as measured by an observer, in a frame of reference in which he is at rest, is always positive), singularities are inevitable once a process of collapse has started and a "point of no return" has been reached. (Subsequent theorems by Penrose and Hawking have succeeded in relaxing the original conditions of Penrose.)

The essential reason for the occurrence of singularities in general relativity is that every force which operates against collapsing to a singularity in the Newtonian theory (such as pressure or rotation) only adds to the inertia of the system and enhances the very gravitational force which is the cause of the collapse.

Effects derived from an ultimate quantal description of matter and fields may intervene and prevent the collapse to a literal point singularity. But these effects are not expected to become operative before the linear dimensions become comparable to the Planck length,

$$\left(\frac{\hbar G}{c^3}\right)^{1/2} = 1.6 \times 10^{-33} \text{ cm.} \tag{41}$$

(where h is the Planck constant divided by 2π), and the density of the matter will be as high as 10^{93} gm/cm^3. For all "practical" purposes, a state of such high density may well be considered as a "singularity."

While it cannot be doubted that an eventual understanding of the phenomena which will occur at the singularities predicted by general relativity will lead to deeper insights into the origin of the universe, it is certainly reasonable to pursue meantime the consequences which may follow from accepting the reality of the singularities in the Friedmann models. But in pursuing these consequences, we do not preclude the possibility that the initial singularity of our universe may have been of a different kind. Indeed, we shall give reasons for believing that the initial and the final singularities may be of quite different kinds if our universe should happen to be a closed one. Also, we shall find that if we drop the assumption of isotropy and retain only the assumption of homogeneity, the general theory of relativity predicts singularities of a kind very different from those of the Friedmann models.

G. The microwave background

If one grants, as it appears one must, that the universe began in an initial singular state, then it becomes possible to speak of an *age* for the universe; and the determination of this age has been one of the prime concerns in current studies in cosmology.

The expansion of the universe, as epitomized in the Hubble relation, enables one to obtain an estimate: the inverse of the Hubble constant $H(= R^{-1}dR/dt)$ is of the dimensions of a time and is clearly a measure of its age. With the present estimate of the value of H, the Hubble time, τ, is

$$\tau = H^{-1} = 20 \text{ billion years.}$$

But as figure 9 demonstrates, the Hubble time is necessarily an overestimate of the "true" age. To obtain a better estimate of the age, it is necessary that we take into account other aspects of the astronomical universe derived from other sources. A detailed discussion of these other sources is beyond the scope of this account, but we shall consider two of these which are of particular relevance to our present measure of the universe: the present temperature of the universal microwave background and the abundance of helium as of primordial origin.

If the universe did begin with an initial singularity, we may justifiably infer that in the beginning it was radiation-dominated and that it was then characterized by the highest temperatures and densities that one can contemplate, and under circumstances when the notions of temperature and thermal equilibrium are pertinent; and, further, we may assume that the temperature fell, initially, very rapidly. (Justifications for these statements will be given in Section H.)

In the very early stages of the universe, we may broadly distinguish three epochs: an earliest epoch when matter was present in forms of which we have hardly the first glimmerings from the most recent discoveries in the domain of elementary-particle physics; a second epoch when the principal constituents, besides radiation, were protons, neutrons, electrons, positrons, neutrinos, and antineutrinos, all highly relativistic (*i.e.*, moving with velocities very nearly that of light), which terminated with the synthesis primarily of helium (and a possible trace of deuterium); and a third epoch when the mixture of radiation, protons, helium nuclei, and electrons (in sufficient numbers to ensure the electrical neutrality of the matter) cooled to a temperature in the range 3000°–5000° K. At the temperature reached during the last epoch, electrons and protons began to combine to form atomic hydrogen. This was a crucial moment in the history of the universe, for up until this moment the opacity of the matter to the radiation that was present was sufficiently high to entrap it effectively, and the temperature of the radiation and the temperature of the matter kept apace. But, once atomic hydrogen became the principal constituent, matter suddenly became transparent to the radiation, with the result that, from this moment on, matter and radiation each began to go their own way: they had been decoupled. Thus the era of radiation domination had ended, and the era of matter domination began.

Figure 9. Demonstration that the age of the universe, t_0, is always less than the Hubble time, τ, which is determined by the tangent to the $R(t)$ curve.

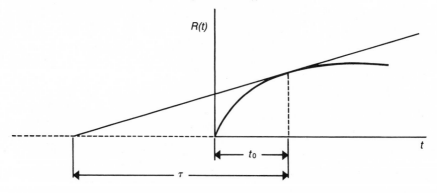

As far as the radiation is concerned, its history, subsequent to its decoupling from matter, was uneventful: it simply cooled as the universe expanded. This cooling was *adiabatic* in that the process of cooling was unattended by any addition of heat from extraneous sources. The radiation cooled in the same way that air contained in a balloon cools when it is rapidly expanded ("rapidly" only to ensure that no heat from the outside comes in).

From the fact that the energy-density of thermal radiation varies as the fourth power of the temperature, and the further fact that the number of photons per unit volume varies as the third power of the temperature, one can conclude that the temperature of the radiation, after its decoupling from matter, falls off inversely as the radius of the universe while retaining the thermal, Planckian character of its spectral distribution at all times. It is in this context that the discovery of the universal microwave radiation of 3° K by Penzias and Wilson is relevant. The inference that this radiation is the same which has adiabatically cooled from an initial temperature of 3000°–5000° K would appear justified, particularly in view of the very high degree of isotropy of the radiation. A corollary of this inference is that the radius of the universe at the time matter and radiation were decoupled was some 1,000–2,000 times smaller than it is at present. Conversely, from the near-perfect isotropy of the microwave radiation, we may conclude that the assumptions of homogeneity and isotropy, on which the Friedmann models are predicated, were valid at this time.

As we have stated, the history of the radiation after the "recombination era" has been uneventful. But with matter it has been otherwise. Clusters of galaxies, distributions of stars, and all the other agglomerations of matter which constitute the present astronomical universe have been formed since that time. While all these things were happening, the total number of photons (N_γ) and nucleons (N_B = the number of protons and neutrons bound in all the atomic nuclei) in the universe have remained unchanged. The ratio of these two numbers can be estimated from our knowledge of the temperature of the microwave radiations (which pervades the entire universe) and of the mean density of the matter in the universe. The uncertainty in this ratio is almost entirely due to the uncertainty in our knowledge of $\bar{\rho}$; but within the limits of its uncertainty, the estimated ratio of N_γ to N_B is $\sim 10^9$—a number which plays an important role in tracing the history of the universe to earlier eras. Again, accepting the Friedmann model, one can ascertain (with the estimated values of $\bar{\rho}$ and H) that the decoupling between the matter and the radiation took place some 300,000 years after the initial singularity.

H. The synthesis of helium and the age of the universe

The discovery of the 3° K microwave radiation and its near-perfect isotropy give one the confidence to extrapolate further back in time to explore whether nucleosynthesis (*i.e.*, the synthesis of the elements) could have taken place at earlier epochs when the temperatures and the densities were sufficiently high to have made it possible. (One has in mind a temperature of the order of $10^{10°}$ K and an energy-density equivalent to a mass density of 10^5 gm/cm^3.)

It has long been known that any appreciable synthesis of the elements beyond helium cannot be accomplished in the rapidly cooling environment of an expanding universe. At the same time, investigations pertaining to the evolution of the stars had shown that, while the elements beyond helium could well be synthesized in the interiors of stars, in a certain mass range, during the later phases of their evolution, it is necessary to assume that there was an abundant supply of hydrogen and helium even before the galaxies and the stars were formed. And the fact that helium is present with an abudance of 25 percent by weight in all cosmic sources (including the "first generation" of stars that were born in the Galaxy) is taken as further evidence for the belief that hydrogen and helium are of primordial origin. It is now generally believed that the synthesis of a requisite amount of helium, in the early universe, is a necessary condition for a cosmological model to be "viable."

We shall now outline the basic principles on which a theory of nucleosynthesis in the early universe is developed and the empirical information which it is necessary to incorporate in the considerations.

The following conservation laws are always assumed:

(a) *The conservation of the net charge.* While particles and antiparticles (such as electrons and positrons, protons and antiprotons) of equal and opposite charges can be created or annihilated in pairs, the net electric charge can never change.

(b) *The conservation of the baryon number.* We include among baryons, protons (p), neutrons (n), and other somewhat heavier (unstable) particles called hyperons. Baryons and antibaryons can be created or annihilated in pairs; and baryons can decay into other baryons even as a free neutron decays into a proton (with the emission of an electron with a half-life of eleven minutes). However, the total number of baryons *minus* the total number of antibaryons must never change. By assigning to each baryon a number $+1$ and to each antibaryon the number -1, we obtain the rule that the total baryon number can never change.

(c) *The conservation of lepton number.* The leptons are the light negatively charged particles, the electron and the muon; the electrically neutral particle of zero mass called the neutrino; and their antiparticles, the positron, the antimuon, and the antineutrino. Despite their zero mass and zero charge, neutrinos carry energy and momentum (like the photons). We assign to each lepton a number $+1$, and to each antilepton a number -1; and the rule, again, is that the lepton number can never change.

In determining the content of the universe in very early times, the conservation laws we have stated are of crucial importance, for, since the net charge, the baryon number, and the lepton number are conserved, they must have had, from the very beginning, the same values as they have at present. Further, since the number of photons per unit volume, as well as the net charge, the number of baryons, and the number of leptons, all vary as the inverse cube of the radius of the universe, it follows that the charge, the baryon number, and the lepton number *per* photon retain the same values at all times. (Strictly, the ratios which retain the same values are: charge to "entropy," baryon number to entropy, and lepton number to entropy; but the conditions under which the conservation laws will be applied, the replacement of entropy by the number of photons is an adequate approximation.) We now turn to what these values are at present.

There can have been no appreciable net charge at any time: an appreciable charge will tear apart every material object. Accordingly, we may safely assume that the net charge per photon has always been zero.

As for the baryon number per photon, we know that its present value is $N_B/N_\gamma \simeq 10^{-9}$. (Actually, this ratio is uncertain by a factor of five, but this uncertainty is not significant for our present purposes.) The fact that N_B/N_γ is so "small" has an important consequence. At sufficiently high temperatures, we can have particles and antiparticles of all sorts. But as they can be created or annihilated only in pairs, it follows that they will not contribute to the baryon (or, for that matter, to the lepton) number. The very small value of the ratio, $N_B/N_\gamma \simeq 10^{-9}$, implies that the contribution of the free baryons (mainly protons and neutrons) to the energy density will be negligible under the circumstances. And this, in fact, will be the case till the onset of the recombination era: the subsequent adiabatic cooling of the radiation ("going its own way") will inaugurate the matter-dominated era. (The importance of the ratio $N_B/N_\gamma \simeq 10^{-9}$ for nucleosynthesis in the early universe was first recognized by P. J. E. Peebles.)

There is some ambiguity in ascertaining the lepton-number density. The electrical neutrality of the universe ensures that the number of electrons (free or otherwise), must equal the number of protons (bound in all the atomic nuclei). But the neutrino and the antineutrino must also be included in counting the leptons; and we have now no effective way of determining the cosmic density of the neutrinos. The lepton number, N_L, per photon is not too relevant to our present considerations, but it is unlikely that N_L/N_γ is substantially different from N_B/N_γ; and we shall assume that N_L/N_γ is comparable to N_B/N_γ.

We shall now consider how, with our present information, we can ascertain how far nucleosynthesis can have proceeded in the early universe, and, in particular, how much helium could have been synthesized.

Consider a time when the temperature was $10^{11\circ}$ K. At this temperature, besides radiation, the only particles that can be present are electrons, positrons, neutrinos, and antineutrinos: antiparticles of other sorts cannot be created by the thermal photons at $10^{11\circ}$ K; at this temperature, the energy-density contributed by the radiation, the leptons, and the antileptons present will be equivalent to a mass density of 3.8×10^9 gms/cm^3.

Under these conditions, even the neutrinos will be effectively trapped in spite of their exceedingly small interaction with matter and radiation. Accordingly, thermal equilibrium among all the constituents will prevail, and in fact they will all be present in about equal numbers. Since $N_B/N_\gamma \simeq 10^{-9}$, the free protons and neutrons will not make any significant contribution to the prevailing energy density. Nevertheless, the relative proportion in which they will be present will be determined by statistical considerations and by the fact that the neutrons, relative to the protons, are at a higher energy level; at $10^{11\circ}$ K they will be present in about equal numbers.

Essentially the same situation as we have described will prevail until the temperature has fallen to $10^{10\circ}$ K and the energy density is the mass equivalent of 3.8×10^5 gms/cm^3. However, at this density, the matter (consisting principally of electrons and positrons) and the radiation become transparent to the neutrinos, and the neutrinos will begin to "go their way," adiabatically cooling as the universe expands. But the neutrinos will continue to

Figure 10. The shifting neutron-proton balance and the synthesis of helium. The abundance of neutrons as a percentage of all nuclear particles is shown as a function both of temperature and of time. The part of the curve marked "thermal equilibrium" describes the period in which densities and temperature are so high that thermal equilibrium is maintained among all particles; the neutron fraction here can be calculated from the neutron-proton difference, using the rules of statistical mechanics. The part of the curve marked "neutron decay" describes the period in which all neutron-proton conversion processes have ceased, except for the radioactive decay of the free neutron. The intervening part of the curve depends on detailed calculations. The dashed part of the curve shows what would happen if nuclei were somehow prevented from forming. Actually, at a time somewhere within the period indicated by the arrow marked "era of nucleosynthesis," neutrons are rapidly assembled into helium nuclei, and the neutron-proton ratio is frozen at the value it has at that time. This curve can also be used to estimate the fraction (by weight) of cosmologically produced helium: for any given value of the temperature or the time of nucleosynthesis, it is just twice the neutron fraction at that time.

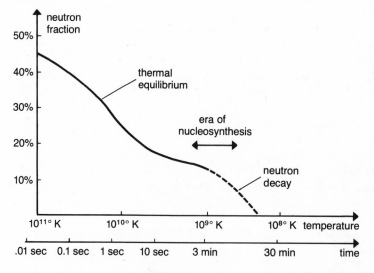

contribute to the energy density since their temperatures will not be very significantly different from that of the radiation and of the electrons and the positrons. Also, at this lower temperature the ratio of the number of free neutrons to the number of free protons will have fallen to $\frac{1}{3}$.

When the temperature falls to $3 \times 10^{9\circ}$ K, the radiation is no longer at a high enough temperature to create electron-positron pairs. Consequently, at this temperature, besides radiation only neutrons, protons, and electrons will be present with a total number density corresponding to $N_B/N_\gamma \simeq 10^{-9}$; and with a neutron/proton ratio 1:5 (appropriate to the lower temperature). Also, at this temperature, the neutrons and the protons will begin to combine to form deuterons. But the deuterons, because of their small binding energy, will be too short-lived to provide "stepping stones" for further nucleosynthesis. However, the situation will drastically change as the temperature continues to fall; for then, in spite of their low binding energy, deuterons in sufficient numbers will exist to initiate a chain of nuclear reactions ending in the synthesis of helium nuclei, which are very stable. At the same time, the rate of expansion of the universe will be such that the radioactive decay of the neutron to become a proton will begin to compete. The net result of the various competing processes is that at a temperature close to $10^{9\circ}$ K (how close depends on the precise value of N_B/N_γ), all the free neutrons that are present will effectively be "locked up" in helium nuclei (leaving possibly a minute amount of deuterons). Figure 10 illustrates (in somewhat greater detail) the sequence of events we have described.

By detailed calculations along the lines outlined, one can seek initial parameters (*e.g.*, $\bar{\rho}$, H, q, etc.) for the universe, on the Friedmann models, which will lead one to a consistent description of all the facts including the primordial abundances of helium and deuterium that are observed. And these attempts have been successful enough to support the belief that the universe is open and that its age is seventeen billion to eighteen billion years.

Epilogue

On the conceptual side, the most significant result which has emerged from our discussion of relativistic cosmology is that the universe began with an initial singularity and, if the universe is closed, will end in a future singularity. And, as we have pointed out, the singularity theorems of Penrose and Hawking require that we confront this prospect regardless of whether or not the Friedmann models provide the basis for an exact extrapolation to the past and to the future. The confrontation raises many complex and difficult issues. In this concluding section, we shall no more than raise the curtain on what these issues may be.

An obvious first question concerns the nature of the singularities that may arise if we consider cosmological models more general than Friedmann's. This question can be answered, in part, by seeking cosmological models which are homogeneous but not necessarily isotropic. It happens that a complete classification of all possible homogeneous cosmological models (which include the Friedmann models as special cases) can be given, and there is, in principle, no difficulty in exploring all of these models. One particular class of these models which has been investigated in some detail (by I. M. Khalatnikov, E. M. Lifshitz, V. A. Belinsky, C. Misner, and others) is an anisotropic modification of the Friedmann models. In this class of models, the anisotropy is measured by the ratios of the circumferences of the universe in three mutually perpendicular directions. In these models, if we follow the evolution of the universe backward (or, forward) in time, we approach the singularity through a sequence of "eras" in which the axis which is the longest is different. Further, during a given era, the ratio of the two remaining axes alternates several times. And what is perhaps the most interesting feature of this evolution is that the frequency with which one era follows another increases indefinitely as the singularity is approached. As Charles Misner has dramatically expressed, "the Universe is meaningfully infinitely old because infinitely many things have happened since the beginning." This curious "mixmaster" behavior, as the singularity is approached, has sometimes been considered as a key to an understanding of the homogeneity and the isotropy of our universe in the belief that some dissipative mechanism (derived, perhaps, from neutrino viscosity or particle production) could, under the circumstances, have smoothed out all initial inhomogeneities and anisotropies as a prelude to the present isotropic state. Quite apart from whether such dissipative mechanisms could have operated, the question whether the universe was, at the very beginning, *isotropic* or *chaotic* is a fundamental one and raises issues of a different sort.

According to those who have advocated an initial state of chaos, the initial singularity was not a uniform one (in the sense that the singularity in the Friedmann models can be described as "uniform"); and that it has come to appear so is because dissipative effects have smoothed out all initial inhomogeneities and anisotropies and prepared the way for isotropy before the nucleosynthesis era. It was also thought that these same considerations will account for the present "large" value of the ratio $N_\gamma/N_B \simeq 10^9$. And, finally, in order not to impose what may appear as *ad hoc* restrictions on the initial singularity, it was conjectured that the chaos at the initial singularity was, in some appropriate sense, *maximal.*

An opposite view (which appears to the writer as a more reasonable one) has been advocated by Penrose. His argument is a very simple one (or, so it appears): all thermodynamic considerations lead one to postulate an evolution in which a system initially very regular (*i.e.*, in a state of zero entropy) becomes progressively irregular (increasing the entropy as required by thermodynamics); and, *therefore*, the present high degree of isotropy of the universe can only mean that the universe was even less inhomogeneous and anisotropic than it is at present. Further, according to Penrose, the ratio $N_\gamma/N_B \simeq 10^9$ is not really large compared to what it might have been had the universe been chaotic at the outset. Penrose's argument is that, had the geometry of space-time corresponded to an initial state of "maximal" inhomogeneity (as the advocates of chaotic cosmology would apparently wish to have), one should expect for N_γ/N_B a value more in the neighborhood of 10^{40}. In other words, the problem is not why the entropy per baryon is so large, it is, rather, why it is so small.

An immediate consequence of the foregoing remarks is that, should our universe be closed, the future singularity must be, fundamentally, quite different from the initial singularity. In the beginning, there were no stars and no galaxies. But now they are here. In addition, the present astronomical universe must be populated by innumerable black holes large ($\sim 10^6$–10^9 solar masses) and small (~ 1 solar mass); and the coalescence of these black holes, as the future singularity is approached, will result in the production of an enormous amount of entropy. Therefore, it even might be that at the final singularity, the chaos is maximal.

There is another class of questions, the elucidation of which will be necessary before we can clarify the issues we have raised in the preceding paragraphs. These questions concern the physical processes which may occur (or must occur) as the singularity is approached.

We have so far considered only densities and temperatures at which nucleosynthesis may be expected to happen. These conditions are not extreme in any sense: the densities considered are comparable to (in fact, much less than) the densities we are familiar with in common atomic nuclei. But the singularities place no limit on the densities we may—indeed, must —contemplate. The questions which now arise are of several kinds. However, we should be aware that the physical conditions we are asked to contemplate transcend our experience by so many orders of magnitude that the questions we ask may be as meaningless as Werner Heisenberg's famous hypothetical query: "What is the color of an electron?" Nevertheless, we have no choice but to formulate questions as a prelude to exploring the vast unknown domain.

It is generally thought that quantal effects will require modifications of the general theory of relativity when we wish to discuss phenomena which may occur (rather, will occur!) in regions whose linear dimensions are of the order of the Planck length ($= (\hbar G/c^3)^{\frac{1}{2}} \simeq 1.6 \times 10^{-33}$ cm) and in intervals of time of the order of Planck length/velocity of light ($= 5.3 \times 10^{-44}$ sec).

Now, we are generally accustomed to having "clocks" which provide the basis for measurements of time intervals that are short compared to the durations in which the phenomena we are interested in take place: we have atomic clocks based on the frequencies of the characteristic spectral radiation of atoms or molecules, and we can contemplate clocks based on the γ-radiations of atomic nuclei or even on the half-lives of unstable particles such as the muons. Must we then presuppose that particles exist whose mean lives are short compared to 10^{-44} sec? Or, is this question meaningless?

It appears, however, that in the framework of what we already know, we may ask if there can be creation of particles at cosmological singularities even as they occur at the horizons of black holes, and if such particle creation can prevent the ultimate collapse to a point singularity. Recent investigations by L. Parker, J. Hartle, Ya. Zeldovich, and others have answered the first question in the affirmative, but the answer to the second question does not seem to be unique. Regardless of the final outcome of these investigations, it would appear that the occurrence of cosmological singularities in the framework of general relativity raises some of the deepest questions in current physical thought.

The Social Sciences Since the Second World War—Part One

Daniel Bell

Though Daniel Bell has had a mixed career in journalism and the academy, he claims to have received his education primarily by teaching, having had what he calls "the good fortune to teach at three good universities"—Chicago, Columbia, and Harvard. Since 1969 he has been professor of sociology at Harvard.

Professor Bell is author of *Marxian Socialism in the United States* (1952); *Work and Its Discontents* (1956); *The End of Ideology* (1960); *The Reforming of General Education* (1966); *The Coming of Post-Industrial Society* (1973); and *The Cultural Contradictions of Capitalism* (1976). With Irving Kristol he is coeditor of *Confrontation* (1969) and *Capitalism Today* (1971). He is at present at work on *Teletext and Technology,* concerning the new networks of knowledge and information in post-industrial society and *The Return of the Sacred,* the argument on the future of religion.

From 1964 to 1966, he served as a member of the President's Commission on Technology, Automation and Economic Progress; from 1966 to 1974, as Chairman for the Commission on the Year 2000, with the American Academy of Arts and Sciences; and since 1976 as the United States representative on the Advisory Committee of the OECD project, "Inter-Futures." With Kristol, he was the founder, and coeditor for almost ten years, of *The Public Interest*. He continues as chairman of its publication committee.

In February 1971 Karl Deutsch of Harvard University and two associates published a study in *Science* magazine listing sixty-two "advances in social science" from 1900 to 1965. Their intention was to study the conditions for "creative success in the social sciences," but to do so, of course, they had to demonstrate that such successes had indeed occurred.

The criterion of achievement was that a theory, or a finding, put forth a "new perception of relationships"; or stipulated verifiable propositions of the "if ... then" form; or produced "a substantial impact that led to further knowledge." After compiling the list (and checking these judgments with those of individuals in other fields), they concluded:

1. There *are* such things as social science achievements and social inventions, which are almost as clearly defined and as operational as technological achievements and inventions.
2. These achievements have commonly been the result of conscious and systematic research and development efforts by individuals or teams working on particular problems in a small number of interdisciplinary centers.
3. These achievements have had widespread acceptance or major social effects in surprisingly short times; median times are in the range of ten to fifteen years, a range comparable with the median times for widespread acceptance of major technological inventions.[1]

What is striking about the list (*see* Tables 1 and 2) is that the early achievements are quite theoretical and, in the jargon of the field, largely qualitative—such as the theory of bureaucracy associated with Max Weber, or the revolutionary-vanguard role of the mobilized party initiated by V. I. Lenin, or the psychoanalytic and depth psychology of Freud, Jung, and Adler—while the later achievements, or even the later developments of early findings, are (with almost the sole exception of the anthropological structuralism of Claude Lévi-Strauss) primarily innovations of mathematical and statistical techniques, or theories derived from quantitative analysis, such as information theory or growth models in economics. Indeed, as the authors write:

Quantitative problems or findings (or both) characterized two-thirds of all advances, and five-sixths of those were made after 1930 (Table 1,

column 7). Completely nonquantitative contributors—the recognition of
new patterns without any clear implication of quantitative
problems—were rare throughout the period and extremely rare since
1930.

This is, surely, one of the reasons why the social sciences, in the period after 1940, acquired new prestige and influence. With the rapid advance in sophisticated new techniques, particularly after the introduction of the computer, theories were no longer simply ideas or rhetoric but propositions that could be stated in empirical and verifiable form. To use the jargon again, social sciences were becoming "hard," like the natural sciences.

A second factor conjoined. This was the halo effect of science, particularly because of its crucial role in World War II. One need go back only twenty-five more years, to World War I, for an instructive contrast. At that time, Thomas Alva Edison had been appointed head of the Navy consulting board. As his biographer Matthew Josephson tells the story, Edison decided that they ought to have a physicist on the board, because they might need someone to deal with mathematical or statistical questions should they arise; but since the Navy did not have a classification of physicist, the man who was appointed was paid as a chemist. James B. Conant tells a similar story. Conant, before becoming president of Harvard, had been a chemist. At the time of the U.S. entry into World War I, Conant was president of the American Chemical Society. In that capacity he went to Newton D. Baker, then Secretary of War, and offered his services and those of the members of the Society to the war effort. Baker thanked him for his patriotism, told him he would inquire into the need, and when Conant returned a week later, he was told that the services of the Society were unnecessary because the War Department already had a sufficient number of chemists.

During World War II the Manhattan Project produced the atomic bomb; the Radiation Laboratory at MIT developed radar (which had been invented by the British); the need for "number crunching" speeded the development of the electronic computer; and the mobilization of thousands of scientists produced hundreds of new devices for the war effort.

The simple thought occurred to many: if the widespread mobilization of science, and the concentration on some specific objectives, could produce scientific and technological breakthroughs, why could not a similar mobilization—the building of interdisciplinary teams—produce similar results in the social sciences? An example was at hand: the mobilization of the economy for war. The experience of mobilization had produced a wide and varied number of new experiences: the planning for production, the allocation of material, new psychological selection and testing procedures, psychological warfare, studies of the means of maintaining soldier and civilian morale, and dozens of other organized research and managerial efforts. Why could not a sustained effort, underwritten by large-scale expenditures, now advance the social sciences in the way that the natural sciences had

text continued on p. 150

141

Table 1. Basic Innovations in Social Science, 1900-65

Abbreviations in column 1: An, anthropology; Ec, economics; Math, mathematics; Phil, philosophy, logic, and history of science; Pol, politics; Psy, psychology; Soc, sociology.

Contribution 1	Contributor 2	Time 3	Place 4
1. Theory and measurement of social inequalities (Ec)	V. Pareto C. Gini	1900 1908	Lausanne, Swit. Cagliari, It. Padua, It. Rome, It.
2. Sociology of bureaucracy, culture, and values (Soc)	M. Weber	1900–21	Freiburg, Ger. Heidelberg, Ger. Munich, Ger.
3. Theory of one-party organization and revolution (Pol)	V. I. Lenin	1900–17	Shushenskoe, Siberia London, Eng. Munich, Ger.
4. Psychoanalysis and depth psychology (Psy)	S. Freud C. G. Jung A. Adler	1900–25 1910–30 1910–30	Vienna, Aus.
5. Correlation analysis and social theory (Math)	K. Pearson F. Edgeworth R. A. Fisher	1900–28 1900–30 1920–48	London, Eng. Oxford, Eng. Cambridge, Eng. Harfenden, Eng.
6. Gradual social transformation (Pol)	B. Webb S. Webb G. B. Shaw H. G. Wells	1900–38	London, Eng.
7. Elite studies (Soc)	G. Mosca V. Pareto H. D. Lasswell	1900–23 1900–16 1936–52	Turin, It. Lausanne, Swit. Chicago, Ill.
8. Unity of logic and mathematics (Phil)	B. Russell A. N. Whitehead	1905–14	Cambridge, Eng.
9. Pragmatic and behavioral psychology (Psy)	J. Dewey G. H. Mead C. Cooley W. I. Thomas	1905–25 1900–34 1900–30 1900–40	Ann Arbor, Mich. Chicago, Ill. Ann Arbor, Mich. Chicago, Ill. New York, N.Y.
10. Learning theory (Psy)	E. L. Thorndike C. Hull *et al.*	1905–40 1929–40	New York, N.Y. New Haven, Conn.
11. Intelligence tests (Psy)	A. Binet L. Terman C. Spearman	1905–11 1916–37 1904–27	Paris, Fr. Stanford, Calif. London, Eng.
12. Role of innovations in socioeconomic change (Ec)	J. A. Schumpeter W. F. Ogburn A. P. Usher J. Schmookler	1908–14 1946–50 1922–30 1924 1966	Vienna, Aus. Cambridge, Mass. New York, N.Y. Cambridge, Mass. Minneapolis, Minn.
13. Conditioned reflexes (Psy)	I. Pavlov	1910–30	Leningrad, U.S.S.R.
14. Gestalt psychology (Psy)	M. Wertheimer K. Koffka W. Koehler	1912–32	Berlin, Ger.
15. Sociometry and sociograms (Soc)	J. L. Moreno	1915 1934–43	Innsbruck, Aus.
16. Soviet type of one-party state (Pol)	V. I. Lenin *et al.*	1917–21	Leningrad, U.S.S.R.
17. Large-scale nonviolent political action (Pol)	M. K. Gandhi	1918–34	Ahmedabad, India

In column 6, + N indicates a larger number of collaborators with a less crucial share in the work. Abbreviations in column 7: QFE, quantitative findings explicit; QPE, quantitative problems explicit; QPI, quantitative problems implied; Non-Q, predominantly nonquantitative.

Type of support 5	No. of workers 6	Quantitative aspects 7	Years until impact 8
University chairs	1 + N	QFE	25
University chair with research support	1	QPI	20 ± 10
Underground party	1 + N	QPI	10 ± 5
University institute of psychology	1 + N	Non-Q	30 ± 10
University chairs	1 + N	QFE	25 ± 15
Fabian society	4 + N	QPE	35 ± 5
University institutes	1 + N	QFE	40 ± 10
University institute	2	QPE	30
University chairs	1	Non-Q	20 ± 10
Teachers college, Institute of human relations	1 + N	QFE	20 ± 5
Testing organizations	1 + N	QFE	15 ± 5
University chair and research program	1 + N	QPI	40
Imperial medico-surgical academy	1 + N	QPI	20 ± 10
University chairs	3 + N	Non-Q	25 ± 5
University chair	1	QFE	10
Politburo	1 + N	QPI	5 ± 5
Political movement and institute (ashram)	1 + N	Non-Q	15 ± 10

Contribution 1	Contributor 2	Time 3	Place 4
18. Central economic planning (Ec)	Q. Krassin G. Grinko	1920–26	Moscow, U.S.S.R.
19. Social welfare function in politics and economics (Ec)	A. C. Pigou K. Arrow	1920–56 1951	London, Eng. Stanford, Calif.
20. Logical empiricism and unity of science (Phil)	M. Schlick R. Carnap O. Neurath P. Frank L. Wittgenstein H. Reichenbach C. Morris	1921–38 1921 1936–50	Vienna, Aus. Cambridge, Eng. Berlin, Ger. Chicago, Ill. Cambridge, Mass.
21. Quantitative mathematical studies of war (Pol)	L. F. Richardson Q. Wright	1921–55 1936–66	London, Eng. Chicago, Ill.
22. Projective tests (Psy)	H. Rorschach H. Murray	1923	Herisau, Swit. Cambridge, Mass.
23. Sociology of knowledge and science (Soc)	K. Mannheim R. K. Merton D. deS. Price	1923–33 1937 1950–60	Heidelberg, Ger. Frankfurt, Ger. Princeton, N.J. New Haven, Conn.
24. Quantitative political science and basic theory (Pol)	C. Merriam S. Rice H. Gosnell H. D. Lasswell	1925–36	Chicago, Ill.
25. Functionalist anthropology and sociology (An)	A. R. Radcliffe-Brown B. Malinowski T. Parsons	1925 1925–45 1932–50	Cape Town, S. Afr. Sidney, Aus. Chicago, Ill. Oxford, Eng. London, Eng. Cambridge, Mass.
26. Ecosystem theory (Soc)	R. Park E. W. Burgess	1926–38	Chicago, Ill.
27. Factor analysis (Math)	L. Thurstone	1926–48	Chicago, Ill.
28. Operational definitions (Phil)	P. W. Bridgman	1927–38	Cambridge, Mass.
29. Structural linguistics (Math)	R. Jakobson and Prague circle N. Chomsky	1927–67 1957–	Brno, Czech. Cambridge, Mass. Cambridge, Mass.
30. Economic propensities, employment, and fiscal policy (Ec)	J. M. Keynes	1928–44	Cambridge, Eng.
31. Game theory (Math)	J. v. Neumann O. Morgenstern	1928–44 1944–58	Berlin, Ger. Princeton, N.J.
32. Peasant and guerrilla organization and government (Pol)	Mao Tse-tung	1929–49	Kiangsi, P. R. China Yenan, P. R. China Peking, P. R. China
33. Community studies (Soc)	R. Lynd H. Lynd L. Warner C. Kluckhohn	1929–62 1941	New York, N.Y. Chicago, Ill.

Type of support 5	No. of workers 6	Quantitative aspects 7	Years until impact 8
Government institute	1 + N	QFE	7 ± 6
University chairs	1 + N	QPE	40 ± 10
Vienna circle and university chairs	3 + N	QPI	20 ± 5
University chairs			
University chair and research program	1 + N	QFE	25 ± 10
Cantonal mental institute University chair	1	Non-Q	15 ± 5
University chairs, institutes, and programs	1 + N	Non-Q	10
University chairs	3 + N	QFE	15 ± 5
University chairs and travel grants	1 + N	Non-Q	20 ± 10
University chairs	2 + N	QFE	25 ± 5
University chair	1 + N	QFE	15 ± 10
University chair	1	QPI	15 ± 5
University chairs and programs	1 + N	QPE	20 ± 10
University chair	1 + N	QFE	6 ± 4
University chairs and institute	2 + N	QFE	10 ± 5
Political movement	1 + N	QPI	15 ± 10
University chairs	2	QFE	20 ± 5

Contribution 1	Contributor 2	Time 3	Place 4
34. Culture and personality and comparative child rearing (An)	R. Benedict	1930	New York, N.Y.
	M. Mead	1930	
	G. Gorer		
	A. Kardiner	1939	
	J. Piaget	1940–60	Geneva, Swit.
	E. Erikson	1950	Cambridge, Mass.
	J. Whiting	1953	Cambridge, Mass.
	I. Child		New Haven, Conn.
35. Economics of monopolistic competiton (Ec)	E. H. Chamberlin	1930–33	Cambridge, Mass.
	J. Robinson		Cambridge, Eng.
36. Authoritarian personality and family structure (Psy)	M. Horkheimer	1930–32	Frankfurt, Ger.
	H. Marcuse		
	E. Fromm		
	T. Adorno *et al.*	1950	Stanford, Calif.
	A. Mitscherlich	1962	Frankfurt, Ger. Heidelberg, Ger.
37. Large-scale sampling in social research (Math)	M. Hansen	1930–53	Washington, D.C.
38. Laboratory study of small groups (Psy)	K. Lewin	1932–36	Cambridge, Mass.
	R. Lippitt		
	R. Likert		
	D. Cartwright		
39. National income accounting (Ec)	S. Kuznets	1933–40	Philadelphia, Pa.
	C. Clark		Cambridge, Eng.
	U.N. Statistical Office	1953	Washington, D.C. New York, N.Y.
40. General systems analysis (Phil)	L. v. Bertalanffy	1936	Vienna, Aus.
	N. Rashevsky		Chicago, Ill.
	J. G. Miller	1956	Ann Arbor, Mich.
	A. Rapoport		
	R. W. Gerard		
	K. Boulding		
41. Attitude survey and opinion polling (Psy)	G. Gallup	1936	Princeton, N.J.
	H. Cantril	1937–52	
	P. F. Lazarsfeld	1940	New York, N.Y.
	A. Campbell	1942	Ann Arbor, Mich.
42. Input-out analysis (Ec)	W. Leontief	1936–53	Cambridge, Mass.
43. Linear programming (Ec)	L. Kantorovich	1938–50	Leningrad, U.S.S.R.
	J. B. Souto	1941	Buenos Aires, Arg.
	G. B. Dantzig	1948	Washington, D.C.
	R. Dorfman	1958	Berkeley, Calif.
44. Content analysis (Pol)	H. Lasswell	1938–56	Chicago, Ill.
	I. deS. Pool		
	B. Berelson		
	P. Stone	1961–66	Cambridge, Mass.
45. Operant conditioning and learning; teaching machines (Psy)	B. F. Skinner	1938–58	Bloomington, Ind. Cambridge, Mass.
46. Statistical decision theory (Math)	A. Wald	1939–50	New York, N.Y.
47. Operations research and systems analysis (Math)	P. M. S. Blackett	1941–50	London, Eng.
	P. Morse	1941–58	Cambridge, Mass.
	R. Bellman		
48. Scaling theory (Psy)	L. Guttman	1941–54	Ithaca, N.Y.
	C. Coombs		Ann Arbor, Mich.

Type of support 5	No. of workers 6	Quantitative aspects 7	Years until impact 8
University chairs, research projects, and travel grants	3 + N	Non-Q	20 ± 10
University chairs	1	QPE	10 ± 5
Institute for social research and university	3 + N	QPI	20 ± 5
Government office	N	QFE	5
University and research institutes	1 + N	QPI	10 ± 5
Public research institutes and university chairs	1 + N	QFE	10 ± 5
University research institutes	4 + N	QPI	15 ± 5
University and research institutes, commercial organizations	3 + N	QFE	5
University chair	1 + N	QFE	15
University research institutes and government office	1 + N	QFE	10 ± 5
University institute	2	QFE	10
University chairs	1 + N	QPE	15
University chair	1 + N	QPE	15 ± 5
Government research institutes	N	QPE	5
University chairs	3 + N	QFE	10 ± 5

Contribution 1	Contributor 2	Time 3	Place 4
49. Quantitative models of nationalism and integration (Pol)	K. Deutsch B. Russett R. L. Merritt	1942–67	Cambridge, Mass. New Haven, Conn.
50. Theories of economic development (Ec)	P. Rosenstein-Rodan R. Prebisch R. Nurkse W. A. Lewis G. Myrdal A. O. Hirschman R. F. Harrod E. Domar H. Chenery	1943–58	London, Eng. Santiago, Chile New York, N.Y. Manchester, Eng. Stockholm, Swed. New Haven, Conn. Oxford, Eng. Baltimore, Md. Stanford, Calif.
51. Computers (Math)	V. Bush S. Caldwell D. P. Eckert J. W. Mauchly	1943–58	Cambridge, Mass. Philadelphia, Pa.
52. Multivariate analysis linked to social theory (Soc)	S. Stouffer T. W. Anderson P. Lazarsfeld	1944–54	Washington, D.C. Cambridge, Mass. New York, N.Y.
53. Information theory, cybernetics, and feedback systems (Math)	C. Shannon N. Wiener	1944–58	Cambridge, Mass. Orange, N.J.
54. Econometrics (Ec)	J. Tinbergen P. Samuelson E. Malinvaud	1935–40 1947 1964	The Hague, Neth. Cambridge, Mass. Paris, Fr.
55. Cognitive dynamics of science (Phil)	J. B. Conant I. B. Cohen T. Kuhn D. deS. Price	1946–64	Cambridge, Mass. Berkeley, Calif. New Haven, Conn.
56. Computer simulation of economic systems (Ec)	L. Klein G. Orcutt	1947–60	Philadelphia, Pa. Madison, Wis.
57. Structuralism in anthropology and social science (An)	C. Levi-Strauss	1949–66	Paris, Fr.
58. Hierarchical computerized decision models (Math)	H. Simon	1950–65	Pittsburgh, Pa.
59. Cost-benefit analysis (planned programming and budgeting) (Pol)	C. Hitch	1956–63	Santa Monica, Calif.
60. Computer simulation of social and political systems (Pol)	W. McPhee H. Simon A. Newell I. Pool R. Abelson	1956–66 1958–64	Pittsburgh, Pa. Cambridge, Mass. New Haven, Conn.
61. Conflict theory and variable sum games (Psy)	A. Rapoport	1960–	Ann Arbor, Mich.
62. Stochastic models of social processes (Math)	J. S. Coleman	1965	Baltimore, Md.

Type of support 5	No. of workers 6	Quantitative aspects 7	Years until impact 8
University chairs	$1 + N$	QFE	20 ± 5
Government offices, U.N. regional commission, university chairs	$6 + N$	QFE	10 ± 5
University and government research laboratories	N	QFE	10 ± 5
Government and university research institutes	$3 + N$	QFE	5
University research institute and Bell Laboratories	$2 + N$	QFE	10 ± 5
Government institute and university chairs	$1 + N$	QFE	10 ± 5
University chairs	$3 + N$	Non-Q	15
Research institutes	$2 + N$	QFE	5
Museum (government)	$1 + N$	QPI	15 ± 5
University research institute	$1 + N$	QPE	10
Government-related research institute	$3 + N$	QFE	7
University chairs and research institutes	$2 + N$	QPE	5 ± 3
University research institute	$1 + N$	QFE	2
University and research institute	$1 + N$	QFE	5

text continued from p. 141

made their advance, particularly in physics and chemistry, in the years after World War I?

A third factor was fortuitous: the extraordinary transformation of universities in the U.S. after World War II. First there was the GI Bill which paid for college schooling of war veterans and brought millions of young men into the colleges and universities. Second was the demographic impact of the baby boom in the immediate postwar years which, following the ebbing of the first wave, produced a new tide of students for the schools. The expansion of the universities expanded the professoriate and the number of persons engaged in research.

The fourth factor brought all the others together: the fact that in the decades following World War II, the United States became the paramount power in the world and then found itself engaged in a Cold War with the Soviet Union for political dominance. A scientific rivalry, particularly in space exploration, intensified as the two countries competed for prestige. In mundane fact this meant that a huge research-and-development effort was now underwritten for the first time by the government and, in auxiliary instances, by the major foundations. The government needed foreign-area political, economic, and language specialists on the Soviet Union, China, Southeast Asia, Africa, the Middle East, Latin America, etc. The military needed not only weapons experts but individuals who could do systems analysis and operations research as well as the new kind of detailed logistical planning. The universities and businesses needed large numbers of specialists, particularly in such fields as economics, psychology, and political science, where the expansion was greatest.

Finally the rediscovery of social problems, particularly in the 1960s, focussed renewed attention on the social sciences. There were the problems of discrimination, poverty, broken families, poor housing environments, race riots, ecological and environmental problems, and the like. And the Kennedy and Johnson administrations responded with extraordinary rapidity in the adoption of social programs that required the "expert advice" of social science.

For all these reasons, the social sciences have been in the forefront of public attention and expectations in the past thirty or so years in a way that had never been true before in their history—short as it is.*

None of this would have been possible without the sense that a set of genuine intellectual advances had taken place in the social sciences which,

---

* The simplest way of establishing lineage is by patrilineal descent. In economics, the grandfathers—Adam Smith, Thomas Malthus, and David Ricardo, *c.* 1776–1810; the fathers—Alfred Marshall and Léon Walras, 1870–90. In sociology, the grandfathers—Auguste Comte, Karl Marx, and Herbert Spencer, *c.* 1850–70; the fathers—Émile Durkheim and Max Weber, 1890–1915. In psychology, the grandfathers—Hermann Helmholz, Ernst Weber, and Gustav Fechner, *c.* 1839–60; the fathers—Wilhelm Wundt, William James, and Sigmund Freud, 1879–1910. In anthropology, the grandfathers—Edward Burnett Tylor and James George Frazer, 1879–1900; the fathers—Franz Boas and Bronisław Malinowski, 1910–20. The dates are somewhat arbitrary, representing the period of major work and the establishment of reputation.

Table 2. Major Social Science Contributions by Field and Focus, 1900-65

Field	Total	Major contributions		Focus on theory		Focus on method		Focus on results	
	1900 to 1965	1900 to 1929	1930 to 1965	1900 to 1929	1930 to 1965	1900 to 1929	1930 to 1965	1900 to 1929	1930 to 1965
Psychology	13	7	6	6	3	6	6	6	6
Economics	12	5	7	4	5	4	6	5	7
Politics	11	7	4	7	2	2	4	4	4
Mathematical statistics	11	4	7	2	5	4	7	4	6
Sociology	7	6	1	4	1	5	1	6	1
Philosophy	5	3	2	3	2	2	2	0	1
Anthropology	3	1	2	1	2	0	2	1	2
Total	62	33	29	27	20	23	28	26	27

for the first time, were equipped to set forth theoretical and practical knowledge. While the source of many of these reorganizations or break-throughs of knowledge antedates the postwar period, the attention to the social sciences and the claims made by the social sciences were largely during the postwar period, and one is therefore justified in considering the period between 1945 and 1970 as a single period in which a set of promises were made—in disciplines, in methodology and techniques, and in social programs—which indicated that the social sciences had come of age. Given the fact, as we shall show, that many of these promises were not realized, it would be useful, even if only schematically as this must be, to review the major claims of the social sciences during this period.

Economics

In the postwar period, especially in the 1960s during the Kennedy adminis-tration, economists were regarded as individuals who had the "right an-swers" not only in managing the economy, but in the formulation of other social programs as well. The symbolic recognition of the status of economics came in 1969 when a Nobel Prize in Economics was established (the first prizes were awarded in 1901), and Ragnar Frisch of Norway and Jan Tinbergen of The Netherlands were jointly rewarded for their indepen-dent work in econometrics. The influence of economics has persisted in the Carter administration: of the fifteen cabinet-rank officials, four have Ph.D.'s in economics.*

---

* The four: W. Michael Blumenthal, Treasury; Juanita M. Kreps, Commerce; James R. Schlesinger, Energy: F. Ray Marshall, Labor. In addition, the Secretary of Defense, Harold Brown, has an academic degree and a Ph.D. in physics and was also president of the California Institute of Technology.

There were six areas in which economics forged ahead steadily during this period:

a) *The Keynesian revolution.* In a charming memoir about his economic upbringing and education, Paul Samuelson, who won the Nobel Prize in Economics in 1970, remarked: "The great romance in the life of any economist of my generation must necessarily have been the Keynesian revolution.... Economics itself was a sleeping princess waiting for the invigorating kiss of Maynard Keynes." And in a eulogy Samuelson wrote in 1946 on the death of Keynes, he remarked:

> ... It is quite impossible for modern students to realize the full effect
> of what has been advisably called "The Keynesian Revolution," upon
> those of us brought up in the orthodox tradition. What beginners
> today often regard as trite and obvious was to us puzzling, novel, and
> heretical. . . .
>
> The *General Theory* caught most economists under the age of 35 with
> the unexpected virulence of a disease first attacking and decimating an
> isolated tribe of South Sea islanders. Economists beyond 50 turned out
> to be quite immune to the ailment. With time, most economists
> in-between began to run the fever, often without knowing or admitting
> their condition.[2]

The heart of Keynes's *Theory,* as it affected public policy, was the argument that a return to economic equilibrium (or a recovery from a depression) was not automatic in the capitalist economic system, even after a "wringing out" of "over-production," or a fall in the money-wage rate (which was difficult anyway), but could be managed by government intervention. There were two elements to the Keynesian diagnosis. One was that savings in the system did not automatically flow into investments, even if the interest rate was high. A second was that the level of economic activity, and hence of employment, depended on the level of aggregate demand. The heart of the Keynesian prescription, therefore, is what is called today "demand management." The mechanism is government fiscal policy, *i.e.,* the level of taxes and the degree of government spending.

b) *National income accounts.* The letters GNP and the term gross national product have passed so quickly into common usage that it is difficult to realize how recent was their adoption. In point of time, the collection of economic data to build a full set of national income accounts and to assess the gross national product was first proposed by Pres. Franklin D. Roosevelt in his budget message of 1945. Actually, the conceptual work and the empirical steps in this accounting were first done in the 1930s by Simon S. Kuznets (who won the Nobel Prize in 1971) in Pennsylvania and Colin Clark in Cambridge, England.

Gross national product is simply the sum total of the monetary value of all goods and services produced by a nation's economy during a single year. It consists, essentially, of two parts: one is the demand for goods and services at all stages of production—from raw materials to finished goods—as reflected in the prices of these goods and services; the other is the income, or the monies paid out to the individuals producing these goods and services. As final totals, the two sides match.

The national income accounts are like a set of building blocks of the economic system. They show what proportions of the total national product go for raw materials, domestic or imported, the cost of intermediate products and services, such as fabricating and finishing, and the totals of the final demands. Along the way, one can calculate the value added at each stage of the process. On the other side of the ledger, we can calculate the proportion of GNP going to individuals for personal consumption, the amounts taken by government and business corporations, and the like.

Each year's figures give us the *level* of economic activity; year-to-year figures allow us to measure the rate of growth, the rate of productivity, and the like. Since every major business corporation plans ahead to some extent —as to capital expansion, degree of inventory, amount of working capital, supply of labor, and the like—the forecasts of GNP clearly affect their plans and their judgments as to what decisions to make. For the government, the GNP is the basic tool to measure the level of employment, the unused capacity of the economy, and the expected degree of economic activity in order to set targets for growth, levels of unemployment, or inflation.

c) *Input-output analysis,* developed by Wassily Leontief (who won the Nobel Prize in 1973) is the physiology of the economic system—the interconnected transactions and flows between industries, and the effects of the shifts in the inputs or outputs of each industry on every other.

The input-output table—the idea in principle goes back to the *Tableau Économique* of the Physiocrats in late eighteenth-century France—is a rectangular grid, the heart of which is a square matrix of 81×81 rows and columns, providing a total of 6,561 cells which would be the "beehive" of the economy. Each row is an industry, and the table shows the interindustry transactions, the sales and purchases of each industry to the other, that tie together the highly differentiated system as a whole.

For purposes of analysis, the eighty-one industries are grouped into seven basic sectors, such as basic metal (*e.g.,* steel); basic nonmetal (*e.g.,* glass, paper, wood, plastic); energy (*e.g.,* oil, natural gas, coal); final metal (*e.g.,* automobiles, aircraft); final nonmetal (*e.g.,* shoes, clothing, furniture), and so on. There are, in addition, ten columns on the right which integrate these transactions into the GNP, such as personal consumption from each industry, investment, new construction, and so forth. Two rows at the bottom specify the imports in each row and the value added by the industry.

Within each cell are a number of input-output coefficients. Thus, one can tell at a glance the ratio of the dollar-flow input in each cell to the total output of the entire sector within which that industry is classified.

As one would imagine, the number of computations to chart these interindustry transactions, or the value added by each industry to a finished product, or the proportion of inputs of each cell to the sector whole, is staggering. When Leontief began this task in the late 1930s, it took about five years to complete the table for the economy, an effort which made the exercise primarily a tool for retrospective analysis. With the introduction of high-speed computers, the input-output table became a major tool for planning and analysis. Thus, with a complete table, one could quickly calculate what the effects would be of a five-fold increase in the price of oil on *all other* industries and sectors of the economy. In this way, the input-output table allows for an "isotope trace" of different measures, governmental and otherwise, on the "physiology" of the system as a whole.

d) *Mathematical analysis and econometric models.* Mathematical analysis is primarily an expression of *relations between variables* (*e.g.*, consumption and investment, wages and prices) in algebraic or some other mathematical notation. It does not necessarily involve numbers or amounts, *i.e.*, the magnitudes of these variables. The analyst is seeking a precise way to formulate these relationships and to manipulate them mathematically to see how they change under stipulated conditions. Econometrics begins with the statistical *aggregation of quantities, i.e.,* the sum totals of specific indices or variables, though when these aggregates are put into a model of the economy they are expressed as coefficients or magnitudes of these variables, and the model itself is then put into mathematical form.

Mathematics has a long history in economics. William Stanley Jevons, when he proposed the theory of marginal analysis, used calculus to measure the incremental changes in prices. Léon Walras, when he wrote his *Elements of Pure Economics* (1874), used mathematics to demonstrate his general economic equilibrium theory, *i.e.*, the way in which relative prices clear all markets simultaneously. But mathematics was usually regarded as a kind of shorthand, rather than as a way of expressing underlying structures or relations. Alfred Marshall, whose *Principles of Economics* (1890) codified the classical approach and informed all economic analysis until Keynes, insisted that mathematics was secondary and that all economic propositions should be put into literary form. For illustrative purposes, he used geometrical diagrams (*e.g.*, supply-and-demand curves, or product elasticities at different price levels), and he felt that these alone were sufficient.

Modern mathematical analysis begins with Paul Samuelson's *Foundations of Economic Analysis* (1947), originally his Ph.D. thesis in 1941; he argued that economics could only advance by putting literary expressions into mathematical propositions. Mathematics, Samuelson insisted, overcomes ambiguities which are inherent in literary expression and allows the economist to "manipulate" the variables more readily and with a greater degree of vigor. As Samuelson wrote in his memoir:

> ... to a person of analytical ability, perceptive enough to realize that mathematical equipment was a powerful sword in economics, the world of economics was his oyster in 1935. The terrain was strewn with

beautiful theorems begging to be picked up and arranged in unified order. Only the other day I read about the accidental importation into South America of the African honey bee, with the resulting decimation of the local varieties. Precisely this happened in the field of theoretical economics: the people with analytical equipment came to dominate in every dimension of the vector the practitioners of literary economics.[3]

In his *Foundations,* for example, Samuelson established a formal mathematical model of the Keynesian "multiplier and accelerator" effects (*i.e.,* the "velocities" of income spent in consumption, or capital spent on investment) and, by choosing a variety of different "values" (*i.e.,* magnitudes) for the parameters (*i.e.,* the limiting variables) in the model, he was able to show the different scale of effects when individuals had different "propensities to consume" (*i.e.,* to spend and save different proportions of their incomes) or business firms made investments in different kinds of plants (*i.e.,* the extra acceleration of that spending).

An indicator of the spread of this mode of analysis is that while thirty years ago graduate students in economics did little or no mathematics, a graduate student today would not be admitted unless he or she were proficient in advanced algebra and calculus; and, while Samuelson's *Foundations* was difficult for his contemporaries, a graduate student is now expected to handle its mathematical reasoning with relative ease.*

Econometrics is the empirical application of economic theory through statistical inference and mathematical models. Statistical analysis in U.S. economics began principally with Wesley Clair Mitchell of Columbia University in the 1920s, through the National Bureau of Economic Research. A student of Thorstein Veblen, Mitchell was skeptical of orthodox economic theory, which seemed to be abstract and deductive, and he decided that one could only understand an economy by the empirical study of actual activities. He began by charting business cycles, and to do so he, along with such students of his as Arthur F. Burns, began to construct statistical indexes of different time-series (*e.g.,* retail sales, money supply, inventories) to see which were leading indicators of upswings and downswings and which were lagging indicators. Out of this pioneering work came the construction of aggregate indexes such as the consumer price index† and, from the work of Simon Kuznets, the national income accounts.

---

* I am indebted in this discussion to the essay on Paul Samuelson by William Breit and Roger Ransom in *The Academic Scribblers: American Economists in Collision* (New York: Holt, Rinehart & Winston, 1971).

† How can one lump together, say, apples and pears, clothing and automobiles? Because each can be expressed as a price per unit, and thus given a homogeneous form, one can weight the relative importance of the different purchases in a consumer's "market basket," and then aggregate these different prices and weights into a single index number. A single "normal" year is picked as the base, and the number for that year is called 100. Subsequent price changes are expressed in index number terms relative to that base year, so that a 10-percent increase in the cost of the items in that market basket makes the next year's numbers on the consumer price index 110.

A model is a representation of a reality. One can have a physical model, such as a small-scale model of an airplane, or the pictorial model of an atom, or a mathematical model, which translates relationships (*e.g.*, the price level, the interest rate, unemployment, and gross national product) into variables and writes mathematical equations for their relationships. The first U.S. economist to do model building was Lawrence Klein of the University of Pennsylvania Wharton School. In his first models, Klein used only twelve equations to represent the components of final demand, such as consumption, fixed investment, inventories, and the like. A contemporary model, such as that of Otto Eckstein of Harvard (the DRI model, from his Data Resources, Inc. company), has a total of 898 variables, most of which are expressed as ratios, square roots, and logarithms and are related through 800 equations.

The DRI model has 165 exogenous variables, which are factors outside the system, such as taxes, government outlays, and the like, and 733 endogenous variables, which are factors that relate to each other usually through market transactions. The DRI model, for example, has four broad sectors for fiscal policy, monetary policy, foreign sector, and supply. The fiscal policy variables correspond to the broad divisions of the national income accounts. The exogenous variables are government spending, foreign transfers, and the like. Endogenous spending variables are "transfer payments" (*e.g.*, social security) and the like. On the supply side, production is seen as the key determinant of investment and employment. The model uses an input-output matrix of seventy-five industries to produce a generated output series.

By running the 800 equations through a computer (using statistical aggregates on a quarterly basis), the econometric models seek to predict the major variables of economic activity for a year ahead and even for each quarter. These basic variables would be real gross national product, non-residential fixed investment, industrial production, consumer prices, wholesale prices, corporate profits, unemployment, and the like. The forecasts have become the basis of policy decisions by government, corporations, financial institutions, and the like.

e) *Growth models.* One should distinguish between theories of economic development and growth models. Theories of economic development are judgments about the most appropriate ways to spur economic development in a society and have been related directly to policy issues, particularly of the less developed nations. Growth models are an attempt to add a dynamic dimension to economic theory, which has been largely based on static considerations.

After World War II, many economists turned to the empirical question of how to spur economic development in a nation. The typical issues were: should one invest first in heavy industry (as the Soviet Union had done) or in agriculture? should one make heavy investment in human resources (*i.e.*, education) or bring in outside capital and skills? should there be balanced growth, between regions or economic sectors, or unbalanced growth, allowing any leading sector to develop even at the expense of others?

Much of the early writing concentrated on the role of planning and the adoption of government plans, and considerable ingenuity went into the development of these plans, as related by W. Arthur Lewis, one of the pioneers of the field, in his informative *The Theory of Economic Growth* (1955). But after a decade of work most of the theorizing in the field had diminished because of the realization that economic development was inextricably tied to political and social factors, and no satisfactory theory of these relationships had emerged.

Growth models, on the other hand, have sought to take neoclassical economic theory, which begins with fixed constants of capital and labor, and introduce a systematic theory of change. The major effort, whose pioneers have been Edward Denison and Robert M. Solow, has been to build a theory of technological change into the models of economic interactions.

f) *Welfare economics* is a field which has sought to define the optimal allocation of goods and services within equilibrium conditions. The famous theorem of Vilfredo Pareto, called "Pareto optimality," states that a distribution is optimal when at least one person is made better off, with no one being worse off. All other modes become *redistributive*. In game theory terms, this states that if one wins and another loses, it is a zero-sum game. However, if everybody wins, even in differential amounts, or no one loses, it is a nonzero-sum game. Much of the work in the field is highly theoretical. During the postwar years, there were two significant developments. One was the work of Kenneth J. Arrow, *Social Choice and Individual Values* (1951, originally his Ph.D. thesis, which, along with his work on equilibrium analysis, won him the Nobel Prize in Economics in 1972); the other was the book by John Rawls, *A Theory of Justice* (1971), which, though a work of political philosophy, drew much of its analysis of distributive justice from the welfare economics of the Indian economist Amartya K. Sen, now at Oxford University.

The Arrow volume establishes the fact that individuals can scale their preferences (*i.e.,* order their choices or buying decisions or voting preferences) in a rationally defensible way, but if certain conditions are observed, such as majority rule or transitivity (*i.e.,* if I prefer *A* to *B*, and *B* to *C*, logically I should prefer *A* to *C*), it is logically impossible to have a combined *social* choice (or, technically, a group welfare function) which assembles the discordant preferences of diverse individuals into a single, rationally ordered scale. The practical effect of Arrow's demonstration is to prove that theoretically there cannot be a single social choice that would satisfy or be approved by all the participants in a group or a society. What it means is that, if individuals are to work out discordant preferences peacefully, there will have to be bargaining and trade-offs, in which one group of individuals forgoes some preferences in order to achieve others.

Since many goods in the society are public goods, that is, not divisible into individual portions like private goods—a road is a public good, a weapons system is a public good—the problem of how to reach rational decisions in these matters becomes a vexing one. In this area, there has grown up a large literature under the rubric of "public choice," and individuals associated with these themes are such writers as Anthony Downs, James Buchanan, Gordon Tullock, Mancur Olson, and James Coleman.

If one reviews the promise of economics in this period, it added up to the belief that economists had learned how to manage (if not plan) an economy; that the business cycle was largely obsolete, since the government could flatten out the peaks and raise the troughs; that full employment was a possibility; that economic growth could be maintained; and that the "Keynesian revolution" had given economists the theoretical and practical tools to achieve all these goals.

Modeling the mind and society

The second great domain of promise for the social sciences in the post-World War II era came in the expectation that some new master sciences would arise which would allow the social sciences to understand the cognitive processes of the mind and to create control systems for the modeling and subsequent management of society. These ambitions are associated with a number of intellectual developments, principally *cybernetics, information theory, structural linguistics, artificial intelligence and automata theory,* and *general systems theory.* Since these developments weave in and out of each other, an effort to sort them out in some schematic form would miss the integrative hopes that underlie them—though there never was a single unified theory that sought to integrate these ideas in a formal discipline—so my presentation, necessarily, will be discursive.

Cybernetics is associated with the name of MIT mathematician Norbert Wiener, who in 1948 published a book entitled *Cybernetics: or Control and Communication in the Animal and the Machine.* Wiener thought he had coined the word from the Greek root *kybernētēs,* meaning a helmsman, or pilot, or a steersman of a vessel. Actually, the word occurs often in Plato, *kybernētikē,* as a subdivision of *technai,* as the art of steersmanship, and denotes for Plato the art of guiding men in society, *i.e.,* the art of government. In 1834 André-Marie Ampère, the eponymous source of our measure of electricity, wrote an ambitious *Essay on the Philosophy of the Sciences* and, in dealing with the management of government, he translated the Greek word into French as *cybernétique.* Ironically, Wiener's book first appeared in French, having been commissioned initially by a French publisher.

Wiener, who did not know of these antecedents, explained that his choice of the word was suggested by the precedent of James Watt in calling a mechanical regulator a "governor." Since he was dealing primarily with servomechanisms, *i.e.*, those that involved a feedback and readjustment to circumstances, Wiener used the term "steersman," or cybernetics.

The principle of cybernetics is suggested by the term. It is a set of control mechanisms to keep a machine or a system on its course, to allow for readjustments to the initial paths or to new paths where there have been deflections or obstacles, and to adapt the mechanism to the goals that have been set. Much of the theory went back to Wiener's practical experience in both world wars of establishing automatic gun controls, as in an anti-aircraft gun seeking to follow a plane taking a weaving or evasive course. The underlying elements are energy and information. The motor of the machine is operated by energy, but signals are given (information) which allow the machine to make the necessary corrections.

The heart of cybernetic theory is that of a "feedback loop," meaning information returned to the control source (by sensors or similar devices) and its readjustment mechanisms. The system is adaptive and homeostatic, having the tendency to maintain stability or equilibrium. More generally, it is a theory of communication and control. Cybernetics thus is not a single field but a theory which finds application in a number of diverse fields.

As the French writer George T. Guilbaud of l'École Pratique des Hautes Études in Paris, has put it:

> Cybernetics is not electronics, nor neurology, nor sociology; nor is it a theory peculiar to any of these fields. It simply borrows problems from these and other fields, hoping that the solution it discovers may have some useful applications. . . . The position of cybernetics is rather analogous to that of statistics, which finds its use in extremely diverse fields (psychology, sociology, astronomy, economics, biology, and so on) and derives its name from the one specialized application—the study of human societies or states—with which it has never lost contact despite its rise to independence.[4]

Information theory arose out of the work of Claude E. Shannon of MIT and Bell Laboratories. Its initial purpose was to design telephone switching circuits which would increase the channel capacity of the transmission system. But information theory quickly came to the algebra of logic, which is the algebra of choice, or the range of alternative possibilities in the routing of a message. The parlor game of "Twenty Questions" is often taken as a conventional illustration of how one narrows a range of possibilities by asking a yes or no question that divides a response into equally likely groups. As Shannon points out, in the article "Information Theory" that he wrote for the 14th edition of the *Encyclopædia Britannica:*

> The writing of English sentences can be thought of as a process of choice: choosing a first word from possible first words with various probabilities; then a second, with probabilities depending on the first; etc. This kind of statistical process is called a stochastic process, and

information sources are thought of, in information theory, as stochastic processes.

The information rate of written English can be translated into bits (binary digits of 1–0), and if each letter in the language occurred with equal frequency in a message, there would be 4.76 bits per letter. But since the frequencies are obviously disparate (E is highly common, for example, while Q and X are not), the actual rate is one bit per letter. Technically, English is said to be 80 percent "redundant," a fact that can be immediately ascertained by the ease of deciphering a sentence from which various vowels or consonants have been deleted. This is the basis of certain speed-writing courses, or the telegraphic transmissions of foreign correspondents, who save words and speed up transmission by compressing words (*e.g.,* compresng wrds) in their telegraphic copy.

By knowing the statistical structure of a language, one can derive a general formula which determines the rate at which information is produced by a stochastic process and, by proper encoding, create huge savings in transmission time. Transmission was the impetus to the formulation of information theory, but the core of the concept is the idea of coding, and the engine of the concept is the statistical theory which determines how a message should be encoded. Messages have to go through channels and inevitably become distorted by noise and other forms of distortion that arise from the physical property of the channel (*e.g.,* the copper telephone wire, or even optical fiber). What Shannon found was that it was possible to encode (*i.e.,* compress) a message so that it could be accurately transmitted even if the channel of communication was faulty, so long as there was enough capacity in the channel.

What is striking is how quickly the mathematical theory of communication took hold and spread into so many diverse fields. Randall L. Dahling, who has traced this process, points out:

> Dr. Shannon first set forth his theory in two articles which appeared in the *Bell System Technical Journal* in July and October of 1948. Here, he set down a unified theory of signal transmission based on the concept that transmitted information may be considered statistically and its probabilities figured. . . .
>
> The importance of the idea was instantly perceived. Other scientists started discussing it immediately, and, within a few months following its publication, new articles making use of the theory began to appear at an ever-increasing rate. At first, these new articles were restricted to communication engineering, but by November 1949, the theory had been applied to psychology (by F. C. Frick and G. A. Miller in the *Psychological Review*). Then in August 1950, H. Jacobson applied the theory in physiology and later extended it to optics (in *Science* on the informational capacity of the human ear, August 4, 1950; and on the informational capacity of the human eye, in *Science,* March 16, 1951). By November of 1950, the theory had established itself in physics (by

Dennis Gabor in *Phil. Mag.*), and in the same month it was carried to linguistics (by O. H. Strauss in the *Journal of the Acoustical Society of America*). In December of the same year, it was written about from biological and sociological viewpoints (by Nicholas Rashevsky in the *Bulletin of Mathematics and Biophysics*). By 1951, it was being discussed in statistical journals (by G. A. Barnard, in *J. Royal Statistical Society*) and still it continued to spread rapidly.[5]

Why the idea took hold so rapidly is fairly clear. The work was at the focal point of a number of intersecting needs, prompted by the demands of the military and of business in communication, automation, and computation. The theoretical and statistical underpinnings seemed to mesh with the more general theory of Wiener's *Cybernetics,* a work which, after its publication in English in 1948, went through seven printings in one year. What the work of Shannon and Wiener seemed to promise was the long-sought-for move toward a unified theory of physical and human behavior (at least in physiology, psychology, and linguistics) through the concept of information.

Linguistic theory is the third leg on which these new ambitions were rising, particularly in the work of Noam Chomsky at MIT. Chomsky's initial work was in structural linguistics, an effort to demonstrate that language, though the most widely dispersed of all human "artifacts" (*i.e.,* the existence of dozens of major streams of language, such as the Indo-European, Uralic-Altaic, Hamito-Semitic, Tai and Sino-Tibetan, and about 3,000 distinct languages, let alone dialects), has a basic syntactical structure (*i.e.,* word orders that control meaning) and that in every language there is a "deep structure" of a few rules which generate all other rules of grammar. While Chomsky began in structural linguistics, his work led him into fundamental issues in epistemology and psychology; one of the crucial debates in the postwar years was the argument between B. F. Skinner (and other behaviorists) and Chomsky on the way in which languages are acquired.

For Skinner, who is an empiricist, a child learns a language in associative building blocks, responding to stimuli, and having its efforts rewarded by response. Through conditioning, through reinforcement (*i.e.,* reward), and through stimulus generalization (*i.e.,* the widening of associations), a child learns a language.

For Chomsky, language acquisition is innate. As he has argued, a person's knowledge of a language is not "representable as a stored set of patterns, overlearned through constant repetition and detailed training, with innovation being at most a matter of 'analogy.' " Instead, "a person who knows a language has represented in his brain some very abstract system of underlying structures along with an abstract system of rules that determine, by free iteration, an infinite range of sound-meaning correspondence. Possession of this grammar is a fact which psychology and neurophysiology must ultimately account for."

For Chomsky, the "underlying deep structures [of syntax] vary slightly, at most, from language to language," and the structure of mind is such that a human being can, without knowing or having heard a large number of cases, grasp the rule which makes intelligible the structure of the language he or she is hearing, or speaking. As Chomsky argues:

> This is what one would expect . . . since it is difficult to imagine how operations of this type could be abstracted from data. There is certainly no process of generalization or association of any kind known to psychology or philosophy, or any procedure of analysis that is known in linguistics that can come close to determining structures of this kind. Again, it is to be expected that these operations and their general properties will be uniform across languages, and this seems to be the case.[6]

The combination of cybernetics, information theory, and Chomskyian linguistics had its most direct impact in the fields of cognitive psychology and in "artificial intelligence," or the theory and practice of logical automata, more popularly, if crudely, called "thinking machines." Ideally, it was hoped that information theory and linguistics would allow the psychologists to learn how the mind worked (and, as an analogue, to trace out these patterns in neurophysiological terms), enabling logicians and computer specialists to write programs that would allow the computer to become a general problem solver, rather than being just an incredibly fast idiot machine capable only of following detailed instructions.

Warren McCulloch, a neurophysiologist, sought to show that the central nervous system does have the kind of connectivity that cybernetic theory presupposed, and that the mind, when it "sees," does not simply reflect what is out there, as if the eye were a camera, but selects elements from perceptual experience to synthesize or cognize what it sees. As Stephen Toulmin, who has written an appreciation of both Wiener and McCulloch, has observed:

> The task of imagining how a machine might be devised that could match the mental performances of a man was a task of exact mathematical analysis, demanding formal ingenuity and precision of a positively baroque order. The task of seeing how the formal analysis of such mechanisms might then be used to throw light on the actual working of the human brain—in particular, upon its role in regulating human behavior—was one for clinical understanding, philosophical reflectiveness, and speculative imagination. At this point, the respective skills of Wiener the mathematician and McCulloch the psychiatrist and neurologist matched one another admirably. Norbert Wiener had the formal virtuosity to transform the mathematical analysis of the electronic control and communication systems developed during the Second World War into a general and abstract theory of self-correcting, quasi-intelligent mechanisms and interconnecting systems. The idea of "negative feedback"—already implicit in the original design for the steam-engine governor and used by Claude

Bernard in the 1860's as a crucial element in a new style of physiological explanation—could thus be extended to yield a general account of self-controlling, or cybernetic, mechanisms. Meanwhile, all Warren McCulloch's empirical familiarity with the actual relations between brain and behavior—ranging from neuroanatomical studies on the structure and interconnections of the cerebral cortex in the higher apes to the accumulated clinical experience of human neurological disorders during his years as a psychiatrist—put him in a special position to judge how these new styles of mathematical and physiological analysis could be used to unravel the actual neurophysiological interactions within the brain.[7]

The major effort to combine information theory with cognitive psychology was made by George A. Miller of Harvard (now at Rockefeller University). In a classic article, seductively entitled "The Magical Number Seven, Plus or Minus Two," Miller suggests that there may be an intrinsic reason why the number seven is so appealing to us. Apart from the whimsy, Miller points out that on single-dimension stimuli (*e.g.*, pitch, loudness, points on a line), the span of absolute judgment that individuals possess in the number of discriminations they can make, or the amount of information that one can transmit, or the span of immediate memory, is about seven distinguishable alternatives—a rather small and limiting number for information processing. As Miller writes:

> There seems to be some limitation built into us either by learning or by the design of our nervous systems, a limit that keeps our channel capacities in this general range. On the basis of the present evidence it seems safe to say that we possess a finite and rather small capacity for making such unidimensional judgments and that this capacity does not vary a great deal from one sensory attribute to another. . . .
>
> There is a clear and definite limit to the accuracy with which we can identify absolutely the magnitude of a unidimensional stimulus variable. I would propose to call this limit *the span of absolute judgment*, and I maintain that for unidimensional judgments this span is usually somewhere in the neighborhood of seven.

Yet, in daily life we can identify accurately any one of several hundred faces, or any one of several thousand words, and the question is how are we able to overcome these limitations of perceptual and discriminatory capacities. What happens, says Miller, is that human beings have the capacity for recoding, or the ability to "embed" the bits of information they receive into larger and larger chunks. A man beginning to learn a telegraph code hears each dot and dash as a separate chunk, but then the sounds become recognized as letters—parts of larger chunks of words.

Miller, one of the most graceful writers in psychology, began his essay with the fascinating question why the history of human culture seems to have been so preoccupied with the "magical" number seven—the seven wonders of the world, the seven seas, the seven levels of hell, the seven days of the week, the win-or-lose of point seven in gambling dice—and though it may be only metaphoric to suggest some innate limit on our capacity to discriminate or to hold in our heads no more than seven distinctions (plus or minus two, as the statistical variance of the span), the more useful finding, which Miller derived from information theory, was not only the breakdown of information into bits as a way of measuring perceptual and discriminatory abilities, but the phenomenon of "recoding." For, as Miller points out:

> ... recoding is an extremely powerful weapon for increasing the amount of information we can deal with. In one form or another we use recoding constantly in our daily behavior. ... Our language is tremendously useful for repackaging material into a few chunks rich in information ... the kind of linguistic recoding that people do seems to me to be the very lifeblood of the thought processes.[8]

Miller has also tried to show that the writing of computer programs illuminates the way individuals think. In computer programs, main routine operations are often interrupted to perform subroutines (additional side problems, such as incidental computations, in order to proceed with the main problem); and programs that allow this are called "recursive." A nonrecursive program is one where the computer does not return to the original routines, or other subroutines, and this process of failing re-entry is likely to clobber the machine's memory. Miller points out that individuals use subroutines in their own cognitive operations, both recursive and nonrecursive, and the question is which do they use and how?

> One way to investigate this question presents itself in the realm of language. It is a feature of natural language—by "natural language" I mean the languages we ordinarily use in speaking to one another, as opposed to the "artificial languages" that we have developed for mathematics, logic, computer programming, and so on—that sentences can be inserted inside of sentences. For example, "The king who said, 'My kingdom for a horse,' is dead" contains the sentence, "My kingdom for a horse" embedded in the middle of another sentence, "The king is dead."
>
> Think of a listener as processing information in order to understand this sentence. Obviously, his analysis of one sentence must be interrupted while he analyzes the embedded sentence. When he finishes analyzing the embedded sentence, he must then resume his analysis of the original sentence. Here we have all the elements present in a computer subroutine.

Miller notes that even though such sentences are grammatical, they are difficult to follow or understand, and this suggests that our ability to use subroutines which refer to themselves must be rather limited.* But the intention in comparing cognitive operations with computer programs is to show that "often very general principles . . . govern the operation of any device, living or nonliving, capable of performing the operation in question. It is not a matter of reducing men to machines, but of discovering general principles applicable to men and machines alike. And this is the exciting prospect that I wish to display for your consideration."[9]

The idea of "artificial intelligence" was stimulated by the British mathematician Alan Mathison Turing, who during World War II was the principal designer of the "Ultra" machine which broke the German transmission codes. He raised the question whether a computing machine can think, or, to avoid the anthropomorphism inherent in such a statement, whether machines can be programmed to behave in the way we behave when we say we are thinking. John von Neumann, the great mathematician who was responsible for some of the major developments in electronic computers, went further and, in his paper, "The General and Logical Theory of Automata" (1951), laid down the conditions whereby automata, using digital (all-or-none) or analogical procedures, could engage in reasoning similar to formal logic and the means whereby automata could produce automata, or become, in effect, self-reproducing machines.

Von Neumann's program was very broad, but in the 1950s and 1960s a sustained effort was made, principally by Marvin Minsky and his associates at MIT, to write computer programs that would "reason," *i.e.*, prove mathematical theorems, untangle linguistic difficulties, and solve problems. The crucial step in the development of artificial intelligence was breaking away from the idea that a computer could solve a problem only when every single step in the procedures—and therefore the solution—is clearly specified by the programmer. On that basis, of course, a computer is simply a rapid tool for human use, and no more. What artificial-intelligence programmers proposed to do was to write a set of general rules into the program which would allow the computer to make analogies, or to follow steps of formal logic, or to analyze and break down complicated statements for purposes of computation, and to employ "heuristics" in the instructions to the computer. A computer is ruled by an algorithm which is an instruction for procedure, or a decision rule. In the most mechanical algorithm, a computer might go through every cell in a memory, or make every permutation

---

* To illustrate the difficulty of these recursive sentence-clauses, Miller begins generating a nest within a nest within a nest:

The question, of course, is whether we can do this more than once, that is to say, recursively. Let us try: *"The person who cited, 'The King who said, "My kingdom for a horse" is dead,' as an example is a psychologist."* Most people find that just on the borderline of intelligibility: if I had not prepared you for it, you probably would not have understood. Let us go one step more: *"The audience who just heard, 'The person who cited, "The king who said, 'My kingdom for a horse,' is dead," as an example is a psychologist,' is very patient."* By now you should be ready to give up. If not, of course, I could go on this way indefinitely.

and combination possible, in order to pick out the correct answer. But for some problems, this would take considerable time, even for a high-speed computer. Heuristics simply means a command to make probable judgments based on comparisons of likeness or similarity, or some similar rule which would make a search procedure more rapid. It is, in effect, a procedure for skipping, or jumping about, the way a mind grasps for clues, in order to combine the relevant steps for coming to a solution.

This is the basis of the checkers, and now the chess, programs that are stored in computers. But it also underlies the effort to have the computer "read" verbal statements of a problem and translate these into mathematical terms. Minsky gives an example of a program called "Student," created by Daniel Bobrow at MIT.

> The remarkable thing about Student is not so much that it
> understands English as that it shows a basic capacity for understanding
> anything at all. When it runs into difficulty, it asks usually pertinent
> questions. Sometimes it has to ask the person operating the computer,
> but often it resolves the difficulty by referring to the knowledge in its
> files. When, for instance, it meets a statement such as "Mary is twice as
> old as Ann was when Mary was as old as Ann is now," the program
> knows how to make the meaning of "was when" more precise by
> rewriting the statement as two simple sentences: "Mary is twice as old
> as Ann was X years ago. X years ago Mary was as old as Ann is now."[10]

The promise of artificial intelligence is not as bright today as it seemed fifteen or twenty years ago, when the enthusiasm was first kindled. Yet, it is always difficult to quell the flame of true believers; nor can one, should one, rule out a field by fiat because its initial claims may not have been realized. It is a question we shall return to in a later section.

Holistic visions

In anthropology and sociology, three movements dominated the field in the quarter century after the war.

In anthropology, there was the new interdisciplinary study called "culture and personality." One can go back to Ruth Benedict's *Patterns of Culture* (1934) for the seminal idea of this. Each culture, Benedict sought to demonstrate, has a basic configuration, and one can describe cultures in terms of their integrative principles. The idea was drawn, specifically, from Oswald Spengler's *Decline of the West* (1926–28), in which Western culture was called Faustian, and Arabic culture Magian. It was similar to Pitirim Sorokin's argument, in *Social and Cultural Dynamics* (4 vol., 1937–41), that cultural mentalities could be divided into the "ideational" and the "sensate" and that history was an alternation between these two ideal types. Essential to all these holistic conceptions was the idea that a single thread ran through all dimensions of a culture, so that the Faustian, or the sensate, elements impregnated all aspects of life, from science through the arts, values, and life-styles. In principle, it was an extension of Marx's belief that the dominant mode of production suffused all other aspects of a society so that, as in capitalism, where workers were treated as commodities—as objects for sale—all other elements, including art, became commodities as well.

While Marx, Spengler, and Sorokin painted their strokes on a broad historical canvas over long periods of time, Benedict sought to apply the idea of "integration" to individual cultures, seeing in each some single principle which defined them through some dominant cultural pattern. Her two modal types were Apollonian and Dionysian, terms she took from Friedrich Nietzsche's *Birth of Tragedy* (1872) to describe two fundamental views of the world. For her, the Pueblo Indians of the North American Southwest were Apollonian because of their harmonious way of life, whereas the Kwakiutl peoples of the Pacific Northwest were Dionysian in the fever pitch of frenzy and ecstasy that marked their rituals. A third culture, the Dobu, were repressed, hostile, inimical to one another; Benedict gave them no metaphorical designation, though at one point she compared their temperament with that of the early American Puritans.

The idea that there were discernible cultural patterns quickly led to the idea that these had to be embodied in the personality attributes of the individuals composing the culture. Especially after World War II, a large number of anthropologists and psychologists—Lloyd Warner, Alfred I. Hallowell, Melford Spiro, and others—began studying cultures in these terms. In some situations, such as the cooperative work of the anthropologist Cora Du Bois and the psychoanalyst Abram Kardiner with the people of Alor, Kardiner analyzed "blind" a set of projective tests (Rorschach, Thematic Apperception) and anthropological field protocols to make various judgments on the culture which were matched, independently, by Du Bois's description of the people.

The idea of "culture and personality" merged, quickly, into the study of "national character." The theme was put forth that individuals in a nation exhibited certain unitary patterns which were also embodied in the modal personality traits of its people. Benedict did a study of the Japanese, *The Chrysanthemum and the Sword* (1946); Erich Fromm did an analysis of the "anal-sadistic" features of German character, which predisposed the German people to authoritarianism, in his book *Escape from Freedom* (1941); Theodor W. Adorno, drawing on unpublished work of the Frankfurt Institute of Social Research, *Authority and the Family*, wrote *The Authoritarian Personality* (1950) with Nevitt Sanford and Elsie Frenkel-Brunswick, two psychologists, seeking to uncover the latent dispositions to Fascism in American society; the anthropologists Margaret Mead and Geoffrey Gorer did studies of the Russian character in which they argued that early patterns of infant swaddling led to a character that was extreme in its explosiveness and repression; Henry Dicks, a British psychiatrist, and Nathan Leites, a political scientist, psychoanalytically trained, sought to identify the salient characteristics of Bolshevik personality. For more than two decades, anthropology, personality theory, and to some extent sociology were dominated almost entirely by the field of "culture and personality." Yet by the 1970s, the field had all but completely disappeared. Why this happened is a fascinating intellectual puzzle, and we shall return to it in the next section.

The second promise was in sociology, where a similar "functionalist" emphasis (but deriving more directly from the work of Émile Durkheim, and indirectly from the functionalism of Bronisław Malinowski) dominated the field until the early 1970s. The leading figure, and a powerful theorist, was Talcott Parsons of Harvard. For Parsons, a society was integrated through its "value system" and these values, expressed as norms governing behavior, or prescribing the roles individuals played, legitimated the basic modes of conduct in society. Thus, American society would be characterized as valuing instrumental activism and achievement—elements drawn from the Protestant heritage with its this-worldly orientation (as against quietism, or pietism, or the otherworldly orientations of Buddhist and non-Western societies) and its Calvinist injunction to strive and work. In the work of Robert K. Merton of Columbia, these ideas were applied to the ways in which different "roles" were patterned in the social structure.

But Parsons had a far greater ambition: to create a general theory of social action. In this respect, Parsons went farther than any sociologist of his time and, in so doing, revealed the limits, and weakness, of that approach.

To write a general theory, one must be able to define the complete range of types of action (technically, to close a system), so that one can make deductive statements about the kinds of action (*e.g.*, a revolution) and the conditions under which they might occur. It is a model drawn from science, in particular from classical mechanics. To do this, Parsons had to achieve two theoretical goals.

The first was to define a set of terms that could give one an exhaustive range of possible combinations of action (in the sense that Newtonian mechanics provides the least number of laws from which one can deduce all possible future states of the celestial system). Sociology, up to the turn of the twentieth century, was cast largely in historical terms, *e.g.*, Marx's notion of social evolution of the modes of production from slavery to feudalism to capitalism. But Marx assumed a determinate pattern to this evolution in which socialism was the natural successor to capitalism. This assumed, first, that the Western pattern (based either on the development of rationality, or Hegel's ideas of consciousness, or man's technical mastery of nature and economic production) was the mode all other civilizations would follow, and second, that the *marche générale* of history was more or less inexorable.

If such a determinism did not exist, then one was left, as with Wilhelm Dilthey, in the swamp of historical relativism.

The first generation of sociologists (*i.e.*, Ferdinand Tönnies, Émile Durkheim, and Max Weber) sought to escape from this deterministic philosophy of history, or inconclusive relativism, by seeking to define some modal, ahistorical types of social relationships, such as *Gemeinschaft* and *Gesellschaft*, or organic and mechanical solidarity, or traditional and rational actions, by which social patterns could be classified. The basic contrast was between close-knit, face-to-face, primordial and undifferentiated groups (kin or tribe or small neighborhoods) and the impersonal, associational, differentiated type of urban society.

For Parsons this typology was too simple, and he sought to substitute for it what he called (in *The Social System,* 1951) the basic "pattern variables,":

Norms: universalistic or particularistic
Statuses: achieved or ascribed
Obligations: specific or diffuse
Emotions: neutral or affective

Norms are universalistic when a merit system open to all is used, while criteria are particularistic when some groups are singled out for more favorable treatment than others, *e.g.,* affirmative action. Statuses or positions are either achieved on the basis of individual ability, or ascribed, either because of birth, as in hereditary systems, or through assignment, as where quotas apply. In a similar way, societies may be seen as predominantly of one kind or mixtures in the way they employ these different values. The United States and Britain, for example, may differ because of the way in which social mobility in the United States is more open (universalistic) and that of Britain more circumscribed (particularistic). The point of this scheme is that one has an exhaustive vocabulary for dealing with all kinds of social situations and types of societies.

Parsons went even further, in that (together with Edward A. Shils and the collaboration of Harvard colleagues, such as the anthropologist Clyde Kluckhohn and the psychologist Gordon W. Allport) he sought to write a general theory of action which would have the effect of constructing an all-embracing system for the analysis of social actions, in the way Léon Walras had constructed a general equilibrium theory for economics. One crucial consideration that governs this intention has to be understood. A general theory is not a descriptive set of statements, or a summary of empirical knowledge about action. It is an analytical framework which would allow the social scientist a way of sorting out different kinds of action, of understanding the levels of complexity, and of making relevant comparisons of seemingly disparate phenomena. The model again is classical mechanics. But in the logic of that mode, the scientist does not deal with concrete bodies, but with aspects, or properties, of *all* bodies taken as a single whole. Thus Galileo, in dealing with the law of falling bodies, did not, could not, describe the trajectory of a *single* body (it is subject to too many contingent vicissitudes) but described the properties of *any* body during a fall, such as mass, acceleration, velocity, etc. In the same way, a general theory does not deal with concrete societies but with society as an analytical abstraction and with the properties of society as analytical dimensions. In the Parsons scheme, there is a cultural system (having four dimensions — cognitive, expressive, evaluative, and transcendental), a social system with four dimensions, a personality system, and an organism system. One could say, for example, that the four dimensions of the cultural system could just as easily be denoted as science, art, philosophy, and religion. But to do so would be to treat these as independent entities, whereas Parsons is interested in seeing the way in which they are attributes of a single cultural system.

In a similar way, Parsons endeavored to show how any social unit sought to maintain its stability, or equilibrium, by fulfilling four functions — of goal definition, integration, adaptiveness, and management of tensions — and that the different institutions of society — the economy, government, cultural institutions — had become specialized in undertaking one or another of these functions.

Before any criticisms are leveled — and many of these are trivial ones or of a know-nothing sort, using the epithet "jargon," a term which would not be applied, for example, to the technical vocabulary of poetic analysis — the intentions have to be understood. Marx had sought to write a general theory of society using such terms as "substructure and superstructure," "mode of production," "class struggle," and the like. Marx assumed that the secret of society lay in the underlying class divisions as rooted in the structure of production, and he had few ways of accounting for the autonomy or variation of political and cultural systems. (Thus Imperial Germany, the Weimar Republic, Nazi Germany, and the postwar Federal Republic were all, in their economic mode, capitalist, yet the political structures were highly variant.) Max Weber sought to provide an analytical framework by dealing primarily with the types of rational and nonrational action in society. Parsons went furthest in the logic of an *ahistorical* analysis by seeking to write a complete morphology of society. The enormous effort, over a thirty-five-year period, is one of his huge contributions to social science.

There is a sense, however, in which the effort may have been a failure. The reason may lie less in the level of abstraction than in the recalcitrance of sociology to the model which guided Parsons's effort, that of classical mechanics. Economics, for example, does not deal with concrete items — such as steel, tin, or rubber — other than translating these into abstract categories such as "production function" (the varied mix of capital and labor at relative prices) or "propensities to consume," and further making them homogeneous and linear by converting these into a single metric — money — and still further manipulating the exchange ratios in theoretical analysis. Such terms as investment, prices, or consumption apply to all societies, but equally one can see how these are exchanged to form an interconnected system. Sociology has terms that are general, such as power, authority, and status, but it is difficult to put these into metrics of exchange, and one can create only formal typologies, such as Montesquieu's classification of aristocracy, republics and monarchies, or contemporary usages of democracy—authoritarian, totalitarian, and the like. In short, a general theory, even if it creates a successful vocabulary that allows us to see the full range of human action, lacks a means of actually showing the processes of exchange, and, even assuming that societies or institutions seek to maintain an equilibrium or homeostatic balance, the means of analyzing these processes are perhaps only metaphorical.

Structural-functionalist sociology has been charged (*see* Alvin Gouldner's *The Coming Crisis of Western Sociology,* 1970) with being politically conservative because of its focus on integration and equilibrium. But problems of structural-functionalist analysis, au fond, are really epistemological and philosophical. They lie at the heart of the issue whether a social science, particularly sociology, can ever have a general theory of society or create a closed system. Marx sought to create a general theory, which was functionalist in its way, since he assumed that every society hangs together by some inner principle, which for him was the mode of production. Parsons took the same logic to its limit by seeking to create a comprehensive morphology of social institutions and social actions. The effort was an honorable one. More, it is one of the great intellectual feats of that generation. But the failure, perhaps, to fulfill the promise does not indicate a lack of greatness; it shows that the reach may be, necessarily, greater than the grasp.

A third major promise was evident in the social sciences, particularly in the 1960s. This was the effort to use social science for social-policy purposes. Since the efforts were so diverse, and many of them were simply empirical— *i.e.,* involved the use of techniques for purposes of investigation and analysis without relating these to any body of theory—it would be difficult to compile an inventory of these efforts, even the significant inquiries. I can briefly indicate the intentions and nature of these movements.

a) *Social indicators.* The example of the economists, in setting up, after World War II, a system of macroeconomic accounts, inevitably turned the attention of the sociologists to the question whether a similar system of social indicators could be created, and even whether these indicators could be integrated into a set of social accounts similar to the national economic accounts. Thus, for example, the question was posed: we know how much money is being spent for doctors, nurses, and hospitals, but is the country "healthier" or not? Or, we know how much money is spent for schools and teachers, but do students know more? Or, we have had large-scale migrations from farms to cities, and vast regional shifts around the country; are such migrations disrupting families? is there a relation between migration rates and crime, and so forth? In 1966 the U.S. Department of Health, Education, and Welfare set up a panel on social indicators headed by Daniel Bell and William Gorham, who was later succeeded by Alice Rivlin, with Mancur Olson as staff director. A document by that panel, entitled "Toward a Social Report," was published in 1966, in the closing days of the Johnson administration. Since then there have been many efforts to develop social indicators of different kinds for environmental adequacy, quality of life, and the like. For various reasons—and these are discussed in the next section—the results have been mixed and the promises largely unfulfilled.

b) *Social forecasting.* In 1965 the American Academy of Arts and Sciences set up a Commission on the Year 2000 chaired by Daniel Bell. It had thirty members, including Wassily Leontief, Zbigniew Brzezinski, Daniel P. Moynihan, Robert C. Wood, and other individuals who went on to government service in various positions. After two book publications, *Towards the Year 2000* (1968), edited by Bell, and *The Year 2000* (1967), edited by Herman Kahn and Anthony Wiener, which was sponsored by the Commission, ten work groups were set up to explore various issues, from the structure of the U.S. government (resulting in a book edited by Harvey S. Perloff, *The Future of the United States Government Toward the Year 2000*, 1971) to questions of values and rights, the life-cycle, the future of computers, cultural institutions, and the like.

The "Futurist" movement spread rapidly and widely.* Parallel movements began in England, France, and Poland. Large numbers of organizations have devoted themselves to systematic forecasting. The World Future Society, an organization of 25,000 members, has become a clearing house for various studies and speculations. Again, the results have fallen far short of the promises, a question to be discussed in the next section.

c) *Social evaluation.* Today social evaluation has become an established feature of government policy. When billions of dollars are spent for government programs, it is inevitable that the government will also want to know how well the programs are working and to what extent policy can be guided by research results.

The foremost example of social evaluation—and the one that has received the most attention for a decade—is the so-called "Coleman Report," by James S. Coleman, then at Johns Hopkins University and now at the University of Chicago, on the effect of segregated school environments on the achievement levels of minority pupils in the elementary and high schools of the country.

The Civil Rights Act of 1964 contained a section, virtually unnoticed, which instructed the Commissioner of Education to conduct a survey on "the lack of availability of equal educational opportunities," by reason of race, religion or national origin. Over a two-year period, Coleman and his associates tested nearly 600,000 children (in five different grades) in 4,000 schools in all 50 states and the District of Columbia, while questioning 60,000 teachers and the principals in these schools as well. The 737 page report, *Equality of Educational Opportunity*, was published by the U.S. Government Printing Office in 1966.

The report made two points: minority children have a serious educational deficiency at the start of school, in grade one, which is obviously not a

---

* *See* "The Planning of the Future," by Bertrand de Jouvenel in *The Great Ideas Today, 1974.*

result of school; and they have an even more serious deficiency at the end of school, in grade twelve, which is obviously in part a result of the school. What made this startling, and quite grave, was the premise which Coleman (and implicitly a liberal society) had: namely, that schools are successful only insofar as they reduce the dependence of a child's opportunities upon his social origins. The effectiveness of schooling was to be measured by its ability to overcome the differences in the starting point of children from different social groups, and the schools were not doing this.

In proof of these conclusions, Coleman pointed out—by the matching of different schools, and by the multivariate analysis of different factors—that such elements as per pupil expenditure, books in the library, and a host of similar facilities and curricular measures had virtually no relation to achievement if the "social" environment of the school, *i.e.*, the educational backgrounds of other students and teachers, is held constant. This led Coleman to argue that *"the sources of inequality of educational opportunity appear to lie first in the home itself and the cultural influences immediately surrounding the home; then they lie in the schools' ineffectiveness to free achievement from the impact of the home, and in the schools' cultural homogeneity which perpetuates the social influences of the home and its environs."*[11]

The curious fact is that at first the Coleman Report went virtually unnoticed. There was no story in the *New York Times* or other national media. The first discussion appeared in the public policy quarterly *The Public Interest* and was soon followed in various educational magazines and then, quickly, in the foundations and the black community itself. One crucial element of the report was singled out for special attention—the discussion of the cultural homogeneity of the schools. And the response, particularly of the black community, was: if this is the case, then de facto segregation of schools (which are a product of residential, not legal, segregation) had to be ended; and the principal means would have to be the busing of black children to white schools and vice versa.

Busing became one of the most vitriolic and divisive issues in community political life. Entire cities, such as Boston, Detroit, and Los Angeles, were torn apart by the issue. Little or no attention was paid to Coleman's other major point, the problem of the initial home environments of minority children, a question that had been raised in 1965 by the "Moynihan Report" on the black family, when Moynihan was assistant secretary of labor in the Johnson administration, nor to the fact that busing alone might not be sufficient. As Coleman wrote in an article in *The Public Interest:*

> It is not a solution simply to pour money into improvement of the physical plants, books, teaching aids, of schools attended by educationally disadvantaged children. For other reasons, it will not suffice merely to bus children or otherwise achieve pro forma integration. (One incidental effect of this would be to increase the segregation within schools, through an increase in tracking.)

The only kinds of policies that appear in any way viable are those which do not seek to improve the education of Negroes and other educationally disadvantaged at the expense of those who are educationally advantaged. This implies new kinds of educational institutions, with a vast increase in expenditures for education—not merely for the disadvantaged, but for all children. The solutions might be in the form of educational parks, or in the form of private schools paid by tuition grants (with Federal regulations to insure racial heterogeneity), public (or publicly-subsidized) boarding schools (like the North Carolina Advancement School), or still other innovations.[12]

One can leave aside the viability of these specific proposals. The point is that Coleman, as a sociologist, approached the problem in terms of the complete social environment of the disadvantaged child—family, home, and school. But the report became the focus of a political division on one issue alone—that of busing. The Coleman Report was probably the most massive social science report in American society in the last several decades. Its findings and its fate are instructive.

Difficulties and disappointments

If one reviews the major theoretical advances in the social sciences from 1940 to 1970, almost all of them have been qualified to some extent, substantially or otherwise.

In economics, Keynesian theory has come increasingly under attack. One reason has been its neglect of monetary theory. To the neoclassical economists of Alfred Marshall's time, the level of economic activity was measured, and to some extent controlled, by monetary measures and monetary policy. To the Keynesians, or at least to the extremists among them, money did not matter. Since they saw, in the depression years, a weak link between the changes in the stock of money and the level of aggregate demand, they argued that monetary policy had little or no impact on the level of economic activity. In the last decade this argument has been hotly challenged by Milton Friedman and his followers. A second factor has been the argument that "macroeconomic" policy is too clumsy a means of managing, or as the saying goes, "fine-tuning," an economy. Thus, economists returned to "microeconomics," or the behavior of individuals and firms, and are seeking, through the analysis of the *expectations* of these units, to understand the relationship between micro- and macro- activity. A third argument is that Keynesian economics, by concentrating largely on effective demand, assumed that supply would simply be a response to changes in demand; yet the argument is now made that changes in supply (*e.g.*, investment in new energy sources, or substitutions of limited metals or minerals) is more a function of government policy, or of long-run expectations, and that Keynesian theory has not been equipped to deal with these questions.

The crucial problem has been the intractability of inflation. Keynesian economics had won its spurs by being able to suggest measures to aid recovery from recession. President Kennedy's tax cut in the 1962 budget, suggested by Walter Heller, was taken as proof of the efficacy of Keynesian measures. Yet Keynesian theory, seemingly, has been unable to account for inflation, and this has given rise to the monetarist counterattack. We shall return to this question in the second part of this article on new directions in the social sciences.

The use of GNP measures to assess economic growth has been questioned, for reasons that are quickly apparent in the nature of the measuring instruments. For one thing, GNP is a measure of transactions *in the market* and necessarily cannot take into account services in the household (*e.g.*, the work of the wife) or consumption on a farm, which may enhance a family's well-being but which is not registered in the market. (As Arthur C. Pigou, the successor to Marshall at Cambridge and one of the founders of modern welfare economics, once remarked: "If a widowed vicar has a housekeeper, and pays her a wage, that is an addition to the national income. If the vicar then marries the housekeeper, it is a subtraction from the national income.") The second reason is that GNP is simply an *addition* of all goods and services and makes no distinction among them. Thus, if a plant spills wastes in a river, which then has to be cleaned up, the subsequent costs of reducing pollution become an addition to GNP. In recent years economists such as James Tobin of Yale University have sought to create a modified GNP by making such subtractions which presumably do not actually increase the quality of life by an index of net national welfare. But the conceptual difficulties of defining quality and welfare have been quite great.

Econometric models have become more complicated and are employed more widely than ever before, but the problem of accuracy of forecasts bedevils the model makers. There are two reasons for this: one is that the important variables are exogenous, *i.e.*, stand outside the system, such as political decisions, and these are difficult to account for; two, the rising degrees of uncertainty (as people seek different ways to defend themselves against inflation) introduce perturbations in the economy, and the models cannot easily follow these at times wildly fluctuating effects. (I shall expand on this somewhat, in the concluding paragraphs of this section, which deal with some of the theoretical limits of the social sciences.)

While modeling the economy has proved recalcitrant, modeling the mind has been even more so. If there is a single term that can sum up the problem, it is "complexity." The number of cells in the human body is somewhere on the general order of 10^{15} or 10^{16}. The number of neurons in the central nervous system is somewhere on the order of 10^{10}. As John von Neumann remarked: "We have absolutely no past experience with systems of this degree of complexity." Whether we can master such complexity is moot. Language, too, has presented some unforeseen hurdles. When linguists began to discover basic *syntactical* rules of word order, mathematicians and computer scientists thought it would be a comparatively simple matter to do machine translation, whereby computers would be able, automatically, to translate one language into another. But natural languages, while following syntactical rules that can be duplicated by constructed or machine languages, present *semantic* difficulties (meaning, nuance, ambiguity, inflection) that are not easily assimilated from one language to another. Idiom alone can be defeating. The popular story is that the phrase "out of sight, out of mind" was translated into Chinese and then translated back literally as "invisible idiot." While a phrasebook of idioms might be programmed into a computer, the larger problems of ambiguity and nuance are not so easily solved, and, except for some simple and highly denotative language sets, or some highly specialized scientific terminology, the idea of machine translation has been all but completely abandoned by linguists today.

If complexity has been the stone of stumbling in the cognitive fields, simplicity has been the undoing of some of the sociological theories. One reason why the large field of "culture and personality" has almost completely evaporated has been the difficulty, in large and complex societies (and on examination many "primitive" societies have proven to be very complex, too, especially in their elaborate kinship structures), of identifying cultural patterns in metaphorical and holistic terms. What strikes one, in looking at any society, is the contrasting patterns that seemingly exist at the same time, or succeed each other so as to question the stability of a culture pattern. Thus, in reading travelers' accounts of England, one is told that the English are practical, matter-of-fact, and utilitarian and that they are law-abiding and well-behaved; yet other accounts will emphasize the romanticism and tradition-bound nature of English life, its conservatism, and still others will center on the boisterousness and roistering of the squirearchy and gentry. Each may be a partial perspective, or each of the generalizations may be true of a particular period of time. But a generalization, to make sense, or to be scientific, must be invariant, that is, must hold true for a sustained period, or else one has to know the principle of change. Either the generalizations are wrong, or we do not know the principle of change.

In a different sense, the Parsonian scheme has proven to be too formalistic. It is a very comprehensive grid and gives us a vocabulary of analysis, but in and of itself it is too removed from an empirical or historical reality to give us a point of re-entry. From a different point of view, this writer, in *The Cultural Contradictions of Capitalism* (1976), has questioned whether one can look at a society in holistic terms. The argument put forth is that societies are disjunctive, for two reasons. One is that, if one looks at the economic, political, and cultural realms, each is ruled by different axial principles that often are antagonistic to each other. Thus, in modern Western societies, the economy is ruled by a principle of efficiency, specialization, and maximization, in which individuals are treated, segmentally, in terms of their roles. The axial structure is bureaucratization. In the polity, however, the axial principle is equality—equality before the law, equality of opportunity, and even, in some demands, equality of outcomes, while the structural principle is one of participation. Inherently, there is a tension between bureaucracy and participation, and this tension has framed Western society for the past seventy years. The axial principle of culture is that of self-realization and, at the extreme, self-gratification, and this emphasis on being considered a whole person, and the hedonism which the culture promotes, clashes with the efficiency principle and even with the work ethic of the economy.

If one looks at social change, there is a different disjunction. In the techno-economic realm, there is a "linear" principle, because of the clear rule of substitution: if a machine, a tool, or a product is cheaper, better, more efficient or extracts more energy, one uses this in place of the previous item. But in culture there is no linear principle, or even no "progress." Boulez does not replace Bach; the two coexist. Culture widens the moral and expressive repertoire of mankind. Yet, if this is true, then culture and economics do not match, and the idea of thinking of civilizations as wholes, of a Greek or Roman or modern world, in Hegel's terms, or the successive modes of production in Marx's scheme of social evolution, or the various Spenglerian or Toynbean terms, is wrong. If this theory of disjunctions is true, we need different schemes to group together different time periods of history.

Efforts to use social science for policy purposes have come up against methodological, as well as evident political, difficulties. In the area of social indicators, a major problem is conceptual. If one asks, as I did earlier, whether a country is healthier or not, what does one mean by "health"? The quick and conventional response is that people live longer. But the difficulty with that answer is that the longer the individual lives, the greater the marginal increment of time spent in hospitals, and medical costs, thus, go up even higher. How does one aggregate different diseases and illnesses along a single dimension? In a realistic sense, one cannot. Economics is relatively simpler because one can, as I pointed out earlier, convert apples and pears, potatoes and automobiles to a single metric—money—and weight the units. But what metric is available for health, and how does one weight the different components? Or, if we ask whether there is more crime or less in the country, what then? It would seem to be a simple problem. Yet—apart from the crimes that are not reported—the conceptual question is how does one aggregate and weight the number of murders, rapes, assaults, thefts, burglaries, and so forth into a single index? One way is to adopt "shadow prices." In the case of crime, it would be "time." How many years in jail does a murderer get, a rapist, a burglar, etc.? The difficulty here is the variability of the sentencing. So, for conceptual reasons, social indicators have not fared so well in recent years.

Social forecasting has encountered a different order of difficulty. This can be best understood by making a distinction, somewhat arbitrary to be sure, between prediction and forecasting. Prediction is an effort to identify a spot or a single event: who will win a next election? who will succeed Brezhnev? will the Chilean dictatorship fall? But since such events are subject to so many contingencies or imponderables, prediction is rarely possible or, if it is, it is a function of close intelligence, or of inside information. Social forecasting is the effort to establish relevant social frameworks, or major structural relationships, so that one can stipulate what kinds of problems may arise in a succeeding time period.

Some of these frameworks are demographic. Thus, we know that in almost all of Latin America, Asia, and Africa, the proportion of individuals under seventeen years of age is between 40 and 50 percent of the population. In the Western industrialized countries, the proportion is between 20 and 27 percent. What this would indicate—and one can take Mexico as a prime example—is that in the next decade there will be a doubling of the entry rate into the labor force or into the higher schools similar to the bulge of young people which swept through the Western countries in the 1960s. How will that economy absorb that large new cohort of young persons? Or, in the Soviet Union, we know that the birth rate in the Asian areas is almost twice that of the European areas. Within a decade and a half, the Russians will be in a minority within the Soviet Union. Three out of every ten Soviet soldiers will be Moslem. How will the Soviet planners meet this problem? Will they seek to bring the large, surplus populations from Central Asia to European Russia, risking ethnic tensions as a consequence? Or will they site new plants and equipment in the Asian areas, thus creating huge new problems of capital investment and risking the loss of political controls? In short, we can identify problems, but we do not know what the responses, largely political, will be.

In a different set of social frameworks, we can show that in the Western societies there is a move away from manufacturing, or the production of goods, to services, just as in the previous fifty years there was a move away from agriculture to industry. In the United States, for example, it is likely that, by the year 2000, only 10 percent of the labor force will be industrial workers. If this seems low, the fact is that today only 17 percent of the labor force is engaged in factory work, and, given the introduction of microprocessors and numerical control machine tools into production, the rate of displacement may quicken. If 10 percent seems low, who might have predicted, fifty years ago, that only 4 percent of the U.S. labor force today would be in agriculture, producing food for the United States and for other parts of the world as well? Thus, the shift from an industrial to a post-industrial framework is a shift in the structural arrangements of society.

The limits of social science

If one reflects on the promises and disappointments of the social sciences in the quarter century since the end of World War II, it should not be a counsel for despair, but a realization of the limits of a *social* science. One can put it in these formal terms:

a) A theory or a model is, necessarily, a simplification of reality. No theory or model can completely represent a multifarious reality in all its diversity and variety. To think that one can do this is to be guilty of what A. N. Whitehead called "the fallacy of misplaced concreteness." To that extent, any theory is inherently bound to be somewhat inadequate in dealing with a specific reality, especially a social reality.

b) A science—any science—can only deal with classes of events, not with particulars. And a science can find the reality it is dealing with more tractable to the extent that it is abstract, homogeneous, with properties statable in linear terms, since the mathematics of nonlinear equations is extremely limited. The simplicity of physics or chemistry is that it deals with elements that are homogeneous within any class, since the chemical properties of any molecule of water are the same for every other molecule of water. But social science questions often hinge on particular situations or particular events, such as the will and character of individuals. As Sidney Hook pointed out in *The Hero in History* (1943), there are "event-making" men, and it is not true that events always cast up the right man at the right time. Without the iron will of Lenin, it is not necessarily true that the October Revolution would have happened. If Charles de Gaulle had not replaced the weak Guy Mollet and Mollet's weak successors as premier of France in 1958, the revolt of the French Army in Algeria against the French government might have taken a successful course.

c) Most events, even in the physical world, are not completely deterministic but stochastic, *i.e.,* they involve random or chance probability. We do not live completely in a Newtonian universe, either in the micro-phenomena of quantum physics or in the social world. A new mathematics to deal with probability has developed rapidly in the last several decades. John von Neumann at one point thought that the prediction of weather would be possible because sophisticated computers would be able to compute all the interacting variables in the atmosphere in "real time." Yet as Tjalling C. Koopmans, who won the Nobel Prize in Economics in 1975, has pointed out, beyond a certain threshold the introduction of added complexity makes the resulting answers less and less reliable. Thus, paradoxically, an effort to obtain complete information can be self-defeating.

What have emerged, in the quarter century since the end of World War II, are striking advances in methodology and technique. This has been so in game theory, in decision theory, and in utility theory, all of which are ways of ordering problems and, more importantly, ways of clarifying choices. In economics, there have been advances in cost-benefit analysis and in linear programming (which allows for more rational scheduling, or allocation of tasks). In sociology, there has been the development of multiple regression, which provides the analyst with a technique for sorting out the various background factors which may have entered or affected a result and the amount of variance attributable to each (*e.g.*, if one were charting social mobility, one could seek to assess the relative weights and influence of parents' class, cultural advantages, the years of schooling, family size, IQ, or other factors which might affect an individual's chance to get ahead), and of network analysis, which shows the way "chains of opportunity," or "vacancy chains" (in housing, or in the "bumping" of jobs by seniority in plant lay-offs), affect an entire network or chain of other persons, and the like.

Technique by itself, of course, no matter how sophisticated, is useless if it cannot be applied. And in one sense the advances in methodologies and techniques have outstripped our theories; or, to put it a different way, there is a mismatch in that the theories are not often put, or sometimes cannot be put, in forms that are testable. But one reason has been that, in sociology at least, many of these theories have been put in grand or either/or terms, whereas the problems, when one is closer to the actual terrain, are often not either/or, but how much more or less, or how does one explain the *variations* among persons. If one makes the loose (and, in the end, vacuous) statement that poverty breeds crime, it is best to consider not whether that is true, but who among the poor commit crimes, who do not, and why. Putting forth a proposition or a theory in stark chiaroscuro terms often commands attention, but it is not the most effective way of going about the understanding of a problem.

The first part of this review has attempted to look at the major statements that held promise in the social sciences in the quarter century since the end of World War II. In the 1970s there have been a number of new and significant turns in the social sciences, among them some radical new departures, such as sociobiology, some a breaking apart of economics, and the development of many new approaches, particularly in the field of microeconomics. In sociology, we have seen a revival of neo-Marxism and a turn to hermeneutics, or interpretative sociology, as against the positivism of a previous period. And in psychology and anthropology, there has been an upsurge of structuralism, in the new appreciation of Jean Piaget and the starburst emergence of Claude Lévi-Strauss as a major figure. It is with these developments that Part Two will deal.

---

[1] Karl W. Deutsch, John Platt, and Dieter Senghaas, "Conditions Favoring Major Advances in Social Science," *Science*, 5 February 1971, Vol. 171, no. 3970, pp. 450-59. (Quotations from p. 450.)

[2] Paul A. Samuelson, "Economics in a Golden Age: A Personal Memoir," in *The Twentieth-Century Sciences*, ed. Gerald Holton (New York: W. W. Norton, 1972) pp. 155-70. (Quotations from pp. 159, 166.) Reprinted also in *The Collected Scientific Papers of Paul A. Samuelson*, eds. Hirokai Nagatami and Kate Crowley (Cambridge, Mass.: MIT Press 1977) pp. 881-96.

[3] Ibid. (Holton, p. 160).

[4] George T. Guilband, *What Is Cybernetics?*, trans. Valerie MacKay (New York: Grove Press, 1960), pp. 5-6. I am indebted to M. Guilband for the references to Plato and Ampère.

[5] Randall L. Dahling, "Shannon's Information Theory: The Spread of an Idea," in *Studies in the Utilization of Behavioral Science*, Vol. II (Institute for Communications Research, Stanford University, 1962). The first popular exposition of Shannon's work, it might be noted, was by Francis Bello, "The Information Theory," in *Fortune*, December 1953.

[6] Noam Chomsky, "The General Properties of Language," in *Brain Mechanisms Underlying Speech and Language*, ed. Frederic L. Darley (New York and London: Grune and Stratton, 1967), p. 81. For Chomsky's discussion of Skinner, *see* review of B. F. Skinner's *Verbal Behavior in Language*, reprinted in *The Structure of Language*, eds. Jerry A. Fodor and Jerrold J. Katz (Englewood Cliffs, N. J.: Prentice-Hall, 1964). Chomsky's *Language and Mind* is his most comprehensive and, for the layman, the clearest statement of his position (New York: Harcourt, Brace & World, 1968).

[7] Stephen Toulmin, "Norbert Wiener and Warren McCulloch," in *Makers of Modern Thought* (New York: American Heritage Publishing Co., 1972), pp. 489-90.

[8] George A. Miller, "The Magical Number Seven, Plus or Minus Two," in *The Psychological Review*, Vol. 63, no. 2, March 1956, pp. 90, 95. Reprinted in George A. Miller, *The Psychology of Communication* (New York: Basic Books, 1967), Chap. 2.

[9] George A. Miller, "Computers, Communication and Cognition," in *The Psychology of Communication*, pp. 112-13, 117.

[10] *See* Marvin Minsky, "Artificial Intelligence," in *Information,* a Scientific American book (San Francisco: W. H. Freeman and Co., 1966), pp. 204-7.

[11] James S. Coleman, "Equal Schools or Equal Students?," *The Public Interest*, no. 4, Summer 1966, pp. 73-74.

[12] Ibid., p. 74.

PART THREE

The Contemporary Status of a Great Idea

On the Idea of Beauty

Donald Merriell

Born in Istanbul in 1952 of American and Canadian parents, Donald
Merriell did most of his undergraduate work at St. John's College in
Santa Fe, New Mexico, but received his honors B.A. in philosophy from
St. Michael's College at the University of Toronto in 1975. Later that
same year he came to Chicago to work with the Institute for
Philosophical Research as a writer and as assistant editor of *The Great
Ideas Today*.

In 1977 Mr. Merriell entered the Ph.D. program of the Centre for
Religious Studies at the University of Toronto. His field of interest is the
doctrine of the Church Fathers and the medieval theologians, with
emphasis on St. Thomas Aquinas's treatment of the image of God in
man—a study of what he says might be termed "theological
aesthetics."

Mr. Merriell was a National Merit scholar during his years at St.
John's. In his doctoral work he has been awarded a Connaught Entry
Scholarship from the University of Toronto, as well as Ontario
government scholarships.

While at St. John's College, he edited the literary magazine *au verso*.
An accomplished musician, he has sung with the choirs of the Roman
Catholic cathedrals in both Toronto and Chicago and thinks everyone
should sing. It is, he declares, "much better for the health than
jogging."

Mirabell: Nay, 'tis true: You are no longer handsome when you've lost your lover; your beauty dies upon the instant: For beauty is the lover's gift; 'tis he bestows your charms. . . .
Mrs. Millamant: O the vanity of these men! — Fainall, d'ye hear him? If they did not commend us, we were not handsome! Now you must know they could not commend one, if one was not handsome. Beauty the lover's gift!—Lord, what is a lover, that it can give?. . . . One no more owes one's beauty to a lover, than one's wit to an echo.

—William Congreve: *The Way of the World*

In this passage from William Congreve's play we have a statement of a dispute that for ages has accompanied man's interest in beauty. It is a dispute concerning the determination of what is beautiful and the part which man's appreciation of beauty plays in this determination. Mirabell suggests that it is the individual's appreciation that determines what is beautiful. A woman is beautiful, he says, as long as she has a lover in whose eyes she is the vision of beauty, and she ceases to be beautiful when her lover no longer cares for her. The implication is that beauty is determined by the beholder who is able to judge of it simply by consulting his own feelings. He has no need to look beyond these, no reason to doubt his subjective response. Nor will he be surprised to find that beauty is one thing for him, another thing for someone else. He will recognize that what is beautiful in one man's eyes may be plain in another's.

Mrs. Millamant objects to Mirabell's theory of beauty. Beauty in her view is not created by the individual; rather, a thing's beauty must be determined before the individual can find cause to appreciate it. It follows that to appreciate beauty is simply to reflect it, and to judge it is to echo it with conscious affirmation of its existence. Beauty is therefore in the eye of the beholder only as in the glass of a mirror: just as the mirror is not the source of its image, so the beholder's eye does not determine beauty. In this view of the matter, beauty is one thing for all people, although many may fail to appreciate it—the mirror of the eye also has its faults, its coarseness, and its distortions. But failures on the part of the beholder do not lessen the beauty of the thing, they only diminish the beholder's enjoyment of it. Appreciation varies from one man to the next, but beauty remains unaffected by these differences of taste.

In dealing with the dispute to which these two views give rise, it will be best if we formulate the issue simply as whether aesthetic judgment is objective or not. To claim that aesthetic judgment is objective is, strictly speaking, to hold that it has universal validity. An aesthetic judgment is either right or wrong in such terms and its validity recognizes no distinction of persons, nations, or epochs. Thus, it cannot be right for one person alone; if it is right for one person, it is right for all. This does not mean that all people will immediately agree that such and such is truly beautiful; no more would all people readily grasp the truth of a complex theorem of mathematics. According to the objectivist position, however, if the judgment were correct, those who did not admit it would be in a state of ignorance or error.

Against the objectivist position it is maintained that aesthetic judgment is subjective. A man may be considered eccentric or abnormal on account of his tastes, the subjectivist argument runs, but it is meaningless to call him mistaken. There is no basis for applying the terms "right" and "wrong" to aesthetic judgment. There is no value that is not created by the individual, whether other individuals join him in affirming it or not. Therefore, no one is entitled to say that another's judgment is wrong. Aesthetic judgment is fundamentally a private affair, say the subjectivists. It may happen that a group, even a majority of all men, finds a certain thing beautiful, but numbers do not give any greater authority to the taste of the group. Value remains the creation of individuals, even though they act in concert. Subjectivists maintain that there is no contradiction between a judgment that "X is beautiful," and a judgment that "X is not beautiful"; objectivists maintain that such a situation involves both contradiction and error.

In stating the issue with which we are concerned, we give the adjectives "objective" and "subjective" in their common meaning. An "objective" statement is one whose validity is independent of bias, idiosyncrasy, and capriciousness. To claim that aesthetic judgment is objective is not to say, of course, that every aesthetic judgment is in fact free of bias, idiosyncrasy, and capriciousness. It is to say that the validity of the aesthetic judgment is not affected by these factors. "Subjective" is used in the common sense of the opposite to "objective." A person is said to be "subjective" when he makes bias, idiosyncrasy, or capriciousness the foundation of his judgment. If aesthetic judgment is subjective, the validity of the judgment is limited to the sphere of the individual and those who share his slant.

It is important to have this clear, because in the language of philosophers today, "objective" and "subjective" have meanings which are derived from the division which they have made between object and subject. Philosophers distinguish two poles in the act of cognition: the subject, which knows, and the object, which is known. There has been debate in the field of aesthetics as to the *location* of beauty—whether it is in the object or in the subject—but that is not our issue; we are concerned with the *judgment* of beauty, and the sense of the controversy on this topic is captured by the more usual meaning of "objective" and "subjective."

There are many versions of the subjectivist position in our sense of the term and some share little common ground with others. Nevertheless, we can list four general points to which all who take this position subscribe. These are that:

1. Aesthetic judgment is not valid universally. A judgment holds for the speaker and may hold for others, but there is no contradiction if another person asserts the contrary.
2. Aesthetic judgment is relative to the individual's response in an aesthetic situation. There is no basis for aesthetic judgment beyond the individual's feelings and perceptions (although these feelings and perceptions may be shared by a group).
3. Aesthetic judgments are deceptive in their form—they have the appearance of objective statements. The predicative form suggests that there is some well-defined quality (designated by some name such as beauty) that is properly attributed to certain objects and wrongly attributed to others. It is impossible, however, to discover such a quality, because the aesthetic predicate is merely a name that covers a very diverse class of subjective responses.
4. Aesthetic judgments have no normative force. An aesthetic judgment may enjoy a widespread acceptance, but such acceptance does not indicate any special authority. Although almost all men may happen to agree with a certain judgment, the fact of these numbers is no proof that the few who have not voiced their opinion will agree or that the few who disagree ought to change their minds. An aesthetic standard has no compelling authority. It is simply a type of statistical average of the preferences of a group.

In these four points we have the minimal subjectivist position. Briefly, it says that beauty is basically in the eye of the beholder and that each person may call beautiful whatsoever he pleases.

On the objectivist side there is also a great diversity of theories, although there is general agreement on four basic points that counter the subjectivist position. The points are that:

1. Aesthetic judgment is valid universally. It is either right or wrong. If disagreement arises, contradiction is real and cannot be accepted.
2. Aesthetic judgment is not relative to an individual's response. A person's feelings and perceptions may lead him to make an incorrect judgment, but as such it has no validity. The basis for aesthetic judgment is the same, whatever the differences between individuals or groups.

3. Aesthetic judgments are objective statements indicating a proper connection between subject and predicate. Agreement does not exist among the objectivists on the character of the predicate—some say it is a real property of objects, some say it is a particular state of consciousness—but it is agreed that the predicate is definite, fixed. There are cases in which it is proper to attach the predicate to the subject and cases in which it is inappropriate to do so. In either case the predicative form in the judgment is not misleading.

4. Aesthetic judgments have a normative force. They demand the assent of all men under the presumption of truth. If they are wrong, their demand is wrong; if they are right, their demand is right. Disagreement is a fact, but it is unacceptable. We are obliged to give reason for our difference of opinion, if we have one, which otherwise will be laid to ignorance. It is the duty of every man who wishes to speak out on matters of taste to educate himself in the discernment of aesthetic excellence.

These four points sum up the general position of the objectivists. This position is, in general, that in each instance all men will agree in the judgment of beauty, or that if they do not it betokens a failure or mistake of judgment on the part of one or more of them.

We will examine a limited number of authors to give an idea of the subjectivist and objectivist positions as they have been presented in the literature on the subject. These authors are but a few among the many on both sides of the issue who could be discussed. They divide as follows:

Subjectivists:

Montaigne	George Boas
Spinoza	Charles Mauron
Francis Jeffrey	Thomas Munro
George Santayana	A. J. Ayer
John Dewey	Charles L. Stevenson
Clive Bell	Friedrich Kainz
Curt J. Ducasse	Albert Hofstadter
David W. Prall	

Objectivists:

Plato	Francis Hutcheson
Aristotle	David Hume
Epictetus	Edmund Burke
Cicero	Joshua Reynolds
Marcus Aurelius	Immanuel Kant
Plotinus	Goethe
Augustine	Schiller
Thomas Aquinas	Hegel
Shaftesbury	Arthur Schopenhauer

John Ruskin	C. E. M. Joad
Edgar Allan Poe	R. G. Collingwood
Grant Allen	Heidegger
Herbert Spencer	DeWitt Parker
Bernard Bosanquet	Thomas E. Jessop
Tolstoy	C. I. Lewis
George E. Moore	Harold Osborne
I. A. Richards	Monroe C. Beardsley
Benedetto Croce	Karl Aschenbrenner
Jacques Maritain	Guy Sircello
Étienne Gilson	Francis Kovach

In speaking of the authors within these two groups, we assume that the terms aesthetic judgment, beauty, and taste share common ground. The word "aesthetic" as we use it today is an invention of the eighteenth century; no one prior to that time spoke of "aesthetic judgment." "Taste" and "beauty" are words that have a much longer history. We find the insights of the ancients on the problem of aesthetic judgment in their discussions of beauty and the fine arts. Later authors are not always willing to concede that aesthetic judgment is identical with the judgment of beauty. There is a tendency to limit the aesthetic to the field of the fine arts, where beauty is considered to be only one type of artistic excellence. Some authors make beauty broad enough to embrace all artistic excellence. In spite of these discrepancies of terminology, it is evident that most authors are referring to the same field (or some portion of it) when they take a position on the issue we are examining. It is valuable to compare their arguments, even though one may be talking about roses, another about movies. Although the context may be limited, the arguments usually hang on general principles that apply to all cases of aesthetic judgment (with whatever range we wish to permit to the term aesthetic).

The subjectivist side

One of the points of the subjectivist position is that aesthetic judgment is relative to the response of the individual in an aesthetic situation. Relativism admits of different degrees. Some subjectivists take relativism to the extreme: each person is free to set his own values according to his feelings. A more moderate relativism draws attention to the importance of group, community, and culture in the individual's creation of values. Members of a group often share the same tastes, and the group will often elevate a common preference to the position of a standard for all its members. Standards may even express the consensus of the majority of mankind. Such standards, however, merely express facts—so many people do, in fact, find such things beautiful without giving reasons why everyone ought to agree.

We examine the spectrum of subjectivist theories. First we take up the extreme relativists, then the moderate relativists. The latter we divide into two sets, of which the first emphasizes the importance of particular groups and the second emphasizes the judgment of the majority.

Extreme relativism

Although Spinoza had no interest in aesthetics, his dismissal of beauty is a classic expression of the subjectivist position. In an appendix to the first book of his *Ethics* he exposes the teleological assumptions that form the basis of most of our terms of value, such as good and evil, beauty and ugliness, order and disorder. Such language hides the true nature of the universe from us, Spinoza claims. This, he argues, is completely determined from the beginning. Hence things do not seek their goals; perfection exists at the source rather than at the end. Nor have things been made for our pleasure and convenience, though we persist in believing that God made the world for a purpose and that the purpose is mainly ourselves. "All final causes are nothing but human fictions," Spinoza says.[1] Therefore, aesthetic judgment is but a misbegotten enterprise that comes of supposing that what we imagine has some external reality. Beauty and ugliness are among a set of notions that "are nothing but modes in which the imagination is affected in different ways, and nevertheless they are regarded by the ignorant as being specially attributes of things."[2] According to Spinoza, we believe that things themselves are beautiful because we imagine that things are oriented by nature to our well-being and pleasure. In fact, Spinoza claims, beauty is but a projection of our pleasure onto the world and has no real significance, for one person finds pleasure in a thing that arouses another's distaste. "All these things," he writes,

> sufficiently show that every one judges things by the constitution of his brain, or rather accepts the affections of his imagination in the place of things. It is not, therefore, to be wondered at, as we may observe in passing, that all those controversies which we see have arisen amongst men, so that at last scepticism has been the result. For although human bodies agree in many things, they differ in more, and therefore that which to one person is good will appear to another evil, that which to one is well arranged to another is confused, that which pleases one will displease another.[3]

This is as much as to say that aesthetic judgment is really a report of the differing pleasures of individuals. If that is so, and inasmuch as differences between individuals are irreducible, there is no reason to expect a reconciliation of aesthetic judgments.

Curt J. Ducasse, a contemporary philosopher of the analytic school, holds that aesthetic judgment is subjective because aesthetic value is determined by each individual's feelings. He subscribes to the old opinion that "man is the measure of all things."[4] This he interprets to mean that no man can force his standards on another. Ducasse defines fine art in terms of feelings as a process of conscious objectification of feeling in a perceptual medium, and aesthetic experience for him is roughly the reverse process, an extraction of the feeling embodied in the medium.[5] Ducasse is not speaking strictly about the artist's feeling, however. "Aesthetic contemplation . . . might be described as a 'listening' for the feeling impact—for the emotive reverberations—of the object attended to," he writes.[6] In his view, there is no necessity that any one object should awaken the same emotional responses in all men. Ducasse is skeptical of the notion of a "social objectivity" of expression in the work of art.[7] Whereas Tolstoy urged that art be evaluated in terms of its capacity to communicate the artist's feeling, Ducasse believes that the success of communication can only be ascertained roughly, "since there is no way of comparing directly the feeling the artist seeks to express with the feeling the spectator obtains."[8] Besides, he argues, the evaluation of the success of expression is not really a measure of aesthetic value but of artistic skill. According to Ducasse, aesthetic value is synonymous with beauty, in its widest sense. "One of the most notorious facts about beauty is its variability," he says.[9] He defines beauty in terms of the pleasure that results from certain feelings. "'Beautiful,'" he writes,

> is an adjective properly predicable only of objects, but what that
> adjective does predicate of an object is that the feelings of which it
> constitutes the aesthetic symbol for a contemplating observer, are
> pleasurable. Beauty being in this definite sense dependent upon the
> constitution of the individual observer, it will be as variable as that
> constitution.[10]

It follows from this that not even the best critic has the right to consider his own taste authoritative. There is no justification for the leap from the study of aesthetic preferences to the proposal of universally valid norms of taste. All men may happen to agree on the beauty of an object, but no one can rightfully say that all men *ought* to hold that opinion. Aesthetic judgment rests upon the individual's taste; his only standard is his own feeling.

Subjectivists often do not define the feelings which cause an individual to call one thing beautiful and another ugly. However, some subjectivists think that certain feelings are proper to aesthetic experience and that these aesthetic emotions are the proper basis of aesthetic judgment. They remain subjectivists because they do not believe that every person will experience these emotions in the same situations, or should. Clive Bell, the twentieth-century critic of art and literature, insists that it is wrong to judge a work of art by cut-and-dried canons, because he thinks we can only appraise the work if we are open to the emotions it arouses. A sincere aesthetic judgment is faithful to the judge's genuine feelings of the moment, Bell indicates, not to his preconceived notions. However, not all emotions are proper to the aesthetic experience, since emotion also occurs outside of aesthetic experience. Bell suggests that there is a characteristic quality belonging to those objects that arouse genuine aesthetic emotion: "significant form." This term is mainly applicable to the visual arts, but Bell considers it a synonym for beauty in general. With respect to painting, he defines significant form as "combinations of lines and colors that provoke esthetic emotion."[11]

Bell seems almost to propose an objective criterion for beauty, but there are no formulae for significant form. He concludes that there is no sure way to discriminate the pure aesthetic emotion from cheaper thrills. Furthermore, one object will arouse aesthetic emotion in one person and fail to arouse it in another. The critic has a greater sensitivity to significant form and his proper business is to serve as a "signpost" to real art.[12] Moreover, if he is good at his job, he does not force his own opinions on his listeners, but "puts them in a state to appreciate the work of art itself."[13] Nevertheless, the critic can offer no guarantee of his judgment. In the end, he can only say with honesty that this or that has pleased or elevated him at some time. Feeling remains the basis of aesthetic judgment:

> We have no other means of recognizing a work of art than our feeling
> for it. The objects that provoke esthetic emotion vary with each
> individual. Esthetic judgments are, as the saying goes, matters of taste;
> and about tastes, as every one is proud to admit, there is no disputing.[14]

Francis Jeffrey, editor of the influential *Edinburgh Review* during the first three decades of the nineteenth century, was opposed to the idea that there exists a special faculty of aesthetic feeling. Jeffrey claimed that the diversity of taste is "conclusive against the supposition of beauty being a real property of objects, addressing itself to the power of taste as a separate sense or faculty."[15] It was a common supposition in the eighteenth century that there is a special faculty of taste that serves as a sort of sixth sense by which we perceive beauty, just as we perceive color by our faculty of sight. Jeffrey denied the existence of such a faculty and explained the sense of beauty solely in terms of mental association. "The power of taste is nothing more than the habit of tracing those associations, by which almost all objects may be connected with interesting emotions," he wrote.[16] Not all emotions that are pleasurable are relevant to the judgment of beauty, only the emotions of sympathy for our fellow men.

> The beauty which we impute to outward objects, is nothing more than
> the reflection of our own inward emotions, and is made up entirely of
> certain portions of love, pity, and affection, which have been connected
> with these objects and still as it were belong to them, and move us
> anew whenever they are presented to our observation.[17]

These emotions of sympathy are reflected by the process of association in the objects of our world, Jeffrey believed. Some objects are natural signs of certain emotions. For example, thunder is sublime because we naturally associate its powerful sound with a feeling of helpless terror. Nevertheless, no object arouses exactly the same emotional state in any two men; therefore, one man sees beauty where another does not. One essay of Jeffrey's concludes with a statement that expresses relativism:

> If things are not beautiful in themselves, but only as they serve to
> suggest interesting conceptions to the mind, then every thing which
> does in point of fact suggest such a conception to any individual, is
> beautiful to that individual; and it is not only quite true that there is
> no disputing about tastes, but that all tastes are equally just and
> correct, in so far as each individual speaks only of his own emotions.[18]

Tempering this conclusion, Jeffrey allowed that men's tastes could be ranked in terms of intensity of feeling: a deep, vital sense of beauty gives more pleasure than a shallow, dull one. He even thought tastes might be compared in terms of public acceptability. Still, although it might be shallow and idiosyncratic, one man's taste was in his view as valid as another's.

Probably the most extreme statement of the subjectivist thesis is the emotivist theory of value. While most of the subjectivists consider that aesthetic judgment is relative to the individual's feelings, the emotivists insist that aesthetic judgment is not so much a report of the individual's feelings as the direct outpouring of his emotions. A. J. Ayer, among contemporary philosophers, first presented this theory, although it appeared as a marginal corollary to his positivist analysis of language; Charles L. Stevenson filled in the defense where Ayer left off.[19] Ayer himself took his inspiration from the discussion of the emotive use of language in I. A. Richards and C. K. Ogden's book, *The Meaning of Meaning* (1923). Richards and Ogden distinguished between the symbolic, or referential, use of words and their emotive use. Some expressions serve no referential purpose at all, they argued, and among these are the basic terms of ethics and aesthetics.

> When we say . . . "*This* is red," the addition of "is red" to "this" does
> symbolize an extension of our reference, namely, to some other red
> thing. But "is good" has no comparable *symbolic* function; it serves only
> as an emotive sign expressing our attitude to *this*, and perhaps evoking
> similar attitudes in other persons, or inciting them to actions of one
> kind or another.[20]

Emotive language in itself simply releases emotions and may also be intended to unleash emotions in other people, Ogden and Richards went on to say. It shares none of the symbolic character of a real statement since it has no referential significance or verifiability.[21]

With the aid of this distinction between symbolic and emotive language, Ayer drew the conclusion that "ethical judgments have no validity."[22] He thought that the terms peculiar to judgments of value are of no empirical significance and add nothing to the grammatical subjects of the statements in which they occur. Therefore, value judgments are not real propositions, and "since the expression of a value judgment is not a proposition, the question of truth or falsehood does not here arise."[23] Evaluative language is not really concerned with statement. It is more akin to exclamations like "Wow!" and "Ugh!" Ayer claims that evaluative terms

> are mere pseudo-concepts. The presence of an ethical symbol in a proposition adds nothing to its factual content. Thus if I say to someone, "You acted wrongly in stealing that money," I am not stating anything more than if I had simply said, "You stole that money." In adding that this action is wrong I am not making any further statement about it. I am simply evincing my moral disapproval of it.[24]

Ayer and Stevenson both deny that aesthetic judgments are real statements. If this is so, it is meaningless to decide whether such judgments are valid. Clearly an outburst of emotion, even if it takes on a verbal form, cannot claim validity if it says nothing about anything.

Ayer and Stevenson distinguish their emotivist theory from more moderate subjectivist theories of value. Ayer refers to his position as "radical subjectivism," in contradistinction to "orthodox subjectivism," which holds that judgments are empirical statements about men's likes and dislikes.[25] Both Ayer and Stevenson agree that a sentence of the type "X is good," cannot be translated by a simple "I like X." Ayer denies that value judgments report either qualities of things or mental states of the speaker:

> In saying that a certain type of action is right or wrong, I am not making any factual statement, not even a statement about my own state of mind. I am merely expressing certain moral sentiments.[26]

Stevenson develops this argument against the type of relativism that turns the aesthetic judgment into a factual report of personal opinions which could only be supported by factual evidence that the persons in question do in fact hold these opinions. In contrast, emotivism proposes that aesthetic judgment is the expression of attitudes and emotions, not of opinions. Therefore, an emotivist would try to back up an aesthetic judgment with reasons that "support an approval by reinforcing it."[27] The real purpose of such argumentation, according to the emotivists, is not logical persuasion but the infection of the audience with the emotion evinced by the speaker. "Ethical terms," Stevenson says, "are *instruments* used in the complicated interplay and readjustment of human interests."[28] Evaluative language, in other words, is manipulative, not referential. The emotivists are actually trying to account for the expectation usually associated with aesthetic and ethical judgments, which is that other people will agree with what is being said, but they end by denying that the concept of validity, the basis for the normative force of any statement, applies at all to such statements. Aesthetic judgment cannot be objective if it has only rhetorical force.

Moderate relativism: (1) with respect to particular groups

On the subjectivist side, recognition of the importance of the similarities between men for the formation of taste tends to make for a more moderate relativism. George Boas, another contemporary, brings to aesthetics the theory of cultural relativism—all standards are relative to some culture of a particular time and place. Boas argues that aesthetic judgment follows guidelines established by the group to which the individual belongs. Each group establishes standards of taste that have validity for the group's members. "There will always be standards in a social group which, though they are not pervasive, will nevertheless be binding on all members of the group," Boas says.[29] Standards are indications of the value attached to various things. Boas defines value in terms of the satisfaction of interests, with the result that the object of interest becomes a multivalent thing and its values shift with the changing interests that individuals have in it.[30] Different people see different things in one work of art. There is no absolute standard of objectivity, Boas maintains, because our perceptions actually help to shape our world, "not only by selecting some features and neglecting others, but by actually modifying their quality."[31] What is more, while our perceptions differ widely, our emotional responses are even more various. "It is . . . this singularity of feeling which accounts for the hopeless diversities in taste," Boas argues.[32] Hence, a person's aesthetic judgment is "purely autobiographical" and "authoritative only to men like himself."[33] Such authority is largely based on peer pressure: there is value in conformity for those who have to work with others in order to reach their own goals. But tastes are also dictated to a great degree by convenience. And no standards of taste can resist the changes that history unfolds.

> Standards emerge out of the confusion of appetites and acquire
> authority; they are neither omnipresent nor omnipotent. Their
> compulsive force is achieved by historical accident. . . .[34]

Boas has chronicled one example of the rise and fall of aesthetic standards in an account of the career of the "Mona Lisa" in the critical opinion of subsequent centuries.[35] There is no objective standpoint from which one could criticize the revolutions of taste, he claims, for value is a product that changes with each age, each culture, each group. One group's values are no less genuine than another's.

Following Boas, Bernard C. Heyl proposes that aesthetic judgment is properly founded neither on the aesthetic object nor on the feelings of the individual. Relativism based on subjective feelings, he claims, destroys the basis of criticism by confusing liking with valuing. Heyl insists that an aesthetic judgment must be a responsible appraisal, not merely a report of one's likes and dislikes. Responsibility consists in the elucidation of the standards under which one is operating, with the acknowledgment that these standards are relative to a particular culture and period. "Values are largely conditioned by and relative to specific cultural groups and periods," Heyl states.[36] Aesthetic judgment is valid only within the limit of the group.

In order that successful communication and a reasonable amount of agreement in regard to critical systems and to specific evaluations may occur, sufficient similarity in cultural environment, in philosophical outlook, and in psychological temperament must exist.[37]

According to Heyl, relativism does not imply that all standards are of equal worth, for within the limits of the cultural group the "competent critic . . . may pronounce *definitive* judgment upon those *inferior* ones which depend upon crude and untrained experience, hasty intuitions, and cultural ignorance."[38] Exactly how the inferior standards are to be distinguished from the superior is a difficult problem, Heyl admits. When the best critics differ, it is impossible to choose between them. Heyl sees no reason why we should have to choose:

When the experiences and appraisals of judicious critics diverge, why conclude that one or the other is wrong rather than that each is accurately describing his own experience and that the valuable experiences of equally sensitive individuals necessarily differ in fundamental ways?[39]

Once again aesthetic judgment is autobiography, although Heyl values only the judgments of pedigreed critics.

Albert Hofstadter, a philosopher who has worked mainly in the field of aesthetics, attempts to formulate a relativism that allows aesthetic judgment a more general validity. Like Heyl, he insists that an aesthetic judgment must specify the group for which it is meant to hold. A specified judgment has a type of universal validity by virtue of the fact that any person can check to see whether the majority of the specified group's members actually accepts the judgment.[40] An aesthetic judgment becomes, in Hofstadter's words, "a kind of 'market research study' statement."[41] Hofstadter, however, wants to know not only whether certain aesthetic features sell well with certain groups, but whether there is some group that has the right to set the trends in consumption for all others. Is there some standard public that has authority to set values? Hofstadter looks for this ideal public, but he is unwilling to grant that even the assemblage of the greatest artists and critics of all ages, were they to reach a consensus, would constitute a group that would be above questioning. In the end, our only recourse is to turn to our own judgment. We can make our judgment more universal, Hofstadter suggests, if we widen our experience to embrace the outlooks of many different groups. "In this process we try to make our own nature a more refined and more sensitive instrument capable of responding better to the esthetic state of affairs than it would if less developed, and we judge the object on the basis of our recording of its sentiment-arousing capacity," he writes.[42] Hofstadter's is a relativism of a refined sort, in which the determination of aesthetic value varies with the critic's concept of the ideal public which he is attempting to embody in himself.

Moderate relativism: (2) *with respect to the majority*

We have divided moderate relativism into two types. The first makes aesthetic judgment relative to the members of some particular group, the second claims that the authority of aesthetic judgments extends over a majority of all mankind. According to this second type of relativism, men share a lot in common including a number of aesthetic preferences which are so widespread that they have the character of standards. These standards, however, are not prescriptive; they do not require all men to uphold them. A majority of mankind confirms the standard, but there are always individuals who do not share the same preference; these individuals have the right to stick to their own tastes. Aesthetic judgment is thus still relative to the individual, but to the individual who has much in common not only with some limited group but with all other men.

George Santayana wanted to put aesthetics on firm footing by investigation of the psychological elements of aesthetic experience common to all men. Such an approach would "reveal the roots of conscience and taste in human nature and enable us to distinguish transitory preferences and ideals, which rest on peculiar conditions, from those which springing from those elements of mind which all men share, are comparatively permanent and universal."[43] In *The Sense of Beauty* Santayana lays out the common elements of beauty, but it is his thesis that beauty really has no such "elements" (in the sense of real constituent parts of objects), that its real foundation is in man's consciousness. He defines beauty as "value positive, intrinsic, and objectified."[44] We do not uncover value in the objects of the external world, he argues. Value is a phenomenon of the emotional part of man, but aesthetic value (which Santayana generally identified with beauty) is inseparably tied to our perceptions. We naturally think of beauty as a quality of objects because it is tied to the perceptions which give us objects.

Of course, men do not all see beauty in the same things. Because beauty in Santayana's view depends essentially on the quality of the immediate experience of the individual, one person's sense of beauty may not agree with another's. Nor is one person's taste better than another's, although a person's judgment may be disqualified if he makes it in accordance with his opinions or interests rather than his actual feeling. Santayana stresses the ultimate authority of the individual's pleasure:

> The test is always the same: Does the thing itself actually please? If it
> does your taste is real: it may be different from that of others, but it is
> equally justified and grounded in human nature.[45]

If a man's taste is genuine, Santayana advises him to stick fast by it. He may find many other people share his preference, for men are fundamentally similar, according to Santayana, although he believed that human nature is strictly an abstraction. "Real and objective beauty" has no more (and no less) significance than "an affinity to a more prevalent and lasting susceptibility, a response to a more general and fundamental demand," he says.[46] "More general and fundamental" does not mean "universal," and there is no reason why all men ought to experience the same feeling in a given situation. Common ground can be found at the roots of our preferences, but Santayana considers it a mistake to speak "of what ought to please, rather than of what actually pleases."[47]

Santayana's aesthetic is distinguished by an American spirit of democracy and the ideas of pragmatist philosophy. He was opposed to the elitist notion that beauty is mainly the province of the fine arts, because he thought beauty (as aesthetic value) was everywhere that men find pleasure in their perceptions. Nevertheless, aesthetic judgment is for him not simply a report of immediate likes and dislikes; it is a reflective development of the immediate feeling. Aesthetic judgment is an ongoing process of perception; we are dealing with a "critical perception" or a "perceptual criticism."[48] Thus, in Santayana's view, the aesthetic judgment embraces not only the unmediated moment of the aesthetic experience, but also the wider context of the individual's past and future. "Reflection refines particular sentiments by bringing them into sympathy with all rational life."[49] Reflection does not reject the immediate experience; it reveals the grounds of the experience in the individual's nature. Santayana thinks that this nature is above all a rational nature, although the individual may not be the most rational of men. A strong, lively pleasure is the response not only of the creature of the moment, he holds, but of the creature who has lived through a continuous flow of experience.

Furthermore, Santayana holds that the future serves to test the value of our tastes to other areas of our lives. It gives us an idea of what tastes are beneficial for us.

> Good taste is indeed nothing but a name for those appreciations which
> the swelling incidents of life recall and reinforce. Good taste is that
> taste which is a good possession, a friend to the whole man.[50]

Santayana gives us a pragmatic test for good taste (although it may not be especially practicable). It recalls Jeffrey's ranking of tastes according to their vitality: a more intense and vital taste is more desirable, although its vitality gives it no special authority over the tastes of other men. Santayana believes that the vitality of a man's taste arises from its consonance with the entire life of the individual and the community of his fellow men. Every experience of intrinsic (rather than instrumental) value is an aesthetic experience, and in Santayana's opinion we are called to take pleasure in every moment of consciousness.[51] However, we do not share the same experience, and we may find pleasure in different things, but in the long run our experience will tend to confirm certain pleasures as more appropriate than others to the rational life. A different pleasure's intrinsic value can never be denied, however, nor can it be dismissed as wrong. Aesthetic judgment never possesses a normative force.

Thomas Munro, the founder of the American Society for Aesthetics, has suggested applying the scientific method to aesthetics, to establish it on a firmer basis. According to his plan in *Scientific Method in Aesthetics,* descriptive method would formulate generalizations based on the observation of men's responses in aesthetic situations. These generalizations would mostly have to be limited in their applicability to specified social and cultural groups. They would be possible because all men share common characteristics, and a certain continuity of interchange maintains itself between past and present, between one individual and another. "General standards of value are, and always must be, used by every one, as a means of bringing to bear the past experience of himself and others," Munro writes.[52] But such standards, even those limited to some particular group, would only be scientific hypotheses that would function as predictions of the probable responses of men in a certain aesthetic situation.

> What binding force, as a standard, would a generalization of this sort have on any individual who chose to differ from it? None whatever as a moral obligation, or as a sign that he was necessarily mistaken in judgment or inferior in taste. It would have no more coercive effect than a "law" of hygiene has in making individuals conform to it; rather much less, since the effects predicted would be vastly more contingent and uncertain.[53]

For Munro, such a "law" of aesthetics is no standard in the normative sense but merely a statistical average that indicates a fairly high probability that any randomly picked individual will share this taste.

In his classic work on aesthetics, *Art as Experience,* John Dewey takes a strong position against the judging of beauty or aesthetic value by rules or standards. Many of the authors on the objectivist as well as the subjectivist side of the issue we are considering have preached against the concept of absolute rules of art. Among them, the more moderate have granted that rules have some usefulness in the formation of critical judgments. Dewey admits that rules have some significance for the education of taste, directing the inexperienced to works of more lasting value. He insists, however, that these rules must not possess an authoritative force, lest they interfere with the direct experience of the work of art. Dewey holds that every work of art is a unique thing which we can appreciate genuinely only if we leave ourselves open to the moment of encounter. Dewey rejects the notion that criticism is a judicial "process of acquittal or condemnation on the basis of merits and demerits."[54] Criticism is not concerned primarily with values but with the "objective properties of the object under consideration," he claims.[55] Dewey does not accept the common subjectivist opinion that critical judgments are strictly autobiographical. Any evaluative judgment must be backed by the evidence of the object itself. Nevertheless, the emphasis of the object must be understood in the light of Dewey's brand of empiricism: experience is a fundamental unity, which we divide, after the fact, into subject and object, "organism and environment."[56] There is no real separation between the spectator and the work of art in the moment of experience. On these grounds, Dewey objects to the phrase, "objectified pleasure," which Santayana used, for the words seem to him to imply that aesthetic experience is a sort of projection of the subject's feelings into the otherwise inert object.[57] Yet Dewey also objects to the theory, common among the objectivists, that the concrete object simply impresses its form upon our mind and senses in the instant of experience. Criticism reflects the complete experience of the critic, he maintains; it is the duty of such a critic to pronounce judgment on the basis of a faithful attention to his immediate experience with its ramifications in both his internal and external worlds.

In an earlier work, *Experience and Nature,* Dewey stresses the element of reflection in aesthetic experience even more markedly than does Santayana. Experience is ongoing and continuous, in Dewey's view. There is the moment of direct pleasure in the object and then there are the moments of the aftertaste, of comparison, of critical reflection. There are alternate "perchings and flights" in the flow of experience, moments of consummation and moments of a more instrumental nature that are directed to other moments in the past and the future.[58] According to Dewey, however, it is not a matter of black and white; each moment is both consummatory and instrumental, although one aspect usually dominates the other. We have moments of "critical appreciation" and moments of "appreciative, warmly emotionalized criticism," as he put it.[59] Value has its source in the moment of unmediated appreciation. Nothing can impeach the value of the moment's pleasure, but recollection and reflection can add a new value (positive or negative) to the first moment, and cultivation of taste makes for a deeper, more enduring pleasure. "The result is a distinction between the apparent and the real good," Dewey concludes.[60] Dewey considers that "great art" is distinguished by its instrumental capacity to spark new moments of consummation in the life of the individual and in the lives of his fellows.[61] Nevertheless, not all men will respond to such a work of art, and they are not culpable of any failure of perception or feeling. "There is a constitution common to all normal individuals,"[62] Dewey asserts, but he adds that men make different use of it in the course of their lives. While criteria can be formulated to guide men in the perception of works of art, "such criteria are not rules or prescriptions."[63] Dewey firmly believed in the instrumental value of aesthetic judgments for the direction of perception and appreciation. He thought, however, that another person might find value in some aspect we never dreamed of, and he did not believe that our appraisals and standards should ever be set up as "dictations of what the attitude of any one should be."[64]

Summary

Some of the positions on the subjectivist side are more extreme than others, but all uphold the autonomy of the individual in the act of aesthetic judgment and insist that no one has the right to dictate to him what his taste should be. It is allowed that one individual has much in common with others, because he belongs to various social and cultural groups, and that very often he will share a common taste with other members. Some subjectivists even grant a limited binding power to the standards of the group. None maintains, however, that aesthetic judgment generically possesses any basis for claims of authority. Dispute may be interesting and educational, but there are no grounds for a real settlement of differences. Subjectivists find no sense in the words "right" and "wrong" when they are applied to aesthetic judgments. Subjectivists spend a good deal of time demolishing the myth that aesthetic judgment is simply an objective report of a world of ordered value common to all of us. Although some try to hide the bluntness of the conclusion, the subjectivist position essentially reduces aesthetic judgment to autobiography, a state of affairs which Anatole France has straightforwardly expressed:

> We are locked into our persons as into a lasting prison. The best we can do, it seems to me, is gracefully to recognize this terrible situation and to admit that we speak of ourselves everytime that we have not the strength to be silent.
>
> To be quite frank, the critic ought to say: "Gentlemen, I am going to talk about myself on the subject of Shakespeare, or Racine, or Pascal, or Goethe."[65]

The objectivist side

According to the objectivist position, aesthetic judgments are either right or wrong. The objectivist's task is to show why this is so. He must show how it is possible for one judgment to be correct and others to be incorrect. Such a demonstration usually entails an analysis of aesthetic judgment and the establishment of some criteria for making correct aesthetic judgments. The objectivist claims that these criteria hold for all times and places and that aesthetic judgment is objective because such criteria exist.

In order to understand the process of aesthetic judgment we must consider the complete set of objects and functions that make up the aesthetic experience. To begin with, there is generally some aesthetic object that is actually present to the human subject in the moment of experience, although this object may be partially the creation of the subject's imagination. Then there is the human subject, whose experience will vary in relation to a number of internal and external conditions. Aesthetic judgment usually follows upon some set of aesthetic experiences in which interaction has occurred between the object and the subject. This interaction involves two sets of processes. One set is composed of the cognitive functions of seeing, hearing, imagining, intuiting, conceiving, and reasoning. These are processes of apprehension by which the subject becomes *aware* of the aesthetic object. The other set consists of appetitive processes such as feelings of pleasure and pain, emotional responses, desires and inclinations, and directions.* Through these functions the subject *reacts* to the object, experiencing either attraction or repulsion.

Most objectivists base their theories of aesthetic judgment upon an understanding of aesthetic experience that emphasizes one or the other of these two sets of processes. Some objectivists stress the appetitive processes. They think that aesthetic judgment is objective because it is based upon a certain appetitive response to the aesthetic object. Other objectivists stress the cognitive processes and claim that aesthetic judgment is objective because it is based on a certain state of cognitive activity occasioned by the aesthetic object. There are a few objectivists who cannot be said to lay a greater emphasis on either the appetitive or the cognitive processes.

Appetitive basis for the objectivist position

Those objectivists who base their arguments on an analysis of aesthetic experience that emphasizes the appetitive side of the experience generally focus on one of the two major divisions of the appetitive processes. The first division comprises the immediate responses of attraction and repulsion, including the simple feelings of pleasure and pain and the more complex responses that we call emotions. That these feelings and emotions experienced by all men form the basis for the objectivity of aesthetic judgment is the belief of Burke and Hume, among others. The second division consists of principles that give direction and guidance to the attractions and repulsions we feel toward objects. That these—principles of morality or ethics, the ideas and habits that make our actions good or virtuous—constitute the basis of aesthetic judgments is contended by Ruskin and Kant.

Emphasis on emotions

In his *Philosophical Enquiry into the Origin of Our Ideas of the Sublime and Beautiful,* Burke, the famous jurist whose interests went further than the law, examines the sense of beauty. By way of a preface, Burke later added to this work an essay, "On Taste," in which he endeavored to establish the critic's authority to dictate tastes. Burke's fundamental thesis was that all men by nature share a common constitution. Therefore, he argued, there are certain things that affect all men with pleasurable feelings of the same sort, and we call such things beautiful.

Although Burke believed that beauty was a property of objects, he thought that the defining mark of beauty was its effect on the human mind. Things of beauty naturally arouse in the mind a pleasurable emotion of affection, tenderness, and love, he held. He devoted much of the *Philosoph-*

---

* The distinction between cognitive and appetitive faculties belongs to the Aristotelian tradition of philosophy. Unfortunately there is no word in common English usage for the highly useful term, "appetitive."

ical Enquiry to a detailed exposition of the qualities of objects that arouse this emotion.

This work maintains that there are laws of nature which govern the relationship between beautiful objects and the minds of men. "Natural objects affect us, by the laws of that connexion, which Providence has established between certain motions and configurations of bodies, and certain consequent feelings in our minds," Burke says.[66] He recognized the fact that people do disagree about beauty, but laws of nature admit of exceptions with no detriment to their validity. Burke believed that in most cases men do experience the same feeling of pleasure in the presence of beauty. Therefore, the critic's business is not to instill an artificial taste in the audience but to demonstrate the beauties that are fit by nature to give him pleasure. The appreciation of beauty is not meant to be forced, Burke points out:

> Who ever said, we *ought* to love a fine woman, or even any of these beautiful animals, which please us? Here, to be affected, there is no need of the concurrence of the will.[67]

To discern beauty according to Burke is to feel and consequently recognize the emotions that beauty naturally awakens in our minds.

Like Burke, Hume makes feeling the key to beauty, but he also equates the feeling of beauty with beauty itself. Beauty is a certain feeling, a state of the mind, he asserts, although "it must be allowed, that there are certain qualities in objects which are fitted by nature to produce those particular feelings."[68] For Hume, beauty is a feeling of pleasure. It is a feeling that can be aroused merely by the appearances of things to our senses, but Hume traces the feeling of beauty primarily to the working of the imagination. Beauty in most cases is the pleasure we find in the usefulness of the object, Hume claims; but in most cases this is not the pleasure enjoyed in the actual use of the object. It is more common to feel beauty when we can appreciate the object only in our imagination, for the object may not be ours to use. According to Hume's definition of beauty, we may enjoy a vicarious pleasure in another's good by imagining how good it is. If the object is fit to please its possessor by its usefulness, "it is sure to please the spectator, by a delicate sympathy with the possessor."[69] To use Hume's own example, a man may take pleasure in the sight of his native Scottish plain, "overgrown with furze and broom," on which he is standing, but if his thoughts should wander south to some "hill cover'd with vines or olive-trees," it would be natural for him to find more beauty in that southern hill.[70] For, by sympathy with its owner, this Scotsman derives a certain pleasure from the fertility and bounty of that distant soil.

Hume admitted that the same thing might please one man and not another, giving rise to differences of taste, but in "Of the Standard of Taste" he argues that things tend to have the same effect on all men. Like Burke, Hume believed that it is natural to feel the pleasure of beauty in certain situations. Therefore, he thought standards of taste could be formulated similar to laws of nature: they would, he said, be "general observations, concerning what has been universally found to please in all countries."[71] Unhappily, most men were limited by prejudice and provinciality in his view.

> Thus, though the principles of taste be universal, and nearly, if not entirely, the same in all men, yet few are qualified to give judgment on any work of art, or establish their own sentiment as the standard of beauty.[72]

Among the other defects that can obstruct the discernment of beauty, Hume thought, were that the critic's senses might be suffering some disorder; his concentration might be poor; he might be experiencing a period of emotional unbalance; and he might have little skill in the analysis of the object's structure. Nevertheless, accepting the difficulties of critical judgment, Hume insisted that "the different degrees of taste would still have subsisted, and the judgment of one man been preferable to that of another," had no man discovered and published the standards of taste.[73]

Hume had only one difficulty with the objectivist thesis: he saw no way to settle differences of taste rooted in differences of cultural and psychological type.[74] He could not account for such differences in terms of errors of judgment, for it seemed to him that one people naturally found pleasure in things that gave no pleasure to another people. But these differences of taste did not threaten the more universal standards of taste, in Hume's opinion. Perhaps we see here the difficulty of maintaining the objectivist position when aesthetic experience is identified primarily with the feeling of pleasure, for such an analysis of aesthetic experience seems more often to lead to a subjectivist conclusion.

Emphasis on principles of morality

John Ruskin devoted two volumes of his work, *Modern Painters,* to the exposition of a theory of aesthetic experience that equates the appreciation of beauty with the love of God the Creator. In effect, Ruskin's theory is a refinement of Hume's definition of beauty in terms of the pleasure we find in the usefulness of a thing. Ruskin distinguished two senses of "useful." In the first sense, a thing is useful if it contributes merely to the support of man's existence; in the second and more important sense, it is useful if it helps man to fulfill the purpose of his existence. That purpose, Ruskin insisted, is to contemplate the glory of God and to lead a life that gives glory to God.[75] Therefore, a thing of beauty is a joy forever and not a thing of fleeting pleasure, for beauty serves to reveal God and to show man how to find happiness.

In Ruskin's plan, the perception of beauty is the moral perception of the divine nature as it is reflected in the world. In order to perceive the reflection of God's perfection in his creation we must strive to be perfect ourselves. The artist especially must be a man of pure heart. As Ruskin puts it, "a painter of saints must be a saint himself."[76] Man's perfection is to live according to the moral law that is the true foundation of all religion. Ruskin says that a good moral character is the chief condition of the appreciation of beauty.[77] The essence of the moral life is the love of God and the love of his creatures. Thus, the perception of beauty in Ruskin's words, "is altogether moral, an instinctive love and clinging to the lines of light. Nothing but love can read the letters, nothing but sympathy catch the sound."[78] If we are to see a thing's beauty, we must first love that thing.

Ruskin thought that aesthetic judgment involves a degree of reflection because the pleasures of the moment are not always the effect of beauty. A man can be deceived by his immediate impressions; he must reflect whether the impressions of the moment present beauty or not. Ruskin agrees with Burke that it may seem odd to tell another person that he *ought* to prefer the smell of violets to that of roses, but he insists that "it is the duty of men to prefer certain impressions of sense to others."[79] It was natural, he thought, for men to find some things beautiful—those things that help man reach his fulfillment. "Men have no right to think some things beautiful," he writes, "and no right to remain apathetic with regard to others."[80] It is man's duty to find beauty only in those things that are consonant with the divine and moral perfection of his heart.

Kant's defense of the objectivity of aesthetic judgment appears in his *Critique of Judgment.** After a lengthy analysis of aesthetic experience, Kant concludes that aesthetic judgment is objective because beauty is the symbol of the ideas of morality. The cultivation of morals is the necessary condition of good taste, he argues.

According to Kant, a man pronounces a judgment that this thing or that is beautiful with the tacit understanding that his judgment is right and that other men ought to agree with him. If to call a thing beautiful meant nothing more than to say that it pleases him, a man would not demand such agreement. Kant thought that the grammatical form of the aesthetic judgment was significant. Although he did not think beauty was really a property of objects, he suggested that a man "speaks of beauty as if it were a property of things" because he means that the thing he calls beautiful ought to give pleasure to all men.[81] To predicate beauty of a thing is to make an objective statement which is universally valid—it is either right or wrong.

On first analysis, beauty is simply the feeling of pleasure, according to Kant. However, like Ruskin, he wished to refine the concept of pleasure. Pleasure, Kant asserts, is often confused with the gratification of the senses or the satisfaction of our desires. Pure pleasure is a feeling that arises when the mind finds rest and peace in itself. In the moment of aesthetic experience the mind is free from the turmoil of seeking things to satisfy our desires and gratify our senses. We find rest from the bustle and the concern of the practical world in the pleasure of beauty; we find surcease, in aesthet-

---

* *Great Books of the Western World*, Vol. 42.

ic experience, even from the pursuit of knowledge, for knowledge, too, involves us with things. Our knowledge, our desires, our senses all essentially bring us into the world where one thing jostles the next. Aesthetic pleasure does not itself arise from this constant motion of things, Kant insists. Only when we step back from the daily bustle of the world and let our minds rest upon the form of some object with no intent to analyze or make use of it does pleasure pure and simple arise in us.

According to Kant, any one who experiences such pleasure believes — rightly — that all men should find pleasure in the form of the object in which his mind has found rest. For this reason the person calls the object beautiful. Commonly, we say that a thing pleases us when it satisfies a desire or charms the senses, but Kant contends that this is loose usage. The pleasure that moves us to call something beautiful has nothing to do with our individual inclinations.[82] It is a pleasure that all men should feel in the same situation.

Kant was not content to leave his analysis with the conclusion that beauty is determined by pleasure. He went on to examine the state of mind that gives rise to the feeling of pleasure. In the experience of beauty the mind rests in itself. It contemplates form alone and is not concerned to know or make use of the object to which the form belongs. Kant explains that when a man turns his mind to the form of an object, he becomes aware of a design and order in the object. However, he can never know the design as a real character of the object, for Kant thought that it was impossible for us to have certain knowledge of any order in the universe beyond the order of mechanical causality. When we become aware of the form and design of an object, we are no longer engaged in acquiring knowledge of things. We have entered the world of the imagination, according to Kant, a world ruled by an order different from the order of mechanical causality.

When a man calls something beautiful, what happens, according to Kant, is that the contemplation of the thing's form gives him an intuition of life within himself. Man cannot prove that there is design in things outside his mind. When his imagination finds design in an object, what happens is that his mind confronts itself. Suddenly the mind realizes that it is playing beyond the limits of knowledge. As it contemplates the form of some object, it senses that the order it is finding in the object is a reflection of the order that exists in itself. According to Kant, man cannot prove that this order exists in the thing, but he can see such order as the principle that rules his mind. It is this intuition of the purposeful harmony which rules his consciousness that gives a man the pleasure that makes him speak of the beauty of things.

Thus the beautiful is for Kant the form that symbolizes the order that guides man's life. This order is basically the moral order by which man freely chooses to act according to a rational purpose. According to Kant's theory of knowledge, we cannot have certain and scientific knowledge of the ideas of morality because our knowledge does not go beyond the limits of the spatio-temporal world that is completely determined by mechanical causality. We cannot know with certitude that we are free, or that God exists, or that there is a moral law. Nevertheless, we are confronted with the freedom of the moral order when we come to act. Assuming the inescapability of freedom in our lives, Kant had earlier demonstrated the ideas of morality in his _Critique of Practical Reason._* However, he felt that there must be some link between the deterministic world of space and time that man knows and the moral order in which he lives. Kant found that link in the aesthetic experience. When we consider the form of some physical object, its design in space and time, we are, he argued, finding a symbolic expression for the ideas of the moral order that governs our lives. To see beauty in a thing is to feel an intimation of a benevolent purpose, an intelligent design that guides the universe. Beauty's peculiar character is never to be more than an intimation of freedom in a world that can never be proved to include freedom.

Aesthetic judgment is objective, Kant maintains, because the forms of certain things symbolize the ideas of the moral order. The moral order is universal and hence the universal validity of aesthetic judgment.

> The beautiful is the symbol of the morally good, and only in this light (a point of view natural to every one, and one which every one exacts from others as a duty) does it give us pleasure with an attendant claim to the agreement of every one else. . . .[83]

Other men ought to feel pleasure in the contemplation of the thing we call beautiful because they ought to recognize the moral order intimated by the thing's form. To perceive beauty truly implies a sensitivity to moral ideas, Kant argues. Therefore, he concludes, "the true propaedeutic for laying the foundations of taste is the development of moral ideas and the culture of the moral feeling."[84]

Cognitive basis for the objectivist position

Many authors who have supported the objectivist position have concluded that aesthetic judgment is objective because aesthetic experience is fundamentally a type of cognition or knowledge. Some of these objectivists, among them Arthur Schopenhauer and Benedetto Croce, identify aesthetic experience with a _special_ mode of cognition that differs from the normal modes of cognition by which we are aware of the world. A second approach is exemplified by the theories of Francis Hutcheson, Guy Sircello, and C. I. Lewis, who claim that aesthetic experience is a _normal_ mode of cognition of certain special qualities of things. Finally, some objectivists hold that aesthetic experience is essentially the highest level of operation of the normal modes of cognition. Among those who have equated aesthetic experience with a _perfected_ state of cognition are Aquinas, Plotinus, and Aristotle.

---

* _GBWW_, Vol. 42

A special mode of cognition

In a major section of his work, *The World as Will and Idea*, Schopenhauer argues that a man knows beauty when he attains the vision of the reality that lies behind the world of the senses. In our everyday life we are caught up in the changes of the world that our senses present to us. We know things only by an analytical dissection of them, and we ourselves are torn apart by the desires they arouse in us. Schopenhauer thought that behind this world of strife there was a reality that did not change, the reality of the eternal Ideas. Aesthetic experience is the gateway to this realm of tranquillity, Schopenhauer claimed. "The object of aesthetical contemplation is not the individual thing, but the Idea in it which is striving to reveal itself," he writes.[85] Such a heavenly vision gives us the pleasure that we associate with beauty.

Schopenhauer's measure of beauty is the degree to which a thing succeeds in revealing the Idea within itself. The Ideas do not change, but some men are too engrossed in the everyday world to perceive them. Therefore, men see beauty according to the "measure of their intellectual worth."[86] Art can serve to make the Ideas more manifest and thus to educate taste. According to Schopenhauer, the man who has a vision of the Ideas is a good judge of beauty.

To Croce's analysis of aesthetic experience we owe the still fashionable statement that art is expression. Croce claimed that aesthetic experience is essentially artistic vision. Nature is not in itself beautiful; the artist's eye makes it so.[87] Beauty is primarily the excellence of the work of art, but Croce argued that the work of art properly exists in the imagination of the artist and of the lover of art. What we are accustomed to call the work of art, the physical object, is merely a medium that allows the artist to share the work of art with others.

According to Croce, art is an act of the imagination by which a man suddenly finds the expression he has been looking for, the expression that allows him to see an order among the data presented to his imagination. It is a moment of intuition in which the artist's mind captures in expressive form a "synthesis of the various, or multiple, in the one."[88] The excellence of art—which equals beauty, in Croce's system—may be defined "as *successful expression*, or rather, as *expression* and nothing more, because expression when it is not successful is not expression."[89] The act of intuition in which the imagination gives birth to expression is a special mode of cognition that is different from the ordinary modes of cognition by which we perceive and know the world. It gives us entry to the world of design and form that lives in the imagination.

Croce argued that the objective basis for aesthetic judgment is the determination of whether the work of art is expressive or not. To tell whether the artist has achieved successful expression, we must try to step into his shoes and reproduce his state of imagination. This may be a difficult task,

Croce admitted, involving careful historical research into the outlook and attitude of the artist. Granting that it is possible to recreate in ourselves the condition of the artist's imagination, we must then see whether we experience the flash of intuition and expression that constitutes the artistic vision. If we fail to see the vision, Croce said, either we have failed to reproduce the imaginative conditions or the artist in fact has given us a sham. Croce assumed that the imagination is fundamentally the same in all men, so that all men can share in the artist's vision if it is genuine. According to Croce, if a work of art is beautiful, all who deny it are in error, because they have failed to see the artist's vision.

Cognition of special qualities

In 1725 the British philosopher Francis Hutcheson published *An Inquiry into the Original of Our Ideas of Beauty and Virtue,* one of the earliest works of modern philosophy to deal with the questions of aesthetics. Hutcheson proposed the theory (to which Francis Jeffrey later objected so strenuously) that we have a special sense of beauty. Beauty is not a quality of objects, Hutcheson claimed, in agreement with Hume and Kant, but an idea in the mind. However, it is an idea that arises in the mind only in the presence of a certain quality of objects, for the sense of beauty, as Hutcheson defined it, is a "passive power of receiving ideas of beauty from all objects in which there is uniformity amidst variety."[90] Like Kant, Hutcheson connected beauty with the design and order of the thing, but he believed that uniformity amidst variety was a real property of objects.

To judge correctly that a thing is beautiful, according to Hutcheson, we must actually have perceived that it possesses uniformity amidst variety. All men are born with the sense of beauty that responds to uniformity amidst variety. It may seem difficult on this assumption to account for all the mistakes that men make in the judgment of beauty, but Hutcheson points out some sources of error.

Because pleasure accompanies the idea of beauty, it is easy to confuse beauty with advantage and utility, which also cause pleasure. Also, the association of ideas can make us find beauty in things that are not beautiful in their own right.[91] Hutcheson's answer to those who are misled in these ways is simply to open their eyes and look for the uniformity amidst variety that is the source of beauty.

In 1975 Guy Sircello, a professor of philosophy at the University of California at Irvine, published a short book, *A New Theory of Beauty,* in which he defined beauty with remarkable precision and originality.[92] Sircello argued that beauty belongs to things although it is not exactly a quality of things. If someone were to ask us why we find a certain thing beautiful, we would answer that it is beautiful in respect to certain of its qualities. In Sircello's analysis the thing is beautiful because it possesses these qualities to a high degree. For instance, we would find a house beautiful in the clear light of a winter afternoon because its colors are so vivid and its design so distinct. Sircello would add that a certain shade of paint in a bright light might make the house ugly because it would then be garish to a high degree. Certain qualities contribute to the beauty of a particular thing when they are present to a high degree; other qualities detract from it. According to Sircello, to judge beauty is to balance the relevant qualities against each other to determine whether it is appropriate to call the thing beautiful, ugly, or indifferent.

Because aesthetic judgment is simply a matter of perceiving certain qualities which things possess, Sircello thinks it might seem difficult to explain how there comes to be so much disagreement about whether a thing is beautiful or not. Sircello points out that one man may notice certain qualities, while another man may concentrate on others. Also, a man may not have a sufficiently wide experience to decide whether a certain quality is present in a certain thing to a high degree rather than to a normal degree. When we see how easy it is to go wrong, "it comes to seem almost miraculous that there exists as much agreement in judgments of beauty as there does," Sircello concludes.[93]

Although Sircello argues that beauty is solely determined by the qualities of a thing, he holds that there is a necessary connection between beauty and pleasure. We are necessarily pleased when we perceive beauty, he says. He explains that it is naturally pleasant to be able to see things clearly, even things of no special notice. To see a thing of beauty is pleasant not only because we are seeing something clearly, but because we see a thing that itself stands out clearly by virtue of the qualities which make for its beauty. Such clarity in the thing makes for a greatly heightened clarity of perception and consequently a higher degree of pleasure.[94] This argument of Sircello's has some points of resemblance to Aquinas's dictum that the beautiful is that which pleases when seen (*pulchra sunt quae visa placent*), although Sircello takes the opportunity to qualify and elaborate that scholastic thesis.

As part of his theory of value philosopher C. I. Lewis gives an analysis of aesthetic value in which he argues for the objectivity of aesthetic judgment. According to Lewis, aesthetic judgment is a predication of value. Lewis distinguishes different modes of value. Value is first of all a quality of our experience. Lewis names this "intrinsic value."[95] Value also belongs to the objects we experience. This value Lewis labels "inherent value." A thing's inherent value is objective; it is not determined by any person's feelings or opinion. Lewis warns that to fail to see this independence of inherent value leads to "the conception of value as subjective and merely relative to particular persons and occasions, and hence of value-predications as merely 'emotive,' non-cognitive and lacking any objective truth or falsity."[96]

Aesthetic value is one type of inherent value, so it is a property of things; but in Lewis's system a property is defined in terms of its effect on men, its ability to give men a certain type of experience. To deny any implication of subjectivism in his definition, he adds that

a property defined as a potentiality of experience is independent and
objective in the sense that any potentiality of a thing depends on what
it would, could, might lead to, but not necessarily on what it does effect
in actual fact.[97]

A thing that has aesthetic value has an inherent ability to give lasting
pleasure to its viewer. In Lewis's terms, it has the power to give us experiences that are intrinsically valuable and to continue to give us such experience over the years.

It is not always easy to judge beauty, according to Lewis, because a thing
that possesses aesthetic value will not necessarily cause its proper effect in
us. In order to judge a thing's aesthetic value, there are conditions that the
viewer must meet. With the other objectivists, Lewis stresses that disagree-
ments of taste betray a lack of the experience and skill necessary to discern
beauty. Lewis argues that the pleasure of a moment is not sufficient to
determine whether a thing is beautiful or not. A skilled critic judges from
a great range of experience and knows the signs to look for that tell whether
the thing will be a source of lasting pleasure. Such lasting pleasure is the
ultimate test of the thing's aesthetic value, in Lewis's opinion. The critic's
judgment rests upon his ability to perceive among the qualities of the thing
the signs of the potentiality for this lasting pleasure.

A perfected state of cognition

Aquinas was heir to the classical tradition that associated beauty and goodness. What is beautiful is also good in this tradition, but as Aquinas points
out, the two terms have different meanings. The good is the desirable, and
as such it satisfies desire when it is attained. Beauty is a special sort of
goodness by which a thing that possesses this goodness gives satisfaction
when it is seen. We have already referred to the Thomistic formula: the
beautiful is that which pleases when seen.[98] Beauty is basically defined in
relation to the faculty of vision, by which Aquinas would have us understand not visual perception but *any cognitive act.* Beauty may give us pleasure
through sight or hearing, through imagination or intellect. Aquinas regarded aesthetic experience as cognitive activity that is pleasant in itself.

According to Aquinas, there are certain properties of beauty that a thing
must possess if it is to please when seen. First, it must possess due proportion. In the strict sense, proportion is a mathematical relationship between
quantities, but Aquinas extended the term's range to include any relationship, so that we may even speak of a proportion between God and his
creatures.[99] Every thing of beauty must reveal a proportion proper to its
nature, by which parts are duly ordered to one another and the whole
occupies its proper place in the universe. In one passage Aquinas adds
another property, integrity, or wholeness of the thing, which simply rein-
forces due proportion.[100] The other principal property of beauty is radiance (*claritas*). A painting owes its beauty not only to its proportioned design

but also to its color. Aquinas again extended the application of the term from a brilliance of color that pleases the eye to the light of the divine mind that illumines the object and allows us to understand it. A thing of beauty cannot please the mind unless it is so made that it shines with such light.

These two properties of beauty, due proportion and radiance, please us when we apprehend a thing that possesses them, because it is reason (*ratio*) that both establishes the due proportion and radiance of things and is the foundation and perfection of our ability to perceive and understand things. Like is attracted to like, according to Aquinas's philosophy. Considering due proportion, he explains that it is what beauty consists of,

> . . . for the senses delight in things duly proportioned, as in what is after their own kind—because even sense is a sort of reason [*ratio:* the Latin has both the sense of "reason" and the mathematical sense of "ratio" or "proportion"], just as is every knowing power.[101]

A thing with due proportion pleases our faculties of cognition because the power of reason that underlies all of our cognitive faculties is itself pure ratio or proportion. Reason is essentially a balance, in Aquinas's view. Ugliness upsets the balance while beauty confirms it. Reason itself is the foundation of beauty, because "both the light that makes beauty seen, and the establishing of due proportion among things belong to reason."[102]

Aquinas's theory of the kinship between beauty and our powers of cognition explains his formulaic statement that the beautiful is that which pleases when seen. In his view, pleasure accompanies the attainment and possession of what is good. In aesthetic experience, our faculties of cognition find and dwell upon some object that is especially good for them because it serves to perfect them and bring them to their fullest performance. A thing of great beauty serves to establish a state of great balance in our mind, a state in which the rational character of our cognitive faculties is perfected. For Aquinas, the contemplation of beauty is basically a state of activity in which our powers of perception reach a certain perfection. Beauty is objective because this perfection is the same for all rational beings.

This may be compared to the *Enneads* in which Plotinus conducts the reader in a search for the meaning of beauty. Plotinus begins on the level of physical beauty. The beauty of the human body lies in good proportion, but Plotinus urges us to look higher for the source of this beauty. He points out that beauty passes from the body upon death, although the corpse retains its proportions for some time.[103] Matter in itself has no beauty; all beauty comes from the form or idea that gives shape and unity to the material thing, according to Plotinus. Adapting the Platonic theory of Ideas, he explains that "the material thing becomes beautiful—by communicating in the thought that flows from the Divine."[104] If we are to understand what beauty really is, we must ascend from the level of the physical to the level of the mind and the eternal ideas.

Although there are many points of resemblance between Plotinus and

Aquinas in their theories of beauty, there is a fundamental difference that springs from their divergent views on the way we perceive and know things. For Aquinas, proportion is the key to the understanding of our powers of cognition, and so to the understanding of that which pleases our powers of cognition. For Plotinus, unity is more important than proportion. In the Plotinian theory of knowledge we come to know a thing not by studying the relations of its parts and the relation of the thing to its causes and its effects, but by a vision of the one unchanging idea that gives unity to the material thing which is a copy of it. To reach knowledge we must ascend to the vision of the ideas, according to Plotinus, and through this perfection of our knowledge we come to see the lasting beauty of which material things give us a poor reflection. Schopenhauer's state of aesthetic vision bears a remarkable similarity to Plotinus's vision of beauty, but for Plotinus the vision of beauty is one and the same as the perfection of knowledge.

To judge beauty rightly, according to Plotinus, is to see how perfectly a thing is molded by its idea. Aesthetic education is basically the attainment to the knowledge that the vision of the ideas gives. The student of beauty finds the ideas in his own mind and applies these ideas as a "canon of accuracy."[105] Plotinus's program is not an easy path, for it demands a purification of the soul in order that the student may come to discern the ideas. Still, it is the necessary foundation for an objective aesthetic judgment in Plotinus's theory of beauty.

In the few passages in his works that deal with beauty, Aristotle suggests that aesthetic experience is the discovery of the amazing order and harmony that underlies all the works of nature. Like Plotinus and Aquinas, he admits that mathematics provides the key to the perception of the "order and symmetry and definiteness" that characterize beauty on the basic level of material existence.[106] Like them, he also understands that beauty is more than mathematical order. For Aristotle, the real source of beauty is the fundamental intelligibility of nature. Beneath the often untidy surface of things we find a marvelous order in which each thing plays its part and moves toward its own perfection and the perfection of the whole. To find this order in the smallest thing is to catch a glimpse of beauty, according to Aristotle, and to feel all the delight of discovering meaning where things appear to be confused or dull.

Aristotle associated the curiosity that moves us to look for the meaning of things with the spirit of philosophy. The best expression of his connection of aesthetic experience and philosophy is found in the following passage from his treatise, *On the Parts of Animals:*

> For if some [animals] have no graces to charm the sense, yet even these, by disclosing to intellectual perception the artistic spirit that designed them, give immense pleasure to all who can trace links of causation, and are inclined to philosophy . . . to all at any rate who have eyes to discern the reasons that determined their formation. We therefore must not recoil with childish aversion from the examination

of the humbler animals. Every realm of nature is marvellous: and as
Heraclitus, when the strangers who came to visit him found him
warming himself at the furnace in the kitchen and hesitated to go in, is
reported to have bidden them not to be afraid to enter, as even in
that kitchen divinities were present, so we should venture on the study
of every kind of animal without distaste; for each and all will reveal to
us something natural and something beautiful. Absence of haphazard
and conduciveness of everything to an end are to be found in Nature's
works in the highest degree, and the resultant end of her generations
and combinations is a form of the beautiful.[107]

This is as much as to say that all who observe nature in the spirit of
philosophy will discover its beauty. For, according to Aristotle, beauty is
what is revealed to the mind that seeks to understand things in terms of
their causes and seeks to grasp the design of things. Aristotle claims that
man knows a thing only when he can give reasons that explain it. Therefore,
any one who has discovered the reasons or causes that underlie a thing has
found some beauty.

Men do not always appreciate the "artistic spirit" found in the works of
nature, but the fine arts provide a glimpse of the beautiful order in nature.
As Aristotle explains in the *Poetics*, all men find the greatest pleasure in
learning, and the fine arts give this pleasure to men who might otherwise
have great difficulty in learning.[108] Like nature, the theatre can present
sights that are very unpleasant, but the effect of the play in the end is to
give us new insight into our world. The excellence, or beauty, of a tragedy's
plot lies in the sudden turn of events that gives us insight into the natural
development of an action. According to Aristotle, the incidents of a plot

have the greatest effect on the mind when they occur unexpectedly
and at the same time in consequence of one another; there is more of
the marvellous in them then than if they happened of themselves or
by mere chance.[109]

A comparison of this text and the passage from *On the Parts of Animals* shows
us that the element of haphazard is for Aristotle the bane of both artistic
excellence and nature's beauty. We delight in the sudden discovery of an
intelligibility that connects events and persons in a network of causal relationships, the existence of which was scarcely suspected.

In one place Aristotle argues that one party is right and the other wrong
in disputes concerning good and bad, beautiful and ugly.[110] We have seen
why this is so in the case of the beautiful. According to Aristotle, the good
judge of beauty is simply the man who is moved by the marvelous or
wonderful (*thaumaston*) to discover the order and design that make these
things so marvelous. To learn—that is, to find the causes of a thing—is to
perceive beauty. Aristotle's theory implies that the greater the order that
underlies the object of our contemplation, the greater the illumination and
the delight that we find in the contemplation of it. A thing of beauty

complements our powers of cognition, and its intelligibility perfects our insight into the nature of things.

Mixed cognitive and appetitive basis for the objectivist position

There are some objectivists who cannot be said to give a greater emphasis to either the appetitive or the cognitive side of the aesthetic experience. George E. Moore considered that the cognitive and appetitive functions were equally important in the aesthetic experience. A different approach is taken by Karl Aschenbrenner, who argues that our aesthetic experience falls between the cognitive and the appetitive sides, yet shares some of the characteristics of both sides.

In the section on man's highest good in the *Principia Ethica*, Moore says that aesthetic experience is the most valuable experience to which men can attain.[111] Moore divides aesthetic experience into two components: the cognitive and the emotional. Beauty is not experienced unless both components are at work. Moore suggests that we miss a thing's beauty if we perceive its beauty-making qualities but fail to be moved, and that we abuse the word "beauty" if we are moved without any clear perception of the thing.[112] Beauty is a property that a thing possesses in virtue of certain qualities of the thing, according to Moore. Aesthetic judgment can go wrong on account of errors in our perception of these qualities, and it can also go wrong on account of errors of taste—a failure to be moved when we perceive those qualities that constitute the thing's beauty.[113]

Although a thing's beauty is determined by its qualities, Moore did not believe that we can formulate a definition of beauty in terms of a specific set of qualities.[114] Beauty has to be judged in terms of the experience to which it contributes. Moore defines beauty as "that of which the admiring contemplation is good in itself."[115] For Moore, to determine whether the admiring contemplation is in fact intrinsically good in any particular case entails an examination of the cognitive and emotional elements of the experience. Although he never makes it very clear how a judgment is finally reached, Moore claims that the judgment of the intrinsic value of an aesthetic experience, hence the judgment of beauty, is an objective determination that does not depend on the feelings of any particular person.

Karl Aschenbrenner's work, *The Concepts of Criticism*, published in 1974, is a theory of the critic's use of language that strongly favors his right to speak authoritatively. Aschenbrenner insists that a man who says that something is beautiful usually has his reasons for such a judgment. There are cases where a man may have no reasons and may only be giving vent to his emotions, but Aschenbrenner argues that the emotivist theory fails to explain a more critical judgment. Aschenbrenner makes it clear that he wishes to defend the critic's authority:

> His response may be thought to involve essentially subjective factors, such as emotions, and the satisfaction or frustration of appetitions, but

if the critic's function is identified with these, it seems readily apparent
that he must forfeit any authority such as he may have claimed or
have had attributed to him. His authority can rest only on his capacity
to offer adequate reasons to support the preeminence and authority of
his feelings.[116]

Anyone who wishes others to take him seriously when he expresses an
opinion on the beauty of some object must offer reasons that others can
understand.

A critic's reasons must reflect both the cognitive and the appetitive sides
of his aesthetic experience, according to Aschenbrenner. The key terms in
a critic's argument are not merely descriptive but also carry a certain
evaluative significance. A critic does more than simply point out the lines
and shades of a painting: he tells us that the painting looks washed out or
suggests that it has a paint-by-number appearance. Aschenbrenner claims
that these

characterizations show that the presence of a subject has not merely
been neutrally recorded but has touched deep fibres of the
respondent's being, his feelings, emotions, appetitions, his recollections
of other subjects, his expectations, and so on.[117]

The language of criticism refers to the work of art in terms that have
connotations of value or disvalue and thus are able to give support to the
critic's judgment.

Because of the evaluative tone of the critic's terms, Aschenbrenner says,
"we do not speak of them as true or false: they are either apt or not
apt."[118] These terms do not refer to qualities given immediately to our
senses. Hence, Aschenbrenner argues, a characterization of a work of art
in such terms is not susceptible of empirical verification. Nevertheless, these
terms always refer to the work of art itself, and it is always possible for
others to check and see how fitting the terms are. According to Aschenbrenner's theory, the cognitive and the appetitive elements blend in the critic's
language to make it both deeply personal and also intrinsically communicative.

Summary

Perhaps the crucial concept of the objectivist position is communication. We
have seen that objectivists do not agree about what goes on in the aesthetic
experience, or as to which elements of that experience are critical for
aesthetic judgment. Nevertheless, the objectivists all believe that an aesthetic judgment is essentially communicative. An aesthetic judgment is not the
statement of a merely private response; it is a statement that all men should
experience a similar response in the same situation. An aesthetic judgment
implies that all men should hold it in common and that they would under
proper conditions.

For the objectivists, aesthetic judgment is not a matter of taste. Donald Tovey, the great music critic, has left us a few words that forcefully convey the sense of this tenet:

One of the elementary lessons that people must learn if they are to come to terms with anything outside the most habit-ridden contents of their own minds is that greatness in art is not a matter of taste at all. Nobody ought to say he likes what he does not like; but it is childish to measure great things by one's likes and dislikes. And by continually taking one's temperature in likes and dislikes one develops no fine artistic sensibilities, but merely becomes a chronic aesthetic valetudinarian.[119]

Neither is beauty determined by a person's likes and dislikes, according to the objectivists. An analysis of aesthetic experience reveals the foundation of the objectivity of aesthetic judgment, in their view. Whether that foundation proves to be Kant's intuition of the unchanging principles of morality or Aristotle's insight into the intelligible order of nature, the objectivists all attempt to show that it is not within the individual's province to determine what is beautiful and what is not.

Conclusions

Philosophy has earned a reputation for persistent conflict and confusion, but even philosophers have regarded the field of aesthetics as a hopeless muddle. Theories of aesthetic experience are like the monstrosities of Empedocles's Chaos, in which, for example, the head of an ox and the limbs of a man were joined in sterile union. Through the ages we see the concepts of aesthetic theory separating and reforming in the oddest combinations. There is no such thing as a school of thought in aesthetics. Disciples of the same master suddenly part company when it comes to this subject. An example is the case of the two Thomistic philosophers, Jacques Maritain and Étienne Gilson, who begin to differ widely when they turn to aesthetics. Sometimes it seems as though the complexity of aesthetic experience has led many to pick some ideas from one source and others from another.

Perhaps all parties would agree on Aquinas's definition of beauty as that which pleases when seen; but the agreement is minimal, if it exists at all. If beauty is understood loosely, so that we may include those who prefer to speak of aesthetic value, almost everyone would agree that it is necessary to perceive the thing in some fashion in order to judge a thing's beauty, and that it is odd to feel no pleasure if one affirms the thing's beauty. However, agreement ceases as soon as we ask what is meant by perception or pleasure.

Aesthetics is a complex subject because so much seems to be involved in aesthetic experience. To understand aesthetic experience, one must understand how our powers of perception function and also how our emotions and our will both work. It is not surprising that it is difficult to grasp many theories of aesthetics, because these theories often presuppose a knowledge of other branches of learning beyond what we possess.

An analysis of aesthetic experience is more important for the defense of the objectivist position than it is for the subjectivist one. Objectivists must indicate a foundation for aesthetic judgment to which all men can have recourse, and the exposition of this foundation usually focuses on certain elements of the aesthetic experience which are prior to the formulation of the judgment. But it is difficult for the objectivist to present a picture of aesthetic experience that will convince his audience. Furthermore, he must face the problem of the divergence of tastes that confronts any theory which emphasizes that it is natural to experience things in a certain way. Most objectivists respond convincingly to this problem. Their major trouble remains the presentation of a convincing theory of aesthetic experience.

The difficulties the subjectivist position faces are even more formidable. It has been noted that not many persons can be found to defend such a position. At least that is the case among the authorities of the past and the present. The subjectivist position has gained more adherents in learned circles in modern times, but one cannot say that they are dominant even in these circles. Subjectivists must answer the objection that their position destroys the authority of critics. They must explain why anyone on their terms should have the slightest respect for another's judgment in matters of beauty. Some subjectivists may be quite willing to ignore the critics, but such a consequence has probably served to deter many persons from holding the subjectivist position. Also, one may turn on the subjectivist and ask why we should listen to what he says if the subject of aesthetics is largely a matter of subjective opinion. Whether these charges are fair or not, it seems that they have served to turn many people back toward the objectivist camp.

Perhaps the only immediate conclusion to draw from all this is that beauty is not determined by the beholder and yet is not entirely independent of him. The best theories of aesthetic judgment are those that somehow avoid the two extremes: on the one hand, the extreme denial, that all judgments of beauty are simply expressions of personal taste and say nothing at all about the character of the object judged or appreciated; on the other hand, the extreme affirmation, that beauty is plainly present in the object for all to see and that those who fail to see it are simply blind to its presence. Avoiding these two extremes, the soundest theories are those that maintain that good taste is somehow a cultivated appreciation of the quality of the object judged, while at the same time also admitting that cultivation does not make anyone an absolute arbiter of taste. The judgment that a given thing is beautiful, or that one thing is more beautiful than another, seems to have less objectivity than the judgment that a given thing has certain measurable physical properties, or that one thing has these properties to a higher degree than another. It is easy to see that the latter judgments should be able to command universal assent from all competent observers, but this is not so in the case of aesthetic judgments. That they do not command universal assent is an undeniable fact. Those who think they should command universal assent because beauty is in the object for all to see often fail to explain why everyone does not see it. In spite of this, there are grounds for thinking that the ideal of universal assent to aesthetic judgments cannot be dismissed as illusory. In other words, the aesthetic judgment is not subjective, as are such statements as, "I like lavender better than pink," or "I get more pleasure from standing on the seashore than I do from standing on a mountain top." Such judgments are entirely personal predilections, the sort of tastes about which there is no disputing because they are in fact nothing more than autobiographical statements. A difference of opinion about whether a sketch by Leonardo da Vinci has more beauty than a kindergarten child's drawing is more arguable; it is worth disputing, for one judgment may have more truth than the others. It may not be easy to settle such a dispute, but the basis for the truth of one aesthetic judgment as opposed to others in this case is the objective superiority of the one work to the other.

---

[1] Spinoza, *Ethics*, Part I, Appendix; *Great Books of the Western World*, Vol. 31, p. 370.

[2] Ibid., p. 371.

[3] Ibid., p. 372

[4] Curt John Ducasse, *The Philosophy of Art* (New York: The Dial Press, 1929), p. 8.

[5] Ibid., p. 174. Ducasse draws upon the Greek for a term to designate this process of extraction—"ecpathy." It is meant to contrast with the special term "empathy," the key term of another aesthetic theory, according to which the spectator is really aware of his own feelings as he contemplates the aesthetic object.

[6] Ducasse, *Art, the Critics, and You* (New York: Oskar Piest, 1944), p. 73.

[7] Ducasse, *Philosophy of Art*, p. 274.

[8] Ducasse, *Art, the Critics, and You*, p. 125.

[9] Ibid., p. 87.

[10] Ducasse, *Philosophy of Art*, p. 284.

[11] Clive Bell, "Significant Form," in *Introductory Readings in Aesthetics*, ed. John Hospers (New York: The Free Press, 1969), p. 89.

[12] Cf. Bell, "Criticism," in *Since Cézanne* (Freeport, N. Y.: Books for Libraries Press, 1922), p. 155.

[13] Ibid.

[14] Bell, "Significant Form," p. 88. Notice that Bell seems to consider that to judge that a thing is a work of art is equivalent to ascribing aesthetic goodness to it. To be a real work of art is to be a good work of art—a common identification.

[15] Francis Lord Jeffrey and Archibald Alison, *Essays on Beauty and Taste* (London: Ward, Lock, & Co., 1879), p. 11.

[16] Ibid., p. 15.

[17] Ibid., p. 27.

[18] Ibid., pp. 59–60.

[19] It is primarily a theory of ethical language, but it was explicitly intended to cover aesthetic terms of value as well. It has certainly had its effect on the discussion of aesthetics since its debut.

[20] I. A. Richards and C. K. Ogden, *The Meaning of Meaning* (London: Kegan Paul, Trench, Trubner & Co., 1936), p. 125.

[21] Ibid., p. 149.

[22] A. J. Ayer, *Language, Truth and Logic* (London: Victor Gollancz, 1946), p. 110. Ayer devotes only a small section of his book to the language of ethical and aesthetic judgments. He openly admits that his systematic reasons played a part in his espousal of the emotivist theory of value: he had classified all verifiable propositions as either analytic or synthetic, and he was left with judgments of value which could be classified neither as analytic nor as synthetic. Hence his solution: they simply aren't verifiable propositions.

[23] Ibid., p. 22. Charles L. Stevenson tempers this assertion, claiming that it is best to retain sentences of the sort, "It is true that X is good." However, he reinterprets the notions of true and false so that they do not necessarily imply that the primary sentence, "X is good," has any cognitive function. "That's true," may be simply an indication that a person shared the *attitude* of the first speaker. Cf. Charles L. Stevenson, *Facts and Values, Studies in Ethical Analysis* (New Haven: Yale University Press, 1963), pp. 214–20.

[24] Ayer, op. cit., p. 107.

[25] Ibid., p. 109.

[26] Ibid., p. 107.

[27] Stevenson, op. cit. p. 83.

[28] Ibid., p. 17.

[29] George Boas, "Cultural Relativism and Standards," in *Vision and Action; Essays in Honor of Horace M. Kallen on his 70th Birthday*, ed. Sidney Ratner (New Brunswick, N. J.: Rutgers University Press, 1953), p. 127.

[30] Boas, *Wingless Pegasus, A Handbook for Critics* (Baltimore: The Johns Hopkins Press, 1950), p. 19. Value is predicated of objects, of course, and Boas does not neglect this aspect of objectivication. Cf. ibid.: "One is interested *in* something; one has a desire *for* something. . . . That is why we transfer the word 'value' and its derivatives to the object satisfying our interest."

[31] Ibid., p. 116.

[32] Ibid., p. 193.

[33] Boas, *A Primer for Critics* (Baltimore: The Johns Hopkins Press, 1937), p. 149.

[34] Ibid., p. 141.

[35] Boas, "The Mona Lisa in the History of Taste," in *Aesthetics and the Philosophy of Criticism*, ed. Marvin Levich (New York: Random House, 1963).

[36] Bernard C. Heyl, *New Bearings in Esthetics and Art Criticism* (New Haven: Yale University Press, 1943), p. 141.

[37] Ibid., p. 140.

[38] Ibid., p. 143.

[39] Ibid., p. 138.

[40] Albert Hofstadter, "On the Grounds of Esthetic Judgment," in *Contemporary Studies in Aesthetics*, ed. Francis J. Coleman (New York: McGraw-Hill, 1968), p. 169. Hofstadter distinguishes between "universality of appeal" and "critical universality." A relativist's specified judgment lays claim only to the second universality, since all men can agree to its truth if it is explicitly limited to some definite group and expressed in terms of probability.

[41] Ibid., p. 171. A metaphor related to the term "aesthetic consumption" which is applied to the spectator's end of the aesthetic business.

[42] Ibid., p. 175.

[43] George Santayana, *The Sense of Beauty* (New York: Charles Scribner's Sons, 1936), p. 6.

[44] Ibid., p. 38.

[45] Ibid., p. 62.

[46] Ibid., p. 99.

[47] Ibid., p. 96.

[48] Cf. ibid., p. 6; also, Santayana, *Reason in Art*, Vol. 4 of *The Life of Reason* (New York: Charles Scribner's Sons, 1905), p. 192.

[49] Santayana, *Reason in Art*, p. 192.

[50] Ibid., pp. 206–7.

[51] Cf. *Sense of Beauty*, pp. 23–24. It is interesting to compare C. S. Peirce's classificatory suggestions that aesthetics is prior to ethics because aesthetics deals with ultimate values whereas ethics deals with the means of attaining these values.

[52] Thomas Munro, *Scientific Method in Aesthetics* (New York: W. W. Norton & Co., 1928), p. 92.

[53] Ibid., p. 97.

[54] John Dewey, *Art as Experience* (New York: Minton, Balch, & Co., 1934), p. 299.

[55] Ibid., p. 308.

[56] Ibid., p. 246.

[57] Ibid., p. 248. Santayana subscribes to a similar empiricism, but he tends toward the idealist position, which threatens an engulfment of the object's reality in the activity of mind.

[58] Dewey, *Experience and Nature* (Chicago: Open Court, 1925), p. 400. Dewey acknowledges his borrowing of William James's words.

[59] Ibid., p. 401.

[60] Ibid., p. 427.

[61] Ibid., p. 365.

[62] Dewey, *Art as Experience*, p. 245.

[63] Ibid., p. 309.

[64] Ibid.

[65] Anatole France, "La vie littéraire" in *Critical Theory Since Plato*, ed. Hazard Adams (New York: Harcourt Brace Jovanovich, 1971), p. 671.

[66] Edmund Burke, *A Philosophical Enquiry into the Origin of Our Ideas of the Sublime and Beautiful*, 2nd ed. (London: R. & J. Dodsley, 1759), p. 311.

[67] Ibid., p. 204.

[68] David Hume, "Of the Standard of Taste," in *Gateway to the Great Books*, Vol. 5, p. 109.

[69] Hume, *A Treatise of Human Nature*, ed. L. A. Selby-Bigge (Oxford: Clarendon Press, 1888), pp. 576–77.

[70] Ibid., p. 364.

[71] Hume, "Of the Standard of Taste," p. 106.

[72] Ibid., p. 114.

[73] Ibid., p. 110.

[74] Ibid., pp. 115–16.

[75] John Ruskin, *Modern Painters*, Vol. 2 (New York: Charles E. Merrill & Co., 1891), pp. 8–9.

[76] Ibid., p. 285.

[77] Ibid., p. xviii.

[78] Ibid., p. 309.

[79] Ibid., p. 49.

[80] Ibid., p. 47.

[81] Immanuel Kant, *The Critique of Judgment*, in *GBWW*, Vol. 42, p. 480.

[82] Ibid., p. 479.

[83] Ibid., p. 547.

[84] Ibid., p. 549.

[85] Arthur Schopenhauer, *The World as Will and Idea*, Vol. 1 (New York: Charles Scribner's Sons, 1883), p. 270.

[86] Ibid., p. 302.

[87] Benedetto Croce, *Aesthetics* (New York: The Noonday Press, 1922), p. 99.

[88] Ibid., p. 20.

[89] Ibid., p. 79.

[90] Francis Hutcheson, "An Inquiry into the Original of Our Ideas of Beauty and Virtue" (1725), in *Aesthetic Theories: Studies in the Philosophy of Art*, eds. Karl Aschenbrenner and Arnold Isenberg (Englewood Cliffs, N. J.: Prentice-Hall, 1965), p. 97.

[91] Ibid., p. 98.

[92] Guy Sircello, *A New Theory of Beauty* (Princeton, N. J.: Princeton University Press, 1975).

[93] Ibid., p. 113.

[94] See the last three chapters of Sircello for this argument.

[95] C. I. Lewis, "An Analysis of Knowledge and Valuation" (1946), in Aschenbrenner and Isenberg, op. cit., p. 460.

[96] Ibid.

[97] Ibid.

[98] Thomas Aquinas, *Summa Theologica*, I, 5, 4, ad 1; *GBWW*, Vol. 19, p. 26.

[99] Ibid., I, 12, 1, ad 4; Vol. 19, p. 51.

[100] Ibid., I, 39, 8, resp., Vol. 19, p. 211.

[101] Ibid., I, 5, 4, ad 1; Vol. 19, p. 26.

[102] Ibid., II-II, 180, 2, ad 3; Vol. 20, p. 609.

[103] Plotinus, *Enneads*, 6.7.22; *GBWW*, Vol. 17, p. 33; cf. also 1.6.1; p. 21.

[104] Ibid., 1.6.2; *GBWW*, p. 22.

[105] Ibid., 1.6.3; *GBWW*, p. 22.

[106] Aristotle, *Metaphysics*, XIII (1078a37–1078b1); *GBWW*, Vol. 8, p. 610.

[107] Aristotle, *On the Parts of Animals,* I (645a7–25); *GBWW,* Vol. 9. pp. 168–69.

[108] Aristotle, *Poetics* (1448b8–17); *GBWW,* Vol. 9. p. 682.

[109] Ibid., (1452a1–11); *GBWW,* p. 686.

[110] *See* Aristotle, *Metaphysics,* XI (1062b33–1063a9); *GBWW,* Vol. 8, pp. 590–91 for a refutation of subjectivism.

[111] George Edward Moore, *Principia Ethica* (Cambridge University Press, 1951). Many of Moore's arguments have been transferred from ethics to aesthetics and widely used in the aesthetics of this century, although he also made some direct statements on matters of aesthetics in the course of his work.

[112] Ibid., p. 192.

[113] Ibid., pp. 192–93. Moore calls these two sorts of failure "errors of judgment" and "errors of taste."

[114] Ibid., pp. 202.

[115] Ibid., p. 201.

[116] Karl Aschenbrenner, *The Concepts of Criticism* (Dordrecht, Holland: D. Reidel, 1974), p. 24.

[117] Ibid., pp. 26–27.

[118] Ibid., p. 130.

[119] Donald Francis Tovey, *Essays in Musical Analysis,* Vol. 3 (Oxford University Press, 1959), p. 298.

PART FOUR

A Special Feature

Great Books of Science in the Twentieth Century: Physics

Gerald Holton and Katherine Sopka

Gerald Holton is Mallinckrodt Professor of Physics and professor of the history of science at Harvard University. Since 1976 he has also acted as visiting professor at the Massachusetts Institute of Technology.

He has long been interested in the history and philosophy of science, serving on the National Science Foundation Advisory Panel for History and Philosophy of Science from 1963 to 1965, and on its Advisory Committee on Ethical and Human Implications of Science and Technology from 1973 to 1978. A prolific author, he has written *Thematic Origins of Scientific Thought: Kepler to Einstein* (1978) and *The Scientific Imagination: Case Studies* (1978) among other works.

Professor Holton was founder and editor in chief (1957–63) of *Daedalus,* the quarterly journal of the American Academy of Arts and Sciences. He serves on the American Council of Learned Societies Committee on the *Dictionary of Scientific Biography* and is editor in chief of a series of scientific classics for Dover Publications.

Katherine Russell Sopka received her B.A. and M.A. degrees in physics from Radcliffe College of Harvard University. She has been a research fellow in the history of science and physics departments at Harvard since 1976 when she received her Ph.D. in the history of science and education as an advisee of Professor Holton. Her Ph.D. thesis, *Quantum Physics in America, 1920–1935,* is to be published in 1980.

About ten years ago, Mark Van Doren wrote in the pages of *The Great Ideas Today* on the question of what works of literature might be included in *The Great Books of the Western World* if someday the series were to be extended to works written in the twentieth century. He made a good case for the candidacy of fifty-six books by twenty-nine authors, from Albert Camus and Anton Chekhov to H. G. Wells and William Butler Yeats. In the process he was able to summarize the chief content of certain works by these authors—drama, lyric poetry, novels, and short stories—and he could count on his readers to understand and sympathize with almost every aspect of that presentation.

Our task is immensely more difficult, and perhaps this accounts for the fact that until now nobody has been so foolhardy as to attempt to write in these pages on the question of what might be the great books of twentieth-century science. The difficulty is not merely that it is virtually impossible to summarize any science book for the general reader in a few lines. Nor is it the case that science books as such are missing from the set of *GBWW*. In fact, a good fraction of its authors are concerned with scientific matters, among them Aristotle, Ptolemy, Copernicus, Bacon, Descartes, Newton, Huygens, Lavoisier, Faraday, Darwin, and Freud. But the volume on Freud is the only example of a work published in the twentieth century.

Of course, in our century one might expect more "great books" in science than in any other area, for the discovery of a work's greatness requires historic distance, and in the rapidly moving field of science a span of ten years now should give us the distance equivalent to a hundred years in a previous century. Repeated studies have shown that a publication in the hard sciences has to be satisfied with whatever references subsequent papers might make to it during the following two or three years, because it will be quickly absorbed or dissolved in the constantly increasing flood of new articles. Only a few of all the references made in contemporary scientific literature are to articles seven years old or more. In a curious way, yesterday's excitement will, tomorrow, turn out to be prehistoric. Thus, if the judgment of quality depends on perspective, nothing should be easier than to make such retrospective judgments in science.

But there are offsetting effects which make such judgments far more difficult than in the case of literature. One effect is obvious enough: in a field in which "progress" is cumulative and rapid, there is no reason why a given book should remain long enough before the eyes of its intended public to become endowed with lasting meaning. The very word "classical" has a slightly pejorative connotation in science, as in "classical mechanics." It indicates a field in which the techniques work very well, but which now is known to be a special case in a more interesting and complex total field. Classical mechanics works well enough for, say, understanding the simpler phenomena of planetary motion; but it is quite too limited to deal with the phenomena in the planetary atmosphere, or even in a single atom. If you should hear someone exclaiming with delight that he has found a "classic" book of science, you are more likely to be listening to a book collector than to a research scientist.

With the increase in the pace of research in modern times, the reference to *any* book becomes rarer and rarer in science literature. A study of the references made in *Physical Review* articles to books shows that they rank a poor third (only about 6 percent), behind journal citations and private communications, unpublished or to be published. Even these books are, more often than not, edited volumes, conference proceedings, and the like. When the diffusion and use of information reaches a speed high enough, it obviously depresses the usefulness of a slower vehicle (*i.e.,* the book).

We shall look in more detail at the consequences of the changing nature of the process of communication in science. But here we might at least record that now even the professional journals are frequently arriving on the scene at a relatively late stage. This is because a large proportion of the research results have been widely communicated before publication in an informal way either through the distribution by the authors of preprints, an invention that traces back to the laboratory of Enrico Fermi in the 1930s, or simply by use of the telephone. Some science journals are now publishing the abstracts of forthcoming articles as a separate journal, thereby providing a summary of the chief results that are to be published some months hence. To a working scientist, an important result that has not yet been published is far more intriguing than a work everyone has had ample opportunity to study.

Occasionally the pace gets so fast that it is oppressive. Edward U. Condon, referring to the period when the new quantum mechanics was developed — when the profession was less than one tenth its present size — wrote: "Great ideas were coming out so fast in that period (1926–27) that . . . one had intellectual indigestion most of the time that year, and it was discouraging."

The scientific professional journal, rather than the book, is thus the obvious medium of choice for publication in our time, even though it has limits, costs, and difficulties that everyone is well acquainted with. Ironically, the chief complaint now is that most journals are too slow in publishing, and indeed it now may take a half a year or more to see one's work in print, whereas in 1900 it might have taken six weeks. Another great complaint is expense, because most of the major scientific journals require "page charges" from their authors to help meet the very high cost of printing scientific materials. More rarely, people refer to the loss of personal style when conciseness of expression, adhering to editorial directives, and the need to reach one's peers quickly and unambiguously serve to shave off all "embellishments." There is, of course, also a loss of historical perspective, since the article typically addresses itself to the field at the moment of writing. Rarely is there time and space for more than predominantly analytical treatments of a well-set problem. Last but not least, journal articles are rarely reviewed after publication, unlike books. (In the *Humanities Index*, about half the articles listed from the world literature are, in fact, book reviews.) In the absence of such reviews, criticism of bad work usually comes down simply to neglect of it; the inadequate work of science is one that just disappears into silence more quickly than the adequate one.

The dissemination of scientific ideas

And yet, we shall argue, for the sake of science and culture as a whole there have to be "great books" even in our time. Moreover, there *are* books that can make a reasonable claim to belong in that category. But before we can make our argument, we must look at more details, attentive to the sociology of the profession. We must define the universe within which great books might be written and read in modern science. As it happens, the statistical facts about current or recent scientific and technical literature are not difficult to find; at least this is true for the United States, and the case is similar in other countries since the amount of activity in science in a country depends chiefly on its GNP.[1]

Until the end of the medieval period and prior to the invention of printing, publication in science was analogous to publication in any field at the time; it occurred via incunabula or letters circulated in a small group. Since science depends on consensus-seeking debate and clarification, all within a network of contemporaries with whom one may have been directly in touch before, the rate of advance was clearly slow, and to a large degree it was set by the difficulty of communication.

The effect of printing on science was much larger than on most other fields of learning. It was, for example, the availability of books by Kepler, Tycho Brahe, and Galileo, in the first part of the seventeenth century, with their different options for the understanding of cosmological questions, that allowed debate on such questions among learned men throughout Europe to maintain its vigor. It has been argued, and we believe correctly, that the printed book was a precondition for modern science to take off and grow. Indeed, the excitement caused by the ideas coming through books caused the next step, the step which ironically, in our time, is leading to the eclipse of the place of the book in precisely the most active fields of science. That step was the response, in the mid-seventeenth century, to the need for face-to-face discussions about new scientific ideas and for reaching out quickly and cheaply to even more interested persons beyond the circle of the immediate interest group. This was accomplished by two inventions, by the societies founded to pursue scientific demonstrations and debate, and by the first scientific journals distributed by these societies to spread discussion beyond them.

A convenient date for this transition is 1665, the start of the publication *Philosophical Transactions* of the newly founded Royal Society of London. The model was soon imitated in other parts of Europe and eventually in the United States, where the American Philosophical Society and the American Academy of Arts and Sciences were both founded in the eighteenth century. Thereafter the spread of information accelerated. Derek Price of Yale University has pointed out that in about 1750 there were some ten science journals in the world; by the end of the eighteenth century there were about one hundred; in the mid-nineteenth century there were about one thousand; by the end of that century, there were about ten thousand. With striking regularity, the number of journals increased by a factor of ten every half century.[2]

This quantitative growth in the number of outlets for publishing and reading entailed all sorts of qualitative changes: interesting and useful new findings proliferated at a rate roughly proportional at any given time to the size of the then existing body of knowledge, thereby adding to it and further increasing the metabolism of the growing organism. The total pool of persons working on scientific and technical problems was increasing in proportion; taking over from the original societies or academies, separate professional specialty societies were founded to organize regular meetings and publish science journals in limited areas of interest. Teamwork, either directly under one roof or by virtue of membership in an "invisible college" of like-minded investigators, became more and more prominent. The further distribution of published articles through the authors' mailing of a few dozen or a couple of hundred reprints became routine, and preprint distribution became organzied.

There are now about two million scientists and engineers in the United States alone; this includes persons working in such varied fields as physics and psychology, civil engineering and statistics, sociology, economics, and medicine. The communication of scientific and technical information itself is a major industry; an estimated ten billion dollars is spent in the United States every year for preparing, publishing, distributing, and getting access to the published literature.

In this setting, a strong incentive has asserted itself to specialize on relatively narrow, analytical problems on which progress is likely to be possible within a short time, rather than to engage in the kind of large-scale synthetic publication which might take years, and for which there is not the ready-made core of an invisible college of readers, such as the list of paid-up subscribers of a science journal. Most of these scientists and engineers, fortunately, do not publish, and those who do are most likely to publish only a couple of articles per lifetime. It has been estimated that 10 percent of the authors write 90 percent of the papers and that only about 20,000 scientists are actually doing almost all of the really significant work, although it would be quite wrong to think that the rest could be dispensed with. Including scholarly, trade, and technical journals, the universe of publishing outlets and reading materials available in the United States alone is now more than 8,000 scientific and technical journals, of which 2,000 are "scholarly" (at least refereed before articles are accepted, with one-quarter to three-quarters of the articles submitted not being published). Some 2,500 more publications are conference proceedings each year, and there are annually about 16,000 doctoral dissertations.

It is clear that for a typical researcher, the problem of keeping up with the flow of publications has become practicably unmanageable unless one sticks rather closely to a limited field. Even there, the size of the publishing universe and the cost per subscription are conspiring to make the search for new solutions attractive. (The average subscription price for journals in the United States is $20 for an individual, but it can be as high as $100 or more, and for a specialty journal such as *Nuclear Physics,* A and B Series, it is now over $1,500 per year.) Hence, photocopying is widely resorted to. In 1976 libraries photocopied 850 million pages in the United States, most of which was science-technical literature. And thanks to an arrangement set up by the Association of American Publishers, one now can do without an individual subscription to a journal, paying instead to receive reprints of specialized articles, assembled to one's particular research interests. Clearly such a subscriber must take energetic measures to avoid becoming ever more narrowly focussed, since he stands to lose even a scanning acquaintance with findings, ideas, and techniques outside his current interest.

If the exponential increase in the number and output of scientists has brought with it so many discomforting side effects, would it not make more sense to proceed on a less explosive, more linear growth pattern? Even if scientists had that choice, which clearly is not the case, it can be argued that scientific effort *has* to be exponential in order for scientific growth to remain constant (linear) in terms of substantive scientific innovation. In a fascinating although idiosyncratic book, Nicholas Rescher supports this "seemingly shocking contention." His measure of substantive contribution is in terms of the number of honors, citations in major synoptic handbooks and monographs, and the like. He insists that "the progress of science as an intellectual discipline—a progress to be adjudged solely in terms of the really major, absolutely first-rate achievements of scientific inquiry—[has] advanced at a linear rate, notwithstanding the exponential growth of the scientific enterprise in the scale of the efforts involved and the correlatively exponential production of purely routine results." The exponential growth with a doubling time of output of around fifty years (where output refers to the total flood of publications) has served to keep science merely at a constant pace of progress. Conversely, Rescher argues, if the output should become linear rather than exponential with time, the rate of forward progress would decrease and science would wither.[3]

If such considerations are sound, they would help to explain the urge to increase scientific output, the demoralization of the scientific community in a period of stagnant levels of funding, and even the reward structures that encourage article production rather than books. The American Association for the Advancement of Science has long had an annual prize for the best major research paper (books do not qualify), and even that was recently changed to reward the much briefer research reports that fill the back pages of the journal *Science*. Prizes for books are very rare among scientific organizations; the American Institute of Physics has a book prize, but it usually goes to a text or popular-level summary. Harriet Zuckerman has pointed out that "since Nobel awards are made for conceptual contributions only when these are validated by the discovery of 'new facts,' ideas that unify large bodies of data without directly giving rise to a new discovery—of the sort represented by Darwin's principles of evolution and Cannon's concept of homeostasis—do not qualify."[4]

Of course, books in science and technology do get written, and more and more every year. In the United States alone, 15,000 hardcover titles were published each year in the mid-1970s—about one book per 150 scientists.[5] But here again we see evidence of increasing specialization. The number of copies that each book sold on the average has dropped just in the last fifteen years or so, from about 2,500 per title to about 800 per title (with a correspondingly large jump in the sales price per copy in such a market). Again, evidence points to the fact that the typical scientist is primarily a member of a small network of researchers, one that has been estimated to number "at the most around two hundred members, and concerned with a fairly narrow range of closely related problems." The actual membership in such a network changes rapidly, but "it is these problem networks which appear to be the basic agents of innovation and of social control in science."[6]

An experimental inquiry

With these considerations in mind, it was initially tempting to turn down the kind invitation of the editor of this volume to write an essay on the great books of twentieth-century science, analogous to that published earlier on literature—or, failing that, to think through why there are no great books of science, or very few of them in this century, if this is the case. In either case the task seemed enormous: to scan the tide of publications for the few great books it might contain, or to make a sociological model of a fiercely publishing set of individuals who cannot produce such books at all.

It did seem worth making an experiment, however. We identified some fifty prominent scientists, historians of science, and sociologists of science, and asked them to answer this question: "Which of the books published since around the turn of the century in the natural sciences or mathematical sciences would you consider to be worthy of the term 'classic,' in the sense of a great book that defined or transformed a field?"

The result was surprising. The great majority responded and the list of proposed candidates came to about 200 books, with considerable overlap or multiple nominations. Moreover, many letters went on at length to indicate that the question had been thought novel and intriguing.

With this encouragement, we began to organize our own search. Clearly it could not be an exercise in recognizing past excellence, if only because of the large problem of ahistoricity. For example, around the turn of the century one of the categories by which science publications were abstracted was "steam turbines." At this end of the same century, we did not want lightly to assume the burden of looking for the great book on steam turbines. We knew that for the purposes of this article we would have to remain bound within the historic "success" of science as we now see it to have developed. (In this, of course, we share the burden of Whiggishness that encumbers any other list of "great books" in any field. Where is the great book of the Inca's myths?) Least of all did we want to make a list of what historians of the twentieth century "should" read, or simply stage a popularity contest of works in our time.

What we could do was simply this: we could identify categories that differentiate types of books that had major importance and search out possible exemplars for these categories. If there should be a suitable consensus in the definition of these categories and exemplars, then and only then would the time have come to attempt to make a list of "greats."

This decision led naturally to a second one. If the categories were correctly identified for one field, they would, with very high probability, make sense in any other scientific field. For our task, it would be wiser to concentrate on one field instead of spreading out to all the various specialties of science. If there were different criteria within any field that made a book important, we would be more likely to discover and test them by looking at a manageable number within that field.

Trained as physicists and historians of science, we naturally chose physics as the subject of our study. This left a large pile of books in other fields which had some claim to greatness in the minds of our correspondents and which we would perhaps like to reread some day. Here, for the record, is the list of these which we shall then leave without discussing them.

Astronomy:

Chandrasekhar, S., *An Introduction to the Study of Stellar Structure* (1939).

Eddington, A. S., *The Internal Constitution of the Stars* (1926).

Hubble, E. P., *The Realm of the Nebulae* (1936).

Poincaré, H., *Les Méthodes nouvelles de la mécanique céleste* [The New Methods of Celestial Mechanics], 3 vols. (1892, 1893, 1899).

Biological sciences:

Cannon, W. B., *The Wisdom of the Body* (1932).

Carson, R., *Silent Spring* (1962).

Dobzhansky, T., *Genetics and the Origin of Species* (1937).

Fisher, R. A., *The Genetical Theory of Natural Selection* (1930).

Henderson, L. J., *The Fitness of the Environment* (1913), and *The Order of Nature* (1917).

Huxley, J., *Evolution: The Modern Synthesis* (1942).

Loeb, J., *The Mechanistic Conception of Life* (1912).

Mayr, E., *Systematics and the Origin of Species* (1942).

Monod, J., *Chance and Necessity* (1971).

Morgan, T. H., *The Theory of the Gene* (1926).

Morgan, T. H.; Sturtevant, A. H.; Muller, H. J.; and Bridges, C. B., *The Mechanism of Mendelian Heredity* (1915).

Sherrington, C. S., *The Integrative Action of the Nervous System* (1906), and *Man on His Nature* (1940).

Simpson, G. G., *Tempo and Mode in Evolution* (1944).

Thompson, D'A., *On Growth and Form* (1917).

Watson, J. D., *Molecular Biology of the Gene* (1965).

Wilson, E. O., *Sociobiology* (1975).

Chemistry:

Hinshelwood, C. N., *The Kinetics of Chemical Change in Gaseous Systems* (1926).

Lewis, G. N., *Valence and the Structure of Atoms and Molecules* (1923).

Geology:

Wegener, A. L. *Die Entstehung der Kontinente und Ozeane* [The Origin of Continents and Oceans] (1915).

Mathematics:

von Neumann, J., and Morgenstern, O., *The Theory of Games and Economic Behavior* (1944).

Whitehead, A. N., and Russell, B., *Principia Mathematica* [Principles of Mathematics] (1910–13).

Note: Kurt Gödel would be listed here, but for the fact that his contribution —as is also the case with others in the century—did not come through a book publication.

Psychology:

Freud, S., *Vorlesungen zur Einführung in die Psychoanalyse* [A General Introduction to Psychoanalysis] (1917) and *Die Traumdeutung* [The Interpretation of Dreams] (1900).

Pavlov, I. P., *Conditioned Reflexes* (1927).

General:

Poincaré, H., *La Science et l'hypothèse* [Science and Hypothesis] (1906).
Whitehead, A. N., *Science and the Modern World* (1925).
Wiener, N., *Cybernetics* (1948).
Wittgenstein, L., *Tractatus Logico-Philosophicus* (1922).

The criteria of greatness

The criteria for determining greatness seem to us to be five in number—
though, to be considered seriously, a book would have to have more than
one qualifying attribute, or else rank exceedingly high within its own category:

1. *A book that introduces an idea that later comes to be part of the accepted body of*
   understanding in a major branch of science. It should combine important
   novelty and fecundity with regard to later developments. For reasons
   discussed above, it is now quite unlikely for this to be done through the
   book; it is accomplished through the journal article. But there are exceptions, as we shall see, *e.g.,* the doctorate theses of Marie Curie and of
   Louis de Broglie.
2. *A book that refines, shapes, and disseminates new ideas of major importance to*
   specialists and students in its own discipline. An example would be Arnold
   Sommerfeld's *Atombau und Spektrallinien* [Atomic Structure and Spectral
   Lines]. Another version of a great book under this heading would be one
   that has done the same major service, not so much for the specialists in
   the discipline as for those in allied disciplines or closely related sciences.
   Examples are *The Origin of Spectra,* by Foote and Nohler, which has been
   credited with bringing Niels Bohr's ideas to chemists, or the enormously
   influential book by Linus Pauling and E. B. Wilson, *Introduction to Quantum*
   Mechanics, with Applications to Chemistry.
3. *A book that assumes the position of the definitive, comprehensive treatment of ideas*
   already in circulation on a sizeable area of science, usually one that also gives new
   perspectives and an account of the personal insights of the author. Examples we
   shall give will be Hans Bethe's "Bible," for about a decade after its
   publication, and John H. Van Vleck's *Theory of Electric and Magnetic Suscep-*
   tibilities.
4. *A textbook that becomes an integral part of the training of a generation or more of*
   aspirants to the discipline. An example is Floyd Richtmyer's *Introduction to*
   Modern Physics.

Before we turn to the fifth and most important category, we should note
that almost by definition, the books in these four categories, in a rapidly
moving science, become outdated and forgotten by most scientists within a
rather brief period, no matter how prominent they may be upon publication. We shall therefore make an effort to locate such books in the frame-

work of their own time—for example, by looking at evidences of contemporaneous acceptance, as indicated by reviews following publication. Again, because of the speed of transformation of the discipline, some books of extraordinary importance will be found to have reached only relatively few persons in their own time before being absorbed into more ordinary sequels, as nova stars disperse after a show of luminosity.

5. *A book that not merely introduces major new ideas but frames these in a new view, both in the field of science and of the place of science in the larger culture.* This is the level that the books of Copernicus, Galileo, and Newton attained. Even though one can read such works as contributions to a specific science, they bring with them a grand, synoptic, and unifying vision that synthesizes the thinking of a period or a field, or that provides the basis upon which such a synthesis is achieved in time. These are therefore cultural products that have immense power over the human imagination long after publication.

Books in this last category, of course, not only determine the direction of scientific progress but also embody the contemporary notion of scientific progress. We may postulate that during a period of history in which the very possibility of a grand, synthesizing function of science seems remote, it would be highly unlikely that a book on this high level would be even attempted. It may well be that the virtual absence of such books in our time is closely linked to the analytical and positivistic spirit which has prevailed in the West since the early part of this century. If so, we may possibly look forward at some future time to a different cultural condition. Having come, in field after field, upon a sense of the inadequacy of this positivistic temper —as seen in a variety of ways, from the sense that there exists a need for the study of ethical and human-value impacts of scientific and technological growth, to the attempts that are being made, for better or worse, to redirect research into areas of higher social "payoffs"—we suspect that the definition of "scientific progress" is already undergoing a transformation.

If this diagnosis is correct, it would help to explain the recent scarcity of major synthesizing works, while at the same time it might encourage one to predict the possibility of a different state of affairs in times to come. Therefore, it will be appropriate to make two brief excursions, one to give some examples of the "missing" great books of science in the fifth category in the last decades, the other to consider the conception of scientific progress which, if it really is changing, should give us some hope for the future.

There are now very few, if any, scientists who, from a firsthand experience of what scientists really do and think and hope to find in the end, present a book-length account of research such as some decades ago was not difficult to find. Where is the whole tradition of philosophically sophisticated scientists who shared their views on the aims, powers, limits, and "natural-philosophy" element of the enterprise, readably and without condescension while addressing themselves to a wide public? One thinks here of the great books by Whewell, Helmholtz, Mach, Haeckel, Loeb, and Poincaré, to name just a few. Until a generation ago, no one who claimed to be intellectually civilized would have dreamed of turning his back on what these men were saying. Such scholars, in turn, saw it as their business to give a humanistically informed account of the process, state, and ambitions of their science. Today, few of the best can persuade themselves even to write a generally readable account of their own technical specialty work. Books like those of Jacques Monod and Sir Peter Medawar are quite rare (and almost all are done in the biological sciences).

The overwhelming majority of students and laymen, even the intellectually most alert, have read nothing by scientists except school texts and perhaps James Watson's *The Double Helix*. We do not believe they have lost interest in science. On the contrary, the desire to understand the place and thrust of scientific development leads them to the kind of substitute literature that has filled the vacuum—a variety of views at secondhand, sometimes verging on science fiction, and of course the arguments against science and technology by eloquent writers.

All this is not accidental. The demise of a whole genre of essential works that so many of us read in the past has identifiable causes. Perhaps this is not a time for giants, even in science itself. Moreover, even the very good scientists today have so little practice in writing outside their professional journals that they often verge on the unreadable when they are persuaded to turn to the larger public.

But chiefly we are dealing here with a change in role perception. For better or worse, the premier scientist thinks of himself no longer as a *Kulturträger* ("upholder of civilization"), with all the obligations and civilizing functions that this implied. It is difficult enough to deal adequately with the complex demands of the day-to-day job. The bright prospects that beckon in his laboratory pull him in one direction, the murky and clamorous issues of science and public policy try to engage him on the other side, and relative to these forces the needs of making unifying connections between science and society or science and the humanities lose their appeal.

If we are right that there have recently been signs of a change—caused not primarily by scientists themselves but by the public—we might see again a renaissance of attention among the potential authors of our "missing books." Our interest in such books leads us therefore to the examination of the idea of "scientific progress" itself.

Scientific progress

It is fairly widely admitted that we are in the midst of a reexamination of this conception, though the discussion, while vigorously pursued during the past decade or two, seems to have gone as far as it could with the intellectual tools it has called forth. One can, however, begin to clarify and distinguish a set of notions, and test some hypotheses. For example:

1. Since Leibniz, the key concept is not scientific understanding itself but *change* of scientific understanding. Changes appear to be relatively easy to determine, but some appealing measures of change are soon found to be far more problematic than they appear at first (as shown by critiques of the largely quantitative *Science Indicators*). The change in any specific field by itself is as useless a concept as the absolute motion of a planet; that motion has no meaning until one sees that it takes place in an interlocking system of reference frames—the solar system, the Galaxy, the cluster of galaxies.

2. "Progressive" change or development is consequently a doubly sophisticated notion, and recent attempts to ascertain the progressiveness of "rational reconstructions" fail insofar as they do not deal with actual scientific developments. Properly viewed, "progressiveness" is, rather, an indicator of both the direction of change and the quality of the work—for instance, success in adding to the store of analytical or phenomenic results, or in the simplification or synthesis (unification) of the underlying conceptual framework.

3. Most examples of progressive change take place within a conceptual framework that is in large part determined by its thematic content. One well-known example is the long development from Kepler through the late nineteenth century representing the modern stage of the mechanization of the world picture, with its dominant themata of classical causality, the efficacy of mechanistic models, and the primacy of force, matter, and structure.

4. We need a name for the conceptual framework within which development takes place. The term "scientific world picture" suggests itself. Even better would be the German *Weltbild*, as used by Planck, Mach, Einstein, and Schrödinger, among others. A testable model of "progress" within a given Weltbild should be possible, based on the historical record of scientific work.

5. The hypothesis that scientific progress takes place with respect to the expectations and internal limits of a given Weltbild "relativizes" the concept of progress, but without denying in any way that progress can be cumulative and perhaps even quantifiable. In addition, a number of questions urge themselves—whether the rate of progess is linear or accelerating or decelerating, how varieties of style of thought are fostered or discouraged by the prevailing Weltbild, whether the logic of individual discovery is accommodated by a Darwinian type of model, and so forth.

6. More important questions arise from the perspective of singling out the most seminal books of our time, when we go on to ask what the effect is of a *change* in the Weltbild. The struggle between competing Weltbilder is easily documented—in nineteenth- and twentieth-century physics

—in the competition between the mechanistic, energistic-phenomenal-istic, electromagnetic, relativistic, and quantum-mechanical Weltbilder. The spectrum of themata in each Weltbild can be laid out and points of conflict identified (*e.g.*, causal vs. statistical lawfulness). But equally important, the successful, or "successor," Weltbild can also be examined to see how its sway over the phenomena compares with that of its predecessor. If there should appear in it discontinuities of both idea and practice with respect to its predecessor, leaving no ground of comparison between them, that would rule out the concept of progress as commonly accepted. On the other hand, if there are important continuities, the radical step of giving up the concept of progress would be unnecessary.

7. In our opinion, the discontinuities, in the actual course of modern science, are far fewer than the continuities. That is due to the fact that a Weltbild is not single valued, but is sufficiently rich and structured. The new Weltbild tends to incorporate or accommodate the old range of practical or technical applicability, and usually absorbs or carries over many themata from the thematic spectrum of the predecessor. (Thus, in modern physics, most of the themata of the mechanistic Weltbild persist in the current Weltbild and are constantly and promi-nently used.) This makes the total effect within science of a change from one Weltbild to the next evolutionary, cumulative, and hence progres-sive—rather than "revolutionary," discontinuous, and hence incom-mensurable.

8. As progress of science is embedded in the conception of the Weltbild, the scientific world picture itself is part of a large cluster existing along-side the social and humanistic presuppositions and ideals of the time, with their own traditions of "progress". All these together form compo-nents of an overarching, time-honored, but recently much neglected conception, namely, of the *Weltanschauung*, or general world view. (One can draw here upon the important literature of that concept, from Wilhelm von Humboldt and Friedrich Schleiermacher to Wilhelm Dil-they, from Karl Jaspers to Ernst Topitsch, and from Philipp Frank to the present.)

9. The interaction at a given time between the scientific world picture and the other components making up the more general world view has feedback effects on the notion of scientific progress. Well-known exam-ples are the impact of Darwinian and Freudian conceptions on contem-porary culture, or conversely, the recently surfacing effect which chang-ing social attitudes toward risk and limits have had on laboratory work in biomedical sciences. These are illustrations, too, of problems that arise when two or more concepts of "progress" come into conflict.

10. It may be argued that the definition of scientific progress in our time is therefore shifting, for better or worse, away from the Ptolemaic model in which science itself has been at the center. It is moving instead

to a cluster-of-galaxies model. In this the progressiveness of a particular scientific research program takes on meaning both with reference to the scientific Weltbild, in which the research is embedded, and also with reference to the general world view, of which the scientific Weltbild is a part.

11. Clearly, when the contemporary scientific Weltbild is not isolated from the general world view but exists in strong interaction with it, good scientific progress is not only likely to occur (as could be, for a time, even in a condition of relative isolation), but is likely to yield writings that transcend the disciplinary boundaries and speak to a wide audience beyond the profession itself. That is just the kind of work which, for about half a century, has been most conspicuous by its rarity.

Physics

Admitting, therefore, the likely absence of members of this fifth category, the stage has now been set for the presentation of our candidates for some version of "great book" status in physics, as one representative science, in the twentieth century. It was very tempting to arrange these books along main axes of development, such as experimental versus theoretical science, or with an eye to thematic opposites such as the triumph of atomicity in electricity, energy, and matter versus the triumph of mathematization and formalization in physics. But, on balance, the most reasonable order to adopt has seemed one that follows rather closely the historical development of the branches of physics in this century: thermodynamics and statistical mechanics; electron theory; radioactivity; the old quantum theory; relativity; quantum mechanics; and a last category of special cases (textbooks, and "one-of-a-kind" books). There are thirty-nine books to be discussed, and in each case, as noted above, mention has been made of the contemporary view of the books. The esteem in which these books are held now is indicated by the fact that the "votes" of our correspondents serve to supplement our own judgment of these books' historic importance.

1. Thermodynamics and statistical mechanics

Max Planck, *Vorlesungen über Thermodynamik* [Lectures on Thermodynamics].

Few figures in the recent history of physics have influenced the course of its development more profoundly than Max Planck. Few treatises in physics have reached such a wide audience as his *Vorlesungen über Thermodynamik*.

Planck was born in 1858. He completed his doctoral work at the University of Munich in 1879 with a dissertation on the second law of thermodynamics. In 1888 he was appointed assistant professor at the University of Berlin and director of the newly established Institute for Theoretical Physics at that institution. He remained there until 1926 and died in 1947. Thus, his lifetime spanned the years in which theoretical physics emerged as a professional discipline. He witnessed and participated in the remarkable scientific developments of the first half of the twentieth century. In 1918 he was awarded the Nobel Prize for Physics "in recognition of the services he rendered to the advancement of Physics by his discovery of energy quanta" —a concept that in fact stems from one of his publications in 1900.

His earlier work showed his power. The first edition of Planck's *Vorlesungen über Thermodynamik* was published in 1897—close enough to 1900 to stretch the point. The eleventh German edition appeared in 1966. In the meantime it had been translated into Russian (1900), French (1913), Spanish (1922), Japanese (1932), and three times into English between 1903 and 1927.

In the preface which Planck wrote for the first edition he stated:

> The often-repeated requests either to publish my collected papers on Thermodynamics, or to work them up into a comprehensive treatise, first suggested the writing of this book. Although the first plan would have been the simpler, especially as I found no occasion to make any important changes in the line of thought of my original papers, yet I decided to rewrite the whole subject matter, with the intention of giving at greater length, and with more detail, certain general considerations and demonstrations too concisely expressed in these papers. My chief reason, however, was that opportunity was offered of presenting the entire field of Thermodynamics from a uniform point of view.

Planck's treatment of the subject of thermodynamics differed from those of earlier and contemporary thermodynamicists, such as Joule, Clausius, Boltzmann, and Helmholtz, in that Planck avoided using any mechanical theory for the nature of heat. During the years when Planck was issuing new editions on the average of one every five years, each publication was very useful to those seeking to learn the latest perspective on thermodynamics from a highly authoritative source. In retrospect, the set of individual editions provides a comprehensive, if individual, view of the evolution of thermodynamics.

In terms of our evaluation criteria, there are few books of twentieth-century physics that rate as highly as does this and another one by Planck, *Wärmestrahlung* (Heat Radiation), to be discussed below. They are distinguished for innovative material, both factual and perspective; for prompt, wide, and long-term dissemination within the discipline; for the authoritative didactic role they have played; for the fecundity of their content; and for their historical significance from the present-day perspective.

J. W. Gibbs, *Elementary Principles of Statistical Mechanics*.
Josiah Willard Gibbs (1839–1903), America's first and in his time lone

theoretical physicist, worked in practical isolation in New Haven at Yale University during the final decades of the nineteenth century and until his death in 1903. By reading and correspondence Gibbs kept in touch with developments in Europe, where he had studied between the time of taking his Ph.D. at Yale in 1863 (the first doctorate of engineering to be conferred in the U.S.) and his return there in 1869. His work was much better known in Europe. In the United States there were few if any who could comprehend him. His classic monograph on thermodynamics, "On the Equilibrium of Heterogeneous Substances," published originally in the relative obscurity of the *Transactions of the Connecticut Academy of Arts and Sciences*, was well known in Europe through its translations into French by Henri Louis Le Chatelier and into German by Friedrich Wilhelm Ostwald. Gibbs himself took the initiative of sending copies of his papers to a sizable international list of fellow scientists.

Gibbs was long interested in the connections between statistical mechanics and thermodynamics. But he published virtually nothing on this topic until 1902, when his book, *Elementary Principles in Statistical Mechanics, Developed with Especial Reference to the Rational Foundation of Thermodynamics*, was published in New York by Charles Scribner's Sons and in London by Edward Arnold. According to Martin Klein, Gibbs's biographer in the *Dictionary of Scientific Biography:*

> The principal theme of Gibbs's book is the analogy, as he
> describes it, between the average behavior of a canonical ensemble
> of systems and the behavior of a physical system obeying the laws
> of thermodynamics. . . .
>
> Gibbs was very much aware of the gaps in his statistical mechanics.
> He had supplied a "rational foundation" for thermodynamics in
> statistical mechanics to the extent that thermodynamic systems could be
> treated as if they were conservative mechanical systems with a finite
> number of degrees of freedom. He could not incorporate the
> phenomena of radiation that were of so much interest at the turn of
> the century, nor could he surmount the long-standing difficulties
> associated with the theorem of the equipartition of energy. . . .
>
> Despite these difficulties Gibbs's work in statistical mechanics
> constituted a major advance. His methods were more general and
> more readily applicable than Boltzmann's and eventually came to
> dominate the whole field. Gibbs did not live to see the real successes of
> statistical mechanics, for his fatal illness came within a year of the
> publication of his book.

In 1902 G. H. Bryan, reviewing Gibbs's book in *Nature,* commented:

> By clothing the investigation in new language, under the title of
> "Statistical Dynamics," [Gibbs] has presented it in a form in which it
> can be studied quite independently of any molecular hypothesis as a
> purely mathematical deduction from the fundamental principles of
> dynamics. . . .

The book became known for both its content and its style. Almost thirty years later, when J. R. Oppenheimer was reviewing Dirac's book *The Principles of Quantum Mechanics,* he likened it to Gibbs's *Statistical Mechanics,* saying:

> In some very fundamental respects Dirac's book is like Gibbs's *Elementary Principles of Statistical Mechanics:* It is clear, with a clarity dangerous for a beginner; deductive, and in its foundations abstract; its argument is predominantly analytical; the virtual contact with experiment is made quite late in the book.

Erwin Schrödinger, *Statistical Thermodynamics.*

Erwin Schrödinger (1887–1961) was one of the architects of quantum mechanics in the 1920s, his name being virtually synonymous with wave mechanics. In 1927 he succeeded Max Planck in the chair of theoretical physics at the University of Berlin and remained there until 1933 when, upset by the injustices to which he saw many of his colleagues subjected, he accepted a position at the University of Oxford. Homesick for Austria (Schrödinger was born in Vienna), he left Oxford in 1936 for a post at the University of Graz. But the political situation deteriorated there also, and he was dismissed without notice in 1938. Fortunately, he was then able to return to Oxford, and ultimately he was appointed to the newly established Dublin Institute for Advanced Studies.

Schrödinger stayed in Dublin at the Institute from 1939 to 1956. There he was able to continue his work, and the presence of a steady stream of visiting physicists helped to overcome his isolation.

During those years Schrödinger broadened his perspective to include "a thorough study of the foundations of physics and their implications for philosophy and for the development of a world view," as noted by Armin Hermann in his biographical sketch of Schrödinger in the *Dictionary of Scientific Biography.*

Between January and March of 1944 Schrödinger delivered a course of seminar lectures at the Institute's School of Theoretical Physics entitled *Statistical Thermodynamics.* The nine sections, as published by Cambridge University Press in 1946, filled a mere eighty-eight pages.

Statistical Thermodynamics was clearly addressed to mature physicists. Schrödinger had worked and published in this area before becoming involved in quantum theory. In these lectures he revisited what for him was old territory, with new insights gained since the advent of quantum mechanics. His treatment was immediately appreciated by fellow physicists. Max Born, writing in *Nature* in 1944, decribed the as yet unpublished work as "not an ordinary text-book ... but an informal communication of ideas, fascinating [and] amusing."

2. Electron theory

J. J. Thomson, *Conduction of Electricity Through Gases.*

J. J. Thomson's book, *Conduction of Electricity Through Gases*, was initially published by the Cambridge University Press in 1903. By the time the second edition appeared in 1906, the first had been translated into German and published by B. J. Teubner of Leipzig. Many years later a two-volume, third edition was prepared by Thomson, aided by his son G. P. Thomson.

In the preface to the first edition, Thomson described the work as an endeavor

> to develop the view that the conduction of electricity through gases is due to the presence in the gas of small particles charged with electricity, called ions, which under the influence of electric forces move from one part of the gas to another. My object has been to show how the various phenomena exhibited when electricity passes through gases can be coordinated by this conception rather than to attempt to give a complete account of the very numerous investigations which have been made on the electrical properties of gases; I have therefore confined myself for the most part to those phenomena which furnish results sufficiently precise to serve as a test of the truth of this theory. The book contains the subject-matter of lectures given at the Cavendish Laboratory, where a good deal of attention has been paid to the subject and where a considerable number of physicists are working at it.

At the time of writing, Thomson was Cavendish Professor of Experimental Physics at the University of Cambridge, a post he had held since 1884 when he succeeded Lord Rayleigh, who in turn had been successor of James Clerk Maxwell in this prestigious position. Thomson was a successful leader of laboratory activity. Under him the Cavendish Laboratory came to be a mecca for young physics students of several nations. These were called research students and they were admitted for the first time in 1895. Most of them spent two years with Thomson. Among those from the early years who later became well known were Ernest Rutherford, Paul Langevin, C. T. R. Wilson, and Theodore Lyman.

Thomson visited the United States twice, lecturing in 1896 at Princeton University and in 1903 at Yale. Both occasions resulted in the publication of books based on Thomson's lectures. They were *The Discharge of Electricity Through Gases* (1898), and *Electricity and Matter* (1904).

Conduction of Electricity Through Gases was concerned with the same general topics as were those lectures, but in this case the presentation was more comprehensive. Among the topics covered were the determination of the ratio of charge to mass of charged particles by means of magnetic deflection; producing ionization by heat, light, or the action of Röntgen rays; the nature of rays from radioactive substances; and the effect of pressure on gaseous discharge.

One of the most important of Thomson's results was the clear identification of cathode rays (*i.e.*, rays which emanate from the negative electrode in a discharge tube and cause fluorescence when they strike the glass walls of such tubes) as consisting of negatively charged particles of very small mass — "electrons." The nature of these rays had long been the subject of controversy. Some, like Philipp Lenard, had held them to be electromagnetic in nature, akin to ultraviolet light. Thomson was awarded the Nobel Prize for Physics in 1906 "in recognition of the great merits of his theoretical and experimental investigations on the conduction of electricity by gases."

Thomson's book was highly regarded from the start and quickly earned a reputation as an indispensable work. That it is still considered a classic is attested by the respondents to our letter of inquiry for nominations of books.

H. A. Lorentz, *The Theory of Electrons and Its Application to the Phenomena of Light and Radiant Heat.*

Lorentz was born in The Netherlands in 1853, received his education in that country, and in 1877 became professor of theoretical physics at the University of Leiden, where he had just two years before earned his Ph.D. summa cum laude. His dissertation dealt with physical optics from the viewpoint of Maxwell and Helmholtz.

Lorentz's most original contribution to theoretical physics was his theory of the electron, which he published in a series of papers beginning in 1892. By 1904 he had largely completed this undertaking.

Lorentz's biographer, Russell McCormmach, commenting in the *Dictionary of Scientific Biography,* says that "for Lorentz, as for others, the electron theory opened up a vast number of new experimental and theoretical directions. Much of the physics community now looked to Leiden for guidance. . . . Lorentz' electron theory became widely adopted, especially on the Continent around 1900."

In 1902 Lorentz shared the Nobel Prize for Physics with Pieter Zeeman "in recognition of the extraordinary service they rendered by their researches into the influence of magnetism upon radiation phenomena." In the biography of Lorentz prepared for the volume *Nobel Lectures in Physics, 1901–1921* it is said that

> from Lorentz stems the conception of the electron: his view that this
> minute electrically charged particle plays a role during electromagnetic
> phenomena in ponderable matter made it possible to apply molecular
> theory to the theory of electricity, and to explain the behavior of light
> waves passing through moving transparent bodies. . . . It may well be
> said that Lorentz was regarded by all theoretical physicists as the
> world's leading spirit, who completed what was left unfinished by
> predecessors and prepared the ground for the fruitful reception of the
> new ideas based on quantum theory.

In the spring of 1906 Lorentz accepted an invitation to deliver a series of lectures at Columbia University, for which he made his first visit to the

United States. The text of these lectures was published in 1909 as *The Theory of Electrons and its Application to the Phenomena of Light and Radiant Heat.* The lectures dealt with the theory of free electrons, the emission and absorption of heat, the theory of the Zeeman effect, the propagation of light in a body composed of molecules, the theory of the inverse Zeeman effect, and optical phenomena in moving bodies.

A. P. Wills, professor of physics at Columbia University, reviewed Lorentz's work for *Science* in 1910. "It was naturally expected," he wrote

> that this book by an author who is himself responsible for a large part
> in the remarkable development of the modern theory of electrons,
> would prove of absorbing interest to physicists and to those in general
> who have any knowledge of the importance and fascination of the
> subject. As was expected, this is the case. . . . Throughout, the reader
> meets with the usual clear methods of exposition so characteristic of all
> the author's writings.

The book is still in print to this day, having been thumbed over by students and researchers for decades.

Robert A. Millikan, *The Electron: Its Isolation and Measurement and the Determination of Some of Its Properties.*

Soon after the completion of his studies on the photoelectric effect in 1916, Robert A. Millikan wrote *The Electron: Its Isolation and Measurement and the Determination of Some of Its Properties,* issued in 1917 by the University of Chicago Press and by the Cambridge University Press in Great Britain. Millikan included a detailed, firsthand description of the research he had been carrying out over the preceding decade at the University of Chicago on the determination of the unit of electric charge by means of his oil-drop method, and on the photoelectric effect in which electrons are ejected from a metallic surface under illumination of suitable wavelength. These were indeed two first-rate experimental achievements, for which Millikan received the Nobel Prize for Physics in 1923.

In this book Millikan presented his results not in isolation but within the context of the time, beginning with a historical discussion of the emergence of the concept of a unit of electric charge in the 1890s and the early work of J. J. Thomson and others. Basing his conclusions on his own published papers (often by quoting from them at great length), he included a refutation of the subelectron advanced by Felix Ehrenhaft and a description of the emerging ideas on the structure of atoms and the nature of radiant energy based on the work of Bohr, Planck, Einstein, and others. Millikan's own work was related to all of these, and it appears all the more noteworthy when viewed in that broad perspective.

Millikan brought out an updated second edition of *The Electron* in 1924. In 1935 it was further expanded and modernized and given a new title,

Electrons (+ *and* −), *Protons, Photons, Neutrons, Cosmic Rays.* By that time Millikan had engaged in cosmic ray investigation, though with results that were not as triumphant as his early ones on electric charge and photoelectric phenomena. The final revision of the work, *Electrons* (+ *and* −), *Protons, Photons, Neutrons, Cosmic Rays,* appeared in 1947 when Millikan was seventy-nine years old.

Edward U. Condon, in his discussion of the 1935 edition in *Review of Scientific Instruments,* wrote:

> It is safe to say that the whole of the present generation of American physicists has derived inspiration from Millikan's famous little red book *The Electron.* Now we have a second edition that is double the size of the old book and tells a moving dramatic story that carries us through the recent experimental discoveries of new fundamental particles. The same vivid writing which made Millikan's first edition a classic is here so that professors who have brilliant undergraduates to be lured into physics can do no better than to feed them on this book. Likewise any of my own generation, approaching that senility of thirty-five which has been so touchingly portrayed by Ring Lardner, may become young again by reading this book. Millikan's youthful enthusiasm is extremely contagious.

Nevertheless, as Millikan's most important scientific work was done before 1920, it is the 1917 edition of *The Electron* that is considered the "classic" version. In recognition of this, it was reproduced in facsimile by the University of Chicago Press in 1963.

3. Radioactivity

Marie Curie, *Recherches sur les substances radioactives* [Investigations of Radioactive Substances].

Few if any doctoral theses, before or since, have received attention comparable with that accorded Marie Curie's *Recherches sur les substances radioactives.* This slim volume, less than 100 pages in length, was published in Paris by Gauthier-Villars in 1903, about the time that Mme. Curie was awarded her doctorate of science by the University of Paris. By the end of 1904 there had been printed a slightly revised edition in French, and translations also appeared in both English and German. In more recent times the English version has been reprinted twice in the United States, first in 1961 and again in 1971.

The dissemination of the work in English began within weeks of its original appearance in French. Mme. Curie's public defense of her thesis took place on June 25. On August 21 *The Chemical News* of London began serialized publication, which was completed on December 4. In 1904 these installments were reprinted as a separate pamphlet, *Radioactive Substances.*

The German translation, issued in 1904, was done by the distinguished physicist W. Kaufman, who also added an introduction and a list of journal

publications related to radioactivity. Further testimony to the book's importance in German scientific circles is the fact that it was issued as the first
volume of a new Vieweg series of scientific and mathematical monographs,
entitled *Die Wissenschaft*, under the direction of E. Wiedemann.

Unusual as it may be for a doctoral thesis to be so widely and promptly
disseminated, it is not surprising when we consider the situation with respect to radioactivity that prevailed in 1903. Although radioactivity was
discovered by Henri Becquerel in 1896, little or no follow-up work was done
before 1898; even then, investigators were few and far between, literally, in
a geographical sense. Five years later, in 1903, interest in radioactivity,
based on results already published in scientific journals, was high among
members of the international scientific community. The Curie thesis was
the first monographic treatment of the subject, and included a survey of the
work of others as well as a presentation of the experimental results obtained
by Pierre and Marie Curie. These were notable in their own right and for
the theoretical interpretations which the Curies largely left to others.

During 1903 the work on radioactivity done by the Curies was accorded
public international acclaim on at least three occasions. Pierre was invited
to describe their work in a talk before the Royal Institution in London
delivered in June, just one week before Marie received her degree with the
citation "très honorable." In November they were jointly awarded the Davy
Medal by the Royal Society of London. Also in November, the Nobel Prize
Committee announced that the 1903 Prize for Physics would be awarded
jointly to Becquerel and the Curies for their discoveries in the field of
radioactivity.

By 1904 the original Curie thesis was no longer unique as a publication
in the field of radioactivity. In that year Ernest Rutherford brought out the
first edition of his more comprehensive treatment, entitled *Radioactivity*, and
works by other authors such as F. Soddy also appeared.

The study of radioactivity continued for a decade or more to provide a
series of new and illuminating discoveries which required further, up-to-
date publications, among which were later editions of Rutherford's *Radioactivity* and Marie Curie's own *Traité de radioactivité* [Treatise on Radioactivity]
(1910), a two-volume work corresponding to the lecture course she gave at
the Sorbonne after Pierre's death. This latter Curie work is regarded by
some as a classic in its own right.

Ernest Rutherford's books on radioactivity.
In the early years of the twentieth century interest in the topic of radioactivity was high, and Ernest Rutherford was recognized throughout the
world of physics as one of the most active and productive investigators in
this recently emerging field.

Rutherford was born in New Zealand in 1871 and received his basic
scientific education there. A scholarship enabled him to join the Cavendish

Laboratory at the University of Cambridge in 1895, where his first work on radioactivity was done under J. J. Thomson. Rutherford continued his investigations, particularly on the nature of radioactive emanations, at McGill University in Montreal. He was made professor of physics there in 1898 at the age of twenty-seven, apparently as the result of Thomson's testimonial: "I have never had a student with more enthusiasm or ability for original research than Mr. Rutherford."

Rutherford, an outgoing person who traveled widely, was well known in contemporary scientific circles when his book *Radioactivity* was first published in 1904. Carl Barus, commenting in a 1905 issue of *Science* upon other books on that topic which had appeared in recent years, stated:

> But Mr. Rutherford's book is on quite a different scale from most of these, and written in a way that betrays consummate mastery of the subject. One would have been grateful if he had given us merely a systematic account of his own researches. The book before us does much more than this, presenting a readable and most painstaking digest of the subject as a whole, or at least that splendid part of it which owes its development chiefly to English genius.

In a review of Marie Curie's *Recherches sur les substances radioactives,* also in *Science* but a year earlier, R. A. Millikan said:

> Of the half dozen books which have recently appeared on radioactivity, two are of commanding importance, for they contain the records of the epoch-making work of the two investigators to whom we are most largely indebted for our present knowledge of the phenomena in question, E. Rutherford and Mme. Curie. Of these two wholly dissimilar treatments the former is the more comprehensive and perhaps the more suggestive; for, from beginning to end it is a presentation of a well-developed theory of the cause and nature of radioactivity. Facts are everywhere grouped about, and fitted into, and interpreted in the light of this theory.

Among the topics set forth by Rutherford were: the experimental aspects of radioactivity (results and techniques), the nature of the emanated rays, the theory of atomic disintegration, and the application of arguments based on radioactivity to the determination of the age of the Earth and the Sun.

A second edition of this work was published in 1905. It contains in the preface an apology by Rutherford for the shortness of time elapsed between editions, but with the explanation that

> though only a year has passed since the book first made its appearance, the researches that have been carried out in that time have been too numerous and of too important a character to permit the publishing of a mere reprint, unless the author were to relinquish his purpose of presenting the subject as it stands at the present moment.

Carl Barus, reviewing this new edition in *Science,* noted that

> among the more conspicous novelties are the chapters on the
> transformation products of uranium, thorium, actinium, radium and
> on the rate of emission of energy.

In 1913 a new volume by Rutherford, *Radioactive Substances and Their Radiations,* brought the discussion of radioactivity up to that date. Among the new material now incorporated by Rutherford were further information on the behavior of α, β, and γ rays as they passed through matter, new methods for counting individual particles, the resolution of β rays from radium C into several homogeneous components, and the recognition of thirty-two radiation products of disintegration, an increase of twelve over what was known in 1905.

It was not until 1930 that Rutherford got around to publishing a sequel, *Radiations from Radioactive Substances.* He was aided in the new enterprise by James Chadwick and C. D. Ellis, whose names appear with him. The reception was again excellent at every level. For example, when Enrico Fermi and his younger colleagues at the University of Rome decided to go into nuclear physics research, this was the book they chose for their self-tutoring seminar. Although several other treatises on radioactivity had appeared by that time, "Rutherford, Chadwick, and Ellis," as it is referred to far more often than by its formal title, remained the standard text on radioactivity for many years. In the reviews, it is interesting to note the repeated reference to the lack of mathematics needed to follow the book. This was probably the last time in the twentieth century that physicists could delve into a new and exciting topic without the need for sophisticated mathematical tools.

Frederick Soddy, *The Chemistry of the Radio-Elements.*

Frederick Soddy (1877–1956) was trained as a chemist at the University of Oxford, where he received a first-class honors degree in 1898. His involvement with the burgeoning new field of radioactivity came largely as the result of work done with Ernest Rutherford at McGill University in Montreal, where Soddy had secured a position as demonstrator in 1900. As noted by Soddy's biographer, Thaddeus J. Trenn, in the *Dictionary of Scientific Biography:*

> Soddy developed with Lord Rutherford during 1901–1903 the
> disintegration theory of radioactivity, confirmed with Sir William
> Ramsay in 1903 the production of helium from radium, advanced in
> 1910 the *concept* of isotope, proposed in 1911 the alpha-ray rule leading
> to the full displacement law of 1913, and was the 1921 Nobel laureate
> in chemistry, principally for his investigations into the origin and
> nature of isotopes.

At the time when Soddy wrote his two-part work, *The Chemistry of the Radio-Elements,* he was a lecturer in physical chemistry and radioactivity at the University of Glasgow, an appointment he had received in 1904.

While physicists and laymen tend to think of radioactivity as being chiefly in the domain of physics, it has chemical aspects as well, not only in terms of the deeper understanding of the nature of elements and the make-up of the periodic table, but also because investigations into radioactivity involved the use of both established and novel chemical techniques for separation and recognition.

It was to this aspect that Soddy addressed himself. What became the first volume of a two-part publication began with the 1911 appearance of Soddy's *Chemistry of the Radio-Elements.* Soddy indicated the scope of his presentation in the opening paragraph:

> Radioactivity has introduced into the science of chemistry a new conception. The radioactive elements are radioactive because they are in progress of spontaneous change. The chemistry of the radio-elements is concerned largely with the nature of the products of these changes, their isolation and separate identification.

B. B. Boltwood, reviewing this publication in *Science* in 1912, remarked:

> It contains the essence of a new branch of science, radiochemistry, and Mr. Soddy has succeeded in collecting together and presenting in a relatively small space, and in a very impressive and convincing manner, much that has previously been accessible only in scattered scientific publications of his own and of other workers in this field of scientific inquiry. . . . Mr. Soddy has provided us with a very valuable book of its kind, unique in respect to the field it covers. It need scarcely be added that no one who desires to work intelligently in this modern branch of chemistry can well afford to be without it.

A German translation of this monograph, *Die Chemie der Radioelemente,* was prepared by Max Iklé and published in 1912, and a second English edition was published in 1915.

In 1914 there appeared *The Chemistry of the Radio-Elements Part II: The Radio-Elements and the Periodic Law,* another slim pamphlet. By this time, through the work of Soddy and others, the components of the various radioactive disintegration series had become unmistakably recognized as chemically indistinguishable from known elements. Thus Soddy could set forth confidently the periodic law: when an atom emits an α particle, its chemical nature changes to that of the element two places lower (or to the left) in the periodic table; when an atom emits a β particle, it is transformed into the element one place higher (or to the right) in the periodic table.

Although chemically indistinguishable from the familiar elements, the new atoms produced through radioactive decay were often physically quite different. For example, most of them were unstable. In order to take these differences into account, Soddy proposed the use of the word "isotope" (*i.e.,* "same place") to characterize the subsets of atoms belonging in a particular box in the periodic table. This was a very important step forward for basic understanding and for simplifying the nomenclature involved. For example, the chemically indistinguishable "ionium," "thorium," and "radio-thorium" could now all be called isotopes of thorium. Similarly, "mesothorium I" was recognized as an isotope of radium. In all, thirty-four radioactive products could be reclassified as ten isotopes of familiar elements.

Again the reviewers praised Soddy's book, and again a German translation was prepared by Max Iklé.

Soddy's presentation of the accumulated information on radioactive decay products in this two-part work was the culmination of years of investigation by many researchers. Soddy provided the perspective to illuminate the facts of radioactivity and also to integrate them into the established chemical framework.

The book itself had no multiple editions, perhaps just because the ideas set forth were promptly assimilated. When techniques were subsequently developed for the electromagnetic separation of isotopes, the results were readily understood in terms of the nomenclature and laws Soddy had proposed. Even the diagramatic presentation of radioactive decay series, which Soddy introduced, became a universal teaching tool without general recognition of where it had originated.

Thus, we rate *The Chemistry of the Radio-Elements* high with regard to innovation, interdisciplinary impact, fecundity, and long-term appreciation. This is undoubtedly the most important of Soddy's many writings, which ranged from the scientific (technical and popular) to works on economics and on science and society.

4. The old quantum theory

Max Planck, *Vorlesungen über die Theorie der Wärmestrahlung* [Lectures on the Theory of Heat Radiation].

In addition to Max Planck's, *Vorlesungen über Thermodynamik* which we have already discussed as a putative classic of twentieth-century physics, his *Vorlesungen über die Theorie der Wärmestrahlung* stands out as at least an equally important and influential treatise. It also evolved through several editions (five between 1906 and 1923, with a sixth in 1966), and was likewise pedagogical, being based on Planck's lectures at the University of Berlin. But the fact that it was virtually the first book that used quantum-theoretical argument, coupled with the fact that Planck himself had been responsible for the introduction of the quantum concept, confers a special status on this book. As his biographer, H. Kangro, commented: "Planck's contribution to the theory of heat radiation comprised the adroit combination of his studies on irreversibility with the new electrodynamics." One of the earliest reviews of the book, in the 1906 volume of the *Beiblätter der Annalen der Physik* [Supplement to the Annals of Physics] was by young Albert Einstein. He wrote an extensive analysis, and expressed his admiration for the exposition as a "wonderfully clear and unified whole."

Planck's book played a significant role in the dissemination of quantum theory, particularly in the United States, where from about 1910 on several universities began offering a graduate level course in physics which specifically referred to the use of Planck's *Wärmestrahlung*. When the English edition, *The Theory of Heat Radiation,* was published in 1913, translator Morton Masius wrote in his preface:

> The profoundly original ideas introduced by Planck in the endeavor to reconcile the electromagnetic theory of radiation with the experimental facts have proven to be of greatest importance in many parts of physics. Probably no single book since the appearance of Clerk Maxwell's *Electricity and Magnetism* has had a deeper influence on the development of physical theories.

Arnold Sommerfeld, *Atombau und Spektrallinien* [Atomic Structure and Spectral Lines].

Arnold Sommerfeld's *Atombau und Spektrallinien* was first published in 1919. Second, third, and fourth editions followed rapidly in 1921, 1922, and 1924. An English translation of the third edition and a French translation were both published in 1923. Following the advent of quantum mechanics, Sommerfeld brought out in 1929 a volume entitled *Wellenmechanischer Ergänzungsband* [Supplementary Volume on Wave Mechanics]. One reviewer, John Slater, in 1930 regarded this as "the most successful book on that very new subject which has yet appeared." It was promptly published in English. In its fifth edition, *Atombau* became a two-volume work, the first dealing largely with empirical facts and older theory appearing in 1931, the second, an updated version of the *Ergänzungsband,* in 1939. Each of the successive editions of this work was widely and warmly reviewed.

That this was an extraordinary publication is evident from stories about its early distribution. Few copies of the first edition reached the United States. Three American physicists who appear to have owned copies of the first edition were P. W. Bridgman, A. H. Compton, and I. Langmuir. Langmuir cited *Atombau,* 1919, in one of his papers. Compton was reported by Carl Eckart to have told him that he had brought the first copy to the United States when he returned from Cambridge in 1920. Karl Compton, however, in his presidential address to the American Association for the Advancement of Science in 1936 stated:

> I well remember when the first copy of Sommerfeld's *Atombau und Spektrallinien* came to America in the possession of P. W. Bridgman. Until later copies arrived, he knew no peace and enjoyed no privacy, for he was besieged by friends wanting to read the book—which he would not allow out of his possession.

The subsequent editions, and their English translations when available, were commonly used in American university courses for graduate students. It was regarded as a feather in one's cap to have one's work cited in *Atombau,* and a few Americans, such as E. C. Kemble and F. W. Loomis, were among the earliest to achieve this status.

Sommerfeld, who had been responsible for extending the Bohr atomic theory to include elliptic orbits, brought together in his book all the material then known to pertain to atomic structure as revealed by spectroscopic evidence. In the years before 1925 it held a unique place as a reference book as well as a textbook. In the post-quantum mechanical years, the fifth and last edition was valued as a work that bridged the old and new theories and bore the characteristic Sommerfeld style and clarity. In the words of John Slater in 1940:

> No one who followed atomic theory and spectroscopy in their earlier days can forget the part which Sommerfeld's *Atombau* played in the development of physics. For a number of years it was practically the physicist's bible; all that was true and valuable could be found in it. As each new edition came out, it was scanned to see what were the latest developments, and to read Professor Sommerfeld's beautifully clear exposition of things which might have been confusing and difficult to read in the original papers.

Further evidence of its recognized place in the dissemination of quantum theory can be seen in the fact that virtually every American theoretical physicist who became professionally active during the early 1920s, as well as others trained in Europe, when interviewed by the American Physical Society's Project on the History of Quantum Physics, spoke of having used the *Atombau* as his introduction to the serious study of quantum theory. Finally, of all the works suggested by respondents to our letter asking for nominations of twentieth-century books to be considered as "great," *Atombau* was included on about one-quarter of the lists, an unusual percentage.

From the perspective of our criteria, *Atombau* rates especially high as a work that was widely disseminated and kept in print through five editions spanning twenty years. It played a strong didactic role among young persons entering the field and among established physicists seeking to keep abreast of latest developments. While little or no material not already published elsewhere was contained in it, *Atombau* served the valued function of organizing and giving perspective to the latest development.

Its up-to-dateness and its authority, indicated by the frequent application of the words "yearbook" and "bible" to describe it, were the outstanding characteristics that ensured its usefulness. Its style enhanced this usefulness and made it universally admired in the physics profession.

Niels Bohr, *The Theory of Spectra and Atomic Constitution.*
The Theory of Spectra and Atomic Constitution was first published by the Cambridge University Press in 1922, the year in which Bohr was awarded the Nobel Prize for Physics "for his service in the investigation of the structure of atoms and of the radiation emanating from them." The content of the book, however, had come into being gradually during the preceding decade and was based on lecture presentations. (Bohr never did write a book about his theory.)

The first part, "On the Spectrum of Hydrogen," called Essay 1 in the book, is a translation of a historic address given before the Physical Society of Copenhagen on December 20, 1913 and subsequently printed in *Fysik Tidsskrift* [Journal of Physics]. In it Bohr set forth his bold assumptions on the orbital structure of the hydrogen atom and the attendant energy levels associated with radiation, relating his ideas to those of Planck and Rutherford. This was the launching of the "Bohr model" of the atom.

The second part of the book, Essay 2, "On the Series Spectra of the Elements," is a translation of an address before the Physical Society in Berlin on April 27, 1920, later printed in *Zeitschrift für Physik* [Journal of Physics]. It covers the related developments of the intervening years and introduces the correspondence principle to bridge the gap between quantum theory and classical electrodynamics.

The third part, Essay 3, "The Structure of the Atom and the Physical and Chemical Properties of the Elements," was originally an address before a joint meeting of the Physical and Chemical Societies of Copenhagen, October 18, 1921 and printed in *Fysik Tidsskrift*. It set forth the way that Bohr's theory could be used to understand the structure of the periodic table.

These essays were translated into English by A. D. Udden, a young American physicist who had come to study at Bohr's Institute during 1921–22. A German translation was published in 1922. Two years later, a second edition of the original book was issued by the Cambridge University Press in which the three essays were left intact but an appendix was added by Bohr to give a brief account of recent developments.

Throughout his presentation Bohr stressed the difficulties and the tentative nature of his theory. In the preface to the first edition he stated:

It . . . may be said that hitherto every progress in the problem of
atomic structure has tended to emphasize the well-known "mysteries"
of the quantum theory more and more. I hope the exposition in these
essays is sufficiently clear, nevertheless, to give the reader an
impression of the peculiar charm which the study of atomic physics
possesses just on this account.

The "peculiar charm" of the "old quantum theory"—the phrase adopted when quantum mechanics arrived a few years later—is nowhere better displayed than in this book, which stands as a progress report of the decade

1913–22 of the work of one of the seminal figures in the history of physics.

By 1923 Bohr's ideas on atomic structure were well known among physicists and chemists throughout the international scientific community. In the fall of 1923 he made a trip to the United States during which he lectured at a number of universities, met with individual physicists, and addressed a meeting of the American Physical Society in Chicago. His Institute for Theoretical Physics at the University of Copenhagen had become the place to go for aspiring theoretical physicists from many nations in the early 1920s. Bohr's ideas were also being assimilated during this period by chemists, at least by those in the United States.

Bohr's *Theory of Spectra and Atomic Constitution* was warmly received internationally. In his review of the second edition of Bohr's book (1925), R. H. Fowler was moved to say:

> If this interpretation of the situation is correct, and we may write *Finis*
> to the central orbit theory, a superficial feeling of disappointment is
> perhaps inevitable, but still more certainly unjust. Every valuable
> theory in process of development must raise hopes that are naturally
> extravagant. We have only to contemplate for a moment the successes
> of the theory, and the beautiful correlations it has introduced into such
> a wide range of physical and chemical properties—to read once again
> Prof. Bohr's book—to lose all feelings of disappointment, and rest
> convinced that the theory, like the nuclear theory from which it
> springs, will remain a fundamental link in the chain of physical science.

Herein lies the value of this book from the perspective of today. It not only traces the development of the Bohr atomic theory but summarizes its achievements and its limitations in the final years of its ascendancy. Furthermore, even today the Bohr theory continues to live in the pages of those books which introduce young physicists and chemists to their science.

Louis de Broglie, *Recherches sur la théorie des quanta* [Investigations on Quantum Theory].

As a student at the University of Paris in the early 1920s, Louis de Broglie was not in the mainstream of activity related to the development of quantum theory that was taking place in Copenhagen and in Munich. He was, however, far from being a typical student; he was older (twenty-eight in 1920) than most as a result of the wartime interruption of his studies. His brother, Maurice, eighteen years his senior, was an established experimental physicist with his own laboratory working in the field of X-rays, and Louis had been allowed to participate to some extent. Also, Maurice had been present at the first Solvay Congress in 1911, where quanta were the principal topic of discussion among the leading theoretical physicists of Europe gathered for the Congress. Maurice was responsible for preparing the proceedings of the Congress for publication and showed the proofs to his brother Louis. As a result, so much enthusiasm was generated in the younger man that he decided to devote himself "to the study of these mysterious quanta," according to his scientific autobiography (as yet unpublished). A voracious reader, Louis de Broglie familiarized himself with the works of Poincaré, Planck, and Einstein. He was especially fascinated by Einstein's work on the theory of relativity and on the dual nature of light. All this awakening of de Broglie's interest took place before he left for military service in October 1913, a service that was not completed until August 1919.

The work that brought the younger de Broglie to the attention of the international community was his *Recherches sur la théorie des quanta* (Paris: Masson et Cie, 1924). It was his doctoral thesis, in which he set forth the startling idea that material particles, such as electrons, have a wave as well as corpuscular nature, analogous to the duality that was becoming generally accepted at that time for photons of light. Some discussion of these ideas had already been published by de Broglie in the *Comptes Rendus* in the autumn of 1923, following what de Broglie called "a sudden illumination" in the summer of 1923. But it was in his thesis that de Broglie gave their more complete development. He suggested that these particle waves should be detectable experimentally and have the wavelength $\lambda = h/mv$, where h is Planck's constant and mv is the momentum of the particles.

This was truly an innovative concept, and one that members of the scientific community initially greeted with interest coupled with skepticism. De Broglie's thesis supervisor, Paul Langevin, was among those who hesitated to accept the wave picture. Langevin sent a copy of de Broglie's thesis to Einstein before the thesis defense took place on November 25, 1924. Einstein responded favorably and called attention to de Broglie's work in a communication to the Berlin Academy in January 1925.

Before the decade of the '20s was over, de Broglie's conception had been absorbed into the wave mechanics of Schrödinger, experimental confirmation had been achieved in the experiments of Clinton Davisson and Lester Germer in the United States and of George P. Thomson in England, and the Nobel Prize for Physics had been awarded in 1929 to de Broglie "for his discovery of the wave nature of electrons."

Over the years, de Broglie has written a number of publications explicating the evolution of his ideas. Among those that have been translated into English are *Matière et lumière* (1937), translated as *Matter and Light: the New Physics* (1939), and *La physique nouvelle et les quanta* (1937), translated as *The Revolution in Physics: A Non-Mathematical Survey of Quanta* (1953). Especially during the last twenty-five years, de Broglie has become more vocal about his misgivings concerning the so-called Copenhagen interpretation of quantum theory, and has interested himself in the writings of those physicists who today support the concept of hidden variables.

It appears that de Broglie's thesis as such may not have had a very wide circulation, although it was translated into German in 1927 by Walther

Becker and published as *Untersuchungen zur Quantentheorie* [Investigations on Quantum Theory]. We have found no evidence of any translation into English.

In considering de Broglie's thesis as a classic of twentieth-century physics, the argument rests on its innovative material, its fecundity in stimulating the work of other physicists, and its historical significance as viewed from the present. However, the rapidity of advance of the science, which it helped to spur, prevented the book from achieving a large circulation of its own.

5. Relativity

Hermann Weyl, *Raum, Zeit, Materie* [Space, Time, Matter].

Hermann Weyl received his mathematical training in the early years of the twentieth century at the University of Göttingen with David Hilbert, and is now considered to have been Hilbert's most gifted student. Weyl, however, after receiving his Ph.D. in 1910, went on to penetrate fields untouched by his master. These included areas of mathematics and mathematical physics. Physicists involved with the new relativity and quantum theories were fortunate to have a mathematician of Weyl's stature interest himself in their concerns.

Weyl came to write two books which have long been recognized as classics in mathematical physics—studied perhaps more by physicists than by mathematicians. *Raum, Zeit, Materie,* published in 1918, had its inception in a series of lectures Weyl gave at the Eidgenössische Technische Hochschule in Zürich in the summer of 1917. Weyl was at the time professor of mathematics at the University of Zürich. In the preface to the first edition, Weyl wrote:

> Although very recently a whole series of more or less popular
> introductions into the general theory of relativity has appeared,
> nevertheless a systematic presentation was lacking. . . . it was my wish to
> present this great subject as an illustration of the intermingling of
> philosophical, mathematical and physical thought, a study which is dear
> to my heart. This could be done only by building up the theory
> systematically from the foundations, and by restricting attention
> throughout to the principles. But I have not been able to satisfy these
> self-imposed requirements: the mathematician predominates at the
> expense of the philosopher.

The work itself is divided into four chapters: "Euclidean Space: Its Mathematical Form and Its Role in Physics"; "The Metrical Continuum"; "Relativity of Space and Time"; and "General Theory of Relativity."

This was a very active publication in the sense that it was reprinted (but called a second edition) soon after it appeared initially; then in 1919 a third edition appeared with significant revision based on recent results achieved by Weyl and others; in 1920 the fourth edition came out, and the fifth in 1923. An English translation of this fourth edition was made by Henry L. Brose and published in 1922 as *Space, Time, Matter.*

In the early 1920s this work by Weyl, and Pauli's *Relativitätstheorie* [Theory of Relativity], were regarded as the most authoritative and comprehensive treatments of relativity theory then available. The reviewer of Weyl's book in *Nature* in 1922 began by saying: "Professor Weyl's work is the standard treatise on the general theory of relativity. It is the most systematic and penetrating book on the subject; it is also by far the most difficult." But apparently Weyl's approach was attractive to this reviewer (identified only as A. S. E.) who went on to say:

> We think . . . that Weyl, more than other continental writers, approaches the outlook natural to an English student. The subtle distinctions between the Cambridge and the continental schools survive the revolution which has overtaken scientific thought. Even with Einstein we feel a need to anglicise his mode of thought, and this is still more necessary with some other German writers. But Weyl strikes just the right note for us; and though he is often too far ahead for us to follow, we pay him the (perhaps doubtful) compliment of claiming him as one of our own school of thought.

If this is true, then Weyl played a significant role in opening relativity theory to a wider audience.

The English translation was printed in the United States for the first time in 1950 by Dover Publications, with a new preface by Weyl himself, in which he remarked on the intervening developments that would be introduced if he were to rewrite the book; but he said, "relativity theory as expounded in this book deals with the space-time aspect of classical physics. Thus, the book's contents are comparatively little affected by the stormy development of quantum physics during the last three decades."

This work by Weyl and his *Gruppentheorie und Quantenmechanik* [Group Theory and Quantum Mechanics], to be discussed later, have become integral parts of the literature of twentieth-century physics. They stand as landmarks in the mathematization of physics. At the time when they were written, much of the trouble physicists were having in coping with new theories was due to the physicists' unfamiliarity with some areas of mathematics. Weyl, as a mathematician interested in physics, served an interdisciplinary role at a time when, as the expression went at the time, "physics had become too important to be left to the physicists."

Albert Einstein, *Über die Spezielle und die Allgemeine Relativitätstheorie* [Relativity: The Special and General Theory].
This book, considered to be a popular presentation ("gemeinverständlich") by Albert Einstein, was published for the first time in 1917 by Friedrich Vieweg and Son as part of a series entitled "Tagesfragen aus den Gebieten der Naturwissenschaft und der Technik" [Current Questions in the Areas of Science and Technology]. By 1920 the publication was in its

seventh edition. It was translated into English as *Relativity: The Special and General Theory, A Popular Exposition* (1920) with an appendix on "The Experimental Confirmation of the General Theory of Relativity."* This referred to the British efforts to test the general theory during the eclipse of 1919, which Einstein graciously acknowledged in this appendix with the words:

> We are indebted to the Royal Society and to the Royal Astronomical Society for the investigation of this important deduction [that during an eclipse the light reaching the Earth from a star close to the Sun in angular measurement would show a bending toward the Sun]. Undaunted by the war and by difficulties of both a material and a psychological nature aroused by the war, these societies equipped two expeditions—to Sobral (Brazil), and to the island of Principe (West Africa)—and sent several of Britain's most celebrated astronomers (Eddington, Cottingham, Crommelin, Davidson), in order to obtain photographs of the solar eclipse of May 29, 1919. . . .
>
> The results of the measurements confirmed the theory in a thoroughly satisfactory manner.

Einstein's preface to the 1916 German edition as included in the English translation, seems worth quoting in full here, since it exhibits the Einstein flair and explains well the scope of the book.

> The present book is intended, as far as possible, to give an exact insight into the theory of Relativity to those readers who, from a general scientific and philosophical point of view, are interested in the theory, but who are not conversant with the mathematical apparatus of theoretical physics. The work presumes a standard of education corresponding to that of a university matriculation examination, and, despite the shortness of the book, a fair amount of patience and force of will on the part of the reader. The author has spared himself no pains in his endeavor to present the main ideas in the simplest and most intelligible form, and on the whole, in the sequence and connection in which they actually originated. In the interest of clearness, it appeared to me inevitable that I should repeat myself frequently, without paying the slightest attention to the elegance of presentation. I adhered scrupulously to the precept of that brilliant theoretical physicist, L. Boltzmann, according to whom matters of elegance ought to be left to the tailor and the cobbler. I make no pretence of having withheld from the reader difficulties, which are inherent to the subject. On the other hand I have purposely treated the empirical physical foundations of the theory in a "step-motherly" fashion, so that readers unfamiliar with physics may not feel like the wanderer who was unable to see the forest for the trees. May the book bring some one a few happy hours of suggestive thought!

---

* Cf. *The Great Ideas Today, 1961,* pp. 421–78.

The text is organized into three parts: "The Special Theory of Relativity"; "The General Theory of Relativity"; and "Considerations on the Universe as a Whole." Each of these is subdivided into little chapters of not more than four or five pages (in some cases only one) apiece. In all likelihood this was a great help to the reader both in digesting of the material and because it made for easy location of specific passages.

Albert Einstein, *The Meaning of Relativity.*

The Meaning of Relativity was not written as a book. It was, rather, the printing in translation of four lectures which had been delivered at Princeton University when Einstein visited that institution in 1921 while visiting the United States for the first time, touring on behalf of the cause of raising funds for the establishment of the Hebrew University in Jerusalem. At that time Einstein's name and his association with the term "relativity" were well known even to the man in the street, chiefly owing to the confirmation of Einstein's theoretical prediction during the solar eclipse of 1919, which had been widely reported in the popular press.

In scientific circles in the United States, interest in the new theory and in the man responsible for it was, of course, keen. Despite the overall nonscientific and nonacademic nature of his visit, Einstein met with a large number of the members of the American physics community and visited a number of their universities and laboratories. But it was Princeton which received the largest share of his time and attention during this visit. He was awarded an honorary doctorate by Princeton and delivered (in German) four lectures there, one each on "Space and Time in Pre-Relativistic Physics" and "The Theory of Special Relativity" and two on the "The General Theory of Relativity." Edwin P. Adams, a member of the physics department at Princeton, prepared the English translation, published in 1922. The German text was published in 1922 as *Vier Vorlesungen über Relativitätstheorie gehalten im Mai 1922 an der Universität Princeton* [Four Lectures on the Theory of Relativity Delivered in May 1922 at Princeton University]. In 1925 Gauthier-Villars of Paris published a French translation by Einstein's old friend from the Bern days, Maurice Solvine. Between 1945 and 1953 three more editions of the English version were published.

Obviously the entire content of relativity theory as it stood in 1921 could not be encompassed in four lectures or a 123-page printed version, but this presentation was admired as one that "does succeed in making clear the general ideas and in setting before the reader the spirit and trend of the argument and in leading him to see much of the detail of the whole theory," as noted by R. D. Carmichael in his review for *Science* in 1923. In *Physikalische Zeitschrift*, the reviewer termed it "the most condensed presentation," and a "master example of how much can be said with few words, in contrast with many learned tomes where the opposite is the case."

Its basic content was still held in high esteem in 1950 when the reviewer,

Leverett Davis, Jr., in *Review of Scientific Instruments* lauded it and added: "The title describes this material very well indeed, provided one regards it as referring to the foundations rather than the implications of the theories."

Wolfgang Pauli, *Relativitätstheorie* [Theory of Relativity].

Wolfgang Pauli's monograph, *Relativitätstheorie,* published in 1921, was originally conceived as an article for the *Encyklopädie der mathematischen Wissenschaften* [Encyclopedia of Mathematical Sciences], edited by Felix Klein. Klein had asked Arnold Sommerfeld to write an article on relativity theory for the forthcoming volume of the *Encyklopädie.* Sommerfeld, in turn, entrusted the task to one of his young students, Wolfgang Pauli.

Pauli succeeded so well in carrying out his assignment that Sommerfeld urged that it also be made available outside the framework of the *Encyklopädie,* since at that time there was a high demand ("apparently insatiable," wrote Sommerfeld) for accounts of the theory of relativity. Thus a special edition in book form was published with a preface by Sommerfeld in which he said:

> Although Herr Pauli was still a student at the time, he was not only familiar with the most subtle arguments in the Theory of Relativity through his own research work, but was also conversant with the literature of the subject.

In addition Sommerfeld wrote to Einstein that Pauli's article was "simply masterful." Einstein, in turn, wrote of Pauli's article in *Die Naturwissenschaften:*

> No one studying this mature, grandly conceived work would believe that the author is a man of twenty-one. One wonders what to admire most, the psychological understanding of the development of ideas, the sureness of mathematical deduction, the profound physical insight, the capacity for lucid, systematical presentation, the knowledge of the literature, the complete treatment of the subject matter, [or] the sureness of critical appraisal. (English translation from Wolfgang Pauli: *Collected Papers.*)

Pauli's article showed for the first time his skill in the art of presenting science, demonstrated again in 1926 and 1933 in the articles on quantum theory and wave mechanics which Pauli prepared for the *Handbuch der Physik,* and brought him to the attention of the older, established members of the physics community.

According to Pauli himself, writing thirty-five years later when an English edition was being prepared, "it was the aim of the article to give a complete review of the whole literature on relativity theory existing at that time." The article as prepared for the *Encyklopädie* consisted of five parts: the foundation of the special theory of relativity, mathematical tools, special theory of relativity: further elaborations, general theory of relativity, and theories on the nature of charged particles.

M. Fierz, writing recently in the *Dictionary of Scientific Biography*, said of Pauli's article that

> despite the necessary brevity of discussion, the monograph is a superior introduction to the special and general theories of relativity; it is in addition a first-rate historical document of science, since, together with H. Weyl's *Raum, Zeit, Materie (Space, Time, Matter)*, it is the first comprehensive presentation of the mathematical and physical ideas of Einstein, who himself never wrote a large work about his theory.

It appears that Pauli himself acknowledged the historical importance which the work acquired. When the English edition of *Theory of Relativity* was being prepared by Gerald Field of the University of Birmingham in 1956, Pauli wrote a preface in which he explained that, although thirty-five years had elapsed between the dates of the two versions, it was decided not to update and revise the original text. Pauli wrote:

> I decided . . . in order to preserve the character of the book as an historical document, to reprint the old text in its original form, but to add a number of notes at the end of the book which refer to certain passages in the text. These notes give to the reader selected information about the later developments connected with relativity theory, and also my personal views upon some controversial questions [the likelihood of the ultimate success of unified field theories, for example].

Pauli's article, "Relativitätstheorie," originally destined to be merely part of the fifth volume of an encyclopedic publication, received immediate appreciation and widespread dissemination as an independent work. Its lasting value is certified by its reissue thirty-five years after original publication. It remains a leading text on relativity to the present time, and is an excellent example of a work that carries the author's perspective and serves to explicate material already in circulation among scientists.

6. Quantum mechanics

Hermann Weyl, *Gruppentheorie und Quantenmechanik* [Group Theory and Quantum Mechanics].

In our earlier discussion of Hermann Weyl's *Raum, Zeit, Materie* we mentioned Weyl's reference in 1950 to "the stormy development of quantum physics during the last three decades." Weyl had closely followed this stormy development, and in his book, *Gruppentheorie und Quantenmechanik* (1928), he contributed to the literature a masterful presentation of one of quantum theory's mathematical aspects, group theory. It was an aspect that was almost totally unfamiliar to quantum physicists of the late 1920s who sometimes used the term *Gruppenpest* to describe its role (and their reaction to it). At least one autodidactic group of young American physicists, namely, W. P. Allis, N. H. Frank, and J. A. Stratton, all of whom were instructors at the Massachusetts Institute of Technology at the time, met regularly during the academic year 1928–29 to try and help each other cope with the contents and techniques of group theory. In recent times, of course, group theory has become part of the standard repertoire of theoretical physicists everywhere.

Weyl's *Gruppentheorie und Quantenmechanik* went into a second edition in 1931. This was translated into English by H. P. Robertson of Princeton University and also published in 1931.

Weyl's book, though admired for its elegance, was difficult going for its early readers. Gregory Breit wrote in the *Physical Review* in 1929 that it

> gives a mathematically elegant presentation of quantum mechanics. . . .
> The importance of the book is a sufficiently detailed discussion of the
> connection between quantum mechanics and a well-worked-out branch
> of mathematics. This makes it possible to present the subject more
> elegantly than has been done without groups. The treatment although
> logical and clear is not easy to follow.

According to his preface for the second edition, Weyl now was adopting "a more thoroughly *elementary* standpoint" and incorporating pedagogical improvements derived from his experience as professor of mathematical physics at Princeton University 1928–29 (when H. P. Robertson was his assistant) and at other American institutions where he had lectured.

As was the case with Weyl's earlier volume *Raum, Zeit, Materie*, his *Gruppentheorie und Quantenmechanik* has become an integral part of the literature of twentieth-century mathematical physics.

Werner Heisenberg, *The Physical Principles of the Quantum Theory*.
When Werner Heisenberg came to the United States in the spring of 1929 he held the rank of professor of theoretical physics at the University of Leipzig, a post to which he had been appointed in 1927 at the age of twenty-five. He had developed the matrix-mechanics form of quantum mechanics in 1925. His doctorate had been earned at the University of Göttingen under Max Born in 1924. Then Heisenberg did postdoctoral work at Niels Bohr's Institute of Theoretical Physics in Copenhagen, acknowledged as the center for quantum theoretical study and a magnet for young persons concerned with its development.

Heisenberg traveled widely in the United States that spring of 1929, visiting several universities and meeting informally with the growing number of American quantum theorists scattered from coast to coast. It was a pleasant experience for the "fair-haired boy" of quantum mechanics, who later wrote in his book *Physics and Beyond: Encounters and Conversations* (1971):

> The New World cast its spell on me right from the start. The carefree attitude of the young, their straightforward warmth and hospitality, their gay optimism—all this made me feel as if a great weight had been lifted from my shoulders. Interest in the new atomic theory was keen, and since I had been invited by a fairly large number of universities in many parts of the country, I became acquainted with many different aspects of American life. Wherever I stayed for more than a few days, I struck up new acquaintanceships that started with tennis, boating or sailing parties and quite often ended in long discussions of recent developments in atomic physics.

Heisenberg's principal academic stop during this trip was the University of Chicago, where he delivered a series of lectures concerned with the various facets of the new quantum mechanics: its mathematical apparatus, its experimental support, its physical concepts, including especially his uncertainty principle. As for the tenor of his presentation, Heisenberg wrote in the preface to the subsequently published version of these lectures:

> On the whole the book contains nothing that is not to be found in previous publications, particularly in the investigations of Bohr. The purpose of the book seems to me to be fulfilled if it contributes somewhat to the diffusion of that "Kopenhagener Geist der Quantentheorie," if I may so express myself, which has directed the entire development of modern atomic physics.

The rather short book, published by the University of Chicago Press in 1930 under the title *The Physical Principles of the Quantum Theory,* included an appendix, "The Mathematical Apparatus of the Quantum Theory," which was more detailed than the development given in the lectures themselves.

Heisenberg's lectures, having been delivered in German, were published in Germany as *Die physikalischen Prinzipien der Quantentheorie* (1930). The English translation was made by Carl Eckart and F. C. Hoyt, both members of the University of Chicago physics department, who had been closely following the development of quantum theory. Hoyt had studied with Bohr at Copenhagen in prequantum mechanical years. Eckart had surprised the world of physics by showing in 1926 the equivalence of the matrix and wave mechanics versions of quantum mechanics. The surprise was due not so much to the results, which were independently and almost simultaneously achieved by Erwin Schrödinger, but to the fact that a then obscure young American should have come up with so important a result. A French translation was published in 1932 with a preface written by Louis de Broglie.

The published versions of Heisenberg's lectures at the University of Chicago were widely distributed and received warm praise by reviewers in the *Astrophysical Journal* (E. U. Condon), *Physical Review* (J. C. Slater), *Nature* (twice by unidentified reviewers), and *Physikalische Zeitschrift* (E. Hückel). Slater noted that:

> Heisenberg has assembled and developed mathematical treatments of many of the advanced parts of quantum mechanics, greatly superior to those which have appeared before. As one would expect, the discussion of general matrix and transformation theory, and of electromagnetic fields, are particularly valuable. This mathematical material will probably prove for many readers to be almost as useful as the discussion of the physical meaning of quantum theory.

Condon hailed its "beautifully clear account of that part of the theory which is concerned with the explanation of the wave-particle dilemma in atomic physics in terms of the 'uncertainty principle.' "

The Physical Principles of the Quantum Theory was highly valued in its own time as a presentation of the current state of quantum theory by one of the great architects of its latest, most successful version. Today, almost half a century later, it remains one of the most important expositions of the status of quantum theory to appear after the arrival of quantum mechanics.

P. A. M. Dirac, *The Principles of Quantum Mechanics.*

P. A. M. Dirac was born in 1902. He trained originally as an electrical engineer at the University of Bristol. It is said that the Depression-related lack of a job resulted in continued years of study by Dirac in mathematics, first at the University of Bristol, later at St. John's College, Cambridge, under R. H. Fowler. Dirac received his Ph.D. in 1926, just as the new quantum mechanics was arriving on the scene.

Dirac's contributions to quantum mechanics were published in a series of highly esteemed papers in the *Proceedings of the Royal Society of London,* beginning in November 1925. Especially noteworthy were those on the relativistic theory of the electron, which appeared in 1928. In general, Dirac's work in quantum mechanics was characterized by the use of an abstract mathematical formalism known as transformation theory and by the fact that it was entirely consistent with relativity theory.

In 1930 the Clarendon Press of Oxford published Dirac's book *The Principles of Quantum Mechanics,* which was rapidly disseminated and favorably received by reviewers. It was quickly translated into German as *Die Prinzipien der Quantenmechanik* by W. Bloch (1930) and into French as *Les Principes de la mécanique quantique* by A. Proca and J. Ullmo (1931). It has since gone through three more editions in English, in 1935, 1947, and 1958.

In 1931 an unidentified reviewer in *Nature* wrote of it as follows:

> The original writings of this author have prepared us for a logical and original mode of approach to the difficult problems in atomic physics.

His method has the character of a new physical principle. He bids us throw aside preconceived ideas regarding the nature of phenomena and admit the existence of a substratum of which it is impossible to form a picture. We may describe this as the application of "pure thought" to physics, and it is this which makes Dirac's method more profound than that of others. . . . It is, even yet, too early to say exactly along what lines the quantum theory will finally develop. Dirac has contributed largely to the detail of the new theory, but the most important contribution he makes is in the mode of approach; he introduces a new attitude of mind towards the investigation of nature, and the interest lies in watching the development and progress of his ideas. There can be no doubt that his work ranks as one of the high achievements of contemporary physics.

J. Robert Oppenheimer's review of Dirac's book in 1931 in *Physical Review* contains the following comments:

A book on quantum mechanics written by Dirac must be of great and in many ways unique interest to physicists. . . . The fact that a book on quantum mechanics must necessarily be largely an account of Dirac's own work, assures us that his account will be unitary and coherent, and that it will be given in just those terms which have shown themselves most useful to the understanding and the development of the theory. . . . In some very fundamental respects Dirac's book is like Gibbs's *Elementary Principles of Statistical Mechanics:* it is clear, with a clarity dangerous for a beginner, deductive, and in its foundation abstract; its argument is predominantly analytical; the virtual contact with experiment is made quite late in the book. . . . Dirac's axioms,—and, in fact, most of his earlier chapters—have an extreme generality, but because the meaning of any equation, in physics, is ultimately to be derived from the numbers given by specific observations, they have also a higher grade of abstractness. This is the price that must be paid for the generality. And Dirac's book will be for many of us so satisfying, that we shall be glad to pay it.

For all its good points, Dirac's book was not the lasting solution to how quantum mechanics should be presented. Aside from its difficulty, especially for those not fully initiated into mathematical abstraction, it did have its drawbacks. John von Neumann, in the introduction to his own *Mathematical Foundations of Quantum Mechanics,* remarked of Dirac's book:

Dirac, in several papers, as well as in his recently published book, has given a representation of quantum mechanics which is scarcely to be surpassed in brevity and elegance, and which is at the same time of invariant character. . . . The method of Dirac . . . (and this is overlooked today in a great part of quantum mechanical literature, because of the clarity and elegance of the theory) in no way satisfies the requirements of mathematical rigor—not even if these are reduced in a natural and proper fashion to the extent common elsewhere in theoretical physics.

Nevertheless, Dirac's book occupies a special place in the evolution of quantum mechanics. His contributions to quantum theory received particular recognition with the awarding to him of the Nobel Prize for Physics in 1933, an award he shared with Schrödinger.

Eugen Wigner, *Gruppentheorie und ihre Anwendung auf die Quantenmechanik der Atomspektren* [Group Theory and Its Application to the Quantum Mechanics of Atomic Spectra].

Wigner's *Gruppentheorie und ihre Anwendung auf die Quantenmechanik der Atomspektren* was published in 1931. At that time group theory, as applied to quantum mechanics, was by no means generally accepted. In a review of the work in *Physical Review* in 1931, E. L. Hill noted that "theoretical physicists seem to be pretty well divided into two camps, one of which has championed the theory of groups while the other has consistently refused to use it."

In his book, Wigner carefully interwove the mathematical elements of group theory with the physical aspects of atomic spectra, showing how the power and generality of group theory could be advantageously applied to problems which involved formidable computational difficulties when approached from more familiar and elementary methods. An example of the way group theory could relate to and surpass more elementary techniques occurs in Wigner's discussion of the Slater determinant. Of this, Hill said Slater's method was "developed originally by means of the most direct and elementary mathematical methods suited to the problem, one finds it here in a refined and spiritualized form."

In 1944 Wigner's book was "published and distributed [in the U.S.] in the public interest by authority of the Alien Property Custodian." By the time the English-language, "expanded and improved" edition, *Group Theory and Its Application to the Quantum Mechanics of Atomic Spectra,* translated by J. J. Griffin, was published in 1959, Wigner (now Eugene P.) could write in his preface that

> when the original German version was first published in 1931, there was a great reluctance among physicists toward accepting group theoretical arguments and the group theoretical point of view. It pleases the author that this reluctance has virtually vanished in the meantime and that in fact, the younger generation does not understand the causes and the basis for this reluctance.

Wigner noted that Max von Laue had been an early exponent of the use of group theoretical methods. He credited von Laue's encouragement as an important factor in the publication of the first edition.

The principal results achieved by Wigner and presented in his book were first published in the *Zeitschrift für Physik* in 1926 and early 1927, stimulated by the investigations by Heisenberg and Dirac on the quantum theory of assemblies of identical particles. In preparing the 1959 edition, new material developed in the intervening years by Wigner and others was added to the original text. The book has been, over the years, probably the most popular group theory text among physicists.

Wigner was born in Budapest in 1902. He was trained as an engineer at the Technische Hochschule [Technical Institute] in Berlin, but turned early to theoretical physics. He came to Princeton University in 1930 as a lecturer in mathematical physics and was soon promoted to a professorship. His work on group theory and general symmetry consideration is world renowned. In 1963 he was awarded the Nobel Prize for Physics "for his contributions to the theory of the atomic nucleus and the elementary particles, particularly through the discovery and application of fundamental symmetry principles." Wigner's book on group theory rates high in terms of innovation, not only because it includes material developed originally by him but also by virtue of his perspective of an engineer turned mathematical physicist, in contrast to that of some other authors of books on group theory who were primarily "pure" mathematicians. Its longevity is in part a fruit of the achievement of the gradual winning over of physicists to the use of group theoretical methods.

John H. Van Vleck, *The Theory of Electric and Magnetic Susceptibilities.*
John H. Van Vleck's book *The Theory of Electric and Magnetic Susceptibilities* was first published in 1932 by the Clarendon Press of Oxford University. As of this writing it is still in print in its original edition.

In one coherently written volume, Van Vleck brought together the known facts pertaining to the electric and magnetic properties of many substances, the partial explanation of these properties in terms of the older theories—classical and early quantum—and their more recent, very successful explanation within the new quantum mechanics.

Van Vleck was, however, more than an organizer and synthesizer in this field. The contributions to the modern understanding of magnetism made by him and some of the young persons who worked with him as doctoral or postdoctoral students, first at the University of Wisconsin and from 1934 on at Harvard University, spanned many years. Those accomplished prior to 1932 were included in his volume published that year, which also contained hints of some that were to come. His contributions in the field of magnetism were honored in 1977 with the award of the Nobel Prize for Physics to Van Vleck, together with one of his former students, Philip Anderson, and N. F. Mott.

The fact that the book was written so soon after the advent of quantum mechanics permitted it to demonstrate for the first time the validity of quantum mechanics when applied to a different set of considerations from those which had given rise to it, namely spectroscopic studies. Thus Van Vleck's book, aside from its own intrinsic value, served to strengthen the place of quantum mechanics in theoretical physics.

Soon after its publication, Van Vleck's careful and thorough treatment of his subject was commended by reviewers on both sides of the Atlantic, among whom were Wolfgang Pauli in *Die Naturwissenschaften* [The Natural Sciences], George Uhlenbeck in *Physical Review*, and "E. C. S." (undoubtedly Edmund C. Stoner, a British authority on magnetism) in *Nature*.

Philip Anderson, in a retrospective talk published in 1967 in *Physics Today*, commented:

> It is a pleasant and fascinating task to go back and reread that book. One sees how even those basic ideas originated by others are illuminated and their bare bones fleshed out by Van's special point of view. . . . Another [useful and important thing] is that the book is not "dated"; it does not attempt or accept a wrong explanation for anything, but leaves subjects open for further ideas. A contribution deserving special mention is the only really clear exposition in existence of the meaning of Maxwell's equations in a medium, in terms of the actual atoms and molecules and the real microscopic electromagnetic fields.

While the book, by the character of its treatment and the relative narrowness of its focus, could never claim the attention of a multitude of readers, its apparent timelessness over almost half a century is all the more noteworthy. In 1933 Wolfgang Pauli commended it as part handbook, part textbook, and so it has continued to be regarded up to the present.

Johann von Neumann, *Mathematische Grundlagen der Quantenmechanik* [Mathematical Foundations of Quantum Mechanics].
In 1932 *Mathematische Grundlagen der Quantenmechanik* by Johann von Neumann was published as Volume 38 of the series *Die Grundlehren der mathematischen Wissenschaften,* edited by R. Courant. In 1943 the first American edition was "published and distributed in the public interest by authority of the U.S. Alien Property Custodian." In 1955 *Mathematical Foundations of Quantum Mechanics,* a translation made by Robert Beyer with von Neumann's cooperation, was published.

At the time of its initial publication in 1932, the author was already a member of the Princeton community, having accepted a position at the University in 1930. When the Institute for Advanced Study opened in 1933, von Neumann became, at age thirty, its youngest permanent member.

Von Neumann was born in Budapest in 1903. His mathematical genius manifested itself early and he received private tutoring by university professors. By the age of nineteen he was publishing original papers in mathematics. He taught at Berlin and at Hamburg before leaving Europe for the United States.

Von Neumann was well established in mathematics when quantum mechanics came upon the scene. To oppose the general confusion which attended its rapid development, von Neumann set out to provide quantum mechanics with a rigorous and logical foundation through axiomatization. According to his biographer, J. Dieudonné, in the *Dictionary of Scientific Biography:*

> Von Neumann showed that mathematical rigor could be restored by taking as basic axioms the assumptions that the states of a physical system were points of a Hilbert space and that the measurable quantities were Hermitian (generally unbounded) operators, densely defined in that space. This formalism, the practical use of which became available after von Neumann had developed the spectral theory of unbounded Hermitian operators (1929), has survived subsequent developments of quantum mechanics and still is the basis of nonrelativistic quantum theory. . . .
>
> [In *Grundlagen*, he] discussed the much-debated question of "causality" versus "indeterminancy" and concluded that no introduction of "hidden parameters" could keep the basic structure of quantum theory and restore "causality."

This is a result that is often quoted in recent years by opponents of the hidden-variable concept, although its adherents do not regard it as the final word, by any means.

In the preface to the English edition of this work, von Neumann himself said that

> the object of this book is to present the new quantum mechanics in a unified representation which, so far as it is possible and useful, is mathematically rigorous.

He added that he would omit applications of quantum mechanics to particular problems (a task being satisfactorily treated by others) but would present the mathematical tools necessary for the theory of Hilbert space and Hermitian operators.

This was not an easy book for physicists, especially those of the '30s, to follow. We suspect many took the attitude that they were grateful to von Neumann for putting quantum mechanics on a solid, mathematically sound basis, but they would go on tending to their business of applying quantum mechanics (more confidently, perhaps) to particular situations.

The principal contribution of von Neumann's *Grundlagen* is the mathematical rigor it brought to quantum mechanics. It demonstrated to physicists that previously unfamiliar mathematics was profoundly relevant to physics. Mathematicians were alerted to the applicability of topics from "pure" mathematics, such as Hermitian operators, in another discipline. Von Neumann's presentation was innovative, authoritative, and interdisciplinary and it has achieved a position of usefulness and widespread respect.

Wolfgang Pauli, *Die allgemeinen Prinzipien der Wellenmechanik* [The General Principles of Wave Mechanics].

We have already discussed Pauli's *Relativitätstheorie*, which was prepared in 1921 for the *Encyklopädie der mathematischen Wissenschaften* and which marked Pauli's debut into the scientific community. Pauli's second survey, prepared for the *Handbuch der Physik*, XXIII [Handbook of Physics], was published in 1926. It included his own exclusion principle—the basis of his Nobel Prize in 1945—which states that no two electrons in a single atom can have identical sets of quantum numbers; but chiefly it was a survey of the quantum theory as it stood in 1925. That article was of great interest when it appeared, but with the coming of quantum mechanics so soon after it was written, it was almost immediately outdated. Incidentally this fate was also shared by John H. Van Vleck's *Quantum Principles and Line Spectra.* Although eclipsed at their time, these two works retain considerable historical interest today.

Pauli's *Die allgemeinen Prinzipien der Wellenmechanik* was yet another of his masterful survey articles written as part of a larger publication. It appeared in the *Handbuch der Physik*, XXIV in 1933. Pauli's biographer in the *Dictionary of Scientific Biography,* M. Fierz, refers to Pauli's 1926 article as "the Old Testament" and the 1933 article as "the New Testament," and provides the following comments on the latter publication:

> A student at the time, the author [Fierz] well remembers meeting
> Hermann Weyl on the street and his saying, "What Pauli has written
> on wave mechanics is again outstanding!" This judgment of a
> connoisseur is still valid today: the same article, twenty-five years later,
> was used unchanged in the new handbook (1958). Pauli's presentation
> was thoroughly modern and well thought out, considering that such
> articles frequently become outdated after only a few years.

In addition, Pauli's article received further circulation as a separate monograph, and in 1950 it was "published and distributed in the public interest by authority of the Alien Property Custodian" through J. W. Edwards of Ann Arbor, Michigan.

This article by Pauli, 190 pages long, is divided into two parts, the first corresponding to the nonrelativistic theory, the second to the relativistic theory; the former refers to the development begun by Schrödinger and continued by others, the latter is due principally to Dirac. The years 1926–32 constituted a period of concentrated, momentous development in quantum physics. Pauli's *Handbuch* article organizes beautifully the course of this development.

> Linus Pauling and E. Bright Wilson, *Introduction to Quantum Mechanics: with Applications to Chemistry*; and Linus Pauling, *The Nature of the Chemical Bond, and the Structure of Molecules and Crystals: An Introduction to Modern Structural Chemistry*.

Linus Pauling was one of the first American chemists to study quantum mechanics. While a doctoral candidate at the California Institute of Technology in the early 1920s he had learned about the old quantum theory through Sommerfeld's *Atombau* in a course taught by the physical chemist Richard Tolman. After receiving his Ph.D. in 1925, he visited and studied at Munich, Zürich, and Copenhagen on a Guggenheim Fellowship. He became sufficiently proficient in the new quantum mechanics to begin applying it to problems of molecular structure.

Pauling returned to Caltech as assistant professor of theoretical chemistry in the fall of 1927. He immediately began giving a course in quantum mechanics which became the basis for the book he later wrote with E. Bright Wilson, *Introduction to Quantum Mechanics: with Applications to Chemistry* (New York and London: McGraw-Hill Book Co., Inc., 1935).

Wilson had come to Caltech in 1931 to study with Pauling after receiving his M.A. in chemistry at Princeton University, where he studied quantum mechanics with E. U. Condon in a course that used Dirac's recently published book, *The Principles of Quantum Mechanics*. Wilson took Pauling's course in quantum mechanics for chemists during his first year at Caltech and served as Pauling's grader for that course the following year. Pauling invited Wilson to collaborate with him in the writing of a textbook. Wilson accepted and recalled later that he wrote about one-third of the manuscript.

As indicated by the title, the Pauling and Wilson text was written primarily for chemists. But, according to the preface, it was also aimed at experimental physicists and beginning students of theoretical physics. With a three-part audience such as this, the authors did not assume a high degree of mathematical sophistication on the part of the students and took pains to work out the mathematical details of the topics they presented. Their stated aim was "to produce a textbook of practical quantum mechanics . . . [and] to provide for the reader a means of equipping himself with a practical grasp of this subject, so that he can apply quantum mechanics to most of the chemical and physical problems which may confront him."

The book proved to be remarkably durable and helpful for subsequent generations of science students. Pauling recently noted: "the President of McGraw-Hill told me that this book is the oldest one of of their books still in print (that is, without having been revised)."

Pauling continued to develop his approach to molecular structure through the use of quantum mechanics, publishing (in either the *Journal of the American Chemical Society* or the *Journal of Chemical Physics*) a series of seven papers between 1931 and 1933 on "The Nature of the Chemical Bond." These became the basis for the Nobel Prize for Chemistry that was awarded to Pauling in 1954.

Pauling's concept of chemical valence was the outgrowth of earlier work by Walter Heitler and Fritz London. It was also independently advanced by John C. Slater; hence it is frequently called the Heitler-London-Pauling-Slater (or H-L-P-S) model. The H-L-P-S model for chemical valence viewed the individual electrons in a molecule as localized to particular atoms in atomic orbitals which had definite shapes and formed "pair bonds." Thus the concept of "directed valence" was introduced. In order to account for the shapes of some molecules, certain of the atomic orbitals must be regarded as "hybridized" between the s and p states, for example. Associated "resonance energies" can be calculated for particular molecules and, in many cases, could be shown to agree with experimentally determined values.

In the fall semesters of 1937–39 Pauling gave courses on this topic at Cornell University which were subsequently organized and published as a book entitled *The Nature of the Chemical Bond, and the Structure of Molecules and Crystals: An Introduction to Modern Structural Chemistry* (Ithaca, New York: Cornell University Press; London: Oxford University Press, 1939). This book was less taxing mathematically for the reader than the earlier volume on quantum mechanics and was a worthy successor to G. N. Lewis's *Valence and the Structure of Atoms and Molecules* (1923), N. V. Sidgwick's *Electronic Theory of Valency* (1927) and *Some Physical Properties of the Covalent Link in Chemistry* (1933). It has also become a valued text.

Its third (1960) edition had the honor of ranking first by a wide margin among the forty-two "most cited books" during the period 1961–72 (with 1,514 citations in journal literature, as monitored by the *Science Citation Index* publication *Current Contents* (January 2, 1974).

Joseph Mayer, in a review of 1939 in *Review of Scientific Instruments*, commented that:

> The book presents a qualitative and quantitative description of the
> information gained by the application of quantum mechanical methods
> to the empirical knowledge of the chemist.

Mayer noted, however, that there was another, Hund-Hückel-Mulliken, valence model using molecular orbitals which Pauling did not mention at all, and he added:

> This consistent limitation to one of the possible viewpoints, or
> approximation methods, of polyatomic systems is both a strength and a
> weakness of the book. . . . Such criticisms would, perhaps, be trivial,

were they not aggravated by the very excellence of the presentation in this book. It is unfortunate that this treatise will almost certainly tend to fix, even more than has already been done by the author's excellent papers, the viewpoint of most chemists on this, and *only* this one, approach to the problem of the chemical bond. It appears likely that the H-L-S-P method will entirely eclipse, in the minds of the chemists, the single electron molecular orbital picture, not primarily by virtue of its greater applicability or usefulness, but solely by the brilliance of its presentation.

The first edition of Pauling's book sold out quickly, and in less than a year Pauling brought out a second, enlarged and updated version.

7. Special cases: one-of-a-kind books

A few more books must be mentioned which cannot be placed in any of our previous categories, but which in each case played an important role in the evolution of modern physical thought.

Jean Perrin, *Brownian Movement and Molecular Reality* and *Les Atomes*.
These two works by Jean Perrin were particularly influential for the dissemination and general acceptance of the atomicity of matter. This ancient notion was given scientific standing by John Dalton in the early nineteenth century, but it had been the subject of years of controversy, with such established scientists as Wilhelm Ostwald and Ernst Mach among its adversaries.

Perrin's earlier work describing his own research, "Mouvement brownien et réalité moléculaire," first appeared in 1909 as a 114-page article in *Annales de chimie et de physique*. It was quickly translated and published in book form, both in German and in English.

Perrin (Nobel laureate in physics in 1926) became a spokesman for atomic theory and wrote a more popular presentation, *Les Atomes*, first published in 1913. There, Perrin set forth a general survey of all existing evidence lending support to the existence of atoms, from chemistry, radioactivity, and electricity, in addition to that produced by his own Brownian motion studies. The book, a huge popular success that saw many editions and translations, brought to the intelligent layman the vision of atomism already established among scientists.

P. W. Bridgman, *The Logic of Modern Physics*.
With the rise of relativity and quantum mechanics, the fundamental conceptual foundations of their discipline troubled many members of the scientific community. P. W. Bridgman, one who felt such "disquietude" acutely, undertook—as he said, essentially for himself—the search for a satisfactory way of thinking that would not only be appropriate for the already established body of science but also would be able to accommodate

the new discoveries and theories being revealed in the early twentieth century.

Bridgman's book, *The Logic of Modern Physics,* published in 1927, found widespread and predominantly enthusiastic response among his scientific colleagues. The salient feature of Bridgman's outlook, idiosyncratic but probably influenced by Stallo and to some degree by Mach, was the introduction of "operational" definitions—*i.e.,* such that "the concept is synonymous with the corresponding set of operations." This notion became a key feature of discussion on philosophy of science, at least in the United States, and influenced the presentation and treatment of subject matter in many fields, among them economics, psychology, and cosmology.

Those of us who learned our physics from the generation of scientists initially influenced by Bridgman's book now clearly recognize the importance of Bridgman's place in the perspective of physics as taught from the late 1930s on.

H. A. Bethe, Articles on nuclear physics in *Reviews of Modern Physics.*
Among these one-of-a-kind works we also nominate Hans Bethe's articles on nuclear physics which were published in the journal *Reviews of Modern Physics* in 1936 and 1937. While not comprising a book in the strict sense of that term, these articles share enough of the usual characteristics of books to merit consideration here. Besides, they served the function of a needed book which did not exist and were enormously influential on the audience for which they were written. They are to this day still known affectionately as the "Bethe Bible."

There were three articles in all under the general title "Nuclear Physics": "Stationary States of the Nuclei" (with R. F. Bacher as coauthor); "Nuclear Dynamics, Theoretical"; "Nuclear Dynamics, Experimental" (with M. S. Livingston as coauthor). Their total length was more than 450 pages, and they were characterized by Bethe's clarity of understanding and exposition.

The nucleus was the new frontier of physics in the 1930s. At that time, fundamental particles were being discovered and experimental techniques were being developed. Theoreticians in the United States were busy trying to assimilate the flow of information, but were handicapped by the absence of broad presentations that would organize the welter of material scattered throughout the research journals of the world of physics. Bethe, having recently come to the United States from Europe, where he had known the theorists in Germany, in Rome, and in England, perceived this need and prepared these articles. They came to be heavily relied on by workers in nuclear physics as well as by students wishing to enter the field.

Erwin Schrödinger, *What is Life? The Physical Aspect of the Living Cell.*
In 1943 at the Dublin Institute for Advanced Studies Erwin Schrödinger, addressing a general scientific audience, delivered a series of lectures which were published the following year as *What Is Life? The Physical Aspect of the*

Living Cell.* In a mere ninety-two pages, Schrödinger, who had formulated wave mechanics in 1926, examined how quantum physics might be applied to the biological process of growth.

His analysis, though outmoded today, was enormously appealing and influenced many, including Francis Crick (as recorded in J. D. Watson's *The Double Helix*), to study biology. Hence it can be said that Schrödinger played a role in stimulating the recent great advances of molecular biology.

8. Special cases: textbooks

In scientific literature, textbooks occupy a unique and important place. In their own time they are the means by which aspirants to a scientific profession come to know their discipline, and by which they are in a manner shaped in conformity with the prevailing attitudes. Historically, textbooks provide insight into the scientific thinking of their period, or of a particular established scientist, and elucidate the background from which their student users went on to make subsequent progress.

With these considerations in mind, we list, together with some of their characteristics, those physics textbooks which seem to us to have been especially important in the early training of physicists since the first quarter of the century.

Floyd K. Richtmyer, *Introduction to Modern Physics:* an intermediate level and still current text which aims not only to impart information but also to help the student develop an appreciation of how modern theoretical understanding has evolved from the time of the Greeks up through the "classical" physics of the nineteenth century; has enjoyed remarkable longevity, with six editions published between 1928 and 1969.

Max Born, *Atomic Physics:* published in 1935, an updated version of previously published and then suppressed lectures in German; largely descriptive yet serving as an introduction to the theoretical advances of the previous decade by one who contributed heavily to those advances.

Robert Bruce Lindsay and Henry Margenau, *Foundations of Physics:* written in 1936 by two authors who shared special concern for the philosophical foundations and implications of modern physics, with the aim of filling the gap between popular discussions of recent advances in physics and rigorous theoretical textbooks; it is credited with shaping the tastes and skills of many physical scientists during their formative period.

Edwin C. Kemble, *The Fundamental Principles of Quantum Mechanics, with Elementary Applications* (1937): written by America's first quantum theorist, who was greatly influenced by the "operational" attitude of his Harvard University colleague, P. W. Bridgman. With commendable mathematical

---

* Reprinted in *GIT, 1967,* pp. 372–425.

rigor, the book stressed the difficulties and weaknesses, as well as the successes, of quantum mechanics.

Enrico Fermi, *Thermodynamics:* based on lectures given at Columbia University in the summer of 1936 while the author was visiting the United States; exhibits well Fermi's pedagogical skill in presenting basic thermodynamic principles with applications in physics and chemistry to students at the intermediate level.

L. D. Landau and E. M. Lifshitz, *Statistical Physics* (1958): translation by E. and R. F. Peierls of a textbook (one of several excellent ones by these authors) written for students in the U.S.S.R. Widely used as text and reference on classical and quantum statistics, and in a recent survey, one of forty-two "most cited books" in physics and chemistry for the period 1961–72.

Leonard I. Schiff, *Quantum Mechanics:* intended as a text on the graduate level, and as a reference book, it explains the physical concepts of quantum mechanics, describes the mathematical formalism, and presents illustrative examples of both ideas and methods. It is a well-remembered book in the training of a considerable number of today's physicists.

Richard P. Feynman, *The Feynman Lectures on Physics:* a three-volume work (published 1963–65) based on lectures to freshmen and sophomores at the California Institute of Technology. Rich, up-to-date treatment of modern ideas in physics for well-prepared students, presented in the euphoric and brilliant style of the author, and fondly recalled today for the role it played in their education by many young physicists today.

The number of candidates on our list for consideration as great books of twentieth-century physics has thus almost reached forty. The list could easily become half again as long were we to add all the other suitable entries that also suggested themselves on the basis of our criteria. But we have already given a sufficient number and variety of examples to demonstrate the different types of books that play, or have played, an important role in the development of modern physics. Nevertheless, let us mention, for the record, a few more by author and title only:

Bragg, Wm. H., and Bragg, Wm. L., *X-Rays and Crystal Structure* (1915).
Condon, E. U., and Shortley, G. H., *The Theory of Atomic Spectra* (1935).
Courant, R., and Hilbert, D., *Methoden der mathematischen Physik* [Methods of Mathematical Physics] 2 vols. (1931 and 1937).
Einstein, A., and Infeld, L., *The Evolution of Physics* (1938).
Fermi, E. *Nuclear Physics* [notes compiled by three students in a course given by Fermi at the University of Chicago] (1949).
International Critical Tables (1926–1930).

Kayser, H. J. G., *Handbuch der Spektroskopie* [Handbook of Spectroscopy] 2 vols. (1900 and 1902).

Purcell, E. M., *Electricity and Magnetism* [the Berkeley physics course, Vol. 2] (1965).

Slater, J. C., and Frank, N. H., *Introduction to Theoretical Physics* (1933).

Smyth, Henry De. W., *Atomic Energy for Military Purposes* (1945).

Tolman, R. C., *The Principles of Statistical Mechanics* (1938).

We recall having read somewhere that any compiler of the "best" of any large category of things begins with enthusiasm but ends in frustration— frustration because such a task turns out to allow too many different solutions, no one of them indubitably more authoritative than the others. Perhaps this attempt of ours to explore and illustrate the criteria for making choices will ease the work of those who, some day, may undertake to put together a list of the "best" in twentieth-century science. At any rate, far from feeling frustrated, we have been left by this exercise with the kind of warm feeling one takes away from a visit at a house full of brilliant and lively people.

It is quite likely that many of these will turn up on any future list of great books. On that score, however, we have precisely the opinion Mark Van Doren expressed in his article on great books of the twentieth century in literature:

I am not deciding, I am suggesting. I am guessing what books of recent or present time will live. Or perhaps I am only saying what books I hope will live for the simple reason that I especially like and respect them.

---

[1]The data that follow are based on *Statistical Indicators of Scientific and Technical Communication, 1960-1980,* Vol. 1, A Summary Report for the National Science Foundation (Rockville, Maryland: King Research, Inc., Center for Quantitative Sciences, 1978). Among the many historical and sociological analyses of science communications, *see* for example D. J. de S. Price, *Science Since Babylon* (New Haven, Conn.: Yale University Press, 1961), and Price, *Little Science, Big Science* (New York: Columbia University Press, 1963); Diana Crane, *Invisible Colleges: Diffusion of Knowledge in Scientific Communities* (Chicago: The University of Chicago Press, 1972); and Henry W. Menard, *Science: Growth & Change* (Cambridge, Mass.: Harvard University Press, 1971).

[2]*See* footnote 1, Price, *Science Since Babylon.*

[3]Nicholas Rescher, *Scientific Progress: A Philosophical Essay on the Economics of Research in Natural Science* (Oxford: Basil Blackwell, 1978).

[4]Harriet Zuckerman, *Scientific Elite: Nobel Laureates in the United States* (New York: The Free Press, 1977), p. 53.

[5]*The Social Indicators 1976,* taking a narrower view than does *Statistical Indicators* (footnote 1) of scientific and technical book publication, counts only 4,700 titles per year in 1975, omitting medicine.

[6]M. J. Mulkay, "Sociology of the Scientific Research Community," Chapter 4 in *Science, Technology and Society: A Cross-Disciplinary Perspective,* eds. Ina Spiegel-Rösing and Derek J. de S. Price (London and Beverly Hills: Sage Publications, 1977), p. 110.

PART FIVE

Reviews of Recent Books

Reviews of Recent Books

We commence this year a new department of *The Great Ideas Today,* one in which we offer reviews of books that have appeared during the past year or so that may be of interest to our readers. It is not the purpose of these reviews to recommend the reading of these books, still less to urge that they be purchased; such matters are left to the determination of our readers. The aim is merely to note that certain works which have recently been published contribute something to the tradition of the Great Books, either by extending and updating the discussion of the issues those books contain—a discussion to which the *Syntopicon* provides a guide—or, on the other hand, by distorting and obscuring the same issues (as sometimes happens) so that they require to be restated and clarified. In either case our readers may think there is good reason to do their own reading of the works reviewed, and may wish to have them in their libraries. We can learn much even from error, if error it be.

As the reviews to be offered are likely to be lengthy, the number of works taken up each year will necessarily be small. This year there are only two of them: *The Life of the Mind* (2 vols.), by Hannah Arendt and *On Human Nature,* by Edward O. Wilson. These books, both of which were published last year, are not the only recent works that bear on the tradition of the Great Books, of course. Among other writings that we would like to have considered in this issue are *Lying,* by Sissela Bok—a book that examines the discussion of its subject by many *GBWW* authors—and *Inventing America,* by Garry Wills, which offers a new reading of the Declaration of Independence, one of the American State Papers in *GBWW,* Vol. 43. Unfortunately, there was not room in this issue to give these works the kind of attention they deserve.

Our reviewer this year is William Gorman, formerly a contributing editor of *The Great Ideas Today* and before that the general editor of the *Syntopicon*. Mr Gorman is a philosopher by training (he has been a student also of criticism and of music) who has taught at both the University of Chicago and St. John's College, Annapolis, Maryland. He has been a member of the Ford Foundation's Basic Ideas Program of

the Fund for the Republic, was at one time associate director of the Institute for Philosophical Research, and for many years has been associated as a fellow and consultant to the Center for the Study of Democratic Institutions. Readers will recall the summaries of Great Books arguments on *Syntopicon* subjects that have appeared in past issues of *The Great Ideas Today*; these were Mr. Gorman's work. Other readers may know *The American Testament* (1975), a study of classic American political documents, which he wrote with Mortimer J. Adler. Few reviewers could be found who are more conversant with the Great Books or more practiced in the art of neutral analysis when presented with serious argument; none could have taken more care with his assignment or striven harder to be just in speaking of the writings on which he was asked to comment here.

The Life of the Mind

by Hannah Arendt

Hannah Arendt was one of the most distinguished refugees from Nazidom. During her life in America, from 1940 to her sudden death in 1975, with a base at the New School for Social Research in New York City, she published nine works in what she here describes as "the relatively safe fields of political science and theory." It is a characterization that hardly catches what was special about those books, since without exception they involved a confrontation with some of the darkest and most tormenting events of our times, a passionate effort to probe for the meaning of those events, and a sustained search for positions in political philosophy that might prove regenerative. Indeed, those books, despite their relative opacity, won her an inner circle of devotees, a considerable academic and lay readership, and invitations to special lectureships at eminent universities.

Arendt's last work, with which we deal here, was in its main lines delivered as the prestigious Gifford Lectures at the University of Aberdeen in 1973–74.[1] These lectures, which Arendt describes as being concerned with "rather awesome matters," the mental activities of thinking and willing, have now been issued by her devotees in two volumes which she did not live to see, nor was she able to write a third volume devoted to the act of judging which would have been the work's concluding part.

The mood of the two volumes that we have is gloomy, even morbid. In her introduction to the first of them, Arendt issues a kind of obituary for things that have "come to an end." Among these is "the basic distinction between the sensory and the suprasensory." Among them also are "God, metaphysics, and philosophy." All these deaths, which are taken as factual, serve to define what Arendt calls "our present situation." For this, she wishes to take some responsibility. "I have clearly joined the ranks," she writes, "of those who for some time now have been attempting to dismantle metaphysics, and philosophy with all its categories, as we have known them from their beginnings in Greece until today" (I: 212). Perhaps that explains the depressing quality of the work. Dismantling the already dead is something of a gloomy task.

Not unconnected is another general characteristic of these volumes. Arendt's pages are literally packed with short quotations plucked from the works of all those dead theologians, metaphysicians, and philosophers.[2] It is impossible to exaggerate how the very momentum of her thinking about thinking and willing depends on this. Her continual takings from various literary works are so frequent and so random as to be dizzying; to follow her, one must endeavor to keep straight in one's own mind all the diverse materials she has consulted and of which she makes some use. Such a task, which would at best be difficult, is further complicated by the fact that in a disconcertingly large number of cases her quick, spasmodic interpretations of text quoted seem arbitrary, and often, when the context is consulted, prove demonstrably wrong.[3]

Arendt is aware of how pervasive is her use of short texts taken out of the literature of philosophy from the pre-Socratics to Heidegger and Merleau-Ponty. In the last paragraphs of the volume on thinking, she speaks of the literature in which the deadly "metaphysical fallacies" are committed, as containing "important hints of what this curious out-of-order activity called thinking may be all about" (I: 211). She had once characterized her way of reading as "*Perlenfischerei.*"[4] Here, at the close of the book on thinking, she sets down the song from *The Tempest* beginning "Full fathom five thy father lies . . ."[5] and writes:

> . . . What you then are left with [after "dismantling"] is still the past,
> but a *fragmented* past, which has lost its certainty of evaluation. . . . It is
> with such fragments from the past, after their sea-change, that I have
> dealt here. . . . If some of my listeners or readers should be tempted to
> try their luck at the technique of dismantling, let them be careful not
> to destroy the "rich and strange," the "coral" and the "pearls," which
> can probably be saved only as fragments. (I: 212)

Diving, then, into the watery grave of dead philosophies, Arendt discovers pearly short texts. If they seem not to mean what they meant before they were "fragments," it is because they have "suffered a sea-change."

Volume I: Thinking

The volume on thinking begins with an epigraph by Martin Heidegger, a four-point declaration about what "thinking" does not do. In Heidegger's words, "thinking does not bring knowledge as do the sciences . . . does not produce usable practical wisdom . . . does not solve the riddles of the universe . . . does not endow us directly with the power to act." Clearly, the questions then are: What *does* thinking do? What *is* it, anyway?

According to Arendt, it is the activity of a mental faculty that differs from the mental *cognitive* faculty. It was, so to speak, "discovered" by Immanuel Kant, even though, as Arendt never tires of repeating throughout the volume, Kant "remained less than fully aware of the extent to which he had liberated reason, the ability to think."[6] Arendt writes, further:

> Crucial for our enterprise is Kant's distinction between *Vernunft* and
> *Verstand,* "reason" and "intellect". . . . the distinguishing of the two

faculties, reason and intellect, coincides with a distinction between two
altogether different mental activities, thinking and knowing, and two
altogether different concerns, meaning, in the first category, and
cognition, in the second. (I: 13–14)

In fact, the entire volume on thinking is controlled by the thesis, derived
from her special interpretation of Kant, that the mind has two diverse
faculties: one a cognitive faculty questing for *truth,* the other not a cognitive
faculty but one that quests for *meaning.* But what does Arendt mean by
"truth," and what does she mean by "meaning"?

"Truth is what we are compelled to admit," she says. "That truth compels
with the force of necessity (*anagkē*), which is far stronger than the force of
violence (*bia*), is an old *topos* in Greek philosophy, and it is always meant as
a compliment to truth that it can compel men with the irresistible force of
Necessity." To which she adds a rather silly sentence from a second order
eighteenth-century Physiocrat with a melodious name: " 'Euclid,' as Mercier
de la Rivière once noted, 'is a veritable despot; the truths he has transmitted
to us are laws veritably despotic' " (I: 60).

Now, that "it is in the nature of truth to necessitate the mind" may be
analogous metaphorically to a projectile being "necessitated" to describe a
parabolic path or some similar mechanical law, but metaphorical comparisons between the force of truth and the rule of despots are not only dubious
but diseased. In fact, Arendt's willingness to bring in such political meta-
phors and her reiterations of truth as "compelling" seem obsessive and
imply a fanatic loyalty to absolute freedom. Surely, the sane feeling about
a Q.E.D. at the end of a Euclidean or Newtonian proposition is a feeling of
pleasure, not some sort of shudder that a measure of "freedom" has been
lost.

Yet it is quite right to insist, as Arendt does, that philosophy has more
than once been seduced by mathematics. This happened when German
philosophers failed to see the "liberating" effects of Kant's insights, she
points out, and thus they pursued "the Cartesian ideal of certainty as
though Kant had never existed, they believed in all earnest that the results
of their speculations possessed the same kind of validity as the results of
cognitive processes" (I: 16).

What Arendt has added here is something very good as far as it goes. It
is true that the Greeks inserted into the history of philosophy an ideal goal
for philosophy of certain knowledge (*epistēmē*) which they derived from an
understandable near ecstasy about mathematics. It is true that Aristotle,
though he did not practice philosophy in accord with it, wrote the *Posterior
Analytics* as an exercise in the logic of mathematics, proceeding from axioms
and definitions by sound reasoning to certain "compelling" conclusions, to
the end that he might state the conditions governing the quest in *all* disciplines for certain knowledge or *epistēmē*.[7] Arendt is right that the vision of
such a goal for the questing of the human intellect persisted and haunted

modern philosophy. It presided over the great dogmatic, rationalistic philosophies of the seventeenth century, particularly those of Descartes, Leibniz, and Spinoza, the last set forth in mathematical style. It presided over Kant's astonished admiration for the certitudes of Newton's *Mathematical Principles of Natural Philosophy*, leading him to so construct the mind as to make such an achievement intelligible and the pretenses or goals of the dogmatic philosophers impossible. Arendt is also right when she says that the post-Kantian German idealists, Hegel and the post-Hegelians, ignored Kant's *Critique of Pure Reason* and proffered big, closed "systems" in which Thought as it were encompassed Being—systems presented as *the* Truth. And Arendt is eminently right in declaring that, at least in a general way (since all these "great" philosophers have professorial followers), the systems of the dogmatic rationalists and the spectacular idealists are, except for pearly fragments, dead.

But she could have made the good point she does without making the bad one that in her view leads to it. In *The Unity of Philosophical Experience* (1937), Étienne Gilson, whose writings Arendt knew and respected, undertook to show "that the history of philosophy makes philosophical sense," and defined "its meaning in regard to the nature of philosophical knowledge itself." He proceeded in this book to trace the formation and subsequent breakdown of every great system of thought from the medieval to the modern. But he did not thereby conclude that philosophy was barren, still less that philosophy was dead. Such a conclusion, he argued, was always the preface to some new philosophical contention. "The so-called death of philosophy being regularly attended by its revival," he wrote, "some new dogmatism should now be at hand." To which he added that "the first law to be inferred from philosophical experience is: *Philosophy always buries its undertakers.*" Arendt, however, shows no sign of remembering this "first law." She thus leaves herself subject to the rule he states.

A book by Mortimer Adler published in 1965 shows likewise that it is possible to expose philosophy's errors without deciding that philosophy itself *is* error. Entitled *The Conditions of Philosophy: Its Checkered Past, Its Present Disorder, and Its Future Promise*, this book contains, in the same sense that Gilson's book did, broad philosophical judgments on the history of philosophy which make Arendt's good point without making her bad one. Adler contends, as I have contended, that the course of philosophy has persistently been harmed by the assumption that *epistēmē* (certain, indubitable, incorrigible, "compelling" knowledge) was an attainable ideal. He points out what he takes to be "the baleful influence" of mathematics on philosophy. He urges that there is "a moderate or weaker sense of the word 'knowledge' equally applicable to the disciplines of history, science, and philosophy." "Knowledge in this moderate sense," Adler says, might be best thought of as reasonable and reasoned "opinions" (*doxa*), expressed in "propositions which are (1) testable by reference to evidence, (2) subject to rational criticism, and either (3) corrigible and rectifiable or (4) falsifiable."

In the few pages which Arendt devotes to modern science, the product of the cognitive faculty that "quests for truth," she shows herself thoroughly aware that such science does not claim that it attains truth in the highest possible mode, that it consists of a sequence of provisional "verities," all far short of the compelling certitude Kant excitedly thought Newton had reached. Why did it not occur to Arendt to examine the possibility that philosophy, after critical reflection on its history, is quite capable of seeing that it, too, cannot attain knowledge and truth in the highest possible mode, but that it is not therefore a futile undertaking?

There is no contradiction involved in the assertions (1) that the human intellect—one power, not split into two faculties with two different sorts of desire—naturally, ineluctably, and ineradicably desires fundamental truth about what is, and (2) that it yet cannot attain such truth in the certain sense of *epistēmē*. The discovery of (2) does not lead to philosophy's obituary, but only to its speculative extension.

As for the rest, while Arendt tells us that "this distinction between truth and meaning seems to me to be . . . decisive for any inquiry into the nature of human thinking," and while she asserts that "a clear-cut line of demarcation between these two altogether different modes cannot be found in the history of philosophy," her own effort to formulate such a distinction is an exercise in confusion (I: 57–58). An instance of this occurs when she credits some "occasional remarks" by Aristotle in his *On Interpretation* with being "exceptions" to the no clear-cut line to be "found in the history of philosophy." She cites a passage from that work in which Aristotle distinguishes between sentences that have meaning but do not have either truth or falsity in them (predicable of them). As an example of the latter, Aristotle submits the meaningful kind of sentence which is a prayer. Elsewhere he offers other examples of meaning sentences—*e.g.*, those that express a question or a command. The distinction he is making is perfectly clear, but Arendt's use of it is not. For what is at stake in *her* distinction between "truth" and "meaning" is a distinction between sentences in science that have *both* meaning and truth or falsity in them, and sentences—products of "thinking"—that, though they have the same grammatical and logical form as those scientific sentences, nevertheless have *only* meaning in them, and have neither truth nor falsity. These are quite different, needless to say, from prayers, questions, commands, and the like.[8] And the confusion is not resolved when a few pages later Arendt writes, Anselm's "ontological demonstration of the existence of God, [though] not valid and in this sense not true . . . is full of meaning" (I: 61). What apart from its validity Anselm's demonstration could mean, except in some historical or psychological terms with which philosophy as such has nothing to do, is impossible to guess.

There are various places in this volume where things are said that lead one to think "meaning" is something ineffable. At I: 65, Arendt is enthusiastic about Kant's assertion that "pure reason [the noncognitive faculty that *thinks*] is in fact occupied with nothing but itself. It can have no other vocation." At I: 123, "thinking is out of order because the quest for meaning produces no end result that will survive the activity, that will make sense after the activity has come to its end." In that same place, I: 123, "the only possible metaphor one may conceive of for the life of the mind [she means the thinking faculty of the mind] is the sensation of being alive . . . *without thinking the human mind is dead.*" One is tempted to think that for Arendt the quest for meaning is in truth something quixotic, intrinsically hopeless, but an adventure needed lest the mind die. At I: 166–67, Arendt speaks of the "helplessness of the thinking ego to give an account of itself." Though one had been given to think that thinking had as its *purpose* a "quest for meaning," one is told at I: 129, that "our question, What makes us think?, does not ask for either causes or purposes." Near the end Arendt writes:

> As I approach the end of these considerations, I hope that no reader expects a conclusive summary. For me to make such an attempt would stand in flagrant contradiction to what has been described here. If thinking is an activity that is its own end and if the only adequate metaphor for it . . . is the sensation of being alive, then it follows that all questions concerning the aim or purpose of thinking are as unanswerable as questions about the aim or purpose of life. (I: 197)

One had been told that the aim or purpose of "thinking" was to find "meaning." Here one is told that questions about the aim or purpose of thinking are unanswerable. Perhaps one should not be surprised, therefore, if one feels that one has failed in the quest for Arendt's meaning of meaning.

Volume I is an elaborate "thought-experiment" (Arendt's term) in splitting the human intellect into two radically diverse faculties. The confusion to which it leads tends to confirm the opposite thesis—that the human intellect is something single, by nature in quest of truth, whatever its capacity may be for perfect attainment.

Volume II: Willing

Volume II, *Willing,* is easier to come to terms with than Volume I. It is not overridden by a dubious thesis about truth and meaning. Arendt decided "to analyze the Will in terms of its history," and she finds well-marked periods in that history. She finds paradigmatic authors and stays with them; there is very little of the astonishing intercalation of brief texts characteristic of Volume I and far less digressiveness. There is, of course, one carryover from Volume I. Arendt is "thinking" about what various authors "thought" about the faculty of will and its freedom or unfreedom. But neither they, as they say what they "think," nor she, as she unmistakably reveals which "thinkers" seem to her to be, so to speak, "right," are to be bound by the constraints of "truth" or the burden of supporting argument, these being requirements that, her first volume has argued, can and must be put aside.

Since Arendt professes no theory of willing and assumes no position with respect to it, one can just indicate here what she takes to be the main lines of the history of willing. It is something of a drama. "Prior to the rise of Christianity we nowhere find any notion of a mental faculty corresponding to the 'idea' of Freedom," she asserts (II: 6). She has a sound section on Aristotle's notion of "choice" (*proairesis*), treated "as a kind of forerunner of the Will," but she follows Gilson's observation "that Aristotle speaks neither of liberty nor of free will . . . the term itself is lacking."[9] "Choice" appears to have been taken in the classical period of Greek philosophy as a given fact of experience; nothing problematic was cast up by the assertion of that fact.

The "discovery" of the will and of a whole host of thorny theological issues about its freedom arose from the religious experiences and conversions of St. Paul and St. Augustine, Arendt tells us. St. Paul in his Letter to the Romans dramatically reports inner conflicts and tormenting impotence of will; Augustine both reports and then proceeds to the philosophical analysis of his conflictful experience on the way to conversion. In recognition of this, the sections in chapter 2 on St. Paul ("and the impotence of the Will") and on Augustine ("the first philosopher of the Will"), though separated by the brief discussion of Epictetus's manual for training the will to avoid misery, are the central parts of Arendt's second volume.[10] She especially delights in expounding Augustine's *Confessions,* which she admires because they "are almost entirely non-argumentative and rich in what we today would call 'phenomenological' descriptions."

In chapter 3, Arendt jumps some 800 years of history to encounter two Christian theologians who do not write "phenomenologically" at all and are exceedingly "argumentative." Sections 11 and 12 of Volume II are devoted to "Thomas Aquinas and the Primacy of Intellect" and to "Duns Scotus and the Primacy of the Will." The differences between Aquinas and Scotus over the intellect and the will and their interrelations in human free acts have long since been researched and analyzed in monographs by Gilson and others. In her thirty-four pages on the two, Arendt is far from being a reliable expositor.[11] But she does contribute emotions—something like animosity or even repugnance, to Aquinas[12]—and total, almost breathless admiration for Scotus (indeed, if she could permit herself to say so, she clearly "thinks" Scotus has a "true" doctrine). This last may be in part because she has perceived, though she does not acknowledge, that in Aquinas's doctrine, while the soul blessed by grace is preeminently free, yet it loses freedom of exercise in the will and cannot *not* will to look and rejoice; whereas Scotus holds that even then, while the will cannot turn away *if* it wills, yet it retains the power not to will—which is about as extreme an assertion of the will's autonomy as is possible to find.

The last chapter, "Conclusions," is in the main concerned with "the uncertain destinies of the willing faculty at the close of the modern age."

The featured authors are Nietzsche (Section 14: "His Repudiation of the Will") and Heidegger (Section 15: "His Will-not-to-Will"). Both are described as embarked on an archaizing search for companionship with the pre-Socratics. The quotations from Nietzsche are, it will surprise no one, exciting. Those from Heidegger are true to his famous (or infamous) opacity.[13] Heidegger's "so-called reversal (*Kehre*) or 'turn-about,'" and his later first and second turnings, and his still later "reinterpretation" of his turnings—all leading him to some sort of rest in "the Will-*not*-to-Will"—are dealt with by Arendt as though Heidegger were somewhere underground sending up oracles. This reader found the atmosphere around the tripod very smoky.

The connection to the last section of the book is somewhat unclear. It is something like this: having so long considered what has been "thought" about "willing," what can we learn about it from the great moments of *action*—moments of "revolution"—and of the founding of cities? All these themes of these last twenty-three pages are familiar from Arendt's earlier political books. But they are ardently, movingly renewed. Her reflections on the biblical and the Roman foundation legends (and in the latter case, her pages on Virgil) are deeply imaginative and beautiful.

*   *   *

This reviewer has felt compelled to express dismay at Arendt's ambitions, audacities, even arrogance, because of his judgment that they have involved her in errors, major and minor. But there is another way of taking her book that would better emphasize its importance, a way more consistent with her own manner—intensely individual, unaccountable, quasi-solipsistic—of "thinking" about thinking and willing. Given that manner, it is decidedly not patronizing or impious (in the Virgilian sense) to read the book as Arendt's end-of-her-life account of the life of *her* mind on "the awesome subjects" of thinking and willing. To be sure, there is nothing overtly autobiographical in her style. Yet, she has given herself no ground for complaint if one reads her book as something like a memoir, for "our present situation," on the meaning of the death of philosophy.

The book *is* such a memoir and, because of Arendt's stature as a life-long, passionate student of Greek and German philosophy, it is a memoir that matters. Its somewhat extravagant morbidity can and should provoke those who care about the past, present, and future of the stubbornly persistent philosophic enterprise. The book's many moments of intellectual passion should be moving, in several senses of the word, to minds young and old, whatever their present philosophical prepossessions. It is difficult for this reader, for example, to feel anything but revulsion for Hegel. Yet, I am caught by Arendt's pages about him, in which he is a fallen hero who ultimately failed "to reconcile the two mental activities, thinking and willing, with their opposing time concepts" (II: 47). Arendt's pages of excited sympathy with Augustine's powerful mind are moving also. Her pages of reverence for the legendary Socrates say things freshly—no mean accomplishment. And for one last example, it is proper to be provocatively saddened by her near ecstasy about Scotus's view of the human will, followed, in her history of the will, by her manifestly dismayed incomprehension of Heidegger's late sinking into a "Will-*not*-to-Will" (at all).

Generally, then, whether taken as her Gifford Lectures or as a sui generis memoir, or as both, Arendt's *The Life of the Mind* is, as the French would say, with a certain ambiguity in the adjective, *un livre formidable*.

---

[1] *The Life of the Mind, Volume I: Thinking; Volume II: Willing* (New York: Harcourt Brace Jovanovich, 1978).

[2] Fair warning of this habit occurs early. Volume I, for example, contains on page 8, Cato, Carnap, Heidegger, Aristotle, Wittgenstein, and Hegel; on page 9, Heidegger, Nietzsche, Hegel, Kant, Moses Mendelssohn, and Richard McKeon.

[3] There is no space in this review to submit numerous examples of such "demonstrations." However, one instance can be referred to. On page II: 18, Arendt refers to a text at the end of Book XII, Chap. 20, in Augustine's *City of God*. On the last page of Volume II on willing, that same text is used as somehow sealing what the whole volume has led to. The fact is that if one reads the whole of Augustine's short chap. 20, it is *strictly impossible* to read the fragment Arendt quotes as meaning what she has it meaning.

[4] Elisabeth Young-Bruehl to the Editor of the *New York Review of Books*, 25 January 1979.

[5] *Full fathom five thy father lies,*
    Of his bones are coral made,
   Those are pearls that were his eyes.
   Nothing of him that doth fade
   But doth suffer a sea-change
      Into something rich and strange.

[6] An astonishing number of passages could be assembled in which Arendt cites a brief text from a philosopher as illuminating, only to add that *he* did not quite see the light in it that *she* sees. Against the charge of arrogance, the reply would have to be that since the philosopher's enterprise was essentially wrong-headed he therefore *could* fail to understand himself as well as Arendt does, who knows it to be wrong-headed.

[7] *See* Mortimer J. Adler, *The Conditions of Philosophy* (New York: Atheneum, 1965), pp. 247–48.

[8] There is an example of another kind of confusion in this paragraph of Arendt's. She speaks of this passage from Aristotle as "an occasional remark" that remained without significance for Aristotle's later philosophy. This is just one of those many instances, referred to in footnote 6, wherein a great philosopher does not see in his propositions what Arendt sees. In point of fact, in the sentence that immediately follows what Arendt quotes—a sentence that Arendt omits—Aristotle writes: "Let us pass over all such [*i.e.*, sentences expressing prayers, questions, commands, and the like] since their study more properly belongs to the province of rhetoric or poetry."

Further, by reference to her assertion about "what cannot be found in the history of philosophy," this distinction of Aristotle's is amply and firmly followed up in the medieval treatise of Thomas of Erfurt, *On the Modes of Signification*, and firmly followed up by contemporary British linguistic analysts.

[9] Étienne Gilson, *The Spirit of Mediaeval Philosophy*, (New York, 1949), p. 307.

[10] The sections on St. Paul and Augustine are amplifications of themes stated in an essay Arendt wrote in the 1950s entitled "What Is Freedom," Chap. 4 in *Between Past and Future* (New York: Viking Press, 1961). Those themes had been set forth, and in the same terms, in Chap. 15, "Free-Will and Christian Liberty," especially footnote 12, of the book by Gilson previously cited. Her debt to this is unacknowledged by Arendt either in the older essay or here.

[11] There is no space in this review for extended support of this charge, but one example may be offered. At II: 119 Arendt writes: "It is obvious that Being, Thomas' first principle, is simply a conceptualization of Life and the life instinct." This is one of the silliest things ever said in the history of metaphysics. One is tempted to recall what Gilson said of Kant: "Though he busied himself with questions about metaphysics, he had no metaphysical interests of his own ... indeed we should remember that what he knew about metaphysics was mere hearsay."

[12] Thomas's literary form, the "article," often admired as one of the few beautiful forms for philosophical writing, drives Arendt wild. Her mania about "compulsion," noted in earlier pages in Volume I, breaks out when she speaks of Thomas's "kind of sheer rational demonstration, usually iron-clad" in which "no rhetoric, no kind of persuasion is ever used; the reader is compelled as only truth can compel." To which she adds that "the trust in compelling truth, so general in medieval philosophy, is boundless in Thomas" (II: 115). It is pretty strong in Arendt's hero, Duns Scotus, too, though she does not say so.

[13] For example, at II: 174, Arendt writes, by way of expounding a point of Heidegger's: "The first demand Being makes of man is to think out the 'ontological difference,' that is, the difference between the sheer isness of beings and the Being of this isness itself, the Being of Being."

On Human Nature

by Edward O. Wilson

Professor Wilson, in his preface to this third book of what we are told is a trilogy, strikes a modest tone. "I might easily be wrong," he says, "in any particular conclusion, in the grander hopes for the role of the natural sciences, and in the trust gambled on scientific materialism."[1] It is hard to know what to make of such a statement. On the record to date Professor Wilson is decidedly not a modest man. Certainly it is not every decade that someone discovers, invents, or fabricates a "new science," and having done so, goes on almost at once to urge that this new science holds hope, perhaps the only hope, for a solution to grave problems in the human condition. To find a precedent for that, one would have to go back past Herbert Spencer —in his fashion a sociobiologist, though one who is no longer read—to Auguste Comte. Not that Comte is now much read either. Nevertheless, in a manner that prefigures Professor Wilson he proclaimed the end of the prior theological and metaphysical stages of the sciences and of society. On the arrival of the third and final "Positivistic" stage, Comte offered a new science which he first called "social physics" and later "sociology." He was worried that the demolition of traditional religion would entail a loss in social cohesion which the natural and social sciences might not be able to make up for. Thus he earnestly, albeit absurdly, proposed a new secular religion of humanity, complete with a catechism of Positive religion, a hierarchical priesthood, and a new Positivistic calendar to go along with instructions for the worship on given days of mankind's benefactors in chapels that displayed their busts. In defense of his formulation, Comte wrote:

> If we have been accustomed to deplore the spectacle, among the
> artisan class, of a workman occupied during his whole life in nothing
> but making knife handles or pinheads, we may find something quite as
> lamentable in the intellectual class, in the exclusive employment of the
> human brain in resolving equations or classifying insects. The moral
> effect is, unhappily, analogous in the two cases. It occasions a miserable
> indifference about the general course of human affairs.

We are reminded in reading this that the first book in Professor Wilson's trilogy is *The Insect Societies*. He is, after all, Curator of Entomology at the Museum of Comparative Zoology, Harvard University. But, whether with Comte's admonition in mind or not, he has not been indifferent to human affairs. The third volume of his trilogy, as its title indicates, is devoted to the subject of human nature.

In his preface, Wilson speaks of the book as:

> not a work of science; [but] a work about science, and about how far the natural sciences can penetrate into human behavior before they will be transformed into something new. It examines the reciprocal impact that a truly evolutionary explanation of human behavior must have on the social sciences and humanities. [This book] may be read for information about behavior and sociobiology, which I have been careful to document. But its core is a speculative essay about the profound consequences that will follow as social theory at long last meets that part of the natural sciences most relevant to it. (p. xi)

As it turns out, and when one takes into account the structure of the book, especially its being framed by a first chapter on "Dilemma" and a last chapter on "Hope," the work as a whole is hortatory and, in its last chapter, positively homiletic.

The volume has nine chapters. The seven between the first and last divide clearly into a first set of three chapters and a subsequent set of four. The first set consists of three smallish chapters on "Heredity," "Development," and "Emergence." They are intended to show, in a general way, the scope of the impact of evolutionary processes on "human nature." Familiar enough evidence is adduced, though in a scrambled way, from the usual disciplines, from the study of animals but especially of primate behavior, through genetics to the latest results in molecular biology. Predictions of what future scientific work will bring forth are generously made and, somewhat illicitly, entered into the argument. The central aim of these three chapters is contained in the very definition given to the term "human nature" in Wilson's rather curious glossary at the end of the book. That glossary has this entry:

> *Human nature.* In the broader sense, the full set of innate behavioral predispositions that characterize the human species; and in the narrower sense, those predispositions that affect social behavior.

The aim, then, is to display the range of constraints upon the leading of a human life that are placed by physically transmitted, ineradicable traits. That man is elaborately preprogrammed before he sets forth on a human life is the burden of the message.

An effort is made in these three chapters to support Wilson's contention that the argument there is the work of a new science, sociobiology, but it is difficult for this reasonably literate layman to see how that is so. At the very least, as Colin Beer, a *New York Times* reviewer of his book, has said, it seems that "objections can be raised to Professor Wilson's touting of sociobiology as a new discipline [since] what is sound science in his enterprise is a continuation of traditional Darwinian biology."[2]

There can be no valid complaint against biological studies which seek to discover genuine, physically inherited constraints that severely limit the scope of human choice. Human freedom (which a Harvard colleague of Wilson's has striven to take us "beyond"[3]) has never been presented, except by certain contemporary existentialist philosophers, as something absolute, something unlimited.

On the other hand, the merest tyro in a high school seminar could not help asking: "But, then, are we not at all free?" And in fact Wilson, while emphasizing and doubtless exaggerating the degree and kinds of constraints physically inherited, is at pains to stress—throughout his book, and critically in the last chapter—that preprogramming is something substantially, even astonishingly, less in the human being than in any other animal species. He even fervently affirms that somehow, because perhaps of the size of the human brain, many options are still open, options that can firmly enough be taken so that they can be culturally, not physically, transmitted.

Beyond any doubt, the tyro's plaintive question about human freedom is important. In this connection, Professor Stuart Hampshire was mistaken in his own review of Wilson's book when he wrote: "The question of whether there is a sense in which the multiply varied human responses must be assumed to be determined, even though they are probably incalculably complex, Wilson leaves to one side, wisely."[4] Professor Hampshire is wrong on two counts: (1) it would not have been wise to leave that question to one side; it would be, in my understanding of the structure and the importance of the argument, not only unwise but inexcusable; (2) in fact, Professor Wilson does confront the question of human freedom (*see* pp. 71–77). But the jejune quality of his treatment seems to have led Hampshire, who has written a complex philosophical book on individual freedom,[5] to miss the fact that Wilson has given the question a comically evasive answer.

Wilson's position on what he calls "the paradox of determinism and free will" can be fairly presented in a brief way. He first discusses two cases, that of a coin flipped and that of a honeybee propelled into the air. Wilson's scientific materialism leads him to consider these two trajectories to be determined and so intrinsically predictable. But, in fact, he says, even with all the resources and measuring tools of modern science brought to bear, we can know the destiny of the coin only to a limited extent. Similarly, with the same resources "we might predict the flight path of the bee with an accuracy that exceeds pure chance," though far from perfectly. However, this need not bother the bee, since "in her own 'mind' the bee, who is isolated permanently from such human knowledge, will always have free will." Then, coming to a third case, that of an individual man, Wilson says:

> When human beings ponder their own central nervous systems, they
> appear at first to be in the same position as the honeybee. Even
> though human behavior is enormously more complicated and variable
> than that of insects, theoretically it can be specified. Genetic constraints

and the restricted number of environments in which human beings can live limit the array of possible outcomes substantially. But only techniques beyond our present imagining could hope to achieve even the short-term prediction of the detailed behavior of an individual human being, and such an accomplishment might be beyond the capacity of any conceivable intelligence.... It may be a law of nature that no nervous system is capable of acquiring enough knowledge to significantly predict the future of any other intelligent system in detail. Nor can intelligent minds gain enough self-knowledge to know their own future, capture fate, and in this sense eliminate free will. (pp. 73–74)

Thus an individual man's course of action, while not really free (something not even dreamable to a true believer in a philosophy of scientific materialism), is yet so complex as to defy effective scientific prediction, a fact which makes it possible for a man to feel as "free" as a bee. It is hard to imagine that the tyro will be able to take much comfort from this curious sense of freedom.

After these three chapters on general theory, Wilson invites the reader "to reconsider four of the elemental categories of behavior, aggression, sex, altruism, and religion, on the basis of sociobiological theory." There is room here only to indicate the kind of "advice to humans" that emerges from the sociobiological account of these four "elemental categories." Something more must be said about religion, however, not just because Wilson's account of it has a certain surprising originality, but because it provides the main transition to the chapter on (human) "Hope," circling back to the first chapter on (the human) "Dilemma."

Wilson holds that "the human forms of aggressive behavior are species-specific: although basically primate in form, they contain features that distinguish them from aggression in all other species." He declares Freud, Konrad Lorenz, and Erich Fromm to be flatly wrong in their position that "a widespread unitary aggressive instinct exists." He himself has a far more modulated view, contending that "no fewer than seven categories [of aggression] can be distinguished," and within the space given by a short chapter he illustrates that diversity from research in zoology and ethology.

Of course in the end he comes to human war. He has two exciting biological terms (*hypertrophy* and *autocatalysis*) explained in the glossary, as pivots for his discussion: "The practice of war is a straightforward example of a hypertrophied biological predisposition." By this he means, as he explains, that war is an enormous enlargement of aggression in the way "an elephant's tusk represents the hypertrophic enlargement and change in shape through evolution of a tooth that originally had an ordinary form." Then again, Wilson says, "the evolution of warfare" is an "autocatalytic reaction that could not be halted by any people, because to attempt to reverse the process unilaterally was to fall victim. A new mode of natural selection was operating at the level of entire societies" (p. 116).

Whether such terminology really adds anything to some familiar Darwinian ideas is open to doubt. There is in any case nothing startling about the advice that Wilson offers on the basis of these propositions to human beings who have hitherto brooded about war and peace without the aid of sociobiology. We are told merely that "to provide a more durable foundation for peace, political and cultural ties can be promoted that create a confusion of cross-binding loyalties." The word "confusion" aside, this would appear only to be what men have known since the time of Homer, though the knowledge has perhaps not done them very much good.

There are too many pieces of research and of speculation in the brief chapter on "Sex" to summarize here. The "profound consequences" of the subject mentioned by Wilson in his preface may be briefly commented upon. For example, this text:

> In full recognition of the struggle for women's rights that is now
> spreading thoughout the world, each society must make one or the
> other of the three following choices: [1] *Condition its members so as to
> exaggerate sexual differences in behavior. . . .* [2] *Train its members so as to
> eliminate all sexual differences in behavior. . . .* [3] *Provide equal opportunities
> and access but take no further action.* (pp. 132–33)

Wilson's comment on this trinity of options is as follows:

> From this troubling ambiguity concerning sex roles one firm
> conclusion can be drawn: the evidences of biological constraint alone
> cannot prescribe an ideal course of action. However, they can help us
> to define the options and to assess the price of each. (p. 134)

Such a conclusion seems fair enough. Whatever the terms in which we understand these three alternatives, if persuasive help about the costs of any one of them can be offered by evolutionary biology, it should be sought and used. But that our understanding would thereby be raised to the level of a new science is something else again.

The pattern is the same in Wilson's admittedly speculative position about homosexuality:

> There is, I wish to suggest, a strong possibility that homosexuality is
> normal in a biological sense, that it is a distinctive beneficent behavior
> that evolved as an important element of early human social
> organization. Homosexuals may be the generic carriers of some of
> mankind's rare altruistic impulses.

Once again, if this hypothesis, at present something fanciful, were to receive some measure of plausibility on the evidence, then such evidence should enter into deliberations about latter-day, complex social organization. But there already exist sciences of this. The same can be said about the suggestion that it is to evolutionary biology that we must turn for a revolution of current issues about the future of the family.

Coming to "Altruism," Wilson offers a small chapter culled from a 1975 article written for the *New York Times Magazine,* doubtless solicited by an editor's query: "What's new in the new science of sociobiology?" It is obvious that after chapters on "Aggression" and "Sex" — relatively well-established subjects in evolutionary biology — Wilson is moving on here to a subject not so submissive to the methods of empirical scientific materialism, a tendency that reaches its climax in chapter 8 on "Religion."

The cue to the chapter on "Altruism" is in its opening sentence, which takes off from a text by Tertullian, who it is true was given to expressing himself in somewhat violent terms. Wilson writes:

'The blood of martyrs is the seed of the church.' With that chilling
dictum the third-century theologian Tertullian confessed the
fundamental flaw of human altruism, an intimation that the purpose of
sacrifice is to raise one human group over another. (p. 149)

Now that is not at all what Tertullian meant, of course. And such a misconstruction of his meaning, as well as of the whole literature of martyrology, tells practitioners of the humanities a good deal about Wilson's abilities to build a bridge between the "two cultures" — a construction that Wilson several times claims can find its foundations in the new science of sociobiology.

There is more. After examples of what he calls "hard-core altruism" in the behavior of certain birds, social insects, and chimpanzees, Wilson introduces the term "soft-core altruism" to characterize altruism that is "ultimately selfish," because of its expectation of reciprocation and reward. He writes:

A key question of social theory, then, must be the relative amounts of
hard-core as opposed to soft-core altruism. . . . The distinction is
important because pure, hard-core altruism based on kin selection is
the enemy of civilization. . . . My own estimate of the relative
proportions of hard-core and soft-core altruism in human behavior is
optimistic. Human beings appear to be sufficiently selfish and
calculating to be capable of indefinitely greater harmony and social
homeostasis. This statement is not self-contradictory. True selfishness, if
obedient to the other constraints of mammalian biology, is the key to a
more nearly perfect social contract. (pp. 156–57)

And so, from a shaky, ill-articulated distinction between two kinds of altruism, followed by a short miscellany of examples from bird, insect, and mammalian life, there emerges a position about "the social contract" — a subject by no means clearly within the range of sociobiology, and one in any case that other disciplines are already adequate to deal with.

Decidedly the most problematic of the four categories discussed is that of religious behavior. Wilson remarks at the beginning of chapter 8 that "the predisposition to religious belief is the most complex and powerful force in the human mind and in all probability an ineradicable part of human nature." Later, he speaks of "religion [as] one of the major categories of behavior undeniably unique to the human species." These considerations lead him to state that "religion constitutes the greatest challenge to human sociobiology and its most exciting opportunity to progress as a truly original theoretical discipline." In response, and with full admission of the many cultural forms religion has taken, he declares "that religious practices can be mapped onto the two dimensions of genetic advantage and evolutionary change."

There can be no following out that mapping here. But Wilson's conclusions should be recorded. "The mind," he writes, "is predisposed—one can speculate that learning rules are physiologically programmed—to participate in a few processes of sacralization which in combination generate the institutions of organized religion." And again, "the readiness to be indoctrinated [is] a neurologically based learning rule that evolved through the selection of clans competing one against the other."[6] The underlying contention is that the "processes of sacralization," of which myth-making is the most powerful, confer biological advantage upon a "clan" in the strictest Darwinian sense. Wilson's discussion of sacralizing processes for the most part touches primitive religions, magic, witchcraft, and tribal rituals. But there is no indication that the so-called higher religions would cause him to alter his speculative hypothesis in any significant way.

The book's big moment comes when Wilson, impressed with the emotional powers of religious commitment and ceremonies and the cohesive results of religious mythopoeic power, asks whether those powers cannot be appropriated, or expropriated, or transmogrified by scientific materialism. This is something of a novelty in the old quarrel between science and religion. In Wilson's own words:

[Scientific materialism] presents the human mind with an alternative mythology that until now has always, point for point in zones of conflict, defeated traditional religion. Its narrative form is the epic . . . the evolutionary epic. . . . Most importantly, we have come to the crucial stage in the history of biology when religion itself is subject to the explanations of the natural sciences. As I have tried to show, sociobiology can account for the very origin of mythology by the principle of natural selection acting on the genetically evolving material structure of the human brain.

If this interpretation is correct, the final decisive edge enjoyed by scientific naturalism will come from its capacity to explain traditional religion, its chief competitor, as a wholly material phenomenon. Theology is not likely to survive as an independent intellectual discipline. But religion itself will endure for a long time as a vital force in society. Like the mythical giant Antaeus who drew energy from his mother, the earth, religion cannot be defeated by those who merely cast it down. The spiritual weakness of scientific naturalism is due to

the fact that it has no such primal source of power. While explaining
the biological sources of religious emotional strength, it is unable in its
present form to draw on them. . . . So the time has come to ask: Does a
way exist to divert the power of religion into the services of the great
new enterprise that lays bare the sources of that power? We have
come back at last to the second dilemma in a form that demands an
answer. (pp. 192–93)

This ending of the chapter on "Religion," with its query about "diverting
the power of religion," leads to the final chapter on "Hope," wherein the
two dilemmas set forth in chapter 1 about the present human condition are,
if not to be resolved, at least removed as causes for despair.

Again, the account of the two dilemmas is best given in Wilson's words:

To the extent that the new naturalism is true, its pursuit seems certain
to generate two great spiritual dilemmas. The first is that no species,
ours included, possesses a purpose beyond the imperatives created by
its genetic history. . . . The first dilemma, in a word, is that we have no
particular place to go. The species lacks any goal external to its own
biological nature. . . . The danger implicit in the first dilemma is the
rapid dissolution of transcendental goals toward which societies can
organize their energies. Those goals . . . have faded; they went one by
one like mirages, as we drew closer. In order to search for a new
morality based upon a more truthful definition of man, it is necessary
to look inward, to dissect the machinery of the mind and to retrace its
evolutionary history. But the effort, I predict, will uncover the second
dilemma, which is the choice that must be made among the ethical
premises inherent in man's biological nature. (pp. 2–5)

In the chapter on "Hope," the address to the first dilemma is brief,
perhaps because Wilson construes his whole book as leading to it:

The intellectual solution of the first dilemma can be achieved by a
deeper and more courageous examination of human nature that
combines the findings of biology with those of the social sciences. The
mind will be more precisely explained as an epiphenomenon of the
neuronal machinery of the brain. (p. 195)

Wilson's somewhat patronizing glossary contains no entry for "epiphenomenon." To grasp what it is that he so confidently predicts, it should
be noted that something may be called epiphenomenal if it is secondary and
derivative, bearing to the primary phenomenon the relation that, say, the
hum of a motor has to the work the motor actually does. No more reductive
position can be taken than that the mind of man is entirely epiphenomenal,
a kind of hum emitted by the working brain.

The importance of pausing on Wilson's extreme of reductive materialism
is that it perforce rearouses, or should rearouse, our sense of what man has
made of man in the whole Western tradition, pre-Darwin and post-Darwin.

No one, Descartes in a special way excepted, ever denied that man was (generically) an animal. The major question has always been: Do the wondrous achievements of the mind of man and of the intellectualized imagination suggest, or not, that man is different in kind, not just in degree, from the other animals? Darwin gave one answer, influential because of his eminence in theorizing about the descent of man, though it may not have been the strongest answer possible since philosophy was not his forte. In our time, many scientists and ordinary laymen consider the question answered by the picturesque, though paltry, linguistic achievements of chimpanzees and great apes taught by patient and ingenious humans. That day which Wilson predicts, when the epiphenomenality of the mind is finally determined, would, if it arrived, of course settle the matter, since if the only explanation for man's achievements is that he has a much larger brain, the difference between him and other animals would then be established as a difference of degree. In the meantime, it is simply foolish to think that the fundamental question about human nature has been resolved.[7]

Concluding his remarks on the first dilemma, Wilson writes:

> By a judicious extension of the methods and ideas of neurobiology,
> ethology, and sociobiology a proper foundation can be laid for the
> social sciences, and the discontinuity still separating the natural sciences
> on the one side and the social sciences and humanities on the other
> might be erased. (p. 195)

The reference here is, of course, to the recent controversy about *The Two Cultures*, conducted by C. P. Snow and F. R. Leavis.[8] What is claimed is that a new science is being discovered which will bridge the gap between those "cultures."

Sociologists, political scientists, and economists must make their own sort of comment on the gulf-bridging potential of sociobiology, since they are never quite sure which side of the gulf they are on. But a brief comment from practitioners of the humanities may be in order.

Earlier in the book Wilson writes: "The key to the emergence of civilization is *hypertrophy,* the extreme growth of pre-existing structures." The example given there, and likewise in the glossary, is of the elephant's tusk, which resulted from something having gone wrong in a process that was only meant to produce a decent-sized tooth. This concept of "hypertrophy"—surely in biology referring to a derangement, to something pathological—is many times resorted to, for its explicative power, throughout Wilson's book. The climax occurs in the last chapter:

> Human nature is, moreover, a hodgepodge of special genetic
> adaptations to an environment largely vanished, the world of the
> Ice-Age hunter-gatherer. Modern life, as rich and rapidly changing as
> it appears to those caught in it, is nevertheless only a mosaic of
> cultural hypertrophies of the archaic behavioral adaptations. (p. 196)

The implications of this are obvious. Attentive observers from the side of the humanities will realize that all their cultural "heroes"—in philosophy, theology, literature, music, painting, sculpture and architecture, and indeed in the natural sciences, which can soundly be taken as part of the humanities—are, in Wilson's view, hypertrophous.[9]

Wilson's is surely the ugliest, and perhaps the most arrogant and foolish, broad characterization of the "heroes" who came along somewhat after the Ice-Age hunter-gatherers that comes to mind. This commentator is tempted to find in that characterization a touch, so to speak, of madness. The temptation can be avoided by recalling that there has always been something heady in the man who discovers a new science, whether genuine or spurious.[10] Indeed, Beer, who suggested in the review cited earlier that "objections can be raised to Professor Wilson's touting of sociobiology as a new discipline," because "what is sound science in his enterprise is just a continuation of traditional Darwinian biology," went on to say: "The rest is a kind of gerrymandering that smacks of a hypertrophy of the territorial imperative." That is a rather complicated put-down, combining a term from political science, Wilson's own favorite term "hypertrophy," and the title of an overnoticed popular book on reasons for animal (and human) aggression. But, complicated or not, it may be taken as a decisive judgment.

It will be recalled that Wilson wrote, as quoted earlier: "Effort [to solve the first dilemma] will uncover the second dilemma, which is the choice that must be made among the ethical premises inherent in man's biological nature." Three choices that will probably emerge are briefly suggested. They are startlingly unstartling.

[First:] In the beginning the new ethicists will want to ponder the cardinal value of the survival of human genes in the form of a common pool over generations. . . . A more detached view of the long-range course of evolution should allow us to see beyond the blind decision-making process of natural selection and to envision the history and future of our own genes against the background of the entire human species. A word already in use intuitively defines this view: nobility. Had dinosaurs grasped that concept they might have survived. They might have been us.

[Second:] I believe that a correct application of evolutionary theory also favors diversity in the gene pool as a cardinal value . . . [though this is] a contingent primary value until such time as an almost unimaginably greater knowledge of human heredity provides us with the option of a democratically contrived eugenics.

[Third:] Universal human rights might properly be regarded as a third primary value . . . [not] through obedience to an abstract principle of unknown extraneous origin, but because we are mammals . . . [the suggestion being that] the true reason for the universal rights movement [comes from] an understanding of its raw biological causation [rather than from] any rationalization contrived by culture to reinforce and euphemize it. (pp. 196–99)

Beyond those three "cardinal" or "primary" values there are "secondary values . . . defined to a large extent by our most intense emotions." Seven such emotions are named. But the evolutionary bioethicist is not yet in a position to make prescriptions regarding them, since though "there is a neurophysiology of such responses" it remains "to be deciphered, and their evolutionary history awaits reconstruction." It will be, one is tempted to suggest, a long wait.

One further thing in the last chapter arises from Wilson's acknowledgment that his "own reasoning follows in a direct line from the [scientific] humanism of the Huxleys, Waddington, Monod, Pauli, Dobzhansky, Cattell and others." He has an explanation of what is new with himself. The others paid little or no attention to the biological and biosociological significance of religion. They thus missed the enormous, indeed, the critical importance for "hope" of the possibility that the "energies" released hitherto by religion's mythopoeic power "can be shifted in new directions when scientific materialism itself is accepted as the more powerful mythology."

Wilson ends his book appropriately with two lines from Aeschylean Prometheus: "I caused mortals to cease foreseeing doom, I placed in them blind hopes." This evocation may make some readers wonder what effect, if any, his efforts are likely to have.

Suppose the negative judgments delivered by Beer, Hampshire, and this commentator are correct. Would that mean that Wilson's new science will only have a short run? Certainly not. What will happen to a new stream entering the academic whirlpool is as unpredictable as the flight of a honeybee.

Suppose Wilson is wrong, as in his preface he said he might easily be, in his grand hopes for the "role of the natural sciences, and in the trust gambled on scientific materialism." Would that mean no good could come from his enterprise? Decidedly not. The so-called Great Conversation has had many fine comic moments—moments in which errors fervently made about important subjects have led the conversation to courses where at least a "hum" of truth was heard or reheard. Professor Wilson's book *On Human Nature* could, indeed should, reinvigorate attention to the many tough issues its subject involves.

---

[1] *On Human Nature* (Cambridge, Mass.: Harvard University Press, 1978). The first two books of the trilogy are: *The Insect Societies* (1971) and *Sociobiology: The New Synthesis* (1975). Mr. Wilson speaks of it as a "trilogy that unfolded without my being consciously aware of any logical sequence," but the last chapter of his first book was called "The Prospect of a Unified Sociobiology" and the last chapter of the second book, "Man: From Sociobiology to Sociology."

[2] Colin Beer, review of *On Human Nature*, in *The New York Times Book Review*, November 26, 1978. Professor Beer, a member of the Institute of Animal Behavior, Newark College of Arts and Sciences, Rutgers University, took note of a hastily put together anthology, entitled *The Sociobiology Debate*, ed. Arthur L. Caplan (New York: Harper & Row, 1978). That his claim of a new science has given Professor Wilson considerable acclaim is indicated by the appearance of such a book.

[3] This reference to B. F. Skinner's absurd book, entitled *Beyond Freedom and Dignity,* prompts one to call attention to what Professor Wilson has to say about that book: "These are powerful ideas, with seductive precedents in the physical sciences, and they have resulted in substantial advances in the study of animal and human behavior. The central idea of the philosophy of behaviorism, that behavior and the mind have an entirely materialist basis subject to experimental analysis, is fundamentally sound" (p. 65). In any opinions about Professor Wilson's trilogy, this judgment must be kept in mind.

[4] Stuart Hampshire, "The Illusion of Sociobiology," *The New York Review of Books,* 25, no. 15 (October 12, 1978). If there is to be a mature continuation of "The Sociobiology Debate" (*see* footnote 2 above), Hampshire's discussion should be a central piece. In an admirably long, admirably serious and polite review-article, Hampshire, holding that "the argument of [Wilson's] book, and the philosophical assumptions behind it, seem to me misconceived and wrong," nevertheless tries to teach Professor Wilson that human beings have a whole langue, totally different from Wilson's language, in which they construe one another as involved in relations wherein intentions, purposes, deliberations, and choices—relations influenced in their occurrence and intelligibility by elaborate social contexts—are the relevant causal factors. Hampshire's incisive objections to Wilson's sociobiology appear formidably sound, but it does not seem likely that Wilson will respond to them, partly because of his evangelical preoccupations, and partly because his limited scientific education has left him seriously incompetent to confront philosophical queries about the adequacy of his quite extreme "scientific materialism."

[5] Stuart Hampshire, *Freedom of the Individual* (New York: Harper & Row, 1965).

[6] In his review (*see* footnote 4), Stuart Hampshire singles out things from chapter 8 on "Religion" to illustrate his complaint that "Wilson's scientific materialism stops short of being materialistic enough." Hampshire writes: "The concept of indoctrination, I think, has no place in a physical science.... One man's indoctrination is another man's learning, according to the evaluations of the propositions learned: do they have a different physical basis?" Or again: "Sacralization is not a concept that can be fitted into physical theory, if only because no criterion or sufficient test of whether a process is a process of sacralization is to be found in observable behavior. The thought of the subject is essential, as it also is essential to distinguishing indoctrination from other learning processes." It should be noted that Professor Wilson is apparently unaware that he trangresses the bounds of "scientific materialism" in his speculations about religion.

[7] In a recent book, the editor in chief of *Great Ideas Today* reviewed the literature on this "fundamental question" from the Greek philosophers and biologists all the way to "Turing's machine" in our time. *See* Mortimer J. Adler, *The Difference of Man and the Difference It Makes* (New York: Holt, Rinehart and Winston 1967).

Mr. Adler's review of the literature is lucid and comprehensive. But he offers something more: a structuring of the old controversy that would enable the contemporary argument to be well-joined—well-joined by scientists and philosophers, it should be added— for Mr. Adler argues that the question of "the nature of man" is one that both disciplines must deal with.

Professor Wilson is not likely to enter the argument as he pursues the promises of the new science he is founding. As a manifestly dogmatic materialist, he will not be able to see that he should do so.

[8] Once again, there is a recent book which reviews and analyzes the several major moments in Western civilization when cultures have been in conflict. *See* Otto A. Bird, *Cultures in Conflict: An Essay in the Philosophy of the Humanities* (Notre Dame, Indiana: University of Notre Dame Press, 1976). Professor Bird's book furnishes a rich context for, and penetrating insights into, the questions of what is at stake in a conflict of cultures.

[9] One can find the word in the *Oxford English Dictionary.*

[10] Examples of the tendency towards "hypertrophic imperialism" on the part of new science inventors can be found in the book cited in footnote 8.

Additions
to the
Great Books Library

Thucydides

J. B. Bury

Editor's Introduction

John Bagnell Bury (1861–1927) was a classicist and historian of phenomenal energy and erudition—his bibliography comprises 369 known items, and he was master of as many as a dozen languages—who for a quarter of a century was Regius professor of modern history at the University of Cambridge, and who in the course of his life produced writings of the first distinction in classics, philology, and history, while serving simultaneously as editor of some of the major scholarly publications of his time.

His preparation for these accomplishments was begun early. Born in Monaghan, Ireland, to parents who were both well-read (his father was a prominent Anglican clergyman), he was taught both Latin and Greek before he was ten, at which time he is said to have been able to answer any question in Greek grammar which his tutor at Foyle College, Londonderry, could think to put to him. In 1878 he entered Trinity College, Dublin, where he won every prize that was offered in classics, and from which he graduated with honors in 1882. Three years later he was made a fellow of the College on the strength of a study of the odes of Pindar, perhaps the most difficult of Greek poets to elucidate, and in 1893, when he had turned his attention to history and published a major work on the later Roman Empire (for which he taught himself both Russian and Hungarian), he was appointed to a chair at Trinity. He was made Regius professor at Cambridge in 1902, succeeding Lord Acton, himself a man of formidable learning who had owned a library of nearly 60,000 volumes.

Bury's historical interests were chiefly though by no means exclusively Roman. His history of the later Roman Empire was followed by a study of the Empire from its beginnings to the time of Marcus Aurelius, and after that he produced an updated version of Gibbon's *Decline and Fall* with notes and appendixes incorporating recent research (1896–1900). Later, he wrote a history of the Eastern Empire and still later a study of Rome from Theodosius I to the death of Justinian. Among his contributions to other subjects were *The Invasion of Europe by the Barbarians* (1928), and *History of the Papacy in the 19th Century (1864–1878)* (1930), both published posthumously.

Amidst these labors Bury found time also to edit the *Cambridge Ancient History* and to plan the *Cambridge Medieval History*. In addition, he edited five volumes of *Byzantine Texts* which are thought to be among the finest examples of Byzantine studies. In these he was an early champion of the idea that philosophy, art, culture, and architecture are valid representations of a civilization's history, and that studies of them are part of the historian's proper business.

The best known of Bury's writings are his *History of Freedom of Thought* (1914) and *The Idea of Progress* (1920), both of which reached wide audiences in their day, along with a *History of Greece to the Death of Alexander the Great* (1900) which at once became a standard text and is still available in a popular edition. In all of these works Bury displayed a clarity of thought and a trenchancy of expression which make interesting and readable the treatment they offer of their subjects, to which, in fact, they may still serve in each case as a very good introduction.

The study of the Thucydides reprinted here was one—actually, two—of a group of lectures which Bury gave at Harvard University in 1908 and which he subsequently published as *The Ancient Greek Historians*. In these lectures he endeavored, as he said, "to bring into a connected view the principles, the governing ideas, and the methods of the Greek historians, and to relate them to the general movements of Greek thought and history." To this he added that, as a Hellenist, he would be happy if he succeeded "in illustrating the fact that, as in poetry and letters generally, as in art, as in philosophy and in mathematics, so too in history, our debt to the Greeks transcends calculation." For, he said, "they were not the first to chronicle human events, but they were the first to apply criticism. And that means, they originated history." Other lectures in the volume were devoted to Herodotus (see *Gateway to the Great Books,* Vol. 6, pp. 360–83) and the predecessors of Herodotus, and to the successors of Thucydides, among them Xenophon and Polybius, as well as to the Roman historians—Cato, Sallust, Livy, Tacitus, and others—whose conception of their task was derived from the Greeks.

Thucydides

His life and the growth of his work

Thucydides belonged by descent to the princely family of Thrace into which Miltiades, the hero of Marathon, had married. He was thus a cousin of the statesman Cimon, and he inherited a rich estate with gold mines in Thrace. And so, while he was an Athenian citizen and connected with a distinguished family of Athens, he had an independent *pied à terre* in a foreign country. His mind was moulded under the influence of that intellectual revolution which we associate with the comprehensive name of the Sophists, the illumination which was flooding the educated world of Hellas with the radiance of reason. Without accepting the positive doctrines of any particular teacher, he learned the greatest lesson of these thinkers: he learned to consider and criticize facts, unprejudiced by authority and tradition. He came to be at home in the "modern" way of thinking, which analysed politics and ethics, and applied logic to everything in the world. We might illustrate how intense and deep-reaching the sophistic movement was, in the third quarter of the fifth century, by pointing to the difference between Herodotus and Thucydides. If you took up the two works without knowing the dates of their composition, you would think there might be a hundred years' development between Sophocles and Euripides.

Thucydides must have been at least twenty-five years old, some think he was as much as forty, when the Peloponnesian war broke out in 431 B.C. At the very beginning he formed the resolution to record it, and in the first years of the war, at least, the composition of the history was nearly contemporary with the events. In 424 B.C. he was elected to the high office of a strategos and appointed to command in Thrace; and the loss of Amphipolis led to his condemnation and banishment. For twenty years he did not see Athens, and, while he probably lived for the most part on his Thracian estate, he also travelled to collect material for his work. It seems certain that he visited Sicily, for his narrative of the Athenian expedition could not have been written by one who had not seen Syracuse with his own eyes.[1] After the end of the war he was allowed to return to Athens in 404 B.C. (by the decree of Oenobius). He did not die before 399 B.C.; perhaps he was no longer alive in 396 B.C.; and he left his book unfinished.[2]

It is evident how these biographical facts, and they are almost all we know about the man, bear upon his historical work. His family connexion at Athens provided him, perhaps, with exceptional facilities for obtaining authentic information, while his military training and experience qualified him to be the historian of a war. His second home in Thrace gave him an interest independent of Athens, and helped him to regard the Athenian empire with a certain detachment which would have been less easy for one who was a pure-blooded citizen and had no home outside Attica. His banishment operated in the same direction, and afforded him opportunities for intercourse with the antagonists of his country. The intellectual movement which invaded Athens when he was a young man was a condition of his mental growth; if

---

[1] That he knew Sparta is a legitimate inference from i. 10. 2, and 134. 4.

[2] There were conflicting stories as to the manner and the place of his death. His tomb, which may have been a cenotaph, was shown at Athens, in the burying-place of the family of his kinsman Cimon, near the Melitid gate.

he had belonged to an earlier generation, he could not have been Thucydides.

But if all these circumstances helped and conditioned the achievements of a profoundly original mind, which always thought for itself, we must seek the stimulus which aroused the historical faculty of Thucydides in—the Athenian empire. If it was the wonder of the Greek repulse of the Persian hosts that inspired the epic spirit of Herodotus, it was the phenomenon of the Empire of Athens, a new thing in the history of Hellas, —an empire governed by a democracy, a new thing in the history of the world—that captured the cooler but intense interest of Thucydides. He did not take up his pen to celebrate; his aim was to understand,—to observe critically how that empire behaved in the struggle which was to test its powers. It has not, I think, been sufficiently realised what an original stroke of genius it was to form the idea of recording the history of the war at the very moment of its outbreak. Contemporary history in the strictest meaning of the term was thus initiated. Thucydides watched the events for the purpose of recording them; he collected the material while it was fresh from the making. Further, he designed a history which should be simply a history of the war and of the relations of the militant states, which should confine itself to its theme, and not deviate into geography or anthropology or other things. Thus he was the founder of "political" history in the special sense in which we are accustomed to use the term.

Widely divergent views are held as to the way in which the work of Thucydides was constructed and the stages by which it reached its final though incomplete state. This question is not one of merely meritorious curiosity which may be left to the commentator as his exclusive concern; it affects our general conception of the historian's point of view, as well as his art, and no study of Thucydides can evade it.

The history falls into two parts. The first ends with the Fifty Years' Peace of 421 B.C., which at the time seemed to conclude the war and terminate the author's task. The second part is formally introduced by a personal explanation, in which Thucydides announces the continuation of his subject down to the capture of Athens in 404 B.C. He explains that though we may divide the whole period 431–404 B.C. into three parts—the first war of ten years, then seven years of hollow truce, and then a second war,—the truer view is that there was only one war lasting twenty-seven years, for the hollow truce was truly nothing less than war. This passage was written after 404 B.C. and naturally suggests that Thucydides had only recently recognised that the indecisive war which he had recorded was only a portion of a greater and decisive war, and had determined to extend the compass of his work to the whole twenty-seven years. On the other hand, his statements[3] seem to make it evident that during his banishment he had followed the course of events and travelled with a view to continuing his work. This continuation was prompted by the Athenian expedition to Sicily, and was intended to be the history of what then seemed to him a second war. I conclude then that there were three stages in his plan. After the Fifty Years' Peace of 421 B.C., his book was to be simply a history of the war of ten years. The course of the Sicilian expedition began a new war which he determined also to record, as a chronologically separate episode. Then the catastrophe of 404 B.C. set in a new light the significance of all that had happened since the original outbreak of hostilities in 431 B.C., and imparted to the whole series of events a unity of meaning which they would hardly have acquired if the struggle had been terminated in 404 B.C. not by the fall of Athens but by a second edition of the Fifty Years' Peace. Hence Thucydides rose to the larger conception of producing a history of the whole period of twenty-seven years.

Accordingly he found on his return to Athens that he had three things to do. He had to compose the history of the ambiguous

---

[3] v. 26.

interval between the Fifty Years' Peace and the Sicilian war. Secondly, he had to work up the rough copy and material of the last ten years. This was done[4] fully and triumphantly for the Sicilian episode, but of the rest we only possess the unrevised draft of the years 412 and 411, known as Book VIII., for which, perhaps in respect to its literary shape, and certainly in respect to its matter (by means of supplementary information procurable at Athens), much had to be done. In the third place, it was desirable and even necessary to make some additions and alterations in the original, completed but still unpublished, history of the first ten years, so as to bring it internally as well as externally into the light of the higher unity. This was a natural thought, and it appears to me the only hypothesis that explains the facts without constraint.

His principles of historiography: accuracy and relevance

In his Introduction Thucydides announces a new conception of historical writing. He sets up a new standard of truth or accurate reproduction of facts, and a new ideal of historical research; judged by which, he finds Herodotus and the Ionian historians wanting. He condemns them expressly for aiming at providing "good reading," as we should say, rather than facts, and for narrating stories, the truth of which cannot possibly be tested. He does not seek himself to furnish entertainment or to win a popular success, but to construct a record which shall be permanently valuable because it is true. He warns his readers that they will find nothing mythical in his work. He saw, as we see, that the mythical element pervaded Herodotus (of whom, evidently, he was chiefly thinking) no less than Homer. His own experience in ascertaining *contemporary* facts taught him, as nothing else could do, how soon and how easily events are wont to pass into the borders of myth; he learned thereby the most effective lesson of scepticism in regard to historical tradition. It was indeed of inestimable

importance for the future of history that Thucydides conceived the new idea of recording the war at its commencement. It made all the difference to his work that he formed the resolve in 431 B.C. and not after the war was over.

Writing the history of the present is always a very different thing from writing the history of the distant past. The history of the distant past depends entirely on literary and documentary sources; the history of the present always involves unwritten material as well as documents. But the difference was much greater in the days of Thucydides than it is now. To-day a writer sitting down to compose a history of his own time would depend mainly on written material,—on official reports, official documents of various kinds, and on the daily press. He would supplement this, so far as he could, by information derived personally from men of affairs, or by his own experience if he had witnessed or taken part in public events; but the main body of his work would depend on written sources. The ancient historian, on the contrary, in consequence of the comparative paucity of official reports and the absence of our modern organization for collecting and circulating news, would have to be his own journalist and do all the labour of obtaining facts orally from the most likely sources; and his success might largely depend on accidental facilities. His work would rest mainly on information obtained orally by his own inquiries, supplemented by such documents as were available, such as texts of treaties or official instructions or letters; whereas the modern work is based principally on printed or written information, supplemented by such private information as may be accessible. It is clear that the ancient conditions made the historian's task more difficult, and demanded from him greater energy and initiative. Few things would be more interesting than a literary diary of Thucydides, telling of his interviews with his informants and showing his ways of collecting and sifting his

---

[4] Perhaps before his return.

material. But it was part of his artistic method to cover up all the traces of his procedure, in his finished narrative. He had to compare and criticize the various accounts he received of each transaction; but his literary art required that he should present the final conclusions of his research without indicating divergences of evidence. It is probable that he suppressed entirely details about which he could not satisfy himself. He was very chary of mentioning reports or allegations concerning which he felt in doubt; in the few cases in which he disclaims certainty we may suppose that he accepted the statement as probable.[5] He does not name his informants; nor does he even tell us on what occasions he was himself an eye-witness of what he describes. We may make guesses, but we can only speak with assurance of the operations which he conducted as strategos.

We are able, however, to gain a slight glimpse into the historian's workshop because some parts of his work have been left incomplete. The eighth Book is only a preliminary draft. In it we find accounts emanating from different informants, Athenian and Peloponnesian, written out so as to form a continuous narrative, yet containing contradictions as to matters of fact as well as differences in tendency. It is possible, for instance, to detect that some of the Peloponnesian informants were favourable to Astyochus the Lacedaemonian commander, and others were not. It is evident that we have material which has only been provisionally sifted. Again, the texts of the three successive treaties of alliance between Persia and Sparta are given *verbatim*,[6] and if we consider the transitory significance of the first two, it seems improbable that Thucydides intended to reproduce them *in extenso* in his final draft. They were material—material, according to a plausible conjecture, furnished by Alcibiades. These facts, and the unsatisfactory nature of the account of the oligarchic revolution, as compared with the finished portions of the work, confirm what the style and the absence of speeches had long ago suggested, that Book VIII. was a first draft which,

if the writer had lived, would have appeared in a very different shape.

In the fifth Book it may also be shown that there was still revision to be done, though this section was in a more advanced state than Book VIII. Here we find a whole series of documentary texts. Now it was not in accordance with the artistic method of Thucydides, or of ancient historians in general, to introduce into the narrative matter heterogeneous in style; and it is almost incredible that he would have admitted texts not written in Attic Greek. We must, I think, conclude that we have here material which was to be wrought in during a final revision.

In the finished part of the history we can sometimes penetrate to the source of information. It is easy to see that he consulted Plataeans as to the siege of Plataea, and that he received information from Spartans as well as from Athenians about the episode of Pylos and Sphacteria. We can sometimes divine that he has derived his statements from the official instructions given to military commanders; and it has been acutely shown that his enumeration of the allies of the two opposing powers at the beginning of the war was based on the instrument of the Thirty Years' Peace. Sometimes the formulae of decrees or treaties peer through the Thucydidean summary.

We have then to take the finished product, which Thucydides furnishes, on trust. We have not any considerable body of independent evidence for testing his accuracy, but so far as we can test it by the chance testimonies of original documents, he comes out triumphantly (in those parts which he completed), and there can be no question that the stress which he laid on accuracy was not a phrase.[7] The serious criticisms which can be brought

---

[5] For instance: of the answer of the oracle to the Spartans, i. 118.3; of the motives of Archidamus, ii. 18. 5; of the end of Nicias, vii. 86.

[6] viii. 18, 37, 58.

[7] Some errors are due not to the author but to very early scribes. For instance, Andocides in i. 51, Methone for Methana in iv. 45. It is unquestionable that he makes grave topographical mistakes in his

against him in regard to facts concern not what he states but what he omits to state. For instance, the important measure which Athens adopted in 424 B.C. of raising the tribute of the subject states is passed over entirely, though it is a pertinent fact in the story of the war; we have learned it in recent years by the discovery of parts of the stone decree. We cannot discern his reasons for recounting some passages of military history at great length and passing over others (such as the attempt of Pericles on Epidaurus) with a bare mention. But in other cases his silence is a judgment. He rejects, for instance, by ignoring, the connexion which the gossip of the Athenian streets alleged between the private life of Pericles and the origin of the war. But it must be allowed in general that, in omitting, Thucydides displays a boldness and masterfulness on which no modern historian would venture.[8]

His omissions are closely connected with a general feature of his work. If the first fundamental principle of his ideal of history was accuracy, the second was relevance; and both signify his rebound from Herodotus. Discursiveness as we saw was the very life-breath of the epic history of Herodotus; the comprehensiveness of the Ionian idea of history enabled him to spread about through a wide range, to string on tale to tale, to pile digression on digression, artfully, yet as loosely as the structure of his Ionic prose. Thucydides conceived the notion of political history, and he laid down for himself a strict principle of exclusion. His subject is the war, and he will not take advantage of opportunities to digress into the history of culture. He excludes geography, so far as brief notices are not immediately necessary for the explanation of the events recorded. He disdains personal gossip and anecdotes; he had no use for the spicy memoirs of Ion and Stesimbrotus. He rigidly abstains from dropping any information about the private life of Pericles, Cleon, or any other politician; and the exception which he makes in the case of Alcibiades only serves to show the reason for the rule; because those sides of the life of Alcibiades

which Thucydides notices had, in his view, distinct political consequences in determining the attitude of the Athenians towards him. Further, he excludes the internal history of the states with whose political interrelations he is concerned, except when the internal affected directly, or was bound up with, the external, as in the case of the plague and of the domestic seditions. He does not give any information about the political parties at Athens, though some of his statements imply their existence, till he comes to the oligarchical revolution. His outlook, as Wilamowitz has observed, is not bounded by the Pnyx, but by the Empire.

There are, of course, digressions in Thucydides, but with hardly an exception they are either closely relevant or introduced for some special purpose.

The history of the growth of the Athenian empire is in form an excursus; but we might fairly say that it properly belongs to the prolegomena; it is distinctly relevant to the subject of the book, and had the special purpose of supplementing and correcting Hellanicus. The digression on the fortunes of Pausanias is also a relevant, though certainly

---

account of the episode of Pylos-Sphacteria. He has completely misconceived the size of the entrances to the bay, and he gives the length of Sphacteria as 15 stades, whereas it is really 24. These errors have led Grundy to deny that Thucydides had ever visited the spot; while R. M. Burrows (who has shown that the whole narrative is otherwise in accordance with the topography) think that his measurements were wrong. My view is that he first wrote the story from information supplied by eye-witnesses who gave him a general, though partly inaccurate, idea of the place, and that he afterwards tested it on the spot and probably added local touches, but omitted to revise the errors of distance. We have a somewhat similar case in the description of New Carthage by Polybius. It is indeed possible that the blunder in the length of the island may have been exaggerated by a scribe's pen.

[8] Thus no modern historian, probably, would have omitted to note the psephisma of Charinus, which followed up the decrees excluding Megara from the markets of Athens and her empire, by excluding Megarians on penalty of death from the very soil of Attica. Thucydides would have said that it did not affect the outbreak of the war.

not necessary, explanation of the Athenian demand that the Lacedaemonians should expel a pollution; but the account, which follows, of the later career of Themistocles is wholly unconnected with the Peloponnesian war. I will however show hereafter that the author had a special motive in introducing it. The valuable chapter on early Athens, with its archaeological evidence,[9] is strictly to the point, for its purpose is to illustrate the historian's acute remark that the distress of the country people at coming to live in the city was due to habits derived from the early history of Attica. A sketch of the early history of Sicily was almost indispensable for the elucidation of the narrative; a knowledge of the island and its cities could not be taken for granted in the Athenian public. The description of the Odrysean kingdom of Sitalces[10] was unquestionably due to the author's personal interest in Thrace; but it had the object of suggesting a contrast between the power and resources of Thrace and Scythia with those of the Greek states.

The story of the fall of the Athenian tyrants (in Book VI.), which is an excursus in the true sense of the word, was introduced to correct popular errors. The other passage in which Thucydides seems for a moment non-Thucydidean is where he sketches the history of the fair of Delos, quotes from a Homeric hymn, and deviates into the history of culture. I cannot help suspecting that here too he is correcting some current misapprehension. If he may legitimately be criticized for turning aside from his subject to correct errors which may seem trivial enough, and if he is sometimes reprimanded for having elsewhere captiously noted a couple of small blunders in Herodotus, it must be remembered that it was of importance to illustrate his doctrine that tradition cannot be taken on trust, and that the facile methods of current historiography inevitably led to inaccuracy.

The digressions then in Thucydides which can fairly be called digressions are different in character from the digressions and amplitudes of Herodotus. The critic Dionysius considered it a point of inferiority in Thucydides, as compared with Herodotus, that he pursued his subject steadily and kept to his argument, without pausing by the way and providing his readers with variety; and he supposed that in "the two or three places" where the historian did digress, his motive was to relieve the narrative by a pleasant pause. The criticism would have been more elucidating if Dionysius had pointed out that, while Herodotus was influenced by the epic, the artistic method of Thucydides must rather be compared with that of the drama. Thucydides adheres as closely to his argument as a tragic poet, and such variety as was secured in tragedy by interjection of choral odes, he obtains by the speeches which he intersperses in the narrative. His first consideration was accuracy; he had to follow events and not to mould them into correspondence with an artistic plan, and his strict chronological order excluded devices of arrangement. But occasionally we can detect deliberate management for the sake of a calculated effect. It may be pointed out that the long section on the origin and growth of the Athenian empire, placed where it is, between the two Assemblies at Sparta, has the effect of interrupting a series of speeches which coming together would have been excessively long. Again, it has been well shown by Wilamowitz-Möllendorff how the delays of Archidamus, in the first invasion of Attica, in the hope that Athens might give in at the last moment, are reflected in the form of the narrative, which is arranged to produce the impression of a slow and halting march; and the archaeological deviation into the early history of Athens has the value of assisting in this artistic effect.

Modern criticisms on his competence

In common with other ancient historians, Thucydides may be taken to task for not hav-

---

[9] A part of it would naturally have appeared in a footnote, had footnotes been then in use.

[10] ii. 96–7; cp. ii. 29.

ing recognised the part played in human affairs by economic facts and commercial interests. That he was not blind to economic conditions is shown by the leading significance he attributes to want of material resources in the early Greek communities; and he fully realises the importance of finance. But it may be said that he should have furnished a detailed explanation and analysis of the commercial basis on which the Athenian power rested, and of the mercantile interests of other states which were affected and endangered by her empire. It is however only in quite recent times that economical and commercial factors in historical development have begun to receive their due, and, perhaps it may be said, rather more than their due. They have come so much to the front that some writers are tempted to explain all historical phenomena by economic causes. This illustrates how the tendencies of the present react upon our conceptions of the past. These factors, of such immense importance in the present age, certainly did not play anything like the same part in the ancient world, and if the ancient historians considerably underrated them, we may easily fall into the error of overrating them. We may be sure that the interests of Athens presented themselves to statesmen, as to Thucydides, primarily under the political, and not the economical, point of view. Thucydides created political history; economic history is a discovery of the nineteenth century.

Perhaps the gravest accusation which has been brought against the competency of Thucydides is that he misunderstood, if he did not intentionally misrepresent, the causes of the Peloponnesian war. The charge has been formulated and pressed in different ways by a German and by an English scholar. Their indictments do not appear to me to be successful. The historian's account, which can only be refuted by proofs of internal discrepancy or of insufficiency, seems to be both consistent and, with certain reserves, adequate.

It will not be amiss to make a preliminary observation on two words which Thucydides uses in the sense of cause—$\alpha\grave{\iota}\tau\acute{\iota}\alpha$ and

$\pi\rho\acute{o}\phi\alpha\sigma\iota\varsigma$. $\alpha\grave{\iota}\tau\acute{\iota}\alpha$ has almost the same history as the Latin equivalent, *caussa*. Its proper sense was "grievance" or "ground of blame," "charge," and in Thucydides it generally[11] either means this or, even when we can most appropriately translate it by cause, implies a charge or imputation. $\pi\rho\acute{o}\phi\alpha\sigma\iota\varsigma$ is an alleged reason, which may be either true or false; ultimately it became virtually restricted to a false or minor reason, and so equivalent to "pretext." In Thucydides it is not so restricted; he employs it in both ways. And from meaning an alleged reason, it is evident how easily it could come to mean a reason, whether alleged or not; in other words, a "motive" or an "occasion," so that here it approximated very closely to the sense of "cause." This various use of the word does not imply any confusion of thought; we use the word "reason" with similar elasticity; the context decides the sense.

When a war breaks out, there are two things to be explained which must be kept distinct: why the aggressors go to war at all, and why they go to war at the time they actually do. This distinction is crucial, for instance, in the case of the outbreak of the Franco-Prussian war of 1870. In some cases, the answer to both questions is the same; there may be no reason for the war, beyond the particular circumstances which lead immediately to its declaration. In the case of the Peloponnesian war, Thucydides is careful to insist that this was not so. There was a permanent motive for hostility, of such a kind that war, sooner or later, might be counted on as a certainty; there were also particular transactions which determined its actual outbreak at a particular moment. When the Lacedaemonians took steps to break the peace, of course they did not mention the permanent and really impelling motive, namely, jealousy of Athenian aggrandisement, but rested their declaration on certain recent actions on the part of Athens. Thucydides puts it thus: "The true motive ($\pi\rho\acute{o}\phi\alpha\sigma\iota\varsigma$), though it was not expressed in words, I consider to

---

[11] But cp. iv. 87. 4.

have been the fear which the growth of the Athenian power caused to the Lacedaemonians; but the publicly alleged grounds of complaint ($\alpha\iota\tau\iota\alpha\iota$) which provoked the war I will proceed to explain," and he enters upon the stories of Corcyra and Potidaea. Thucydides accepted the convictions expressed both by the Corcyraean ambassador in his speech at Athens and by Pericles that a war was unavoidable, and that it was merely a question how long it might be postponed; and we certainly cannot prove that this judgment was wrong.

The distinction then between the real motive of the Lacedaemonians, in the absence of which they would not have declared war, and the particular actions which brought matters to a head and determined the beginning of a war at a certain date, is perfectly clear and valid. The further question can be raised, whether in his account of the affairs which moved the Peloponnesian alliance to hostile action at a given moment, Thucydides estimated rightly their proportional gravity. The charge is that he has not given its due importance to the Megarian business, whether failing to realise its meaning, or deliberately keeping it in the background in order to devolve the responsibility for the war from the shoulders of Pericles who was responsible for the Megarian policy. The second insinuation I need not consider; for I will show hereafter that the historian's attitude to Pericles and his policy is detached. I will only observe here that if he had wished to shield that statesman from the alleged responsibility, it was clumsy of him not to suppress or explain away the fact that in the final negotiations the Lacedaemonians made Megara the test-question, and said they would be satisfied if Athens yielded on that point.

This ultimatum of the Lacedaemonians may indeed appear, at first sight, inconsistent with the subordinate rôle which the Megarian grievance plays in the historian's narrative of the circumstances which led to the war; and it has been urged that instead of keeping it in the background he ought to have assigned it the most prominent place in the foreground. But a careful examination will show, I think, that the narrative is completely consistent, and embodies a closely reasoned account of the causes and motives at work.

The most casual reader receives the unmistakable impression that the Corinthians were the prime instigators of the war, driving the Lacedaemonians into action. The two affairs in which their interests were exclusively involved, the affair of Corcyra and the affair of Potidaea, are those which the author designates as the direct occasion of the war; and the leading part taken by Corinth is emphasized by the reproduction of two Corinthian speeches, voicing Peloponnesian dissatisfaction. If the deepest concern of Corinth was the action which Athens had taken in regard to Megara by excluding her from the markets of the Athenian empire, and thereby threatening her with economic ruin, then it must be allowed that Thucydides was entirely misinformed. In their speeches at Sparta, the Corinthian envoys do not mention the Megarian name, and the author expressly states that their eagerness to have war declared immediately was due to their anxiety for Potidaea. Can we discover any proof as to the real interest of Corinth in the Megarian question?

When the Corcyraean affair occurred, Corinth was so far from being anxious for war that she did all she could to secure the goodwill and neutrality of Athens. And she did not come with her hands empty. She did not merely urge her claims on Athenian gratitude for past services. She proposed a deal (433 B.C.). Some time before this, Athens had already initiated new designs on Megara by a decree excluding Megarian wares from Athens itself. Corinth now said to her in effect: Leave us a free hand in dealing with Corcyra, and we will leave you a free hand in dealing with Megara. The Corinthian ambassador put this diplomatically, at least in his speech before the popular Assembly.[12] He did not say: You have improper designs on

---

[12] i. 42. 2.

Megara, and we will connive. He said: Your conduct in regard to Megara has been open to suspicion; you can allay these suspicions by doing what we ask. It came to the same thing.

This proposition on the part of Corinth shows that in her eyes the independence of Megara was not of crucial importance. Her interests there weighed much less than her interests elsewhere. It was the alliance of Athens with Corcyra, followed by the affair of Potidaea, that determined the collision of Corinth with Athens, and it was this collision that precipitated a war which would in any case have come later. The Megarian decrees did not determine the action of Corinth, and it was Corinth's action which was decisive. On the other hand, once war was decided on by Corinth and the war-party at Sparta, the grievance of Megara formed an imposing item in the list of Peloponnesian complaints and the general indictment of Athenian policy. In this indictment, the alliance of Athens with Corcyra, though it had been the first of the effective causes which led to the war, could not appear at all; it could not be represented as either illegal or immoral. The attack on Potidaea could form a count; but it arose out of a complicated situation, and a great deal could be said on both sides. It was therefore an obvious stroke of diplomatic tactics to move the Megarian question into the foremost place, and represent the cruelty of Athens to Megara as the principal of her offences. The Lacedaemonians said: Yield on this question and there will be no war. It was a demand which no proud state, in the position of Athens, could have granted, and concession would have been simply an invitation for further commands. The reply was: We deny your right to dictate; but we are perfectly willing to submit all your complaints to arbitration in accordance with the instrument of the Thirty Years' Peace.

This is a perfectly consistent and intelligible account of the origin of the war; is there any reason for supposing that it is not true? The only positive evidence to which an appeal can be made for rejecting it is that of Aristophanes, who attributes the outbreak to the second Megarian decree. This was the natural, superficial view, on account of the prominence which had been given to that decree in the final negotiation; and it is not inconsistent with the Thucydidean account, in so far as that, if Athens had yielded, the war might have been avoided, or rather postponed. Further: in evaluating the statement of the comic poet, which doubtless reflected the current opinion of the Athenian market-place, we must not leave out of account the Athenian feeling against the war a year or so after it had broken out, a feeling which sought to lay the entire blame on Pericles and wove legends round the Megarian decree.[13] But the popular opinion, expressed by Aristophanes, does not really contradict the causal perspective of Thucydides. It was precisely the notion which in the given circumstances was most likely to be left in the popular mind, if the occurrences were such as Thucydides represents them.

There is another consideration which must not be neglected. Unless we hold the doctrine that all the speeches are entirely free inventions of his own, as purely Thucydidean throughout in argument as they are in style,—a doctrine which is untenable in face of his express statement,—and that he adapted the speeches of the first Book to a preconceived construction of his own, the speeches were a most important part of his material for forming his conclusion as to the causes and motives of the war. He probably heard those delivered at Athens; he was informed of the tenor or heads of those delivered at Sparta; and he has reproduced the drift of these important pieces of evidence. Both in what they say, and in what they do not say, they bear out the justice of his construction and his perspective.

It is a distinct question, What were the guiding motives of the Athenian policy in

---

[13] We do not know whether the Megarian business figured in the *Dionysalexandros* of Cratinus (430–29 B.C.), which satirised Pericles as being the cause of the war.

regard to Megara? Thucydides does not consider it, because it did not seem to him to have determined the outbreak of the war, and was therefore, in a narrow sense, irrelevant; a modern historian would not venture to treat it in this way. The object of Athens was undoubtedly to recover control of the Megarid which she had in recent times won and lost; and, to do this without violating the Thirty Years' Peace, she resorted to economical pressure which would starve her neighbour into voluntary submission. Megara had a double value. Her control would give Athens the power of blocking the land route between the Peloponnesus and Boeotia, and would also secure to her a direct access to the Corinthian Gulf, for her commerce or her troops.[14] We cannot say which of these consequences of the geographical position of Megara counted more with Athenian statesmen, in their unarmed aggression against a neighbour with whom their relations had long been unfriendly; whether they were actuated rather by the "long view" of the use of a port on the Corinthian Gulf, for adding a western to their eastern empire, or by the more obvious view of erecting a barrier against the Peloponnesus. At Sparta, we may be sure, it was the second danger which would create more alarm. But however this may be, there is nothing to show that if there had been no affair of Corcyra and no affair of Potidaea, the Megarian question by itself would have caused the outbreak of the war at the time.

But the criticism to which Thucydides has been exposed illustrates the disadvantages of his method, when it is pressed too far. His principle is to mention only effective policies, and to mention them for the first time when they begin to become effective. If Megara was a pawn in Athenian schemes of aggrandisement in western Greece, it was never moved; and in saying nothing of this aspect of the Megarian question, the historian is true to his method. If, in 433 B.C. or before, some Athenian politicians had their eyes on Sicily and Italy, the policy had no results till 427

B.C., and therefore in passing over with a bare mention the fact that Athens, in accepting the Corcyraean proposals in 433 B.C., recognised Italy and Sicily as within the range of her interests, he is again true to his method.

His treatment of non-contemporary history

Thucydides not only showed Greece how contemporary history should be studied and recorded; he also gave a specimen of a new way of handling the history of past ages. He prefixed to his work a general sketch of the history of Hellas which Dionysius of Halicarnassus, who by no means appreciated its merits, justly described as equivalent to an independent work. This sketch is amazing in its power and insight. We must remember that it is confined strictly to one side of the historical development. It is intended to answer a definite question: how it was that before quite recent times no large and powerful state had arisen in Greece; and to explain the small scale of the military and political enterprises of the past. It does not touch on constitutional history at all, and the "period of the tyrants" is only emphasized because their nonaggressive policy was a relevant point in the exposition. Within the limits to which it strictly adheres, this outline is a most closely reasoned argument and was the revelation of a totally new way of treating history. We cannot endorse it all; and of the Homeric and pre-Homeric civilisation in Greece we have come to know within the last thirty years more than Thucydides could discover. But criticism of details is not the point; his sketch remains a shining example of sheer historical insight and grasp. Rising with easy mastery over the mass of legends and details

---

[14] F. M. Cornford has ably explained the geographical importance of the Megarid as a commercial route between East and West, taking as his text what he calls Bérard's "law of isthmuses"; and those who do not accept his inferences as a criticism of Thucydides must recognise the value of his investigation.

which constituted the ill-ordered store of Greek tradition, he constructs a reasoned march of development, furnishing the proofs of his conclusions. He draws broad lines of historical growth, elicits general and essential facts from the multitude of particulars, and characterizes periods by their salient features. He calls attention to the importance of considering conditions of culture, and suggests the text for a history of Greek civilisation. He turns the daylight of material conditions on the mythical period, and discovers in the want of resources the key to certain sides of the development of Hellas.

He accepts, of course, like Herodotus and every one else, the actual existence of heroes such as Pelops, Agamemnon, Minos, for whom the genealogies seemed to vouch.[15] He did not question the fact of the Trojan war; but he inferred that such a fact meant the eminence of a leading state in Greece at the time, and showed that an examination of the traditions about it pointed to a general lack of resources. He accepted Minos; and his instinct in emphasizing the Cretan thalassocracy seems to be justified by the recent discoveries in Crete. When he comes to a later time, he seizes with a sure eye as the greatest and most important fact of the two centuries before the Persian war the revival of nautical powers and the growth of navies.

In his acute arguments he employs methods which may be called modern. For instance, he points to the culture of backward parts of Greece as a survival of a culture which at one time in the past prevailed generally. He quotes Homer as a witness for the conditions of his own age without any reserve; but when he quotes him in evidence for facts about the Trojan war, he adds a clause of caution. His proof of a Carian population in the islands is not literary but archaeological—Carian tombs which were discovered in his own day when Delos was purified.

The outline of the growth of the Athenian empire after the Persian wars is an exercise of a different kind. No history of this period existed except what was furnished by the brief chronicle of Hellanicus. The account of Thucydides is an original contribution and embodies the results of his own inquiries. He comments on the work of Hellanicus, noticing its inadequacy and alleging that it was chronologically inaccurate. Hellanicus, as we saw, found a place for every event in an archon year, and I gave an instance of the errors into which he fell through pretending to know too much. Thucydides gives no absolute dates and very few chronological indications of any kind. It looks at first sight as if Hellanicus might have retorted on Thucydides that he had a curious notion of chronological precision. But the point of the Thucydidean criticism was just this, that there were no certain or sufficient data for such precision, and that the chronological exactness of Hellanicus was an illusion. We may suspect further that in the order in which he placed some of the events, he corrected his predecessor. How far his corrections, for which he must have relied on the memories of older men, were right, we cannot say. But in any case, here too, he gave his contemporaries a salutary lesson in scepticism. He pointedly abstains from referring at all to the archon years.[16] In his view the ar-

---

[15] He takes a matter-of-fact account of the establishment of the Pelopid dynasty in Argolis from some previous writer, i. 9. 2. A Peloponnesian on ancient Argive history suggests Acusilaus. We should expect a man interested in history like Thucydides to have read all or most of the historical works which then existed. The only particular works he mentions (besides Homer) are the συγγραφὴ Ἀττική of Hellanicus and the *Apology* of Antiphon; but he refers generally to the works of poets and prose writers on early Greece, and of prose writers he was here thinking chiefly of Herodotus, whom he admittedly criticizes elsewhere. It has been conjectured with much probability that in writing the early chapters of Book VI. on the colonisation of Sicily he used the history of Antiochus of Syracuse (Wölfflin). He cannot have failed to know the books of Ion of Chios and Stesimbrotus, which must have been read with avidity at Athens.

[16] In the Pentekontaëteriis. He is careful to mark the beginning of the Peloponnesian war (ii. 2) by the archon, the Spartan ephor, and the Ar-

chon years, which ran from July to July, were inconvenient and unsuitable for a chronicle of military events, and liable to lead to serious inaccuracies. For this reason he based his own military history on the natural division of the year into summer and winter. That strict chronology was indispensable for accurate history, Thucydides was fully convinced. He proved it by casting his own work into the form of annals. He was an artist, and he could not have failed to see as clearly as his critics (like Dionysius of Halicarnassus) that the annalistic frame was an awkward impediment to any plan of artistic construction. The two claims of chronological accuracy and a pleasing literary arrangement are not irreconcilable, as other historians, like Gibbon, have shown; but Thucydides did not attempt to combine them, and it was characteristic that he should have preferred the demand of historical precision to the exigencies of literary art. His artistic powers were displayed not in the architecture of his work, but in a certain dramatic mode of treatment which will be considered hereafter.

The speeches

The historian has to do more than chronicle events. It is his business to show why things happened and to discover the forces which were at work. In order to understand the meaning of historical facts, he has to measure the characters and penetrate the motives of the actors, as well as to realise the conditions in which they acted. A psychological reconstruction is thus always involved in history, a reconstruction carried out in the mind of the individual historian, and necessarily affected by his personal temperament and his psychological ability. Some one has said that a writer who could draw a perfectly true and adequate portrait of Napoleon's complex character would be a man whose own soul was a counterpart of Napoleon's. This of course is an extreme way of putting the case, for there is such a thing as psychological imagination. But the subjective process can never be

eliminated. It has different aspects in the cases of contemporary and non-contemporary historians. The contemporary historian lives in the same milieu, in the same sphere of ideas, and thus has more points of common sympathy with the political actors of his time; but, on the other hand, he cannot generally avoid the bias of personal views of his own. The historian of a past epoch may hope to be more impartial, but he cannot hope to divest himself, beyond a certain point, of the standards and measures of his own age; they are inwoven in the tissue of his mind and they must affect his attempts to reconstruct the past.

Thucydides has concealed this inevitable subjective element by his dramatic method. The persons who play leading parts in the public affairs which he relates reveal their characters and personalities, so far as is required, by their actions and speeches. The author, like a dramatist, remains in the background, only sometimes coming forward to introduce them with a description as brief as in a playbill, or to indicate what men thought about them or the impression they made on their contemporaries. His rule is to commit himself to no personal judgments, and to this rule there are very few exceptions.

The characters of some of the political personages are partly indicated in the speeches, of which I must now speak. They are an essential feature of the Thucydidean art. Herodotus had set the example, but Thucydides used speeches for different purposes and on a different scale, and adapted them to a different method. He states explicitly how the speeches are to be taken and what they represent. In some cases he heard speeches

give priestess of Hera (this last dating, which he puts first, shows the influence of Hellanicus, which has also been conjectured in iv. 133). Similarly, when he starts afresh after the Ten Years' War, the date is marked by archon and ephor, v. 25. But we may legitimately criticize him for not having indicated formally the chronology of the four years (435-2) which are treated in Book 1. A date is obviously wanted in c. 24.

delivered, but it was impossible for him to remember them accurately; and in other cases he had to depend on the oral reports of others. His general rule was to take the general drift and intention of the speaker, and from this text compose what he might probably have said. It is clear that this principle gave great latitude to the author, and that the resemblances of the Thucydidean speeches to those actually spoken must have varied widely according to his information. They are all distinctly Thucydidean in style, just as the various characters in a play of Euripides all use similar diction. Homogeneity in style was a canon of most ancient men of letters; they shrank from introducing lengthy quotations or inserting the *ipsissima verba* of documents. Occasionally Thucydides has probably indicated personal mannerisms. For instance, in a speech of Alcibiades there are one or two expressions which are intended to suggest his characteristically "forcible" style. But this has been done with great reserve. Thucydides in his portraiture does not depend on mannerisms. The speeches of Pericles produce the effect of the lofty earnestness of a patriotic statesman who is somewhat of an idealist; the speech of Cleon is that of a bullying pedagogue. But the diction is the same. So in Aeschylus, the nurse maunders, though she speaks Aeschylean; and the *naïveté* of the policeman in Sophocles is sufficiently revealed though he does not speak a policeman's language.

But though Thucydides is always Thucydides, yet within the compass of his style there are remarkable variations. It is outside my scope to enter upon this subject in any detail; to do justice to the styles of the writers who come before us would require another set of lectures. But in the case of Thucydides, I suspect that his different styles have a certain meaning for the treatment of his subject. It is patent to any reader that there is a difference between the narrative and the speeches, and that there are marked differences in the speeches themselves. Obscurity is a reproach which has constantly been brought against

him and of which he cannot be acquitted. But it is not true of his work as a whole. The narrative is generally clear and straightforward. If it stood alone, we should never dream of describing him as obscure. Nor is this description true of the speeches indiscriminately. Some are lucid and simple; others excessively obscure; in others again we have perfectly simple passages beside sections which, with Dionysius, we may designate as conundrums or as darker than dark sayings of Heracleitus.[17] I have taken obscurity and difficulty—difficulty which the Greeks felt no less than we—as a rough test of distinction. But on what does this difficulty depend? It depends on stylistic technique. There is no doubt that Thucydides was influenced by the rhetorical school of Gorgias, though he was not dominated by it. He modified it by peculiarities of his own; but the affinity is unmistakably shown in the artificial balancing of clauses, the artificial verbal antitheses, the poetical phrase. Generally he keeps this tendency well in hand, but in some passages he deliberately allows it to run riot, and then he becomes obscure because the grammatical constructions have to be twisted unnaturally to subserve verbal effects. Some of these crooked passages produced upon a Greek ear almost the effect of dithyrambs released from the bonds of metre. Dionysius in his instructive criticism takes two passages as conspicuous for this fault (as he considered it),—the dialogue of the Athenian and Melian diplomatists, and the reflexions upon the psychological and social aspects of civil sedition. Both might be described as elaborate studies in this kind of technique—the "obscure and contorted style." It is unnecessary, nor have I time, to illustrate it at length, but I will give one brief example. It is said in the Funeral Oration of Pericles, about sol-

---

[17] It has been rightly pointed out by Mahaffy that it is a misapprehension to explain the obscurities of Thucydides as due to condensation of thought. He is "condensed in expression but not in thought" (*Greek Literature*, ii. 1. 112).

diers who had fallen in battle: οἷς ἐνευδαι-
μονῆσαί τε ὁ βίος ὁμοίως καί ἐν-
τελευτῆσαι ξυνεμετρήθη. To express the
meaning in tolerable English we have to
render somewhat like this: "Whose days were
so measured that the term of their happiness
was also the term of their life." But this is a
paraphrase, and it does not give the effect of
the Greek. The literal translation is: "For
whom life was made commensurate, to be
happy in and to die in, alike." (Even this fails
to bring out the force of the aorist tense
ἐνευδαιμονῆσαι which suggests the familiar Greek saying, that a man's life cannot be
judged happy till after his death.) But if the
English is obscure and intolerable, to a
Greek ear, such as that of Dionysius, the
Greek was hardly less so.

Now is there any significance in this remarkable variation in style? Is it purely capricious? Does Thucydides break into di-
thyrambic prose just when, and simply
because, he is in the mood? Such caprice
would not be artistic, and it would not be
Greek. If the difference in style corresponded to the distinction between narrative and
speeches, the explanation would be ready.
The speeches, in any case, serve the artistic
purpose of pauses in the action; they introduce the variety which Herodotus
secured by digressions; they fulfil somewhat
the function of choruses in the drama. And
so we should not be surprised to find a corresponding variety in the diction and technique. But the difference in style extends into
the speeches themselves.

The explanation which I would submit to
you is that when Thucydides adopts what we
may fairly call his unnatural style, when he is
involved and obscure, he is always making
points of his own. In support of this view, I
allege the following considerations. (1) The
meditation on the party-struggles in Greek
states, though not a speech, belongs to this
category. It interrupts the action; it is, in fact,
a speech of the author. And it is one of the
flagrant examples of the unnatural style, and
is commented on, as such, by Dionysius. Here

then the author undisguisedly adopts this
style for his own reflexions. (2) Secondly, take
the Melian dialogue. Now whether we think,
as some do, that such a conference was never
held, or believe—and this is my opinion—
that it was held, all agree that the actual conversation is in the main fictitious. I will return
to this dialogue in another connexion. I
would point out now that it is a clear case in
which the unnatural style is employed for a
political study of the author. Contrast it, as
Dionysius contrasts it, with another dialogue,
that between Archidamus and the Plataeans.
This is in the natural style, and obviously
gives the simple tenor of what passed on the
occasion. (3) My third proof lies in the contrast between two of the speeches of Pericles.
The speech he delivered before the war is so
lucid and straightforward in style as to have
satisfied Dionysius; and at the same time it is
perfectly appropriate to the situation, and no
doubt gives the general drift of the Periclean
argument. On the other hand, the speech
which he delivers in self-defence, when he
became unpopular, is marked in part by
those obscurities which excited the censure
of Dionysius, and is also distinguished by unsuitable statements which could not have
been addressed by any statesman to a public
whose favour he desired to recover.

I infer that when Thucydides writes in the
unnatural style, he intends the reader to understand that he has here to do with the
author himself—that the author is making
points. When he writes in the natural style,
he is producing documentary evidence. The
speech of Pericles on the eve of the war is
virtually a document.

Let me make an application of this inference, which I think has some interest. The
Epitaphios of Pericles is composed on the
whole in the unnatural style. It enshrines, as
I believe, some utterances of Pericles himself;
but the style is generally contorted and obscure, though we forgive, or may even find a
certain pleasure in, this, so lofty is the spirit
and so fine the thoughts. Now it is to be noted
that, unlike other speeches, this funeral ad-

dress does not cast any direct light on the events of the war, and that its tone is out of keeping with the occasion. There was no great action, no conspicuous deed of valour, in the first year of the war, yet this oration over the Athenians who fell in it is pitched in a key which would be appropriate to the burial of the heroes of a Thermopylae. My view is that Thucydides has seized this occasion to turn the light on Pericles himself. The Athens which Pericles here depicts is an ideal; and the purpose of the historian is to bring out the fact that he was an idealist. The very incongruity between the occasion and the high-pitched strain of the orator heightens the calculated impression that Pericles, along with his political wisdom, possessed an imagination which outranged realities.

If you were asked to translate into ancient Greek "he is an idealist," you could not, I think, find a more exact equivalent than ζητεῖ ἄλλο τι, ὡς ἔπος εἰπεῖν, ἢ ἐν οἷς ζῶμεν. ["You seek, one might say, a world quite unlike that in which we live."] This expression is applied by Cleon (in his speech about Mytilene[18]) to the Athenians in general, to whom it was hardly appropriate; it was, I take it, a covert hit at the *êthos* and character of Pericles. Now both this speech of Cleon and the counter-speech of Diodotus are, by my criterion, largely composed of matter which is purely Thucydidean. The speech of Diodotus contains, you remember, reflexions on the general theory of punishment—the earliest discussion of the subject in literature; and we know from other evidence that this was a question which had a special interest for Pericles. I venture therefore to think that one of the points which Thucydides wishes to make in these speeches is, that the more lenient treatment of the rebels of Mytilene was in accordance with the *spirit* of Periclean policy. With the spirit; but it might have been argued that it was not in accordance with the letter and the logic; and this, I think, is one of the points which Cleon's speech intended to suggest. It is notable that while the speaker makes, as I think, an oblique hit at Periclean

idealism, and strikes an anti-Periclean note in his dispraise of knowledge and criticism, at the same time he iterates phrases which occur in the Periclean speeches: "Empire means tyranny"; "Do not play the virtuous." Thucydides is here studying not only the contrast between the two politicians, but also the difficulties inherent in the Periclean imperialism.

Dramatic treatment of the *historiae personae*

The speeches in general served two purposes. In the first place they were used by the author to explain the facts and elements of a situation, as well as underlying motives and ideas. In some cases the speech was only a dramatic disguise of a study of his own. Thus, the characters of two protagonist cities, Athens and Sparta, are delineated in a speech of a third party, the Corinthians: the author of this famous comparison was unquestionably Thucydides himself. But in other cases he uses the actual expositions of politicians,—genuine political documents so far as the main tenor went,—as the most useful means of explaining a situation. The comparative advantages of the two contending powers for the coming war are stated in two speeches from opposite points of view.[19] The prospects and difficulties of the Sicilian expedition are set forth by the same means.

The speeches had the second function— and here I return to the point from which I set out—of serving the objective dramatic method of indicating character which Thucydides chose to adopt. The speeches of Pericles, Cleon, Brasidas, Nicias, and Alcibiades, taken in conjunction with their actions, reveal as much of their characters as seemed to the author necessary for the matter in hand; that is, those sides of their nature which in his opinion governed their public actions or

---

[18] iii. 38. 7.

[19] In the second speech of the Corinthians and the first of Pericles.

affected their political influence. The general plan was that the men, as well as the events, should speak or be made to speak for themselves, with little or no direct comment from the writer.

This method produced the illusion that the actors showed themselves to the reader independently of the author. It really meant that the author had framed a psychological estimate of them, as a dramatist constructs his characters: an estimate founded on his knowledge of their actions, but nevertheless no more than his own subjective interpretation. The reader is here almost as completely in the author's hands as in a drama. He has not the means of forming a corrective judgment for himself; for he does not know how the historian has arrived at his results.

The application of the method may be observed in the cases of Cleon and Nicias. Thucydides held a distinct view of the character of Cleon as a politician. He allows us to see it reflected from Cleon's actions and from the opinions of people about him. When he describes Cleon as an influential leader of the demos, who was very violent, namely in manner and speech, he only states a fact which was undoubtedly notorious and admitted. The oration of Cleon on the Lesbian question exhibits his fashion of rating the people like a pedagogue. The drastic judgment that, if Cleon's command at Pylos ended in disaster, this would be a great blessing, for it would rid the city of Cleon, is not recorded as the historian's own sarcasm; it is mentioned as the opinion of some people at Athens. But as the people who thought so are called "sensible" ($\sigma\omega\phi\rho\text{ο}\nu\epsilon\varsigma$), the disguise is here very thin; the writer permits his own assent to be visible. No reader of the scenes in which Cleon appears would be left in any doubt that Cleon in the author's estimation was a pestilent demagogue; but in one passage[20] Thucydides entirely abandons his dramatic reserve and ascribes the worst motives to the politician for his unwillingness to bring the war to a close.

The portrait of Nicias, the conscientious patriot, an embodiment of respectability,

cautious and experienced, but unendowed with first-rate talent, afraid of responsibility, afraid of the Ecclesia, is perhaps the most successful achievement of Thucydides in dramatic art. All this comes out in his actions and speeches. But in this case too the author once comes forward himself and directly construes the motives which actuated Nicias in working in the interests of peace. They were of a selfish nature: he thought of his own reputation; he desired "while he had suffered no reverses and was held in repute, to preserve his good fortune; he wished for rest himself as well as to give the people rest; he hoped to leave his name to posterity as of one who had never brought calamity on the city; and he thought that the best means to secure this was to trust as little as possible to fortune and to keep out of danger, which would be avoided by peace." The irony is unmistakable. Again, in the last scene, when Nicias has been executed at Syracuse, the historian appears before the curtain for a moment and pronounces an epitaph, the point of which posterity has frequently misunderstood. It is generally taken as an encomium; it is really *malice*. In my opinion, says Thucydides, Nicias deserved such an end less than any other Athenian, considering his conventional virtue. In other words, a man of such conventional virtue was unsuited for such an unconventional end. That is irony of a kind in which Thucydides rarely indulges; behind it lurks the suppressed judgment that Athens was unfortunate in the trust which she reposed in Nicias, the model of irreproachable respectability.

In the case of Alcibiades the historian dwells on the extravagance and display of his private life, because they had a direct influence on the feelings of the Athenians towards him, and affected his public career and the course of the war. But here too the character is revealed in actions and words; insolence and ambition come out in his orations, and as I have already observed, some strong

---

[20] v. 16. 1

phrases seem to be characteristic of his manner. Thucydides refrains from commenting on his character, but points out his services and shows that the Athenians regarded him with a suspicious apprehension which prevented them from profiting by his ability.

In the cases of Themistocles, Pericles, and Antiphon, the author departs from his usual practice, and gives characterising judgments of his own. In the case of Themistocles this might be considered a necessary exception, as he does not come into the main narrative and cannot reveal himself dramatically. The same reason might be held partly to apply to Pericles, since the greater part of his lifework was over when he comes on the stage. The favourable notice of Antiphon's ability might also be explained by the fact that he had hardly appeared in the political arena before the year of the revolution, and his appearance then was so brief. The eulogy on Antiphon indeed has a personal note, which betrays perhaps a friendship. It is, however, futile to seek to explain or explain away these exceptions. The truth is that in general Thucydides is dramatic, but he has not carried his method to extremes.

It is noteworthy that nearly all the judgments which he pronounces concern intelligence and political ability. This is the case with Themistocles, Pericles, Antiphon, Theramenes, and Hermocrates. They all receive greater or less praise for political capacity, which in the case of Themistocles is said to have amounted to genius.

The case of Hyperbolus demands a few words, because it illustrates the method of Thucydides and his political leanings. In the years between the Fifty Years' Peace and the Sicilian Expedition, the division of parties under the opposing leaders Nicias and Alcibiades paralysed the foreign policy of Athens and hindered continuity of action. The situation was so serious that the only way out seemed that proposed by the demagogue Hyperbolus—a trial of ostracism, which would expel one of the rivals and secure unity. Alcibiades frustrated this device by combining, if not with his rival, at least with a

sufficiently large oligarchical faction, to procure the ostracism of Hyperbolus. Thucydides does not say a word about this affair, though of course he was perfectly aware of the facts, and though they had an immediate bearing on the foreign policy of Athens. We must suppose that as the purpose of the ostracism was defeated and the relative positions of the two leaders were not altered by the vote, he considered it superfluous to record the occurrence. It will be admitted, however, that a modern historian who allowed himself such an omission or carried his principle of exclusion so far, would not escape censorious criticism. But in another connexion, Thucydides refers to the ostracism, without dating it, or in any way suggesting its significance. Hyperbolus was killed in 411 B.C. at Samos. Thucydides records this and mentions that Hyperbolus had been ostracized. This is the only place where he names the demagogue, who in the years following Cleon's death had been one of the most influential speakers in the Ecclesia. We might suspect that in ignoring this politician, just as he ignored men of the same type like Eucrates and Lysicles, he exercised a reserve which was equivalent to an adverse criticism, a negative expression of contempt; but no doubt is permitted by the words in which he paints his memory black. Hyperbolus was ostracized, we are told, not because he was esteemed dangerous, but because he was an unprincipled scoundrel and a disgrace to the city. The same epithet ($\mu o \chi \theta \eta \rho \acute{o} s$) is here applied to Hyperbolus which was applied to him by Aristophanes.[21] We may note how Thucydides violates here his own principle of relevance. At this moment, Hyperbolus is not interesting or important, and in holding up his character to reprobation the historian is deviating from his narrative. Again, what he says of the cause of the ostracism is untrue. Hyperbolus was not ostracized because he was a disgrace to the city, whether he was so or not. He would not have been ostracized if the supporters of Alcibiades had not been

---

[21] *Knights*, 1304.

instructed to write his name on the sherds instead of that of the virtuous Nicias. We know very little about Hyperbolus; but this judgment of Thucydides cannot be taken as objective or impartial. It is quite clear that he had a profound antipathy to popular leaders like Cleon and Hyperbolus, and that he was incapable of doing them whatever justice they deserved. And such antipathy is sufficient to account for the treatment of Cleon, without invoking a further motive of personal resentment for any part Cleon may have taken in procuring the condemnation of the historian.[22]

Rationalistic view of history

It is by his practice of allowing his characters to reveal themselves by their actions and words, while keeping himself in the background, although he does not adhere to this plan with pedantic consistency, that the art of Thucydides may be appropriately called dramatic. The description of "dramatic" has indeed been claimed for his history on another ground. It has been thought that he viewed the whole war under the scheme of a tragedy, in which the Sicilian expedition was the *peripeteia* or "reversal" of fortune for Athens. This idea has recently been developed in a new shape by Mr. F. M. Cornford, in a brilliant study which seeks to establish that the historian read Aeschylean conceptions into the events of the war and mounted it, like a tragedy, with the dark figures of Tyche, Hybris, Peitho, and Eros, moving in the background and prompting the human actors. That such a conception should be read by an ingenious scholar in a work which impresses the ordinary reader as entirely matter of fact in its treatment of political transactions, illustrates what a wonderful book the history of Thucydides is. The truth is, I think, that the style of Thucydides was influenced by the Attic drama, no less than by the rhetoric of Gorgias, and it is one of the merits of Mr. Cornford's monograph to have illustrated this influence. But that the tragic phrases and reminiscences, and the occasional use of

tragic irony, cannot be held to have more than a stylistic significance, and that Thucydides did not intend to cast the war into the typical scheme of a tragic development, will be apparent if we consider his own clear statements.

His view of the causes of the collapse of Athens displays the difference between his own outlook on human affairs and that of Herodotus. The older historian pourtraying the collapse of the Persian power discerns, in the development of the plot, imminent above the actors a superhuman control and the occult operation of nemesis. The only external influence recognised by the younger writer appears in the form of the incalculable element which he calls *Tyche*, Chance. Herodotus interpreted history and life, in the sense that the decline of a state or of a man from a post of commanding eminence was due to the action of a supernatural power which would not tolerate the exaltation which invariably leads to immoderate elation of soul and often to acts of insolence and rashness. In one of the speeches in Thucydides this anthropopathic idea is translated into the dry formula: "It is the nature of human things to decline." But it can hardly be said that he believed unreservedly in this principle (which may be found in Ionian philosophers) as a certain fact. And his analysis of the course of the war and his explanation of its issue show that the operation of the incalculable element of chance need not be decisive. It contributed to the decline of the Athenian power, but that power might have survived and defied its outrages, if it had not been for human mismanagement.

In the early stage of the war there were two cases of the play of the incalculable. There was first of all the plague. But though severe, maiming and weakening more than anything else the offensive power of the State for years to come, it was not crushing, it did not spell doom; one of its gravest conse-

---

[22] F.M. Cornford touches on this point in his *Thucydides Mythistoricus*. I think he is right. The hypothesis of personal spite is superfluous.

quences was the psychical effect upon the Athenians, for which Pericles suffered. The other surprise of fortune was a kind one, the combination of circumstances which helped the Athenians to their stroke of luck at Pylos. This elated them, as the pestilence had cast them down. Instead of grasping the opportunity of making advantageous terms and bringing to an end a war which they would gladly have concluded on any terms a few years before, they were incited to hopes of new conquest. But the consequences were by no means disastrous; the Peace of 421 B.C. left the balance of power much the same.

They had recovered from the effects of the plague and the war when they undertook the conquest of Sicily in 415 B.C. The catastrophe of that enterprise was the beginning of a gradual decline, which was determined by domestic dissensions in Athens, and afterwards by the intervention of Persia. A modern historian has designated the Sicilian expedition as an act of insanity, an instance of a whole people gone mad, analogous to the case of England in the Crimean war. But this was not the opinion of Thucydides. He says, and he is speaking in his own name, that it was not an error of judgment in the design or in the calculation of strength, and would have been a success, if it had been properly supported and carried out. The verdict of the modern writer was influenced partly by ethical considerations; the verdict of Thucydides did not take ethics into account; he only contemplates the question whether, judging the strength of Athens and the resistance offered to her, the ambition of extending her empire to Sicily was reasonable or foolish. The failure of the enterprise and the reverses of the ensuing years he imputes to the dissensions at home; and in the same way he explains mismanagement in the earlier period of the war by the jealousies of rival politicians. In other words, the key to the decline of Athenian power was the fact that Pericles had no successors. The city began to fall away from her eminence when her government was no longer controlled by an able leader. Even after the Sicilian expedition, the situation might have been retrieved; for there was a man marked out to be a leader like Pericles, if the Athenians had trusted him. This was Alcibiades. That this was the view which Thucydides formed of Alcibiades can, I think, admit of little doubt. The distrust of the Athenians, he says, contributed heavily to the fall of the city; Alcibiades conducted the war with masterly ability.[23] In other words, things would have turned out very differently, if the conduct of affairs had been entrusted to him. The distrust is attributed to the somewhat insolent display and splendour of his private life, which excited envy and the suspicion of tyrannical designs. Nicias taunts him with this λαμπρότης, Alcibiades glories in it.[24] Now the career of Alcibiades had remarkable points of resemblance with that of a great Athenian statesman of a former age, Themistocles. They were both banished from Athens; both conspired with her enemies against her; and Alcibiades like Themistocles became a trusted adviser of the Persians. But another point of likeness is indicated by Thucydides, λαμπρότης. It is not for nothing that he describes Themistocles and Pausanias as the most magnificent or luxurious of the Greeks of their time (λαμπροτάτους). That was a weak point in the case of Themistocles as in that of Alcibiades; it led to the suspicion of tyranny. This parallel suggests that one motive of the digression on Themistocles was to point it. At all events it throws light on the view of the historian. Athens produced three men who had the faculty, which cannot be learned by study, for guiding the affairs of a great state, Themistocles, Pericles, and Alcibiades. Two of them fell into the snare of luxurious splendour, which ruined their careers. Pericles avoided that pitfall, and won and retained the public confidence. This contrast, I would observe, gives special point to a famous phrase in the *Epitaphios*. Pericles himself was φιλόκαλος μετ' εὐτελείας (one who cultivated refinement without ex-

---

[23] vi. 15.
[24] vi. 12; 16.

travagance), he was not λαμπρός (lavish) he indulged his private tastes without undue or obtrusive expense.

This analysis, which is furnished by the historian's own comments, eliminates entirely the dim superstitious notions of doom and nemesis, which do duty for Providence in Herodotus and dispense the spectator from any deeper study of the course and causes of events. Thucydides deals with purely human elements; human brains bear the ultimate responsibility. There is nothing mysterious about the fact that events cannot be foreseen. The course of events, says Pericles, may sometimes be as incalculable by reason as the thoughts of a man's mind. Thucydides does not regard the plague as a divine dispensation. It was simply an occurrence which could not be foreseen, exactly as you may not foresee the moves of your enemy. Herodotus credits the oracles with mysterious knowledge; Thucydides occasionally refers to oracles, but their sole significance for him lies in the physical effect they produce on those who believe them. Of the oracle which predicted that the war would last twenty-seven years, he drily observes that it is the only one to which people who put their faith in oracles can point as having been certainly fulfilled. Here he was at the same standpoint as Anaxagoras and Pericles.[25] The philosophers who had established the reign of law had not written in vain for Thucydides. Chance means for him the same kind of thing that it means for us; it does not signify the interference of an external will or caprice; it simply represents an element which cannot be foretold. He recognises the operation of the unknown; he does not recognise the presence of "things occult." And he reduces the unknown to its minimum of significance for human life. The great philosopher, Democritus of Abdera, had said: "Chance is an idol which men fashioned to excuse their own mental incapacity. As a matter of fact chance seldom conflicts with wisdom. In most affairs of life, an intelligent mind can exercise clairvoyance with success.[26] These words of Democritus might serve as a motto for Thucydides.

The elements for the conception of the war as a tragedy, in the proper sense of the word, were absent from his interpretation of the course of history. There was no mysterious controlling force, no doom or retribution, no inevitable decree of fate, no moral principle at stake. The lessons which the catastrophe conveyed were not moral or cathartic. The war was full of instructive lessons for statesmen and generals; but those lessons were assuredly of a very different order from the lessons of Aeschylus and Sophocles. And the occasional use of phraseology, which the tragedians charged with meaning, should not mislead us. Just as a writer of the present day who is completely innocent of any traffic with the supernatural may employ such terms as fate, doom, nemesis, so Thucydides could borrow the personified abstractions of tragedy for purposes of expression, without meaning to suggest anything occult. If I say that I have been prompted to do something by an imp of mischief or by a demon of unrest, you will not impute to me a belief in demons or imps. If Thucydides has sometimes expressed psychological observations in the language of tragic poets, this does not prove that he looked at history from a tragic poet's point of view.

Political analysis

Attempts have inevitably been made to peer behind the scenes and discover the personal political views or tendencies of this singularly reserved historian. Dionysius, a critic who is usually instructive though never profound and often obtuse, stigmatizes in Thucydides a lack of patriotism so marked as to amount

---

[25] He speaks indeed strangely of the frequency of solar eclipses during the war (i. 23. 3), as if they had some significance for the human race; we may wonder what comment Anaxagoras would have made.

[26] Democritus, in Mullach, *Frag. Phil.* 167. Thucydides observes *sub persona Hermocratis* (iv. 62. 4) that in war the incalculable element has its uses; it is the same for both and conduces to caution and prudence.

to positive ill-will both towards Greece and towards Athens. "He began at a point where the Greek world had begun to decline. A Greek and Athenian should not have done this, especially one who was no outcast but had been honoured by the Athenians with high command. He was so malicious that he imputed to his own city the open causes of the war, though he might have found means to attach the responsibility to other cities. He could have *begun* not with the Corcyraean affair but with the supreme successes of his country after the Persian war, and could have shown that it was through jealousy and fear, the consequence of these successes, that the Lacedaemonians, alleging other reasons, began the war." When this criticism is examined, it will be found that it mainly touches the *arrangement* of the first Book, but it shows that the narrative produced upon Dionysius the impression that Thucydides was unpatriotic.

On the other hand, it is held by some modern critics that the account of the beginnings and first years of the war is virtually a defence of the policy of Pericles, and it is even insinuated that the author manipulated facts, concealing some and mitigating others, with the purpose of presenting that policy in a favourable light. This view evidently contradicts that of Dionysius; it implies that Thucydides sympathized with Athens during the Periclean régime and at the outbreak of the war.

The fact that the narrative can convey two such contradictory impressions is a certificate of the author's critical impartiality. The censure of Dionysius is based on the conventional principle of later times that it is a historian's duty to be patriotic at all costs, to sacrifice his critical judgment; and it is superfluous to refute his charge of ill-will. On the other hand, the theory that Thucydides was an unreserved admirer of Pericles and deliberately intended to exalt and defend his policy, almost as a partisan, has some *prima facie* plausibility, and, as it has a direct bearing on the writer's attitude to history and politics, we must consider it more particularly.

We have seen how Thucydides speaks in the highest terms of the political ability of Pericles, and was convinced that, if he had lived or had a successor as able as himself, the war would have terminated favourably for Athens. But this general conviction would be quite compatible with discriminating criticism. The tribute which he has paid to Pericles does not imply that he saw eye to eye with the statesman in all things or held his political faith. There are proofs, in my opinion, that he exercised here, as in the other cases, a cold independent judgment, and had no scruples in exhibiting weak points.

The speeches of Pericles claim our special attention. I may begin by pointing out that the praise which Pericles bestows in the *Epitaphios*[27] on the democratic constitution of Athens, implying that it was an ideal form of government, is not in accordance with the view of Thucydides, who expressly states that in his opinion the short-lived *politeia* which was established in Athens after the fall of the Four Hundred was not merely superior to democracy, but was the only good constitution that Athens had enjoyed in his lifetime. In other words, he did not consider democracy a good constitution. In the second place, we may feel confident that the eloquent and fascinating portrait of Athens, drawn by Pericles, did not in the historian's opinion correspond to reality. It was the Periclean ideal. And Thucydides knew perfectly well that the claim that Athens was the school of liberal education for Greece would have been scouted by other states; and, as a matter of fact, it did not become anything of the kind till after the Peloponnesian war. Again, it seems more than doubtful whether Thucydides approved of the Periclean policy of bringing all the inhabitants of Attica into the city. The length at which he dwells on the unpleasant consequences of this arrangement, his pains in showing how distasteful it was to the people, suggest that he considered it a measure of highly questionable wisdom.

He certainly looked on Pericles as the most

[27] ii. 37.

successful statesman who had recently guided the counsels of Athens. But he saw him, like all his other *dramatis personae*, in a dry light, and, as I have suggested, he has presented one side of the statesman's mind with a certain veiled irony.

The dramatic detachment of Thucydides readily produced the impression that he was unpatriotic. He allows every party to state their case as strongly and persuasively as possible. But while he wrote not as a patriot but as a historian, it is Athens, not Sparta, the Athenian Empire, not the Peloponnesian Confederacy, in which the interest of the narrative centres throughout. As to the questions at stake and the issues involved in the war, what we may hope to discover is not what political views the historian held, but *what was his attitude of mind in observing political events.*

His interest centres in the Athenian empire. In the passage in which he offers a general explanation of the result of the war he writes from the Athenian side entirely. Now as to the nature of the Athenian empire he has no illusions. In the first Book he unfolds the unscrupulous way in which it was acquired, with perfect candour. He states that it was generally unpopular, and he allots a speech to an indictment of it by one of the subject states. That it was a despotism based not on right but on might is not merely alleged by the opponents of Athens but is emphasized by Athenian speakers. The Athenian diplomatist who spoke at the Congress of Sparta characterizes it without any reserve as having been won from motives of self-confidence and ambition; and the justification assigned is that it is a law of human nature that the weaker should be constrained by the stronger. Pericles is still more candid and emphatic. "The Empire you possess," he says, "is a tyranny; it may have been unjust to acquire, it is perilous to relinquish it." Again: "That man is truly wise who incurs odium for the highest stakes. Hatred does not balance the present magnificence and the future fame." Here power, wealth, and glory are

assigned as a justification of an unjustly gotten and unpopular empire. Arguing against the peace-party—οἱ ἀπάγμονες—who have scruples about justice, Pericles takes the same line, though with more cynicism, as a modern British chauvinist contemptuous of those whom he calls the Little Englanders. He sneers at their conscience, which, he suggests, is a cloak for cowardice. Alcibiades in advocating the Sicilian expedition points out the necessity to imperial states of an active and aggressive policy. Hermocrates, the enemy of Athens, does not complain of such a policy on grounds of morality; he says: "I can fully pardon the Athenians for their grasping policy; I do not blame those who seek empire, but those who are ready to submit; for it has always been the natural instinct of man to rule him who yields and to resist the aggressor."

The excuse which both Hermocrates and Athenians urge for the acquisition of empire is the instinct of human nature. But Pericles also attempted what may be called a justification on higher grounds. In the Funeral Oration he draws a picture of the grandeur and the *culture* of Athens. There, he so much as says, is the ideal which our city, by winning power and wealth, through an empire which was certainly *not* built on foundations of justice, has realised for the admiration and imitation of Hellas. Such things cannot be achieved by timid justice and stay-at-home piety. This is the *leit-motif* of the Funeral Oration.

Thus the historian kept before himself, and keeps before us, the fact that the empire cannot be defended on grounds of justice, that it could not be maintained except by *force majeure,* and that if slavery was an extreme word for the condition of the subject states, they were generally reluctant under the yoke. It is further to be observed that when Thucydides makes occasional reflexions of his own, he never takes justice or morality into account, from which we may infer that in his estimation those conceptions did not illuminate the subject. He recognised that the ideal of justice was an actual psychological force and could not be neglected by statesmen, any more than popular religion. But he did not consider it worth while to apply the standard of justice in estimating political transactions, just as he did not ask whether an action was pleasing to the gods.

The speech of Diodotus, advocating lenient treatment for the rebels of Mytilene, is interesting in this connexion. As the speaker played no part in history except here, the harangue must be introduced solely for the sake of its arguments. Its chief interest is that it repudiates the intrusion of justice into the question; the speaker reproaches Cleon for having dragged in so irrelevant a consideration, and bases his own view entirely on reasons of state. Thucydides with his usual reticence abstains from comment, though the tone of his narrative suggests that he sympathized with the lenient policy; but the fact that he chose these speeches of Cleon and Diodotus for working up, and that he has worked them up largely in the style which he employs when he is not documentary, shows that *his interest lay in the logic of policy.*

In the light of the debate on Mytilene we may consider the notorious debate of the Athenian and Melian representatives. Melos, you remember, was an independent state. Athens had made an attempt to force her into her empire in 426 B.C.; the idea was not resumed til 416 B.C., but in the meantime the relations of the two states had been hostile. When the expedition reached the island, the generals sent envoys to demand submission. They were admitted to a round-table conference with members of the Melian government, and Thucydides gives in the form of a dialogue what purposes to be the tenor of the debate. That such a conference was held, there cannot be a reasonable doubt, nor is it improbable that Thucydides had something to work upon. There is no difficulty in supposing that he might have heard enough from some one who knew to furnish him with a text.

The note of the dialogue is the elimination of justice from the discussion, by the Athenians. "Lass unsern Herr Gott aus dem Spass." The field of the argument is confined to policy and reason of state. When the Melians essay to find an issue from this restricted ground by observing that, being innocent of wrong, they expect a heaven-sent chance to intervene in their favour, the Athenians retort that gods as well as men recognise it to be a law of nature that the weaker should be ruled by the stronger. Now this is nothing more than what had already been said by Hermocrates and the Athenian envoy at Sparta. The attitude of the Athenians on the occasion is exactly the same as that of Diodotus in arguing for leniency towards Mytilene. Both alike are ruthlessly realistic; both alike refuse to consider any reason but reason of state. The conscience and feelings of the readers of Thucydides have been shocked by the tone of the Athenians at Melos because they sympathize with Mytilene. Yet Diodotus in 427 B.C. regarded Mytilene just as Athens in 416 B.C. regarded Melos, merely as a pawn in the game of empire. It is also important to observe that the discussion in the Melian council-chamber before the siege has nothing to do with the rigorous treatment of the people after the capture of the city. A few years before, Athens had meted out the same treatment to Scione; all the adult males were killed, the women and children enslaved. Thucydides makes no comment in either case. But if Athens had contented herself with reducing Melos to the condition of a tributary, the notorious dialogue would have been equally to the point. The policy of annexing Melos was one thing, the policy of punishing was another; Thucydides does not express his views on either. But it has been supposed by various critics that he introduced a cynical dialogue for the purpose of holding up to obloquy the conduct of Athens, and even of making it appear an ill-omened prelude to the disastrous expedition against Sicily. This theory will not, in my opinion, bear examination. Thucydides, as we have seen, did not consider that the Sicilian expedition was ill-advised in principle, and he does not hint that any consequences, bad or good for Athens, ensued from the conquest of Melos.

The truth is, I think, that Thucydides took the opportunity of the round-table conference to exhibit, pure and unvarnished, the springs of political action. The motives and arguments of the Athenians, whether wisely or unwisely applied in this particular case, were nothing new; they were the same which lay at the foundation of all their empire-building. This was the first case of a new annexation since the outbreak of the war, and it was the first occasion offered to the historian to analyse imperial policy from the point of view of aggression; he had already examined it from the point of view of preservation. The Melian dialogue only develops more undisguisedly and expressly—and the circumstance that no public was present gave the author the artistic pretext for candour—what is to be found in all the argumentative speeches: that not justice but reason of state is the governing consideration which guides the action of cities and claims the interest of historians.

We are now in a position to understand the attitude of Thucydides. *His object is to examine and reveal political actions from an exclusively political point of view.* He does not consider moral standards; his method is realistic and detached; he takes history as it is and examines it on its own merits. This detached analytical treatment is illustrated by the earliest political prose pamphlet we possess, written by a contemporary of the historian in the early years of the war; I mean the short tract on the Athenian Constitution. The author was an oligarch and declares without reserve his personal hostility to the democracy; but it is not a polemical work. He detaches himself from his own feelings, places himself at the point of view of democrats, and examines democracy exclusively in this light. Applying his acute logic, he demonstrates that the institutions of Athens could hardly be improved upon. The writer is intellectually al-lied to Thucydides in the detachment of his attitude and the logical restriction of the issue under a particular point of view.

Now when Thucydides offers reflexions *in propria persona* on events, his criticisms, on the policy of Athens, for instance, or on the value of an Athenian politician, are generally determined by the consideration whether they were conducive to success or failure in the war. In his appreciation of Brasidas, he places himself at the point of view of Sparta, and recognises that this general's conduct, policy, and character were conducive to the extension of Spartan power in competition with Athens. He takes the objects of the conflicting states as given, without approving or condemning; and in recording acts and methods his rare verdicts of praise or blame are confined to the question whether those acts and methods were calculated to achieve their object; just as in characterizing a man he refers only to his intellectual powers. He offers no opinion whether the aims were justifiable or admirable; he applies no ethical standard to policies or politicians.

Of course, he was full conscious of ethical questions which arise in connexion with high politics, and these questions raise their heads in the dramatic parts of the work. In the speeches, justice and expediency are frequently distinguished and opposed. A speaker, for example, according to circumstances, is concerned to show that a course which is just is also expedient, or that expedience ought to be preferred to justice. Sometimes the consideration of justice is briefly dismissed as irrelevant. It appears as a psychical factor actually operative in international transactions, a principle to which at least homage of the lips was paid, by which praise and blame were popularly awarded, and which therefore had to be taken into account. But its rôle was slight and subordinate: the dramatist could not ignore it, though he allows it as small a range as he can; the thinker dismissed it.

There is not, so far as I can discover, any reason for believing that Thucydides thought or intended to suggest that an un-compromising policy of self-interest con-duced to the fall of the Athenian empire, or that her wrong and unwise actions were wrong and unwise because they were guided by considerations of expediency alone. There is no ground for supposing that he would have had a thought of censure, if he had lived in our own days, for statesmen like Cavour and Bismarck and Disraeli, who were guided exclusively by reason of state, and are therefore blamed by moralists for having debased the moral currency in Europe. If, instead of a history, Thucydides had written an analytical treatise on politics, with particular reference to the Athenian empire, it is probable that he would occupy a different place from that which he holds actually in the world's esteem; he would have forestalled the fame of Machiavelli.

Thucydides simply observes facts; Ma-chiavelli lays down maxims and prescribes methods; but the whole innuendo of the Thucydidean treatment of history agrees with the fundamental postulate of Ma-chiavelli, the supremacy of reason of state. To maintain a state, said the Florentine thinker, "a statesman is often compelled to act against faith, humanity, and religion." In Thucydides, reason of state appears as actu-ally the sovran guide in the conduct of affairs. But the essential point of comparison is that both historians, in examining history and politics, abstracted from all but political con-siderations, and applied logic to this restrict-ed field. Machiavelli—the true Machiavelli, not the Machiavelli of fable, the *scelerum in-ventor Ulixes*—entertained an ideal: Italy for the Italians, Italy freed from the stranger: and in the service of this ideal he desired to see his speculative science of politics applied. Thucydides had no political aim in view; he was purely a historian; his interest was to investigate the actual policy of Athens in maintaining and losing her empire. But it was part of the method of both alike to elimi-nate conventional sentiment and morality.

A certain use of the term ἀρετή by Thu-cydides has an interest in this connexion. It is sometimes said that he did not assign great importance to the action and rôle of in-dividuals. This seems to me a mistake, due to the circumstance that he does not draw per-sonal portraits in the manner of subsequent historians. For it is evident that he consid-ered the brains and wisdom of him whom he calls "the first man" as largely responsible for the success of Athenian policy before the Peloponnesian war. We can read between the lines that in his view the Peisistratids, The-mistocles, and Alcibiades were also forces which counted for a great deal. The pre-emi-nent significance of the individual was a tenet of Machiavelli and his contemporaries (a classical feature of the Renaissance); it was a prince, an individual brain and will, to which he looked for the deliverance and regenera-tion of Italy. Both writers conceived the in-dividual, as a political factor, purely from the intellectual side. Now Thucydides has used ἀρετή in his notice of the oligarch Antiphon, to express the intelligence, dexterity, and will-power of a competent statesman, in sharp contradistinction to the conventional ἀρετή of the popular conception. The only appropriate equivalent by which we can render in a modern language this Thucydi-dean ἀρετή is a key-word of Machiavelli's system, *virtù*, a quality possessed by men like Francesco Sforza and Cesare Borgia.

It must be understood that this attitude of Thucydides only concerns international poli-tics, the subject of his work. Domestic politics lie, except incidentally, outside his scope. When he turns aside to describe the disinte-grating influence of party faction on the in-ternal conditions of Greek states, he recog-nises the important operation of ethical beliefs and religious sanctions in holding a society together. But where national aims are at stake and international rivalries are in mo-tion, no corresponding beliefs and sanctions appear, possessing the same indefeasible val-ue for the success and prosperity of a state. There is irony in his remark that the Lace-daemonians, after the first war had come to an end, ascribed their own want of success to the fact that they had refused the Athenian proposition to submit the Peloponnesian grievances to arbitration, in accordance with the Thirty Years' Peace. It is noteworthy that in the Funeral Oration of Pericles, where he pourtrays the qualities of his countrymen, there is not a single word about those conventional virtues in which Nicias shone. The Athenians are praised for their political intelligence and versatility, for their adventurous activity, for enlightened freedom in their intercourse with strangers, and for other excellent things. Not a word is said of their piety, and they were certainly pious. We are told that they have accomplished much and reached the heights by their own talents and their own toil. There is not a word, not a single perfunctory phrase, of assistance or favour from heaven. Of religion, or of morality in the conventional sense, there is not a syllable from the beginning to the end of this brilliant speech. Pericles could hardly have avoided at least some conventional reference to the gods, in the speech he actually delivered at the sepulture; that Thucydides overlooked it is significant.

If this appreciation of the historian is sympathetic, I hope you will not suppose that I belong to the band of devotees who make a cult of Thucydides and can see no defects in their idol. Such devotees existed in ancient as well as in modern times, and the historian's ancient indiscriminating admirers received a very proper rebuke from Dionysius of Halicarnassus. I have already suggested that he carried his method of exclusion and omission too far. His treatment of individuals displays a more serious limitation in his idea of historical reconstruction. Thucydides does not seem to have grasped fully that in estimating the action of an individual in history his whole character must be taken into account; he is a psychical unity, and it is not possible to detach and isolate certain qualities. Psychological reconstruction is one of the most important as well as delicate problems which encounter the historian, and

Thucydides failed to realise all that it means. In his impatience of biographical trivialities, he went to the extreme of neglecting biography altogether. Take, for instance, his silence concerning the personality of Pericles. This statesman was one of the forces which operated in bringing about the war, and to understand his actions we want to know more about his personality. Thucydides is content to note his consummate political ability and his indifference to money, and to indicate his idealism. This does not enable us to realise what manner of man Pericles was; we still feel, and modern criticism illustrates this, that he is in many respects an unknown or at least ambiguous quantity.

The work of Thucydides has limitations which we must beware of underrating; but it marks the longest and most decisive step that has ever been taken by a single man towards making history what it is to-day. Out of the twilight in which Herodotus still moved wondering, he burst into the sunlight where facts are hard, not to wonder but to understand. With the Greeks historical study never acquired the scientific character which it was reserved for the nineteenth century to impress upon it. But within the limits of the task he attempted Thucydides was a master in the craft of investigating contemporary events, and it may be doubted whether within those limits the nineteenth century would have much to teach him. If he had admitted his readers into the secrets of his workshop, if he had more clearly displayed his raw material and shown how he arrived at his conclusion, if he had argued and discussed, he might have exercised a greater influence than he did on the *methods* of subsequent Greek historians. His incomplete work, posthumously published, had an immediate and far-reaching result in establishing political history; and men of the younger generation received a stimulus from him. But, although the value and greatness of his work were at once recognised, and he always remained the one and undisputed authority on the period he had treated, yet, for several centuries after his immediate successors, his history seems to have been little read except by scholars; he was a great name, not a living influence as a teacher or a model. His style, with its "old-fashioned and wilful beauty," repelled, and other ideals of history, sharply opposed to his, came into fashion. It was not till the first century B.C., with the return to Attic models, that the interest in his work revived; and from that time we can trace his influence on leading writers down to one of the latest Byzantine historians, Critobulus. But this influence was of a superficial kind; it concerned style and phraseology; it was generally a mere mechanical imitation. And the historians whom he would himself have most esteemed were not those who came under his own influence.

Lives of the Poets

Samuel Johnson

Editor's Introduction

The *Lives of the Poets* were written by Samuel Johnson in the final years of his life, after he had long been established as the "great Cham of literature." They were "his very favourite work," James Boswell informs us, and Boswell himself considered them "the richest, most beautiful and indeed most perfect production of Johnson's pen." They came as the culmination of his lifelong study of poetry, of delight in it and criticism of it, and indeed of talk about it. For Boswell tells us that "those who lived most in intimacy with him, heard him upon all occasions, when there was a proper opportunity, take delight in expatiating upon the various merits of the English Poets: upon the niceties of their characters, and the events of their progress through the world which they contributed to illuminate."

The work for Johnson was an occasional one in that it owed its inception to the initiative of three London booksellers, who had conceived the project of publishing a set of the works of the English poets. They then approached Johnson with an offer to write a preface and life for any of the poets they selected for publication. Of the fifty-two poets whose works were finally included, only five were there at Johnson's urging (and of these five only Thomson is now much remembered). Johnson began work upon them in the first half of 1777; the first four volumes appeared in 1779 and the remaining six in 1781 under the title, *Prefaces Biographical and Critical to the Works of the English Poets*, by Samuel Johnson, LL.D. Because of Johnson's contribution the venture proved a great publishing success. His own work was soon published independently under the title it bears today.

Johnson was born at Lichfield, Staffordshire, September 18, 1709. His father, sheriff of the city at the time of Samuel's birth, was a prominent, though never very successful, bookseller. In his father's shop the boy soon became a helper and began the voracious and wide-range reading that he continued throughout his life. By the time he entered Pembroke College, Oxford, at the age of nineteen, he was better read than some of the tutors. Poverty compelled him to leave college after thirteen months and, without a degree, he returned home. The business was in decline, and on his father's death in 1731, upon marrying a woman twenty years older who brought him a dowry of £700, he set up a school of his own, where he offered to board young gentlemen and teach them Latin and Greek. But after two years he had attracted so few young gentlemen that he had to admit failure.

Determined to achieve his ambition of becoming a scholar and writer, Johnson set forth for London in 1737 in the company of David Garrick, the future actor and theater manager, who had been one of his few pupils. His first literary work was as a journalist for the newly founded *Gentleman's*

Magazine, for which he wrote odes, epigrams, and reviews, as well as a series of short biographies. In 1738, at the age of twenty-nine, he wrote and published his first substantial poem, *London,* an imitation of the Latin satirist Juvenal. The poem was well received, winning praise from Alexander Pope, and quickly sold out three editions. The first of Johnson's prose works to win acclaim was a life of his friend Richard Savage, actor, playwright, and poet, and was praised by Henry Fielding, the novelist, as the "best treatise in the language on the excellencies and defects of human nature."

The opportunity to win fame in scholarship as well as literature came in 1746, just nine years after Johnson's coming to London. A syndicate of booksellers asked him to compile a dictionary of the English language. He accepted and published his *Plan of a Dictionary* the following year. But the remuneration he received was insufficient for his support, and to supplement his income he inaugurated the *Rambler,* a twopenny sheet published twice a week and containing a single anonymous essay. The *Dictionary* occupied Johnson and his staff for eight and one-half years. Published in 1755 in two volumes, it contained some 40,000 words with a wealth of literary illustration and precision of definition.

The *Dictionary* brought him increased fame, but did little to ease his financial situation, and in 1756 he was arrested for debt. Need compelled him to accept much hack work, yet he continued to produce works of both literature and scholarship. In 1759 appeared *The Prince of Abissinia,* better known as *Rasselas,* an account of imaginary travels in Ethiopia and Egypt that explore and expose the vanity of man's search for happiness—in fictional form Johnson's own spiritual autobiography. Then in 1765 he published his long promised edition of the works of Shakespeare. His financial worries had come to an end finally in 1762, when the king conferred upon him an annual pension of £300.

Johnson enjoyed and exulted in what he called "colloquial entertainment." In taverns and clubs, several of which he founded, he met frequently with his many friends and soon became the established center of literary and artistic London. Evidence of his power and fame as a conversationalist has been preserved for posterity as a result of his meeting with Boswell on May 16, 1763. The young Scotsman was then only twenty-two, whereas Johnson was fifty-three. From then until his death Johnson enjoyed warm companionship and the never flagging admiration of Boswell. To that love, as well as to Boswell's interest and abilities, readers owe one of the greatest biographies of any language or time. Johnson died in 1784, three years after the publication of the *Lives.*

Of all the fifty-two *Lives* Johnson considered the *Life* of Cowley his best, largely because of its dissertation upon the Metaphysical Poets. That part of the work on Cowley is reprinted here, along with the better portion of the *Lives* of Dryden and Pope, some selections from the *Life* of Milton (to whose politics and religion Johnson was profoundly opposed), and a short section from the *Life* of Gray.

From the Life of Cowley

Cowley, like other poets who have written with narrow views and, instead of tracing intellectual pleasure to its natural sources in the mind of man, paid their court to temporary prejudices, has been at one time too much praised and too much neglected at another.

Wit, like all other things subject by their nature to the choice of man, has its changes and fashions, and at different times takes different forms. About the beginning of the seventeenth century appeared a race of writers that may be termed the metaphysical poets, of whom in a criticism on the works of Cowley it is not improper to give some account.

The metaphysical poets were men of learning, and to shew their learning was their whole endeavour; but, unluckily resolving to shew it in rhyme, instead of writing poetry they only wrote verses, and very often such verses as stood the trial of the finger better than of the ear; for the modulation was so imperfect that they were only found to be verses by counting the syllables.

If the father of criticism has rightly denominated poetry τέχνη μιμητική, *an imitative art,* these writers will without great wrong lose their right to the name of poets, for they cannot be said to have imitated any thing: they neither copied nature nor life; neither painted the forms of matter nor represented the operations of intellect.

Those however who deny them to be poets allow them to be wits. Dryden confesses of himself and his contemporaries that they fall below Donne in wit, but maintains that they surpass him in poetry.

If Wit be well described by Pope as being 'that which has been often thought, but was never before so well expressed, they certainly never attained nor ever sought it, for they endeavoured to be singular in their thoughts, and were careless of their diction. But Pope's account of wit is undoubtedly erroneous; he depresses it below its natural dignity, and reduces it from strength of thought to happiness of language.

If by a more noble and more adequate conception that be considered as Wit which is at once natural and new, that which though not obvious is, upon its first production, acknowledged to be just; if it be that, which he that never found it, wonders how he missed; to wit of this kind the metaphysical poets have seldom risen. Their thoughts are often new, but seldom natural; they are not obvious, but neither are they just; and the reader, far from wondering that he missed them, wonders more frequently by what perverseness of industry they were ever found.

But Wit, abstracted from its effects upon the hearer, may be more rigorously and philosophically considered as a kind of *discordia concors**; a combination of dissimilar images, or discovery of occult resemblances in things apparently unlike. Of wit, thus defined, they have more than enough. The most heterogeneous ideas are yoked by violence together; nature and art are ransacked for illustrations, comparisons, and allusions; their learning instructs, and their subtilty surprises; but the reader commonly thinks his improvement dearly bought, and, though he sometimes admires, is seldom pleased.

From this account of their compositions it will be readily inferred that they were not successful in representing or moving the affections. As they were wholly employed on something unexpected and surprising they had no regard to that uniformity of sentiment, which enables us to conceive and to excite the pains and the pleasure of other

---

* Concordant discord.

minds: they never enquired what on any occasion they should have said or done, but wrote rather as beholders than partakers of human nature; as beings looking upon good and evil, impassive and at leisure; as Epicurean deities making remarks on the actions of men and the vicissitudes of life, without interest and without emotion. Their courtship was void of fondness and their lamentation of sorrow. Their wish was only to say what they hoped had been never said before.

Nor was the sublime more within their reach than the pathetick; for they never attempted that comprehension and expanse of thought which at once fills the whole mind, and of which the first effect is sudden astonishment, and the second rational admiration. Sublimity is produced by aggregation, and littleness by dispersion. Great thoughts are always general, and consist in positions not limited by exceptions, and in descriptions not descending to minuteness. It is with great propriety that subtlety, which in its original import means exility of particles, is taken in its metaphorical meaning for nicety of distinction. Those writers who lay on the watch for novelty could have little hope of greatness; for great things cannot have escaped former observation. Their attempts were always analytick: they broke every image into fragments, and could no more represent by their slender conceits and laboured particularities the prospects of nature or the scenes of life, than he who dissects a sunbeam with a prism can exhibit the wide effulgence of a summer noon.

What they wanted however of the sublime they endeavoured to supply by hyperbole; their amplifications had no limits: they left not only reason but fancy behind them, and produced combinations of confused magnificence that not only could not be credited, but could not be imagined.

Yet great labour directed by great abilities is never wholly lost: if they frequently threw away their wit upon false conceits, they likewise sometimes struck out unexpected truth: if their conceits were far-fetched, they were often worth the carriage. To write on their plan it was at least necessary to read and think. No man could be born a metaphysical poet, nor assume the dignity of a writer by descriptions copied from descriptions, by imitations borrowed from imitations, by traditional imagery and hereditary similes, by readiness of rhyme and volubility of syllables.

In perusing the works of this race of authors the mind is exercised either by recollection or inquiry; either something already learned is to be retrieved, or something new is to be examined. If their greatness seldom elevates their acuteness often surprises; if the imagination is not always gratified, at least the powers of reflection and comparison are employed; and in the mass of materials, which ingenious absurdity has thrown together, genuine wit and useful knowledge may be sometimes found, buried perhaps in grossness of expression, but useful to those who know their value, and such as, when they are expanded to perspicuity and polished to elegance, may give lustre to works which have more propriety though less copiousness of sentiment.

This kind of writing, which was, I believe, borrowed from Marino and his followers, had been recommended by the example of Donne, a man of very extensive and various knowledge, and by Jonson, whose manner resembled that of Donne more in the ruggedness of his lines than in the cast of his sentiments.

When their reputation was high they had undoubtedly more imitators than time has left behind. Their immediate successors, of whom any remembrance can be said to remain, were Suckling, Waller, Denham, Cowley, Cleiveland, and Milton. Denham and Waller sought another way to fame, by improving the harmony of our numbers. Milton tried the metaphysick style only in his lines upon Hobson the Carrier. Cowley adopted it, and excelled his predecessors, having as much sentiment and more musick. Suckling neither improved versification nor abounded in conceits. The fashionable style remained chiefly with Cowley: Suckling could not reach it, and Milton disdained it.

From the Life of Milton

In the examination of Milton's poetical works I shall pay so much regard to time as to begin with his juvenile productions. For his earlier pieces he seems to have had a degree of fondness not very laudable: what he has once written he resolves to preserve, and gives to the publick an unfinished poem, which he broke off because he was 'nothing satisfied with what he had done,' supposing his readers less nice than himself. These preludes to his future labours are in Italian, Latin, and English. Of the Italian I cannot pretend to speak as a critick, but I have heard them commended by a man well qualified to decide their merit. The Latin pieces are lusciously elegant; but the delight which they afford is rather by the exquisite imitation of the ancient writers, by the purity of the diction, and the harmony of the numbers, than by any power of invention or vigour of sentiment. They are not all of equal value; the elegies excell the odes, and some of the exercises on Gunpowder Treason might have been spared.

The English poems, though they make no promises of *Paradise Lost,* have this evidence of genius, that they have a cast original and unborrowed. But their peculiarity is not excellence: if they differ from verses of others, they differ for the worse; for they are too often distinguished by repulsive harshness; the combinations of words are new, but they are not pleasing; the rhymes and epithets seem to be laboriously sought and violently applied.

That in the early parts of his life he wrote with much care appears from his manuscripts, happily preserved at Cambridge, in which many of his smaller works are found as they were first written, with the subsequent corrections. Such reliques shew how excellence is acquired: what we hope ever to do with ease we may learn first to do with diligence.

Those who admire the beauties of this great poet sometimes force their own judgement into false approbation of his little pieces, and prevail upon themselves to think that admirable which is only singular. All that short compositions can commonly attain is neatness and elegance. Milton never learned the art of doing little things with grace; he overlooked the milder excellence of suavity and softness: he was a 'Lion' that had no skill 'in dandling the Kid.'

One of the poems on which much praise has been bestowed is *Lycidas;* of which the diction is harsh, the rhymes uncertain, and the numbers unpleasing. What beauty there is we must therefore seek in the sentiments and images. It is not to be considered as the effusion of real passion; for passion runs not after remote allusions and obscure opinions. Passion plucks no berries from the myrtle and ivy, nor calls upon Arethuse and Mincius, nor tells of 'rough satyrs and fauns with cloven heel.' 'Where there is leisure for fiction there is little grief.'

In this poem there is no nature, for there is no truth; there is no art, for there is nothing new. Its form is that of a pastoral, easy, vulgar, and therefore disgusting: whatever images it can supply are long ago exhausted; and its inherent improbability always forces

343

dissatisfaction on the mind. When Cowley tells of Hervey that they studied together, it is easy to suppose how much he must miss the companion of his labours and the partner of his discoveries; but what image of tenderness can be excited by these lines!

We drove a field, and both together heard
What time the grey fly winds her sultry horn,
Battening our flocks with the fresh dews of night.

We know that they never drove a field, and that they had no flocks to batten; and though it be allowed that the representation may be allegorical, the true meaning is so uncertain and remote that it is never sought because it cannot be known when it is found.

Among the flocks and copses and flowers appear the heathen deities, Jove and Phœbus, Neptune and Æolus, with a long train of mythological imagery, such as a College easily supplies. Nothing can less display knowledge or less exercise invention than to tell how a shepherd has lost his companion and must now feed his flocks alone, without any judge of his skill in piping; and how one god asks another god what is become of Lycidas, and how neither god can tell. He who thus grieves will excite no sympathy; he who thus praises will confer no honour.

This poem has yet a grosser fault. With these trifling fictions are mingled the most awful and sacred truths, such as ought never to be polluted with such irreverent combinations. The shepherd likewise is now a feeder of sheep, and afterwards an ecclesiastical pastor, a superintendent of a Christian flock. Such equivocations are always unskillful; but here they are indecent, and at least approach to impiety, of which, however, I believe the writer not to have been conscious.

Such is the power of reputation justly acquired that its blaze drives away the eye from nice examination. Surely no man could have fancied that he read *Lycidas* with pleasure had he not known its author.

Of the two pieces, *L'Allegro* and *Il Penseroso*, I believe opinion is uniform; every man that reads them, reads them with pleasure. The author's design is not, what Theobald has remarked, merely to shew how objects derived their colours from the mind, by representing the operation of the same things upon the gay and the melancholy temper, or upon the same man as he is differently disposed; but rather how, among the successive variety of appearances, every disposition of mind takes hold on those by which it may be gratified.

The *chearful* man hears the lark in the morning; the *pensive* man hears the nightingale in the evening. The *chearful* man sees the cock strut, and hears the horn and hounds echo in the wood; then walks 'not unseen' to observe the glory of the rising sun or listens to the singing milk-maid, and view the labours of the plowman and the mower; then casts his eyes about him over scenes of smiling plenty, and looks up to the distant tower, the residence of some fair inhabitant: thus he pursues rural gaiety through a day of labour or of play, and delights himself at night with the fanciful narratives of superstitious ignorance.

The *pensive* man at one time walks 'unseen' to muse at midnight, and at another hears the sullen curfew. If the weather drives him home he sits in a room lighted only by 'glowing embers'; or by a lonely lamp outwatches the North Star to discover the habitation of separate souls, and varies the shades of meditation by contemplating the magnificent or pathetick scenes of tragick and epick poetry. When the morning comes, a morning gloomy with rain and wind, he walks into the dark trackless woods, falls asleep by some murmuring water, and with melancholy enthusiasm expects some dream of prognostication or some musick played by aerial performers.

Both Mirth and Melancholy are solitary, silent inhabitants of the breast that neither receive nor transmit communication; no mention is therefore made of a philosophical friend or a pleasant companion. The seriousness does not arise from any participation of calamity, nor the gaiety from the pleasures of the bottle.

The man of *chearfulness* having exhausted the country tries what 'towered cities' will afford, and mingles with scenes of splendor, gay assemblies, and nuptial festivities; but he mingles a mere spectator as, when the learned comedies of Jonson or the wild dramas of Shakespeare are exhibited, he attends the theatre.

The *pensive* man never loses himself in crowds, but walks the cloister or frequents the cathedral. Milton probably had not yet forsaken the Church.

Both his characters delight in musick; but he seems to think that chearful notes would have obtained from Pluto a compleat dismission of Eurydice, of whom solemn sounds only procured a conditional release.

For the old age of Chearfulness he makes no provision; but Melancholy he conducts with great dignity to the close of life. His Chearfulness is without levity, and his Pensiveness without asperity.

Through these two poems the images are properly selected and nicely distinguished, but the colours of the diction seem not sufficiently discriminated. I know not whether the characters are kept sufficiently apart. No mirth can, indeed, be found in his melancholy; but I am afraid that I always meet some melancholy in his mirth. They are two noble efforts of imagination.

The greatest of his juvenile performances is the *Mask of Comus,* in which may very plainly be discovered the dawn or twilight of *Paradise Lost.* Milton appears to have formed very early that system of diction and mode of verse which his maturer judgement approved, and from which he never endeavoured nor desired to deviate.

Nor does *Comus* afford only a specimen of his language: it exhibits likewise his power of description and his vigour of sentiment, employed in the praise and defence of virtue. A work more truly poetical is rarely found; allusions, images, and descriptive epithets embellish almost every period with lavish decoration. As a series of lines, therefore, it may be considered as worthy of all the admiration with which the votaries have received it.

As a drama it is deficient. The action is not probable. A Masque, in those parts where supernatural intervention is admitted, must indeed be given up to all the freaks of imagination; but so far as the action is merely human it ought to be reasonable, which can hardly be said of the conduct of the two brothers, who, when their sister sinks with fatigue in a pathless wilderness, wander both away in search of berries too far to find their way back, and leave a helpless Lady to all the sadness and danger of solitude. This however is a defect over-balanced by its convenience.

What deserves more reprehension is that the prologue spoken in the wild wood by the attendant Spirit is addressed to the audience; a mode of communication so contrary to the nature of dramatick representation that no precedents can support it.

The discourse of the Spirit is too long, an objection that may be made to almost all the following speeches; they have not the spriteliness of a dialogue animated by reciprocal contention, but seem rather declamations deliberately composed and formally repeated on a moral question. The auditor therefore listens as to a lecture, without passion, without anxiety.

The song of Comus has airiness and jolity; but, what may recommend Milton's morals as well as his poetry, the invitations to pleasure are so general that they excite no distinct images of corrupt enjoyment, and take no dangerous hold on the fancy.

The following soliloquies of Comus and the Lady are elegant, but tedious. The song must owe much to the voice, if it ever can delight. At last the Brothers enter, with too much tranquillity; and when they have feared lest their sister should be in danger, and hoped that she is not in danger, the Elder makes a speech in praise of chastity, and the Younger finds how fine it is to be a philosopher.

Then descends the Spirit in form of a shepherd; and the Brother, instead of being in haste to ask his help, praises his singing, and enquires his business in that place. It is remarkable that at this interview the Brother is taken with a short fit of rhyming. The Spirit relates that the Lady is in the power of Comus, the Brother moralises again, and the Spirit makes a long narration, of no use because it is false, and therefore unsuitable to a good Being.

In all these parts the language is poetical and the sentiments are generous, but there is something wanting to allure attention.

The dispute between the Lady and Comus is the most animated and affecting scene of the drama, and wants nothing but a brisker reciprocation of objections and replies, to invite attention and detain it.

The songs are vigorous and full of imagery; but they are harsh in their diction, and not very musical in their numbers.

Throughout the whole the figures are too bold and the language too luxuriant for dialogue: it is a drama in the epick style, inelegantly splendid, and tediously instructive.

The *Sonnets* were written in different parts of Milton's life upon different occasions. They deserve not any particular criticism; for of the best it can only be said that they are not bad, and perhaps only the eighth and the twenty-first are truly entitled to this slender commendation. The fabrick of a sonnet, however adapted to the Italian language, has never succeeded in ours, which, having greater variety of termination, requires the rhymes to be often changed.

Those little pieces may be dispatched without much anxiety; a greater work calls for greater care. I am now to examine *Paradise Lost*, a poem which, considered with respect to design, may claim the first place, and with respect to performance the second, among the productions of the human mind.

By the general consent of criticks the first praise of genius is due to the writer of an epick poem, as it requires an assemblage of all the powers which are singly sufficient for other compositions. Poetry is the art of uniting pleasure with truth, by calling imagination to the help of reason. Epick poetry undertakes to teach the most important truths by the most pleasing precepts, and therefore relates some great event in the most affecting manner. History must supply the writer with the rudiments of narration, which he must improve and exalt by a nobler art, must animate by dramatick energy, and diversify by retrospection and anticipation; morality must teach him the exact bounds and different shades of vice and virtue; from the policy and the practice of life he has to learn the discriminations of character and the tendency of the passions, either single or combined; and physiology must supply him with illustrations and images. To put these materials to poetical use is required an imagination capable of painting nature and realizing fiction. Nor is he yet a poet till he has attained the whole extension of his language, distinguished all the delicacies of phrase, and all the colours of words, and learned to adjust their different sounds to all the varieties of metrical modulation.

Bossu is of opinion that the poet's first work is to find a *moral*, which his fable is afterwards to illustrate and establish. This seems to have been the process only of Milton: the moral of other poems is incidental and consequent; in Milton's only it is essential and intrinsick. His purpose was the most useful and the most arduous: 'to vindicate the ways of God to man'; to shew the reasonableness of religion, and the necessity of obedience to the Divine Law.

To convey this moral there must be a *fable*, a narration artfully constructed so as to excite curiosity and surprise expectation. In this part of his work Milton must be confessed to have equalled every other poet. He has involved in his account of the Fall of Man the events which preceded, and those that were to follow it: he has interwoven the whole system of theology with such propriety that every part appears to be necessary, and scarcely any recital is wished shorter for the sake of quickening the progress of the main action.

The subject of an epick poem is naturally an event of great importance. That of Milton is not the destruction of a city, the conduct of a colony, or the foundation of an empire. His subject is the fate of worlds, the revolutions of heaven and of earth; rebellion against the Supreme King raised by the highest order of created beings; the overthrow of their host and the punishment of their crime; the creation of a new race of reasonable creatures; their original happiness and innocence, their forfeiture of immortality, and the restoration to hope and peace.

Great events can be hastened or retarded only by persons of elevated dignity. Before the greatness displayed in Milton's poem all other greatness shrinks away. The weakest of his agents are the highest and noblest of human beings, the original parents of mankind; with whose actions the elements consented; on whose rectitude or deviation of will depended the state of terrestrial nature and the condition of all the future inhabitants of the globe.

Of the other agents in the poem the chief are such as it is irreverence to name on slight occasions. The rest were lower powers;

> *of which the least could wield*
> *Those elements, and arm him with the force*
> *Of all their regions;*

powers which only the controul of Omnipotence restrains from laying creation waste, and filling the vast expanse of space with ruin and confusion. To display the motives and actions of beings thus superiour, so far as human reason can examine them or human imagination represent them, is the task which this mighty poet has undertaken and performed.

In the examination of epick poems much speculation is commonly employed upon the *characters*. The characters in the *Paradise Lost* which admit of examination are those of angels and of man; of angels good and evil, of man in his innocent and sinful state.

Among the angels the virtue of Raphael is mild and placid, of easy condescension and free communication; that of Michael is regal and lofty, and, as may seem, attentive to the dignity of his own nature. Abdiel and Gabriel appear occasionally, and act as every incident

requires; the solitary fidelity of Abdiel is very amiably painted.

Of the evil angels the characters are more diversified. To Satan, as Addison observes, such sentiments are given as suit 'the most exalted and most depraved being.' Milton has been censured by Clarke for the impiety which sometimes breaks from Satan's mouth. For there are thoughts, as he justly remarks, which no observation of character can justify, because no good man would willingly permit them to pass, however transiently, through his own mind. To make Satan speak as a rebel, without any such expressions as might taint the reader's imagination, was indeed one of the great difficulties in Milton's undertaking, and I cannot but think that he has extricated himself with great happiness. There is in Satan's speeches little that can give pain to a pious ear. The language of rebellion cannot be the same with that of obedience. The malignity of Satan foams in haughtiness and obstinacy; but his expressions are commonly general, and no otherwise offensive than as they are wicked.

The other chiefs of the celestial rebellion are very judiciously discriminated in the first and second books; and the ferocious character of Moloch appears, both in the battle and the council, with exact consistency.

To Adam and to Eve are given during their innocence such sentiments as innocence can generate and utter. Their love is pure benevolence and mutual veneration; their repasts are without luxury and their diligence without toil. Their addresses to their Maker have little more than the voice of admiration and gratitude. Fruition left them nothing to ask, and Innocence left them nothing to fear.

But with guilt enter distrust and discord, mutual accusation, and stubborn self-defence; they regard each other with alienated minds, and dread their Creator as the avenger of their transgression. At last they seek shelter in his mercy, soften to repentance, and melt in supplication. Both before and after the Fall the superiority of Adam is diligently sustained.

Of the *probable* and the *marvellous*, two parts of a vulgar epick poem which immerge the critick in deep consideration, the *Paradise Lost* requires little to be said. It contains the history of a miracle, of Creation and Redemption; it displays the power and the mercy of the Supreme Being: the probable therefore is marvellous, and the marvellous is probable. The substance of the narrative is truth; and as truth allows no choice, it is, like necessity, superior to rule. To the accidental or adventitious parts, as to every thing human, some slight exceptions may be made. But the main fabrick is immovably supported.

It is justly remarked by Addison that this poem has, by the nature of its subject, the advantage above all others, that it is universally and perpetually interesting. All mankind will, through all ages, bear the same relation to Adam and to Eve, and must partake of that good and evil which extend to themselves.

Of the *machinery*, so called from θεὸς ἀπὸ μηχανῆς, by which is meant the occasional interposition of supernatural power, another fertile topic of critical remarks, here is no room to speak, because every thing is done under the immediate and visible direction of Heaven; but the rule is so far observed that no part of the action could have been accomplished by any other means.

Of *episodes* I think there are only two, contained in Raphael's relation of the war in heaven and Michael's prophetick account of the changes to happen in this world. Both are closely connected with the great action; one was necessary to Adam as a warning, the other as a consolation.

To the compleatness or *integrity* of the design nothing can be objected; it has distinctly and clearly what Aristotle requires, a beginning, a middle, and an end. There is perhaps no poem of the same length from which so little can be taken without apparent mutilation. Here are no funeral games, nor is there any long description of a shield. The short digressions at the beginning of the third, seventh, and ninth books might doubtless be spared; but superfluities so beautiful who would take away? or who does not wish that the author of the *Iliad* had gratified succeeding ages with a little knowledge of himself? Perhaps no passages are more frequently or more attentively read than those extrinsick paragraphs; and, since the end of poetry is pleasure, that cannot be unpoetical with which all are pleased.

The questions, whether the action of the poem be strictly *one*, whether the poem can be properly termed *heroick*, and who is the hero, are raised by such readers as draw their principles of judgement rather from books than from reason. Milton, though he intituled *Paradise Lost* only a 'poem,' yet calls it himself 'heroick song.' Dryden, petulantly and indecently, denies the heroism of Adam because he was overcome; but there is no reason why the hero should not be unfortunate except established practice, since success and virtue do not go necessarily together. Cato is the hero of Lucan, but Lucan's authority will not be suffered by Quintilian to decide. However, if success be necessary, Adam's deceiver was at last crushed; Adam was restored to his Maker's favour, and therefore may securely resume his human rank.

After the scheme and fabrick of the poem must be considered its component parts, the sentiments, and the diction.

The *sentiments*, as expressive of manners or appropriated to characters, are for the greater part unexceptionally just.

Splendid passages containing lessons of morality or precepts of prudence occur seldom. Such is the original formation of this poem that as it admits no human manners till the Fall, it can give little assistance to human conduct. Its end is to raise the thoughts above sublunary cares or pleasures. Yet the praise of that fortitude, with which Abdiel maintained his singularity of virtue against the scorn of multitudes, may be accommodated to all times; and Raphael's reproof of Adam's curiosity after the planetary motions, with the answer returned by Adam, may be confidently opposed to any rule of life which any poet has delivered.

The thoughts which are occasionally called forth in the progress are such as could only be produced by an imagination in the highest degree fervid and active, to which materials were supplied by incessant study and unlimited curiosity. The heat of Milton's mind might be said to sublimate his learning, to throw off into his work the spirit of science, unmingled with its grosser parts.

He had considered creation in its whole extent, and his descriptions are therefore learned. He had accustomed his imagination to unrestrained indulgence, and his conceptions therefore were extensive. The characteristick quality of his poem is sublimity. He sometimes descends to the elegant, but his element is the great. He can occasionally invest himself with grace; but his natural port is gigantick loftiness. He can please when pleasure is required; but it is his peculiar power to astonish.

He seems to have been well acquainted with his own genius, and to know what it was that Nature had bestowed upon him more bountifully than upon others; the power of displaying the vast, illuminating the splendid, enforcing the awful, darkening the gloomy, and aggravating the dreadful: he therefore chose a subject on which too much could not be said, on which he might tire his fancy without the censure of extravagance.

The appearances of nature and the occurrences of life did not satiate his appetite of greatness. To paint things as they are requires a minute attention, and employs the memory rather than the fancy. Milton's delight was to sport in the wide regions of possibility; reality was a scene too narrow for his mind. He sent his faculties out upon discovery, into worlds where only imagination can travel, and delighted to form new modes of existence, and furnish sentiment and action to superior beings, to trace the counsels of hell, or accompany the choirs of heaven.

But he could not be always in other worlds: he must sometimes revisit earth, and tell of things visible and known. When he cannot raise wonder by the sublimity of his mind he gives delight by its fertility.

Whatever be his subject he never fails to fill the imagination. But his images and descriptions of the scenes or operations of Nature do not seem to be always copied from the original form, nor to have the freshness, raciness, and energy of immediate observation. He saw Nature, as Dryden expresses it, 'through the spectacle of books'; and on most occasions calls learning to his assistance. The garden of Eden brings to his mind the vale of Enna, where Proserpine was gathering flowers. Satan makes his way through fighting elements, like Argo between the Cyanean rocks, or Ulysses between the two *Sicilian* whirlpools, when he shunned Charybdis 'on the larboard.' The mythological allusions have been justly censured, as not being always used with notice of their vanity; but they contribute variety to the narration, and produce an alternate exercise of the memory and the fancy.

His similes are less numerous and more various than those of his predecessors. But he does not confine himself within the limits of rigorous comparison: his great excellence is amplitude, and he expands the adventitious image beyond the dimensions which the occasion required. Thus, comparing the shield of Satan to the orb of the Moon, he crowds the imagination with the discovery of the telescope and all the wonders which the telescope discovers.

Of his moral sentiments it is hardly praise to affirm that they excel those of all other poets; for this superiority he was indebted to his acquaintance with the sacred writings. The ancient epick poets, wanting the light of Revelation, were very unskilful teachers of virtue: their principal characters may be great, but they are not amiable. The reader may rise from their works with a greater degree of active or passive fortitude, and sometimes of prudence; but he will be able to carry away few precepts of justice, and none of mercy.

From the Italian writers it appears that the advantages of even Christian knowledge may be possessed in vain. Ariosto's pravity is generally known; and, though the *Deliverance of*

Jerusalem may be considered as a sacred subject, the poet has been very sparing of moral instruction.

In Milton every line breathes sanctity of thought and purity of manners, except when the train of the narration requires the introduction of the rebellious spirits; and even they are compelled to acknowledge their subjection to God in such a manner as excites reverence and confirms piety.

Of human beings there are but two; but those two are the parents of mankind, venerable before their fall for dignity and innocence, and amiable after it for repentance and submission. In their first state their affection is tender without weakness, and their piety sublime without presumption. When they have sinned they shew how discord begins in mutual frailty, and how it ought to cease in mutual forbearance; how confidence of the divine favour is forfeited by sin, and how hope of pardon may be obtained by penitence and prayer. A state of innocence we can only conceive, if indeed in our present misery it be possible to conceive it; but the sentiments and worship proper to a fallen and offending being we have all to learn, as we have all to practise.

The poet whatever be done is always great. Our progenitors in their first state conversed with angels; even when folly and sin had degraded them they had not in their humiliation 'the port of mean suitors'; and they rise again to reverential regard when we find that their prayers were heard.

As human passions did not enter the world before the Fall, there is in the *Paradise Lost* little opportunity for the pathetick; but what little there is has not been lost. That passion which is peculiar to rational nature, the anguish arising from the consciousness of transgression and the horrours attending the sense of the Divine Displeasure, are very justly described and forcibly impressed. But the passions are moved only on one occasion; sublimity is the general and prevailing quality in this poem—sublimity variously modified, sometimes descriptive, sometimes argumentative.

The defects and faults of *Paradise Lost,* for faults and defects every work of man must have, it is the business of impartial criticism to discover. As in displaying the excellence of Milton I have not made long quotations, because of selecting beauties there had been no end, I shall in the same general manner mention that which seems to deserve censure; for what English man can take delight in transcribing passages, which, if they lessen the reputation of Milton, diminish in some degree the honour of our country?

The generality of my scheme does not admit the frequent notice of verbal inaccuracies which Bentley, perhaps better skilled in grammar than in poetry, has often found, though he sometimes made them, and which he imputed to the obtrusions of a reviser whom the author's blindness obliged him to employ. A supposition rash and groundless, if he thought it true; and vile and pernicious, if, as is said, he in private allowed it to be false.

The plan of *Paradise Lost* has this inconvenience, that it comprises neither human actions nor human manners. The man and woman who act and suffer are in a state which no other man or woman can ever know. The reader finds no transaction in which he can be engaged, beholds no condition in which he can by any effort of imagination place himself; he has, therefore, little natural curiosity or sympathy.

We all, indeed, feel the effects of Adam's disobedience; we all sin like Adam, and like him must all bewail our offences; we have restless and insidious enemies in the fallen angels, and in the blessed spirits we have guardians and friends; in the Redemption of mankind we hope to be included: in the description of heaven and hell we are surely interested, as we are all to reside hereafter either in the regions of horrour or of bliss.

But these truths are too important to be new: they have been taught to our infancy; they have mingled with our solitary thoughts and familiar conversation, and are habitually interwoven with the whole texture of life. Being therefore not new they raise no unaccustomed emotion in the mind: what we knew before we cannot learn; what is not unexpected, cannot surprise.

Of the ideas suggested by these awful scenes, from some we recede with reverence, except when stated hours require their association; and from others we shrink with horrour, or admit them only as salutary inflictions, as counterpoises to our interests and passions. Such images rather obstruct the career of fancy than incite it.

Pleasure and terrour are indeed the genuine sources of poetry; but poetical pleasure must be such as human imagination can at least conceive, and poetical terrour such as human strength and fortitude may combat. The good and evil of Eternity are too ponderous for the wings of wit; the mind sinks under them in passive helplessness, content with calm belief and humble adoration.

Known truths however may take a different appearance, and be conveyed to the mind by a new train of intermediate images. This Milton has undertaken, and performed with pregnancy and vigour of mind peculiar to himself. Whoever considers the few radical positions which the Scriptures afforded him will wonder by what energetick operations he expanded them to such extent and ramified them to so much variety, restrained as he was by religious reverence from licentiousness of fiction.

Here is a full display of the united force of study and genius; of a great accumulation of materials, with judgement to digest and fancy to combine them: Milton was able to select from nature or from story, from ancient fable or from modern science, whatever could illustrate or adorn his thoughts. An accumulation of knowledge impregnated his mind, fermented by study and exalted by imagination.

It has been therefore said without an indecent hyperbole by one of his encomiasts, that in reading *Paradise Lost* we read a book of universal knowledge.

But original deficience cannot be supplied. The want of human interest is always felt. *Paradise Lost* is one of the books which the reader admires and lays down, and forgets to take up again. None ever wished it longer than it is. Its perusal is a duty rather than a pleasure. We read Milton for instruction, retire harassed and overburdened, and look elsewhere for recreation; we desert our master, and seek for companions.

Another inconvenience of Milton's design is that it requires the description of what cannot be described, the agency of spirits. He saw that immateriality supplied no images, and that he could not show angels acting but by instruments of action; he therefore invested them with form and matter. This being necessary was therefore defensible; and he should have secured the consistency of his system by keeping immateriality out of sight, and enticing his reader to drop it from his thoughts. But he has unhappily perplexed his poetry with his philosophy. His infernal and celestial powers are sometimes pure spirit and sometimes animated body. When Satan walks with his lance upon the 'burning marle' he has a body; when in his passage between hell and the new world he is in danger of sinking in the vacuity and is supported by a gust of rising vapours he has a body; when he animates the toad he seems to be mere spirit that can penetrate matter at pleasure; when he 'starts up in his own shape,' he has at least a determined form; and when he is brought before Gabriel he has 'a spear and a shield,' which he had the power of hiding in the toad, though the arms of the contending angels are evidently material.

The vulgar inhabitants of Pandæmonium, being 'incorporeal spirits,' are 'at large though without number' in a limited space, yet in the battle when they were overwhelmed by mountains their armour hurt them, 'crushed in upon their substance, now grown gross by sinning.' This likewise happened to the uncorrupted angels, who were overthrown 'the sooner for their arms, for unarmed they might easily as spirits have evaded by contraction or remove.' Even as spirits they are hardly spiritual, for 'contraction' and 'remove' are images of matter; but if they could have escaped without their armour, they might have escaped from it and left only the empty cover to be battered. Uriel, when he rides on a sun-beam, is material; Satan is material when he is afraid of the prowess of Adam.

The confusion of spirit and matter which pervades the whole narration of the war of heaven fills it with incongruity; and the book in which it is related is, I believe, the favourite of children, and gradually neglected as knowledge is increased.

After the operation of immaterial agents which cannot be explained may be considered that of allegorical persons, which have no real existence. To exalt causes into agents, to invest abstract ideas with form, and animate them with activity has always been the right of poetry. But such airy beings are for the most part suffered only to do their natural office, and retire. Thus Fame tells a tale and Victory hovers over a general or perches on a standard; but Fame and Victory can do no more. To give them any real employment or ascribe to them any material agency is to make them allegorical no longer, but to shock the mind by ascribing effects to nonentity. In the *Prometheus* of Æschylus we see Violence and Strength, and in the *Alcestis* of Euripides we see Death, brought upon the stage, all as active persons of the drama; but no precedents can justify absurdity.

Milton's allegory of Sin and Death is undoubtedly faulty. Sin is indeed the mother of Death, and may be allowed to be the portress of hell; but when they stop the journey of Satan, a journey described as real, and when Death offers him battle, the allegory is broken. That Sin and Death should have shewn the way to hell might have been allowed; but they cannot facilitate the passage by building a bridge, because the difficulty of Satan's passage is described as real and sensible, and the bridge ought to be only figurative. The hell assigned to the rebellious spirits is described as not less local than the residence of man. It is placed in some distant part of space, separated from the regions of harmony and order by a chaotick waste and an unoccupied vacuity; but Sin and Death worked up a 'mole of aggregated soil,' cemented with asphaltus, a work too bulky for ideal architects.

This unskilful allegory appears to me one of the greatest faults of the poem; and to this there was no temptation, but the author's opinion of its beauty.

To the conduct of the narrative some objections may be made. Satan is with great expectation brought before Gabriel in Paradise, and is suffered to go away unmolested. The creation of man is represented as the consequence of the vacuity left in heaven by the expulsion of the rebels; yet Satan mentions it as a report 'rife in heaven' before his departure.

To find sentiments for the state of innocence was very difficult; and something of anticipation perhaps is now and then discovered. Adam's discourse of dreams seems not to be the speculation of a new-created being. I know not whether his answer to the angel's reproof for curiosity does not want something of propriety: it is the speech of a man acquainted with many other men. Some philosophical notions, especially when the philosophy is false, might have been omitted. The angel in a comparison speaks of 'timorous deer,' before deer were yet timorous, and before Adam could understand the comparison.

Dryden remarks that Milton has some flats among his elevations. This is only to say that all the parts are not equal. In every work one part must be for the sake of others; a palace must have passages, a poem must have transitions. It is no more to be required that wit should always be blazing than that the sun should always stand at noon. In a great work there is a vicissitude of luminous and opaque parts, as there is in the world a succession of day and night. Milton, when he has expatiated in the sky, may be allowed sometimes to revisit earth; for what other author ever soared so high or sustained his flight so long?

Milton, being well versed in the Italian poets, appears to have borrowed often from them; and, as every man catches something from his companions, his desire of imitating Ariosto's levity has disgraced his work with the 'Paradise of Fools'; a fiction not in itself ill-imagined, but too ludicrous for its place.

His play on words, in which he delights too often; his equivocations, which Bentley endeavours to defend by the example of the ancients; his unnecessary and ungraceful use of terms of art; it is not necessary to mention, because they are easily remarked and generally censured, and at last bear so little proportion to the whole that they scarcely deserve the attention of a critick.

Such are the faults of that wonderful performance *Paradise Lost;* which he who can put in balance with its beauties must be considered not as nice but as dull, as less to be censured for want of candour than pitied for want of sensibility.

Of *Paradise Regained* the general judgement seems now to be right, that it is in many parts elegant, and every-where instructive. It was not to be supposed that the writer of *Paradise Lost* could ever write without great effusions of fancy and exalted precepts of wisdom. The basis of *Paradise Regained* is narrow; a dialogue without action can never please like an union of the narrative and dramatick powers. Had this poem been written, not by Milton but by some imitator, it would have claimed and received universal praise.

If *Paradise Regained* has been too much depreciated, *Sampson Agonistes* has in requital been too much admired. It could only be by long prejudice and the bigotry of learning that Milton could prefer the ancient tragedies with their encumbrance of a chorus to the exhibitions of the French and English stages; and it is only by a blind confidence in the reputation of Milton that a drama can be praised in which the intermediate parts have neither cause nor consequence, neither hasten nor retard the catastrophe.

In this tragedy are however many particular beauties, many just sentiments and striking lines; but it wants that power of attracting attention which a well-connected plan produces.

Milton would not have excelled in dramatick writing; he knew human nature only in the gross, and had never studied the shades of character, nor the combinations of concurring or the perplexity of contending passions. He had read much and knew what books could teach; but had mingled little in the world, and was deficient in the knowledge which experience must confer.

Through all his greater works there prevails an uniform peculiarity of *Diction,* a mode and cast of expression which bears little resemblance to that of any former writer, and which is so far removed from common use that an unlearned reader when he first opens his book finds himself surprised by a new language.

This novelty has been, by those who can find nothing wrong in Milton, imputed to his laborious endeavours after words suitable to the grandeur of his ideas. 'Our language,' says Addison, 'sunk under him.' But the truth is, that both in prose and verse, he had formed his style by a perverse and pedantick principle. He was desirous to use English words with a foreign idiom. This in all his prose is discovered and condemned, for there judgement operates freely, neither softened by the beauty nor awed by the dignity of his thoughts; but such is the power of his poetry that his call is obeyed without resistance, the reader feels himself in captivity to a higher and a nobler mind, and criticism sinks in admiration.

Milton's style was not modified by his subject: what is shown with greater extent in *Paradise Lost* may be found in *Comus.* One source of his peculiarity was his familiarity with the Tuscan poets: the disposition of his words is, I think, frequently Italian; perhaps sometimes combined with other tongues. Of him, at last, may be said what Jonson says of Spenser, that 'he wrote no language,' but has formed what Butler calls 'a Babylonish Dialect,' in itself harsh and barbarous, but made by exalted genius and extensive learning the vehicle of so much instruction and so much pleasure that, like other lovers, we find grace in its deformity.

Whatever be the faults of his diction he cannot want the praise of copiousness and variety; he was master of his language in its full extent, and has selected the melodious words with such diligence that from his book alone the Art of English Poetry might be learned.

After his diction something must be said of his versification. 'The measure,' he says, 'is the English heroick verse without rhyme.' Of this mode he had many examples among the Italians, and some in his own country. The Earl of Surrey is said to have translated one of Virgil's books without rhyme, and besides our tragedies a few short poems had appeared in blank verse; particularly one tending to reconcile the nation to Raleigh's wild attempt upon Guiana, and probably written by Raleigh himself. These petty performances cannot be supposed to have much influenced Milton, who more probably took his hint from Trisino's *Italia Liberata;* and, finding blank verse easier than rhyme, was desirous of persuading himself that it is better.

'Rhyme,' he says, and says truly, 'is no necessary adjunct of true poetry.' But perhaps of poetry as a mental operation metre or musick is no necessary adjunct; it is however by the musick of metre that poetry has been discriminated in all languages, and in languages melodiously constructed with a due proportion of long and short syllables metre is sufficient. But one language cannot communicate its rules to another; where metre is scanty and imperfect some help is necessary. The musick of the English heroick line strikes the ear so faintly that it is easily lost, unless all the syllables of every line co-operate together; this co-operation can be only obtained by the preservation of every verse unmingled with another as a distinct system of sounds, and this distinctness is obtained and preserved by the artifice of rhyme. The variety of pauses, so much boasted by the lovers of blank verse, changes the measures of an English poet to the periods of a declaimer; and there are only a few skilful and happy readers of Milton who enable their audience to perceive where the lines end or begin. 'Blank verse,' said an ingenious

critick, 'seems to be verse only to the eye.'

Poetry may subsist without rhyme, but English poetry will not often please; nor can rhyme ever be safely spared but where the subject is able to support itself. Blank verse makes some approach to that which is called the 'lapidary style'; has neither the easiness of prose nor the melody of numbers, and therefore tires by long continuance. Of the Italian writers without rhyme, whom Milton alleges as precedents, not one is popular; what reason could urge in its defence has been confuted by the ear.

But whatever be the advantage of rhyme I cannot prevail on myself to wish that Milton had been a rhymer, for I cannot wish his work to be other than it is; yet like other heroes he is to be admired rather than imitated. He that thinks himself capable of astonishing may write blank verse, but those that hope only to please must condescend to rhyme.

The highest praise of genius is original invention. Milton cannot be said to have contrived the structure of an epick poem, and therefore owes reverence to that vigour and amplitude of mind to which all generations must be indebted for the art of poetical narration, for the texture of the fable, the variation of incidents, the interposition of dialogue, and all the stratagems that surprise and enchain attention. But of all the borrowers from Homer, Milton is perhaps the least indebted. He was naturally a thinker for himself, confident of his own abilities and disdainful of help or hindrance; he did not refuse admission to the thoughts or images of his predecessors, but he did not seek them. From his contemporaries he neither courted nor received support; there is in his writings nothing by which the pride of other authors might be gratified or favour gained, no exchange of praise nor solicitation of support. His great works were performed under discountenance and in blindness, but difficulties vanished at his touch; he was born for whatever is arduous; and his work is not the greatest of heroick poems, only because it is not the first.

From the Life of Dryden

Of the person of Dryden I know not any account; of his mind the portrait which has been left by Congreve, who knew him with great familiarity, is such as adds our love of his manners to our admiration of his genius.

> He was, we are told, of a nature exceedingly humane and compassionate, ready to forgive injuries, and capable of a sincere reconciliation with those that had offended him. His friendship, where he professed it, went beyond his professions. He was of a very easy, of very pleasing access; but somewhat slow, and, as it were, diffident in his advances to others: he had that in his nature which abhorred intrusion into any society whatever. He was therefore less known, and consequently his character became more liable to misapprehensions and misrepresentations: he was very modest, and very easily to be discountenanced in his approaches to his equals or superiors. As his reading had been very extensive, so was he very happy in a memory tenacious of *every thing that he had read. He was not more possessed of* knowledge than he was communicative of it; but then his communication was by no means pedantick or imposed upon the conversation, but just such, and went so far as, by the natural turn of the conversation in which he was engaged, it was necessarily promoted or required. He was extreme ready, and gentle in his correction of the errors of any writer who thought fit to consult him, and full as ready and patient to admit of the reprehensions of others in respect of his own oversights or mistakes.

To this account of Congreve nothing can be objected but the fondness of friendship; and to have excited that fondness in such a mind is no small degree of praise. The disposition of Dryden, however, is shewn in this character rather as it exhibited itself in cursory conversation, than as it operated on the more important parts of life. His placability and his friendship indeed were solid virtues; but courtesy and good-humour are often found with little real worth. Since Congreve, who knew him well, has told us no more, the rest must be collected as it can from other testimonies, and particularly from those notices which Dryden has very liberally given us of himself.

The modesty which made him so slow to advance, and so easy to be repulsed, was certainly no suspicion of deficient merit, or unconsciousness of his own value: he appears to have known in its whole extent the dignity of his character, and to have set a very high value on his own powers and performances. He probably did not offer his conversation, because he expected it to be solicited; and he retired from a cold reception, not submissive but indignant, with such reverence of his own greatness as made him unwilling to expose it to neglect or violation.

His modesty was by no means inconsistent with ostentatiousness: he is diligent enough to remind the world of his merit, and expresses with very little scruple his high opinion of his own powers; but his self-commendations are read without scorn or indignation: we allow his claims, and love his frankness.

Tradition, however, has not allowed that his confidence in himself exempted him from jealousy of others. He is accused of envy and insidiousness; and is particularly charged with inciting Creech to translate Horace, that he might lose the reputation which Lucretius had given him.

Of this charge we immediately discover that it is merely conjectural: the purpose was such as no man would confess; and a crime that admits no proof, why should we believe?

He has been described as magisterially presiding over the younger writers, and assuming the distribution of poetical fame; but

he who excels has a right to teach, and he whose judgement is incontestable may, without usurpation, examine and decide.

Congreve represents him as ready to advise and instruct; but there is reason to believe that his communication was rather useful than entertaining. He declares of himself that he was saturnine, and not one of those whose spritely sayings diverted company; and one of his censurers makes him say,

Nor wine nor love [*Nor love nor wine*] *could ever see*
   me gay;
To writing bred, I knew not what to say.

There are men whose powers operate only at leisure and in retirement, and whose intellectual vigour deserts them in conversation; whom merriment confuses, and objection disconcerts; whose bashfulness restrains their exertion, and suffers them not to speak till the time of speaking is past; or whose attention to their own character makes them unwilling to utter at hazard what has not been considered, and cannot be recalled.

Of Dryden's sluggishness in conversation it is vain to search or to guess the cause. He certainly wanted neither sentiments nor language; his intellectual treasures were great, though they were locked up from his own use. 'His thoughts,' when he wrote, 'flowed in upon him so fast, that his only care was which to chuse, and which to reject'. Such rapidity of composition naturally promises a flow of talk, yet we must be content to believe what an enemy says of him, when he likewise says it of himself. But whatever was his character as a companion, it appears that he lived in familiarity with the highest persons of his time. It is related by Carte of the duke of Ormond that he used often to pass a night with Dryden, and those with whom Dryden consorted: who they were Carte has not told; but certainly the convivial table at which Ormond sat was not surrounded with a plebeian society. He was indeed reproached with boasting of his familiarity with the great; and

Horace will support him in the opinion that to please superiors is not the lowest kind of merit.

*   *   *

Dryden may be properly considered as the father of English criticism, as the writer who first taught us to determine upon principles the merit of composition. Of our former poets the greatest dramatist wrote without rules, conducted through life and nature by a genius that rarely misled, and rarely deserted him. Of the rest, those who knew the laws of propriety had neglected to teach them.

Two *Arts of English Poetry* were written in the days of Elizabeth by Webb and Puttenham, from which something might be learned, and a few hints had been given by Jonson and Cowley; but Dryden's *Essay on Dramatick Poetry* was the first regular and valuable treatise on the art of writing.

He who, having formed his opinions in the present age of English literature, turns back to peruse this dialogue, will not perhaps find much increase of knowledge or much novelty of instruction; but he is to remember that critical principles were then in the hands of a few, who had gathered them partly from the Ancients, and partly from the Italians and French. The structure of dramatick poems was not then generally understood. Audiences applauded by instinct, and poets perhaps often pleased by chance.

A writer who obtains his full purpose loses himself in his own lustre. Of an opinion which is no longer doubted, the evidence ceases to be examined. Of an art universally practised, the first teacher is forgotten. Learning once made popular is no longer learning: it has the appearance of something which we have bestowed upon ourselves, as the dew appears to rise from the field which it refreshes.

To judge rightly of an author we must transport ourselves to his time, and examine what were the wants of his contemporaries, and what were his means of supplying them.

That which is easy at one time was difficult at another. Dryden at least imported his science, and gave his country what it wanted before; or rather, he imported only the materials, and manufactured them by his own skill.

The dialogue on the Drama was one of his first essays of criticism, written when he was yet a timorous candidate for reputation, and therefore laboured with that diligence which he might allow himself somewhat to remit when his name gave sanction to his positions, and his awe of the public was abated, partly by success. It will not be easy to find in all the opulence of our language a treatise so artfully variegated with successive representations of opposite probabilities, so enlivened with imagery, so brightened with illustrations. His portraits of the English dramatists are wrought with great spirit and diligence. The account of Shakespeare may stand as a perpetual model of encomiastick criticism; exact without minuteness, and lofty without exaggeration. The praise lavished by Longinus, on the attestation of the heroes of Marathon by Demosthenes, fades away before it. In a few lines is exhibited a character, so extensive in its comprehension and so curious in its limitations, that nothing can be added, diminished, or reformed; nor can the editors and admirers of Shakespeare, in all their emulation of reverence, boast of much more than of having diffused and paraphrased this epitome of excellence, of having changed Dryden's gold for baser metal, of lower value though of greater bulk.

In this, and in all his other essays on the same subject, the criticism of Dryden is the criticism of a poet; not a dull collection of theorems, nor a rude detection of faults, which perhaps the censor was not able to have committed; but a gay and vigorous dissertation, where delight is mingled with instruction, and where the author proves his right of judgement by his power of performance.

The different manner and effect with which critical knowledge may be conveyed was perhaps never more clearly exemplified than in the performances of Rymer and Dryden. It was said of a dispute between two mathematicians, 'malim cum Scaligero errare, quam cum Clavio recte sapere'; that 'it was more eligible to go wrong with one than right with the other.' A tendency of the same kind every mind must feel at the perusal of Dryden's prefaces and Rymer's discourses. With Dryden we are wandering in quest of Truth, whom we find, if we find her at all, drest in the graces of elegance; and if we miss her, the labour of the pursuit rewards itself: we are led only through fragrance and flowers. Rymer, without taking a nearer, takes a rougher way; every step is to be made through thorns and brambles, and Truth, if we meet her, appears repulsive by her mien and ungraceful by her habit. Dryden's criticism has the majesty of a queen; Rymer's has the ferocity of a tyrant.

As he had studied with great diligence the art of poetry, and enlarged or rectified his notions by experience perpetually increasing, he had his mind stored with principles and observations: he poured out his knowledge with little labour; for of labour, notwithstanding the multiplicity of his productions, there is sufficient reason to suspect that he was not a lover. To write *con amore*, with fondness for the employment, with perpetual touches and retouches, with unwillingness to take leave of his own idea, and an unwearied pursuit of unattainable perfection, was, I think, no part of his character.

His criticism may be considered as general or occasional. In his general precepts, which depend upon the nature of things and the structure of the human mind, he may doubtless be safely recommended to the confidence of the reader; but his occasional and particular positions were sometimes interested, sometimes negligent, and sometimes capricious. It is not without reason that Trapp, speaking of the praises which he bestows on *Palamon and Arcite,* says

Novimus [quidem Angli] judicium Drydeni [popularis nostri] de poemate quodam Chauceri, pulchro sane illo, et admodum [plurimum] laudando, nimirum quod non

modo vere epicum sit, sed *Iliada* etiam atque
Æncida æquet, imo superet. Sed novimus
eodem tempore viri illius maximi non semper
accuratissimas esse censuras, nec ad
severissimam critices normam exactas: Illo
judice id plerumque optimum est, quod nunc
[optimum est plerumque quod ille] prae
manibus habet, et in quo nunc occupatur.*

He is therefore by no means constant to
himself. His defence and desertion of dramatick rhyme is generally known. Spence, in
his remarks on Pope's *Odyssey,* produces what
he thinks an unconquerable quotation from
Dryden's preface to the *Eneid,* in favour of
translating an epick poem into blank verse;
but he forgets that when his author attempted the *Iliad,* some years afterwards, he departed from his own decision, and translated
into rhyme.

When he has any objection to obviate, or
any license to defend, he is not very scrupulous about what he asserts, nor very cautious,
if the present purpose be served, not to en-
tangle himself in his own sophistries. But
when all arts are exhausted, like other hunt-
ed animals, he sometimes stands at bay; when
he cannot disown the grossness of one of his
plays, he declares that he knows not any law
that prescribes morality to a comick poet.

His remarks on ancient or modern writers
are not always to be trusted. His parallel of
the versification of Ovid with that of Claudi-
an has been very justly censured by Sewel.
His comparison of the first line of Virgil with
the first of Statius is not happier. Virgil, he
says, is soft and gentle, and would have
thought Statius mad if he had heard him
thundering out

Quæ superimposito moles geminata colosso.

Statius perhaps heats himself, as he proceeds, to exaggerations somewhat hyperbolical; but undoubtedly Virgil would have been
too hasty if he had condemned him to straw
for one sounding line. Dryden wanted an instance, and the first that occurred was im-
prest into the service.

What he wishes to say, he says at hazard;

he cited *Gorbuduc,* which he had never
seen; gives a false account of Chapman's versification; and discovers in the preface to his
Fables that he translated the first book of
the *Iliad* without knowing what was in the
second.

It will be difficult to prove that Dryden
ever made any great advances in literature.
As having distinguished himself at Westmin-
ster under the tuition of Busby, who advanced his scholars to a height of knowledge
very rarely attained in grammar-schools, he
resided afterwards at Cambridge, it is not to
be supposed that his skill in the ancient languages was deficient compared with that of
common students; but his scholastick acquisitions seem not proportionate to his opportunities and abilities. He could not, like
Milton or Cowley, have made his name illustrious merely by his learning. He mentions
but few books, and those such as lie in the
beaten track of regular study; from which, if
ever he departs, he is in danger of losing
himself in unknown regions.

In his *Dialogue on the Drama* he pronounces
with great confidence that the Latin tragedy
of *Medea* is not Ovid's, because it is not sufficiently interesting and pathetick. He might
have determined the question upon surer
evidence, for it is quoted by Quintilian as the
work of Seneca; and the only line which remains of Ovid's play, for one line is left us, is
not there to be found. There was therefore
no need of the gravity of conjecture, or the
discussion of plot or sentiment, to find what
was already known upon higher authority
than such discussions can ever reach.

His literature, though not always free from
ostentation, will be commonly found either
obvious, and made his own by the art of

* We have known Dryden to claim that a certain
poem of Chaucer's which is certainly beautiful and
much to be praised, was truly an epic and not only
equal but superior to both the *Iliad* and the *Aeneid.*
At the same time we have known that the man's
judgments are not always accurate nor in accord
with the strictest critical standard; he judges that to
be best which he has in hand and with which he is
occupied at the moment.

dressing it; or superficial, which by what he gives shews what he wanted; or erroneous, hastily collected, and negligently scattered.

Yet it cannot be said that his genius is ever unprovided of matter, or that his fancy languishes in penury of ideas. His works abound with knowledge, and sparkle with illustrations. There is scarcely any science or faculty that does not supply him with occasional images and lucky similitudes; every page discovers a mind very widely acquainted both with art and nature, and in full possession of great stores of intellectual wealth. Of him that knows much it is natural to suppose that he has read with diligence; yet I rather believe that the knowledge of Dryden was gleaned from accidental intelligence and various conversation; by a quick apprehension, a judicious selection, and a happy memory, a keen appetite of knowledge, and a powerful digestion; by vigilance that permitted nothing to pass without notice, and a habit of reflection that suffered nothing useful to be lost. A mind like Dryden's, always curious, always active, to which every understanding was proud to be associated, and of which every one solicited the regard by an ambitious display of himself, had a more pleasant, perhaps a nearer, way to knowledge than by the silent progress of solitary reading. I do not suppose that he despised books or intentionally neglected them; but that he was carried out by the impetuosity of his genius to more vivid and speedy instructors, and that his studies were rather desultory and fortuitous than constant and systematical.

It must be confessed that he scarcely ever appears to want book-learning but when he mentions books; and to him may be transferred the praise which he gives his master Charles:

> His conversation, wit, and parts,
> His knowledge in the noblest useful arts,
> Were such, dead authors could not give,
> But habitudes of those that [who] live;
> Who, lighting him, did greater lights receive:
> He drain'd from all, and all they knew,
> His apprehension quick, his judgement true:

> That the most learn'd with shame confess
> His knowledge more, his reading only less.

Of all this however if the proof be demanded I will not undertake to give it; the atoms of probability, of which my opinion has been formed, lie scattered over all his works: and by him who thinks the question worth his notice his works must be perused with very close attention.

Criticism, either didactick or defensive, occupies almost all his prose, except those pages which he has devoted to his patrons; but none of his prefaces were ever thought tedious. They have not the formality of a settled style, in which the first half of the sentence betrays the other. The clauses are never balanced, nor the periods modelled; every word seems to drop by chance, though it falls into its proper place. Nothing is cold or languid; the whole is airy, animated, and vigorous: what is little is gay; what is great is splendid. He may be thought to mention himself too frequently; but while he forces himself upon our esteem, we cannot refuse him to stand high in his own. Every thing is excused by the play of images and the spriteliness of expression. Though all is easy, nothing is feeble; though all seems careless, there is nothing harsh; and though since his earlier works more than a century has passed they have nothing yet uncouth or obsolete.

He who writes much will not easily escape a manner, such a recurrence of particular modes as may be easily noted. Dryden is always 'another and the same'; he does not exhibit a second time the same elegances in the same form, nor appears to have any art other than that of expressing with clearness what he thinks with vigour. His style could not easily be imitated, either seriously or ludicrously; for, being always equable and always varied, it has no prominent or discriminative characters. The beauty who is totally free from disproportion of parts and features cannot be ridiculed by an overcharged resemblance.

From his prose however Dryden derives

only his accidental and secondary praise; the veneration with which his name is pronounced by every cultivator of English literature is paid to him as he refined the language, improved the sentiments, and tuned the numbers of English Poetry.

After about half a century of forced thoughts and rugged metre some advances towards nature and harmony had been already made by Waller and Denham; they had shewn that long discourses in rhyme grew more pleasing when they were broken into couplets, and that verse consisted not only in the number but the arrangement of syllables.

But though they did much, who can deny that they left much to do? Their works were not many, nor were their minds of very ample comprehension. More examples of more modes of composition were necessary for the establishment of regularity, and the introduction of propriety in word and thought.

Every language of a learned nation necessarily divides itself into diction scholastick and popular, grave and familiar, elegant and gross; and from a nice distinction of these different parts arises a great part of the beauty of style. But if we except a few minds, the favourites of nature, to whom their own original rectitude was in the place of rules, this delicacy of selection was little known to our authors: our speech lay before them in a heap of confusion, and every man took for every purpose what chance might offer him.

There was therefore before the time of Dryden no poetical diction: no system of words at once refined from the grossness of domestick use and free from the harshness of terms appropriated to particular arts. Words too familiar or too remote defeat the purpose of a poet. From those sounds which we hear on small or on coarse occasions, we do not easily receive strong impressions or delightful images; and words to which we are nearly strangers, whenever they occur, draw that attention on themselves which they should transmit to things.

Those happy combinations of words which distinguish poetry from prose had been rarely attempted; we had few elegances or flowers of speech: the roses had not yet been plucked from the bramble or different colours had not been joined to enliven one another.

It may be doubted whether Waller and Denham could have over-borne the prejudices which had long prevailed, and which even then were sheltered by the protection of Cowley. The new versification, as it was called, may be considered as owing its establishment to Dryden; from whose time it is apparent that English poetry has had no tendency to relapse to its former savageness.

The affluence and comprehension of our language is very illustriously displayed in our poetical translations of ancient writers: a work which the French seem to relinquish in despair, and which we were long unable to perform with dexterity. Ben Jonson thought it necessary to copy Horace almost word by word; Feltham, his contemporary and adversary, considers it as indispensably requisite in a translation to give line for line. It is said that Sandys, whom Dryden calls the best versifier of the last age, has struggled hard to comprise every book of his English *Metamorphoses* in the same number of verses with the original. Holyday had nothing in view but to shew that he understood his author, with so little regard to the grandeur of his diction, or the volubility of his numbers, that his metres can hardly be called verses; they cannot be read without reluctance, nor will the labour always be rewarded by understanding them. Cowley saw that such 'copyers' were a 'servile race'; he asserted his liberty, and spread his wings so boldly that he left his authors. It was reserved for Dryden to fix the limits of poetical liberty, and give us just rules and examples of translation.

When languages are formed upon different principles, it is impossible that the same modes of expression should always be elegant in both. While they run on together the closest translation may be considered as the best; but when they divaricate each must take its natural course. Where correspondence cannot be obtained it is necessary to be content with something equivalent. 'Translation therefore,' says Dryden, 'is not so loose as paraphrase, nor so close as metaphrase.'

All polished languages have different styles: the concise, the diffuse, the lofty, and the humble. In the proper choice of style consists the resemblance which Dryden principally exacts from the translator. He is to exhibit his author's thoughts in such a dress of diction as the author would have given them, had his language been English: rugged magnificence is not to be softened; hyperbolical ostentation is not to be repressed, nor sententious affectation to have its points blunted. A translator is to be like his author: it is not his business to excel him.

The reasonableness of these rules seems sufficient for their vindication; and the effects produced by observing them were so happy that I know not whether they were ever opposed but by Sir Edward Sherburne, a man whose learning was greater than his powers of poetry, and who, being better qualified to give the meaning than the spirit of Seneca, has introduced his version of three tragedies by a defence of close translation. The authority of Horace, which the new translators cited in defence of their practice, he has, by a judicious explanation, taken fairly from them; but reason wants not Horace to support it.

It seldom happens that all the necessary causes concur to any great effect: will is wanting to power, or power to will, or both are impeded by external obstructions. The exigences in which Dryden was condemned to pass his life are reasonably supposed to have blasted his genius, to have driven out his works in a state of immaturity, and to have intercepted the full-blown elegance which longer growth would have supplied.

Poverty, like other rigid powers, is sometimes too hastily accused. If the excellence of Dryden's works was lessened by his indigence, their number was increased; and I know not how it will be proved that if he had written less he would have written better; or that indeed he would have undergone the toil of an author, if he had not been solicited by something more pressing than the love of praise.

But as is said by his Sebastian,

What had been, is unknown; what is, appears.

We know that Dryden's several productions were so many successive expedients for his support: his plays were therefore often borrowed, and his poems were almost all occasional.

In an occasional performance no height of excellence can be expected from any mind, however fertile in itself, and however stored with acquisitions. He whose work is general and arbitrary has the choice of his matter, and takes that which his inclination and his studies have best qualified him to display and decorate. He is at liberty to delay his publication, till he has satisfied his friends and himself; till he has reformed his first thoughts by subsequent examination, and polished away those faults which the precipitance of ardent composition is likely to leave behind it. Virgil is related to have poured out a great number of lines in the morning, and to have passed the day in reducing them to fewer.

The occasional poet is circumscribed by the narrowness of his subject: whatever can happen to man has happened so often that little remains for fancy or invention. We have been all born; we have most of us been married; and so many have died before us that our deaths can supply but few materials for a poet. In the fate of princes the publick has an interest; and what happens to them of good or evil the poets have always considered as business for the Muse. But after so many inauguratory gratulations, nuptial hymns, and funeral dirges, he must be highly favoured by nature or by fortune who says any thing not said before. Even war and conquest, however splendid, suggest no new images; the triumphal chariot of a victorious monarch can be decked only with those ornaments that have graced his predecessors.

Not only matter but time is wanting. The

poem must not be delayed till the occasion is forgotten. The lucky moments of animated imagination cannot be attended; elegances and illustrations cannot be multiplied by gradual accumulation: the composition must be dispatched while conversation is yet busy and admiration fresh; and haste is to be made lest some other event should lay hold upon mankind.

Occasional compositions may however secure to a writer the praise both of learning and facility; for they cannot be the effect of long study, and must be furnished immediately from the treasures of the mind.

The death of Cromwell was the first publick event which called forth Dryden's poetical powers. His heroick stanzas have beauties and defects; the thoughts are vigorous, and though not always proper shew a mind replete with ideas; the numbers are smooth, and the diction, if not altogether correct, is elegant and easy.

*   *   *

Not long afterwards he undertook perhaps the most arduous work of its kind, a translation of Virgil, for which he had shewn how well he was qualified by his version of the *Pollio*, and two episodes, one of Nisus and Euryalus, the other of Mezentius and Lausus.

In the comparison of Homer and Virgil the discriminative excellence of Homer is elevation and comprehension of thought, and that of Virgil is grace and splendor of diction. The beauties of Homer are therefore difficult to be lost, and those of Virgil difficult to be retained. The massy trunk of sentiment is safe by its solidity, but the blossoms of elocution easily drop away. The author, having the choice of his own images, selects those which he can best adorn; the translator must at all hazards follow his original, and express thoughts which perhaps he would not have chosen. When to this primary difficulty is added the inconvenience of a language so much inferior in harmony to the Latin, it cannot be expected that they who read the *Georgick* and the *Eneid* should be much delighted with any version.

All these obstacles Dryden saw, and all these he determined to encounter. The expectation of his work was undoubtedly great; the nation considered its honour as interested in the event. One gave him the different editions of his author, and another helped him in the subordinate parts. The arguments of the several books were given him by Addison.

The hopes of the publick were not disappointed. He produced, says Pope, 'the most noble and spirited translation that I know in any language.' It certainly excelled whatever had appeared in English, and appears to have satisfied his friends, and, for the most part, to have silenced his enemies. Milbourne, indeed, a clergyman, attacked it; but his outrages seem to be the ebullitions of a mind agitated by stronger resentment than bad poetry can excite, and previously resolved not to be pleased.

*   *   *

In a general survey of Dryden's labours he appears to have had a mind very comprehensive by nature, and much enriched with acquired knowledge. His compositions are the effects of a vigorous genius operating upon large materials.

The power that predominated in his intellectual operations was rather strong reason than quick sensibility. Upon all occasions that were presented he studied rather than felt, and produced sentiments not such as Nature enforces, but meditation supplies. With the simple and elemental passions, as they spring separate in the mind, he seems not much acquainted, and seldom describes them but as they are complicated by the various relations of society and confused in the tumults and agitations of life.

What he says of love may contribute to the explanation of his character:

Love various minds does variously inspire;
It stirs in gentle bosoms [natures] gentle fire,

Like that of incense on the altar [altars] laid;
But raging flames tempestuous souls invade,
A fire which every windy passion blows;
With pride it mounts, or [and] with revenge it glows.

Dryden's was not one of the 'gentle bosoms': Love, as it subsists in itself, with no tendency but to the person loved and wishing only for correspondent kindness, such love as shuts out all other interest, the Love of the Golden Age, was too soft and subtle to put his faculties in motion. He hardly conceived it but in its turbulent effervescence with some other desires: when it was inflamed by rivalry or obstructed by difficulties; when it invigorated ambition or exasperated revenge.

He is therefore, with all his variety of excellence, not often pathetick; and had so little sensibility of the power of effusions purely natural that he did not esteem them in others. Simplicity gave him no pleasure; and for the first part of his life he looked on Otway with contempt, though at last, indeed very late, he confessed that in his play 'there was Nature, which is the chief beauty.'

We do not always know our own motives. I am not certain whether it was not rather the difficulty which he found in exhibiting the genuine operations of the heart than a servile submission to an injudicious audience that filled his plays with false magnificence. It was necessary to fix attention; and the mind can be captivated only by recollection or by curiosity; by reviving natural sentiments or impressing new appearances of things: sentences were readier at his call than images; he could more easily fill the ear with some splendid novelty than awaken those ideas that slumber in the heart.

The favourite exercise of his mind was ratiocination; and, that argument might not be too soon at an end, he delighted to talk of liberty and necessity, destiny and contingence; these he discusses in the language of the school with so much profundity that the terms which he uses are not always understood. It is indeed learning, but learning out of place.

When once he had engaged himself in disputation, thoughts flowed in on either side: he was now no longer at a loss; he had always objections and solutions at command: 'verbaque provisam rem'*—give him matter for his verse, and he finds without difficulty verse for his matter.

In comedy, for which he professes himself not naturally qualified, the mirth which he excites will perhaps not be found so much to arise from any original humour or peculiarity of character nicely distinguished and diligently pursued, as from incidents and circumstances, artifices and surprises; from jests of action rather than of sentiment. What he had of humorous or passionate, he seems to have had not from nature, but from other poets; if not always as a plagiary, at least as an imitator.

Next to argument, his delight was in wild and daring sallies of sentiment, in the irregular and excentrick violence of wit. He delighted to tread upon the brink of meaning, where light and darkness begin to mingle; to approach the precipice of absurdity, and hover over the abyss of unideal vacancy. This inclination sometimes produced nonsense, which he knew, as

Move swiftly, sun, and fly a lover's pace,
Leave weeks and months behind thee in thy race.
　　　　　　Amariel flies . . .
　　To guard thee from the demons of the air;
　　My flaming sword above them do display,
　　All keen, and ground upon the edge of day.

And sometimes it issued in absurdities, of which perhaps he was not conscious:

Then we upon our orb's last verge shall go,
　　And see the ocean leaning on the sky;
From thence our rolling neighbours we shall
　　know,
　　And on the lunar world securely pry.

---

* Horace, *Ars Poetica,* 311. "Words follow easily upon matter that has been prepared."

These lines have no meaning; but may we not say, in imitation of Cowley on another book,

'Tis so like sense *'twill serve the turn as well?*

*   *   *

He had sometimes faults of a less generous and splendid kind. He makes, like almost all other poets, very frequent use of mythology, and sometimes connects religion and fable too closely without distinction.

He descends to display his knowledge with pedantick ostentation; as when, in translating Virgil, he says, 'tack to the larboard'—and 'veer starboard'; and talks, in another work, of 'virtue spooming before the wind.' His vanity now and then betrays his ignorance:

They [And] Nature's king through Nature's opticks view'd;
Revers'd they view'd him lessen'd to their eyes [eye].

He had heard of reversing a telescope, and unluckily reverses the object.

He is sometimes unexpectedly mean. When he describes the Supreme Being as moved by prayer to stop the Fire of London, what is his expression?

A [An] hollow crystal pyramid he takes,
In firmamental waters dipp'd above,
Of this [it] a broad extinguisher *he makes,*
And hoods the flames that to their
quarry strove.

When he describes the Last Day, and the decisive tribunal, he intermingles this image:

When rattling bones together fly,
From the four quarters [corners] of the sky.

It was indeed never in his power to resist the temptation of a jest. In his Elegy on Cromwell:

No sooner was the Frenchman's cause embrac'd,
Than the light Monsieur *the* grave Don *out-weigh'd;*
His fortune turn'd the scale.

He had a vanity, unworthy of his abilities, to show, as may be suspected, the rank of the company with whom he lived, by the use of French words, which had then crept into conversation; such as *fraicheur* for *coolness,* *fougue* for *turbulence,* and a few more, none of which the language has incorporated or retained. They continue only where they stood first, perpetual warnings to future innovators.

These are his faults of affectation; his faults of negligence are beyond recital. Such is the unevenness of his compositions that ten lines are seldom found together without something of which the reader is ashamed. Dryden was no rigid judge of his own pages; he seldom struggled after supreme excellence, but snatched in haste what was within his reach; and when he could content others, was himself contented. He did not keep present to his mind an idea of pure perfection; nor compare his works, such as they were, with what they might be made. He knew to whom he should be opposed. He had more musick than Waller, more vigour than Denham, and more nature than Cowley; and from his contemporaries he was in no danger. Standing therefore in the highest place he had no care to rise by contending with himself; but while there was no name above his own was willing to enjoy fame on the easiest terms.

He was no lover of labour. What he thought sufficient he did not stop to make better, and allowed himself to leave many parts unfinished, in confidence that the good lines would overbalance the bad. What he had once written he dismissed from his thoughts; and, I believe, there is no example to be found of any correction or improvement made by him after publication. The hastiness of his productions might be the effect of necessity; but his subsequent neglect could hardly have any other cause than impatience of study.

What can be said of his versification will be little more than a dilatation of the praise given it by Pope:

Waller was smooth; but Dryden taught to join
The varying verse, the full-resounding line,
The long majestick march, and energy divine.

Some improvements had been already made in English numbers, but the full force of our language was not yet felt: the verse that was smooth was commonly feeble. If Cowley had sometimes a finished line he had it by chance. Dryden knew how to chuse the flowing and the sonorous words; to vary the pauses and adjust the accents; to diversify the cadence, and yet preserve the smoothness of his metre.

Of triplets and alexandrines, though he did not introduce the use, he established it. The triplet has long subsisted among us. Dryden seems not to have traced it higher than to Chapman's *Homer*; but it is to be found in Phaer's *Virgil*, written in the reign of Mary, and in Hall's *Satires*, published five years before the death of Elizabeth.

The alexandrine was, I believe, first used by Spenser, for the sake of closing his stanza with a fuller sound. We had a longer measure of fourteen syllables, into which the *Eneid* was translated by Phaer, and other works of the ancients by other writers; of which Chapman's *Iliad* was, I believe, the last.

The two first lines of Phaer's third *Eneid* will exemplify this measure:

When Asia's [Asia] state was overthrown, and
Priam's kingdom stout,
All guiltless, by the power of gods above was
rooted out.

As these lines had their break or *cæsura* always at the eighth syllable it was thought in time commodious to divide them; and quatrains of lines alternately consisting of eight and six syllables make the most soft and pleasing of our lyrick measures, as

Relentless Time, destroying power,
Which [Whom] stone and brass obey,
Who giv'st to every flying hour
To work some new decay.

In the alexandrine, when its power was once felt, some poems, as Drayton's *Polyolbion*, were wholly written; and sometimes the measures of twelve and fourteen syllables were interchanged with one another. Cowley was the first that inserted the alexandrine at pleasure among the heroick lines of ten syllables, and from him Dryden professes to have adopted it.

The triplet and alexandrine are not universally approved. Swift always censured them, and wrote some lines to ridicule them. In examining their propriety it is to be considered that the essence of verse is regularity, and its ornament is variety. To write verse is to dispose syllables and sounds harmonically by some known and settled rule—a rule however lax enough to substitute similitude for identity, to admit change without breach of order, and to relieve the ear without disappointing it. Thus a Latin hexameter is formed from dactyls and spondees differently combined; the English heroick admits of acute or grave syllables variously disposed. The Latin never deviates into seven feet, or exceeds the number of seventeen syllables; but the English alexandrine breaks the lawful bounds, and surprises the reader with two syllables more than he expected.

The effect of the triplet is the same: the ear has been accustomed to expect a new rhyme in every couplet; but is on a sudden surprised with three rhymes together, to which the reader could not accommodate his voice did he not obtain notice of the change from the braces of the margins. Surely there is something unskilful in the necessity of such mechanical direction.

Considering the metrical art simply as a science, and consequently excluding all casualty, we must allow that triplets and alexandrines inserted by caprice are interruptions of that constancy to which science aspires. And though the variety which they produce may very justly be desired, yet to make our poetry exact there ought to be some stated mode of admitting them.

But till some such regulation can be formed, I wish them still to be retained in their present state. They are sometimes grateful to the reader, and sometimes convenient to the poet. Fenton was of opinion that Dryden was too liberal and Pope too sparing in their use.

The rhymes of Dryden are commonly just, and he valued himself for his readiness in finding them; but he is sometimes open to objection.

It is the common practice of our poets to end the second line with a weak or grave syllable:

> *Together o'er the Alps methinks we fly,*
> *Fill'd [Fired] with ideas of fair* Italy.

Dryden sometimes puts the weak rhyme in the first:

Laugh [Laughed] all the powers that [who] favour
> tyranny,
And all the standing army of the sky.

Sometimes he concludes a period or paragraph with the first line of a couplet, which, though the French seem to do it without irregularity, always displeases in English poetry.

The alexandrine, though much his favourite, is not always very diligently fabricated by him. It invariably requires a break at the sixth syllable; a rule which the modern French poets never violate, but which Dryden sometimes neglected:

And with paternal thunder vindicates his throne.

Of Dryden's works it was said by Pope that 'he could select from them better specimens of every mode of poetry than any other English writer could supply.' Perhaps no nation ever produced a writer that enriched his language with such variety of models. To him we owe the improvement, perhaps the completion of our metre, the refinement of our language, and much of the correctness of our sentiments. By him we were taught 'sapere et fari,' to think naturally and express forcibly. Though Davies has reasoned in rhyme before him, it may be perhaps maintained that he was the first who joined argument with poetry. He shewed us the true bounds of a translator's liberty. What was said of Rome, adorned by Augustus, may be applied by an easy metaphor to English poetry embellished by Dryden, 'lateritiam invenit, marmoream reliquit,' he found it brick, and he left it marble.

From the Life of Pope

Alexander Pope was born in London, May 22, 1688, of parents whose rank or station was never ascertained: we are informed that they were of *gentle blood;* that his father was of a family of which the Earl of Downe was the head, and that his mother was the daughter of William Turner, Esquire, of York, who had likewise three sons, one of whom had the honour of being killed, and the other of dying, in the service of Charles the First; the third was made a general officer in Spain, from whom the sister inherited what sequestrations and forfeitures had left in the family.

This, and this only, is told by Pope; who is more willing, as I have heard observed, to shew what his father was not, than what he was. It is allowed that he grew rich by trade; but whether in a shop or on the Exchange was never discovered, till Mr. Tyers told, on the authority of Mrs. Racket, that he was a linen-draper in the Strand. Both parents were papists.

Pope was from his birth of a constitution tender and delicate; but is said to have shewn remarkable gentleness and sweetness of disposition. The weakness of his body continued through his life, but the mildness of his mind perhaps ended with his childhood. His voice, when he was young, was so pleasing, that he was called in fondness the *little Nightingale.*

Being not sent early to school, he was taught to read by an aunt; and when he was seven or eight years old, became a lover of books. He first learned to write by imitating printed books; a species of penmanship in which he retained great excellence through his whole life, though his ordinary hand was not elegant.

When he was about eight, he was placed in Hampshire under Taverner, a Romish priest, who, by a method very rarely practised, taught him the Greek and Latin rudiments together. He was now first regularly initiated in poetry by the perusal of Ogylby's Homer, and Sandys's Ovid: Ogylby's assistance he never repaid with any praise; but of Sandys he declared, in his notes to the *Iliad,* that English poetry owed much of its present beauty to his translations. Sandys very rarely attempted original composition.

From the care of Taverner, under whom his proficiency was considerable, he was removed to a school at Twyford near Winchester, and again to another school about Hyde-park Corner; from which he used sometimes to stroll to the playhouse, and was so delighted with theatrical exhibitions, that he formed a kind of play from Ogylby's *Iliad,* with some verses of his own intermixed, which he persuaded his school-fellows to act, with the addition of his master's gardener, who personated Ajax.

At the two last schools he used to represent himself as having lost part of what Taverner had taught him, and on his master at Twyford he had already exercised his poetry in a lampoon. Yet under those masters he translated more than a fourth part of the *Metamorphoses.* If he kept the same proportion in his other exercises, it cannot be thought that his loss was great.

He tells of himself, in his poems, that *he lisp'd in numbers;* and used to say that he could not remember the time when he began to make verses. In the style of fiction it might have been said of him as of Pindar, that when he lay in his cradle, *the bees swarmed about his mouth.*

About the time of the Revolution his father, who was undoubtedly disappointed by the sudden blast of popish prosperity, quitted his trade, and retired to Binfield in Windsor Forest, with about twenty thousand pounds; for which, being conscientiously determined not to entrust it to the government, he found no better use than that of locking it up in a chest, and taking from it what his expences required; and his life was long enough to consume a great part of it, before his son came to the inheritance.

To Binfield Pope was called by his father when he was about twelve years old; and there he had for a few months the assistance of one Deane, another priest, of whom he learned only to construe a little of Tully's *Offices*. How Mr. Deane could spend, with a boy who had translated so much of Ovid, some months over a small part of Tully's *Offices*, it is now vain to enquire.

Of a youth so successfully employed, and so conspicuously improved, a minute account must be naturally desired; but curiosity must be contented with confused, imperfect, and sometimes improbable intelligence. Pope, finding little advantage from external help, resolved thenceforward to direct himself, and at twelve formed a plan of study which he completed with little other incitement than the desire of excellence.

His primary and principal purpose was to be a poet, with which his father accidentally concurred, by proposing subjects, and obliging him to correct his performances by many revisals; after which the old gentleman, when he was satisfied, would say, *these are good rhymes.*

In his perusal of the English poets he soon distinguished the versification of Dryden, which he considered as the model to be studied, and was impressed with such veneration for his instructer, that he persuaded some friends to take him to the coffee-house which Dryden frequented, and pleased himself with having seen him.

Dryden died May 1, 1701, some days before Pope was twelve; so early must he therefore have felt the power of harmony, and the zeal of genius. Who does not wish that Dryden could have known the value of the homage that was paid him, and foreseen the greatness of his young admirer?

The earliest of Pope's productions is his *Ode on Solitude*, written before he was twelve, in which there is nothing more than other forward boys have attained, and which is not equal to Cowley's performances at the same age.

His time was now spent wholly in reading and writing. As he read the Classicks, he amused himself with translating them; and at fourteen made a version of the first book of the *Thebais*, which, with some revision, he afterwards published. He must have been at this time, if he had no help, a considerable proficient in the Latin tongue.

By Dryden's Fables, which had then been not long published, and were much in the hands of poetical readers, he was tempted to try his own skill in giving Chaucer a more fashionable appearance, and put January and May, and the Prologue of the Wife of Bath, into modern English. He translated likewise the Epistle of Sappho to Phaon from Ovid, to complete the version, which was before imperfect; and wrote some other small pieces, which he afterwards printed.

He sometimes imitated the English poets, and professed to have written at fourteen his poem upon *Silence*, after Rochester's *Nothing*. He had now formed his versification, and in the smoothness of his numbers surpassed his original: but this is a small part of his praise; he discovers such acquaintance both with human life and public affairs, as is not easily conceived to have been attainable by a boy of fourteen in Windsor Forest.

Next year he was desirous of opening to himself new sources of knowledge, by making himself acquainted with modern languages; and removed for a time to London, that he might study French and Italian, which, as he desired nothing more than to read them, were by diligent application soon dispatched. Of Italian learning he does not appear to have ever made much use in his subsequent studies.

He then returned to Binfield, and delighted himself with his own poetry. He tried all styles, and many subjects. He wrote a comedy, a tragedy, an epick poem, with panegyricks, on all the princes of Europe; and, as he confesses, *thought himself the greatest genius that ever was*. Self-confidence is the first requisite to great undertakings; he, indeed, who forms his opinion of himself in solitude, without knowing the powers of other men, is very liable to errour; but it was the felicity of Pope to rate himself at his real value.

Most of his puerile productions were, by his maturer judgement, afterwards destroyed; *Alcander*, the epick poem, was burnt by the persuasion of Atterbury. The tragedy was founded on the legend of St. Genevieve. Of the comedy there is no account.

Concerning his studies it is related, that he translated Tully on Old Age; and that, besides his books of poetry and criticism, he read Temple's *Essays* and Locke *On Human Understanding*. His reading, though his favourite authors are not known, appears to have been sufficiently extensive and multifarious; for his early pieces shew, with sufficient evidence, his knowledge of books.

He that is pleased with himself, easily imagines that he shall please others. Sir William Trumbal, who had been ambassador at Constantinople, and secretary of state, when he retired from business, fixed his residence in the neighbourhood of Binfield. Pope, not yet sixteen, was introduced to the statesman of sixty, and so distinguished himself, that their interviews ended in friendship and correspondence. Pope was, through his whole life, ambitious of splendid acquaintance, and he seems to have wanted neither diligence nor success in attracting the notice of the great; for from his first entrance into the world, and his entrance was very early, he was admitted to familiarity with those whose rank or station made them most conspicuous.

From the age of sixteen the life of Pope, as an author, may be properly computed. He now wrote his Pastorals, which were shewn to the Poets and Criticks of that time; as they well deserved, they were read with admiration, and many praises were bestowed upon them and upon the Preface, which is both elegant and learned in a high degree: they were, however, not published till five years afterwards.

Cowley, Milton, and Pope, are distinguished among the English Poets by the early exertion of their powers: but the works of Cowley alone were published in his childhood, and therefore of him only can it be certain that his puerile performances received no improvement from his maturer studies.

At this time began his acquaintance with Wycherley, a man who seems to have had among his contemporaries his full share of reputation, to have been esteemed without virtue, and caressed without good-humour. Pope was proud of his notice; Wycherley wrote verses in his praise, which he was charged by Dennis with writing to himself, and they agreed for a while to flatter one another. It is pleasant to remark how soon Pope learned the cant of an author, and began to treat criticks with contempt, though he had yet suffered nothing from them.

But the fondness of Wycherley was too violent to last. His esteem of Pope was such, that he submitted some poems to his revision; and when Pope, perhaps proud of such confidence, was sufficiently bold in his criticisms, and liberal in his alterations, the old scribbler was angry to see his pages defaced, and felt more pain from the detection than content from the amendment of his faults. They parted; but Pope always considered him with kindness, and visited him a little time before he died.

Another of his early correspondents was Mr. Cromwell, of whom I have learned nothing particular but that he used to ride a-hunting in a tye-wig. He was fond, and perhaps vain, of amusing himself with poetry and criticism; and sometimes sent his performances to Pope, who did not forbear such remarks as were now-and-then unwelcome. Pope, in his turn, put the juvenile version of *Statius* into his hands for correction.

Their correspondence afforded the publick its first knowledge of Pope's Epistolary Powers; for his Letters were given by Cromwell to one Mrs. Thomas, and she many years afterwards sold them to Curll, who inserted them in a volume of his Miscellanies.

Walsh, a name yet preserved among the minor poets, was one of his first encouragers. His regard was gained by the Pastorals, and from him Pope received the counsel by which he seems to have regulated his studies. Walsh advised him to correctness, which, as he told him, the English poets had hitherto neglected, and which therefore was left to him as a basis of fame; and, being delighted with rural poems, recommended to him to write a pastoral comedy, like those which are read so eagerly in Italy; a design which Pope probably did not approve, as he did not follow it.

Pope had now declared himself a poet; and thinking himself entitled to poetical conversation, began at seventeen to frequent Will's, a coffee-house on the north side of Russell-street in Covent-garden, where the wits of that time used to assemble, and where Dryden had, when he lived, been accustomed to preside.

During this period of his life he was indefatigably diligent, and insatiably curious; wanting health for violent, and money for expensive pleasures, and having certainly excited in himself very strong desires of intellectual eminence, he spent much of his time over his books; but he read only to store his mind with facts and images, seizing all that his authors presented with undistinguishing voracity, and with an appetite for knowledge too eager to be nice. In a mind like his, however, all the faculties were at once involuntarily improving. Judgement is forced upon us by experience. He that reads many books must compare one opinion or one style with another; and when he compares, must necessarily distinguish, reject and prefer. But the account given by himself of his studies was, that from fourteen to twenty he read only for amusement, from twenty to twenty-seven for improvement and instruction; that in the first part of this time he desired only to know, and in the second he endeavoured to judge.

*   *   *

This year (1715) being enabled to live more by choice, having persuaded his father to sell their estate at Binfield, he purchased, I think only for his life, that house at Twickenham to which his residence afterwards procured so much celebration, and removed thither with his father and mother.

Here he planted the vines and the quincunx which his verses mention; and being under the necessity of making a subterraneous passage to a garden on the other side of the road, he adorned it with fossil bodies, and dignified it with the title of a grotto; a place of silence and retreat, from which he endeavoured to persuade his friends and himself that cares and passions could be excluded.

A grotto is not often the wish or pleasure of an Englishman, who has more frequent need to solicit than exclude the sun; but Pope's excavation was requisite as an entrance to his garden, and, as some men try to be proud of their defects, he extracted an ornament from an inconvenience, and vanity produced a grotto where necessity enforced a passage. It may be frequently remarked of the studious and speculative, that they are proud of trifles, and that their amusements seem frivolous and childish; whether it be that men conscious of great reputation think themselves above the reach of censure, and safe in the admission of negligent indulgences, or that mankind expect from elevated genius an uniformity of greatness, and watch its degradation with malicious wonder; like him who having followed with his eye an eagle into the clouds, should lament that she ever descended to a perch.

*   *   *

The person of Pope is well known not to have been formed by the nicest model. He has, in his account of the Little Club, compared himself to a spider, and by another is described as protuberant behind and before. He is said to have been beautiful in his infancy; but he was of a constitution originally feeble and weak; and as bodies of a tender frame are easily distorted, his deformity was probably in part the effect of his application.

His stature was so low, that, to bring him to a level with common tables, it was necessary to raise his seat. But his face was not displeasing, and his eyes were animated and vivid.

By natural deformity, or accidental distortion, his vital functions were so much disordered, that his life was a *long disease*. His most frequent assailant was the headache, which he used to relieve by inhaling the steam of coffee, which he very frequently required.

Most of what can be told concerning his petty peculiarities was communicated by a female domestick of the Earl of Oxford, who knew him perhaps after the middle of life. He was then so weak as to stand in perpetual need of female attendance; extremely sensible of cold, so that he wore a kind of fur doublet, under a shirt of very coarse warm linen with fine sleeves. When he rose, he was invested in boddice made of stiff canvas, being scarce able to hold himself erect till they were laced, and he then put on a flannel waistcoat. One side was contracted. His legs were so slender, that he enlarged their bulk with three pairs of stockings, which were drawn on and off by the maid; for he was not able to dress or undress himself, and neither went to bed nor rose without help. His weakness made it very difficult for him to be clean.

His hair had fallen almost all away; and he used to dine sometimes with Lord Oxford, privately, in a velvet cap. His dress of ceremony was black with a tye-wig, and a little sword.

The indulgence and accommodation which his sickness required had taught him all the unpleasing and unsocial qualities of a valetudinary man. He expected that every thing should give way to his ease or humour, as a child, whose parents will not hear her cry, has an unresisted dominion in the nursery.

C'est que l'enfant toûjours est homme,
C'est que l'homme est toûjours enfant.

When he wanted to sleep he *nodded in company;* and once slumbered at his own table while the Prince of Wales was talking of poetry.

The reputation which his friendship gave, procured him many invitations; but he was a very troublesome inmate. He brought no servant, and had so many wants, that a numerous attendance was scarcely able to supply them. Wherever he was, he left no room for another, because he exacted the attention, and employed the activity of the whole family. His errands were so frequent and frivolous, that the footmen in time avoided and neglected him; and the Earl of Oxford discharged some of the servants for their resolute refusal of his messages. The maids, when they had neglected their business, alleged that they had been employed by Mr. Pope. One of his constant demands was of coffee in the night, and to the woman that waited on him in his chamber he was very burthensome; but he was careful to recompense her want of sleep; and Lord Oxford's servant declared, that in a house where her business was to answer his call, she would not ask for wages.

He had another fault, easily incident to those who, suffering much pain, think themselves entitled to whatever pleasures they can snatch. He was too indulgent to his appetite; he loved meat highly seasoned and of strong taste; and, at the intervals of the table, amused himself with biscuits and dry conserves. If he sat down to a variety of dishes, he would oppress his stomach with repletion, and though he seemed angry when a dram was offered him, did not forbear to drink it. His friends, who knew the avenues to his heart, pampered him with presents of luxury, which he did not suffer to stand neglected. The death of great men is not always proportioned to the lustre of their lives. Hannibal, says Juvenal, did not perish by a javelin or a sword; the slaughters of Cannæ were revenged by a ring. The death of Pope was imputed by some of his friends to a silver saucepan, in which it was his delight to heat potted lampreys.

That he loved too well to eat, is certain; but that his sensuality shortened his life will not be hastily concluded, when it is remembered that a conformation so irregular lasted six and fifty years, notwithstanding such pertinacious diligence of study and meditation.

In all his intercourse with mankind, he had great delight in artifice, and endeavoured to attain all his purposes by indirect and unsuspected methods. *He hardly drank tea without a stratagem.* If, at the house of his friends, he wanted any accommodation, he was not willing to ask for it in plain terms, but would mention it remotely as something convenient; though when it was procured, he soon made it appear for whose sake it had been recommended. Thus he teazed Lord Orrery till he obtained a screen. He practised his arts on such small occasions, that Lady Bolingbroke used to say, in a French phrase, that *he played the politician about cabbages and turnips.* His unjustifiable impression of the Patriot King, as it can be imputed to no particular motive, must have proceeded from his general habit of secrecy and cunning; he caught an opportunity of a sly trick and pleased himself with the thought of outwitting Bolingbroke.

In familiar or convivial conversation, it does not appear that he excelled. He may be said to have resembled Dryden, as being not one that was distinguished by vivacity in company. It is remarkable, that, so near his time, so much should be known of what he has written, and so little of what he has said: traditional memory retains no sallies of raillery, nor sentences of observation; nothing either pointed or solid, either wise or merry. One apophthegm only stands upon record. When an objection raised against his inscription for Shakspeare was defended by the authority of Patrick, he replied—*horresco referens**—that *he would allow the publisher of a Dictionary to know the meaning of a single word, but not of two words put together.*

He was fretful, and easily displeased, and allowed himself to be capriciously resentful. He would sometimes leave Lord Oxford silently, no one could tell why, and was to be courted back by more letters and messages than the footmen were willing to carry. The table was indeed infested by Lady Mary Wortley, who was the friend of Lady Oxford,

and who, knowing his peevishness, could by no intreaties be restrained from contradicting him, till their disputes were sharpened to such asperity, that one or the other quitted the house.

He sometimes condescended to be jocular with servants or inferiors; but by no merriment, either of others or his own, was he ever seen excited to laughter.

Of his domestick character, frugality was a part eminently remarkable. Having determined not to be dependent, he determined not to be in want, and therefore wisely and magnanimously rejected all temptations to expence unsuitable to his fortune. This general care must be universally approved; but it sometimes appeared in petty artifices of parsimony, such as the practice of writing his compositions on the back of letters, as may be seen in the remaining copy of the *Iliad*, by which perhaps in five years five shillings were saved; or in a niggardly reception of his friends, and scantiness of entertainment, as, when he had two guests in his house, he would set at supper a single pint upon the table; and having himself taken two small glasses would retire, and say, *Gentlemen, I leave you to your wine.* Yet he tells his friends that *he has a heart for all, a house for all, and, whatever they may think, a fortune for all.*

He sometimes, however, made a splendid dinner, and is said to have wanted no part of the skill or elegance which such performances require. That this magnificence should be often displayed, that obstinate prudence with which he conducted his affairs would not permit; for his revenue, certain and casual, amounted only to about eight hundred pounds a year, of which however he declares himself able to assign one hundred to charity.

Of this fortune, which as it arose from publick approbation was very honourably obtained, his imagination seems to have been too full: it would be hard to find a man, so well entitled to notice by his wit, that ever

---

* I shudder to mention it.

delighted so much in talking of his money. In his Letters, and in his Poems, his garden and his grotto, his quincunx and his vines, or some hints of his opulence, are always to be found. The great topick of his ridicule is poverty; the crimes with which he reproaches his antagonists are their debts, their habitation in the Mint, and their want of a dinner. He seems to be of an opinion not very uncommon in the world, that to want money is to want every thing.

Next to the pleasure of contemplating his possessions, seems to be that of enumerating the men of high rank with whom he was acquainted, and whose notice he loudly proclaims not to have been obtained by any practices of meanness or servility; a boast which was never denied to be true, and to which very few poets have ever aspired. Pope never set genius to sale; he never flattered those whom he did not love, or praised those whom he did not esteem. Savage however remarked, that he began a little to relax his dignity when he wrote a distich for *his Highness's dog.*

His admiration of the Great seems to have increased in the advance of life. He passed over peers and statesmen to inscribe his *Iliad* to Congreve, with a magnanimity of which the praise had been compleat, had his friend's virtue been equal to his wit. Why he was chosen for so great an honour, it is not now possible to know; there is no trace in literary history of any particular intimacy between them. The name of Congreve appears in the Letters among those of his other friends, but without any observable distinction or consequence.

To his latter works, however, he took care to annex names dignified with titles, but was not very happy in his choice; for, except Lord Bathurst, none of his noble friends were such as that a good man would wish to have his intimacy with them known to posterity: he can derive little honour from the notice of Cobham, Burlington, or Bolingbroke.

Of his social qualities, if an estimate be made from his Letters, an opinion too favourable cannot easily be formed; they ex-hibit a perpetual and unclouded effulgence of general benevolence, and particular fondness. There is nothing but liberality, gratitude, constancy, and tenderness. It has been so long said as to be commonly believed, that the true characters of men may be found in their Letters, and that he who writes to his friend lays his heart open before him. But the truth is, that such were simple friendships of the *Golden Age,* and are now the friendships only of children. Very few can boast of hearts which they dare lay open to themselves, and of which, by whatever accident exposed, they do not shun a distinct and continued view; and, certainly, what we hide from ourselves we do not shew to our friends. There is, indeed, no transaction which offers stronger temptations to fallacy and sophistication than epistolary intercourse. In the eagerness of conversation the first emotions of the mind often burst out, before they are considered; in the tumult of business, interest and passion have their genuine effect; but a friendly Letter is a calm and deliberate performance, in the cool of leisure, in the stillness of solitude, and surely no man sits down to depreciate by design his own character.

Friendship has no tendency to secure veracity; for by whom can a man so much wish to be thought better than he is, as by him whose kindness he desires to gain or keep? Even in writing to the world there is less constraint; the author is not confronted with his reader and takes his chance of approbation among the different dispositions of mankind; but a Letter is addressed to a single mind, of which the prejudices and partialities are known; and must therefore please, if not by favouring them, by forbearing to oppose them.

To charge those favourable representations, which men give of their own minds, with the guilt of hypocritical falsehood, would shew more severity than knowledge. The writer commonly believes himself. Almost every man's thoughts, while they are general, are right; and most hearts are pure, while temptation is away. It is easy to awaken generous sentiments in privacy; to despise death when there is no danger; to glow with benevolence when there is nothing to be given. While such ideas are formed they are felt, and self-love does not suspect the gleam of virtue to be the meteor of fancy.

If the Letters of Pope are considered merely as compositions, they seem to be premeditated and artificial. It is one thing to write because there is something which the mind wishes to discharge, and another, to solicit the imagination because ceremony or vanity requires something to be written. Pope confesses his early Letters to be vitiated with *affectation and ambition*: to know whether he disentangled himself from these perverters of epistolary integrity, his book and his life must be set in comparison.

One of his favourite topicks is contempt of his own poetry. For this, if it had been real, he would deserve no commendation, and in this he was certainly not sincere; for his high value of himself was sufficiently observed, and of what could he be proud but of his poetry? He writes, he says, when *he has just nothing else to do;* yet Swift complains that he was never at leisure for conversation, because he *had always some poetical scheme in his head.* It was punctually required that his writing-box should be set upon his bed before he rose; and Lord Oxford's domestick related, that, in the dreadful winter of Forty, she was called from her bed by him four times in one night, to supply him with paper, lest he should lose a thought.

He pretends insensibility to censure and criticism, though it was observed by all who knew him that every pamphlet disturbed his quiet, and that his extreme irritability laid him open to perpetual vexation; but he wished to despise his criticks, and therefore hoped that he did not despise them.

As he happened to live in two reigns when the Court paid little attention to poetry, he nursed in his mind a foolish disesteem of Kings, and proclaims that *he never sees Courts.* Yet a little regard shewn him by the Prince of Wales melted his obduracy; and he had not much to say when he was asked by his Royal Highness, *how he could love a Prince while he disliked Kings?*

He very frequently professes contempt of the world, and represents himself as looking on mankind, sometimes with gay indifference, as on emmets of a hillock, below his serious attention; and sometimes with gloomy indignation, as on monsters more worthy of hatred than of pity. These were dispositions apparently counterfeited. How could he despise those whom he lived by pleasing, and on whose approbation his esteem of himself was superstructed? Why should he hate those to whose favour he owed his honour and his ease? Of things that terminate in human life, the world is the proper judge; to despise its sentence, if it were possible, is not just; and if it were just, is not possible. Pope was far enough from this unreasonable temper; he was sufficiently *a fool to Fame,* and his fault was that he pretended to neglect it. His levity and his sullenness were only in his Letters; he passed through common life, sometimes vexed, and sometimes pleased, with the natural emotions of common men.

His scorn of the Great is repeated too often to be real; no man thinks much of that which he despises; and as falsehood is always in danger of inconsistency, he makes it his boast at another time that he lives among them.

It is evident that his own importance dwells often in his mind. He is afraid of writing, lest the clerks of the Post-office should know his secrets; he has many enemies; he considers himself as surrounded by universal jealousy; *after many deaths, and many dispersions, two or three of us,* says he, *may still be brought together, not to plot, but to divert ourselves, and the world too, if it pleases;* and they can live together, and *shew what friends wits may be, in spite of all the fools in the world.* All this while it was likely that the clerks did not know his hand; he certainly had no more enemies than a publick character like his inevitably excites, and with what degree of friendship the wits might live, very few were so much fools as ever to enquire.

Some part of this pretended discontent he learned from Swift, and expresses it, I think, most frequently in his correspondence with him. Swift's resentment was unreasonable, but it was sincere; Pope's was the mere mimickry of his friend, a fictitious part which he began to play before it became him. When he was only twenty-five years old, he related that *a glut of study and retirement had throw him on the world*, and that there was danger lest *a glut of the world should throw him back upon study and retirement*. To this Swift answered with great propriety, that Pope had not yet either acted or suffered enough in the world to have become weary of it. And, indeed, it must be some very powerful reason that can drive back to solitude him who has once enjoyed the pleasures of society.

In the Letters both of Swift and Pope there appears such narrowness of mind, as makes them insensible of any excellence that has not some affinity with their own, and confines their esteem and approbation to so small a number, that whoever should form his opinion of the age from their representation, would suppose them to have lived amidst ignorance and barbarity, unable to find among their contemporaries either virtue or intelligence, and persecuted by those that could not understand them.

When Pope murmurs at the world, when he professes contempt of fame, when he speaks of riches and poverty, of success and disappointment, with negligent indifference, he certainly does not express his habitual and settled sentiments, but either wilfully disguises his own character, or, what is more likely, invests himself with temporary qualities, and sallies out in the colours of the present moment. His hopes and fears, his joys and sorrows, acted strongly upon his mind; and if he differed from others, it was not by carelessness; he was irritable and resentful; his malignity to Philips, whom he had first made ridiculous, and then hated for being angry, continued too long. Of his vain desire to make Bentley contemptible, I never heard any adequate reason. He was sometimes wanton in his attacks; and, before Chandos, Lady

Wortley, and Hill, was mean in his retreat.

The virtues which seen to have had most of his affection were liberality and fidelity of friendship, in which it does not appear that he was other than he describes himself. His fortune did not suffer his charity to be splendid and conspicuous; but he assisted Dodsley with a hundred pounds, that he might open a shop; and of the subscription of forty pounds a year that he raised for Savage, twenty were paid by himself. He was accused of loving money, but his love was eagerness to gain, not solicitude to keep it.

In the duties of friendship he was zealous and constant: his early maturity of mind commonly united him with men older than himself, and therefore, without attaining any considerable length of life, he saw many companions of his youth sink into the grave; but it does not appear that he lost a single friend by coldness or by injury; those who loved him once, continued their kindness. His ungrateful mention of Allen in his will was the effect of his adherence to one whom he had known much longer, and whom he naturally loved with greater fondness. His violation of the trust reposed in him by Bolingbroke could have no motive inconsistent with the warmest affection; he either thought the action so near to indifferent that he forgot it, or so laudable that he expected his friend to approve it.

It was reported, with such confidence as almost to enforce belief, that in the papers intrusted to his executors was found a defamatory Life of Swift, which he had prepared as an instrument of vengeance to be used, if any provocation should be ever given. About this I enquired of the Earl of Marchmont, who assured me that no such piece was among his remains.

The religion in which he lived and died was that of the Church of Rome, to which in his correspondence with Racine he professes himself a sincere adherent. That he was not scrupulously pious in some part of his life, is known by many idle and indecent applications of sentences taken from the Scriptures; a mode of merriment which a good man dreads for its profaneness, and a witty man disdains for its easiness and vulgarity. But to whatever levities he has been betrayed, it does not appear that his principles were ever corrupted, or that he ever lost his belief of Revelation. The positions which he transmitted from Bolingbroke he seems not to have understood, and was pleased with an interpretation that made them orthodox.

A man of such exalted superiority, and so little moderation, would naturally have all his delinquencies observed and aggravated; those who could not deny that he was excellent, would rejoice to find that he was not perfect.

Perhaps it may be imputed to the unwillingness with which the same man is allowed to possess many advantages, that his learning has been depreciated. He certainly was in his early life a man of great literary curiosity; and when he wrote his *Essay on Criticism* had, for his age, a very wide acquaintance with books. When he entered into the living world, it seems to have happened to him as to many others, that he was less attentive to dead masters; he studied in the academy of Paracelsus, and made the universe his favourite volume. He gathered his notions fresh from reality, not from the copies of authors, but the originals of Nature. Yet there is no reason to believe that literature ever lost his esteem; he always professed to love reading; and Dobson, who spent some time at his house translating his *Essay on Man*, when I asked him what learning he found him to possess, answered, *More than I expected.* His frequent references to history, his allusions to various kinds of knowledge, and his images selected from art and nature, with his observations on the operations of the mind and the modes of life, shew an intelligence perpetually on the wing, excursive, vigorous, and diligent, eager to pursue knowledge, and attentive to retain it.

From this curiosity arose the desire of travelling, to which he alludes in his verses to Jervas, and which, though he never found an opportunity to gratify it, did not leave him till his life declined.

Of his intellectual character, the constituent and fundamental principle was Good Sense, a prompt and intuitive perception of consonance and propriety. He saw immediately, of his own conceptions, what was to be chosen, and what to be rejected; and, in the works of others, what was to be shunned, and what to be copied.

But good sense alone is a sedate and quiescent quality, which manages its possessions well, but does not increase them; it collects few materials for its own operations, and preserves safety, but never gains supremacy. Pope had likewise genius; a mind active, ambitious, and adventurous, always investigating, always aspiring; in its wildest searches still longing to go forward, in its highest flights still wishing to be higher; always imagining something greater than it knows, always endeavouring more than it can do.

To assist these powers, he is said to have had great strength and exactness of memory. That which he had heard or read was not easily lost; and he had before him not only what his own meditation suggested, but what he had found in other writers, that might be accommodated to his present purpose.

These benefits of nature he improved by incessant and unwearied diligence; he had recourse to every source of intelligence, and lost no opportunity of information; he consulted the living as well as the dead; he read his compositions to his friends, and was never content with mediocrity when excellence could be attained. He considered poetry as the business of his life, and however he might seem to lament his occupation, he followed it with constancy; to make verses was his first labour, and to mend them was his last.

From his attention to poetry he was never diverted. If conversation offered anything that could be improved, he committed it to paper; if a thought, or perhaps an expression more happy than was common, rose to his mind, he was careful to write it; an independent distich was preserved for an opportunity of insertion, and some little fragments have been found containing lines, or parts of lines, to be wrought upon at some other time.

He was one of those few whose labour is their pleasure; he was never elevated to negligence, nor wearied to impatience; he never passed a fault unamended by indifference, nor quitted it by despair. He laboured his works first to gain reputation, and afterwards to keep it.

Of composition there are different methods. Some employ at once memory and invention, and, with little intermediate use of the pen, form and polish large masses by continued meditation, and write their productions only when, in their own opinion, they have completed them. It is related of Virgil, that his custom was to pour out a great number of verses in the morning, and pass the day in retrenching exuberances and correcting inaccuracies. The method of Pope, as may be collected from his translation, was to write his first thoughts in his first words, and gradually to amplify, decorate, rectify, and refine them.

With such faculties, and such dispositions, he excelled every other writer in *poetical prudence;* he wrote in such a manner as might expose him to few hazards. He used almost always the same fabrick of verse; and, indeed, by those few essays which he made of any other, he did not enlarge his reputation. Of this uniformity the certain consequence was readiness and dexterity. By perpetual practice, language had in his mind a systematical arrangement; having always the same use for words, he had words so selected and combined as to be ready at his call. This increase of facility he confessed himself to have perceived in the progress of his translation.

But what was yet of more importance, his effusions were always voluntary, and his subjects chosen by himself. His independence secured him from drudging at a task, and labouring upon a barren topick: he never exchanged praise for money, nor opened a shop of condolence or congratulation. His poems, therefore, were scarce ever temporary. He suffered coronations and royal marriages to pass without a song, and derived no opportunities from recent events, nor any popularity from the accidental disposition of

his readers. He was never reduced to the necessity of soliciting the sun to shine upon a birthday, of calling the Graces and Virtues to a wedding, or of saying what multitudes have said before him. When he could produce nothing new, he was at liberty to be silent.

His publications were for the same reason never hasty. He is said to have sent nothing to the press till it had lain two years under his inspection: it is at least certain, that he ventured nothing without nice examination. He suffered the tumult of imagination to subside, and the novelties of invention to grow familiar. He knew that the mind is always enamoured of its own productions, and did not trust his first fondness. He consulted his friends, and listened with great willingness to criticism; and, what was of more importance, he consulted himself, and let nothing pass against his own judgement.

He professed to have learned his poetry from Dryden, whom, whenever an opportunity was presented, he praised through his whole life with unvaried liberality; and perhaps his character may receive some illustration, if he be compared with his master.

Integrity of understanding and nicety of discernment were not allotted in a less proportion to Dryden than to Pope. The rectitude of Dryden's mind was sufficiently shewn by the dismission of his poetical prejudices, and the rejection of unnatural thoughts and rugged numbers. But Dryden never desired to apply all the judgement that he had. He wrote, and professed to write, merely for the people; and when he pleased others, he contented himself. He spent no time in struggles to rouse latent powers; he never attempted to make that better which was already good, nor often to mend what he must have known to be faulty. He wrote, as he tells us, with very little consideration; when occasion or necessity called upon him, he poured out what the present moment happened to supply, and, when once it had passed the press, ejected it from his mind; for when he had no pecuniary interest, he had no further solicitude.

Pope was not content to satisfy; he desired

to excel, and therefore always endeavoured to do his best: he did not court the candour, but dared the judgement of his reader, and, expecting no indulgence from others, he shewed none to himself. He examined lines and words with minute and punctilious observation, and retouched every part with indefatigable diligence, till he had left nothing to be forgiven.

For this reason he kept his pieces very long in his hands, while he considered and reconsidered them. The only poems which can be supposed to have been written with such regard to the times as might hasten their publication, were the two satires of *Thirty-eight;* of which Dodsley told me, that they were brought to him by the author, that they might be fairly copied. "Almost every line," he said, "was then written twice over; I gave him a clean transcript, which he sent some time afterwards to me for the press, with almost every line written twice over a second time."

His declaration, that his care for his works ceased at their publication, was not strictly true. His parental attention never abandoned them; what he found amiss in the first edition, he silently corrected in those that followed. He appears to have revised the *Iliad,* and freed it from some of its imperfections; and the *Essay on Criticism* received many improvements after its first appearance. It will seldom be found that he altered without adding clearness, elegance, or vigour. Pope had perhaps the judgement of Dryden; but Dryden certainly wanted the diligence of Pope.

In acquired knowledge, the superiority must be allowed to Dryden, whose education was more scholastick, and who before he became an author had been allowed more time for study, with better means of information. His mind has a larger range, and he collects his images and illustrations from a more extensive circumference of science. Dryden knew more of man in his general nature, and Pope in his local manners. The notions of Dryden were formed by comprehensive speculation, and those of Pope by

minute attention. There is more dignity in the knowledge of Dryden, and more certainty in that of Pope.

Poetry was not the sole praise of either; for both excelled likewise in prose; but Pope did not borrow his prose from his predecessor. The style of Dryden is capricious and varied, that of Pope is cautious and uniform; Dryden obeys the motions of his own mind, Pope constrains his mind to his own rules of composition. Dryden is sometimes vehement and rapid; Pope is always smooth, uniform, and gentle. Dryden's page is a natural field, rising into inequalities, and diversified by the varied exuberance of abundant vegetation; Pope's is a velvet lawn, shaven by the scythe, and levelled by the roller.

Of genius, that power which constitutes a poet; that quality without which judgement is cold and knowledge is inert; that energy which collects, combines, amplifies, and animates; the superiority must, with some hesitation, be allowed to Dryden. It is not to be inferred that of this poetical vigour Pope had only a little because Dryden had more; for every other writer since Milton must give place to Pope; and even of Dryden it must be said, that if he has brighter paragraphs, he has not better poems. Dryden's performances were always hasty, either excited by some external occasion, or extorted by domestick necessity; he composed without consideration, and published without correction. What his mind could supply at call, or gather in one excursion, was all that he sought, and all that he gave. The dilatory caution of Pope enabled him to condense his sentiments, to multiply his images, and to accumulate all that study might produce, or chance might supply. If the flights of Dryden therefore are higher, Pope continues longer on the wing. If of Dryden's fire the blaze is brighter, of Pope's the heat is more regular and constant. Dryden often surpasses expectation, and Pope never falls below it. Dryden is read with frequent astonishment, and Pope with perpetual delight.

This parallel will, I hope, when it is well considered, be found just; and if the reader should suspect me, as I suspect myself, of some partial fondness for the memory of Dryden, let him not too hastily condemn me; for meditation and enquiry may, perhaps, shew him the reasonableness of my determination.

*　　*　　*

The train of my disquisition has now conducted me to that poetical wonder, the translation of the Iliad; a performance which no age or nation can pretend to equal. To the Greeks translation was almost unknown; it was totally unknown to the inhabitants of Greece. They had no recourse to the Barbarians for poetical beauties, but sought for every thing in Homer, where, indeed, there is but little which they might not find.

The Italians have been very diligent translators; but I can hear of no version, unless perhaps Anguillara's Ovid may be excepted, which is read with eagerness. The *Iliad* of Salvini every reader may discover to be punctiliously exact; but it seems to be the work of a linguist skilfully pedantick, and his countrymen, the proper judges of its power to please, reject it with disgust.

Their predecessors the Romans have left some specimens of translation behind them, and that employment must have had some credit in which Tully and Germanicus engaged; but unless we suppose, what is perhaps true, that the plays of Terence were versions of Menander, nothing translated seems ever to have risen to high reputation. The French, in the meridian hour of their learning, were very laudably industrious to enrich their own language with the wisdom of the ancients; but found themselves reduced, by whatever necessity, to turn the Greek and Roman poetry into prose. Whoever could read an author, could translate him. From such rivals little can be feared.

The chief help of Pope in this arduous undertaking was drawn from the versions of Dryden. Virgil had borrowed much of his imagery from Homer, and part of the debt was now paid by his translator. Pope searched the pages of Dryden for happy combinations of heroic diction; but it will not be denied that he added much to what he found. He cultivated our language with so much diligence and art, that he has left in his Homer a treasure of poetical elegances to posterity. His version may be said to have tuned the English tongue; for since its appearance no writer, however deficient in other powers, has wanted melody. Such a series of lines so elaborately corrected, and so sweetly modulated, took possession of the publick ear; the vulgar was enamoured of the poem, and the learned wondered at the translation.

But in the most general applause discordant voices will always be heard. It has been objected by some, who wish to be numbered among the sons of learning, that Pope's version of Homer is not Homerical; that it exhibits no resemblance of the original and characteristick manner of the Father of Poetry, as it wants his awful simplicity, his artless grandeur, his unaffected majesty. This cannot be totally denied; but it must be remembered that *necessitas quod cogit defendit**; that may be lawfully done which cannot be forborne. Time and place will always enforce regard. In estimating this translation, consideration must be had of the nature of our language, the form of our metre, and, above all, of the change which two thousand years have made in the modes of life and the habits of thought. Virgil wrote in a language of the same general fabrick with that of Homer, in verses of the same measure, and in an age nearer to Homer's time by eighteen hundred years; yet he found, even then, the state of the world so much altered, and the demand for elegance so much increased, that mere nature would be endured no longer; and perhaps, in the multitude of borrowed passages, very few can be shewn which he has not embellished.

There is a time when nations emerging from barbarity, and falling into regular subordination, gain leisure to grow wise, and feel the shame of ignorance and the craving pain of unsatisfied curiosity. To this hunger

---

* The necessity that compels is its own defense.

of the mind plain sense is grateful; that which fills the void removes uneasiness, and to be free from pain for a while is pleasure; but repletion generates fastidiousness: a saturated intellect soon becomes luxurious, and knowledge finds no willing reception till it is recommended by artificial diction. Thus it will be found, in the progress of learning, that in all nations the first writers are simple, and that every age improves in elegance. One refinement always makes way for another, and what was expedient to Virgil was necessary to Pope.

I suppose many readers of the English *Iliad*, when they have been touched with some unexpected beauty of the lighter kind, have tried to enjoy it in the original, where, alas! it was not to be found. Homer doubtless owes to his translator many Ovidian graces not exactly suitable to his character; but to have added can be no great crime, if nothing be taken away. Elegance is surely to be desired, if it be not gained at the expence of dignity. A hero would wish to be loved, as well as to be reverenced.

To a thousand cavils one answer is sufficient; the purpose of a writer is to be read, and the criticism which would destroy the power of pleasing must be blown aside. Pope wrote for his own age and his own nation: he knew that it was necessary to colour the images and point the sentiments of his author; he therefore made him graceful, but lost him some of his sublimity.

* * *

After all this, it is surely superfluous to answer the question that has once been asked, Whether Pope was a poet; otherwise than by asking in return, If Pope be not a poet, where is poetry to be found? To circumscribe poetry by a definition will only shew the narrowness of the definer, though a definition which shall exclude Pope will not easily be made. Let us look round upon the present time, and back upon the past; let us enquire to whom the voice of mankind has decreed the wreath of poetry; let their productions be examined, and their claims stated, and the pretensions of Pope will be no more disputed. Had he given the world only his version, the name of poet must have been allowed him: if the writer of the *Iliad* were to class his successors, he would assign a very high place to his translator, without requiring any other evidence of Genius.

From the Life of Gray

G ray's Poetry is now to be considered: and I hope not to be looked on as an enemy to his name, if I confess that I contemplate it with less pleasure than his life.

His *Ode on Spring* has something poetical, both in the language and the thought; but the language is too luxuriant, and the thoughts have nothing new. There has of late arisen a practice of giving to adjectives, derived from substantives, the termination of participles; such as the *cultured* plain, the *daisied* bank; but I was sorry to see, in the lines of a scholar like Gray, the *honied* Spring. The morality is natural, but too stale; the conclusion is pretty.

The poem on the Cat was doubtless by its author considered as a trifle, but it is not a happy trifle. In the first stanza, *the azure flowers* that *blow*, shew resolutely a rhyme is sometimes made when it cannot easily be found. Selima, the Cat, is called a nymph, with some violence both to language and sense; but there is good use made of it when it is done; for of the two lines,

> *What female heart can gold despise?*
> *What cat's averse to fish?*

the first relates merely to the nymph and the second only to the cat. The sixth stanza contains a melancholy truth, that *a favourite has no friend;* but the last ends in a pointed sentence of no relation to the purpose; if *what glistered* had been *gold*, the cat would not have gone into the water; and, if she had, would not less have been drowned.

The *Prospect of Eton College* suggests nothing to Gray which every beholder does not equally think and feel. His supplication to father Thames, to tell him who drives the hoop or tosses the ball, is useless and puerile. Father Thames has no better means of knowing than himself. His epithet *buxom health* is not elegant; he seems not to under-

stand the word. Gray thought his language more poetical as it was more remote from common use: finding in Dryden *honey redolent of Spring*, an expression that reaches the utmost limits of our language, Gray drove it a little more beyond common apprehension, by making *gales* to be *redolent of joy and youth.*

Of the *Ode on Adversity*, the hint was at first taken from *O Diva, gratum quæ regis Antium*[*]; but Gray has excelled his original by the variety of his sentiments, and by their moral application. Of this piece, at once poetical and rational, I will not by slight objections violate the dignity.

My process has now brought me to the wonderful *Wonder of Wonders*, the two Sister Odes; by which, though either vulgar ignorance or common sense at first universally rejected them, many have been since persuaded to think themselves delighted. I am one of those that are willing to be pleased, and therefore would gladly find the meaning of the first stanza of *The Progress of Poetry.*

Gray seems in his rapture to confound the images of *spreading sound* and *running water.* A *stream of musick* may be allowed; but where does *Musick*, however *smooth and strong*, after having visited the *verdant vales, rowl down the steep amain*, so as that *rocks and nodding groves rebellow to the roar?* If this be said of *Musick*, it is nonsense; if it be said of *Water*, it is nothing to the purpose.

The second stanza, exhibiting Mar's car and Jove's eagle, is unworthy of further notice. Criticism disdains to chase a schoolboy to his common places.

To the third it may likewise be objected, that it is drawn from Mythology, though such as may be more easily assimilated to real life. Idalia's *velvet-green* has something of cant. An epithet or metaphor drawn from Nature

---

[*] Horace, Ode 1, 35.1. "O goddess, you who rule Antium."

enobles Art; an epithet or metaphor drawn from Art degrades Nature. Gray is too fond of words arbitrarily compounded. *Many-twinkling* was formerly censured as not analogical; we may say *many-spotted,* but scarcely *many-spotting.* This stanza, however, has something pleasing.

Of the second ternary of stanzas, the first endeavours to tell something, and would have told it, had it not been crossed by Hyperion: the second describes well enough the universal prevalence of Poetry; but I am afraid that the conclusion will not rise from the premises. The caverns of the North and the plains of Chili are not the residences of *Glory and generous Shame.* But that Poetry and Virtue go always together is an opinion so pleasing, that I can forgive him who resolves to think it true.

The third stanza sounds big with *Delphi,* and *Egean,* and *Ilissus,* and *Meander,* and *hallowed fountain* and *solemn sound;* but in all Gray's odes there is a kind of cumbrous splendor which we wish away. His position is at last false; in the time of Dante and Petrarch, from whom he derives our first school of Poetry, Italy was over-run by *tyrant power* and *coward vice;* nor was our state much better when we first borrowed the Italian arts.

Of the third ternary, the first gives a mythological birth of Shakspeare. What is said of that mighty genius is true; but it is not said happily; the real effects of this poetical power are put out of sight by the pomp of machinery. Where truth is sufficient to fill the mind, fiction is worse than useless; the counterfeit debases the genuine.

His account of Milton's blindness, if we suppose it caused by study in the formation of his poem, a supposition surely allowable, is poetically true, and happily imagined. But the *car* of Dryden, with his *two coursers,* has nothing in it peculiar; it is a car in which any other rider may be placed.

The Bard appears, at the first view, to be, as Algarotti and others have remarked, an imitation of the prophecy of Nereus. Algarotti thinks it superior to its original; and, if preference depends only on the imagery and animation of the two poems, his judgement is right. There is in *The Bard* more force, more thought, and more variety. But to copy is less than to invent, and the copy has been unhappily produced at a wrong time. The fiction of Horace was to the Romans credible; but its revival disgusts us with apparent and unconquerable falsehood. *Incredulus odi.**

To select a singular event, and swell it to a giant's bulk by fabulous appendages of spectres and predictions, has little difficulty, for he that forsakes the probable may always find the marvellous. And it has little use; we are affected only as we believe; we are improved only as we find something to be imitated or declined. I do not see that *The Bard* promotes any truth, moral or political.

His stanzas are too long, especially his epodes; the ode is finished before the ear has learned its measures, and consequently before it can receive pleasure from their consonance and recurrence.

Of the first stanza the abrupt beginning has been celebrated; but technical beauties can give praise only to the inventor. It is in the power of any man to rush abruptly upon his subject, that has read the ballad of Johnny Armstrong,

Is there ever a man in all Scotland—

The initial resemblances, or alliterations, *ruin, ruthless, helm or hauberk,* are below the grandeur of a poem that endeavours at sublimity.

In the second stanza *The Bard* is well described; but in the third we have the puerilities of obsolete mythology. When we are told that *Cadwallo hush'd the stormy main,* and that *Modred* made *huge Plinlimmon bow his cloud-top'd head,* attention recoils from the repetition of a tale that, even when it was first heard, was heard with scorn.

The *weaving* of the *winding sheet* he bor-

---

* Horace, *Ars Poetica,* 188. "I don't believe it, but rather abhor it."

rowed, as he owns, from the northern Bards; but their texture, however, was very properly the work of female powers, as the art of spinning the thread of life in another mythology. Theft is always dangerous; Gray has made weavers of his slaughtered bards, by a fiction outrageous and incongruous. They are then called upon to *Weave the warp, and weave the woof,* perhaps with no great propriety; for it is by crossing the *woof* with the *warp* that men *weave* the *web* or piece; and the first line was dearly bought by the admission of its wretched correspondent, *Give ample room and verge enough.* He has, however no other line as bad.

The third stanza of the second ternary is commended, I think, beyond its merit. The personification is indistinct. *Thirst* and *Hunger* are not alike; and their features, to make the imagery perfect, should have been discriminated. We are told, in the same stanza, how *towers* are *fed.* But I will no longer look for particular faults; yet let it be observed that the ode might have been concluded with an action of better example; but suicide is always to be had, without expence of thought.

These odes are marked by glittering accumulations of ungraceful ornaments; they strike, rather than please; the images are magnified by affectation; the language is laboured into harshness. The mind of the writer seems to work with unnatural violence. *Double, double, toil and trouble.* He has a kind of strutting dignity, and is tall by walking on tiptoe. His art and his struggle are too visible, and there is too little appearance of ease and nature.

To say that he has no beauties, would be unjust: a man like him, of great learning and great industry, could not but produce something valuable. When he pleases least, it can only be said that a good design was ill directed.

His translations of Northern and Welsh Poetry deserve praise; the imagery is preserved, perhaps often improved; but the language is unlike the language of other poets.

In the character of his *Elegy* I rejoice to concur with the common reader; for by the common sense of readers uncorrupted with literary prejudices, after all the refinements of subtilty and the dogmatism of learning, must be finally decided all claim to poetical honours. *The Churchyard* abounds with images which find a mirrour in every mind, and with sentiments to which every bosom returns an echo. The four stanzas beginning *Yet even these bones,* are to me original: I have never seen the notions in any other place; yet he that reads them here, persuades himself that he has always felt them. Had Gray written often thus, it had been vain to blame, and useless to praise him.

Popular Scientific Lectures

Ernst Mach

Editor's Introduction

Ernst Mach (1838–1916) was one of the great nineteenth-century European men of science, in a class with Helmholtz, Ostwald (the originator of physical chemistry), Hans Vaihinger, Ludwig Boltzmann, and Max Planck, not to speak of the members, mostly from a later generation, of the Vienna Circle of Positivists—Otto Neurath, Richard von Mises, Philipp Frank, and others —on whom he exerted a powerful influence.

Born at Turas, Moravia, in what is now part of Czechoslovakia, Mach was trained originally as a mathematician and was appointed professor of that subject at the University of Graz in 1864. The greater part of his profession- al life was spent, however, at the University of Prague, where he was professor of physics from 1867 to 1895. Among the researches he under- took were some on the motion of bodies in wind tunnels, in recognition of which the ratio of the speed of a body to the speed of sound in undisturbed air, a matter of importance in the theory of flight, is now called the Mach number. While at Prague he also conducted classic studies in experimental psychology on the perception of bodily rotation. These he described in *Contributions to the Analysis of Sensations* (1886), a work that is regarded as having done much to draw the line between physics and psychology, and in which Mach expounded the doctrine, derived from Hume, that we know nothing of phenomena except as the senses tell us, that all our ideas can be defined in terms of elementary sense data. By thus denying that body and mind are distinct from one another, Mach suggested one of the funda- mental notions of Gestalt psychology.

His best known book is *The Science of Mechanics: A Critical and Historical Account of Its Development* (1883), in which he sought to show that the laws of mechanics are not a priori truths but are derived from common experi- ence, and in which he argued that concepts that are unverifiable by obser- vation have no place in physical science. In the latter category he placed Newton's conceptions of absolute space and time, and his arguments against these notions were subsequently taken up and applied by Einstein, who gave the term Mach's principle to the idea that centrifugal force is not an absolute property of a body in rotation but is an indication rather of the gravitational force of other matter in the universe.

The Science of Mechanics rejects much traditional scientific thought as being full of "metaphysical obscurities," but its examination of the great literature of science is informed and deeply thoughtful. Indeed, Mach was learned in the classics of scientific writing from Archimedes on down, and the book's discussion of its subject, arguably the best thing of its kind ever written, is a model for those conversant with the tradition of the *Great Books*—the work of a well and liberally educated man.

The addresses known as *Popular Scientific Lectures* were first published in 1894. Devoted to a variety of subjects, they had been given by Mach on various occasions in the belief, as he said, that while they could afford "only a *modicum* of instruction," and were perforce restricted "to the exposition of the simplest and the most essential points," yet they could be taken as showing "the substantial sameness of scientific and every-day thought." Thus confronted, Mach believed, "the public . . . loses its shyness towards scientific questions, and acquires an interest in scientific work which is a great help to the inquirer." To which he added that "the latter, in his turn, is brought to understand that his work is a small part only of the universal process of life, and that the results of his labors must redound to the benefit not only of himself and a few of his associates, but to that of the collective whole."

Of the lectures reprinted here, those on "The Economical Nature of Physical Inquiry" and "The Principle of Comparison in Physics" are classics in the philosophy of science. "On Transformation and Adaptation in Scientific Thought" and "The Part Played by Accident in Invention and Discovery" are also philosophical in tone, however, while "Why Has Man Two Eyes?" and "On Symmetry" are analytical in a smaller way.

In 1895 Mach was made professor of the history and theory of inductive philosophy at the University of Vienna, a position he held until 1901. He was then elected to the Austrian House of Peers. As the positivist principles he had expounded could be seen even while he lived to have been adopted by the Vienna Circle of scientists, so after he had died his thought remained alive in the work of what by then were known as the Logical Positivists, of whom Rudolf Carnap and Ludwig Wittgenstein are the best known. Mach may thus be said to have contributed significantly to the main development of scientific theory in this century. An account of this development, "The Philosophy of Science," by Herbert Feigl, who was himself a member of the Vienna Circle in the late 1920s, appeared in *The Great Ideas Today, 1969.*

Why Has Man Two Eyes?

Why has man two eyes? That the pretty symmetry of his face may not be disturbed, the artist answers. That his second eye may furnish a substitute for his first if that be lost, says the farsighted economist. That we may weep with two eyes at the sins of the world, replies the religious enthusiast.

Odd opinions! Yet if you should approach a modern scientist with this question you might consider yourself fortunate if you escaped with less than a rebuff. "Pardon me, madam, or my dear sir," he would say, with stern expression, "man fulfils no purpose in the possession of his eyes; nature is not a person, and consequently not so vulgar as to pursue purposes of any kind."

Still an unsatisfactory answer! I once knew a professor who would shut with horror the mouths of his pupils if they put to him such an unscientific question.

But ask a more tolerant person, ask me. I, I candidly confess, do not know exactly why man has two eyes, but the reason partly is, I think, that I may see you here before me to-night and talk with you upon this delightful subject.

Again you smile incredulously. Now this is one of those questions that a hundred wise men together could not answer. You have heard, so far, only five of these wise men. You will certainly want to be spared the opinions of the other ninety-five. To the first you will reply that we should look just as pretty if we were born with only one eye, like the Cyclops; to the second we should be much better off, according to his principle, if we had four or eight eyes, and that in this respect we are vastly inferior to spiders; to the third, that you are not just in the mood to weep; to the fourth, that the unqualified interdiction of

the question excites rather than satisfies your curiosity; while of me you will dispose by saying that my pleasure is not as intense as I think, and certainly not great enough to justify the existence of a double eye in man since the fall of Adam.

But since you are not satisfied with my brief and obvious answer, you have only yourselves to blame for the consequences. You must now listen to a longer and more learned explanation, such as it is in my power to give.

As the church of science, however, debars the question "Why?" let us put the matter in a purely orthodox way: Man has two eyes, what *more* can he see with two than with one?

I will invite you to take a walk with me. We see before us a wood. What is it that makes this real wood contrast so favorably with a painted wood, no matter how perfect the painting may be? What makes the one so much more lovely than the other? Is it the vividness of the coloring, the distribution of the lights and the shadows? I think not. On the contrary, it seems to me that in this respect painting can accomplish very much.

The cunning hand of the painter can conjure up with a few strokes of his brush forms of wonderful plasticity. By the help of other means even more can be attained. Photographs of reliefs are so plastic that we often imagine we can actually lay hold of the elevations and depressions.

But one thing the painter never can give with the vividness that nature does—the difference of near and far. In the real woods you see plainly that you can lay hold of some trees, but that others are inaccessibly far. The picture of the painter is rigid. The picture of the real woods changes on the slight-

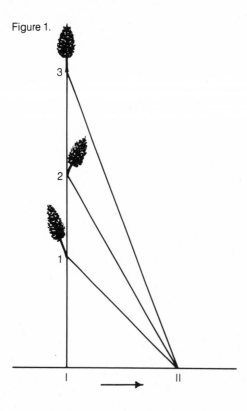

Figure 1.

est movement. Now this branch is hidden behind that; now that behind this. The trees are alternately visible and invisible.

Let us look at this matter a little more closely. For convenience sake we shall remain upon the highway, I, II (fig. 1). To the right and the left lies the forest. Standing at I, we see, let us say, three trees (1, 2, 3) in a line, so that the two remote ones are covered by the nearest. Moving further along, this changes. At II we shall not have to look round so far to see the remotest tree 3 as to see the nearer tree 2, nor so far to see this as to see 1. *Hence, as we move onward, objects that are near to us seem to lag behind as compared with objects that are remote from us, the lagging increasing with the proximity of the objects.* Very remote objects, towards which we must always look in the same direction as we proceed, appear to travel along with us.

If we should see, therefore, jutting above the brow of yonder hill the tops of two trees

whose distance from us we were in doubt about, we should have in our hands a very easy means of deciding the question. We should take a few steps forward, say to the right, and the tree-top which receded most to the left would be the one nearer to us. In truth, from the amount of the recession a geometer could actually determine the distance of the trees from us without ever going near them. It is simply the scientific development of this perception that enables us to measure the distances of the stars.

Hence, from change of view in forward motion the distances of objects in our field of vision can be measured.

Rigorously, however, even forward motion is not necessary. For every observer is composed really of *two* observers. Man has *two* eyes. The right eye is a short step ahead of the left eye in the right-hand direction. Hence, the two eyes receive *different* pictures of the same woods. The right eye will see the near trees displaced to the left, and the left eye will see them displaced to the right, the displacement being greater, the greater the proximity. This difference is sufficient for forming ideas of distance.

We may now readily convince ourselves of the following facts:

1. With one eye, the other being shut, you have a very uncertain judgment of distances. You will find it, for example, no easy task, with one eye shut, to thrust a stick through a ring hung up before you; you will miss the ring in almost every instance.

2. You see the same object differently with the right eye from what you do with the left. Place a lamp-shade on the table in front of you with its broad opening turned downwards, and look at it from above (fig. 2). You will see with your right eye the image 2, with your left eye the image 1. Again, place the shade with its wide opening turned upwards; you will receive with your right eye the image 4, with your left eye the image 3. Euclid mentions phenomena of this character.

3. Finally, you know that it is easy to judge of distances with both eyes. Accordingly your judgment must spring in some way from a

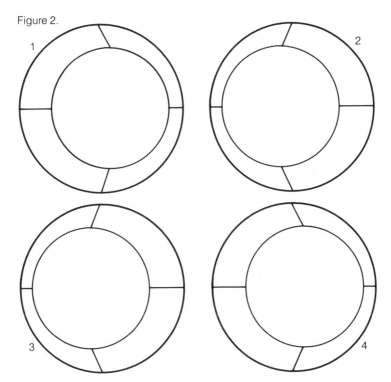

Figure 2.

co-operation of the two eyes. In the preceding example the openings in the different images received by the two eyes seem displaced with respect to one another, and this displacement is sufficient for the inference that the one opening is nearer than the other.

I have no doubt that you, ladies, have frequently received delicate compliments upon your eyes, but I feel sure that no one has ever told you, and I know not whether it will flatter you, that you have in your eyes, be they blue or black, little geometricians. You say you know nothing of them? Well, for that matter, neither do I. But the facts are as I tell you.

You understand little of geometry? I shall accept that confession. Yet with the help of your two eyes you judge of distances? Surely that is a geometrical problem. And what is more, you know the solution of this problem: for you estimate distances correctly. If, then, *you* do not solve the problem, the little

geometricians in your eyes must do it clandestinely and whisper the solution to you. I doubt not they are fleet little fellows.

What amazes me most here is, that you know nothing about these little geometricians. But perhaps they also know nothing about you. Perhaps they are models of punctuality, routine clerks who bother about nothing but their fixed work. In that case we may be able to deceive the gentlemen.

If we present to our right eye an image which looks exactly like the lamp shade for the right eye, and to our left eye an image which looks exactly like a lamp-shade for the left eye, we shall imagine that we see the whole lamp-shade bodily before us.

You know the experiment. If you are practised in squinting, you can perform it directly with the figure, looking with your right eye at the right image, and with your left eye at the left image. In this way the experiment was first performed by Elliott. Improved and perfected, its form is Wheatstone's stereoscope, made so popular and useful by Brewster.

By taking two photographs of the same object from two different points, corresponding to the two eyes, a very clear three-dimensional picture of distant places or buildings can be produced by the stereoscope.

But the stereoscope accomplishes still more than this. It can visualise things for us which we never see with equal clearness in real objects. You know that if you move much while your photograph is being taken, your picture will come out like that of a Hindu deity, with several heads or several arms, which, at the spaces where they overlap, show forth with equal distinctness, so that we seem to see the one picture *through* the other. If a person moves quickly away from the camera before the impression is completed, the objects behind him will also be imprinted upon the photograph; the person will look transparent. Photographic ghosts are made in this way.

Some very useful applications may be made of this discovery. For example, if we photograph a machine stereoscopically, successively removing during the operation the single parts (where of course the impression suffers interruptions), we obtain a transparent view, endowed with all the marks of spatial solidity, in which is distinctly visualised the interaction of parts normally concealed. I have employed this method for obtaining transparent stereoscopic views of anatomical structures.

You see, photography is making stupendous advances, and there is great danger that in time some malicious artist will photograph his innocent patrons with solid views of their most secret thoughts and emotions. How tranquil politics will then be! What rich harvests our detective force will reap!

*   *   *

By the joint action of the two eyes, therefore, we arrive at our judgments of distances, as also of the forms of bodies.

Permit me to mention here a few additional facts connected with this subject, which will assist us in the comprehension of certain phenomena in the history of civilisation.

You have often heard, and know from personal experience, that remote objects appear perspectively dwarfed. In fact, it is easy to satisfy yourself that you can cover the image of a man a few feet away from you simply by holding up your finger a short distance in front of your eye. Still, as a general rule, you do not notice this shrinkage of objects. On the contrary, you imagine you see a man at the end of a large hall, as large as you see him near by you. For your eye, in its measurement of the distances, makes remote objects correspondingly larger. The eye, so to speak, is aware of this perspective contraction and is not deceived by it, although its possessor is unconscious of the fact. All persons who have attempted to draw from nature have vividly felt the difficulty which this superior dexterity of the eye causes the perspective conception. Not until one's judgment of distances is made uncertain, by their size, or from lack of points of reference, or from being too quickly changed, is the perspective rendered very prominent.

On sweeping round a curve on a rapidly moving railway train, where a wide prospect is suddenly opened up, the men upon distant hills appear like dolls. You have at the moment, here, no known references for the measurement of distances. The stones at the entrance of a tunnel grow visibly larger as we ride towards it; they shrink visibly in size as we ride from it.

Usually both eyes work together. As certain views are frequently repeated, and lead always to substantially the same judgments of distances, the eyes in time must acquire a special skill in geometrical constructions. In the end, undoubtedly, this skill is so increased that a single eye alone is often tempted to exercise that office.

Permit me to elucidate this point by an example. Is any sight more familiar to you than that of a vista down a long street? Who has not looked with hopeful eyes time and again into a street and measured its depth? I will take you now into an art-gallery where

I will suppose you to see a picture representing a vista into a street. The artist has not spared his rulers to get his perspective perfect. The geometrician in your left eye thinks, "Ah ha! I have computed that case a hundred times or more. I know it by heart. It is a vista into a street," he continues; "where the houses are lower is the remote end." The geometrician in the right eye, too much at his ease to question his possibly peevish comrade in the matter, answers the same. But the sense of duty of these punctual little fellows is at once rearoused. They set to work at their calculations and immediately find that all the points of the picture are equally distant from them, that is, lie all upon a plane surface.

What opinion will you now accept, the first or the second? If you accept the first you will see distinctly the vista. If you accept the second you will see nothing but a painted sheet of distorted images.

It seems to you a trifling matter to look at a picture and understand its perspective. Yet centuries elapsed before humanity came fully to appreciate this trifle, and even the majority of you first learned it from education.

I can remember very distinctly that at three years of age all perspective drawings appeared to me as gross caricatures of objects. I could not understand why artists made tables so broad at one end and so narrow at the other. Real tables seemed to me just as broad at one end as at the other, because my eye made and interpreted its calculations without my intervention. But that the picture of the table on the plane surface was not to be conceived as a plane painted surface but stood for a table and so was to be imaged with all the attributes of extension was a joke that I did not understand. But I have the consolation that whole nations have not understood it.

Ingenuous people there are who take the mock murders of the stage for real murders, the dissembled actions of the players for real actions, and who can scarcely restrain themselves, when the characters of the play are sorely pressed, from running in deep indignation to their assistance. Others, again, can never forget that the beautiful landscapes of the stage are painted, that Richard III. is only the actor, Mr. Booth, whom they have met time and again at the clubs.

Both points of view are equally mistaken. To look at a drama or a picture properly one must understand that both are *shows*, simply *denoting* something real. A certain preponderance of the intellectual life over the sensuous life is requisite for such an achievement, where the intellectual elements are safe from destruction by the direct sensuous impressions. A certain liberty in choosing one's point of view is necessary, a sort of humor, I might say, which is strongly wanting in children and in childlike peoples.

Let us look at a few historical facts. I shall not take you as far back as the stone age, although we possess sketches from this epoch which show very original ideas of perspective. But let us begin our sight-seeing in the tombs and ruined temples of ancient Egypt, where the numberless reliefs and gorgeous colorings have defied the ravages of thousands of years.

A rich and motley life is here opened to us. We find the Egyptians represented in all conditions of life. What at once strikes our attention in these pictures is the delicacy of their technical execution. The contours are extremely exact and distinct. But on the other hand only a few bright colors are found, unblended and without trace of transition. Shadows are totally wanting. The paint is laid on the surfaces in equal thicknesses.

Shocking for the modern eye is the perspective. All the figures are equally large, with the exception of the king, whose form is unduly exaggerated. Near and far appear equally large. Perspective contraction is nowhere employed. A pond with water-fowl is represented flat, as if its surface were vertical.

Human figures are portrayed as they are never seen, the legs from the side, the face in profile. The breast lies in its full breadth across the plane of representation. The heads of cattle appear in profile, while the horns lie in the plane of the drawing. The principle which the Egyptians followed might be best expressed by saying that their figures are pressed in the plane of the drawing as plants are pressed in a herbarium.

The matter is simply explained. If the Egyptians were accustomed to looking at things ingenuously with both eyes at once, the construction of perspective pictures in space could not be familiar to them. They saw all arms, all legs on real men in their natural lengths. The figures pressed into the planes resembled more closely, of course, in their eyes the originals than perspective pictures could.

This will be better understood if we reflect that painting was developed from relief. The minor dissimilarities between the pressed figures and the originals must gradually have compelled men to the adoption of perspective drawing. But physiologically the painting of the Egyptions is just as much justified as the drawings of our children are.

A slight advance beyond the Egyptians is shown by the Assyrians. The reliefs rescued from the ruined mounds of Nimrod at Mossul are, upon the whole, similar to the Egyptian reliefs. They were made known to us principally by Layard.

Painting enters on a new phase among the Chinese. This people have a marked feeling for perspective and correct shading, yet without being very logical in the application of their principles. Here, too, it seems, they took the first step but did not go far. In harmony with this immobility is their constitution, in which the muzzle and the bamboo-rod play significant functions. In accord with it, too, is their language, which like the language of children has not yet developed into a grammar, or, rather, according to the modern conception, has not yet degenerated into a grammar. It is the same also with their music which is satisfied with the five-toned scale.

The mural paintings at Herculaneum and Pompeii are distinguished by grace of representation, as also by a pronounced sense for perspective and correct illumination, yet they are not at all scrupulous in construction.

Here still we find abbreviations avoided. But to offset this defect, the members of the body are brought into unnatural positions, in which they appear in their full lengths. Abridgements are more frequently observed in clothed than in unclothed figures.

A satisfactory explanation of these phenomena first occurred to me on the making of a few simple experiments which show how differently one may see the same object, after some mastery of one's senses has been attained, simply by the arbitrary movement of the attention.

Look at the annexed drawing (fig. 3). It represents a folded sheet of paper with either its depressed or its elevated side turned towards you, as you wish. You can conceive the drawing in either sense, and in either case it will appear to you differently.

Figure 3.

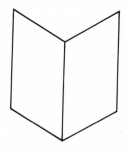

If, now, you have a real folded sheet of paper on the table before you, with its sharp edges turned towards you, you can, on looking at it with one eye, see the sheet alternately elevated, as it really is, or depressed. Here, however, a remarkable phenomenon is presented. When you see the sheet properly, neither illumination nor form presents anything conspicuous. When you see it bent back you see it perspectively distorted. Light and shadow appear much brighter or darker, or as if overlaid thickly with bright colors. Light and shadow now appear devoid of all cause. They no longer harmonise with the body's form, and are thus rendered much more prominent.

In common life we employ the perspective and illumination of objects to determine their forms and position. Hence we do not notice the lights, the shadows, and the distortions. They first powerfully enter consciousness when we employ a different construction from the usual spatial one. In looking at the planar image of a camera obscura we are amazed at the plenitude of the light and the profundity of the shadows, both of which we do not notice in real objects.

In my earliest youth the shadows and lights on pictures appeared to me as spots void of meaning. When I began to draw I regarded shading as a mere custom of artists. I once drew the portrait of our pastor, a friend of the family, and shaded, from no necessity, but simply from having seen something similar in other pictures, the whole half of his face black. I was subjected for this to a severe criticism on the part of my mother, and my deeply offended artist's pride is probably the reason that these facts remained so strongly impressed upon my memory.

You see, then, that many strange things, not only in the life of individuals, but also in that of humanity, and in the history of general civilisation, may be explained from the simple fact that man has two eyes.

Change man's eye and you change his conception of the world. We have observed the truth of this fact among our nearest kin, the Egyptians, the Chinese, and the lake-dwellers; how must it be among some of our remoter relatives,—with monkeys and other animals? Nature must appear totally different to animals equipped with substantially different eyes from those of men, as, for example, to insects. But for the present science must forego the pleasure of portraying this appearance, as we know very little as yet of the mode of operation of these organs.

It is an enigma even how nature appears to animals closely related to man; as to birds, who see scarcely anything with two eyes at once, but since their eyes are placed on opposite sides of their heads, have a separate field of vision for each.

The soul of man is pent up in the prison-house of his head; it looks at nature through its two windows, the eyes. It would also fain

Figure 4.

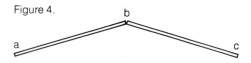

know how nature looks through other windows. A desire apparently never to be fuilfiled. But our love for nature is inventive, and here, too, much has been accomplished.

Placing before me an angular mirror, consisting of two plane mirrors slightly inclined to each other, I see my face twice reflected. In the right-hand mirror I obtain a view of the right side, and in the left-hand mirror a view of the left side, of my face. Also I shall see the face of a person standing in front of me, more to the right with my right eye, more to the left with my left. But in order to obtain such widely different views of a face as those shown in the angular mirror, my two eyes would have to be set much further apart from each other than they actually are.

Squinting with my right eye at the image in the right-hand mirror, with my left eye at the image in the left-hand mirror, my vision will be the vision of a giant having an enormous head with his two eyes set far apart. This, also, is the impression which my own face makes upon me. I see it now, single and solid. Fixing my gaze, the relief from second to second is magnified, the eyebrows start forth prominently from above the eyes, the nose seems to grow a foot in length, my mustache shoots forth like a fountain from my lip, the teeth seem to retreat immeasurably. But by far the most horrible aspect of the phenomenon is the nose.

Interesting in this connexion is the telestereoscope of Helmholtz. In the telestereoscope we view a landscape by looking with our right eye (fig. 5) through the mirror a into the mirror A, and with our left eye through the mirror b into the mirror B. The mirrors A and B stand far apart. Again we see with the widely separated eyes of a giant. Everything appears dwarfed and near us. The distant mountains look like moss-covered stones at our feet. Between, you see the reduced model of a city, a veritable Liliput.

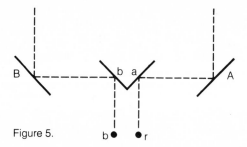

Figure 5.

You are tempted almost to stroke with your hand the soft forest and city, did you not fear that you might prick your fingers on the sharp, needle-shaped steeples, or that they might crackle and break off.

Liliput is no fable. We need only Swift's eyes, the telestereoscope, to see it.

Picture to yourself the reverse case. Let us suppose ourselves so small that we could take long walks in a forest of moss, and that our eyes were correspondingly near each other. The moss-fibres would appear like trees. On them we should see strange, unshapely monsters creeping about. Branches of the oak-tree, at whose base our moss-forest lay, would seem to us dark, immovable, myriad-branched clouds, painted high on the vault of heaven; just as the inhabitants of Saturn, forsooth, might see their enormous ring. On the tree-trunks of our mossy woodland we should find colossal globes several feet in diameter, brilliantly transparent, swayed by the winds with slow, peculiar motions. We should approach inquisitively and should find that these globes, in which here and there animals were gaily sporting, were liquid globes, in fact that they were water. A short, incautious step, the slightest contact, and woe betide us, our arm is irresistibly drawn by an invisible power into the interior of the sphere and held there unrelentingly fast! A drop of dew has engulfed in its capillary maw a manikin, in revenge for the thousands of drops that its big human counterparts have quaffed at breakfast. Thou shouldst have known, thou pygmy natural scientist, that with thy present puny bulk thou shouldst not joke with capillarity!

My terror at the accident brings me back to my senses. I see I have turned idyllic. You must pardon me. A patch of greensward, a moss or heather forest with its tiny inhabitants have incomparably more charms for me than many a bit of literature with its apotheosis of human character. If I had the gift of writing novels I should certainly not make John and Mary my characters. Nor should I transfer my loving pair to the Nile, nor to the age of the old Egyptian Pharaohs, although perhaps I should choose that time in preference to the present. For I must candidly confess that I hate the rubbish of history, interesting though it may be as a mere phenomenon, because we cannot simply observe it but must also *feel* it, because it comes to us mostly with supercilious arrogance, mostly unvanquished. The hero of my novel would be a cockchafer, venturing forth in his fifth year for the first time with his newly grown wings into the light, free air. Truly it could do no harm if man would thus throw off his inherited and acquired narrowness of mind by making himself acquainted with the worldview of allied creatures. He could not help gaining incomparably more in this way than the inhabitant of a small town would in circumnavigating the globe and getting acquainted with the views of strange peoples.

* * *

I have now conducted you, by many paths and byways, rapidly over hedge and ditch, to show you what wide vistas we may reach in every field by the rigorous pursuit of a single scientific fact. A close examination of the two eyes of man has conducted us not only into the dim recesses of humanity's childhood, but has also carried us far beyond the bourne of human life.

It has surely often struck you as strange that the sciences are divided into two great groups, that the so-called humanistic sciences, belonging to the so-called "higher education," are placed in almost a hostile attitude to the natural sciences.

I must confess I do not overmuch believe in this partition of the sciences. I believe that this view will appear as childlike and ingenuous to a matured age as the want of perspective in the old paintings of Egypt does to us. Can it really be that "higher culture" is to be gotten only from a few old pots and palimpsests, which are at best mere scraps of nature, or that more is to be learned from them alone than from all the rest of nature? I believe that both these sciences are simply parts of the same science, which have begun at different ends. If these two ends still act towards each other as the Montagues and Capulets, if their retainers still indulge in lively tilts, I believe that after all they are not in earnest. On the one side there is surely a Romeo, and on the other a Juliet, who, some day, it is hoped, will unite the two houses with a less tragic sequel than that of the play.

Philology began with the unqualified reverence and apotheosis of the Greeks. Now it has begun to draw other languages, other peoples and their histories, into its sphere; it has, through the mediation of comparative linguistics, already struck up, though as yet somewhat cautiously, a friendship with physiology.

Physical science began in the witch's kitchen. It now embraces the organic and inorganic worlds, and with the physiology of articulation and the theory of the senses, has even pushed its researches, at times impertinently, into the province of mental phenomena.

In short, we come to the understanding of much within us solely by directing our glance without, and *vice versa*. Every object belongs to both sciences. You, ladies, are very interesting and difficult problems for the psychologist, but you are also extremely pretty phenomena of nature. Church and State are objects of the historian's research, but not less phenomena of nature, and in part, indeed, very curious phenomena. If the historical sciences have inaugurated wide extensions of view by presenting to us the thoughts of new and strange peoples, the physical sciences in a certain sense do this in a still greater degree. In making man disappear in the All, in annihilating him, so to speak, they force him to take an unprejudiced position without himself, and to form his judgments by a different standard from that of the pretty human.

But if you should ask me now why man has two eyes, I should answer:

That he may look at nature justly and accurately; that he may come to understand that he himself, with all his views, correct and incorrect, with all his *haute politique*, is simply an evanescent shred of nature; that, to speak with Mephistopheles, he is a part of the part, and that it is absolutely unjustified,

For man, the microscopic fool, to see
Himself a whole so frequently.

On Symmetry*

An ancient philosopher once remarked that people who cudgelled their brains about the nature of the moon reminded him of men who discussed the laws and institutions of a distant city of which they had heard no more than the name. The true philosopher, he said, should turn his glance within, should study himself and his notions of right and wrong; only thence could he derive real profit.

This ancient formula for happiness might be restated in the familiar words of the Psalm:

Dwell in the land, and verily thou shalt be fed.

To-day, if he could rise from the dead and walk about among us, this philosopher would marvel much at the different turn which matters have taken.

The motions of the moon and the other heavenly bodies are accurately known. Our knowledge of the motions of our own body is by far not so complete. The mountains and natural divisions of the moon have been accurately outlined on maps, but physiologists are just beginning to find their way in the geography of the brain. The chemical constitution of many fixed stars has already been investigated. The chemical processes of the animal body are questions of much greater difficulty and complexity. We have our *Mécanique celeste*. But a *Mécanique sociale* or a *Mécanique morale* of equal trustworthiness remains to be written.

Our philosopher would indeed admit that we have made great progress. But we have not followed his advice. The patient has recovered, but he took for his recovery exactly the opposite of what the doctor prescribed.

Humanity is now returned, much wiser, from its journey in celestial space, against which it was so solemnly warned. Men, after having become acquainted with the great and simple facts of the world without, are now beginning to examine critically the world within. It sounds absurd, but it is true, that only after we have thought about the moon are we able to take up ourselves. It was necessary that we should acquire simple and clear ideas in a less complicated domain, before we entered the more intricate one of psychology, and with these ideas astronomy principally furnished us.

To attempt any description of that stupendous movement, which, originally springing out of the physical sciences, went beyond the domain of physics and is now occupied with the problems of psychology, would be presumptuous in this place. I shall only attempt here, to illustrate to you by a few simple examples the methods by which the province of psychology can be reached from the facts of the physical world—especially the adjacent province of sense-perception. And I wish it to be remembered that my brief attempt is not to be taken as a measure of the present state of such scientific questions.

* * *

It is a well-known fact that some objects please us, while others do not. Generally speaking, anything that is constructed according to fixed and logically followed rules, is a product of tolerable beauty. We see thus nature herself, who always acts according to fixed rules, constantly producing such pretty

---

* Delivered before the German Casino of Prague, in the winter of 1871.

things. Every day the physicist is confronted in his workshop with the most beautiful vibration-figures, tone-figures, phenomena of polarisation, and forms of diffraction.

A rule always presupposes a repetition. Repetitions, therefore, will probably be found to play some important part in the production of agreeable effects. Of course, the nature of agreeable effects is not exhausted by this. Furthermore, the repetition of a physical event becomes the source of agreeable effects only when it is connected with a repetition of sensations.

An excellent example that repetition of sensations is a source of agreeable effects is furnished by the copy-book of every schoolboy, which is usually a treasure-house of such things, and only in need of an Abbé Domenech to become celebrated. Any figure, no matter how crude or poor, if several times repeated, with the repetitions placed in line, will produce a tolerable frieze.

Also the pleasant effect of symmetry is due to the repetition of sensations. Let us abandon ourselves a moment to this thought, yet not imagine when we have developed it, that we have fully exhausted the nature of the agreeable, much less of the beautiful.

First, let us get a clear conception of what symmetry is. And in preference to a definition let us take a living picture. You know that the reflexion of an object in a mirror has a great likeness to the object itself. All its proportions and outlines are the same. Yet there is a difference between the object and its reflexion in the mirror, which you will readily observe.

Hold your right hand before a mirror, and you will see in the mirror a left hand. Your right glove will produce its mate in the glass. For you could never use the reflexion of your right glove, if it were present to you as a real thing, for covering your right hand, but only for covering your left. Similarly, your right ear will give as its reflexion a left ear; and you will at once perceive that the left half of your body could very easily be substituted for the reflexion of your right half. Now just as in the place of a missing right ear a left ear cannot be put, unless the lobule of the ear be turned upwards, or the opening into the concha backwards, so, despite all similarity of form, the reflexion of an object can never take the place of the object itself.

The reason of this difference between the object and its reflexion is simple. The reflexion appears as far behind the mirror as the object is in front of it. The parts of the object, accordingly, which are nearest the mirror will also be nearest the mirror in the reflexion. Consequently, the succession of the parts in the reflexion will be reversed, as may best be seen in the reflexion of the face of a watch or of a manuscript.

It will also be readily seen, that if a point of the object be joined with its reflexion in the image, the line of junction will cut the mirror at right angles and be bisected by it. This holds true of all corresponding points of object and image.

If, now, we can divide an object by a plane into two halves so that each half, as seen in the reflecting plane of division, is a reproduction of the other half, such an object is termed symmetrical, and the plane of division is called the plane of symmetry.

If the plane of symmetry is vertical, we can say that the body is vertically symmetrical. An example of vertical symmetry is a Gothic cathedral.

If the plane of symmetry is horizontal, we can say that the object is horizontally symmetrical. A landscape on the shores of a lake with its reflexion in the water, is a system of horizontal symmetry.

Exactly here is a noticeable difference. The vertical symmetry of a Gothic cathedral

Figure 6.

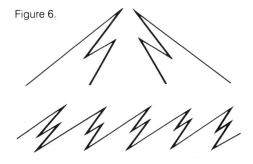

strikes us at once, whereas we can travel up and down the whole length of the Rhine or the Hudson without becoming aware of the symmetry between objects and their reflexions in the water. Vertical symmetry pleases us, whilst horizontal symmetry is indifferent, and is noticed only by the experienced eye.

Whence arises this difference? I say from the fact that vertical symmetry produces a repetition of the same sensation, while horizontal symmetry does not. I shall now show that this is so.

Let us look at the following letters:

d   b

q   p

It is a fact known to all mothers and teachers, that children in their first attempts to read and write, constantly confound **d** and **b**, and **q** and **p**, but never **d** and **q**, or **b** and **p**. Now **d** and **b** and **q** and **p** are the two halves of a *vertically* symmetrical figure, while **d** and **q**, and **b** and **p** are two halves of a *horizontally* symmetrical figure. The first two are confounded; but confusion is only possible of things that excite in us the same or similar sensations.

Figures of two flower-girls are frequently seen on the decorations of gardens and of drawing-rooms, one of whom carries a flower-basket in her right hand and the other a flower-basket in her left. All know how apt we are, unless we are very careful, to confound these figures with one another.

While turning round a thing from right to left is scarcely noticed, the eye is not at all indifferent to the turning of a thing upside down. A human face which has been turned upside down is scarcely recognisable as a face, and makes an impression which is altogether strange. The reason of this is not to be sought in the unwontedness of the sight, for it is just as difficult to recognise an arabesque that has been inverted, where there can be no question of a habit. This curious fact is the foundation of the familiar jokes played with the portraits of unpopular personages, which are so drawn that in the upright position of the page an exact picture of

the person is presented, but on being inverted some popular animal is shown.

It is a fact, then, that the two halves of a vertically symmetrical figure are easily confounded and that they therefore probably produce very nearly the same sensations. The question, accordingly, arises, *why* do the two halves of a vertically symmetrical figure produce the same or similar sensations? The answer is: Because our apparatus of vision, which consists of our eyes and of the accompanying muscular apparatus is itself vertically symmetrical.

Whatever external resemblances one eye may have with another they are still not alike. The right eye of a man cannot take the place of a left eye any more than a left ear or left hand can take the place of a right one. By artificial means, we can change the part which each of our eyes plays. (Wheatstone's pseudoscope.) But we then find ourselves in an entirely new and strange world. What is convex appears concave; what is concave, convex. What is distant appears near, and what is near appears far.

The left eye is the reflexion of the right. And the light-feeling retina of the left eye is a reflexion of the light-feeling retina of the right, in all its functions.

The lense of the eye, like a magic lantern, casts images of objects on the retina. And you may picture to yourself the light-feeling retina of the eye, with its countless nerves, as a hand with innumerable fingers, adapted to feeling light. The ends of the visual nerves, like our fingers, are endowed with varying degrees of sensitiveness. The two retinæ act like a right and a left hand; the sensation of touch and the sensation of light in the two instances are similar.

Examine the right-hand portion of this letter T: namely Γ. Instead of the two retinæ on which this image falls, imagine feeling the object, my two hands. The Γ, grasped with the right hand, gives a different sensation from that which it gives when grasped with the left. But if we turn our character about from right to left, thus: ꓶ, it will give the same sensation in the left hand that it gave before in the right. The sensation is repeated.

If we take a whole T, the right half will produce in the right hand the same sensation that the left half produces in the left, and *vice versa*.

The symmetrical figure gives the same sensation twice.

If we turn the T over thus:⊢, or invert the half T thus: L, so long as we do not change the position of our hands we can make no use of the foregoing reasoning.

The retinæ, in fact, are exactly like our two hands. They, too, have their thumbs and index fingers, though they are thousands in number; and we may say the thumbs are on the side of the eye near the nose, and the remaining fingers on the side away from the nose.

With this I hope to have made perfectly clear that the pleasing effect of symmetry is chiefly due to the repetition of sensations, and that the effect in question takes place in symmetrical figures, only where there is a repetition of sensation. The pleasing effect of regular figures, the preference which straight lines, especially vertical and horizontal straight lines, enjoy, is founded on a similar reason. A straight line, both in a horizontal and in a vertical position, can cast on the two retinæ the same image, which falls moreover on symmetrically corresponding spots. This also, it would appear, is the reason of our psychological preference of straight to curved lines, and not their property of being the shortest distance between two points. The straight line is felt, to put the matter briefly, as symmetrical to itself, which is the case also with the plane. Curved lines are felt as deviations from straight lines, that is, as deviations from symmetry.[1] The presence of a sense for symmetry in people possessing only one eye from birth, is indeed a riddle. Of course, the sense of symmetry, although primarily acquired by means of the eyes, cannot be wholly limited to the visual organs. It must also be deeply rooted in other parts of the organism by ages of practice and can thus not be eliminated forthwith by the loss of one eye. Also, when an eye is lost, the symmetrical

muscular apparatus is left, as is also the symmetrical apparatus of innervation.

It appears, however, unquestionable that the phenomena mentioned have, in the main, their origin in the peculiar structure of our eyes. It will therefore be seen at once that our notions of what is beautiful and ugly would undergo a change if our eyes were different. Also, if this view is correct, the theory of the so-called eternally beautiful is somewhat mistaken. It can scarcely be doubted that our culture, or form of civilisation, which stamps upon the human body its unmistakable traces, should not also modify our conceptions of the beautiful. Was not formerly the development of all musical beauty restricted to the narrow limits of a five-toned scale?

The fact that a repetition of sensations is productive of pleasant effects is not restricted to the realm of the visible. To-day, both the musician and the physicist know that the harmonic or the melodic addition of one tone to another affects us agreeably only when the added tone reproduces a part of the sensation which the first one excited. When I add an octave to a fundamental tone, I hear in the octave a part of what was heard in the fundamental tone. (Helmholtz.) But it is not my purpose to develop this idea fully here. We shall only ask to-day, whether there is anything similar to the symmetry of figures in the province of sounds.

Look at the reflexion of your piano in the mirror.

You will at once remark that you have never seen such a piano in the actual world, for it has its high keys to the left and its low ones

---

[1] The fact that the first and second differential coefficients of a curve are directly seen, but the higher coefficients not, is very simply explained. The first gives the position of the tangent, the declination of the straight line from the position of symmetry, the second the declination of the curve from the straight line. It is, perhaps, not unprofitable to remark here that the ordinary method of testing rulers and plane surfaces (by reversed applications) ascertains the deviation of the object from symmetry to itself.

to the right. Such pianos are not manufactured.

If you could sit down at such a piano and play in your usual manner, plainly every step which you imagined you were performing in the upward scale would be executed as a corresponding step in the downward scale. The effect would be not a little surprising.

For the practised musician who is always accustomed to hearing certain sounds produced when certain keys are struck, it is quite an anomalous spectacle to watch a player in the glass and to observe that he always does the opposite of what we hear.

But still more remarkable would be the effect of attempting to strike a harmony on such a piano. For a melody it is not indifferent whether we execute a step in an upward or a downward scale. But for a harmony, so great a difference is not produced by reversal. I always retain the same consonance whether I add to a fundamental note an upper or a lower third. Only the order of the intervals of the harmony is reversed. In point of fact, when we execute a movement in a major key on our reflected piano, we hear a sound in a minor key, and *vice versa*.

It now remains to execute the experiments indicated. Instead of playing upon the piano in the mirror, which is impossible, or of having a piano of this kind built, which would be somewhat expensive, we may perform our experiments in a simpler manner, as follows:

1) We play on our own piano in our usual manner, look into the mirror, and then repeat on our real piano what we see in the mirror. In this way we transform all steps upwards into corresponding steps downwards. We play a movement, and then another movement, which, with respect to the keyboard, is symmetrical to the first.

2) We place a mirror beneath the music in which the notes are reflected as in a body of water, and play according to the notes in the mirror. In this way also, all steps upwards are changed into corresponding, equal steps downwards.

3) We turn the music upside down and read the notes from right to left and from below upwards. In doing this, we must regard all sharps as flats and all flats as sharps, because they correspond to half lines and spaces. Besides, in this use of the music we can only employ the bass clef, as only in this clef are the notes not changed by symmetrical reversal.

You can judge of the effect of these experiments from the examples which appear in the annexed musical cut (fig. 7). The movement which appears in the upper lines is symmetrically reversed in the lower.

The effect of the experiments may be briefly formulated. The melody is rendered unrecognisable. The harmony suffers a transposition from a major into a minor key and *vice versa*. The study of these pretty effects, which have long been familiar to physicists and musicians, was revived some years ago by Von Oettingen.[2]

Now, although in all the preceding examples I have transposed steps upward into equal and similar steps downward, that is, as we may justly say, have played for every movement the movement which is symmetrical to it, yet the ear notices either little or nothing of symmetry. The transposition from a major to a minor key is the sole indication of symmetry remaining. The symmetry is there for the mind, but is wanting for sensation. No symmetry exists for the ear, because a reversal of musical sounds conditions no repetition of sensations. If we had an ear for height and an ear for depth, just as we have an eye for the right and an eye for the left, we should also find that symmetrical sound-structures existed for our auditory organs. The contrast of major and minor for the ear corresponds to inversion for the eye, which is also only symmetry for the mind, but not for sensation.

By way of supplement to what I have said, I will add a brief remark for my mathematical readers.

---

[2] A. von Oettingen, *Harmoniesystem in dualer Entwicklung*. Leipsic and Dorpat, 1866.

Figure 7.

Our musical notation is essentially a graphical representation of a piece of music in the form of curves, where the time is the abscissæ, and the logarithms of the number of vibrations the ordinates. The deviations of musical notation from this principle are only such as facilitate interpretation, or are due to historical accidents.

If, now, it be further observed that the sensation of pitch is proportional to the logarithm of the number of vibrations, and that the intervals between the notes correspond to the differences of the logarithms of the numbers of vibrations, the justification will be found in these facts of calling the harmonies and melodies which appear in the mirror, symmetrical to the original ones.

*   *   *

I simply wish to bring home to your minds by these fragmentary remarks that the progress of the physical sciences has been of great help to those branches of psychology that have not scorned to consider the results of physical research. On the other hand, psychology is beginning to return, as it were, in a spirit of thankfulness, the powerful stimulus which it received from physics.

The theories of physics which reduce all phenomena to the motion and equilibrium of smallest particles, the so-called molecular theories, have been gravely threatened by the progress of the theory of the senses and of space, and we may say that their days are numbered.

I have shown in another work that the musical scale is simply a species of space—a space, however, of only one dimension, and that, a one-sided one. If, now, a person who could only hear, should attempt to develop a conception of the world in this, his linear space, he would become involved in many difficulties, as his space would be incompetent to comprehend the many sides of the relations of reality. But is it any more justifiable for us, to attempt to force the whole world into the space of our eye, in aspects in which it is not accessible to the eye? Yet this is the dilemma of all molecular theories.

We possess, however, a sense, which, with respect to the scope of the relations which it can comprehend, is richer than any other. It is our reason. This stands above the senses. It alone is competent to found a permanent and sufficient view of the world. The mechanical conception of the world has per-

formed wonders since Galileo's time. But it must now yield to a broader view of things. A further development of this idea is beyond the limits of my present purpose.

One more point and I have done. The advice of our philosopher to restrict ourselves to what is near at hand and useful in our researches, which finds a kind of exemplification in the present cry of inquirers for limitation and division of labor, must not be too slavishly followed. In the seclusion of our closets, we often rack our brains in vain to fulfil a work, the means of accomplishing which lies before our very doors. If the inquirer must be perforce a shoemaker, tapping constantly at his last, it may perhaps be permitted him to be a shoemaker of the type of Hans Sachs, who did not deem it beneath him to take a look now and then at his neighbor's work and to comment on the latter's doings.

Let this be my apology, therefore, if I have forsaken for a moment to-day the last of my specialty.

The Economical Nature of Physical Inquiry*

When the human mind, with its limited powers, attempts to mirror in itself the rich life of the world, of which it is itself only a small part, and which it can never hope to exhaust, it has every reason for proceeding economically. Hence that tendency, expressed in the philosophy of all times, to compass by a few organic thoughts the fundamental features of reality. "Life understands not death, nor death life." So spake an old Chinese philosopher. Yet in his unceasing desire to diminish the boundaries of the incomprehensible, man has always been engaged in attempts to understand death by life and life by death.

Among the ancient civilised peoples, nature was filled with demons and spirits having the feelings and desires of men. In all essential features, this animistic view of nature, as Tylor[1] has aptly termed it, is shared in common by the fetish-worshipper of modern Africa and the most advanced nations of antiquity. As a theory of the world it has never completely disappeared. The monotheism of the Christians never fully overcame it, no more than did that of the Jews. In the belief in witchcraft and in the superstitions of the sixteenth and seventeenth centuries, the centuries of the rise of natural science, it assumed frightful pathological dimensions. Whilst Stevinus,[2] Kepler, and Galileo were slowly rearing the fabric of modern physical science, a cruel and relentless war was waged with firebrand and rack against the devils that glowered from every corner. To-day even, apart from all survivals of that period, apart from the traces of fetishism which still inhere in our physical concepts,[3] those very ideas still covertly lurk in the practices of modern spiritualism.

By the side of this animistic conception of the world, we meet from time to time, indifferent forms, from Democritus to the present day, another view, which likewise claims exclusive competency to comprehend the universe. This view may be characterised as the *physico-mechanical* view of the world. To-day, that view holds, indisputably, the first place in the thoughts of men, and determines the ideals and the character of our times. The coming of the mind of man into the full consciousness of its powers, in the eighteenth century, was a period of genuine disillusionment. It produced the splendid precedent of a life really worthy of man, competent to overcome the old barbarism in the practical fields of life; it created the *Critique of Pure Reason*,[4] which banished into the realm of shadows the sham-ideas of the old metaphysics; it pressed into the hands of the mechanical philosophy the reins which it now holds.

The oft-quoted words of the great Laplace,[5] which I will now give, have the ring of a jubilant toast to the scientific achievements of the eighteenth century: "A mind to which were given for a single instant all the forces of nature and the mutual positions of all its

---

* An address delivered before the anniversary meeting of the Imperial Academy of Sciences, at Vienna, May 25, 1882.

[1] Sir Edward Burnett Tylor, author of *Primitive Culture* (1871).

[2] Simon Stevinus (1548–1620), a mathematician whose work on gravity, refuting the theory that heavy bodies fall faster than light ones, preceded Galileo's.

[3] Tylor, loc. cit.

[4] See *GBWW*, Vol. 42.

[5] *Essai philosophique sur les probabilités*. 6th Ed. Paris, 1840, p. 4. The necessary consideration of the initial velocities is lacking in this formulation.

masses, if it were otherwise powerful enough to subject these problems to analysis, could grasp, with a single formula, the motions of the largest masses as well as of the smallest atoms; nothing would be uncertain for it; the future and the past would lie revealed before its eyes." In writing these words, Laplace, as we know, had also in mind the atoms of the brain. That idea has been expressed more forcibly still by some of his followers, and it is not too much to say that Laplace's ideal is substantially that of the great majority of modern scientists.

Gladly do we accord to the creator of the *Mécanique céleste* the sense of lofty pleasure awakened in him by the great success of the Enlightenment, to which we too owe our intellectual freedom. But today, with minds undisturbed and before *new* tasks, it becomes physical science to secure itself against self-deception by a careful study of its character, so that it can pursue with greater sureness its true objects. If I step, therefore, beyond the narrow precincts of my specialty in this discussion, to trespass on friendly neighboring domains, I may plead in my excuse that the subject-matter of knowledge is common to all domains of research, and that fixed, sharp lines of demarcation cannot be drawn.

The belief in occult magic powers of nature has gradually died away, but in its place a new belief has arisen, the belief in the magical power of science. Science throws her treasures, not like a capricious fairy into the laps of a favored few, but into the laps of all humanity, with a lavish extravagance that no legend ever dreamt of! Not without apparent justice, therefore, do her distant admirers impute to her the power of opening up unfathomable abysses of nature, to which the senses cannot penetrate. Yet she who came to bring light into the world, can well dispense with the darkness of mystery, and with pompous show, which she needs neither for the justification of her aims nor for the adornment of her plain achievements.

The homely beginnings of science will best reveal to us its simple, unchangeable character. Man acquires his first knowledge of nature half-consciously and automatically, from an instinctive habit of mimicking and forecasting facts in thought, of supplementing sluggish experience with the swift wings of thought, at first only for his material welfare. When he hears a noise in the underbrush he constructs there, just as the animal does, the enemy which he fears; when he sees a certain rind he forms mentally the image of the fruit which he is in search of; just as we mentally associate a certain kind of matter with a certain line in the spectrum or an electric spark with the friction of a piece of glass. A knowledge of causality in this form certainly reaches far below the level of Schopenhauer's pet dog, to whom it was ascribed. It probably exists in the whole animal world, and confirms that great thinker's statement regarding the will which created the intellect for its purposes. These primitive psychical functions are rooted in the economy of our organism not less firmly than are motion and digestion. Who would deny that we feel in them, too, the elemental power of a long practised logical and physiological activity, bequeathed to us as an heirloom from our forefathers?

Such primitive acts of knowledge constitute to-day the solidest foundation of scientific thought. Our instinctive knowledge, as we shall briefly call it, by virtue of the conviction that we have consciously and intentionally contributed nothing to its formation, confronts us with an authority and logical power which consciously acquired knowledge even from familiar sources and of easily tested fallibility can never possess. All so-called axioms are such instinctive knowledge. Not consciously gained knowledge alone, but powerful intellectual instinct, joined with vast conceptive powers, constitute the great inquirer. The greatest advances of science have always consisted in some successful formulation, in clear, abstract, and communicable terms, of what was instinctively known long before, and of thus making it the permanent property of humanity. By Newton's principle of the equality of pressure and counterpressure, whose truth all before him had felt, but which no predecessor had abstractly formulated, mechanics was placed by a single stroke on a higher level. Our statement might also be historically justified by examples from the scientific labors of Stevinus, S. Carnot, Faraday, J. R. Mayer, and others.

All this, however, is merely the soil from which science starts. The first real beginnings of science appear in society, particularly in the manual arts, where the necessity for the communication of experience arises. Here, where some new discovery is to be described and related, the compulsion is first felt of clearly defining in consciousness the important and essential features of that discovery, as many writers can testify. The aim of instruction is simply the saving of experience; the labor of one man is made to take the place of that of another.

The most wonderful economy of communication is found in language. Words are comparable to type, which spare the repetition of written signs and thus serve a multitude of purposes; or to the few sounds of which our numberless different words are composed. Language, with its helpmate, conceptual thought, by fixing the essential and rejecting the unessential, constructs its rigid pictures of the fluid world on the plan of a mosaic, at a sacrifice of exactness and fidelity but with a saving of tools and labor. Like a piano-player with previously prepared sounds, a speaker excites in his listener thoughts previously prepared, but fitting many cases, which respond to the speaker's summons with alacrity and little effort.

The principles which a prominent political economist, E. Hermann,[6] has formulated for the economy of the industrial arts, are also applicable to the ideas of common life and of science. The economy of language is augmented, of course, in the terminology of science. With respect to the economy of written intercourse there is scarcely a doubt that science itself will realise that grand old dream of the philosophers of a Universal Real Character. That time is not far distant. Our numeral characters, the symbols of mathematical analysis, chemical symbols, and

musical notes, which might easily be supplemented by a system of color-signs, together with some phonetic alphabets now in use, are all beginnings in this direction. The logical extension of what we have, joined with a use of the ideas which the Chinese ideography furnishes us, will render the special invention and promulgation of a Universal Character wholly superfluous.

The communication of scientific knowledge always involves description, that is, a mimetic reproduction of facts in thought, the object of which is to replace and save the trouble of new experience. Again, to save the labor of instruction and of acquisition, concise, abridged description is sought. This is really all that natural laws are. Knowing the value of the acceleration of gravity, and Galileo's laws of descent, we possess simple and compendious directions for reproducing in thought all possible motions of falling bodies. A formula of this kind is a complete substitute for a full table of motions of descent, because by means of the formula the data of such a table can be easily constructed at a moment's notice without the least burdening of the memory.

No human mind could comprehend all the individual cases of refraction. But knowing the index of refraction for the two media presented, and the familiar law of the sines, we can easily reproduce or fill out in thought every conceivable case of refraction. The advantage here consists in the disburdening of the memory; an end immensely furthered by the written preservation of the natural constants. More than this comprehensive and condensed report about facts is not contained in a natural law of this sort. In reality, the law always contains less than the fact itself, because it does not reproduce the fact as a whole but only in that aspect of it which is important for us, the rest being either intentionally or from necessity omitted. Natural laws may be likened to intellectual type of a higher order, partly movable, partly stereo-

---

[6] Principien der Wirthschaftslehre [*Principles of Economy*], Vienna, 1873.

typed, which last on new editions of experience may become downright impediments.

When we look over a province of facts for the first time, it appears to us diversified, irregular, confused, full of contradictions. We first succeed in grasping only single facts, unrelated with the others. The province, as we are wont to say, is not *clear*. By and by we discover the simple, permanent elements of the mosaic, out of which we can mentally construct the whole province. When we have reached a point where we can discover everywhere the same facts, we no longer feel lost in this province; we comprehend it without effort; it is *explained* for us.

Let me illustrate this by an example. As soon as we have grasped the fact of the rectilinear propagation of light, the regular course of our thoughts stumbles at the phenomena of refraction and diffraction. As soon as we have cleared matters up by our index of refraction we discover that a special index is necessary for each color. Soon after we have accustomed ourselves to the fact that light added to light increases its intensity, we suddenly come across a case of total darkness produced by this cause. Ultimately, however, we see everywhere in the overwhelming multifariousness of optical phenomena the fact of the spatial and temporal periodicity of light, with its velocity of propagation dependent on the medium and the period. This tendency of obtaining a survey of a given province with the least expenditure of thought, and of representing all its facts by some one single mental process, may be justly termed an economical one.

The greatest perfection of mental economy is attained in that science which has reached the highest formal development, and which is widely employed in physical inquiry, namely, in mathematics. Strange as it may sound, the power of mathematics rests upon its evasion of all unnecessary thought and on its wonderful saving of mental operations. Even those arrangement-signs which we call numbers are a system of marvellous simplicity and economy. When we employ the multiplication-table in multiplying numbers of several places, and so use the results of old operations of counting instead of performing the whole of each operation anew; when we consult our table of logarithms, replacing and saving thus new calculations by old ones already performed; when we employ determinants instead of always beginning afresh the solution of a system of equations; when we resolve new integral expressions into familiar old integrals; we see in this simply a feeble reflexion of the intellectual activity of a Lagrange[7] or a Cauchy,[8] who, with the keen discernment of a great military commander, substituted for new operations whole hosts of old ones. No one will dispute me when I say that the most elementary as well as the highest mathematics are economically-ordered experiences of counting, put in forms ready for use.

In algebra we perform, as far as possible, all numerical operations which are identical in form once for all, so that only a remnant of work is left for the individual case. The use of the signs of algebra and analysis, which are merely symbols of operations to be performed, is due to the observation that we can materially disburden the mind in this way and spare its powers for more important and more difficult duties, by imposing all mechanical operations upon the hand. One result of this method, which attests its economical character, is the construction of calculating machines. The mathematician Babbage, the inventor of the difference-engine [the forerunner of the modern calculator], was probably the first who clearly perceived this fact, and he touched upon it, although only cursorily, in his work, *The Economy of Manufactures and Machinery.*

The student of mathematics often finds it hard to throw off the uncomfortable feeling that his science, in the person of his pencil, surpasses him in intelligence,—an impres-

---

[7] Joseph-Louis Lagrange (1736–1813) excelled in all fields of analysis and number theory and analytical and celestial mechanics.

[8] Augustin-Louis Cauchy (1789–1857) pioneered in analysis and the theory of substitution groups.

sion which the great Euler confessed he often could not get rid of. This feeling finds a sort of justification when we reflect that the majority of the ideas we deal with were conceived by others, often centuries ago. In great measure it is really the intelligence of other people that confronts us in science. The moment we look at matters in this light, the uncanniness and magical character of our impressions cease, especially when we remember that we can think over again at will any one of those alien thoughts.

Physics is experience, arranged in economical order. By this order not only is a broad and comprehensive view of what we have rendered possible, but also the defects and the needful alterations are made manifest, exactly as in a well-kept household. Physics shares with mathematics the advantages of succinct description and of brief, compendious definition, which precludes confusion, even in ideas where, with no apparent burdening of the brain, hosts of others are contained. Of these ideas the rich contents can be produced at any moment and displayed in their full perceptual light. Think of the swarm of well-ordered notions pent up in the idea of the potential. Is it wonderful that ideas containing so much finished labor should be easy to work with?

Our first knowledge, thus, is a product of the economy of self-preservation. By communication, the experience of *many* persons, individually acquired at first, is collected in *one*. The communication of knowledge and the necessity which every one feels of managing his stock of experience with the least expenditure of thought, compel us to put our knowledge in economical forms. But here we have a clue which strips science of all its mystery, and shows us what its power really is. With respect to specific results it yields us nothing that we could not reach in a sufficiently long time without methods. There is no problem in all mathematics that cannot be solved by direct counting. But with the present implements of mathematics many operations of counting can be performed in a few minutes which without mathematical meth-

ods would take a lifetime. Just as a single human being, restricted wholly to the fruits of his own labor, could never amass a fortune, but on the contrary the accumulation of the labor of many men in the hands of one is the foundation of wealth and power, so, also, no knowledge worthy of the name can be gathered up in a single human mind limited to the span of a human life and gifted only with finite powers, except by the most exquisite economy of thought and by the careful amassment of the economically ordered experience of thousands of co-workers. What strikes us here as the fruits of sorcery are simply the rewards of excellent housekeeping, as are the like results in civil life. But the business of science has this advantage over every other enterprise, that from *its* amassment of wealth no one suffers the least loss. This, too, is its blessing, its freeing and saving power.

The recognition of the economical character of science will now help us, perhaps, to understand better certain physical notions.

Those elements of an event which we call "cause and effect" are certain salient features of it, which are important for its mental reproduction. Their importance wanes and the attention is transferred to fresh characters the moment the event or experience in question becomes familiar. If the connexion of such features strikes us as a necessary one, it is simply because the interpolation of certain intermediate links with which we are very familiar, and which possess, therefore, higher authority for us, is often attended with success in our explanations. That *ready* experience fixed in the mosaic of the mind with which we meet new events, Kant calls an innate concept of the understanding (*Verstandesbegriff*).

The grandest principles of physics, resolved into their elements, differ in no wise from the descriptive principles of the natural historian. The question, "Why?" which is always appropriate where the explanation of a contradiction is concerned, like all proper habitudes of thought, can overreach itself and be asked where nothing remains to be understood. Suppose we were to attribute to nature the property of producing like effects in like circumstances; just these like circumstances we should not know how to find. Nature exists once only. Our schematic mental imitation alone produces like events. Only in the mind, therefore, does the mutual dependence of certain features exist.

All our efforts to mirror the world in thought would be futile if we found nothing permanent in the varied changes of things. It is this that impels us to form the notion of substance, the source of which is not different from that of the modern ideas relative to the conservation of energy. The history of physics furnishes numerous examples of this impulse in almost all fields, and pretty examples of it may be traced back to the nursery. "Where does the light go to when it is put out?" asks the child. The sudden shrivelling up of a hydrogen balloon is inexplicable to a child; it looks everywhere for the large body which was just there but is now gone.

Where does heat come from? Where does heat go to? Such childish questions in the mouths of mature men shape the character of a century.

In mentally separating a body from the changeable environment in which it moves, what we really do is to extricate a group of sensations on which our thoughts are fastened and which is of relatively greater stability than the others, from the stream of all our sensations. Absolutely unalterable this group is not. Now this, now that member of it appears and disappears, or is altered. In its full identity it never recurs. Yet the sum of its constant elements as compared with the sum of its changeable ones, especially if we consider the continuous character of the transition, is always so great that for the purpose in hand the former usually appear sufficient to determine the body's identity. But because we can separate from the group every single member without the body's ceasing to be for us the same, we are easily led to believe that after abstracting all the members something additional would remain. It thus comes to pass that we form the notion of a substance

distinct from its attributes, of a thing-in-itself, whilst our sensations are regarded merely as symbols or indications of the properties of this thing-in-itself. But it would be much better to say that bodies or things are compendious mental symbols for groups of sensations —symbols that do not exist outside of thought. Thus, the merchant regards the labels of his boxes merely as indexes of their contents, and not the contrary. He invests their contents, not their labels, with real value. The same economy which induces us to analyse a group and to establish special signs for its component parts, parts which also go to make up other groups, may likewise induce us to mark out by some single symbol a whole group.

On the old Egyptian monuments we see objects represented which do not reproduce a single visual impression, but are composed of various impressions. The heads and the legs of the figures appear in profile, the head-dress and the breast are seen from the front, and so on. We have here, so to speak, a mean view of the objects, in forming which the sculptor has retained what he deemed essential, and neglected what he thought indifferent. We have living exemplifications of the processes put into stone on the walls of these old temples, in the drawings of our children, and we also observe a faithful analogue of them in the formation of ideas in our own minds. Only in virtue of some such facility of view as that indicated, are we allowed to speak of *a* body. When we speak of a cube with trimmed corners—a figure which is not a cube—we do so from a natural instinct of economy, which prefers to add to an old familiar conception a correction instead of forming an entirely new one. This is the process of all judgment.

The crude notion of "body" can no more stand the test of analysis than can the art of the Egyptians or that of our little children. The physicist who sees a body flexed, stretched, melted, and vaporised, cuts up this body into smaller permanent parts; the chemist splits it up into elements. Yet even an element is not unalterable. Take sodium.

When warmed, the white, silvery mass becomes a liquid, which, when the heat is increased and the air shut out, is transformed into a violet vapor, and on the heat being still more increased glows with a yellow light. If the name sodium is still retained, it is because of the continuous character of the transitions and from a necessary instinct of economy. By condensing the vapor, the white metal may be made to reappear. Indeed, even after the metal is thrown into water and has passed into sodium hydroxide, the vanished properties may by skilful treatment still be made to appear; just as a moving body which has passed behind a column and is lost to view for a moment may make its appearance after a time. It is unquestionably very convenient always to have ready the name and thought for a group of properties wherever that group by any possibility can appear. But more than a compendious economical symbol for these phenomena, that name and thought is not. It would be a mere empty word for one in whom it did not awaken a large group of well-ordered sense-impressions. And the same is true of the molecules and atoms into which the chemical element is still further analysed.

True, it is customary to regard the conservation of weight, or, more precisely, the conservation of mass, as a direct proof of the constancy of matter. But this proof is dissolved, when we go to the bottom of it, into such a multitude of instrumental and intellectual operations, that in a sense it will be found to constitute simply an equation which our ideas in imitating facts have to satisfy. That obscure, mysterious lump which we involuntarily add in thought, we seek for in vain outside the mind.

It is always, thus, the crude notion of substance that is slipping unnoticed into science, proving itself constantly insufficient, and ever under the necessity of being reduced to smaller and smaller world-particles. Here, as elsewhere, the lower stage is not rendered indispensable by the higher which is built upon it, no more than the simplest mode of locomotion, walking, is rendered superfluous by the most elaborate means of transportation. Body, as a compound of light and touch sensations, knit together by sensations of space, must be as familiar to the physicist who seeks it, as to the animal who hunts its prey. But the student of the theory of knowledge, like the geologist and the astronomer, must be permitted to reason back from the forms which are created before his eyes to others which he finds ready made for him.

All physical ideas and principles are succinct directions, frequently involving subordinate directions, for the employment of economically classified experiences, ready for use. Their conciseness, as also the fact that their contents are rarely exhibited in full, often invests them with the semblance of independent existence. Poetical myths regarding such ideas,—for example, that of Time, the producer and devourer of all things,—do not concern us here. We need only remind the reader that even Newton speaks of an *absolute* time independent of all phenomena, and of an absolute space—views which even Kant did not shake off, and which are often seriously entertained to-day. For the natural inquirer, determinations of time are merely abbreviated statements of the dependence of one event upon another, and nothing more. When we say the acceleration of a freely falling body is 9.810 metres per second, we mean the velocity of the body with respect to the centre of the earth is 9.810 metres greater when the earth has performed an additional 86400th part of its rotation—a fact which itself can be determined only by the earth's relation to other heavenly bodies. Again, in velocity is contained simply a relation of the position of a body to the position of the earth.[9] Instead of referring events to the earth we may refer them to a clock, or even to our internal sensation of time. Now, because all are connected, and each may be made the measure of the rest,

---

[9] It is clear from this that all so-called elementary (differential) laws involve a relation to the Whole.

the illusion easily arises that time has significance independently of all.[10]

The aim of research is the discovery of the equations which subsist between the elements of phenomena. The equation of an ellipse expresses the universal *conceivable* relation between its co-ordinates, of which only the real values have *geometrical* significance. Similarly, the equations between the elements of *phenomena* express a universal, mathematically conceivable relation. Here, however, for many values only certain directions of change are *physically* admissible. As in the ellipse only certain *values* satisfying the equation are realised, so in the physical world only certain *changes* of value occur. Bodies are always accelerated towards the earth. Differences of temperature, left to themselves, always grow less; and so on. Similarly, with respect to space, mathematical and physiological researches have shown that the space of experience is simply an *actual* case of many conceivable cases, about whose peculiar properties experience alone can instruct us. The elucidation which this idea diffuses cannot be questioned, despite the absurd uses to which it has been put.

Let us endeavor now to summarise the results of our survey. In the economical schematism of science lie both its strength and its weakness. Facts are always represented at a sacrifice of completeness and never with greater precision than fits the needs of the moment. The incongruence between thought and experience, therefore, will continue to subsist as long as the two pursue their course side by side; but it will be continually diminished.

In reality, the point involved is always the completion of some partial experience; the derivation of one portion of a phenomenon from some other. In this act our ideas must be based directly upon sensations. We call this measuring.[11] The condition of science, both in its origin and in its application, is a *great relative stability* of our environment. What it teaches us is interdependence. Absolute forecasts, consequently, have no significance in science. With great changes in celestial space we should lose our co-ordinate systems of space and time.

When a geometer wishes to understand the form of a curve, he first resolves it into small rectilinear elements. In doing this, however, he is fully aware that these elements are only provisional and arbitrary devices for comprehending in parts what he cannot comprehend as a whole. When the law of the curve is found he no longer thinks of the elements. Similarly, it would not become physical science to see in its self-created, changeable, economical tools, molecules and atoms, realities behind phenomena, forgetful of the lately acquired sapience of her older sister, philosophy, in substituting a mechanical mythology for the old animistic or metaphysical scheme, and thus creating no end of suppositious problems. The atom must remain a tool for representing phenomena, like the functions of mathematics. Gradually, however, as the intellect, by contact with its subject-matter, grows in discipline, physical science will give up its mosaic play with stones and will seek out the boundaries and forms of the bed in which the living stream of phenomena flows. The goal which it has set itself is the *simplest* and *most economical* abstract expression of facts.

* * *

The question now remains, whether the same method of research which till now we have tacitly restricted to physics, is also applicable in the psychical domain. This question will appear superfluous to the physical inquirer. Our physical and psychical views spring in exactly the same manner from instinctive knowledge. We read the thoughts of

---

[10] If it be objected, that in the case of perturbations of the velocity of rotation of the earth, we could be sensible of such perturbations, and being obliged to have some measure of time, we should resort to the period of vibration of the waves of sodium light,—all that this would show is that for practical reasons we should select that event which best served us as the *simplest* common measure of the others.

[11] Measurement, in fact, is the definition of one phenomenon by another (standard) phenomenon.

men in their acts and facial expressions without knowing how. Just as we predict the behavior of a magnetic needle placed near a current by imagining Ampère's swimmer in the current, similarly we predict in thought the acts and behavior of men by assuming sensations, feelings, and wills similar to our own connected with their bodies. What we here instinctively perform would appear to us as one of the subtlest achievements of science, far outstripping in significance and ingenuity Ampère's rule of the swimmer, were it not that every child unconsciously accomplished it. The question simply is, therefore, to grasp scientifically, that is, by conceptional thought, what we are already familiar with from other sources. And here much is to be accomplished. A long sequence of facts is to be disclosed between the physics of expression and movement and feeling and thought.

We hear the question, "But how is it possible to explain feeling by the motions of the atoms of the brain?" Certainly this will never be done, no more than light or heat will ever be deduced from the law of refraction. We need not deplore, therefore, the lack of ingenious solutions of this question. The problem is not a problem. A child looking over the walls of a city or of a fort into the moat below sees with astonishment living people in it, and not knowing of the portal which connects the wall with the moat, cannot understand how they could have got down from the high ramparts. So it is with the notions of physics. We cannot climb up into the province of psychology by the ladder of our abstractions, but we can climb down into it.

Let us look at the matter without bias. The world consists of colors, sounds, temperatures, pressures, spaces, times, and so forth, which now we shall not call sensations, nor phenomena, because in either term an arbitrary, one-sided theory is embodied, but simply *elements*. The fixing of the flux of these elements, whether mediately or immediately, is the real object of physical research. As long as, neglecting our own body, we employ ourselves with the interdependence of those groups of elements which, including men and animals, make up *foreign* bodies, we are physicists. For example, we investigate the change of the red color of a body as produced by a change of illumination. But the moment we consider the special influence on the red of the elements constituting our body, outlined by the well-known perspective with head invisible, we are at work in the domain of physiological psychology. We close our eyes, and the red together with the whole visible world disappears. There exists, thus, in the perspective field of every sense a portion which exercises on all the rest a different and more powerful influence than the rest upon one another. With this, however, all is said. In the light of this remark, we call *all* elements, in so far as we regard them as dependent on this special part (our body), *sensations*. That the world is our sensation, in this sense, cannot be questioned. But to make a system of conduct out of this provisional conception, and to abide its slaves, is as unnecessary for us as would be a similar course for a mathematician who, in varying a series of variables of a function which were previously assumed to be constant, or in interchanging the independent variables, finds his method to be the source of some very surprising ideas for him.

If we look at the matter in this unbiassed light it will appear indubitable that the method of physiological psychology is none other than that of physics; what is more, that this science is a part of physics. Its subject-matter is not different from that of physics. It will unquestionably determine the relations the sensations bear to the physics of our body. We have already learned from a member of this academy (Hering) that in all probability a sixfold manifoldness of the chemical processes of the visual substance corresponds to the sixfold manifoldness of color-sensation, and a threefold manifoldness of the physiological processes to the threefold manifoldness of space-sensations. The paths of reflex actions and of the will are followed up and disclosed; it is ascertained what region of the brain subserves the function of speech, what region the function of locomotion, etc. That which still clings to our body, namely, our thoughts, will, when those investigations are finished, present no difficulties new in principle. When experience has once clearly exhibited these facts and science has marshalled them in economic and perspicuous order, there is no doubt that we shall *understand* them. For other "understanding" than a mental mastery of facts never existed. Science does not create facts from facts, but simply *orders* known facts.

Let us look, now, a little more closely into the modes of research of physiological psychology. We have a very clear idea of how a body moves in the space encompassing it. With our optical field of sight we are very familiar. But we are unable to state, as a rule, how we have come by an idea, from what corner of our intellectual field of sight it has entered, or by what region the impulse to a motion is sent forth. Moreover, we shall never get acquainted with this mental field of view from self-observation alone. Self-observation, in conjunction with physiological research, which seeks out physical connexions, can put this field of vision in a clear light before us, and will thus first really reveal to us our inner man.

Primarily, natural science, or physics, in its widest sense, makes us acquainted with only the firmest connexions of groups of elements. Provisorily, we may not bestow too much attention on the single constituents of those groups, if we are desirous of retaining a comprehensible whole. Instead of equations between the primitive variables, physics gives us as much the easiest course, equations between *functions* of those variables. Physiological psychology teaches us how to separate the visible, the tangible, and the audible from bodies—a labor which is subsequently richly requited, as the division of the subjects of physics well shows. Physiology further analyses the visible into light and space sensations; the first into colors, the last also into their component parts; it resolves noises into sounds, these into tones, and so on. Unquestionably this analysis can be carried much

further than it has been. It will be possible in the end to exhibit the common elements at the basis of very abstract but definite logical acts of life form,—elements which the acute jurist and mathematician, as it were, *feels* out, with absolute certainty, where the uninitiated hears only empty words. Physiology, in a word, will reveal to us the true real elements of the world. Physiological psychology bears to physics in its widest sense a relation similar to that which chemistry bears to physics in its narrowest sense. But far greater than the mutual support of physics and chemistry will be that which natural science and psychology will render each other. And the results that shall spring from this union will, in all likelihood, far outstrip those of the modern mechanical physics.

What those ideas are with which we shall comprehend the world when the closed circuit of physical and psychological facts shall lie complete before us, (that circuit of which we now see only two disjoined parts,) cannot be foreseen at the outset of the work. The men will be found who will see what is right and will have the courage, instead of wandering in the intricate paths of logical and historical accident, to enter on the straight ways to the heights from which the mighty stream of facts can be surveyed. Whether the notion which we now call matter will continue to have a scientific significance beyond the crude purposes of common life, we do not know. But we certainly shall wonder how colors and tones which were such innermost parts of us could suddenly get lost in our physical world of atoms; how we could be suddenly surprised that something which outside us simply clicked and beat, in our heads should make light and music; and how we could ask whether matter can feel, that is to say, whether a mental symbol for a group of sensations can feel?

We cannot mark out in hard and fast lines the science of the future, but we can foresee that the rigid walls which now divide man from the world will gradually disappear; that human beings will not only confront each other, but also the entire organic and so-called lifeless world, with less selfishness and with livelier sympathy. Just such a presentiment as this perhaps possessed the great Chinese philosopher Licius some two thousand years ago when, pointing to a heap of mould-ering human bones, he said to his scholars in the rigid, lapidary style of his tongue: "These and I alone have the knowledge that we neither live nor are dead."

On Transformation and Adaptation in Scientific Thought*

It was towards the close of the sixteenth century that Galileo with a superb indifference to the dialectic arts and sophistic subtleties of the Schoolmen of his time, turned the attention of his brilliant mind to nature. By nature his ideas were transformed and released from the fetters of inherited prejudice. At once the mighty revolution was felt, that was therewith effected in the realm of human thought—felt indeed in circles far remote and wholly unrelated to the sphere of science, felt in strata of society that hitherto had only indirectly recognised the influence of scientific thought.

And how great and how far-reaching that revolution was! From the beginning of the seventeenth century till its close we see arising, at least in embryo, almost all that plays a part in the natural and technical science of to-day, almost all that in the two centuries following so wonderfully transformed the facial appearance of the earth, and all that is moving onward in process of such mighty evolution to-day. And all this, the direct result of Galilean ideas, the direct outcome of that freshly awakened sense for the investigation of natural phenomena which taught the Tuscan philosopher to form the concept and the law of falling bodies from the *observation* of a falling stone! Galileo began his investigations without an implement worthy of the name; he measured time in the most primitive way, by the efflux of water. Yet soon afterwards the telescope, the microscope, the barometer, the thermometer, the air-pump, the steam-engine, the pendulum, and the electrical machine were invented in rapid succession. The fundamental theorems of dynamical science, of optics, of heat, and of electricity were all disclosed in the century that followed Galileo.

Of scarcely less importance, it seems, was that movement which was prepared for by the illustrious biologists of the hundred years just past, and formally begun by the late Mr. Darwin. Galileo quickened the sense for the simpler phenomena of *inorganic* nature. And with the same simplicity and frankness that marked the efforts of Galileo, and without the aid of technical or scientific instruments, without physical or chemical experiment, but solely by the power of thought and observation, Darwin grasps a new property of *organic* nature—which we may briefly call its *plasticity*.[1] With the same directness of purpose, Darwin, too, pursues his way. With the same

---

* Inaugural Address, delivered on assuming the Rectorate of the University of Prague, October 18, 1883.

The idea presented in this essay is neither new nor remote. I have touched upon it myself on several occasions (first in 1867), but have never made it the subject of a formal disquisition. Doubtless, others, too, have treated it; it lies, so to speak, in the air. However, as many of my illustrations were well received, although known only in an imperfect form from the lecture itself and the newspapers, I have, contrary to my original intention, decided to publish it. It is not my intention to trespass here upon the domain of biology. My statements are to be taken merely as the expression of the fact that no one can escape the influence of a great and far-reaching idea.

[1] At first sight an apparent contradiction arises from the admission of both heredity and adaptation; and it is undoubtedly true that a strong disposition to heredity precludes great capability of adaptation. But imagine the organism to be a plastic mass which retains the form transmitted to it by former influences until new influences modify it; the *one* property of *plasticity* will then represent capability of adaptation as well as power of heredity. Analogous to this is the case of a bar of magnetised steel of high coercive force: the steel retains its magnetic properties until a new force displaces them. Take also a body in motion: the body retains the velocity acquired in (*inherited* from) the interval

candor and love of truth, he points out the strength and the weakness of his demonstrations. With masterly equanimity he holds aloof from the discussion of irrelevant subjects and wins alike the admiration of his adherents and of his adversaries.

Scarcely thirty years have elapsed[2] since Darwin first propounded the principles of his theory of evolution. Yet, already we see his ideas firmly rooted in every branch of human thought, however remote. Everywhere, in history, in philosophy, even in the physical sciences, we hear the watchwords: heredity, adaptation, selection. We speak of the struggle for existence among the heavenly bodies and of the struggle for existence in the world of molecules.

The impetus given by Galileo to scientific thought was marked in every direction; thus, his pupil, Borelli, founded the school of exact medicine, from whence proceeded even distinguished mathematicians. And now Darwinian ideas, in the same way, are animating all provinces of research. It is true, nature is not made up of two distinct parts, the inorganic and the organic; nor must these two divisions be treated perforce by totally distinct methods. Many *sides*, however, nature has. Nature is like a thread in an intricate tangle, which must be followed and traced, now from this point, now from that. But we must never imagine,—and this physicists have learned from Faraday and J. R. Mayer, —that progress along paths once entered upon is the *only* means of reaching the truth.

It will devolve upon the specialists of the future to determine the relative tenability and fruitfulness of the Darwinian ideas in the different provinces. Here I wish simply to consider the growth of natural *knowledge* in the light of the theory of evolution. For knowledge, too, is a product of organic nature. And although ideas, as such, do not comport themselves in all respects like independent organic individuals, and although violent comparisons should be avoided, still, if Darwin reasoned rightly, the general imprint of evolution and transformation must be noticeable in ideas also.

I shall waive here the consideration of the fruitful topic of the transmission of ideas or rather of the transmission of the aptitude for certain ideas. Nor would it come within my province to discuss psychical evolution in any form, as Spencer and many other modern psychologists have done, with varying success. Neither shall I enter upon a discussion of the struggle for existence and of natural selection among scientific theories. We shall consider here only such processes of transformation as every student can easily observe in his own mind.

The child of the forest picks out and pursues with marvellous acuteness the trails of animals. He outwits and overreaches his foes with surpassing cunning. He is perfectly at home in the sphere of his peculiar experience. But confront him with an unwonted phenomenon; place him face to face with a technical product of modern civilisation, and he will lapse into impotency and helplessness. Here are facts which he does not comprehend. If he endeavors to grasp their meaning, he misinterprets them. He fancies the moon, when eclipsed, to be tormented by

---

of time just preceding, except it be changed in the next moment by an accelerating force. In the case of the body in motion the *change* of velocity (*Abänderung*) was looked upon as a matter of course, while the discovery of the principle of *inertia* (or persistence) created surprise; in Darwin's case, on the contrary, *heredity* (or persistence) was taken for granted, while the principle of *variation* (*Abänderung*) appeared novel.

Fully adequate views are, of course, to be reached only by a study of the original facts emphasised by Darwin, and not by these analogies. The example referring to motion, if I am not mistaken, I first heard, in conversation, from my friend J. Popper, Esq., of Vienna.

Many inquirers look upon the stability of the species as something settled, and oppose to it the Darwinian theory. But the stability of the species is itself a "theory." The essential modifications which Darwin's views also are undergoing will be seen from the works of Wallace [and Weismann], but more especially from a book of W.H. Rolph, *Biologische Probleme*, Leipsic, 1882. Unfortunately, this last talented investigator is no longer numbered among the living.

[2] Written in 1883.

an evil spirit. To his mind a puffing locomotive is a living monster. The letter accompanying a commission with which he is entrusted, having once revealed his thievishness, is in his imagination a conscious being, which he must hide beneath a stone, before venturing to commit a fresh trespass. Arithmetic to him is like the art of the geomancers in the Arabian Nights,—an art which is able to accomplish every imaginable impossibility. And, like Voltaire's *ingénu,* when placed in our social world, he plays, as we think, the maddest pranks.

With the man who has made the achievements of modern science and civilisation his own, the case is quite different. He sees the moon pass temporarily into the shadow of the earth. He feels in his thoughts the water growing hot in the boiler of the locomotive; he feels also the increase of the tension which pushes the piston forward. Where he is not able to trace the direct relation of things he has recourse to his yardstick and table of logarithms, which aid and facilitate his thought without predominating over it. Such opinions as he cannot concur in, are at least known to him, and he knows how to meet them in argument.

Now, wherein does the difference between these two men consist? The train of thought habitually employed by the first one does not correspond to the facts that he sees. He is surprised and nonplussed at every step. But the thoughts of the second man follow and anticipate events, his thoughts have become adapted or accommodated to the larger field of observation and activity in which he is located; he conceives things as they are. The Indian's sphere of experience, however, is quite different; his bodily organs of sense are in constant activity; he is ever intensely alert and on the watch for his foes; or, his entire attention and energy are engaged in procuring sustenance. Now, how can such a creature project his mind into futurity, foresee or prophesy? This is not possible until our fellow-beings have, in a measure, relieved us of our concern for existence. It is then that we acquire freedom for observation, and not infrequently too that narrowness of thought which society helps and teaches us to disregard.

If we move for a time within a fixed circle of phenomena which recur with unvarying uniformity, our thoughts gradually adapt themselves to our environment; our ideas reflect unconsciously our surroundings. The stone we hold in our hand, when dropped, not only falls to the ground in reality; it also falls in our thoughts. Iron-filings dart towards a magnet in imagination as well as in fact, and when thrown into a fire, they grew hot in conception as well.

The impulse to complete mentally a phenomenon that has been only partially observed, has not its origin in the phenomenon itself; of this fact, we are fully sensible. And we well know that it does not lie within the sphere of our volition. It seems to confront us rather as a power and a law imposed from without and controlling both thought and facts.

The fact that we are able by the help of this law to prophesy and forecast, merely proves a sameness or uniformity of environment sufficient to effect a mental adaptation of this kind. A necessity of fulfilment, however, is not contained in this compulsory principle which controls our thoughts; nor is it in any way determined by the possibility of prediction. We are always obliged, in fact, to await the completion of what has been predicted. Errors and departures are constantly discernible, and are slight only in provinces of great rigid constancy, as in astronomy.

In cases where our thoughts follow the connexion of events with ease, and in instances where we positively forefeel the course of a phenomenon, it is natural to fancy that the latter is determined by and must conform to our thoughts. But the belief in that mysterious agency called *causality,* which holds thought and event in unison, is violently shaken when a person first enters a province of inquiry in which he has previously had no experience . Take for instance the strange interaction of electric currents and magnets, or the reciprocal action of currents, which seem to defy all the resources of mechanical science. Let him be confronted with such phenomena and he will immediately feel himself forsaken by his power of prediction; he will bring nothing with him into this strange field of events but the hope of soon being able to adapt his ideas to the new conditions there presented.

A person constructs from a bone the remaining anatomy of an animal; or from the visible part of a half-concealed wing of a butterfly he infers and reconstructs the part concealed. He does so with a feeling of highest confidence in the accuracy of his results; and in these processes we find nothing preternatural or transcendent. But when physicists adapt their thoughts to conform to the dynamical course of events in time, we invariably surround their investigations with a metaphysical halo; yet these latter adaptations bear quite the same character as the former, and our only reason for investing them with a metaphysical garb, perhaps, is their high practical value.

Let us consider for a moment what takes place when the field of observation to which our ideas have been adapted and now conform, becomes enlarged. We had, let us say, always seen heavy bodies sink when their support was taken away; we had also seen, perhaps, that the sinking of heavier bodies forced lighter bodies upwards. But now we see a lever in action, and we are suddenly struck with the fact that a lighter body is lifting another of much greater weight. Our customary train of thought demands its rights; the new and unwonted event likewise demands its rights. From this conflict between thought and fact the *problem* arises; out of this partial contrariety springs the question, "Why?" With the new adaptation to the enlarged field of observation, the problem disappears, or, in other words, is solved. In the instance cited, we must adopt the habit of always considering the mechanical work performed.

The child just awakening into consciousness of the world, knows no problem. The bright flower, the ringing bell, are all new to it; yet it is surprised at nothing. The out and out Philistine, whose only thoughts lie in the beaten path of his every-day pursuits, likewise has no problems. Everything goes its wonted course, and if perchance a thing go wrong at times, it is at most a mere object of curiosity and not worth serious consideration. In fact, the question "Why?" loses all warrant in relations where we are familiar with every aspect of events. But the capable and talented young man has his head full of problems; he has acquired, to a greater or less degree, certain habitudes of thought, and at the same time he is constantly observing what is new and unwonted, and in his case there is no end to the questions, "Why?"

Thus, the factor which most promotes scientific thought is the gradual widening of the field of experience. We scarcely notice events we are accustomed to; the latter do not really develop their intellectual significance until placed in contrast with something to which we are unaccustomed. Things that at home are passed by unnoticed, delight us when abroad, though they may appear in only slightly different forms. The sun shines with heightened radiance, the flowers bloom in brighter colors, our fellow-men accost us with lighter and happier looks. And, returning home, we find even the old familiar scenes more inspiring and suggestive than before.

Every motive that prompts and stimulates us to modify and transform our thoughts, proceeds from what is new, uncommon, and not understood. Novelty excites wonder in persons whose fixed habits of thought are shaken and disarranged by what they see. But the element of wonder never lies in the phenomenon or event observed; its place is in the person observing. People of more vigorous mental type aim at once at an *adaptation of thought* that will conform to what they have observed. Thus does science eventually become the natural foe of the wonderful. The sources of the marvellous are unveiled, and surprise gives way to calm interpretation.

Let us consider such a mental transformative process in detail. The circumstance that heavy bodies fall to the earth appears perfectly natural and regular. But when a person observes that wood floats upon water, and that flames and smoke rise in the air, then the contrary of the first phenomenon is presented. An olden theory endeavors to explain these facts by imputing to substances the power of volition, as that attribute which is most familiar to man. It asserted that every substance seeks its proper place, heavy bodies tending downwards and light ones upwards. It soon turned out, however, that even smoke had weight, that it, too, sought its place below, and that it was forced upwards only because of the downward tendency of the air, as wood is forced to the surface of water because the water exerts the greater downward pressure.

Again, we see a body thrown into the air. It ascends. How is it that it does not seek its proper place? Why does the velocity of its "violent" motion decrease as it rises, while that of its "natural" fall increases as it descends. If we mark closely the relation between these two facts, the problem will solve itself. We shall see, as Galileo did, that the decrease of velocity in rising and the increase of velocity in falling are one and the same phenomenon, viz., an increase of velocity towards the earth. Accordingly, it is not a place that is assigned to the body, but an increase of velocity towards the earth.

By this idea the movements of heavy bodies are rendered perfectly familiar. Newton, now, firmly grasping this new way of thinking, sees the moon and the planets moving in their paths upon principles similar to those which determine the motion of a projectile thrown into the air. Yet the movements of the planets were marked by peculiarities which compelled him once more to modify slightly his customary mode of thought. The heavenly bodies, or rather the parts composing them, do not move with constant accelerations towards each other, but "attract each other," directly as the mass and inversely as the square of the distance.

This latter notion, which includes the one applying to terrestrial bodies as a special case, is, as we see, quite different from the conception from which we started. How limited in scope was the original idea and to what a multitude of phenomena is not the present one applicable! Yet there is a trace, after all, of the "search for place" in the expression "attraction." And it would be folly, indeed, for us to avoid, with punctilious dread, this conception of "attraction" as bearing marks of its pedigree. It is the historical base of the Newtonian conception and it still continues to direct our thoughts in the paths so long familiar to us. Thus, the happiest ideas do not fall from heaven, but spring from notions already existing.

Similarly, a ray of light was first regarded as a continuous and homogeneous straight line. It then became the path of projection for minute missiles; then an aggregate of the paths of countless different kinds of missiles. It became periodic; it acquired various sides; and ultimately it even lost its motion in a straight line.

The electric current was conceived originally as the flow of a hypothetical fluid. To this conception was soon added the notion of a chemical current, the notion of an electric, magnetic, and anisotropic optical field, intimately connected with the path of the current. And the richer a conception becomes in following and keeping pace with facts, the better adapted it is to anticipate them.

Adaptive processes of this kind have no assignable beginning, inasmuch as every problem that incites to new adaptation, presupposes a fixed habitude of thought. Moreover, they have no visible end; in so far as experience never ceases. Science, accordingly, stands midway in the evolutionary process; and science may advantageously direct and promote this process, but it can never take its place. That science is inconceivable the principles of which would enable a person with no experience to construct the world of experience, without a knowledge of it. One might just as well expect to become a great musician, solely by the aid of theory, and without musical experience; or to become a painter by following the directions of a textbook.

In glancing over the history of an idea with which we have become perfectly familiar, we are no longer able to appreciate the full significance of its growth. The deep and vital changes that have been effected in the course of its evolution, are recognisable only from the astounding narrowness of view with which great contemporary scientists have occasionally opposed each other. Huygens's wave-theory of light was incomprehensible to Newton, and Newton's idea of universal gravity was unintelligible to Huygens. But a century afterwards both notions were reconcilable, even in ordinary minds.

On the other hand, the original creations of pioneer intellects, unconsciously formed, do not assume a foreign garb; their form is their own. In them, childlike simplicity is joined to the maturity of manhood, and they are not to be compared with processes of thought in the average mind. The latter are carried on as are the acts of persons in the state of mesmerism, where actions involuntarily follow the images which the words of other persons suggest to their minds.

The ideas that have become most familiar through long experience, are the very ones that intrude themselves into the conception of every new fact observed. In every instance, thus, they become involved in a struggle for self-preservation, and it is just they that are seized by the inevitable process of transformation.

Upon this process rests substantially the method of explaining by hypothesis new and uncomprehended phenomena. Thus, instead of forming entirely new notions to explain the movements of the heavenly bodies and the phenomena of the tides, we imagine the material particles composing the bodies of the universe to possess weight or gravity with respect to one another. Similarly, we imagine electrified bodies to be freighted with fluids that attract and repel, or we conceive the space between them to be in a state of elastic tension. In so doing, we substitute for new ideas distinct and more familiar notions of old experience—notions which to a great extent run unimpeded in their courses, although they too must suffer partial transformation.

The animal cannot construct new members to perform every new function that circumstances and fate demand of it. On the contrary it is obliged to make use of those it already possesses. When a vertebrate animal chances into an environment where it must learn to fly or swim, an additional pair of extremities is not grown for the purpose. On the contrary, the animal must adapt and transform a pair that it already has.

The construction of hypotheses, therefore, is not the product of artificial scientific methods. This process is unconsciously carried on in the very infancy of science. Even later, hypotheses do not become detrimental and dangerous to progress except when more reliance is placed on them than on the facts themselves; when the contents of the former are more highly valued than the latter, and when, rigidly adhering to hypothetical notions, we overestimate the ideas we possess as compared with those we have to acquire.

The extension of our sphere of experience always involves a transformation of our ideas. It matters not whether the face of nature becomes actually altered, presenting new and strange phenomena, or whether these phenomena are brought to light by an intentional or accidental turn of observation. In fact, all the varied methods of scientific inquiry and of purposive mental adaptation enumerated by John Stuart Mill, those of observation as well as those of experiment, are ultimately recognisable as forms of one fundamental method, the method of change, or variation. It is through change of circumstances that the natural philosopher learns. This process, however, is by no means confined to the investigator of nature. The historian, the philosopher, the jurist, the mathematician, the artist, the aesthetician, all illuminate and unfold their ideas by producing from the rich treasures of memory similar, but different, cases; thus, they observe and experiment in their thoughts. Even if all sense-experience should suddenly cease, the events of the days past would meet in different attitudes in the mind and the process of adaptation would still continue—a process which, in contradistinction to the adaptation of thoughts to facts in practical spheres, would be strictly theoretical, being an adaptation of thoughts to thoughts.

The method of change or variation brings before us like cases of phenomena, having partly the same and partly different elements. It is only by comparing different cases of refracted light at changing angles of incidence that the common factor, the constancy of the refractive index, is disclosed. And only by comparing the refractions of light of different colors, does the difference, the inequality of the indices of refraction, arrest the attention. Comparison based upon change leads the mind simultaneously to the highest abstractions and to the finest distinctions.

Undoubtedly, the animal also is able to distinguish between the similar and dissimilar of two cases. Its consciousness is aroused by a noise or a rustling, and its motor centre is put in readiness. The sight of the creature causing the disturbance, will, according to its size, provoke flight or prompt pursuit; and in the latter case, the more exact distinctions will determine the mode of attack. But man alone attains to the faculty of voluntary and conscious comparison. Man alone can, by his power of abstraction, rise, in one moment, to the comprehension of principles like the conservation of mass or the conservation of energy, and in the next observe and mark the arrangement of the iron lines in the spectrum. In thus dealing with the objects of his conceptual life, his ideas unfold and expand, like his nervous system, into a widely ramified and organically articulated tree, on which he may follow every limb to its farthermost branches, and, when occasion demands, return to the trunk from which he started.

The English philosopher Whewell has remarked that two things are requisite to the formation of science: facts and ideas. Ideas alone lead to empty speculation; mere facts can yield no organic knowledge. We see that all depends upon the capacity of adapting existing notions to fresh facts.

Over-readiness to yield to every new fact prevents fixed habits of thought from arising. Excessively rigid habits of thought impede freedom of observation. In the struggle, in the compromise between judgment and prejudgment (prejudice), if we may use the term, our understanding of things broadens.

Habitual judgment, applied to a new case without antecedent tests, we call prejudgment or prejudice. Who does not know its terrible power! But we think less often of the importance and utility of prejudice. Physically, no one could exist, if he had to guide and regulate the circulation, respiration, and digestion of his body by conscious and purposive acts. So, too, no one could exist intellectually if he had to form judgments on every passing experience, instead of allowing himself to be controlled by the judgments he has already formed. Prejudice is a sort of reflex motion in the province of intelligence.

On prejudices, that is, on habitual judgments not tested in every case to which they are applied, reposes a goodly portion of the thought and work of the natural scientist. On prejudices reposes most of the conduct of society. With the sudden disappearance of prejudice society would hopelessly dissolve. That prince displayed a deep insight into the power of intellectual habit, who quelled the loud menaces and demands of his bodyguard for arrears of pay and compelled them to turn about and march, by simply pronouncing the regular word of command; he well knew that they would be unable to resist that.

Not until the discrepancy between habitual judgments and facts becomes great is the investigator implicated in appreciable illusion. Then tragic complications and catastrophes occur in the practical life of individuals and nations—crises where man, placing custom above life, instead of pressing it into the service of life, becomes the victim of his error. The very power which in intellectual life advances, fosters, and sustains us, may in other circumstances delude and destroy us.

Ideas are not all of life. They are only momentary efflorescences of light, designed to illuminate the paths of the will. But as delicate reagents on our organic evolution our ideas are of paramount importance. No theory can gainsay the vital transformation which we feel taking place within us through their agency. Nor is it necessary that we should have a proof of this process. We are immediately assured of it.

The transformation of ideas thus appears as a part of the general evolution of life, as a part of its adaptation to a constantly widening sphere of action. A granite boulder on a mountain-side tends towards the earth below. It must abide in its resting-place for thousands of years before its support gives way. The shrub that grows at its base is farther advanced; it accommodates itself to summer and winter. The fox which, overcoming the force of gravity, creeps to the summit where he has scented his prey, is freer in his movements than either. The arm of man reaches further still; and scarcely anything of note happens in Africa or Asia that does not leave an imprint upon his life. What an immense portion of the life of other men is reflected in ourselves; their joys, their affections, their happiness and misery! And this too, when we survey only our immediate surroundings, and confine our attention to modern literature. How much more do we experience when we travel through ancient Egypt with Herodotus, when we stroll through the streets of Pompeii, when we carry ourselves back to the gloomy period of the crusades or to the golden age of Italian art, now making the acquaintance of a physician of Molière, and now that of a Diderot or of a D'Alembert. What a great part of the life of others, of their character and their purpose, do we not absorb through poetry and music! And although they only gently touch the chords of our emotions, like the memory of youth softly breathing upon the spirit of an aged man, we have nevertheless lived them over again in part. How great and compre-

hensive does self become in this conception; and how insignificant the person! Egoistical systems both of optimism and pessimism perish with their narrow standard of the import of intellectual life. We feel that the real pearls of life lie in the ever changing contents of consciousness, and that the person is merely an indifferent symbolical thread on which they are strung.[3]

We are prepared, thus, to regard ourselves and every one of our ideas as a product and a subject of universal evolution; and in this way we shall advance sturdily and unimpeded along the paths which the future will throw open to us.[4]

---

[3] We must not be deceived in imagining that the happiness of other people is not a very considerable and essential portion of our own. It is common capital, which cannot be created by the individual, and which does not perish with him. The formal and material limitation of the *ego* is necessary and sufficient only for the crudest practical objects, and cannot subsist in a broad conception. Humanity in its entirety may be likened to a polyp-plant. The material and organic bonds of individual union have, indeed, been severed; they would only have impeded freedom of movement and evolution. But the ultimate aim, the psychical connexion of the whole, has been attained in a much higher degree through the richer development thus made possible.

[4] C. E. von Baer, the subsequent opponent of Darwin and Haeckel, has discussed the narrowness of the view which regards an animal in its existing state as finished and complete, instead of conceiving it as a phase in the series of evolutionary forms and regarding the species itself as a phase of the development of the animal world in general.

On the Principle of Comparison in Physics*

Twenty years ago when Kirchhoff[1] defined the object of mechanics as the "description, in complete and very simple terms, of the motions occurring in nature," he produced by the statement a peculiar impression. Fourteen years subsequently, Boltzmann,[2] in the life-like picture which he drew of the great inquirer, could still speak of the universal astonishment at this novel method of treating mechanics, and we meet with epistemological treatises to-day, which plainly show how difficult is the acceptance of this point of view. A modest and small band of inquirers there were, however, to whom Kirchhoff's few words were tidings of a welcome and powerful ally in the epistemological field.

Now, how does it happen that we yield our assent so reluctantly to the philosophical opinion of an inquirer for whose scientific achievements we have only words of praise? One reason probably is that few inquirers can find time and leisure, amid the exacting employments demanded for the acquisition of new knowledge, to inquire closely into that tremendous psychical process by which science is formed. Further, it is inevitable that much should be put into Kirchhoff's rigid words that they were not originally intended to convey, and that much should be found wanting in them that had always been regarded as an essential element of scientific knowledge. What can mere description accomplish? What has become of explanation, of our insight into the causal connexion of things?

*　　*　　*

Permit me, for a moment, to contemplate not the results of science, but the mode of its

growth, in a frank and unbiassed manner. We know of only *one* source of *immediate revelation* of scientific facts—*our senses*. Restricted to this source alone, thrown wholly upon his own resources, obliged to start always anew, what could the isolated individual accomplish? Of a stock of knowledge so acquired the science of a distant negro hamlet in darkest Africa could hardly give us a sufficiently humiliating conception. For there that veritable miracle of thought-transference has already begun its work, compared with which the miracles of the spiritualists are rank monstrosities— *communication by language*. Reflect, too, that by means of the magical characters which our libraries contain we can raise the spirits of "the sovereign dead of old" from Faraday to Galileo and Archimedes, through ages of time—spirits who do not dismiss us with ambiguous and derisive oracles, but tell us the best they know; then shall we feel what a stupendous and indispensable factor in the formation of science *communication* is. Not the dim, half-conscious *surmises* of the acute observer of nature or critic of humanity belong to science, but only that which they possess clearly enough to *communicate* to others.

But how, now, do we go about this communication of a newly acquired experience, of a newly observed fact? As the different calls and battle-cries of gregarious animals are unconsciously formed signs for a com-

---

* An address delivered before the General Session of the German Association of Naturalists and Physicians, at Vienna, Sept. 24, 1894.

[1] G. R. Kirchhoff (1824–87), physicist who established the theory of spectrum analysis.

[2] L. E. Boltzmann (1844–1906), physicist celebrated for his role in the development of statistical mechanics.

mon observation or action, irrespective of the causes which produce such action—a fact that already involves the germ of the concept; so also the words of human language, which is only more highly specialised, are names or signs for universally known facts, which all can observe or have observed. If the mental representation, accordingly, follows the new fact at once and *passively*, then that new fact must, of itself, immediately be constituted and represented in thought by facts already universally known and commonly observed. Memory is always ready to put forward for *comparison* known facts which resemble the new event, or agree with it in certain features, and so renders possible that elementary internal judgment which the mature and definitely formulated judgment soon follows.

Comparison, as the fundamental condition of communication, is the most powerful inner vital element of science. The zoölogist sees in the bones of the wing-membranes of bats, fingers; he compares the bones of the cranium with the vertebræ, the embryos of different organisms with one another, and the different stages of development of the same organism with one another. The geographer sees in Lake Garda a fjord, in the Sea of Aral a lake in process of drying up. The philologist compares different languages with one another, and the formations of the same language as well. If it is not customary to speak of comparative physics in the same sense that we speak of comparative anatomy, the reason is that in a science of such great experimental activity the attention is turned away too much from the *contemplative* element. But like all other sciences, physics lives and grows by comparison.

*   *   *

The manner in which the result of the comparison finds expression in the communication, varies of course very much. When we say that the colors of the spectrum are red, yellow, green, blue, and violet, the designations employed may possibly have been derived from the technology of tattooing, or they may subsequently have acquired the significance of standing for the colors of the rose, the lemon, the leaf, the cornflower, and the violet. From the frequent repetition of such comparisons, however, made under the most manifold circumstances, the inconstant features, as compared with the permanent congruent features, get so obliterated that the latter acquire a fixed significance independent of every object and connexion, or take on as we say an *abstract* or *conceptual* import. No one thinks at the word "red" of any other agreement with the rose than that of color, or at the word "straight" of any other property of a stretched cord than the sameness of direction. Just so, too, numbers, originally the names of the fingers of the hands and feet, from being used as arrangement-signs for all kinds of objects, were lifted to the plane of abstract concepts. A verbal report (communication) of a fact that uses only these purely abstract implements, we call a *direct description*.

The direct description of a fact of any great extent is an irksome task, even where the requisite notions are already completely developed. What a simplification it involves if we can say, the fact *A* now considered comports itself, not in *one*, but in *many* or in *all* its features, like an old and well-known fact *B*. The moon comports itself as a heavy body does with respect to the earth; light like a wave-motion or an electric vibration; a magnet, as if it were laden with gravitating fluids, and so on. We call such a description, in which we appeal, as it were, to a description already and elsewhere formulated, or perhaps still to be precisely formulated, an *indirect description*. We are at liberty to supplement this description, gradually, by direct description, to correct it, or to replace it altogether. We see, thus, without difficulty, that what is called a *theory* or a *theoretical idea*, falls under the category of what is here termed indirect description.

*   *   *

What, now, is a theoretical idea? Whence do we get it? What does it accomplish for us?

Why does it occupy a higher place in our judgment than the mere holding fast to a fact or an observation? Here, too, memory and comparison alone are in play. But instead of *a single* feature of resemblance culled from memory, in this case *a great system* of resemblances confronts us, a well-known physiognomy, by means of which the new fact is immediately transformed into an old acquaintance. Besides, it is in the power of the idea to offer us more than we actually see in the new fact, at the first moment; it can extend the fact, and enrich it with features which we are first induced to *seek* from such suggestions, and which are often actually found. It is this *rapidity* in extending knowledge that gives to theory a preference over simple observation. But that preference is wholly *quantitative*. Qualitatively, and in real essential points, theory differs from observation neither in the mode of its origin nor in its last results.

The adoption of a theory, however, always involves a danger. For a theory puts in the place of a fact *A* in thought, always a *different*, but simpler and more familiar fact *B*, which in *some* relations can mentally represent *A*, but for the very reason that it is different, in other relations cannot represent it. If now, as may readily happen, sufficient care is not exercised, the most fruitful theory may, in special circumstances, become a downright obstacle to inquiry. Thus, the emission-theory of light, in accustoming the physicist to think of the projectile path of the "light-particles" as an undifferentiated straight-line, demonstrably impeded the discovery of the periodicity of light. By putting in the place of light the more familiar phenomena of sound, Huygens renders light in many of its features a familiar event, but with respect to polarisation, which lacks the longitudinal waves with which alone he was acquainted, it had for him a doubly strange aspect. He is unable thus to grasp in abstract thought the fact of polarisation, which is before his eyes, whilst Newton, merely by adapting to the observation his thoughts, and putting this question, "*Annon radiorum luminus diversa sunt latera?*"

["Have not the rays of light. . . ?"][3] abstractly grasped polarisation, that is, directly described it, a century before Malus.[4] On the other hand, if the agreement of the fact with the idea theoretically representing it, extends further than its inventor originally anticipated, then we may be led by it to unexpected discoveries, of which conical refraction, circular polarisation by total reflexion, Hertz's waves offer ready examples, in contrast to the illustrations given above.

Our insight into the conditions indicated will be improved, perhaps, by contemplating the development of some theory or other more in detail. Let us consider a magnetised bar of steel by the side of a second unmagnetised bar, in all other respects the same. The second bar gives no indication of the presence of iron-filings; the first attracts them. Also, when the iron-filings are absent, we must think of the magnetised bar as in a different condition from that of the unmagnetised. For, that the mere presence of the iron-filings does not induce the phenomenon of attraction is proved by the second unmagnetised bar. The ingenuous man, who finds in his will, as his most familiar source of power, the best facilities for comparison, conceives a species of *spirit* in the magnet. The behavior of a warm body or of an *electrified* body suggests similar ideas. This is the point of view of the oldest theory, *fetishism*, which the inquirers of the early Middle Ages had not yet overcome, and which in its last vestiges, in the conception of forces, still flourishes in modern physics. We see, thus, the *dramatic* element need no more be absent in a scientific description, than in a thrilling novel.

If, on subsequent examination, it be observed that a cold body, in contact with a hot body, warms itself, so to speak, *at the expense* of the hot body; further, that when the substances are the same, the cold body, which,

[3] Sir Issac Newton, *Optics*, Book Two, Part 1, Qu. 26; GBWW, Vol. 34, p. 524.
[4] E. L. Malus (1775–1812), a French physicist who made important discoveries relating to the polarization of light.

let us say, has twice the mass of the other, gains only half the number of degrees of temperature that the other loses, a wholly new impression arises. The demoniac character of the event vanishes, for the supposed spirit acts not by caprice, but according to fixed laws. In its place, however, *instinctively* the notion of a *substance* is substituted, part of which flows over from the one body to the other, but the total amount of which, representable by the sum of the products of the masses into the respective changes of temperature, remains constant. Black[5] was the first to be *powerfully* struck with this resemblance of thermal processes to the motion of a substance, and under its guidance discovered the specific heat, the heat of fusion, and the heat of vaporisation of bodies. Gaining strength and fixity, however, from these successes, this notion of substance subsequently stood in the way of scientific advancement. It blinded the eyes of the successors of Black, and prevented them from seeing the manifest fact, which every savage knows, that heat is *produced* by friction. Fruitful as that notion was for Black, helpful as it still is to the learner to-day in Black's special field, permanent and universal validity as a *theory* it could never maintain. But what is essential, conceptually, in it, viz., the constancy of the product-sum above mentioned, retains its value and may be regarded as a *direct description* of Black's facts.

It stands to reason that those theories which push themselves forward unsought, instinctively, and wholly of their own accord, should have the greatest power, should carry our thoughts most with them, and exhibit the staunchest powers of self-preservation. On the other hand, it may also be observed that when critically scrutinised such theories are extremely apt to lose their cogency. We are constantly busied with "substance," its modes of action have stamped themselves indelibly upon our thoughts, our vividest and clearest reminiscences are associated with it. It should cause us no surprise, therefore, that J. R. Mayer[6] and Joule,[7] who gave the final blow to Black's substantial conception of

heat, should have re-introduced the same notion of substance in a more abstract and modified form, only applying to a much more extensive field.

Here, too, the psychological circumstances which impart to the new conception its power, lie clearly before us. By the unusual redness of the venous blood in tropical climates Mayer's attention is directed to the lessened expenditure of internal heat and to the proportionately lessened *consumption of material* by the human body in those climates. But as every effort of the human organism, including its mechanical work, is connected with the consumption of material, and as work by friction can engender heat, therefore heat and work appear in kind equivalent, and between them a proportional relation must subsist. Not *every* quantity, but the appropriately calculated *sum* of the two, as connected with a proportionate consumption of material, appears *substantial.*

By exactly similar considerations, relative to the economy of the galvanic element, Joule arrived at his view; he found experimentally that the sum of the heat evolved in the circuit, of the heat consumed in the combustion of the gas developed, of the electromagnetic work of the current, properly calculated,—in short, the sum of all the effects of the battery,—is connected with a proportionate consumption of zinc. Accordingly, this sum itself has a substantial character.

Mayer was so absorbed with the view attained, that the indestructability of *force*, in our phraseology *work*, appeared to him *a priori* evident. "The creation or annihilation of a force," he says, "lies without the province of human thought and power." Joule expressed himself to a similar effect: "It is manifestly

---

[5] Joseph Black (1728–99), discoverer of carbon dioxide, the concept of latent heat, etc.
[6] J. R. Mayer (1814–78), German physicist who contributed importantly to the development of thermodynamic theory.
[7] James P. Joule (1811–89), established that the various forms of energy—mechanical, electrical, and heat—are basically the same (the basis of the first law of thermodynamics).

absurd to suppose that the powers with which God has endowed matter can be destroyed." Strange to say, on the basis of such utterances, not Joule, but Mayer, was stamped as a metaphysician. We may be sure, however, that both men were merely giving expression, and that half-unconsciously, to a powerful *formal* need of the new simple view, and that both would have been extremely surprised if it had been proposed to them that their principle should be submitted to a philosophical congress or ecclesiastical synod for a decision upon its validity. But with all agreements, the attitude of these two men, in other respects, was totally different. Whilst Mayer represented this *formal* need with all the stupendous instinctive force of genius, we might say almost with the ardor of fanaticism, yet was withal not wanting in the conceptive ability to compute, prior to all other inquirers, the mechanical equivalent of heat from old physical constants long known and at the disposal of all, and so to set up for the new doctrine a programme embracing all physics and physiology; Joule, on the other hand, applied himself to the exact verification of the doctrine by beautifully conceived and masterfully executed experiments, extending over all departments of physics. Soon Helmholtz too attacked the problem, in a totally independent and characteristic manner. After the professional virtuosity with which this physicist grasped and disposed of all the points unsettled by Mayer's programme and more besides, what especially strikes us is the consummate critical lucidity of this young man of twenty-six years. In his exposition is wanting that vehemence and impetuosity which marked Mayer's. The principle of the conservation of energy is no self-evident or *a priori* proposition for him. What follows, on the assumption that that proposition obtains? In this hypothetical form, he subjugates his matter.

I must confess, I have always marvelled at the æsthetic and ethical taste of many of our contemporaries who have managed to fabricate out of this relation of things, odious national and personal questions, instead of praising the good fortune that made *several* such men work together and of rejoicing at the instructive diversity and idiosyncrasies of great minds fraught with such rich consequences for us.

We know that still another theoretical conception played a part in the development of the principle of energy, which Mayer held aloof from, namely, the conception that heat, as also the other physical processes, are due to motion. But once the principle of energy has been reached, these auxiliary and transitional theories discharge no essential function, and we may regard the principle, like that which Black gave, as a contribution to the *direct description* of a widely extended domain of facts.

It would appear from such considerations not only advisable, but even necessary, with all due recognition of the helpfulness of theoretic ideas in research, yet gradually, as the new facts grow familiar, to substitute for indirect description *direct* description, which contains nothing that is unessential and restricts itself absolutely to the abstract apprehension of facts. We might almost say, that the descriptive sciences, so called with a tincture of condescension, have, in respect of scientific character, outstripped the physical expositions lately in vogue. Of course, a virtue has been made of necessity here.

We must admit, that it is not in our power to describe directly every fact, on the moment. Indeed, we should succumb in utter despair if the whole wealth of facts which we come step by step to know, were presented to us all at once. Happily, only detached and unusual features first strike us, and such we bring nearer to ourselves by *comparison* with every-day events. Here the notions of the common speech are first developed. The comparisons then grow more manifold and numerous, the fields of facts compared more extensive, the concepts that make direct description possible, proportionately more general and more abstract.

First we become familiar with the motion of freely falling bodies. The concepts of force, mass, and work are then carried over, with appropriate modifications, to the phenomena of electricity and magnetism. A stream of water is said to have suggested to Fourier the first distinct picture of currents of heat. A special case of vibrations of strings investigated by Taylor,[8] cleared up for him a special case of the conduction of heat. Much in the same way that Daniel Bernoulli and Euler constructed the most diverse forms of vibrations of strings from Taylor's cases, so Fourier constructs out of simple cases of conduction the most multifarious motions of heat; and that method has extended itself over the whole of physics. Ohm forms his conception of the electric current in imitation of Fourier's. The latter, also, adopts Fick's theory of diffusion. In an analogous manner a conception of the magnetic current is developed. All sorts of stationary currents are thus made to exhibit common features, and even the condition of complete equilibrium in an extended medium shares these features with the dynamical condition of equilibrium of a stationary current. Things as remote as the magnetic lines of force of an electric current and the streamlines of a frictionless liquid vortex enter in this way into a peculiar relationship of similarity. The concept of potential, originally enunciated for a restricted province, acquires a wide-reaching applicability. Things as dissimilar as pressure, temperature, and electromotive force, now show points of agreement in relation to ideas derived by definite methods from that concept: viz., fall of pressure, fall of temperature, fall of potential, as also with the further notions of liquid, thermal, and electric strength of current. That relationship between systems of ideas in which the dissimilarity of every two homologous concepts as well as the agreement in logical relations of every two homologous pairs of concepts, is clearly brought to light, is called an *analogy*. It is an effective means of mastering heterogeneous fields of facts in unitary comprehension. The path is plainly shown in which *a universal physical phenomenology* embracing all domains, will be developed.

In the process described we attain for the first time to what is indispensable in the direct description of broad fields of fact—the wide-reaching *abstract concept*. And now I must put a question smacking of the schoolmaster, but unavoidable: What is a concept? Is it a hazy representation, admitting withal of mental visualisation? No. Mental visualisation accompanies it only in the simplest cases, and then merely as an adjunct. Think, for example, of the "coefficient of self-induction," and seek for its visualised mental image. Or is, perhaps, the concept a mere word? The adoption of this forlorn idea, which has been actually proposed of late by a reputed mathematician would only throw us back a thousand years into the deepest scholasticism. We must, therefore, reject it.

The solution is not far to seek. We must not think that sensation, or representation, is a purely passive process. The lowest organisms respond to it with a simple reflex motion, by engulfing the prey which approaches them. In higher organisms the centripetal stimulus encounters in the nervous system obstacles and aids which modify the centrifugal process. In still higher organisms, where prey is pursued and examined, the process in question may go through extensive paths of circular motions before it comes to relative rest. Our own life, too, is enacted in such processes; all that we call science may be regarded as parts, or middle terms, of such activities.

It will not surprise us now if I say: the definition of a concept, and, when it is very familiar, even its name, is an *impulse* to some accurately determined, often complicated, critical, comparative, or constructive *activity*, the usually sense-perceptive result of which is a term or member of the concept's scope. It matters not whether the concept draws the attention only to one certain sense (as sight) or to a phase of a sense (as color, form), or is the starting point of a complicated action; nor whether the activity in question (chemi-

---

[8] Brook Taylor (1685–1731), mathematician who first reduced the form of a vibrating string to mechanical principles.

cal, anatomical, and mathematical operations) is muscular or technical, or performed wholly in the imagination, or only intimated. The concept is to the physicist what a musical note is to a piano-player. A trained physicist or mathematician reads a memoir like a musician reads a score. But just as the piano-player must first learn to move his fingers singly and collectively, before he can follow his notes without effort, so the physicist or mathematician must go through a long apprenticeship before he gains control, so to speak, of the manifold delicate innervations of his muscles and imagination. Think of how frequently the beginner in physics or mathematics performs more, or less, than is required, or of how frequently he conceives things differently from what they are! But if, after having had sufficient discipline, he lights upon the phrase "coefficient of self-induction," he knows immediately what that term requires of him. Long and thoroughly practiced *actions*, which have their origin in the necessity of comparing and representing facts by other facts, are thus the very kernel of concepts. In fact, positive and philosophical philology both claim to have established that all roots represent concepts and stood originally for muscular activities alone. The slow assent of physicists to Kirchhoff's dictum now becomes intelligible. They best could feel the vast amount of individual labor, theory, and skill required before the ideal of direct description could be realised.

*   *   *

Suppose, now, the ideal of a given province of facts is reached. Does description accomplish all that the inquirer can ask? In my opinion, it does. Description is a building up of facts in thought, and this building up is, in the experimental sciences, often the condition of actual execution. For the physicist, to take a special case, the metrical units are the buildingstones, the concepts the directions for building, and the facts the result of the building. Our mental imagery is almost a complete substitute for the fact, and by means of it we can ascertain all the fact's

properties. We do not know that worst which we ourselves have made.

People require of science that it should *prophesy,* and Hertz uses that expression in his posthumous *Mechanics.* But, natural as it is, the expression is too narrow. The geologist and the palæontologist, at times the astronomer, and always the historian and the philologist, prophesy, so to speak, *backwards.* The descriptive sciences, like geometry and mathematics, prophesy neither forward or backwards, but seek from given conditions the conditioned. Let us say rather: *Science completes in thought facts that are only partly given.* This is rendered possible by description, for description presupposes the interdependence of the descriptive elements: otherwise nothing would be described.

It is said, description leaves the sense of causality unsatisfied. In fact, many imagine they understand motions better when they picture to themselves the pulling forces; and yet the *accelerations,* the facts, accomplish more, without superfluous additions. I hope that the science of the future will discard the idea of cause and effect, as being formally obscure; and in my feeling that these ideas contain a strong tincture of fetishism, I am certainly not alone. The more proper course is, *to regard the abstract determinative elements of a fact as interdependent,* in a purely logical way, as the mathematician or geometer does. True, by comparison with the will, forces are brought nearer to our feeling; but it may be that ultimately the will itself will be made clearer by comparison with the accelerations of masses.

If we are asked, candidly, when is a fact *clear* to us, we must say "when we can reproduce it by very *simple* and very familiar intellectual operations, such as the construction of accelerations, or the geometrical summation of accelerations, and so forth." The requirement of *simplicity* is of course to the expert a different matter from what it is to the novice. For the first, description by a system of differential equations is sufficient; for the second, a gradual construction out of elementary laws is required. The first discerns at once the connexion of the two expositions. Of course, it is not disputed that the *artistic* value of materially equivalent descriptions may not be different.

Most difficult is it to persuade strangers that the grand universal laws of physics, such as apply indiscriminately to material, electrical, magnetic, and other systems, are not essentially different from descriptions. As compared with many sciences, physics occupies in this respect a position of vantage that is easily explained. Take, for example, anatomy. As the anatomist in his quest for agreements and differences in animals ascends to ever higher and higher *classifications,* the individual facts that represent the ultimate terms of the system, are still so different that they must be *singly* noted. Think, for example, of the common marks of the vertebrates, of the class-characters of mammals and birds on the one hand and of fishes on the other, of the double circulation of the blood on the one hand and of the single on the other. In the end, always *isolated* facts remain, which show only a *slight* likeness to one another.

A science still more closely allied to physics, chemistry, is often in the same strait. The abrupt change of the qualitative properties, in all likelihood conditioned by the slight stability of the intermediate states, the remote resemblance of the co-ordinated facts of chemistry render the treatment of its data difficult. Pairs of bodies of different qualitative properties unite in different mass-ratios; but no connexion between the first and the last is to be noted, at first.

Physics, on the other hand, reveals to us wide domains of *qualitatively homogeneous* facts, differing from one another only in the number of equal parts into which their characteristic marks are divisible, that is, differing only *quantitatively.* Even where we have to deal with qualities (colors and sounds), quantitative characters of those qualities are at our disposal. Here the classification is so simple a task that it rarely impresses us as such, whilst in infinitely fine gradations, in a *continuum of facts,* our number-system is ready beforehand to follow as far as we wish. The co-ordinated facts are here extremely similar and very closely affined, as are also their descriptions which consist in the determination of the numerical measures of one given set of characters from those of a different set by means of familiar mathematical operations —methods of derivation. Thus, the common characteristics of all descriptions can be found here; and with them a succinct, comprehensive description, or a rule for the construction of all single descriptions, is assigned,—and this we call *law.* Well-known examples are the formulæ for freely falling bodies, for projectiles, for central motion, and so forth. If physics apparently accomplishes more by its methods than other sciences, we must remember that in a sense it has presented to it much simpler problems.

The remaining sciences, whose facts also present a physical side, need not be envious of physics for this superiority; for all its acquisitions ultimately redound to their benefit as well. But also in other ways this mutual help shall and must change. Chemistry has advanced very far in making the methods of physics her own. Apart from older attempts, the periodical series of Lothar Meyer and Mendelejeff are a brilliant and adequate means of producing an easily surveyed system of facts, which by gradually becoming complete, will take the place almost of a continuum of facts. Further, by the study of solutions, of dissociation, in fact generally of phenomena which present a continuum of cases, the methods of thermodynamics have found entrance into chemistry. Similarly we may hope that, at some future day, a mathematician, letting the fact-continuum of embryology play before his mind, which the palæontologists of the future will supposedly have enriched with more intermediate and derivative forms between Saurian and Bird than the isolated Pterodactyl, Archaeopteryx, Ichthyornis, and so forth, which we now have—that such a mathematician shall transform, by the variation of a few parameters, as in a dissolving view, one form into another, just as we transform one conic section into another.

Reverting now to Kirchhoff's words, we can come to some agreement regarding their import. Nothing can be built without building-stones, mortar, scaffolding, and a builder's skill. Yet assuredly the wish is well founded, that will show to posterity the complete structure in its finished form, bereft of unsightly scaffolding. It is the pure logical and æsthetic sense of the mathematician that speaks out of Kirchhoff's words. Modern expositions of physics aspire after his ideal; that, too, is intelligible. But it would be a poor didactic shift, for one whose business it was to train architects, to say: "Here is a splendid edifice; if thou wouldst really build, go thou and do likewise."

The barriers between the special sciences, which make division of work and concentration possible, but which appear to us after all as cold and conventional restrictions, will gradually disappear. Bridge upon bridge is thrown over the gaps. Contents and methods, even of the remotest branches, are compared. When the Congress of Natural Scientists shall meet a hundred years hence, we may expect that they will represent a unity in a higher sense than is possible to-day, not in sentiment and aim alone, but in method also. In the meantime, this great change will be helped by our keeping constantly before our minds the fact of the intrinsic relationship of all research, which Kirchhoff characterised with such classical simplicity.

The Part Played by Accident in Invention and Discovery*

It is characteristic of the naïve and sanguine beginnings of thought in youthful men and nations, that all problems are held to be soluble and fundamentally intelligible on the first appearance of success. The sage of Miletus,[1] on seeing plants take their rise from moisture, believed he had comprehended the whole of nature, and he of Samos,[2] on discovering that definite numbers corresponded to the lengths of harmonic strings, imagined he could exhaust the nature of the world by means of numbers. Philosophy and science in such periods are blended. Wider experience, however, speedily discloses the error of such a course, gives rise to criticism, and leads to the division and ramification of the sciences.

At the same time, the necessity of a broad and general view of the world remains; and to meet this need philosophy parts company with special inquiry. It is true, the two are often found united in gigantic personalities. But as a rule their ways diverge more and more widely from each other. And if the estrangement of philosophy from science can reach a point where data unworthy of the nursery are not deemed too scanty as foundations of the world, on the other hand the thorough-paced specialist may go to the extreme of rejecting point-blank the possibility of a broader view, or at least of deeming it superfluous, forgetful of Voltaire's apophthegm, nowhere more applicable than here, *Le superflu—chose très nécessaire.*

It is true, the history of philosophy, owing to the insufficiency of its constructive data, is and must be largely a history of error. But it would be the height of ingratitude on our part to forget that the seeds of thoughts which still fructify the soil of special research, such as the theory of irrationals, the conceptions of conservation, the doctrine of evolution, the idea of specific energies, and so forth, may be traced back in distant ages to philosophical sources. Furthermore, to have deferred or abandoned the attempt at a broad philosophical view of the world from a full knowledge of the insufficiency of our materials, is quite a different thing from never having undertaken it at all. The revenge of its neglect, moreover, is constantly visited upon the specialist by his committal of the very errors which philosophy long ago exposed. As a fact, in physics and physiology, particularly during the first half of this century, are to be met intellectual productions which for naïve simplicity are not a jot inferior to those of the Ionian school, or to the Platonic ideas, or to that much reviled ontological proof.

Latterly, there has been evidence of a gradual change in the situation. Recent philosophy has set itself more modest and more attainable ends; it is no longer inimical to special inquiry; in fact, it is zealously taking part in that inquiry. On the other hand, the special sciences, mathematics and physics, no less than philology, have become eminently philosophical. The material presented is no longer accepted uncritically. The glance of the inquirer is bent upon neighboring fields, whence that material has been derived. The different special departments are striving for closer union, and gradually the conviction is gaining ground that philosophy can consist

---

* Inaugural lecture delivered on assuming the Professorship of the History and Theory of Inductive Science in the University of Vienna, October 21, 1895.
[1] Thales
[2] Pythagoras

only of mutual, complemental criticism, interpenetration, and union of the special sciences into a consolidated whole. As the blood in nourishing the body separates into countless capillaries, only to be collected again and to meet in the heart, so in the science of the future all the rills of knowledge will gather more and more into a common and undivided stream.

It is this view—not an unfamiliar one to the present generation—that I purpose to advocate. Entertain no hope, or rather fear, that I shall construct systems for you. I shall remain a natural inquirer. Nor expect that it is my intention to skirt all the fields of natural inquiry. I can attempt to be your guide only in that branch which is familiar to me, and even there I can assist in the furtherment of only a small portion of the allotted task. If I shall succeed in rendering plain to you the relations of physics, psychology, and the theory of knowledge, so that you may draw from each profit and light, redounding to the advantage of each, I shall regard my work as not having been in vain. Therefore, to illustrate by an example how, consonantly with my powers and views, I conceive such inquiries should be conducted, I shall treat to-day, in the form of a brief sketch, of the following special and limited subject—of *the part which accidental circumstances play in the development of inventions and discoveries.*

*   *   *

When we Germans say of a man that he was not the inventor of gunpowder,[3] we impliedly cast a grave suspicion on his abilities. But the expression is not a felicitous one, as there is probably no invention in which deliberate thought had a smaller, and pure luck a larger, share than in this. It is well to ask, Are we justified in placing a low estimate on the achievement of an inventor because accident has assisted him in his work? Huygens, whose discoveries and inventions are justly sufficient to entitle him to an opinion in such matters, lays great emphasis on this factor. He asserts that a man capable of inventing the telescope without the concurrence of

accident must have been gifted with superhuman genius.

A man living in the midst of civilisation finds himself surrounded by a host of marvellous inventions, considering none other than the means of satisfying the needs of daily life. Picture such a man transported to the epoch preceding the invention of these ingenious appliances, and imagine him undertaking in a serious manner to comprehend their origin. At first the intellectual power of the men capable of producing such marvels will strike him as incredible, or, if we adopt the ancient view, as divine. But his astonishment is considerably allayed by the disenchanting yet elucidative revelations of the history of primitive culture, which to a large extent prove that these inventions took their rise very slowly and by imperceptible degrees.

A small hole in the ground with fire kindled in it constituted the primitive stove. The flesh of the quarry, wrapped with water in its skin, was boiled by contact with heated stones. Cooking by stones was also done in wooden vessels. Hollow gourds were protected from the fire by coats of clay. Thus, from the burned clay accidentally originated the enveloping pot, which rendered the gourd superfluous, although for a long time thereafter the clay was still spread over the gourd, or pressed into woven wicker-work before the potter's art assumed its final independence. Even then the wicker-work ornament was retained, as a sort of attest of its origin.

We see, thus, it is by accidental circumstances, or by such as lie without our purpose, foresight, and power, that man is gradually led to the acquaintance of improved means of satisfying his wants. Let the reader picture to himself the genius of a man who could have foreseen without the help of accident that clay handled in the ordinary manner would produce a useful cooking utensil! The majority of the inventions made in the early stages of civilisation, including language, writing, money, and the rest, could

---

[3] The phrase is, *Er hat das Pulver nicht erfunden.*

not have been the product of deliberate methodical reflexion for the simple reason that no idea of their value and significance could have been had except from practical use. The invention of the bridge may have been suggested by the trunk of a tree which had fallen athwart a mountain-torrent; that of the tool by the use of a stone accidentally taken into the hand to crack nuts. The use of fire probably started in and was disseminated from regions where volcanic eruptions, hot springs, and burning jets of natural gas afforded opportunity for quietly observing and turning to practical account the properties of fire. Only after that had been done could the significance of the fire-drill be appreciated, an instrument which was probably discovered from boring a hole through a piece of wood. The suggestion of a distinguished inquirer that the invention of the fire-drill originated on the occasion of a religious ceremony is both fantastic and incredible. And as to the use of fire, we should no more attempt to derive that from the invention of the fire-drill than we should from the invention of sulphur matches. Unquestionably the opposite course was the real one.[4]

Similar phenomena, though still largely veiled in obscurity, mark the initial transition of nations from a hunting to a nomadic life and to agriculture.[5] We shall not multiply examples, but content ourselves with the remark that the same phenomena recur in historical times, in the ages of great technical inventions, and, further, that regarding them the most whimsical notions have been circulated — notions which ascribe to accident an unduly exaggerated part, and one which in a psychological respect is absolutely impossible. The observation of steam escaping from a tea-kettle and of the clattering of the lid is supposed to have led to the invention of the steam-engine. Just think of the gap between this spectacle and the conception of the performance of great mechanical work by steam, for a man totally ignorant of the steam-engine! Let us suppose, however, that an engineer, versed in the practical construction of pumps, should accidentally dip into water an inverted bottle that had been filled with steam for drying and still retained its steam. He would see the water rush violently into the bottle, and the idea would very naturally suggest itself of founding on this experience a convenient and useful atmospheric steam-pump, which by imperceptible degrees, both psychologically possible and immediate, would then undergo a natural and gradual transformation into Watt's steam-engine.

But granting that the most important inventions are brought to man's notice accidentally and in ways that are beyond his foresight, yet it does not follow that accident alone is sufficient to produce an invention. The part which man plays is by no means a passive one. Even the first potter in the primeval forest must have felt some stirrings of genius within him. In all such cases, the inventor is obliged *to take note* of the new fact, he must discover and grasp its advantageous feature, and must have the power to turn that feature to account in the realisation of his purpose. He must *isolate* the new feature, impress it upon his memory, unite and interweave it with the rest of his thought; in short, he must possess the capacity *to profit by experience.*

The capacity to profit by experience might well be set up as a test of intelligence. This power varies considerably in men of the same race, and increases enormously as we advance from the lower animals to man. The former are limited in this regard almost entirely to the reflex actions which they have inherited with their organism, they are almost totally incapable of individual experience, and considering their simple wants are scarcely in need of it. The ivory-snail (*Eburna spirata*) never learns to avoid the carnivorous Actinia, no matter how often it may wince under the latter's shower of needles, appar-

---

[4] I must not be understood as saying that the fire-drill has played no part in the worship of fire or of the sun.

[5] Compare on this point the extremely interesting remarks of Dr. Paul Carus in his *Philosophy of the Tool*, Chicago, 1893.

ently having no memory for pain whatever. A spider can be lured forth repeatedly from its hole by touching its web with a tuning-fork. The moth plunges again and again into the flame which has burnt it. The humming-bird hawk-moth dashes repeatedly against the painted roses of the wall-paper, like the unhappy and desperate thinker who never wearies of attacking the same insoluble chimerical problem. As aimlessly almost as Maxwell's gaseous molecules and in the same unreasoning manner common flies in their search for light and air stream against the glass pane of a half-opened window and remain there from sheer inability to find their way around the narrow frame. But a pike separated from the minnows of his aquarium by a glass partition, learns after the lapse of a few months, though only after having butted himself half to death, that he cannot attack these fishes with impunity. What is more, he leaves them in peace even after the removal of the partition, though he will bolt a strange fish at once. Considerable memory must be attributed to birds of passage, a memory which, probably owing to the absence of disturbing thoughts, acts with the precision of that of some idiots. Finally, the susceptibility to training evinced by the higher vertebrates is indisputable proof of the ability of these animals to profit by experience.

A powerfully developed *mechanical* memory, which recalls vividly and faithfully old situations, is sufficient for avoiding definite particular dangers, or for taking advantage of definite particular opportunities. But more is required for the development of *inventions*. More extensive chains of images are necessary here, the excitation by mutual contact of widely different trains of ideas, a more powerful, more manifold, and richer connexion of the contents of memory, a more powerful and impressionable psychical life, heightened by use. A man stands on the bank of a mountain-torrent, which is a serious obstacle to him. He remembers that he has crossed just such a torrent before on the trunk of a fallen tree. Hard by trees are

growing. He has often moved the trunks of fallen trees. He has also felled trees before, and then moved them. To fell trees he has used sharp stones. He goes in search of such a stone, and as the old situations that crowd into his memory and are held there in living reality by the definite powerful interest which he has in crossing just this torrent,—as these impressions are made to pass before his mind in the *inverse order* in which they were here evoked, he invents the bridge.

There can be no doubt but the higher vertebrates adapt their actions in some moderate degree to circumstances. The fact that they give no appreciable evidence of advance by the accumulation of inventions, is satisfactorily explained by a difference of degree or intensity of intelligence as compared with man; the assumption of a difference of kind is not necessary. A person who saves a little every day, be it ever so little, has an incalculable advantage over him who daily squanders that amount, or is unable to keep what he has accumulated. A slight quantitative difference in such things explains enormous differences of advancement.

The rules which hold good in prehistoric times also hold good in historical times, and the remarks made on invention may be applied almost without modification to discovery; for the two are distinguished solely by the use to which the new knowledge is put. In both cases the investigator is concerned with some *newly observed* relation of new or old properties, abstract or concrete. It is observed, for example, that a substance which gives a chemical reaction A is also the cause of a chemical reaction B. If this observation fulfils no purpose but that of furthering the scientist's insight, or of removing a source of intellectual discomfort, we have a discovery; but an invention, if in using the substance giving the reaction A to produce the desired reaction B, we have a practical end in view, and seek to remove a source of material discomfort. The phrase, *disclosure of the connexion of reactions*, is broad enough to cover discoveries and inventions in all departments. It embraces the Pythagorean proposition, which is a combination of a geometrical and an arithmetical reaction, Newton's discovery of the connexion of Kepler's motions with the law of the inverse squares, as perfectly as it does the detection of some minute but appropriate alteration in the construction of a tool, or of some appropriate change in the methods of a dyeing establishment.

The disclosure of new provinces of facts before unknown can only be brought about by accidental circumstances, under which are *remarked* facts that commonly go unnoticed. The achievement of the discoverer here consists in his *sharpened attention*, which detects the uncommon features of an occurrence and their determining conditions from their most evanescent marks, and discovers means of submitting them to exact and full observation. Under this head belong the first disclosures of electrical and magnetic phenomena, Grimaldi's observation of interference, Arago's discovery of the increased check suffered by a magnetic needle vibrating in a copper envelope as compared with that observed in a bandbox, Foucault's observation of the stability of the plane of vibration of a rod accidentally struck while rotating in a turning-lathe, Mayer's observation of the increased redness of venous blood in the tropics, Kirchhoff's observation of the augmentation of the D-line in the solar spectrum by the interposition of a sodium lamp, Schönbein's discovery of ozone from the phosphoric smell emitted on the disruption of air by electric sparks, and a host of others. All these facts, of which unquestionably many were *seen* numbers of times before they were *noticed*, are examples of the inauguration of momentous discoveries by accidental circumstances, and place the importance of strained attention in a brilliant light.

But not only is a significant part played in the beginning of an inquiry by co-operative circumstances beyond the foresight of the investigator; their influence is also active in its prosecution. Dufay,[6] thus, whilst following up the behavior of *one* electrical state which he had assumed, discovers the existence of *two*. Fresnel[7] learns by accident that the interfer-

ence-bands received on ground glass are seen to better advantage in the open air. The diffraction-phenomenon of two slits proved to be considerably different from what Fraunhofer[8] had anticipated, and in following up this circumstance he was led to the important discovery of grating-spectra. Faraday's induction-phenomenon departed widely from the initial conception which occasioned his experiments, and it is precisely this deviation that constitutes his real discovery.

Every man has pondered on some subject. Every one of us can multiply the examples cited, by less illustrious ones from his own experience. I shall cite but one. On rounding a railway curve once, I accidentally remarked a striking apparent inclination of the houses and trees. I inferred that the direction of the total resultant *physical* acceleration of the body reacts *physiologically* as the vertical. Afterwards, in attempting to inquire more carefully into this phenomenon, and this only, in a large whirling machine, the collateral phenomena conducted me to the sensation of angular acceleration, vertigo, Flouren's experiments on the section of the semi-circular canals etc., from which gradually resulted views relating to sensations of direction which are also held by Breuer[9] and Brown,[10] which were at first contested on all hands, but are now regarded on many sides as correct, and which have been recently enriched by the interesting inquiries of Breuer concerning the *macula acustica*, and Kreidel's experiments with magnetically orientable crustacea. Not disregard of accident but a direct and purposeful employment of it advances research.

The more powerful the psychical connex-

----

6 Charles Dufay (1698–1739), French chemist.
7 Augustin-Jean Fresnel (1788–1827), French physicist.
8 Joseph von Fraunhofer (1787–1826), Bavarian physicist.
9 Josef Breuer (1842–1925), Austrian physiologist and physician.
10 Alexander Crum Brown (1838–1922), Scottish chemist.

ion of the memory pictures is,—and it varies with the individual and the mood,—the more apt is the same accidental observation to be productive of results. Galileo knows that the air has weight; he also knows of the "resistance to a vacuum," expressed both in weight and in the height of a column of water. But the two ideas dwelt asunder in his mind. It remained for Torricelli to vary the specific gravity of the liquid measuring the pressure, and not till then was the air included in the list of pressure-exerting fluids. The reversal of the lines of the spectrum was seen repeatedly before Kirchhoff, and had been mechanically explained. But it was left for his penetrating vision to discern the evidence of the connexion of this phenomenon with questions of heat, and to him alone through persistent labor was revealed the sweeping significance of the fact for the mobile equilibrium of heat. Supposing, then, that such a rich organic connexion of the elements of memory exists, and is the prime distinguishing mark of the inquirer, next in importance certainly is that *intense interest* in a definite object, in a definite idea, which fashions advantageous combinations of thought from elements before disconnected, and obtrudes that idea into every observation made, and into every thought formed, making it enter into relationship with all things. Thus Bradley,[11] deeply engrossed with the subject of aberration, is led to its solution by an exceedingly unobtrusive experience in crossing the Thames. It is permissible, therefore, to ask whether accident leads the discoverer, or the discoverer accident, to a successful outcome in scientific quests.

No man should dream of solving a great problem unless he is so thoroughly saturated with his subject that everything else sinks into comparative insignificance. During a hurried meeting with Mayer in Heidelberg once, Jolly[12] remarked, with a rather dubious implication, that if Mayer's theory were correct water could be warmed by shaking. Mayer went away without a word of reply. Several weeks later, and now unrecognised by Jolly, he rushed into the latter's presence exclaiming:

"*Es ischt aso!*" (It is so, it is so!) It was only after considerable explanation that Jolly found out what Mayer wanted to say. The incident needs no comment.[13]

A person deadened to sensory impressions and given up solely to the pursuit of his own thoughts, may also light on an idea that will divert his mental activity into totally new channels. In such cases it is a psychical accident, an intellectual experience, as distinguished from a physical accident, to which the person owes his discovery—a discovery which is here made "deductively" by means of mental copies of the world, instead of experimentally. *Purely* experimental inquiry, moreover, does not exist, for, as Gauss says, virtually we always experiment with our thoughts. And it is precisely that constant, corrective interchange or intimate union of experiment and deduction, as it was cultivated by Galileo in his *Dialogues* and by Newton in his *Optics,* that is the foundation of the benign fruitfulness of modern scientific inquiry as contrasted with that of antiquity, where observation and reflexion ofttimes pursued their respective courses like two strangers.

We have to wait for the appearance of a favorable physical accident. The movement of our thoughts obeys the law of association. In the case of meagre experience the result of this law is simply the mechanical reproduction of definite sensory experiences. On the other hand, if the psychical life is subjected to the incessant influences of a powerful and rich experience, then every representative element in the mind is connected with so many others that the actual and natural course of the thoughts is easily influenced and determined by insignificant circumstances, which accidentally are decisive. Hereupon, the process termed imagination produces its protean and infinitely diversified forms. Now what can we do to guide

---

[11] James Bradley (1693–1762), English astronomer who discovered the aberration of starlight.
[12] Philipp Jolly (1809–84), German physicist.
[13] This story was related to me by Jolly, and subsequently repeated in a letter from him.

this process, seeing that the combinatory law of the images is without our reach? Rather let us ask, what influence can a powerful and constantly recurring idea exert on the movement of our thoughts? According to what has preceded, the answer is involved in the question itself. The *idea* dominates the thought of the inquirer, not the latter the former.

Let us see, now, if we can acquire a profounder insight into the process of discovery. The condition of the discoverer is, as James[14] has aptly remarked, not unlike the situation of a person who is trying to remember something that he has forgotten. Both are sensible of a gap, and have only a remote presentiment of what is missing. Suppose I meet in a company a well-known and affable gentleman whose name I have forgotten, and who to my horror asks to be introduced to some one. I set to work according to Lichtenberg's rule, and run down the alphabet in search of the initial letter of his name. A vague sympathy holds me at the letter *G*. Tentatively I add the second letter and am arrested at *e*, and long before I have tried the third letter *r*, the name "Gerson" sounds sonorously upon my ear, and my anguish is gone. While taking a walk I meet a gentleman from whom I receive a communication. On returning home, and in attending to weightier affairs, the matter slips my mind. Moodily, but in vain, I ransack my memory. Finally I observe that I am going over my walk again in thought. On the street corner in question the selfsame gentleman stands before me and repeats his communication. In this process are successively recalled to consciousness all the percepts which were connected with the percept that was lost, and with them, finally, that, too, is brought to light. In the first case—where the experience had already been made and is permanently impressed on our thought—a *systematic* procedure is both possible and easy, for we know that a name must be composed of a limited number of sounds. But at the same time it should be observed that the labor involved in such a combinatorial task would be enormous if the name were long and the responsiveness of the mind weaker.

It is often said, and not wholly without justification, that the scientist has solved a *riddle*. Every problem in geometry may be clothed in the garb of a *riddle*. Thus: "What thing is that *M* which has the properties *A, B, C*?" "What circle is that which touches the straight lines *A, B*, but touches *B* in the point *C*?" The first two conditions marshal before the imagination the group of circles whose centres lie in the line of symmetry of *A, B*. The third condition reminds us of all the circles having centres in the straight line that stands at right angles to *B* in *C*. The *common* term, or common terms, of the two groups of images solves the riddle—satisfies the problem. Puzzles dealing with things or words induce similar processes, but the memory in such cases is exerted in many directions and more varied and less clearly ordered provinces of ideas are surveyed. The difference between the situation of a geometer who has a construction to make, and that of an engineer, or a scientist, confronted with a problem, is simply this, that the first moves in a field with which he is thoroughly acquainted, whereas the two latter are obliged to familiarise themselves with this field subsequently, and in a measure far transcending what is commonly required. In this process the mechanical engineer has at least always a definite goal before him and definite means to accomplish his aim, whilst in the case of the scientist that aim is in many instances presented only in vague and general outlines. Often the very formulation of the riddle devolves on him. Frequently it is not until the aim has been reached that the broader outlook requisite for systematic procedure is obtained. By far the larger portion of his success, therefore, is contingent on luck and instinct. It is immaterial, so far as its character is concerned, whether the process in question is brought rapidly to a conclusion in the brain of one man, or whether it is spun

---

[14] William James (1848–1910), author of *Principles of Psychology* and other works. (See *GBWW*, Vol. 53.)

out for centuries in the minds of a long succession of thinkers. The same relation that a word solving a riddle bears to that riddle is borne by the modern conception of light to the facts discovered by Grimaldi, Römer, Huygens, Newton, Young, Malus, and Fresnel, and only by the help of this slowly developed conception is our mental vision enabled to embrace the broad domain of facts in question.

A welcome complement to the discoveries which the history of civilisation and comparative psychology have furnished, is to be found in the confessions of great scientists and artists. Scientists *and* artists, we might say, for Liebig[15] boldly declared there was no essential difference between the two. Are we to regard Leonardo da Vinci as a scientist or as an artist? If the artist builds up his work from a few motives, the scientist discovers the motives which permeate reality. If scientists like Lagrange or Fourier are in a certain measure artists in the presentation of their results, on the other hand, artists like Shakespeare or Ruysdael are scientists in the insight which must have preceded their creations.

Newton, when questioned about his methods of work, could give no other answer but that he was wont to ponder again and again on a subject; and similar utterances are accredited to D'Alembert and Helmholtz. Scientists and artists both recommend persistent labor. After the repeated survey of a field has afforded opportunity for the interposition of advantageous accidents, has rendered all the traits that suit with the mood or the dominant thought more vivid, and has gradually relegated to the background all things that are inappropriate, making their future appearance impossible; then from the teeming, swelling host of fancies which a free and high-flown imagination calls forth, suddenly that particular form arises to the light which harmonises perfectly with the ruling idea, mood, or design. Then it is that that which has resulted slowly as the result of a gradual selection, appears as if it were the outcome of a deliberate act of crea-

tion. Thus are to be explained the statements of Newton, Mozart, Richard Wagner, and others, when they say that thoughts, melodies, and harmonies had poured in upon them, and that they had simply retained the right ones. Undoubtedly, the man of genius, too, consciously or instinctively, pursues systematic methods wherever it is possible; but in his delicate presentiment he will omit many a task or abandon it after a hasty trial on which a less endowed man would squander his energies in vain. Thus, the genius accomplishes[16] in a brief space of time undertakings for which the life of an ordinary man would far from suffice. We shall hardly go astray if we regard genius as only a slight deviation from the average mental endowment—as possessing simply a greater sensitiveness of cerebral reaction and a greater swiftness of reaction. The men who, obeying their inner impulses, make sacrifices for an idea instead of advancing their material welfare, may appear to the full-blooded Philistine as fools; yet we shall scarcely adopt Lombroso's view, that genius is to be regarded as a disease, although it is unfortunately true that the sensitive brains and fragile constitutions succumb most readily to sickness.

The remark of C. G. J. Jacobi that mathematics is slow of growth and only reaches the truth by long and devious paths, that the way to its discovery must be prepared for long beforehand, and that then the truth will make its long-deferred appearance as if impelled by some divine necessity—all this holds true of every science. We are astounded often to note that it required the combined labors of many eminent thinkers for a full century to reach a truth which it takes us only a few hours to master and which once

---

[15] Justus von Liebig (1803–73), German chemist.
[16] I do not know whether Swift's academy of schemers in Lagado, in which great discoveries and inventions were made by a sort of verbal game of dice, was intended as a satire on Francis Bacon's method of making discoveries by means of huge synoptic tables constructed by scribes. It certainly would not have been ill-placed. (See *GBWW*, Vol. 36.)

acquired seems extremely easy to reach under the right sort of circumstances. To our humiliation we learn that even the greatest men are born more for life than for science. The extent to which even they are indebted to accident—to that singular conflux of the physical and the psychical life in which the continuous but yet imperfect and never-ending adaptation of the latter to the former finds its distinct expession—that has been the subject of our remarks to-day. Jacobi's poetical thought of a divine necessity acting in science will lose none of its loftiness for us if we discover in this necessity the same power that destroys the unfit and fosters the fit. For loftier, nobler, and more romantic than poetry is the truth and the reality.

Young Goodman Brown

Nathaniel Hawthorne

Both of the stories reprinted in *The Great Ideas Today* this year—"Young Goodman Brown," by Nathaniel Hawthorne and "Two Old Men," by Leo Tolstoy—are parables, the one dealing with evil, the other with good (or more strictly love) in the lives of men. In both instances a miracle or at least a supernatural event of some sort seems to take place, an event which we are at liberty to believe does not actually happen, but which, as it is thought to have happened by the persons who witness it, has the same effect on them as if it did. The difference, apart from the fact that the moral principles involved are diametrically opposed, is that in one case the witness is a young man while in the other he is old, and whereas the old man has lived long enough to be able to derive a chastening wisdom from what he thinks he sees, the other is overwhelmed by his experience and driven to incurable despair.

That he is young is the first thing we know about Goodman Brown, who therefore does not himself know what an older person would, or might, which is that there is evil in every human heart. It is in his own, though he has not yet faced it—so at least we gather when at the start of the tale we are told of his "evil purpose," which is to meet the devil in what he does not realize will be a ceremony of initiation into a community of the sinful— and that evil exists as a general thing he is of course aware, as any Puritan would be in seventeenth-century New England, where the story has its setting. But he is not prepared for what he sees, or thinks he sees, in the witches' sabbath at which he finally arrives at night in the deepest part of the woods. For there he finds, or imagines that he finds, a host of spirits gathered that includes all the worthiest and most pious persons of the town, living and dead, as well as the respected leaders of the larger colony and province; and particularly does he find his pretty wife Faith, as young as himself, whom he thinks he has left safely behind at home in her cap with pink ribbons, but who along with him, as it appears, is on this occasion to be formally baptized into the company of the damned.

Does all this really happen? If it does—and even if it does not, but only seems to—what does it mean? The reader is left to guess about these questions, as to the first of which Hawthorne carefully avoids saying—it could have been a dream, perhaps—and as to which the second has no simple answer. The story seems to pose a riddle which Goodman Brown misreads, and which if it were rightly read would allow him a happier existence than the one he subsequently has. But what is the right reading? Not, surely, that evil is unreal, still less that it is unimportant. Yet it can be too important, Hawthorne seems to say, and will be when it takes us by surprise. Only when we have accepted the idea of what the Puritans would have called original sin, the story implies, can we take a cheerful view of human life.

Hawthorne, however, was not himself a very cheerful man. Born in New England, where he lived and died (1804–64), he wrote many stories—*The Scarlet Letter* is the finest and the most famous of them—in which he examined what we may think of as the Puritan conscience, with its deeply rooted sense of sin. These stories made him uncomfortable—"blasted allegories," he called them—because, as often and as variously as he delivered himself of them, he could not rid himself of the painful insight into human nature that gave rise to them. So he preferred, as posterity has not, certain slighter and more genial tales that he also wrote, in which the dark force of his imagination was kept down. It was as if he knew that, having seen what Goodman Brown saw, he was likely to live as Goodman Brown lived, save as he could keep his mind for the most part—but happily for us, not always—on more agreeable things.

"Young Goodman Brown" was probably written about 1829, when Hawthorne was 25. First published by the *New England Magazine* in 1835, it was not reprinted in any collection of his stories until 1846, when it appeared in *Mosses from an Old Manse*—which means that Hawthorne passed it over, for reasons which are unknown, when putting together two earlier collections of what he called *Twice-Told Tales* (1837 and 1842). Among the earliest admirers of the story was Herman Melville, who reviewed the volume in which it appeared, who saw in it a "power of blackness" that he connected with what struck him as Hawthorne's peculiar "calvinistic sense of Innate Depravity and Original Sin, from whose visitations, in some shape or other, no thinking mind is always and wholly free," and who thought it "as deep as Dante." Henry James, too, who wrote the earliest critical biography of Hawthorne, called the tale a "little masterpiece," and said that with "Rappacini's Daughter" it represented "the highest point that Hawthorne reached" in what James called his "stories of fantasy and allegory." Its source, so far as its subject is witchcraft, was probably Cotton Mather's contemporary account of the Salem witchcraft trials of 1692, called *Wonders of the Invisible World*, which Hawthorne is known to have read.

Young Goodman Brown

Young Goodman Brown came forth at sunset into the street at Salem village; but put his head back, after crossing the threshold, to exchange a parting kiss with his young wife. And Faith, as the wife was aptly named, thrust her own pretty head into the street, letting the wind play with the pink ribbons of her cap while she called to Goodman Brown.

"Dearest heart," whispered she, softly and rather sadly, when her lips were close to his ear, "prithee put off your journey until sunrise and sleep in your own bed to-night. A lone woman is troubled with such dreams and such thoughts that she's afeard of herself sometimes. Pray tarry with me this night, dear husband, of all nights in the year."

"My love and my Faith," replied young Goodman Brown, "of all nights in the year, this one night must I tarry away from thee. My journey, as thou callest it, forth and back again, must needs be done 'twixt now and sunrise. What, my sweet, pretty wife, dost thou doubt me already, and we but three months married?"

"Then God bless you!" said Faith, with the pink ribbons; "and may you find all well when you come back."

"Amen!" cried Goodman Brown. "Say thy prayers, dear Faith, and go to bed at dusk, and no harm will come to thee."

So they parted; and the young man pursued his way until, being about to turn the corner by the meeting-house, he looked back and saw the head of Faith still peeping after him with a melancholy air, in spite of her pink ribbons.

"Poor little Faith!" thought he, for his heart smote him. "What a wretch am I to leave her on such an errand! She talks of dreams, too. Methought as she spoke there was trouble in her face, as if a dream had warned her what work is to be done to-night. But no, no; 't would kill her to think it. Well, she's a blessed angel on earth; and after this one night I'll cling to her skirts and follow her to heaven."

With this excellent resolve for the future, Goodman Brown felt himself justified in making more haste on his present evil purpose. He had taken a dreary road, darkened by all the gloomiest trees of the forest, which barely stood aside to let the narrow path creep through, and closed immediately behind. It was all as lonely as could be; and there is this peculiarity in such a solitude, that the traveller knows not who may be concealed by the innumerable trunks and the thick boughs overhead; so that with lonely footsteps he may yet be passing through an unseen multitude.

"There may be a devilish Indian behind every tree," said Goodman Brown to himself; and he glanced fearfully behind him as he added, "What if the devil himself should be at my very elbow!"

His head being turned back, he passed a crook of the road, and, looking forward again, beheld the figure of a man, in grave and decent attire, seated at the foot of an old tree. He arose at Goodman Brown's approach and walked onward side by side with him.

"You are late, Goodman Brown," said he. "The clock of the Old South was striking as I came through Boston, and that is full fifteen minutes agone."

"Faith kept me back a while," replied the young man, with a tremor in his voice, caused by the sudden appearance of his companion, though not wholly unexpected.

It was now deep dusk in the forest, and deepest in that part of it where these two were journeying. As nearly as could be discerned, the second traveller was about fifty years old, apparently in the same rank of life as Goodman Brown, and bearing a considerable resemblance to him, though perhaps more in expression than features. Still they might have been taken for father and son. And yet, though the elder person was as simply clad as the younger, and as simple in manner too, he had an indescribable air of one who knew the world, and who would not have felt abashed at the governor's dinner table or in King William's court, were it possible that his affairs should call him thither. But the only thing about him that could be fixed upon as remarkable was his staff, which bore the likeness of a great black snake, so curiously wrought that it might almost be seen to twist and wriggle itself like a living serpent. This, of course, must have been an ocular deception, assisted by the uncertain light.

"Come, Goodman Brown," cried his fellow-traveller, "this is a dull pace for the beginning of a journey. Take my staff, if you are so soon weary."

"Friend," said the other, exchanging his slow pace for a full stop, "having kept covenant by meeting thee here, it is my purpose now to return whence I came. I have scruples touching the matter thou wot'st of."

"Sayest thou so?" replied he of the serpent, smiling apart. "Let us walk on, nevertheless, reasoning as we go; and if I convince thee not thou shalt turn back. We are but a little way in the forest yet."

"Too far! too far!" exclaimed the goodman, unconsciously resuming his walk. "My father never went into the woods on such an errand, nor his father before him. We have been a race of honest men and good Christians since the days of the martyrs; and shall I be the first of the name of Brown that ever took this path and kept"—

"Such company, thou wouldst say," observed the elder person, interpreting his pause. "Well said, Goodman Brown! I have been as well acquainted with your family as with ever a one among the Puritans; and that's no trifle to say. I helped your grandfather, the constable, when he lashed the Quaker woman so smartly through the streets of Salem; and it was I that brought your father a pitch-pine knot, kindled at my own hearth, to set fire to an Indian village, in King Philip's war. They were my good friends, both; and many a pleasant walk have we had along this path, and returned merrily after midnight. I would fain be friends with you for their sake."

"If it be as thou sayest," replied Goodman Brown, "I marvel they never spoke of these matters; or, verily, I marvel not, seeing that the least rumor of the sort would have driven them from New England. We are a people of prayer, and good works to boot, and abide no such wickedness."

"Wickedness or not," said the traveller with the twisted staff, "I have a very general acquaintance here in New England. The deacons of many a church have drunk the communion wine with me; the selectmen of divers towns make me their chairman; and a majority of the Great and General Court are firm supporters of my interest. The governor and I, too—But these are state secrets."

"Can this be so?" cried Goodman Brown, with a stare of amazement at his undisturbed companion. "Howbeit, I have nothing to do with the governor and council; they have their own ways, and are no rule for a simple husbandman like me. But, were I to go on with thee, how should I meet the eye of that good old man, our minister, at Salem village? Oh, his voice would make me tremble both Sabbath day and lecture day."

Thus far the elder traveller had listened with due gravity; but now burst into a fit of irrepressible mirth, shaking himself so violently that his snake-like staff actually seemed to wriggle in sympathy.

"Ha! ha! ha!" shouted he again and again; then composing himself, "Well, go on, Goodman Brown, go on; but, prithee, don't kill me with laughing."

"Well, then, to end the matter at once,"

said Goodman Brown, considerably nettled, "there is my wife, Faith. It would break her dear little heart; and I'd rather break my own."

"Nay, if that be the case," answered the other, "e'en go thy ways, Goodman Brown. I would not for twenty old women like the one hobbling before us that Faith should come to any harm."

As he spoke he pointed his staff at a female figure on the path, in whom Goodman Brown recognized a very pious and exemplary dame, who had taught him his catechism in youth, and was still his moral and spiritual adviser, jointly with the minister and Deacon Gookin.

"A marvel, truly, that Goody Cloyse should be so far in the wilderness at nightfall," said he. "But with your leave, friend, I shall take a cut through the woods until we have left this Christian woman behind. Being a stranger to you, she might ask whom I was consorting with and whither I was going."

"Be it so," said his fellow-traveller. "Betake you the woods, and let me keep the path."

Accordingly the young man turned aside, but took care to watch his companion, who advanced softly along the road until he had come within a staff's length of the old dame. She, meanwhile, was making the best of her way, with singular speed for so aged a woman, and mumbling some indistinct words—a prayer, doubtless—as she went. The traveller put forth his staff and touched her withered neck with what seemed the serpent's tail.

"The devil!" screamed the pious old lady.

"Then Goody Cloyse knows her old friend?" observed the traveller, confronting her and leaning on his writhing stick.

"Ah, forsooth, and is it your worship indeed?" cried the good dame. "Yea, truly is it, and in the very image of my old gossip, Goodman Brown, the grandfather of the silly fellow that now is. But—would your worship believe it?—my broomstick hath strangely disappeared, stolen, as I suspect, by that unhanged witch, Goody Cory, and that, too, when I was all anointed with the juice of smallage, and cinquefoil, and wolf's bane"—

"Mingled with fine wheat and the fat of a new-born babe," said the shape of old Goodman Brown.

"Ah, your worship knows the recipe," cried the old lady, cackling aloud. "So, as I was saying, being all ready for the meeting, and no horse to ride on, I made up my mind to foot it; for they tell me there is a nice young man to be taken into communion to-night. But now your good worship will lend me your arm, and we shall be there in a twinkling."

"That can hardly be," answered her friend. "I may not spare you my arm, Goody Cloyse; but here is my staff, if you will."

So saying, he threw it down at her feet, where, perhaps, it assumed life, being one of the rods which its owner had formerly lent to the Egyptian magi. Of this fact, however, Goodman Brown could not take cognizance. He had cast up his eyes in astonishment, and, looking down again, beheld neither Goody Cloyse nor the serpentine staff, but this fellow-traveller alone, who waited for him as calmly as if nothing had happened.

"That old woman taught me my catechism," said the young man; and there was a world of meaning in this simple comment.

They continued to walk onward, while the elder traveller exhorted his companion to make good speed and persevere in the path, discoursing so aptly that his arguments seemed rather to spring up in the bosom of his auditor than to be suggested by himself. As they went, he plucked a branch of maple to serve for a walking stick, and began to strip it of the twigs and little boughs, which were wet with evening dew. The moment his fingers touched them they became strangely withered and dried up as with a week's sunshine. Thus the pair proceeded, at a good free pace, until suddenly, in a gloomy hollow of the road, Goodman Brown sat himself down on the stump of a tree and refused to go any farther.

"Friend," said he, stubbornly, "my mind is made up. Not another step will I budge on this errand. What if a wretched old woman do choose to go to the devil when I thought she was going to heaven: is that any reason why I should quit my dear Faith and go after her?"

"You will think better of this by and by," said his acquaintance, composedly. "Sit here and rest yourself awhile; and when you feel like moving again, there is my staff to help you along."

Without more words, he threw his companion the maple stick, and was as speedily out of sight as if he had vanished into the deepening gloom. The young man sat for a few moments by the roadside, applauding himself greatly, and thinking with how clear a conscience he should meet the minister in his morning walk, nor shrink from the eye of good old Deacon Gookin. And what calm sleep would be his that very night, which was to have been spent so wickedly, but so purely and sweetly now, in the arms of Faith! Amidst these pleasant and praiseworthy meditations, Goodman Brown heard the tramp of horses along the road, and deemed it advisable to conceal himself within the verge of the forest, conscious of the guilty purpose that had brought him thither, though now so happily turned from it.

On came the hoof tramps and the voices of the riders, two grave old voices, conversing soberly as they drew near. These mingled sounds appeared to pass along the road, within a few yards of the young man's hiding-place; but, owing doubtless to the depth of the gloom at that particular spot, neither the travellers nor their steeds were visible. Though their figures brushed the small boughs by the wayside, it could not be seen that they intercepted, even for a moment, the faint gleam from the strip of bright sky athwart which they must have passed. Goodman Brown alternately crouched and stood on tiptoe, pulling aside the branches and thrusting forth his head as far as he durst without discerning so much as a shadow. It vexed him the more because he could have sworn, were such a thing possible, that he recognized the voices of the minister and Deacon Gookin, jogging along quietly, as they were wont to do, when bound to some

ordination or ecclesiastical council. While yet within hearing, one of the riders stopped to pluck a switch.

"Of the two, reverend sir," said the voice like the deacon's, "I had rather miss an ordination dinner than to-night's meeting. They tell me that some of our community are to be here from Falmouth and beyond, and others from Connecticut and Rhode Island, besides several of the Indian powwows, who, after their fashion, know almost as much deviltry as the best of us. Moreover, there is a goodly young woman to be taken into communion."

"Mighty well, Deacon Gookin!" replied the solemn old tones of the minister. "Spur up, or we shall be late. Nothing can be done, you know, until I get on the ground."

The hoofs clattered again; and the voices, talking so strangely in the empty air, passed on through the forest, where no church had ever been gathered or solitary Christian prayed. Whither, then, could these holy men be journeying so deep into the heathen wilderness? Young Goodman Brown caught hold of a tree for support, being ready to sink down on the ground, faint and overburdened with the heavy sickness of his heart. He looked up to the sky, doubting whether there really was a heaven above him. Yet there was the blue arch, and the stars brightening in it.

"With heaven above and Faith below, I will yet stand firm against the devil!" cried Goodman Brown.

While he still gazed upward into the deep arch of the firmament and had lifted his hands to pray, a cloud, though no wind was stirring, hurried across the zenith and hid the brightening stars. The blue sky was still visible, except directly overhead, where this black mass of cloud was sweeping swiftly northward. Aloft in the air, as if from the depths of the cloud, came a confused and doubtful sound of voices. Once the listener fancied that he could distinguish the accents of towns-people of his own, men and women, both pious and ungodly, many of whom he had met at the communion table, and had seen others rioting at the tavern. The next

450

moment, so indistinct were the sounds, he doubted whether he had heard aught but the murmur of the old forest, whispering without a wind. Then came a stronger swell of those familiar tones, heard daily in the sunshine at Salem village, but never until now from a cloud of night. There was one voice, of a young woman, uttering lamentations, yet with an uncertain sorrow, and entreating for some favor, which, perhaps, it would grieve her to obtain; and all the unseen multitude, both saints and sinners, seemed to encourage her onward.

"Faith!" shouted Goodman Brown, in a voice of agony and desperation; and the echoes of the forest mocked him, crying, "Faith! Faith!" as if bewildered wretches were seeking her all through the wilderness.

The cry of grief, rage, and terror was yet piercing the night when the unhappy husband held his breath for a response. There was a scream, drowned immediately in a louder murmur of voices, fading into far-off laughter, as the dark cloud swept away, leaving the clear and silent sky above Goodman Brown. But something fluttered lightly down through the air and caught on the branch of a tree. The young man seized it, and beheld a pink ribbon.

"My Faith is gone!" cried he, after one stupefied moment. "There is no good on earth; and sin is but a name. Come, devil; for to thee is this world given."

And, maddened with despair, so that he laughed loud and long, did Goodman Brown grasp his staff and set forth again, at such a rate that he seemed to fly along the forest path rather than to walk or run. The road grew wilder and drearier and more faintly traced, and vanished at length, leaving him in the heart of the dark wilderness, still rushing onward with the instinct that guides mortal man to evil. The whole forest was peopled with frightful sounds—the creaking of the trees, the howling of wild beasts, and the yell of Indians; while sometimes the wind tolled like a distant church bell, and sometimes gave a broad roar around the traveller, as if all Nature were laughing him to scorn. But

he was himself the chief horror of the scene, and shrank not from its other horrors.

"Ha! ha! ha!" roared Goodman Brown when the wind laughed at him. "Let us hear which will laugh loudest. Think not to frighten me with your deviltry. Come witch, come wizard, come Indian powwow, come devil himself, and here comes Goodman Brown. You may as well fear him as he fear you."

In truth, all through the haunted forest there could be nothing more frightful than the figure of Goodman Brown. On he flew among the black pines, brandishing his staff with frenzied gestures, now giving vent to an inspiration of horrid blasphemy, and now shouting forth such laughter as set all the echoes of the forest laughing like demons around him. The fiend in his own shape is less hideous than when he rages in the breast of man. Thus sped the demoniac on his course, until, quivering among the trees, he saw a red light before him, as when the felled trunks and branches of a clearing have been set on fire, and throw up their lurid blaze against the sky, at the hour of midnight. He paused, in a lull of the tempest that had driven him onward, and heard the swell of what seemed a hymn, rolling solemnly from a distance with the weight of many voices. He knew the tune; it was a familiar one in the choir of the village meeting-house. The verse died heavily away, and was lengthened by a chorus, not of human voices, but of all the sounds of the benighted wilderness pealing in awful harmony together. Goodman Brown cried out, and his cry was lost to his own ear by its unison with the cry of the desert.

In the interval of silence he stole forward until the light glared full upon his eyes. At one extremity of an open space, hemmed in by the dark wall of the forest, rose a rock, bearing some rude natural resemblance either to an altar or a pulpit, and surrounded by four blazing pines, their tops aflame, their stems untouched, like candles at an evening meeting. The mass of foliage that had overgrown the summit of the rock was all on fire, blazing high into the night and fitfully illuminating the whole field. Each pendent twig and leafy festoon was in a blaze. As the red light arose and fell, a numerous congregation alternately shone forth, then disappeared in shadow, and again grew, as it were, out of the darkness, peopling the heart of the solitary woods at once.

"A grave and dark-clad company," quoth Goodman Brown.

In truth they were such. Among them, quivering to and fro between gloom and splendor, appeared faces that would be seen next day at the council board of the province, and others which, Sabbath after Sabbath, looked devoutly heavenward, and benignantly over the crowded pews, from the holiest pulpits in the land. Some affirm that the lady of the governor was there. At least there were high dames well known to her, and wives of honored husbands, and widows, a great multitude, and ancient maidens, all of excellent repute, and fair young girls, who trembled lest their mothers should espy them. Either the sudden gleams of light flashing over the obscure field bedazzled Goodman Brown, or he recognized a score of the church members of Salem village famous for their especial sanctity. Good old Deacon Gookin had arrived, and waited at the skirts of that venerable saint, his revered pastor. But, irreverently consorting with these grave, reputable, and pious people, these elders of the church, these chaste dames and dewy virgins, there were men of dissolute lives and women of spotted fame, wretches given over to all mean and filthy vice, and suspected even of horrid crimes. It was strange to see that the good shrank not from the wicked, nor were the sinners abashed by the saints. Scattered also among their pale-faced enemies were the Indian priests, or powwows, who had often scared their native forest with more hideous incantations than any known to English witchcraft.

"But where is Faith?" thought Goodman Brown; and, as hope came into his heart, he trembled.

Another verse of the hymn arose, a slow and mournful strain, such as the pious love,

but joined to words which expressed all that our nature can conceive of sin, and darkly hinted at far more. Unfathomable to mere mortals is the lore of fiends. Verse after verse was sung; and still the chorus of the desert swelled between like the deepest tone of a mighty organ; and with the final peal of that dreadful anthem there came a sound, as if the roaring wind, the rushing streams, the howling beasts, and every other voice of the unconcerted wilderness were mingling and according with the voice of guilty man in homage to the prince of all. The four blazing pines threw up a loftier flame, and obscurely discovered shapes and visages of horror on the smoke wreaths above the impious assembly. At the same moment the fire on the rock shot redly forth and formed a glowing arch above its base, where now appeared a figure. With reverence be it spoken, the figure bore no slight similitude, both in garb and manner, to some grave divine of the New England churches.

"Bring forth the converts!" cried a voice that echoed through the field and rolled into the forest.

At the word, Goodman Brown stepped forth from the shadow of the trees and approached the congregation, with whom he felt a loathful brotherhood by the sympathy of all that was wicked in his heart. He could have well-nigh sworn that the shape of his own dead father beckoned him to advance, looking downward from a smoke wreath, while a woman, with dim features of despair, threw out her hand to warn him back. Was it his mother? But he had no power to retreat one step, nor to resist, even in thought, when the minister and good old Deacon Gookin seized his arms and led him to the blazing rock. Thither came also the slender form of a veiled female, led between Goody Cloyse, that pious teacher of the catechism, and Martha Carrier, who had received the devil's promise to be queen of hell. A rampant hag was she. And there stood the proselytes beneath the canopy of fire.

"Welcome, my children," said the dark figure, "to the communion of your race. Ye have found thus young your nature and your destiny. My children, look behind you!"

They turned; and flashing forth, as it were, in a sheet of flame, the fiend worshippers were seen; the smile of welcome gleamed darkly on every visage.

"There," resumed the sable form, "are all whom ye have reverenced from youth. Ye deemed them holier than yourselves, and shrank from your own sin, contrasting it with their lives of righteousness and prayerful aspirations heavenward. Yet here are they all in my worshipping assembly. This night it shall be granted you to know their secret deeds: how hoary-bearded elders of the church have whispered wanton words to the young maids of their households; how many a woman, eager for widows' weeds, has given her husband a drink at bedtime and let him sleep his last sleep in her bosom; how beardless youths have made haste to inherit their fathers' wealth; and how fair damsels—blush not, sweet ones—have dug little graves in the garden, and bidden me, the sole guest, to an infant's funeral. By the sympathy of your human hearts for sin ye shall scent out all the places—whether in church, bed-chamber, street, field, or forest—where crime has been committed, and shall exult to behold the whole earth one stain of guilt, one mighty blood spot. Far more than this. It shall be yours to penetrate, in every bosom, the deep mystery of sin, the fountain of all wicked arts, and which inexhaustibly supplies more evil impulses than human power—than my power at its utmost—can make manifest in deeds. And now, my children, look upon each other."

They did so; and, by the blaze of the hell-kindled torches, the wretched man beheld his Faith, and the wife her husband, trembling before that unhallowed altar.

"Lo, there ye stand, my children," said the figure, in a deep and solemn tone, almost sad with its despairing awfulness, as if his once angelic nature could yet mourn for our miserable race. "Depending upon one another's hearts, ye had still hoped that virtue were not all a dream. Now are ye undeceived. Evil is

the nature of mankind. Evil must be your only happiness. Welcome again, my children, to the communion of your race."

"Welcome," repeated the fiend worshippers, in one cry of despair and triumph.

And there they stood, the only pair, as it seemed, who were yet hesitating on the verge of wickedness in this dark world. A basin was hollowed, naturally, in the rock. Did it contain water, reddened by the lurid light? or was it blood? or, perchance, a liquid flame? Herein did the shape of evil dip his hand and prepare to lay the mark of baptism upon their foreheads, that they might be partakers of the mystery of sin, more conscious of the secret guilt of others, both in deed and thought, than they could now be of their own. The husband cast one look at his pale wife, and Faith at him. What polluted wretches would the next glance show them to each other, shuddering alike at what they disclosed and what they saw!

"Faith! Faith!" cried the husband, "look up to heaven, and resist the wicked one."

Whether Faith obeyed he knew not. Hardly had he spoken when he found himself amid calm night and solitude, listening to a roar of the wind which died heavily away through the forest. He staggered against the rock, and felt it chill and damp; while a hanging twig, that had been all on fire, besprinkled his cheek with the coldest dew.

The next morning young Goodman Brown came slowly into the street of Salem village, staring around him like a bewildered man. The good old minister was taking a walk along the graveyard to get an appetite for breakfast and meditate his sermon, and bestowed a blessing, as he passed, on Goodman Brown. He shrank from the venerable saint as if to avoid an anathema. Old Deacon Gookin was at domestic worship, and the holy words of his prayer were heard through the open window. "What God doth the wizard pray to?" quoth Goodman Brown. Goody Cloyse, that excellent old Christian, stood in the early sunshine at her own lattice, catechizing a little girl who had brought her a pint of morning's milk. Goodman Brown snatched away the child as from the grasp of the fiend himself. Turning the corner by the meeting-house, he spied the head of Faith, with the pink ribbons, gazing anxiously forth, and bursting into such joy at sight of him that she skipped along the street and almost kissed her husband before the whole village. But Goodman Brown looked sternly and sadly into her face, and passed on without a greeting.

Had Goodman Brown fallen asleep in the forest and only dreamed a wild dream of a witch-meeting?

Be it so if you will; but, alas! it was a dream of evil omen for young Goodman Brown. A stern, a sad, a darkly meditative, a distrustful, if not a desperate man did he become from the night of that fearful dream. On the Sabbath day, when the congregation were singing a holy psalm, he could not listen because an anthem of sin rushed loudly upon his ear and drowned all the blessed strain. When the minister spoke from the pulpit with power and fervid eloquence, and, with his hand on the open Bible, of the sacred truths of our religion, and of saint-like lives and triumphant deaths, and of future bliss or misery unutterable, then did Goodman Brown turn pale, dreading lest the roof should thunder down upon the gray blasphemer and his hearers. Often, awaking suddenly at midnight, he shrank from the bosom of Faith; and at morning or eventide, when the family knelt down at prayer, he scowled and muttered to himself, and gazed sternly at his wife, and turned away. And when he had lived long, and was borne to his grave a hoary corpse, followed by Faith, an aged woman, and children and grandchildren, a goodly procession, besides neighbors not a few, they carved no hopeful verse upon his tombstone, for his dying hour was gloom.

Two Old Men

Leo Tolstoy

Editor's Introduction

In the story that follows by Tolstoy (1828–1910), as in the preceding one by Hawthorne, there is an event (which in fact occurs three times) that is, or seems to be, miraculous, implying the presence of a supernatural power. And again, while we may if we like conclude that this event does not actually happen (all attempts to verify it in the story are frustrated), the person who perceives it, and for whom it seems to be intended, is convinced. He is not himself a young man like Goodman Brown, however, but an old one; he knows or thinks he knows that he has seen not the devil but the hand of God; and the result in him is not despair for other souls but an awareness of his own.

The story is briefly told. Two old peasants, one of them well-to-do, the other "not so well off," decide to make a pilgrimage together to the Holy Land from their Russian village. In the course of their journey they become separated. The poorer one, Elisha, stops one day to assist a needy family in a region where the harvest has failed, and having given them all he has, realizes that he can go no further, he must return home. The rich one, Efím, not realizing what has happened, goes on alone, and in due course arrives in Jerusalem, where he dutifully visits all the holy places. He is surprised at one of them to see the figure of Elisha at the very head of the crowd, too far away to speak to; he sees him a second time and then a third, but can never get close enough to greet him. Unable to understand how his friend could have arrived in Jerusalem before him, he at last starts homeward himself. On the way he stops for lodging at the same farmhouse. The now recovered family can do nothing but talk of the good old man who stopped to help them in their need. Efím spends a sleepless night. "So that is how he got ahead of me," he thinks.

That Tolstoy manages to convey a sense of reality in this — in what is, after all, a parable composed for the sake of an explicit moral stated at its end — is one of those mysteries of genius which is easier to call attention to than to explain. Tolstoy himself does not appear to have doubted that the thing was possible to do. Hawthorne's story is no less fine in its way, but its way is the way that remains conscious of the problems of belief its fantasy creates. Tolstoy ignores these problems, and somehow they never arise. He does not seem to force his meaning from his matter.

This may have been in part because his meaning was something he was eager to propound, as Hawthorne in his own case was not. "Two Old Men" was written in 1885, about five years after Tolstoy's spiritual crisis and religious conversion. By then he had repudiated the great works that had made him famous—*War and Peace* and *Anna Karenina*—as not consistent with the moral purpose to which he had become committed, which was to instill a sense of good in his readers flowing from the love of God and man. That was what in "Two Old Men" and certain other tales of this period he sought to do. They were tales of what he thought of as "universal art," intended for the peasants themselves, whose ideal of serving God and living for others had become Tolstoy's guiding rule. As such, they are to be distinguished from other stories he wrote at approximately the same time, among them "The Death of Ivan Ilich" (*Gateway to the Great Books*, Vol. 3), which were intended for more educated readers, to whom they conveyed a similar message in more sophisticated terms.

None of this moral fervor would serve, however, if Tolstoy had not been the master storyteller that he was. "Two Old Men" as a narrative is managed with the economy of one who knows how little room he needs to leave in such a work for psychology, for description, and for commentary. But it also includes details that no reader of it is ever likely to forget. Among them are the starving little boy who stares not at the man who offers him a piece of bread but at the bread itself, and takes a bite so deep that his nose disappears in the slice; his sister, months later, who shows that she remembers every smallest movement that Elisha made when he entered her house the first time; Elisha himself, coming in from his swarming hives, smiling and talking and gently picking bees out of his beard with his fingers. We are reminded that Hawthorne too is economical in "Young Goodman Brown," which has its own details, such as the pink ribbons in Faith's cap, of which we hear twice on the first page of the story and which are not mentioned again until much later, at an otherwise uncertain moment, they suddenly flutter down from the sky with terrible effect. And we can understand how it is that even those profoundly serious writers who think they have something to say about the nature of the world, or who believe they can tell us how we ought to live, have sought first to make us believe that we are looking in their stories at the world itself, and at life itself, so that, to the extent that we agree with what they tell us, we do so not because they say it, but because we think it true.

Two Old Men

The woman saith unto him, Sir, I perceive that thou art a prophet. Our fathers worshipped in this mountain and ye say, that in Jerusalem is the place where men ought to worship. Jesus saith unto her, Woman, believe me, the hour cometh when neither in this mountain, nor in Jerusalem, shall ye worship the Father. . . . But the hour cometh, and now is, when the true worshippers shall worship the Father in spirit and truth: for such doth the Father seek to be his worshippers.
—John iv. 19-21, 23

I

There were once two old men who decided to go on a pilgrimage to worship God at Jerusalem. One of them was a well-to-do peasant named Efím Tarásich Shevélev. The other, Elisha Bódrov, was not so well off.

Efím was a staid man, serious and firm. He neither drank nor smoked nor took snuff, and had never used bad language in his life. He had twice served as village Elder, and when he left office his accounts were in good order. He had a large family: two sons and a married grandson, all living with him. He was hale, long-bearded, and erect, and it was only when he was past sixty that a little grey began to show itself in his beard.

Elisha was neither rich nor poor. He had formerly gone out carpentering, but now that he was growing old he stayed at home and kept bees. One of his sons had gone away to find work, the other was living at home. Elisha was a kindly and cheerful old man. It is true he drank sometimes, and he took snuff, and was fond of singing; but he was a peaceable man and lived on good terms with his family and with his neighbours. He was short and dark, with a curly beard, and, like his patron saint Elisha, he was quite bald-headed.

The two old men had taken a vow long since and had arranged to go on a pilgrimage to Jerusalem together: but Efím could never spare the time; he always had so much business on hand: as soon as one thing was finished he started another. First he had to arrange his grandson's marriage; then to wait for his youngest son's return from the army, and after that he began building a new hut.

One holiday the two old men met outside the hut and, sitting down on some timber, began to talk.

'Well,' asked Elisha, 'when are we to fulfil our vow?'

Efím made a wry face.

'We must wait,' he said. 'This year has turned out a hard one for me. I started building this hut thinking it would cost me something over a hundred rúbles, but now it's getting on for three hundred and it's still not finished. We shall have to wait till the summer. In summer, God willing, we will go without fail.'

'It seems to me we ought not to put it off, but should go at once,' said Elisha. 'Spring is the best time.'

459

'The time's right enough, but what about my building? How can I leave that?'

'As if you had no one to leave in charge! Your son can look after it.'

'But how? My eldest son is not trustworthy —he sometimes takes a glass too much.'

'Ah, neighbour, when we die they'll get on without us. Let your son begin now to get some experience.'

'That's true enough; but somehow when one begins a thing one likes to see it done.'

'Eh, friend, we can never get through all we have to do. The other day the women-folk at home were washing and house-cleaning for Easter. Here something needed doing, there something else, and they could not get everything done. So my eldest daughter-in-law, who's a sensible woman, says: "We may be thankful the holiday comes without waiting for us, or however hard we worked we should never be ready for it."'

Efím became thoughtful.

'I've spent a lot of money on this building,' he said, 'and one can't start on the journey with empty pockets. We shall want a hundred rúbles apiece—and it's no small sum.'

Elisha laughed.

'Now, come, come, old friend!' he said, 'you have ten times as much as I, and yet you talk about money. Only say when we are to start, and though I have nothing now I shall have enough by then.'

Efím also smiled.

'Dear me, I did not know you were so rich!' said he. 'Why, where will you get it from?'

'I can scrape some together at home, and if that's not enough, I'll sell half a score of hives to my neighbour. He's long been wanting to buy them.'

'If they swarm well this year, you'll regret it.'

'Regret it! Not I, neighbour! I never regretted anything in my life, except my sins. There's nothing more precious than the soul.'

'That's so; still it's not right to neglect things at home.'

'But what if our souls are neglected? That's worse. We took the vow, so let us go! Now, seriously, let us go!'

II

Elisha succeeded in persuading his comrade. In the morning after thinking it well over, Efím came to Elisha.

'You are right,' said he, 'let us go. Life and death are in God's hands. We must go now, while we are still alive and have the strength.'

A week later the old men were ready to start. Efím had money enough at hand. He took a hundred rúbles himself, and left two hundred with his wife.

Elisha, too, got ready. He sold ten hives to his neighbour, with any new swarms that might come from them before the summer. He took seventy rúbles for the lot. The rest of the hundred rúbles he scraped together from the other members of his household, fairly clearing them all out. His wife gave him all she had been saving up for her funeral, and his daughter-in-law also gave him what she had.

Efím gave his eldest son definite orders about everything: when and how much grass to mow, where to cart the manure, and how to finish off and roof the cottage. He thought out everything, and gave his orders accordingly. Elisha, on the other hand, only explained to his wife that she was to keep separate the swarms from the hives he had sold and to be sure to let the neighbour have them all, without any tricks. As to household affairs, he did not even mention them.

'You will see what to do and how to do it as the needs arise,' he said. 'You are the masters and will know how to do what's best for yourselves.'

So the old men got ready. Their people baked them cakes, and made bags for them, and cut them linen for leg-bands.[1] They put on new leather shoes and took with them spare shoes of platted bark. Their families went with them to the end of the village and

---

[1] Worn by Russian peasants instead of stockings.

there took leave of them, and the old men started on their pilgrimage.

Elisha left home in a cheerful mood and as soon as he was out of the village forgot all his home affairs. His only care was how to please his comrade, how to avoid saying a rude word to any one, how to get to his destination and home again in peace and love. Walking along the road, Elisha would either whisper some prayer to himself or go over in his mind such of the lives of the saints as he was able to remember. When he came across any one on the road, or turned in anywhere for the night, he tried to behave as gently as possible and to say a godly word. So he journeyed on, rejoicing. One thing only he could not do, he could not give up taking snuff. Though he had left his snuff-box behind, he hankered after it. Then a man he met on the road gave him some snuff, and every now and then he would lag behind (not to lead his comrade into temptation) and would take a pinch of snuff.

Efím too walked well and firmly, doing no wrong and speaking no vain words, but his heart was not so light. Household cares weighed on his mind. He kept worrying about what was going on at home. Had he not forgotten to give his son this or that order? Would his son do things properly? If he happened to see potatoes being planted or manure carted as he went along, he wondered if his son was doing as he had been told. And he almost wanted to turn back and show him how to do things, or even do them himself.

III

The old men had been walking for five weeks, they had worn out their home-made bark shoes and had to begin buying new ones when they reached Little Russia.[2] From the time they left home they had had to pay for their food and for their night's lodging, but when they reached Little Russia the people vied with one another in asking them into their huts. They took them in and fed them, and would accept no payment; and more than that, they put bread or even cakes into their bags for them to eat on the road.

The old men travelled some five hundred miles in this manner free of expense, but after they had crossed the next province, they came to a district where the harvest had failed. The peasants still gave them free lodging at night, but no longer fed them for nothing. Sometimes even they could get no bread: they offered to pay for it, but there was none to be had. The people said the harvest had completely failed the year before. Those who had been rich were ruined and had had to sell all they possessed; those of moderate means were left destitute, and those of the poor who had not left those parts, wandered about begging, or starved at home in utter want. In the winter they had had to eat husks and goosefoot.

One night the old men stopped in a small village; they bought fifteen pounds of bread, slept there, and started before sunrise to get well on their way before the heat of the day. When they had gone some eight miles, on coming to a stream they sat down, and, filling a bowl with water, they steeped some bread in it and ate it. Then they changed their leg-bands and rested for a while. Elisha took out his snuff-box. Efím shook his head at him.

'How is it you don't give up that nasty habit?' said he.

Elisha waved his hand. 'The evil habit is stronger than I,' he said.

Presently they got up and went on. After walking for nearly another eight miles, they came to a large village and passed right through it. It had now grown hot. Elisha was tired out and wanted to rest and have a drink, but Efím did not stop. Efím was the better walker of the two and Elisha found it hard to keep up with him.

'If I could only have a drink,' said he.

'Well, have a drink,' said Efím. 'I don't want any.'

---

[2] Little Russia is situated in the south-western part of Russia, and consists of the Governments of Kíev, Poltáva, Chernígov, and part of Kharkov and Kherson; it is now generally called the Ukraine.

Elisha stopped.

'You go on,' he said, 'but I'll just run in to the little hut there. I will catch you up in a moment.'

'All right,' said Efím, and he went on along the high road alone while Elisha turned back to the hut.

It was a small hut plastered wih clay, the bottom a dark colour, the top whitewashed; but the clay had crumbled away. Evidently it was long since it had been replastered, and the thatch was off the roof on one side. The entrance to the hut was through the yard. Elisha entered the yard, and saw, lying close to a bank of earth that ran round the hut, a gaunt, beardless man with his shirt tucked into his trousers, as is the custom in Little Russia.[3] The man must have lain down in the shade, but the sun had come round and now shone full on him. Though not asleep, he still lay there. Elisha called to him and asked for a drink, but the man gave no answer.

'He is either ill or unfriendly,' thought Elisha; and going to the door he heard a child crying in the hut. He took hold of the ring that served as a door-handle and knocked with it.

'Hey, masters!' he called. No answer. He knocked again with his staff.

'Hey, Christians!' Nothing stirred.

'Hey, servants of God!' Still no reply.

Elisha was about to turn away, when he thought he heard a groan the other side of the door.

'Dear me, some misfortune must have happened to the people. I had better have a look.'

And Elisha entered the hut.

IV

Elisha turned the ring, the door was not fastened. He opened it and went along up the narrow passage. The door into the dwelling-room was open. To the left was a brick stove; in front against the wall was an icon-shelf[4] and a table before it; by the table was a bench on which sat an old woman, bare-headed and wearing only a single garment. There she sat with her head resting on the table, and near her was a thin, wax-coloured boy, with a protruding stomach. He was asking for something, pulling at her sleeve and crying bitterly. Elisha entered. The air in the hut was very foul. He looked round, and saw a woman lying on the floor behind the stove: she lay flat on the ground with her eyes closed and her throat rattling, now stretching out a leg, now dragging it in, tossing from side to side; and the foul smell came from her. Evidently she could do nothing for herself and no one had been attending to her needs. The old woman lifted her head and saw the stranger.

'What do you want?' said she. 'What do you want, man? We have nothing.'

Elisha understood her, though she spoke in the Little-Russian dialect.

'I came in for a drink of water, servant of God,' he said.

'There's no one—no one—we have nothing to fetch it in. Go your way.'

Then Elisha asked:

'Is there no one among you, then, well enough to attend to that woman?'

'No, we have no one. My son is dying outside, and we are dying in here.'

The little boy had ceased crying when he saw the stranger, but when the old woman began to speak, he began again, and clutching hold of her sleeve cried:

'Bread, Granny, bread.'

Elisha was about to question the old woman, when the man staggered into the hut. He came along the passage clinging to the wall, but as he was entering the dwelling-room he fell in the corner near the threshold, and without trying to get up again to reach the bench, he began to speak in broken words. He brought out a word at a time, stopping to draw breath, and gasping.

'Illness has seized us . . . ,' said he, 'and famine. He is dying . . . of hunger.'

---

[3] In Great Russia the peasants let their shirt hang outside their trousers.

[4] An icon (properly ikón) is a representation of God, Christ, an angel, or a saint, or of a sacred event, usually painted, enamelled, or embossed.

And he motioned towards the boy and began to sob.

Elisha jerked up the sack behind his shoulder and, pulling the straps off his arms, put it on the floor. Then he lifted it on to the bench and untied the strings. Having opened the sack, he took out a loaf of bread and, cutting off a piece with his knife, handed it to the man. The man would not take it, but pointed to the little boy and to a little girl crouching behind the stove, as if to say:

'Give it to them.'

Elisha held it out to the boy. When the boy smelt bread, he stretched out his arms, and seizing the slice with both his little hands, bit into it so that his nose disappeared in the chunk. The little girl came out from behind the stove and fixed her eyes on the bread. Elisha gave her also a slice. Then he cut off another piece and gave it to the old woman, and she too began munching it.

'If only some water could be brought,' she said, 'their mouths are parched. I tried to fetch some water yesterday—or was it to-day—I can't remember, but I fell down and could go no further, and the pail has remained there, unless someone has taken it.'

Elisha asked where the well was. The old woman told him. Elisha went out, found the pail, brought some water, and gave the people a drink. The children and the old woman ate some more bread with the water, but the man would not eat.

'I cannot eat,' he said.

All this time the younger woman did not show any consciousness, but continued to toss from side to side. Presently Elisha went to the village shop and bought some millet, salt, flour, and oil. He found an axe, chopped some wood, and made a fire. The little girl came and helped him. Then he boiled some soup and gave the starving people a meal.

V

The man ate a little, the old woman had some too, and the little girl and boy licked the bowl clean and then curled up and fell fast asleep in one another's arms.

The man and the old woman then began telling Elisha how they had sunk to their present state.

'We were poor enough before,' said they, 'but when the crops failed, what we gathered hardly lasted us through the autumn. We had nothing left by the time winter came, and had to beg from the neighbours and from any one we could. At first they gave, then they began to refuse. Some would have been glad enough to help us but had nothing to give. And we were ashamed of asking: we were in debt all round, and owed money, and flour, and bread.'

'I went to look for work,' the man said, 'but could find none. Everywhere people were offering to work merely for their own keep. One day you'd get a short job and then you might spend two days looking for work. Then the old woman and the girl went begging, further away. But they got very little; bread was so scarce. Still we scraped food together somehow and hoped to struggle through till next harvest, but towards spring people ceased to give anything. And then this illness seized us. Things became worse and worse. One day we might have something to eat, and then nothing for two days. We began eating grass. Whether it was the grass, or what, made my wife ill, I don't know. She could not keep on her legs, and I had no strength left, and there was nothing to help us to recovery.'

'I struggled on alone for a while,' said the old woman, 'but at last I broke down too for want of food, and grew quite weak. The girl also grew weak and timid. I told her to go to the neighbours—she would not leave the hut, but crept into a corner and sat there. The day before yesterday a neighbour looked in, but seeing that we were ill and hungry she turned away and left us. Her husband has had to go away and she has nothing for her own little ones to eat. And so we lay, waiting for death.'

Having heard their story, Elisha gave up the thought of overtaking his comrade that day and remained with them all night. In the morning he got up and began doing the housework, just as if it were his own home. He kneaded the bread with the old woman's help and lit the fire. Then he went with the little girl to the neighbours to get the most necessary things; for there was nothing in the hut, everything had been sold for bread — cooking utensils, clothing, and all. So Elisha began replacing what was necessary, making some things himself and buying some. He remained there one day, then another, and then a third. The little boy picked up strength and whenever Elisha sat down crept along the bench and nestled up to him. The little girl brightened up and helped in all the work, running after Elisha and calling,

'Daddy, daddy.'

The old woman grew stronger and managed to go out to see a neighbour. The man too improved and was able to get about, holding on to the wall. Only the wife could not get up, but even she regained consciousness on the third day and asked for food.

'Well,' thought Elisha, 'I never expected to waste so much time on the way. Now I must be getting on.'

VI

The fourth day was the feast day after the summer fast, and Elisha thought:

'I will stay and break the fast with these people. I'll go and buy them something and keep the feast with them, and to-morrow evening I will start.'

So Elisha went into the village, bought milk, wheat-flour and dripping, and helped the old woman to boil and bake for the morrow. On the feast day Elisha went to church, and then broke the fast with his friends at the hut. That day the wife got up and managed to move about a bit. The husband had shaved and put on a clean shirt which the old woman had washed for him; and he went to beg for mercy of a rich peasant in the village to whom his ploughland and meadow were mortgaged. He went to beg the rich peasant to grant him the use of the meadow and field till after the harvest; but in the evening he came back very sad and began to weep. The

rich peasant had shown no mercy, but had said: 'Bring me the money.'

Elisha again grew thoughtful. 'How are they to live now?' thought he to himself. 'Other people will go haymaking, but there will be nothing for these to mow, their grass land is mortgaged. The rye will ripen. Others will reap (and what a fine crop mother-earth is giving this year), but they have nothing to look forward to. Their three acres are pledged to the rich peasant. When I am gone they'll drift back into the state I found them in.'

Elisha was in two minds, but finally decided not to leave that evening, but to wait until the morrow. He went out into the yard to sleep. He said his prayers and lay down; but he could not sleep. On the one hand he felt he ought to be going, for he had spent too much time and money as it was; on the other hand he felt sorry for the people.

'There seems to be no end to it,' he said. 'First I only meant to bring them a little water and give them each a slice of bread, and just see where it has landed me. It's a case of redeeming the meadow and the cornfield. And when I have done that I shall have to buy a cow for them, and a horse for the man to cart his sheaves. A nice coil you've got yourself into, brother Elisha! You've slipped your cables and lost your reckoning!'

Elisha got up, lifted his coat which he had been using for a pillow, unfolded it, got out his snuff and took a pinch, thinking that it might perhaps clear his thoughts.

But no! He thought and thought, and came to no conclusion. He ought to be going; and yet pity held him back. He did not know what to do. He refolded his coat and put it under his head again. He lay thus for a long time, till the cocks had already crowed once: then he was quite drowsy. And suddenly it seemed as if some one had roused him. He saw that he was dressed for the journey, with the sack on his back and the staff in his hand, and the gate stood ajar so that he could just squeeze through. He was about to pass out when his sack caught against the fence on one side: he tried to free it, but then his leg-band caught on the other side and came undone. He pulled at the sack and saw that it had not caught on the fence, but that the little girl was holding it and crying,

'Bread, daddy, bread!'

He looked at his foot, and there was the tiny boy holding him by the leg-band, while the master of the hut and the old woman were looking at him through the window.

Elisha awoke and said to himself in an audible voice:

'To-morrow I will redeem their cornfield, and will buy them a horse, and flour to last till the harvest, and a cow for the little ones; or else while I go to seek the Lord beyond the sea I may lose Him in myself.'

Then Elisha fell asleep and slept till morning. He awoke early, and going to the rich peasant, redeemed both the cornfield and the meadow land. He bought a scythe (for that also had been sold) and brought it back with him. Then he sent the man to mow, and himself went into the village. He heard that there was a horse and cart for sale at the public-house, and he struck a bargain with the owner and bought them. Then he bought a sack of flour, put it in the cart, and went to see about a cow. As he was going along he overtook two women talking as they went. Though they spoke the Little-Russian dialect, he understood what they were saying.

'At first, it seems, they did not know him; they thought he was just an ordinary man. He came in to ask for a drink of water, and then he remained. Just think of the things he has bought for them! Why, they say he bought a horse and cart for them at the publican's only this morning! There are not many such men in the world. It's worth while going to have a look at him.'

Elisha heard and understood that he was being praised, and he did not go to buy the cow, but returned to the inn, paid for the horse, harnessed it, drove up to the hut, and got out. The people in the hut were astonished when they saw the horse. They thought it might be for them, but dared not ask. The man came out to open the gate.

'Where did you get a horse from, grandfather?' he asked.

'Why, I bought it,' said Elisha. 'It was going cheap. Go and cut some grass and put it in the manger for it to eat during the night. And take in the sack.'

The man unharnessed the horse, and carried the sack into the barn. Then he mowed some grass and put it in the manger. Everybody lay down to sleep. Elisha went outside and lay by the roadside. That evening he took his bag out with him. When every one was asleep, he got up, packed and fastened his bag, wrapped the linen bands round his legs, put on his shoes and coat, and set off to follow Efím.

VII

When Elisha had walked rather more than three miles it began to grow light. He sat down under a tree, opened his bag, counted his money, and found he had only seventeen rúbles and twenty kopéks left.

'Well,' thought he, 'it is no use trying to cross the sea with this. If I beg my way it may be worse than not going at all. Friend Efím will get to Jerusalem without me, and will place a candle at the shrines in my name. As for me, I'm afraid I shall never fulfil my vow in this life. I must be thankful it was made to a merciful Master and to one who pardons sinners.'

Elisha rose, jerked his bag well up on his shoulders, and turned back. Not wishing to be recognized by any one, he made a circuit to avoid the village, and walked briskly homeward. Coming from home the way had seemed difficult to him and he had found it hard to keep up with Efím, but now on his return journey, God helped him to get over the ground so that he hardly felt fatigue. Walking seemed like child's play. He went along swinging his staff and did his forty to fifty miles a day.

When Elisha reached home the harvest was over. His family were delighted to see him again, and all wanted to know what had happened: Why and how he had been left behind? And why he had returned without reaching Jerusalem? But Elisha did not tell them.

'It was not God's will that I should get there,' said he. 'I lost my money on the way and lagged behind my companion. Forgive me, for the Lord's sake!'

Elisha gave his old wife what money he had left. Then he questioned them about home affairs. Everything was going on well; all the work had been done, nothing neglected, and all were living in peace and concord.

Efím's family heard of his return the same day, and came for news of their old man, and to them Elisha gave the same answers.

'Efím is a fast walker. We parted three days before St. Peter's day, and I meant to catch him up again, but all sorts of things happened. I lost my money and had no means to get any further, so I turned back.'

The folks were astonished that so sensible a man should have acted so foolishly: should have started and not got to his destination, and should have squandered all his money. They wondered at it for a while and then forgot all about it; and Elisha forgot it too. He set to work again on his homestead. With his son's help he cut wood for fuel for the winter. He and the women threshed the corn. Then he mended the thatch on the outhouses, put the bees under cover, and handed over to his neighbour the ten hives he had sold him in spring and all the swarms that had come from them. His wife tried not to tell how many swarms there had been from these hives, but Elisha knew well enough from which there had been swarms and from which not. And instead of ten, he handed over seventeen swarms to his neighbour. Having got everything ready for the winter, Elisha sent his son away to find work, while he himself took to plaiting shoes of bark and hollowing out logs for hives.

VIII

All that day while Elisha stopped behind in the hut with the sick people, Efím waited for him. He only went on a little way before he sat down. He waited and waited, had a nap, woke up again, and again sat waiting, but his comrade did not come. He gazed till his eyes ached. The sun was already sinking behind a tree and still no Elisha was to be seen.

'Perhaps he has passed me,' thought Efím, 'or perhaps some one gave him a lift and he drove by while I slept, and did not see me. But how could he help seeing me? One can see so far here in the steppe. Shall I go back? Suppose he is on in front we shall then miss each other completely and it will be still worse. I had better go on, and we shall be sure to meet where we put up for the night.'

He came to a village, and told the watchman, if an old man of a certain description came along, to bring him to the hut where Efím stopped. But Elisha did not turn up that night. Efím went on, asking all he met whether they had not seen a little, bald-headed, old man? No one had seen such a traveller. Efím wondered, but went on alone, saying:

'We shall be sure to meet in Odessa, or on board the ship,' and he did not trouble more about it.

On the way he came across a pilgrim wearing a cassock, with long hair and a skull-cap such as priests wear. This pilgrim had been to Mount Athos, and was now going to Jerusalem for the second time. They both stopped at the same place one night and, having met, they travelled on together.

They got safely to Odessa and there had to wait three days for a ship. Many pilgrims from many different parts were in the same case. Again Efím asked about Elisha, but no one had seen him.

Efím got himself a foreign passport, which cost him five rúbles. He paid forty rúbles for a return ticket to Jerusalem, and bought a supply of bread and herrings for the voyage.

The pilgrim began explaining to Efím how he might get on to the ship without paying his fare, but Efím would not listen. 'No, I came prepared to pay, and I shall pay,' said he.

The ship was freighted and the pilgrims went on board, Efím and his new comrade among them. The anchors were weighed and the ship put out to sea.

All day they sailed smoothly, but towards night a wind arose, rain came on, and the vessel tossed about and shipped water. The people were frightened: the women wailed and screamed and some of the weaker men ran about the ship looking for shelter. Efím too was frightened, but he would not show it, and remained at the place on deck where he had settled down when first he came on board, beside some old men from Tambóv. There they sat silent, all night and all next day, holding on to their sacks. On the third day it grew calm, and on the fifth day they anchored at Constantinople. Some of the pilgrims went on shore to visit the Church of St. Sophia, now held by the Turks. Efím remained on the ship, and only bought some white bread. They lay there for twenty-four hours and then put to sea again. At Smyrna they stopped again, and at Alexandretta; but at last they arrived safely at Jaffa, where all the pilgrims had to disembark. From there still it was more than forty miles by road to Jerusalem. When disembarking the people were again much frightened. The ship was high, and the people were dropped into boats, which rocked so much that it was easy to miss them and fall into the water. A couple of men did get a wetting, but at last all were safely landed.

They went on on foot, and at noon on the third day reached Jerusalem. They stopped outside the city, at the Russian hostel, where their passports were indorsed. Then, after dinner, Efím visited the Holy Places with his companion, the pilgrim. It was not the time when they could be admitted to the Holy Sepulchre, but they went to the Patriarchate. All the pilgrims assembled there. The women were separated from the men, who were all told to sit in a circle, barefoot. Then a monk came in with a towel to wash their feet. He washed, wiped, and then kissed their feet, and did this to every one in the circle. Efím's feet were washed and kissed, with the rest. He stood through vespers and matins, prayed, placed candles at the shrines, handed in booklets inscribed with his parent's names, that they might be mentioned in the church prayers. Here at the Patriarchate food and wine were given them. Next morning they went to the cell of Mary of Egypt, where she had lived doing penance. Here too they placed candles and had prayers read. From there they went to the Monastery of Abraham, and saw the place where Abraham intended to slay his son as an offering to God. Then they visited the spot where Christ appeared to Mary Magdalene, and the Church of James, the Lord's brother. The pilgrim showed Efím all these places, and told him how much money to give at each place. At mid-day they returned to the hostel and had dinner. As they were preparing to lie down and rest, the pilgrim cried out, and began to search his clothes, feeling them all over.

'My purse has been stolen, there were twenty-three rúbles in it,' said he, 'two-ten rúble notes and the rest in change.'

He sighed and lamented a great deal, but as there was no help for it, they lay down to sleep.

IX

As Efím lay there he was assailed by temptation.

'No one has stolen any money from this pilgrim,' thought he, 'I do not believe he had any. He gave none away anywhere, though he made me give and even borrowed a rúble of me.'

This thought had no sooner crossed his mind, than Efím rebuked himself, saying: 'What right have I to judge a man? It is a sin. I will think no more about it.' But as soon as his thoughts began to wander, they turned again to the pilgrim: how interested he seemed to be in money, and how unlikely it sounded when he declared that his purse had been stolen.

'He never had any money,' thought Efím. 'It's all an invention.'

Towards evening they got up, and went to midnight Mass at the great Church of the Resurrection, where the Lord's Sepulchre is. The pilgrim kept close to Efím and went everywhere with him. They came to the Church; a great many pilgrims were there, some Russians and some of other nationalities: Greeks, Armenians, Turks, and Syrians. Efím entered the Holy Gates with the crowd. A monk led them past the Turkish sentinels, to the place where the Saviour was taken down from the cross and anointed, and where candles were burning in nine great candlesticks. The monk showed and explained everything. Efím offered a candle there. Then the monk led Efím to the right, up the steps to Golgotha, to the place where the cross had stood. Efím prayed there. Then they showed him the cleft where the ground had been rent asunder to its nethermost depths; then the place where Christ's hands and feet were nailed to the cross; then Adam's tomb, where the blood of Christ had dripped on to Adam's bones. Then they showed him the stone on which Christ sat when the crown of thorns was placed on His head; then the post to which Christ was bound when He was scourged. Then Efím saw the stone with two holes for Christ's feet. They were going to show him something else, but there was a stir in the crowd and the people all hurried to the church of the Lord's Sepulchre itself. The Latin Mass had just finished there and the Russian liturgy was begining. And Efím went with the crowd to the tomb cut in the rock.

He tried to get rid of the pilgrim, against whom he was still sinning in his mind, but the pilgrim would not leave him, but went with him to the Mass at the Holy Sepulchre. They tried to get to the front, but were too late. There was such a crowd that it was impossible to move either backwards or forwards. Efím stood looking in front of him, praying, and every now and then feeling for his purse. He was in two minds: sometimes he thought that the pilgrim was deceiving him, and then again he thought that if the pilgrim spoke the truth and his purse had really been stolen, the same thing might happen to himself.

X

Efím stood there gazing into the little chapel in which was the Holy Sepulchre itself with thirty-six lamps burning above it. As he stood looking over the people's heads, he saw something that surprised him. Just beneath the lamps in which the sacred fire burns, and in front of every one, Efím saw an old man in a grey coat, whose bald, shining head was just like Elisha Bódrov.

'It is like him,' thought Efím, 'but it cannot be Elisha. He could not have got ahead of me. The ship before ours started a week earlier. He could not have caught that; and he was not on ours, for I saw every pilgrim on board.'

Hardly had Efím thought this, when the little old man began to pray, and bowed three times: once forwards to God, then once on each side—to the brethren. And as he turned his head to the right, Efím recognized him. It was Elisha Bódrov himself, with his dark, curly beard turning grey at the cheeks, with his brows, his eyes and nose, and his expression of face. Yes, it was he!

Efím was very pleased to have found his comrade again and wondered how Elisha had got ahead of him.

'Well done, Elisha!' thought he. 'See how he has pushed ahead. He must have come across some one who showed him the way. When we get out I will find him, get rid of this fellow in the skull-cap, and keep to Elisha. Perhaps he will show me how to get to the front also.'

Efím kept looking out, so as not to lose sight of Elisha. But when the Mass was over the crowd began to sway, pushing forward to kiss the tomb, and pushed Efím aside. He was again seized with fear lest his purse should be stolen. Pressing it with his hand, he began elbowing through the crowd, anxious only to get out. When he reached the open he went about for a long time searching for Elisha both outside and in the Church itself. In the chapels of the Church he saw many people of all kinds, eating, and drinking wine, and reading and sleeping there. But Elisha was nowhere to be seen. So Efím returned to the inn without having found his comrade. That evening the pilgrim in the skull-cap did not turn up. He had gone off without repaying the rúble, and Efím was left alone.

The next day Efím went to the Holy Sepulchre again, with an old man from Tambóv, whom he had met on the ship. He tried to get to the front, but was again pressed back; so he stood by a pillar and prayed. He looked before him, and there in the foremost place under the lamps, close to the very Sepulchre of the Lord, stood Elisha, with his arms spread out like a priest at the altar, and with his bald head all shining.

'Well, now,' thought Efím, 'I won't lose him!'

He pushed forward to the front, but when he got there, there was no Elisha: he had evidently gone away.

Again on the third day Efím looked, and saw at the Sepulchre, in the holiest place, Elisha standing in the sight of all men, his arms outspread and his eyes gazing upwards as if he saw something above. And his bald head was all shining.

'Well, this time,' thought Efím, 'he shall not escape me! I will go and stand at the door, then we can't miss one another!'

Efím went out and stood by the door till past noon. Every one had passed out, but still Elisha did not appear.

Efím remained six weeks in Jerusalem, and went everywhere: to Bethlehem, and to Bethany, and to the Jordan. He had a new shroud stamped at the Holy Sepulchre for his burial, and he took a bottle of water from the Jordan and some holy earth, and bought candles that had been lit at the sacred flame. In eight places he inscribed names to be prayed for, and he spent all his money except just enough to get home with. Then he started homeward. He walked to Jaffa, sailed thence to Odessa, and walked home from there on foot.

XI

Efím travelled the same road he had come by; and as he drew nearer home his former anxiety returned as to how affairs were getting on in his absence. 'Much water flows away in a year,' the proverb says. It takes a lifetime to build up a homestead but not long to ruin it, thought he. And he wondered how his son had managed without him, what sort of spring they were having, how the cattle had wintered, and whether the cottage was well finished. When Efím came to the district where he had parted from Elisha the summer before, he could hardly believe that the people living there were the same. The year before they had been starving, but now they were living in comfort. The harvest had been good, and the people had recovered and had forgotten their former misery.

One evening Efím reached the very place where Elisha had remained behind; and as he entered the village a little girl in a white smock ran out of a hut.

'Daddy, daddy, come to our house!'

Efím meant to pass on, but the little girl would not let him. She took hold of his coat, laughing, and pulled him towards the hut, where a woman with a small boy came out into the porch and beckoned to him.

'Come in, grandfather,' she said. 'Have supper and spend the night with us.'

So Efím went in.

'I may as well ask about Elisha,' he thought. 'I fancy this is the very hut he went to for a drink of water.'

The woman helped him off with the bag he carried, and gave him water to wash his face. Then she made him sit down to table, and set milk, curdcakes, and porridge, before him. Efím thanked her, and praised her for her kindness to a pilgrim. The woman shook her head.

'We have good reason to welcome pilgrims,' she said. 'It was a pilgrim who showed us what life is. We were living forgetful of God and God punished us almost to death. We reached such a pass last summer that we all lay ill and helpless with nothing to eat. And we should have died, but that God sent an old man to help us—just such a one as you. He came in one day to ask for a drink of water, saw the state we were in, took pity on us, and remained with us. He gave us food and drink and set us on our feet again; and he redeemed our land, and bought a cart and horse and gave them to us.'

Here the old woman, entering the hut, interrupted the younger one and said:

'We don't know whether it was a man or an angel from God. He loved us all, pitied us all, and went away without telling us his name, so that we don't even know whom to pray for. I can see it all before me now! There I lay waiting for death, when in comes a bald-headed old man. He was not anything much to look at, and he asked for a drink of water. I, sinner that I am, thought to myself: "What does he come prowling about here for?" And just think what he did! As soon as he saw us he let down his bag, on this very spot, and untied it.'

Here the little girl joined in.

'No, Granny,' said she, 'first he put it down here in the middle of the hut, and then he lifted it on to the bench.'

And they began discussing and recalling all he had said and done, where he sat and slept, and what he had said to each of them.

At night the peasant himself came home on his horse, and he too began to tell about Elisha and how he had lived with them.

'Had he not come we should all have died in our sins. We were dying in despair, murmuring against God and man. But he set us on our feet again; and through him we learned to know God and to believe that there is good in man. May the Lord bless him! We used to live like animals, he made human beings of us.'

After giving Efím food and drink, they showed him where he was to sleep; and lay down to sleep themselves.

But though Efím lay down, he could not sleep. He could not get Elisha out of his mind, but remembered how he had seen him three times at Jerusalem, standing in the foremost place.

'So that is how he got ahead of me,' thought Efím. 'God may or may not have accepted my pilgrimage, but He has certainly accepted his!'

Next morning Efím bade farewell to the people, who put some patties in his sack before they went to their work, and he continued his journey.

XII

Efím had been away just a year and it was spring again when he reached home one evening. His son was not at home, but had gone to the public-house, and when he came back he had had a drop too much. Efím began questioning him. Everything showed that the young fellow had been unsteady during his father's absence. The money had all been wrongly spent and the work had been neglected. The father began to upbraid the son, and the son answered rudely.

'Why didn't you stay and look after it yourself?' he said. 'You go off, taking the money with you, and now you demand it of me!'

The old man grew angry and struck his son.

In the morning Efím went to the village Elder to complain of his son's conduct. As he was passing Elisha's house his friend's wife greeted him from the porch.

'How do you do, neighbor?' she said. 'How do you do, dear friend? Did you get to Jerusalem safely?'

Efím stopped.

'Yes, thank God,' he said. 'I have been there. I lost sight of your old man, but I hear he got home safely.'

The old woman was fond of talking:

'Yes, neighbour, he has come back,' said she. 'He's been back a long time. Soon after

Assumption, I think it was, he returned. And we were glad the Lord had sent him back to us! We were dull without him. We can't expect much work from him any more, his years for work are past; but still he is the head of the household and it's more cheerful when he's at home. And how glad our lad was! He said, "It's like being without sunlight, when father's away!" It was dull without him, dear friend. We're fond of him, and take good care of him.'

'Is he at home now?'

'He is, dear friend. He is with his bees. He is hiving the swarms. He says they are swarming well this year. The Lord has given such strength to the bees that my husband doesn't remember the like. "The Lord is not rewarding us according to our sins," he says. Come in, dear neighbour, he will be so glad to see you again.'

Efím passed through the passage into the yard and to the apiary, to see Elisha. There was Elisha in his grey coat, without any facenet or gloves, standing under the birch trees, looking upwards, his arms stretched out and his bald head shining as Efím had seen him at the Holy Sepulchre in Jerusalem: and above him the sunlight shone through the birches as the flames of fire had done in the holy place, and the golden bees flew round his head like a halo, and did not sting him.

Efím stopped. The old woman called to her husband.

'Here's your friend come,' she cried.

Elisha looked round with a pleased face, and came towards Efím, gently picking bees out of his own beard.

'Good-day, neighbor, good-day, dear friend. Did you get there safely?'

'My feet walked there and I have brought you some water from the river Jordan. You must come to my house for it. But whether the Lord accepted my efforts . . .'

'Well, the Lord be thanked! May Christ bless you!' said Elisha.

Efím was silent for a while, and then added:

'My feet have been there, but whether my soul or another's has been there more truly. . .'

'That's God's business, neighbour, God's business,' interrupted Elisha.

'On my return journey I stopped at the hut where you remained behind . . . .'

Elisha was alarmed, and said hurriedly:

'God's business, neighbour, God's business! Come into the cottage, I'll give you some of our honey.' And Elisha changed the conversation, and talked of home affairs.

Efím sighed, and did not speak to Elisha of the people in the hut, nor of how he had seen him in Jerusalem. But he now understood that the best way to keep one's vows to God and to do His will, is for each man while he lives to show love and do good to others.

PICTURE CREDITS

*Key to abbreviations used to indicate location of pictures on page: r. —right; l. —left; t. —top; b. —bottom; c. —center; * —courtesy. Abbreviations are combined to indicate unusual placement.*

—**FRONTISPIECE** Painting by Barton J. Faist from a portrait by Karsh of Ottawa—Woodfin Camp and Associates —**10, 11, 27, 28, 29** *Hale Observatories —**33** Godfrey Argent —**56** *Ramsay and Muspratt, Oxford —**71** *Crawford Collection, Royal Observatory, Edinburgh; permission of the Astronomer Royal for Scotland —**74** The Metropolitan Museum of Art, Robert Lehman Collection, 1975 —**77** From the original Regiomontanus edition of Peurbach's "Theoricae novae planetarum;" photo, Yale Medical Library —**79** From Copernicus's "De revolutionibus" (1543); photo *Charles Eames —**80** Detail from the frontispiece of J.B. Riccioli's "Almagestum novum" (1651); photo, Houghton Library, Harvard University —**81** From Descartes's "Principia philosophiae" (1644); photo, *Owen Gingerich —**84** From James Clerk Maxwell's "On Physical Lines of Force" (1861) —**134** Figure 9 from "The First Three Minutes: A Modern View of the Origin of the Universe" by Steven Weinberg, © 1977 by Steven Weinberg, Basic Books, Inc., Publishers, New York —**139** *Harvard University News Office —**142-149, 151** "Conditions Favoring Major Advances in Social Science," Karl W. Deutsch, John Platt, Dieter Senghass, *Science,* Vol. 171, pp. 451-455, Table 1 and Table 2, 5 February, 1971 —**184** *Henry J. Feather —**224** (l.) *Harvard University News Office —**306** *J.P.T. Bury —**336** Samuel Johnson, oil painting by Sir Joshua Reynolds, 1765; photo, *the National Portrait Gallery, London —**340** Abraham Cowley, oil painting by Mary Beale; photo, *the Curators of the Bodleian Library, Oxford —**342** John Milton, engraving by W. Faithorne, 1670; photo, *the National Portrait Gallery, London —**356** John Dryden, oil painting by Sir Godfrey Kneller; photo, *the National Portrait Gallery, London —**368** Alexander Pope, oil painting by Charles Jervas; photo, *the Curators of the Bodleian Library, Oxford —**384** Thomas Gray, detail of an oil painting by John Giles Eccardt; photo, the National Portrait Gallery, London —**388** *Osterreichische Nationalbibliothek, Vienna —**444** Photograph by Mathew Brady National Archives, Washington, D.C.; photo, *U.S. Signals Corps —**456** The Bettmann Archive

*T*o extend the tradition of excellence of your Britannica Great Books educational program, you may also avail yourself of other aids for your home reference center.

*T*he following pages feature two companion products—the Britannica 3 bookcase and the Britannica Reading Achievement Program—that are designed to help you and your family.

*S*hould you wish to order them, or to obtain further information, please write to us at

Britannica Home Library Service
Attn: Year Book Department
P. O. Box 4928
Chicago, Illinois 60680

Britannica 3
custom-designed
BOOKCASE

- requires less than 1 x 3-ft. floor space

- laminated pecan finish resists burns, stains, scratches

- Early American styling enriches any setting

- case size: $35^3/_4''$ wide, $9^3/_4''$ deep, $27^5/_8''$ high

The *Britannica* READING ACHIEVEMENT PROGRAM

- classroom tested
- designed by reading experts
- minimum parental help required
- builds reading confidence

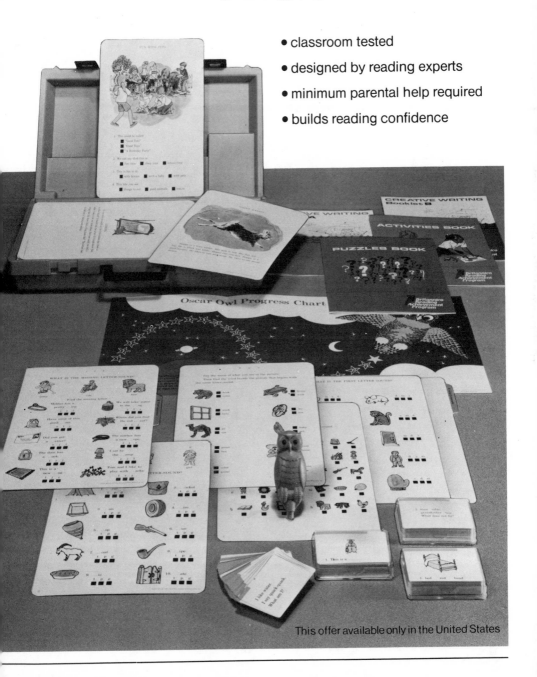

Authors

in Great Books of the Western World

Homer

Aeschylus

Sophocles

Herodotus

Euripides

Thucydides

Hippocrates

Aristophanes

Plato

Aristotle

Euclid

Archimedes

Apollonius

Lucretius

Virgil

Plutarch

Tacitus

Epictetus

Nicomachus

Ptolemy

Marcus Aurelius

Galen

Plotinus

Augustine

Thomas Aquinas

Dante

Chaucer

Machiavelli

Copernicus

Rabelais

Montaigne

Gilbert

Cervantes

Francis Bacon

Galileo

Shakespeare

Kepler